THE NAVY V-12 PROGRAM

THE NAVY

V-12

PROGRAM

Leadership for a Lifetime

James G. Schneider

1987

Houghton Mifflin Company : Boston

Library of Congress Cataloging-in-Publication Data

Schneider, James G.
The Navy V-12 Program.
Includes index.
1. United States. Navy Dept. V-12 Program — History.
2. United States. Navy — History — World War, 1939–1945.
I. Title. II. Title: V-12 Program.
V427.S36 1987   359'.007'1173   87-3684
ISBN 0-395-41932-8

Printed in the United States of America

P 10 9 8 7 6 5 4 3 2 1

Book design by David Ford

To Arthur Stanton Adams
and all of the Navy
and Marine Corps personnel and the civilians
who contributed to the success
of the V-12 program.

What a Naval Officer Should Be

It is by no means enough that an officer of the Navy shall be a capable mariner. He must be that, of course, but also a great deal more. He should be, as well, a gentleman of liberal education, refined manner, punctilious courtesy, and the nicest sense of personal honor.

He should be the soul of tact, patience, justice, firmness and charity. No meritorious act of a subordinate should escape his attention or be left to pass without its reward, if even the reward be only one word of approval. Conversely, he should not be blind to a single fault in any subordinate, though, at the same time, he should be quick and unfailing to distinguish error from malice, thoughtlessness from incompetency, and well-meant shortcoming from the heedless or stupid blunder. As he should be universal and impartial in his remarks and approval of merit, so should he be judicial and unbending in his punishment or reproof of misconduct.

John Paul Jones,
from a statement to the Maritime Commission, 1775

CONTENTS

CONTENTS

PREFACE

THIS VOLUME records the history of the Navy V-12 program, which trained more than sixty thousand Navy and Marine Corps officers in World War II. That exceeded the output of the Naval Academy, Naval Reserve Officers Training Corps (NROTC), and other pre-V-12 programs combined. Aside from a 1945 Navy Department summary, which was immediately stamped "confidential," this story has not been reported in the forty-one years that have elapsed since the program's termination on June 30, 1946.

The nation needs to understand the vital wartime role shouldered by 131 of its colleges and universities and the warm and intelligent program direction given by a specially recruited group of Navy officers. It should also be interested in the success enjoyed in later life and the important contributions made to the country by the V-12 trainees.

For the trainees, the work defines the forest in which they were the trees. (Although only sixty thousand men completed the program, a total of 125,000 were enrolled, seventy thousand at a time.) It is, in part, an anecdotal book that may bring pleasure from the reminiscences of one of the most interesting and effort-filled times of their lives.

The V-12 program did not turn out the "ninety-day wonders" so frequently scorned by enlisted personnel and comedians. Those with seven semesters of college before the program began may have been commissioned in the minimum time of 240 days, whereas those (like myself) who came in with no college experience were closer to "seven-hundred-day wonders."

The unprecedented democratic nature of the selection process for V-12 trainees opened the door of educational opportunity to many young men. For all who successfully completed the V-12 training and its follow-up at midshipmen's, supply, or Marine officer candidate schools or NROTC, the program led to a heavy load of responsibility at a very early age. Many were commissioned at age nineteen (some looked closer to sixteen) and placed in charge of dozens of men up to double their age.

Though it was not an easy role, that early leadership set the future course for most of the V-12s. Their postwar accomplishments have been substantial.

PREFACE

This book does not cover in detail the NROTC program, although that program was technically a part of the V-12 Naval College Training Program beginning on July 1, 1943. NROTC units were in operation in twenty-seven colleges and universities before V-12 began. They continued to operate on their prewar premise of providing an additional flow of naval officers to supplement the limited supply turned out by the U.S. Naval Academy. NROTC students took more specific naval courses, wore the uniforms of midshipmen, and at the completion of their college course were commissioned ensigns without attendance at a midshipmen's school.

Between July 1, 1943, and June 30, 1946, all new entrants into the NROTC program came from the V-12 ranks; trainees were usually selected at the end of their second trimester. At the termination of the V-12 program those who desired to continue and met requisite qualifications were transferred on an inactive basis to NROTC units to complete their training. Since all of the NROTC entrants originated from V-12 during the life of the latter program, most wartime NROTCs will find part of their training covered herein.

The V-12s in medical and dental schools had a program entirely different from that of the typical undergraduate V-12. They selected their own quarters, were paid subsistence, were not required to attend military formations, and were generally free to come and go as they pleased. They were especially set apart by their midshipman's uniforms instead of sailor whites and blues. They were scattered among seventy-three medical and thirty-seven dental schools, with sometimes as few as fifteen V-12s in a school's program. Thus, medical and dental V-12s are not covered in this volume, except for their V-12 premed and predent days when they were part of regular V-12 units, the same as future deck and supply officers.

The approximately two hundred V-12s who attended theological seminaries were quartered and uniformed like the medical and dental students, so no attempt has been made to cover their professional training. But, of course, their undergraduate days in standard V-12 units are covered.

The V-12 program started with high standards of selection, and these tightened as the schedule moved along. Trainees who persevered were given an early background of decision making and responsibility that has served them all their lives.

The Navy, the colleges, and the trainees were not the only beneficiaries of the program. The entire nation has gained from the leadership provided by former V-12s in virtually every field from education and government to business and industry. It's time the nation learned about the Navy V-12 program. That's why this book was written.

1

THE NEED

THE WAR was going badly for the United States and its allies during the first months of 1942. In the Pacific Japan was scoring victory after victory, with every enemy land triumph marking one more place to be retaken and each success of the Japanese navy making our ultimate victory ever more distant.

In the European theater Hitler's forces had control of nearly the entire continent, and the prospect of a total Allied triumph seemed remote. Indeed, while the topic of how long the war would last was a daily conversational theme all across America, the sobering question of whether America and the Allies would even win it was occasionally raised.

Those first months of 1942 were depressing to the American home front. It was not until the Battle of Midway in early June that Americans could reasonably hope for a brighter future. But the Guadalcanal landing in August, with the ensuing months of bloody combat, put a damper on expectations for anything resembling a near-term conclusion of the war.

In formulating the strategy for retaking the Pacific outposts and eventually bringing the war to the Japanese homeland, the Navy began scheduling the necessary ship and aircraft construction. Manning those ships and planes had to be dovetailed with production, and the Navy found that its officer strength would be totally inadequate to meet that huge demand.

Prior to this time the Navy had considered a college degree a *sine qua non* for a commission. With the war clouds gathering, the expanding United States Navy had set up its V-7 officer program in June of 1940 and began in earnest to seek a substantial number of recent college graduates for its commissioned ranks.

The V-7 program enlisted young male graduates who met specified physical qualifications and had the aptitude and mental outlook the Navy deemed necessary in its officers. When space was available, they were called up for active duty and assigned to Naval Reserve midshipmen's schools then operating on the *Prairie State* (the old battleship

THE NEED

Illinois, which was then tied up in the Hudson River at New York City) and at Northwestern University's downtown campus in Chicago.[1]

On January 3, 1942, shortly after the attack on Pearl Harbor, the Navy revised the V-7 program to enlist qualified college juniors and seniors into the inactive reserve. That made the V-7s draft-exempt while completing their regular college work, after which they would be called to active duty and ordered to a midshipmen's school or other officer training program.

When the Navy announced in February of 1942 its V-1 program for college freshmen and sophomores, it offered the student the same general advantages as V-7. But because of academic deficiencies that had turned up in its V-7 officer candidates, the Navy now required its V-1 reservists to take at least one year of college math, one year of college physical science, and "an adequate physical training program." In addition, V-1 reservists had to successfully complete an annual Navy examination to document their progress.[2]

Men who did not finish V-1 (as well as high school graduates) were invited to apply for training as aviation cadets (V-5 program) and, if accepted and successful, were commissioned as ensigns in the flying service.

With the Selective Service call-up age set at twenty, the Navy had effectively ensured a steady flow of qualified officers. But in August of 1942, at the urging of the War Department, strong movements were made toward lowering the draft age to eighteen, and the Navy could foresee its supply of officer material quickly drying up. It was not ready to rely upon the draft for its future officers, so plans began to take shape for the Navy college training program.

Meanwhile, through both patriotism and self-interest, America's colleges and universities had been persistently volunteering their resources to the armed forces and had received only limited acceptance. Indeed, from January 2 to 4, just a month after Pearl Harbor, representatives of one thousand colleges and universities had met in Baltimore to offer their facilities to the federal government for whatever might be their most productive use in the successful prosecution of the war.

Six months later, on July 15 and 16, 1942, members of a limited but representative number of institutions met at the invitation of the American Council on Education (ACE) for the Second Baltimore Conference. They deplored the armed forces' minimal acceptance of their proferred help and urged a coordinated wartime plan for higher education. They also criticized all of the armed services for their fierce and "unseemly" competition during the previous six months in the recruitment of college men with officer potential.

In August, the Committee on the Relationships of Higher Education to the Federal Government, chaired by President Edmund E. Day of

THE NEED

Cornell University and composed of twelve leading college and university presidents, was appointed by the ACE at the request of Paul McNutt, chairman of the War Manpower Commission (WMC).[3] The committee's purpose was to meet with representatives of the War and Navy departments and the WMC to further develop plans for putting campuses and faculties to good use in the war effort.

The act of Congress setting up the WMC gave it control of the Selective Service System and invested the chairman with vast powers. The Army and Navy — with considerable justification — were concerned about the possible intrusion of the WMC into their own domains. Although the infighting between the WMC and the services continued for more than a year, the services were able to avoid significant usurpations by the WMC.

On August 19, 1942, the WMC released the report of its Special Committee on the Utilization of Colleges and Universities for the Purpose of the War. This short-lived committee had been appointed in July to consider the resolutions of the Second Baltimore Conference and the study provided (upon request) by the U.S. Office of Education on the place of colleges in the war effort.

The announced adoption of the committee report by the WMC substantially ended the practice of deferring some young men for vital civilian war-related work and study. The report included this unequivocal statement: "All able-bodied male students are destined for the Armed Forces and responsibility for determining the specific training of such students is a function of the Army and Navy." Although the announcement contained no plan, it did provide the basis for college training programs to be developed jointly by the military and the WMC.

After receiving the early tentative plans of the War Department, the ACE's committee offered a counterproposal for use of colleges and universities. It was submitted to the War and Navy departments on October 14, 1942, and included a number of points that were later adopted by the Navy College Training Program, to wit: (1) that a "broad democratic basis" be used in selecting the trainees, (2) that selection boards include civilian members, and (3) that the training proceed year round. The council's plan received broad approval from the institutions of higher learning.

On October 15, President Franklin D. Roosevelt, in letters to the secretaries of the War and Navy departments, asked the services to "Please have an immediate study made as to the highest utilization of the American colleges. . . . It may be advisable to call in . . . a number of the leading educators. . . . There is an enormous amount of equipment in colleges . . . which the Army and Navy may be able to use without great changes."

Just three days before, in a radio "fireside chat" on October 12, Roo-

THE NEED

sevelt had called for lowering the Selective Service induction age to eighteen. On November 13 he signed into law an amendment to the Selective Training and Service Act that accomplished that goal.

Within two weeks after the letter from the president, the Navy brought to the forefront a committee it had appointed in February to set up the V-1 program. It added three more educators and called it the Navy Advisory Educational Council.[4] With the approval of the ACE, the Navy gave to the Advisory Council the key role in providing the civilian input to assist in planning the college training program.

The Advisory Council met on October 29, 1942, and continued meetings at the call of the Navy. The meetings were held in the Bureau of Naval Personnel (BuPers) offices at the Navy Annex in Arlington, Virginia, and were usually day-long affairs attended by the director of training and some of his key aides. The lunch break was sometimes taken with such high ranking officers as Vice-Admiral Randall Jacobs, the chief of naval personnel.

A member of both the Day Committee on the Relationships of Higher Education to the Federal Government and the Advisory Council, Dr. Rufus C. Harris, then president of Tulane University, recalled, "The Council really did have influence in the shaping of the program. I had never seen the Navy work as effectively with any other committee before that time."[5]

The Council recommended to the Navy that (1) institutions should be widely distributed geographically, and should be carefully chosen by a joint Army/Navy board with civilian representation; (2) each institution selected should be guaranteed at least two hundred men, and "as an administrative necessity," that each institution should be required to accept the men ordered to it, but that each should be allowed to drop trainees who failed to maintain traditional academic standards of the school; (3) students should be selected on the basis of competitive examinations, preferably given at the end of the senior year in high school; (4) the Navy should prescribe the minimum portion of the curricula that was necessary to ensure production of officer material, but should use as far as possible the current curricular organization of the colleges; (5) recruit training should not be a prerequisite for the college program and military training should be kept to a minimum as a part of the physical training program; and (6) men in the V-1 and V-7 programs should be called to active duty on July 1, 1943, and permitted a number of terms of college work inversely proportional to the number already completed.[6]

The Army had been separately developing its college training program. Both the Army and the Navy plans were sent to President Roosevelt in a memorandum dated December 3, 1942. Just two days earlier,

THE NEED

in a letter to BuPers, Roosevelt's naval aide said that the president had been discussing the college plans and had three recommendations: (1) states should be assigned quotas by population; (2) students should be chosen by selection boards composed of one naval officer, one "good-common-sense civilian," and one educator; and (3) the plans presented "a grand chance to save some little colleges, ones with say four hundred to eight hundred students." The president further suggested that the Navy ask the U.S. Office of Education which small colleges "will be put in a bad way as a result of the drafting of the eighteen and nineteen year olds and which are 'worth keeping open.' "[7]

On December 5, 1942, the president issued an important executive order (no. 9279) that banned further enlistments by men aged eighteen to thirty-eight, thus (except for seventeen-year-olds) delegating to the Selective Service System the total responsibility for assignment of men to the various branches of the armed services. The order also provided that the secretary of war and the secretary of the Navy should take whatever steps were necessary to assure that all training programs carried on in nonfederal educational institutions would conform with such policies and regulations as the chairman of the WMC deemed necessary to ensure the efficient utilization of the nation's educational facilities and personnel for the effective prosecution of the war.

Although President Roosevelt had approved both the Army and Navy plans (following their December 3 submission to him), under the terms of executive order no. 9279, the WMC was given control of all educational facilities so the services were compelled to send their college training plans to WMC Chairman Paul V. McNutt for his review before publication. He substituted his own statement for one key paragraph of the announcement, the effect being that the WMC chairman could prescribe the rules and regulations under which institutions of higher learning would be selected, and that he had the ultimate power to decide on the schools to be chosen if the selection committee could not reach a unanimous decision.

Finally, on Saturday, December 12, the armed forces released to the ACE the announcement of the Army Specialized Training Program (ASTP) and the Navy College Training Program. The ACE promptly dispatched it to the educational institutions. The public announcement came the following Thursday, December 17. The ACE happily noted that the Navy's program was substantially in agreement with the ACE's own ideas; it was disappointed that the War Department's was not.[8]

The announcement was called a "joint statement of the Secretary of War and the Secretary of the Navy on utilization of college facilities and specialized training for the Army and Navy." The opening paragraph noted that "the demands of a mechanical war and of steadily growing

THE NEED

armed forces require a flow into the respective services of young men who require specialized educational technical training which could be provided by the colleges and universities."

Appreciation was expressed for the "benefit of fruitful consultation with many educators, and particularly the staff of the War Manpower Commission, the Office of Education, the Committee of the American Council on Education and the Navy Advisory Council on Education [sic]. In the administration of these plans, the Army and Navy are counting on further assistance from the same sources."

The announcement also noted that the ASTP was aimed at "specialized technical training of soldiers on active duty," whereas the Navy program intended to "provide a continuing supply of officer candidates in the various special fields required by the U.S. Navy, Marine Corps and Coast Guard."

The Navy claimed that its plan would permit selection of "the country's best qualified young men on a broad democratic basis, without regard to financial resources, and thus permit the Navy to induct and train young men of superior ability for officers and specialists." It specified that trainees would include "selected high school graduates, or others of satisfactory educational qualifications, having established their proper mental, physical, and potential officer qualifications by appropriate examinations." Enlisted or inducted men then on active duty were included in the program as well as the V-1, V-5, and V-7 reservists. Enlistment of college students under eighteen in the V-1 program would be continued only until March 15, 1943.

The release said that the selection of the institutions would be made by a joint committee made up of representatives of the War Department, the Navy Department, and the WMC. It specifically requested "that institutions do not endeavor themselves to get in touch with government administrative organizations handling the matter" and warned that "no institution will receive any advantage by departing from this procedure."

With that announcement the colleges and universities began scrambling for selection and the Navy stepped up its efforts to assemble the staff necessary to carry out its program.

2

THE PROGRAM
TAKES FORM

TO ARRIVE at the December 1942 announcement of its college training program, the Navy had been working at an accelerated pace since mid-August. At that time, it had become apparent that the draft age would soon be lowered to eighteen, which would curtail its recruitment of officer candidates through the V-1, V-5, and V-7 programs.

The number of officers necessary to man the projected flow of new ships and planes had been determined by the chief of naval operations and the chief of naval personnel. Now came the tasks of recruiting sufficient future officer candidates and training them along with those reservists then in the V-1, V-5, and V-7 pipeline.

Capt. Forrest U. Lake, USN, had been in charge of officer training in BuPers since 1936, and on April 1, 1940, he was appointed director of training, making him responsible for all Navy schooling. Thus, by the fall of 1942 he had been directing the NROTC for six years, during which time he had supervised its expansion from six campuses to twenty-seven. Lake's intimate familiarity with that important officer training program and his contacts with those major institutions gave him a background that was to prove invaluable in establishing the Navy's new college training program.

It is apparent that the Navy carefully listened to the many civilian recommendations that came its way, for, in contrast to the Army Specialized Training Program, the V-12 was planned, announced, and carried out as a *college* program. It left with each school the authority to select its own textbooks, determine course content (within some broad outlines), and establish the level of academic achievement necessary for a trainee to remain in the program. Although the Navy urged that full academic credit be given for the courses, that determination remained with the schools, as did each institution's criteria for the awarding of degrees.

Dr. Rufus C. Harris, who served on three of the key civilian committees involved with the V-12 program, gave Captain Lake full credit for shaping the early outline of the program.[1] Lake was sometimes referred

THE PROGRAM TAKES FORM

to as "the father of the V-12 Program" and was recognized for that work by a commendation from the secretary of the Navy in May of 1945.[2]

In accordance with Navy policy of rotating officers, Lake was reassigned on January 5, 1943. He was succeeded as the director of the training activity by Capt. Bruce Canaga, USN(Ret.), an Annapolis graduate, like Lake. As the officer directly responsible for implementation of the V-12 program, Canaga and his representatives continued to meet regularly with the Navy Advisory Educational Council.

Another important person in the formulation of the structure of the V-12 program was Dr. Joseph W. Barker, dean of the School of Engineering at Columbia University, who since 1941 had been serving as special assistant to the secretary of the Navy. His academic background and his wide college acquaintanceship provided important inputs into the program. He attended most of the meetings of the Advisory Council and was in the thick of the correspondence about the program.

The sudden appearance of this massive training program raised some fundamental problems within the Bureau of Naval Personnel, most of them dealing with jurisdiction. This was a unique program: the men were officer candidates in an enlisted status while attending civilian schools under contract with the Navy.

Selection of the candidates was under the control of the Procurement Division of Officer Personnel, but between the time of enlistment and the later commissioning as an officer (also under Procurement) there were to be extended periods of training, which clearly came under the aegis of the Training Division.

Before he left the Bureau, Captain Lake saw the jurisdictional problems arising, so he issued a memorandum in December stating the quandary and suggesting that the matter be resolved early on.[3]

There followed an exchange of memos between the officers-in-charge of the Procurement Division and the Field Administration Section of the Training Division, each firmly staking out his turf and expecting the other to recognize that the "needs of the service" clearly made the writer's position the superior one.

This conflict was too important to be ignored. It was too explosive to be allowed to simmer. Finally, on January 28, 1943, the assistant chief of naval personnel, Rear Adm. Louis E. Denfeld, USN, approved a "Memorandum Re Procurement-Training Responsibilities," which was expected to be the definitive answer to the knotty problem.[4]

It provided that Procurement was responsible for the selection of the V-12 trainees, but was required to confer with Training as to minimum standards and to "seek and accept" the advice of Training on the methods of selection. Even the appointment of the three-man selection committees was established in a Solomon-like fashion, with Procurement

THE PROGRAM TAKES FORM

choosing the naval officer and the civilian and Training, presumably because of its close ties with academe, selecting the educator.

The memo further noted that both divisions were bound by a joint responsibility to deliver the qualified commissioned officers for which the program was designed. In essence, Procurement selected the men and sent them to the right places and then had nothing further to do with them until commissioning time. Meanwhile, the Training Division would administer the college program in all its facets.

Perhaps the most important part of Denfeld's memorandum was the establishment of a Committee on Procurement-Training Responsibilities, which, as ordered, met at least once a week until the fall of 1944. The committee was composed of the officers-in-charge of the Administration Section and the Standards and Curriculum Section of the Training Division and of the College Programs Section and Field Offices Section of the Procurement Division. A representative of the Manpower Policies Section of the Planning and Control Division was also named, and other representatives from involved sections or divisions were invited to attend from time to time.

The operation of the committee provided a fine channel for solving differences, and apparently worked very well. The fact that any unresolved problems were to be directed to Admiral Denfeld brought considerable reason to the conference table.

To administer the V-12 program, the director of training set up within his Administration Section the College Training Unit, which was to handle the direction and coordination of the program. Of necessity it would work closely with two other sections, the Physical Training Section and the Standards and Curriculum Section.

The College Training Unit was also in nearly constant communication with the Planning and Control Division, the Office of Counsel of the Bureau, the Office of Naval Officer Procurement, the Bureau of Supplies and Accounts, the Bureau of Medicine and Surgery, the commandant of the U.S. Marine Corps, and the training officers of the various naval districts, plus several joint committees established with the Army and the War Manpower Commission. It had a big assignment.

From the time of announcement of the program until the selected start-up date of July 1, 1943, was a bare six months. With so many decisions to be made and so many institutions clamoring for inclusion in the program, the work was cut out for the director of training and the officer-in-charge of the College Training Unit. There was no time to wait until one area was settled before proceeding to the next. Simultaneous action was necessary by all of the participating interests, and each had to assume that the others would diligently and promptly carry out their assigned tasks. Fortunately, they all did.

3

SELECTION
OF SCHOOLS

ALTHOUGH the Navy had asked colleges and universities not to aggressively seek a unit and stated that such action would avail them naught, most schools immediately began planning their political tactics. Life in college America was getting too difficult for institutions to use less than their maximum efforts to secure one of the very desirable college training contracts.

For many schools, the need to maintain solvency and retain faculty members were the primary motivating factors. In other cases, the very existence of the school was at stake. But, in fairness, it must be noted that the patriotic satisfaction of doing their part in the war effort was a most important ingredient for all of the schools.

The small colleges of America had been assured that they would be given full consideration for the program, but their spirits were bolstered by a statement made by Secretary of the Navy Frank Knox. It was reported in the *Des Moines Register* on December 19, 1942: "We will not place at the top of the priority list the large state universities and privately endowed institutions of the country which should be able to carry on unaided. . . . We will give special consideration to the smaller colleges whose financial resources are so meager that their existence may be threatened by the war."[1]

By the end of December an extensive questionnaire developed by the War Manpower Commission had been dispatched to all institutions of higher learning. They were urged to complete and return it promptly. It inquired into the school's facilities, devoting special attention to housing and messing capabilities. By the end of March 1943 more than sixteen hundred questionnaires had been returned. This information was made available to the Army and Navy, and each was free to gather such additional data as it desired. The Navy sought information assistance from at least four other organizations.[2]

The selection process was divided into two stages: (1) an initial classification (based upon information in the questionnaires and the collec-

SELECTION OF SCHOOLS

tive judgment of a special Joint Committee) of about five hundred schools that had the academic, housing, and messing facilities to accommodate a unit; and (2) a final selection (after various inspections of the facilities) of institutions by either the Army or the Navy, or, in the case of some larger schools, by both. Being placed on the preliminary list simply meant that the school could now be inspected by the Army or the Navy, which would then have to determine if the institution was adequate for its needs.

The initial selection of five hundred qualified schools was made by the nine-member Joint Committee for the Selection of Non-Federal Educational Institutions, chaired by Dr. Edward C. Elliott, president of Purdue University, who was then serving as chief of the Division of Professional and Technical Training of the WMC. The committee adopted six principles to guide its selection of schools.[3] The committee's decision for inclusion or exclusion was to be unanimous, according to the ground rules set by the program announcement as amended by WMC Chairman McNutt. If unanimity were not achieved, McNutt alone would make the final choice. The Army and Navy took special care to see that Chairman McNutt did not have to trouble himself with such decisions.

When the Joint Committee placed a school on its preliminary list of five hundred, the institution was notified, raising hope for ultimate selection. This process went on all through February and March, finishing on April 11.

It was also decided that at schools where the Navy had an NROTC unit or the Army had an ROTC unit, the established service was to have the "primary interest." It was agreed that except in cases where the institution could accommodate more than one thousand trainees, the two services would not be present on the same campus. This sharpened the competition for early inspection and selection of potential schools.

Once the five hundred qualified schools had been selected, the Army appeared to move swiftly with its inspections. As a result, the Navy hurriedly called to Washington all of its directors of training of the naval districts for a one-day meeting on February 1, 1943, to explain the V-12 program and the directors' role in the inspection of the subject campuses. The district directors then returned to their headquarters and outlined the program and inspection to the junior officers who would actually conduct them.

The resulting inspections, complicated by the politically inspired need for broad geographical distribution of the schools, were far from uniform. Most were conducted by unqualified officers, who produced a diverse set of recommendations. As a result, BuPers Counsel James A. Fowler, Jr., urged that qualified personnel be sent into the field to settle

SELECTION OF SCHOOLS

questions as to "capacity of the housing and messing facilities and as to the use to be made of the instructional, medical, athletic, and other facilities." A month elapsed before those qualified officers from Planning and Control started this second round of inspections.

It should be stressed that although this was a college program, the Navy's planning did not call for the typical prewar college accommodations: two trainees were now to be put into the space that the college had previously assigned to one civilian student. But the officers knew of the need to provide adequate study space — that consideration was clearly more important in this program than was strict adherence to the Navy's traditional standards of how many men should occupy a given square footage in barracks-type housing.

Doubling the capacity of dormitories meant twice as many toilet facilities ("heads" to the Navy) would be needed, but wartime shortages of fixtures, pipes, and the labor to install them made expansion difficult.

Because the results of the second inspection differed so drastically from the findings of the first, some colleges that were initially told that their facilities were adequate were informed just a few weeks later that serious deficiencies existed that had to be corrected for the institution to meet Navy standards. Often this news was received only a few weeks before the scheduled opening of the program.

In the middle of April the Navy privately circulated to members of the Navy Advisory Educational Council its tentative list of 146 undergraduate V-12 schools, which caused at least one member to question the basis for some of the selections.[4] Aided by the second inspection report, some deletions were made before the Navy awarded the contracts. The final list was whittled down to 131.

In February, the Navy notified some schools of their V-12 selection. The announcement of these choices stirred up more anxiety in the breasts of officials who did not even know if their schools would make the first preliminary list of five hundred.

All kinds of imaginative efforts were forwarded to Washington by the schools in attempts to improve their chances: one offered to build a swimming pool, another promised trainees free use of the town golf course, while many others fired up their congressmen, senators, and other friends in high places to redouble their efforts.

The Joint Committee gave each service forty-five days from the time of the preliminary approval to report whether the school would be used for its college program. Otherwise the institution would be released for other purposes. This put some time pressure on the selection process.

Political influence was felt by the Navy in several ways. There was pressure to select particular schools, to let the schools know as soon as possible whether they had been selected, and to financially assist the

SELECTION OF SCHOOLS

James G. Schneider

Milligan College was the only school in the country in which all students were V-12s. Shown above are the author (left) and his roommate Frank Stephenson behind the sign that clearly identified the school as a Navy unit. Some other schools, such as Carroll College, had as few as nineteen civilian students at one time.

schools to meet the physical standards required for the program. A congressman or senator was not doing his duty to his constituents if he didn't actively support their "most reasonable" request to land a Navy contract for "such a fine and well-qualified school."[5]

A long-time congressman who later served as Republican national chairman, B. Carroll Reece, was undoubtedly helpful in securing the unit for Milligan College, which was located in his district near Johnson City, Tennessee, even though the school was not then an accredited institution and its largest dormitory, three stories tall, had just one central open stairway and no fire escapes.

The Navy helped some schools acquire extremely scarce kitchen equipment to bring their food handling areas up to standards and helped other schools obtain material priorities to quickly build additions to their dining rooms and even new dormitories. Other schools, such as Marquette University, purchased or leased small nearby hotels to house and feed their V-12s.

At Southwestern University in Georgetown, Texas, the prominence of

SELECTION OF SCHOOLS

two-term congressman Lyndon B. Johnson on an important committee that dealt with Navy appropriations put considerable pressure on the Navy to help that school renovate a very substandard men's dormitory. But the Navy would not yield, so Southwestern reluctantly assigned the V-12s to its relatively new girls' dormitory and then launched an appeal to its alumni to raise funds to bring the men's dorm up to standards for occupancy by the women.[6]

At some schools, even the announcement of selection as a V-12 unit caused problems. A unique situation occurred at Gustavus Adolphus College in St. Peter, Minnesota, a Lutheran school with a very conservative social code and a strong clergy-led pacifist influence among its trustees. Just two days after college president Walter Lunden proudly announced the Navy's selection of Gustavus Adolphus for a unit, the board of trustees in special session voted seven to four to terminate further negotiations with the Navy. The next day the official board representative reported to the faculty that "the main reason was the lack of sufficient information by a majority of Board members concerning the details of the program and the fear that the ideals and standards of the college might be adversely affected."[7] An immediate reaction by faculty, students, and alumni necessitated a second special meeting two days later, and the trustees reversed themselves, again by a seven-to-four vote, and agreed to accept the V-12 unit.

When the selection of a school was disclosed by the Navy Department, it was a cause for celebration at all of the schools. When the announcement came that the University of Rochester would have a V-12 unit, the university's chimes rang out with three successive songs: "Anchors Aweigh," "Praise God from Whom All Blessings Flow," and "God Send Us Men."

After the selection of a unit had been publicly announced, a flurry of planning, purchasing, remodeling, and hiring began at each of the 131 colleges and universities. These activities were based solely upon a letter of selection issued by the Navy. The formal Navy contracts had to be negotiated separately for each school. Cost of food, fair rental of the buildings, and rightful compensation for instruction were just a few of the important but highly individual considerations.

The Navy did not announce the complete list of 131 undergraduate V-12 units prior to June 30, 1943. Instead, each successful school announced its own selection, so announcements continued over a four-month period.

The units varied in size from the nearly two thousand V-12s at Dartmouth to the sixty-eight at Webb Institute of Naval Architecture in New York City.

SELECTION OF SCHOOLS

The types of schools ran the gamut from prestigious Ivy League institutions to small, church-aided colleges serving very small areas. The church schools included Roman Catholic, mainline Protestant, Evangelical and Reformed, and Quaker. The state schools included major universities and some narrowly focused state teachers colleges.

Institutions Selected for V-12 Units (1943)

Key to types of training:

B = Basic
E = Engineering
M = Marines
P = Premedical and predental
* = Existing NROTC units

Alabama
Howard College	B

Arizona
Arizona State Teachers College	M,P

Arkansas
Arkansas A & M College	B,M,P

California
California Institute of Technology	E
College of the Pacific	B,M,P
Occidental College	B,M,P
University of California (Berkeley)*	B,E,M,P
University of California (Los Angeles)*	B,P
University of Redlands	B,M
University of Southern California*	B,E,M,P

Colorado
Colorado College	B,M,P
University of Colorado*	B,E,M,P

Connecticut
Trinity College	B,P
Wesleyan University	B,P
Yale University*	B,E,M,P

Florida
University of Miami	B,P

Georgia
Emory University	B,M,P
Georgia School of Technology*	E,M
Mercer University	B,P

Idaho
University of Idaho, Southern Branch	B,P

SELECTION OF SCHOOLS

Illinois

Illinois Institute of Technology	E
Illinois State Normal	B
Northwestern University*	B,E,M,P
University of Illinois	E,P

Indiana

DePauw University	B,P
Indiana State Teachers College	B
Purdue University	B,E,M,P
University of Notre Dame*	B,E,M,P
Wabash College	B

Iowa

Iowa State A & M College	E
St. Ambrose College	B,P
University of Dubuque	B,P

Kansas

Kansas State Teachers College	B
University of Kansas	E,P
Municipal University (Washburn)	B,P

Kentucky

Berea College	B,P
University of Louisville	B,E,P

Louisiana

Louisana Polytechnic Institute	B,M,P
Southwestern Louisiana Institute	B,M,P
Tulane University*	B,E,P

Maine

Bates College	B,P

Maryland

Mount St. Mary's College	B

Massachusetts

College of the Holy Cross*	B,P
Harvard University*	B,P
Massachusetts Institute of Technology	E,P
Tufts College*	B,E,P
Williams College	B,P
Worcester Polytechnic Institute	E

Michigan

Alma College	B,P
Central Michigan College of Education	B
University of Michigan*	B,E,M,P
Western Michigan College	B,M

Minnesota

College of St. Thomas	B
Gustavus Adolphus College	B,M,P
St. Mary's College	B,P
University of Minnesota*	E,P

SELECTION OF SCHOOLS

Mississippi
Millsaps College	B,M,P
Mississippi College	B,P

Missouri
Central College	B,P
Central Missouri State Teachers College	B
Missouri Valley College	B
Northwest Missouri State Teachers College	B
Park College	B
Southeast Missouri State Teachers College	B,P
Westminster College	B,P

Montana
Carroll College	B,P
Montana School of Mines	B,E

Nebraska
Doane College	B
Peru State Teachers College	B

New Hampshire
Dartmouth College	B,E,M,P

New Jersey
Drew University	B
Princeton University	B,M,P
Stevens Institute of Technology	E

New Mexico
University of New Mexico*	B,E,P

New York
Colgate University	B,M,P
Columbia University	E,P
Cornell University	B,E,M,P
Hobart and William Smith Colleges	B,P
Rensselaer Polytechnic Institute*	E
St. Lawrence University	B,P
Union College	B,E,P
University of Rochester	B,E,M,P
Webb Institute of Naval Architecture	E

North Carolina
Duke University*	B,E,M,P
University of North Carolina*	B,M,P

North Dakota
State Teachers College, Dickinson	B
State Teachers College, Minot	B
State Teachers College, Valley City	B

Ohio
Baldwin-Wallace College	B,P
Bowling Green State University	B,M,P
Case School of Applied Science	E
Denison University	B,M,P

SELECTION OF SCHOOLS

John Carroll University	B,P
Miami University	B,M,P
Oberlin College	B,M,P
Ohio Wesleyan University	B,P
Oklahoma	
University of Oklahoma*	E,P
Oregon	
Willamette University	B,P
Pennsylvania	
Bloomsburg State Teachers College	B
Bucknell University	B,E,M,P
Franklin and Marshall College	B,M,P
Muhlenberg College	B,M,P
Pennsylvania State College	B,M
Swarthmore College	B,E,P
University of Pennsylvania*	B
Ursinus College	B,P
Villanova College	B,E,M,P
Rhode Island	
Brown University*	B,E,P
South Carolina	
Newberry College	B
University of South Carolina*	B,E,P
Tennessee	
Carson-Newman College	B,P
Milligan College	B
University of the South	B
Texas	
North Texas Agricultural College	B,M
Rice Institute*	E
Southern Methodist University	E,P
Southwestern University	B,M
Texas Christian University	B,P
University of Texas*	E,P
Vermont	
Middlebury College	B,P
Virginia	
Emory and Henry College	B,P
Hampden-Sydney College	B,P
University of Richmond	B,P
University of Virginia*	B,E,P
Washington	
Gonzaga University	B,P
University of Washington*	B,E,M,P
Whitman College	B,P
West Virginia	
Bethany College	B,P

SELECTION OF SCHOOLS

Wisconsin

Lawrence College	B
Marquette University*	E,P
University of Wisconsin	E

The next step was to enter into contracts with each school. In the interest of fair play and efficiency and to keep the services from vying for favor with the institutions, the Joint Army/Navy Board for Training Unit Contracts had been set up to establish one basic contract for use with all schools. But developing a single contract for use with such diverse institutions was not easy. As with many other committees of the time, the members agreed that their decisions had to be unanimous. Could that be done?

4

A UNIFORM
ARMY/NAVY
CONTRACT

WHILE THE PROCESS of selecting the colleges for both the Army and Navy programs was nearing completion in the early spring of 1943, the start-up date of July 1 was relentlessly drawing closer. Both services recognized that their next formidable task was to contract with hundreds of schools. Ever mindful of the problems associated with the World War I Student Army Training Corps,[1] the armed forces realized the necessity of a uniform and fair approach to the process.

On March 25, 1943, Robert P. Patterson, undersecretary of war, and James Forrestal, undersecretary of the Navy, established a Joint Army and Navy Board for Training Unit Contracts and invested it with general supervision over such contracts to ensure that the terms and provisions "shall be fair and uniform and that there shall be no material differences in the standards applied by the two departments in their contract negotiations."[2]

Robert B. Stewart, controller of Purdue University, who had been serving as a Navy consultant on college contracts, was appointed chairman of the board, an indication of the confidence placed in him by both the Army and the Navy. An impressive man with boundless energy, Stewart was indefatigable in his role as chairman. He traveled to colleges and universities whenever a problem arose. Forrestal had earlier urged him to accept a Navy commission, but Stewart correctly reasoned that his opinions and positions would carry infinitely more weight with the Army and Navy brass as a civilian chairman than as a Navy junior officer.

The chief of the Facilities Branch of the Army Specialized Training Division, Lieutenant Colonel Blake R. Van Leer, who had been dean of the consolidated schools of engineering of the University of North Carolina and North Carolina State College, was selected to represent the Army, and James A. Fowler, Jr., counsel for the Bureau of Naval Personnel, was chosen by the Navy.

A UNIFORM ARMY/NAVY CONTRACT

This Joint Board was directed to (1) approve one or more of the contract forms and determine the extent to which the contract should be observed by the two departments; (2) develop standards for determining rates of payment for facilities and services; (3) keep informed as to the use made of such forms and standards and the rates established in negotiations between the services and the colleges; and (4) decide any questions that might arise in negotiations.

Thus, it was clear that the Joint Board was a policy-maker and an arbitrator, but it was not a negotiator. The actual negotiation of payments to colleges was to be done by each of the services. The Navy experience is covered in the following chapter, "Contracting with the Colleges."

Before establishing the Joint Board, the Navy had gained much helpful experience through its negotiations for training facilities at several dozen colleges and universities in 1942. Since Fowler had been instrumental in drafting the form used there, it was logical for him to proceed with a draft for the Joint Board. He refined the contract into a document entitled "Principles of Contract," which provided the basis for the college contract for both the Army and the Navy. It proposed different methods of compensation for each type of facility or service provided by the colleges.

The plan covered the following:

1. The college would be paid 4 percent per year of the prewar book value of the buildings used for the program. No payment other than maintenance would be made for the use of land, but where fraternity or sorority houses not owned by the college were to be utilized, 5 percent of their book value was authorized.
2. The messing of the trainees was to be paid on a "budgeted cost basis"; that is, payments would be based on expected costs predicated upon the current facts of operation, with sufficiently frequent reviews to correct differences between estimated and actual costs.
3. To avoid potentially huge payments for lightly used stadiums and gymnasiums, the physical training payment was to be determined on a fee basis. Like the messing, fees would be based upon estimated costs and subject to adjustment when the true costs were established. The physical training fees were established at so much per man, per month.
4. Instructional costs proved to be the thorniest problem of all. It was soon realized by the Joint Board that a final determination of instructional fees could not be reached before the opening of the programs. It was decided to pay each school a preliminary set

sum and defer the establishment of the final formula to a later date.

5. Another major problem involved the expenditures required to adapt campus facilities for use by the military. It was agreed that these expenses, called "commissioning expenses" by the Navy, would be rigidly controlled so the government would not pay for a college's deferred maintenance or to bring substandard facilities up to the requirements of the services. The commissioning expenses authorized were usually limited to the purchase of specialized equipment not usable by the college in its normal operations and to plant modifications requested by the services to meet their particular requirements.

Reaching agreement on the principles and the contract form at its meeting of April 28, 1943, the Joint Board next day met separately with Undersecretary Patterson and Undersecretary Forrestal and received their approval. The next step was the important one: getting the colleges and universities to agree. Their sizes, complexity of operation, costs, and fiscal sophistication varied so widely that their acceptance of the principles and forms could be difficult.

But Stewart took care of that. According to W. Glasgow Reynolds of the Counsel's Office, "He sold it to the colleges."[3] As one of their own, Stewart was trusted by the business managers of America's colleges and universities. He assured them that they could secure some cash for operations and rely upon a letter of intent; the formal contract would come later. The pressure of the July 1 start-up date was undoubtedly a major factor in getting their agreement, but the colleges were not completely happy about the uncertainties associated with the use of their facilities. Stewart assured them that they would be treated fairly by the services and they accepted that.

The schools, however, indicated in numerous ways that they felt underrepresented by the three-man Joint Board. At the May 25 meeting of the Joint Board, the Association of American Colleges and Universities indicated its serious disappointment with the contract and objected to the omission of some payment in the contract for the use of student union facilities. The University of Illinois objected to the failure to include the loss of net income as a basis for payment for a school's facilities.

At the next meeting of the Joint Board, on July 6, the chairman requested that the Army and Navy provide board members with a summary analysis of the contract terms for each completed contract. The interchange of information would permit the services to coordinate their practices so that the colleges would be treated more uniformly. In

A UNIFORM ARMY/NAVY CONTRACT

a July 30 memo to the other members of the committee, Stewart noted the need to organize the work of the board to produce a manual that would show college officers how the payments were computed under the contract. This, he said, would allay the "considerable unrest and dissatisfaction in the field."[4]

Stewart's firm hand in directing the work of the Joint Board was clearly indicated by another paragraph in that memo, in which he related that he had taken it upon himself as an individual, "unofficially," to invite some leaders of the college business offices of the nation to be his guests at Purdue University for the "purpose of considering and preparing a tentative draft of the proposed manual of instructions" for the college contract.

Stewart also mentioned that some members of the invited group, "as well as officers of the American Council on Education and some other people in the field of education with whom I have visited," felt that the Joint Board should be enlarged by the addition of a college president, a college dean, an Army Air Corps representative, and a Navy commissioned officer selected by the Bureau of Naval Personnel.

On August 7, Patterson, undersecretary of war, and Forrestal, undersecretary of the Navy, issued a new memorandum superseding the original one of March 25 that established the Joint Board. The new memo enlarged the membership. Stewart, representing both services, was to remain as chairman. Representing educational institutions were Horace Ford, treasurer of Massachusetts Institute of Technology; Dr. Rufus C. Harris, president of Tulane University; and Dr. Robert G. Sproul, president of the University of California at Berkeley. Representing the Navy were Captain Cortlandt C. Baughman, director of training of the Bureau of Naval Personnel, and Fowler. Representing the Army were Colonel W. F. Volandt, assistant chief of air staff, Training Division, and Van Leer. The Joint Board's functions remained as provided at the inception.

Stewart's strong leadership in reforming the membership was well received by the academic community and instilled more confidence that the schools would be fairly treated by the services.

The newly enlarged Joint Board met in the Pentagon on August 18 and 19. It was decided to prepare manuals codifying all of the information and practices relative to contract rates agreed to by the two services. These manuals were to be distributed to the schools in order to avoid mutual misunderstanding, suspicion, and ill will.

The next meeting was set for September 8 and 9 to review and finally adopt the manuals and to authorize their publication to the schools concerned. The members also agreed at the August meeting that the Joint Board should not function in a definitive arbitration capacity

A UNIFORM ARMY/NAVY CONTRACT

Office of Presidents Emeriti, Tulane University

Joint Army and Navy Board for Training Unit Contracts meeting in Washington, D.C., on August 18, 1943. Seated, left to right, are Capt. Cortlandt C. Baughman, director of special activities, Bureau of Naval Personnel; Dr. Rufus C. Harris, president, Tulane University; Col. W. F. Volandt, chief, Procurement Branch, Materiel Division, Office of Assistant Chief of Air Staff; J. A. Fowler, Jr., counsel, Bureau of Naval Personnel; and Dr. Horace G. Ford, treasurer, Massachusetts Institute of Technology. Standing, left to right, are Lt. Col. Theodore D. Palmer, Jr., deputy director, Army Specialized Training Division; Col. Herman Beukema, director, Army Specialized Training Division; Lt. Col. Blake R. Van Leer, chief, Facilities Branch, Army Specialized Training Division; Dr. Robert G. Sproul, president, University of California (Berkeley); Dr. R. B. Stewart, controller, Purdue University; and Mr. Gerard Swope, Jr., assistant counsel, Bureau of Naval Personnel.

involving the setting or adjusting of individual rates, but should direct its attention "to the formulation of proper rules and regulations and the interpretation thereof for the guidance of schools and colleges. The administration of such rules should be left to the respective services in each case."[5]

At the onset of the August meeting, Chairman Stewart emphasized to the new members that "the Joint Board . . . is an Army and Navy Agency. We are responsible to give the two services the best of our ability in order that the services may be protected from the colleges as well as the colleges protected from bad advice in dealing with the services. To

A UNIFORM ARMY/NAVY CONTRACT

that end, I believe it is wise to keep in mind that our purpose is to act for the services — in aiding the services to develop proper bases for a payment which also, of course, should be open and fair to the colleges."[6]

When the Joint Board next met on September 8 and 9, 1943, no agreement had yet been reached on how to compensate the schools for the instructional expenses, but preliminary instructions had been sent to the institutions in the form of Navy V-12 Bulletin No. 80. The first motion passed at the September meeting was to approve an additional 3 percent of all expenditures to cover "a general administrative expense" composed largely of the expenses of the institutional trustees, the president's office, and the business office.

Next, the Joint Board reached the thorny problem of how to compensate schools where some or all of the teaching was done by members of religious societies or orders, who were not paid regular salaries by the schools but who instead received maintenance. By a six-to-two vote, the Joint Board agreed that the basis of the fair and proper allowance in such instances of "maintenance" would be the cash value of the cost of the room, meals, clothing, and other benefits (including an annuity up to $250 per year for retirement and sick benefits) furnished to a member of the society or order.

Those who voted against this proposal preferred an alternate method of instructional compensation based on the salaries paid to lay instructors in the same institution for similar work.

The final work of the meeting was the unanimous approval of the revised copy for publication of the manuals offered by each of the respective services. The *Contract Manual for Navy V-12 Unit* was sent out as Navy V-12 Bulletin No. 90 on September 13, 1943.

In approving the *Contract Manual,* the Joint Board confirmed the preliminary instructions of V-12 Bulletin No. 80, which stated that payment for the instructional costs of the programs would be made by allocating the direct teaching salaries of all instructional personnel between the military trainees and the civilian students actually enrolled in each class. This required considerable record keeping and delayed exact payment until the academic terms were well under way. To alleviate that bookkeeping chore, the method was later changed to a flat fee per man per trimester hour.[7]

In addition to the percentage of direct teaching salaries, the Navy also paid the schools for such indirect teaching costs as library service, supervisory and clerical salaries, furnishing of instructional supplies, services entailed in handling the distribution of textbooks, and maintenance, repair, and depreciation of classroom and laboratory furniture and equipment.[8]

The matter of religious compensation had not been finally resolved,

A UNIFORM ARMY/NAVY CONTRACT

however. The Roman Catholic schools involved in the V-12 program consulted each other and decided to ask for a hearing at the next meeting of the Joint Board, which was held on November 22 and 23, 1943. Appearing before the board to present this first item of business were the executive director of the Jesuit Educational Association, the executive secretary of the National Catholic Education Association, and the comptroller of the University of Notre Dame. Their presentation included a document entitled "The Question of Proper Remuneration for Members of Religious Orders Teaching in Army and Navy Specialized Training Programs."

Following an executive session, the board voted unanimously to amend the appropriate section of the manual approved on September 9 to add an alternative basis for payment. Religious schools were to be paid for instruction provided by nonsalaried members of the order "on the same basis as average salaries actually paid to comparable lay teachers in the same institutions for similar work."[9] The secretary, Colonel Van Leer, was instructed to inform the services that the Joint Board had also recommended a policy for the few cases where an institution's entire teaching staff was composed of members of a religious sect not receiving regular salaries, and for which there was no basis for comparison with lay teachers in the same institution for similar work. The service concerned was authorized to select a nearby institution deemed to be comparable to the one under consideration as a guide in setting the cash equivalent for the work of the religious order instructors.

Various other complaints from the schools were taken to the Joint Board, but only four resulted in formal appeals. All of them came from the Army and Air Force programs; none were from the Navy.

When the Army and Army Air Force drastically reduced their programs in a sudden move in February 1944, steps had to be taken to terminate the school contracts. Those services developed procedures in a manual entitled "Disposition of Excess Property and Unserviceable Property Under War Department Training Contracts," and their procedures were approved by the Joint Board on March 7, 1944.

On May 22, 1944, the chief of naval personnel recommended that the board consider revising the contract to permit fees covering instructional costs to be fixed, rather than attempting to adjust such payments on an actual-cost basis. A subcommittee delegated to explore the matter recommended on June 6 that after July 1, 1944, all instruction costs be computed on a fixed rate per man per term. The change in method of computing instructional rates proved "very satisfactory both to the schools and to the government," according to the final report of the Joint Board on November 30, 1945.

The Joint Board had eighteen meetings during its existence. It ended

A UNIFORM ARMY/NAVY CONTRACT

its affairs on November 30, 1945, with a report to the undersecretary of war and the undersecretary of the Navy.[10]

The Joint Board's efficiency was recognized by both the services and the president. Immediately after its termination all of its members were appointed to the Veterans' Administration's Educational Advisory Committee on the GI Bill of Rights, whose job was to develop the uniform procedures necessary to deal with every institution of higher learning (and trade school) in the nation under the education section of the GI Bill of Rights. This expression of confidence meant more to the Joint Board's members than did the formal "well done" they received.[11]

The Joint Board had indeed done a splendid job for both the colleges and the services.

5

CONTRACTING WITH
THE COLLEGES

war and the undersecretary of the Navy.

PRIOR TO December of 1942 the responsibility for Navy contracts was
scattered among the various bureaus and the Judge Advocate General's Office.[1] Contracts were awarded on a competitive bid basis, and
the legal work was done mainly by Navy officers who had received their
legal education while in the Navy. Most did not have civilian legal experience, which handicapped the Navy in dealing with the new situations
and massive problems brought on by its extremely rapid expansion.

When President Roosevelt in July 1940 selected Frank Knox and
Henry Stimson to be secretaries of the Navy and War departments, respectively, they were instructed to reorganize their departments inter-
nally by function. A month earlier Congress had created a new office of
"undersecretary" of the Navy, but had left the assignment of duties to
the secretary of the Navy. James V. Forrestal, president of the New York
investment firm of Dillon, Read, and Company, was sworn in as undersecretary of the Navy on August 20, 1940, and given responsibilities in
procurement, contract negotiations, taxes, and other legal matters affecting the Navy.

In January of 1942 Secretary Knox commissioned the Chicago-based
management firm of Booz, Frye, Allen, and Hamilton to make a management study of the Navy in order to adapt it to the needs of the rapidly
expanding military force. As a result of this study and the creation of
the office of undersecretary, some of the regular naval establishment.
felt threatened by the new civilian leadership, and the frequent internal
battles that ensued were not always kept within the family. The Bureau
of Supplies and Accounts and the Judge Advocate General's Office
thought their traditional roles were in danger, and they did not easily
give up their authority for contracts.[2]

Forrestal named as his assistants H. Struve Hensel, a member of a
New York City law firm, and W. John Kenney of the Los Angeles bar.
Hensel was directed to make a study of the contracting process. He
found that Congress had approved a negotiated contract procedure

CONTRACTING WITH THE COLLEGES

back in 1939, and had further extended the authority for this procedure in June of 1940. Hence, his recommendation that the legal aspects of procurement be handled by lawyers attached to Forrestal's office immediately aroused the active opposition of Rear Adm. Walter B. Woodson, the judge advocate general, who was reluctant to turn over his authority over the contracting process to newcomers.

Eventually Woodson took the matter to Congress and succeeded in delaying the reorganization of the contracting process, but Forrestal ultimately prevailed by establishing a Procurement Legal Division, which later (1944) became the Office of General Counsel. Under this new arrangement, a civilian lawyer was assigned to work with each naval bureau. On January 19, 1943, James A. Fowler, Jr., a partner in the New York law firm that later became Cahill, Gordon, and Reindel, was named counsel of the Bureau of Naval Personnel. He reported only to the bureau chief and to Undersecretary Forrestal's office, being totally freed from the Office of the Judge Advocate General.[3]

Fowler was a wise choice. He has been described by his associates in the Office of Counsel as "a master public relations man and administrator" and "very dedicated and hard-working," a man who was "very philosophical and enjoyed a good discussion."[4]

Fowler had been brought aboard — as a civilian — in the summer of 1942 when the Navy had started contracting with several dozen colleges for aviation training facilities. In those contracts, the college furnished the physical location for housing, messing, classrooms, and physical training, but the instruction was provided by the Navy. Fowler personally handled the negotiations with many of those schools, but he was severely handicapped by not having his own secretary. He was forced to use whatever time was available from the secretary of Comdr. John Webb of the Division of Planning and Control of the Bureau.

On October 1, 1942, WAVE Kathleen Middleton, a legal secretary from Newark, New Jersey, reported to the Bureau and was assigned to Fowler. Her skills were sufficient for the Navy to have given her the rating of chief yeoman upon enlistment. She made short work of Fowler's backlog and thereafter handled the correspondence and contracts that he dictated after returning from negotiating trips. When he was on the road, however, she had little work.

Always a practical man, Fowler asked Middleton how their procedure could be expedited. She suggested that if she accompanied him on the negotiating trips, the correspondence could be handled immediately, eliminating the delay. That idea was adopted and later, traveling V-12 negotiating parties were usually accompanied by a WAVE yeoman to handle the typing of letters and contracts.[5]

In December of 1942, in preparation for his new legal semiautonomy,

CONTRACTING WITH THE COLLEGES

Fowler brought on board lawyers Gerard Swope, Jr., from General Electric and W. Glasgow Reynolds from the DuPont Company. Swope remained a civilian at that time and became assistant counsel. Reynolds was commissioned a lieutenant, senior grade. Both men had extensive negotiating experience from the civilian side of military contracts, and their expertise was to prove invaluable to the efficient operation of the Office of Bureau Counsel.

Joining the Counsel's Office in 1943 were the following attorneys, all of whom were commissioned Navy officers: Willard Woelper of Newark, John Meck of Dartmouth College, Francis X. Reilly of Massachusetts, Roswell D. Pine of the Dixie Cup Company, and Robert R. Barrett of Buffalo. From New York City came Edward Hidalgo, William Sayre, Paul H. Fox, and John P. Ohl.

Not all of these lawyers were in the Counsel's Office at the same time. For instance, Hidalgo served only briefly, and Fox and Ohl joined at a later date. Only six lawyer-officers handled the initial negotiations for all of the 131 colleges and universities with undergraduate V-12 units.

The Bureau Counsel's Office posed for this photo in July 1945. Note the map showing the location of schools under contract for V-12, V-5, and other Navy programs. Standing (left to right): Lt. Robert Barrett and Comdr. Gerard Swope, Jr., Bureau Counsel. Seated (left to right): Lt.(jg) Paul H. Fox, Lt. Kathleen Middleton, and Lt. Willard Woelper. (*Kathleen Middleton McAlpin*)

Kathleen Middleton McAlpin

CONTRACTING WITH THE COLLEGES

They also were involved with the 110 V-12 medical and dental school contracts, as well as the legal details of contracts with the theological schools.

Using the Navy's 1942 experience in contracting with colleges for flight preparatory and pre-flight schools and the early 1943 negotiations with resort hotels for other Navy training schools, Fowler honed his negotiating team down to three officers. Each team was composed of a lawyer from the Counsel's Office, a specialist from the Finance Section of the Division of Planning and Control, and a representative of the Training Division, usually from the Administration Section, which included the College Training Unit.

The negotiating parties were quite often composed of officers who had worked together previously. Their assignments were usually concentrated in a particular region or regions of the country so they could become more familiar with the individual circumstances of each V-12 contract.

At the start of the V-12 program the Finance Section of the Division of Planning and Control of the Bureau of Naval Personnel was headed by Comdr. John Crawford Webb, USN, a Naval Academy graduate in the class of 1920. Working under him at various times were officers with wide-ranging financial experience. The senior negotiating officer of the Finance Section was Lt. Comdr. F. Vinton Lawrence, Jr., USNR, who was a partner in the New York investment firm of Scudder, Stevens, and Clark. Other officers who served on the negotiating teams were H. T. Healy, a certified public accountant; Robert C. Baker, a banker from Richmond, Virginia; E. G. "Woody" Childers of the Industrial Bank of Commerce of New York; Jack B. Goodwin of the Chase National Bank of New York; and C. F. Gaskill and A. L. Lindley, Jr., of New York.

Due to a shortage of qualified officers for such trips, the Finance Section sometimes hired civilians to represent it. One was Boardman Bump, comptroller and treasurer of Mount Holyoke College, who served on teams working the New England and upstate New York region.[6]

The representative from the College Training Unit of the Administration Section of the Division of Training came from among the officers mentioned in chapter 7, "The CTS in Action." Occasionally other officers were added to the basic party from other sections of Naval Personnel or from the Bureau of Supplies and Accounts. Lt. Jack Adair, a prominent real estate broker from Atlanta, was on many of the negotiating trips.[7]

After the Joint Army and Navy Board for Training Unit Contracts had approved the contract outline on April 28, 1943, Fowler completed the final draft on May 1. On May 4 and 5 in the BuPers conference room at the Arlington Annex, a two-day "Indoctrination Class on Navy College

CONTRACTING WITH THE COLLEGES

Training Program Contract Negotiations" was held for all of the interested personnel from the Office of Counsel, the Finance Section of Planning and Control, and the Administration Section of the Training Division.[8]

The importance of the meeting was established in the opening remarks by Rear Adm. Louis E. Denfeld, USN, the assistant chief of personnel. "Personnel Requirements" was covered by Capt. H. G. Hopwood, USN, director of planning and control; "Selection and Establishment of Naval Training School Locations" was presented by Capt. William W. Behrens, USN, officer-in-charge of the Administration Section and a member of the school selection committee; while Comdr. B. W. Hogan, USN(MC), explained "Medical Services at Contract Schools." "Rate Determination" was discussed by Lt. Wesley S. Hertrais, USNR, of the Finance Section, followed by an hour of study on "Contract Negotiations" before noon of the first day. That was quite a full morning!

A case study of contract negotiations occupied the afternoon and continued into the next morning. In the final afternoon's session Lt. Comdr. H. T. Healy, USNR, of the Finance Section, explained "Rate Redetermination."

Following those two intensive days, the teams were sent out to the field, where they were often joined by officers representing the Naval District's director of training and medical officer.

The scheduling of the negotiating teams was handled by Chief Yeoman Kathleen Middleton, who did such an able job that upon Fowler's recommendation she was sent to officer training for the WAVEs at Mount Holyoke College in June of 1943. When she finished her schooling there, she was commissioned a lieutenant (junior grade) and was reassigned to the Counsel's Office.[9]

Forty-two years later Lt. W. Glasgow Reynolds recalled, "Kay was the den mother of our BuPers Counsel's Office — able — efficient — and so smart you couldn't believe it!"[10]

The first travels of the negotiating parties were to negotiate agreements between the Navy and the V-12 colleges preliminary to the issuance of "letters of intent." All parties realized that it would not be possible to have completed contracts for this large group of colleges by the start-up date of July 1.

Inasmuch as the first round of negotiations involved sending an untried team into the field, Fowler required that all the reports and recommendations come back to him or Swope for final approval before a letter of intent was issued. Such letters became the basis for the eventual contract with the college.

Among the key points to be stressed to the colleges was the necessity

CONTRACTING WITH THE COLLEGES

for the Navy's prior approval for the payment of any commissioning costs. The negotiating team was also asked to observe and report what had to be done at each school to make the program operational there by the start-up date.

The matter of determining the payment for instruction had been deferred to the fall of the year by the Joint Board, so that problem did not immediately face the negotiating teams.

The V-12 program, however, posed a different contract situation than the Navy had experienced with other types of training programs carried out in academic institutions. It was settled that in the V-12 program these institutions would provide all of the instruction and administration of the academic program, and often the supervision of the physical training and the medical care as well. The earlier naval aviation units did not require such services from the colleges. Just the arrangements to provide them for the V-12 program created a multitude of complications, which had to be handled in a rush.

A typical nonstop schedule for a negotiating team was the following:[11]

May 7, 1943	Leave Washington, D.C.
May 8–9	University of Washington, Seattle
May 10–11	University of California, Berkeley
May 12–13	College of the Pacific, Stockton
May 14–15	California Polytechnic Institute, San Luis Obispo
May 16–17	California Institute of Technology, Pasadena
May 17–18	University of Southern California, Los Angeles
May 19–20	Occidental College, Los Angeles
May 20	University of Redlands, Redlands

When the party arrived on a campus, the officer from the Training Division set out to inspect the physical facilities. Among themselves the members of the team referred to this task as "counting the —— -pots." After all, there were certain ratios to be met: one toilet for every fifteen men and one urinal for every ten men in a housing unit.

The lawyer and the finance officer met with the college negotiating team, which usually included the business manager, the dean, the president, the college's attorney, and various other faculty and administration representatives.

The Navy negotiating team was regarded by most colleges as exceedingly tough. The business manager of Berea College in Kentucky, in his report of the June 26, 1943, visit of the Navy V-12 contracting party, was clearly unhappy.[12] The Navy officers were Lt. Mode L. Stone of the College Training Section, Lt.(jg) C. F. Gaskill of the Finance Section,

CONTRACTING WITH THE COLLEGES

Typical of the negotiating parties was this one, which visited St. Lawrence University, Canton, New York, on June 10 and 11, 1943. The members of the party are shown with officers stationed at St. Lawrence. (Left to right): Comdr. Elwin C. Taylor (MC), from the Third Naval District Medical Office; Lt. (jg) Albert L. Morrison, officer-in-charge, St. Lawrence University; Lt. C. B. Reemelin, Training Division, Bureau of Naval Personnel; Ens. William M. Sayre, Office of Bureau Counsel; Virginia Duhigg, Y3/C, Office of Bureau Counsel; Boardman Bump, comptroller and treasurer of Mount Holyoke College, representing the Finance Section of the Division of Planning and Control; and Lt. (jg) Richard E. Bathiany, St. Lawrence University V-12 unit.

and Lt.(jg) John F. Meck, Jr., of the Counsel's Office. In addition, a Lieutenant Ford of the Division of Planning and Control and a Lieutenant Commander Luten from the Bureau of Medicine came along to assist in the inspection.

The negotiating officers had indicated that the Navy's top figure for physical education costs (at any school) was $1.50 a man per month, and suggested that Berea should receive $1.35. Berea's proposed figure was $3.50.

Complained the business manager, "While the manner in which the physical education costs were being estimated seemed to me entirely unfair and unreasonable, after extended discussion it became apparent that no change of attitude on the part of the Navy men would take place.

CONTRACTING WITH THE COLLEGES

They finally agreed that we might receive $1.40 a man a month for this service."

When the program opened on July 1, negotiating parties were still on the road, working out the details of the agreed-upon costs for housing, messing, physical training, and medical service. The reimbursement for instruction awaited the final determination of a formula by the Joint Board. When the instructional payment method was settled in September of 1943 (see chapter 4, "A Uniform Army/Navy Contract"), Forrestal ordered "full speed ahead" to wrap up the final contracts with all 131 schools. The negotiating teams were again sent out under forced draft. A WAVE yeoman accompanied each team and stayed behind to type up the document agreed upon. After obtaining the signatures of the college authorities, she mailed the contract to the Bureau Counsel's Office and then hurried to catch up to the negotiating party at its next stop.

Regarding the WAVE yeomen who traveled with the negotiating parties, Kathleen Middleton McAlpin said, "These young women were exceptional, and performed their duties most ably. They really were super!"[13]

Most of the V-12 contracts were completed in November and December of 1943, but a few weren't put into final form until January 1944.

As the V-12 program moved along, there were various modifications of the contracts, in accordance with the initial understanding that they would be amended to reflect changes in conditions and actual costs.

The principles for termination of contracts were worked out by the Joint Board early in 1944 after the Army discontinued the major portion of its ASTP program. (The Army officially cited "imperative military necessity" as the reason for its abrupt announcement on February 18, 1944, that it was slashing the program by 110,000 of the 140,000 men involved. They were shifted back to line duty. In retrospect, we know that the Army wanted to be at full fighting strength for the impending D-Day landings in Normandy.[14]) When the V-12 termination procedure started in 1945, the negotiating parties again went out to each of the schools. (See chapter 39, "Winding Down.")

The contracting process was regarded as hard but essentially fair by most of the schools involved. The Counsel's Office did a fine job of carrying out the Bureau's intent of sustaining the colleges' initial good feeling toward the Navy. That was important in the smooth operation of the V-12 program.

6

COLLEGE TRAINING
SECTION

EARLY IN 1943, Lt. Comdr. Arthur Stanton Adams, USN(Ret.), was placed in charge of organizing the V-12 program.

Adams had been a member of the U.S. Naval Academy class of 1919, which, due to wartime acceleration, was graduated on June 6, 1918. He ranked 25 out of 199. A popular member of his class, Adams was dubbed "Beany" by his classmates, as both a tribute to his intelligence and a description of his rapidly disappearing hair. The yearbook, the 1919 *Lucky Bag*, reported that Adams was chairman of both the class ring and class pin committees, worked on the *Lucky Bag* and the Academy newspaper, *The Log*, and was leader of the glee club in his senior year. He also participated in the choir and various theatrical productions.[1]

His classmates at the Naval Academy considered him brilliant and exceptionally articulate.[2] But he also had a mischievous spirit, which brought him very close to being denied graduation from the Academy. In the final weeks of their final year, he and Midshipman James L. Holloway, Jr., who later became chief of naval operations, were the architects of an Academy musical review that ridiculed many of the Navy's most revered traditions. They were called in to explain why men who could treat those traditions so lightly were worthy of receiving a commission in the U.S. Navy. Evidently Adams and Holloway were persuasive. In later years they had many laughs over the episode, according to Dr. J. P. Mather, who traveled with the two in 1945 during the expansion of the NROTC program under the so-called Holloway Plan.[3]

Following graduation, Ensign Adams was assigned to the Navy's Submarine School at New London, Connecticut. Also ordered there was his classmate George C. Dyer, who later became president of the class of 1919 after the original president died. At New London, Adams and Dyer became better acquainted, and Adams asked his friend to serve as best man at his wedding.[4]

Adams's strength of character — or stubbornness, according to your viewpoint — was uniquely evident at the time of his wedding in an Epis-

COLLEGE TRAINING SECTION

copal church in Philadelphia in November of 1918. According to best man Dyer, during the Friday night rehearsal when the rector asked the bride, Dorothy Anderson, if she would "love, honor, and obey," she interjected, "No obey." Rejoined Adams, "No obey, no wedding."

The rest of the wedding party retreated to the rear of the church while the principals — the rector, the bride, the bride's mother, and the groom — held a protracted conference. After about twenty minutes of discussion the bride's mother addressed those at the rehearsal: "I am most sorry that this has happened but I guess there is not going to be any ceremony. We thank you very much for being here and I hope you will keep in touch."

Rather than spoil the entire weekend, Dyer decided to go down to Annapolis to see the Navy football game. At the Philadelphia depot on Saturday morning he was flagged down by the bride, who said the wedding would take place at the scheduled time but gave no hint as to who had given in. Dyer noted that "obey" was a part of the ceremony.

In recounting the story of Adams's wedding, Vice Admiral Dyer said, "It showed how he operated. He had a very keen mind, a sense of humor, and a sense of proportion. He did very well in anything he turned his hand to."

The marriage was a good one. When Arthur was running the V-12 program, Dorothy worked as an administrative assistant in another

Arthur Stanton Adams as a senior midshipman.

1919 *Lucky Bag* of the U.S. Naval Academy; courtesy of Rear Adm. Richard Tuggle, USN (Ret.)

office in BuPers. They lunched together daily in the large cafeteria at the Bureau, and the officers serving under Adams often noted how remarkable it was that after so many years of marriage they never seemed talked out. They indulged in animated conversation every lunch hour.[5]

Adams was an honor graduate of the Submarine School. Following that he served afloat in submarines and battleships; his duty included a submarine command.

While in submarine service, Adams, then a lieutenant (junior grade), contracted tuberculosis, which brought an end to his naval service at that time. He was retired on November 25, 1921.[6]

He sought relief in Denver, in accordance with the standard practice of that day. The treatment at the Army's Fitzsimon's General Hospital was successful. Adams soon regained his health and in 1922 taught math and science at East High School in Denver. According to Lynn Adams, his daughter-in-law, Adams tried homesteading near Rand, Colorado, where he built a cabin, moved in his family (which now included an adopted son, John), and started to raise dogs. However, the mountain winter drove him out. That was, perhaps, the only time in his life that Arthur Adams accepted defeat. A year later he was the associate principal of the Pitts School, also in Denver.

In 1924 the young educator moved to California, where two years later he earned his M.A. in physics from the University of California. Returning to Colorado the following year, he spent the next thirteen years as instructor, professor, and assistant to the president at the Colorado School of Mines. He also served as an alderman in Golden and as president of the Board of Control of the nearby Colorado State Industrial School for Boys.[7]

While at Mines, Adams earned his doctorate in metallurgy, published a number of scholarly papers, and coauthored two books, *Fundamentals of Thermodynamics* and *Development of Physical Thought*.[8]

In 1940 he became assistant dean of engineering at Cornell University, and in the summer of 1941 served as acting dean. He was recalled to active Navy duty on November 12, 1941, reporting as a lieutenant (junior grade), but he remained in Ithaca as officer-in-charge of the Navy Officers' Diesel Engineering School at Cornell.[9]

The terms of Adams's recall were set forth in a September 16, 1941, letter from the commandant of the Third Naval District to the chief of the Bureau of Navigation, the forerunner of the Bureau of Naval Personnel. The chief at that time was Chester W. Nimitz. The letter explained:

> Lieut. Adams holds a very important position in the Engineering faculty of Cornell University, which is providing a large number of engineers of vital importance to the Navy, the Army, and to national defense. In addition, he is

COLLEGE TRAINING SECTION

supervising in that section of New York the training of mechanics for defense industries.

. . . Assignment to such active duty would permit Lieut. Adams to continue to live at home, in the climate which has contributed to his present good health, and would also enable him to continue his important work in connection with National Defense and education. Under these circumstances, he would be pleased to be ordered to this duty.

The arrangement meant that Adams could remain in civilian clothes and continue with his duties at Cornell.[10]

On the day after the attack on Pearl Harbor, Adams reported to the dean's office in his uniform as a lieutenant (junior grade)[11] and remained in uniform throughout his service in the war. He was promoted to full lieutenant on January 10, 1942, to rank from January 2.

On June 27, 1942, he was promoted again, this time to lieutenant commander. Later in the year Adams received orders to the Bureau of Naval Personnel to head the Officer Program Unit in the Training Division. On October 26 he was detached at Cornell and a few days later he packed up his 1940 Packard sedan and drove the 362 miles to Washington. Dorothy Adams followed two weeks later by train.

The duties of Adams at the Officer Program Desk in the Training Division were described in an exchange of correspondence in October between Adams's Cornell boss, Dean S. C. Hollister, and Dean Joseph W. Barker of Columbia, who was assistant for educational affairs to the secretary of the Navy. Hollister wrote Dr. Barker complaining about the transfer of Adams, but at the same time listing Adams's outstanding qualifications.

I'm impelled to say to you that Dr. Adams, both in his capacity as Assistant Dean of the College and for nearly two years as Director of the E. S. M. W. T. Program at Cornell University, has through his great personal ability and his fine technical background been able to render to Cornell University and to the College of Engineering a notable contribution. He is a graduate of Annapolis and served with the Navy in the last war. Subsequently he obtained a Master's Degree in Physics from the University of California and a Doctor of Science in Metallurgy at the Colorado School of Mines. He has been here at Cornell for about two and one-quarter years. In that time, he has won the support and loyalty of the staff to an extent that . . . newcomers seldom enjoy. It is because of the attractiveness of his personality and the richness of his academic training and experience that he was able to make the distinguished contribution he has made on this campus.

My earnest hope is that the new service to which he is called, the nature of which I do not as yet know, will offer the full play of his extensive abilities. I am sure that if this is so the Navy will be assured of the same order of distinguished achievement which he has rendered here.[12]

Dean Barker replied:

I really didn't intend to have Adams taken away from you and the work he was doing at Cornell. However, we have had to reorganize the entire Training

COLLEGE TRAINING SECTION

Arthur Stanton Adams after he had been promoted to captain in 1944. Note Naval Academy ring on left hand.

Division in the Bureau of Naval Personnel and one of the principal desks in the new set-up is in charge of all Technical Training of officers. I tried to secure a certain engineering educator to accept a commission and come to Washington for the job but he turned me down.

The situation was critical and while I was trying to get a suitable other man, Captain Lake simply decided to cut the knot by ordering Adams here. It really is a vitally important job. At that desk all decisions [are made] as to where and how the advanced technical training of all our officers will be conducted. The diesel schools are but one example, there are many others to be established. It will call for all the capacities that Adams has.

But Adams was not destined to remain at the Officer Program Desk for very long. The V-12 program was then being developed under the guidance of the Navy Advisory Educational Council, Captain Forrest U. Lake, and Dean Barker.

In January of 1943, Lieutenant Commander Adams was directed to organize the V-12 program. On March 9, 1943, the Bureau formally established "the College Program Unit" under Adams, making it the "centralizing agency" for the administration of the college units. (Al-

COLLEGE TRAINING SECTION

though it was not until May of 1944 that the body's name was changed to "The College Training Section," for simplicity it will hereafter be referred to by the latter name.)[13]

Of all the officers in the rapidly expanding Navy, why was Adams chosen to head this key program? First, he was an Academy man. Undoubtedly the Navy leadership felt that the V-12 program was too important to be put into the hands of a reserve officer who knew little about the traditions, responsibilities, and training of naval officers.

Second, with nearly twenty years of experience in civilian education, he was wise in the ways of academe and knew the standards, protocol, and ways of communication necessary to get things done. Furthermore, he had a wide acquaintanceship in educational circles, which was an important advantage in dealing with more than two hundred and fifty colleges and universities (including professional schools) of different sizes and varying degrees of quality.

Finally, he had friends in the proper places who knew of his abilities and temperament. His classmates from the class of 1919 now held high level assignments in the Navy. Their recommendations of "Beany" were important, as were those of others who had worked with him.

Dr. Edmund E. Day, president of Cornell University, chaired the key committee of the American Council on Education that had worked closely with the Navy in formulating the V-12 program. He no doubt confirmed the high opinion of Adams expressed by Hollister, Cornell's dean of engineering, back in October.

Dean Barker, assistant for educational affairs to the Navy secretary, undoubtedly had a great deal to say about the officer who was to run the V-12 program. He had observed Adams's handling of the Officer Program Desk. The highly complimentary report supplied by his friend "Holly" Hollister must also have had substantial impact.

The unanimous opinion of four officers serving under the five foot, ten inch Adams in the College Training Section: he was a marvelous choice! His right-hand man and the unofficial executive officer of the section, Raymond F. Howes, was full of praise for Adams when interviewed forty years later.[14] When Adams in 1950 became president of the American Council on Education, he offered Howes the same kind of executive officer position and Howes jumped at the opportunity. They always worked well together.

Dr. George Winchester Stone offered this description of Adams: "Few administrators with whom I have come in contact were superior to Arthur S. Adams — bright, perceptive, understanding, with a sense of humor and optimism, and a man of excellent diplomacy."[15]

Adams was recalled as "a brilliant man" and "the greatest administrator I had ever seen" by Dr. Jean Paul Mather, who worked with him at

COLLEGE TRAINING SECTION

the Colorado School of Mines, served in the College Training Section for more than two years, traveled extensively with him in setting up the postwar expansion of the Naval ROTC Program, and later in the 1950s again served under him when Adams was president of the American Council on Education.[16]

Mather also stated that "Adams could work out beautiful compromises, but I never knew him to compromise a principle." He recalled that Adams frequently told his audiences the difference between "training" and "education": "You can train a seal, but you can't educate him."

John Wight, a McGraw-Hill sales representative who had called on Adams at Cornell, remembered him as highly articulate, kindly, and one who never scolded, but led by example. He said Adams was a superior leader.[17]

As officer in charge, Adams was given a free hand in assembling his staff. He was afforded the opportunity of looking over the orders of all naval officers being reassigned anywhere, and he was able to reach into civilian life and secure commissions for the men who accepted his in-

Lt. Raymond F. Howes, assistant to the officer-in-charge of the College Training Section until June 1945 and then officer-in-charge until the end of the program.

Raymond F. Howes

COLLEGE TRAINING SECTION

vitation to join the College Training Section, regardless of the physical condition of the candidate.

The prime example: his choice of Raymond F. Howes, the thirty-nine-year-old director of public information at Cornell. Howes recalled that he received waivers for weight, eyesight, teeth, chest expansion, and other physical standards before he was commissioned. The pharmacist's mate helping with the examination thought Howes might have set a Navy record for waivers![18]

But Adams wanted him, and Adams's authority was sufficient to get him. Lieutenant Howes took the oath in Ithaca on January 30 and went directly to the College Training Section, arriving in Washington on February 1, 1943, without having had to undertake a naval officer indoctrination course. Time did not permit. ·

After earning his B.A. at Cornell in 1924, Howes had become an instructor in English at the University of Pittsburgh, from which he received his M.A. degree in 1926. For the next ten years he taught English at Washington University in St. Louis, becoming assistant professor of English and director of forensics. He was also director of the Washington University News Bureau.

In 1936 Howes moved back to Cornell University, where he served as assistant to the dean of engineering until 1941. He first met Adams when the latter joined Cornell in 1940. Howes was also director of public information and assistant to the provost of Cornell, in addition to being the author or coauthor of four books and numerous magazine articles.

Howes occupied a room in the Adamses' house for the first five months he was in Washington. Thus, until Howes's wife and two boys moved there, he and Adams had a chance to talk over office matters on most evenings as well as during their working days. This closeness of contact no doubt contributed to the smooth working of the V-12 program.

According to other officers in the College Training Section, Howes was ideal in the post of *de facto* executive officer. He complemented Adams, seeing that Adams's directives were carried out in an expeditious manner. Dr. Mather remembered that Howes was effective in calming Adams when the latter occasionally reacted to the frustrations of the job.

When special trouble-shooting jobs arose, Howes was the man called upon. Mather recalled, "Howes handled some nasty situations for Adams." Many times Howes was sent to visit units to see if any basis existed for a disturbing report about the unit or its leadership. His recommendations to Adams were usually approved and carried out immediately.

When speeches on the V-12 program had to be prepared for Adm.

COLLEGE TRAINING SECTION

Randall Jacobs and other high-ranking officers, Howes was frequently given the assignment. He wrote most of Jacobs's widely quoted speech at the first Columbia Conference on May 14 and 15, 1943.[19]

When Adams moved upstairs to become officer-in-charge of the Administration Division in May of 1944, he purposely left Howes in the College Training Section at his same post under the new officer-in-charge, Lt. Comdr. William S. Thomson. That was to assure that the program would be kept on the course charted by Adams.

When Commander Thomson was released to inactive duty at the end of June of 1945, Howes was selected as his replacement. On July 2, 1945, he was designated as officer-in-charge of the College Training Section and was the man who closed up the program. He was thus the only officer who was with the College Training Section from start to finish. His key role is a major reason why the V-12 program always adhered to the principles laid down at the beginning. It was a consistent program.

In organizing the V-12 program, the College Training Section's role was part planner and part coordinator. Many of the key decisions were outside of Adams's control.

For instance, the selection of the V-12 schools was technically the responsibility of the Elliott Committee, a joint Army-Navy-War Manpower Commission group officially titled the Joint Committee for the Selection of Non-Federal Educational Institutions. Capt. William W. Behrens, USN, officer-in-charge of the Administration Section of the Training Division and the officer to whom Adams reported, was a member of the Elliott Committee. But the Committee merely rubber-stamped the agreement already reached between the Army and Navy on the division of schools between their programs.

The final determination of the outline of the Navy program was made by Admiral Jacobs. He had input, however, from many officers, including Captain Behrens; Lt. Comdr. Alvin Eurich of Curriculum and Standards; Capt. John C. Webb of Planning and Control; Bureau Counsel James A. Fowler, Jr.; Dean Joseph Barker, special assistant to Secretary Knox; Rear Adm. Ross T. McIntire, USN(MC), chief of the Bureau of Medicine and Surgery; and Adams.

Other matters that were beyond Adams's control included the negotiation of the contracts between the Navy and the colleges, curriculum matters, the selection of the V-12 candidates, and the development of standards for admission of medical and dental V-12s to the professional schools.

But Adams did have a great deal to do with the type of trainees chosen for the program. According to Howes, it was Adams who decided that many good officer candidates could be found in the enlisted ranks. That

COLLEGE TRAINING SECTION

decision was very important to the success of the V-12 program, for it brought a great deal of maturity and naval tradition into the program from the start.[20]

It was also Adams who insisted that the Navy show an interest in the individual person in the V-12, so that trainees were not treated as a faceless, homogeneous mass of sailors.

Adams had the key responsibility for coordinating the whole venture to see that the jobs assigned to other units were being done promptly and that all would be completed in time to begin the program on the scheduled start-up date of July 1.

Another of Adams's important jobs was to reassure both the colleges and the Navy that each would be treated fairly by the other. Communications given to both parties by Adams and his staff and by Dr. Robert B. Stewart, chairman of the Joint Army and Navy Board for Training Unit Contracts, were instrumental in achieving the mutual confidence so necessary between the Navy and the institutions.

Commander Adams also had to see that the program was organized so that it could be administered in a relatively simple manner after it began actual operation. He could not afford to let impractical or inefficient procedures get in the way.

Secretary of the Navy Frank Knox addressed the V-12s at Middlebury College on August 19, 1943. On the same tour he visited Dartmouth, Colgate, St. Lawrence, and Rochester. Knox and his successor, James V. Forrestal, had a keen interest in the V-12 program.

Middlebury College Archives

COLLEGE TRAINING SECTION

The College Training Section was under careful scrutiny all of the time. Vice Admiral Jacobs delegated most of the day-to-day decision making on policies for V-12 to his assistant chief, Rear Adm. Louis E. Denfeld, but Jacobs continued to keep himself well informed about the program, as his prominent part in both Columbia conferences (May 1943 and May 1944) indicates.

Secretary of the Navy Frank Knox had many friends who were presidents of V-12 colleges, and he was himself a trustee of a V-12 school, Alma College. His frequent appearances at V-12 schools reflected his interest.

Undersecretary James V. Forrestal was also cognizant of all of the major V-12 decisions, and he was pleased with the progress being made. Forrestal, when he was secretary of the Navy, once took a group of V-12s on a Potomac River cruise on the presidential yacht.[21]

Thanks to the leadership of Adams and the careful work of his staff, the V-12 program started smoothly on July 1, 1943. It was a wonderful forty-seventh birthday present for Arthur Stanton Adams. His efforts, and those of his staff, were recognized in a letter of personal commendation from Undersecretary Forrestal. On July 7, Forrestal sent this memorandum to Admiral Jacobs: "The V-12 College Program has been so well set up, and put into operation so smoothly that I think your responsible people deserve a word of commendation." A copy of the letter was placed in Adams's fitness report file.[22]

Adams also received a more tangible reward: he was promoted to full commander, to rank from July 3, 1943.

7

THE CTS
IN ACTION

THE IMPORTANT responsibilities entrusted to the College Training Section required highly skilled personnel. Most were hand-picked by Adams on the basis of his own acquaintanceship with them or the recommendations of his trusted associates. The urgency of getting the program into operation on July 1 guaranteed that they would face months of long work days.

In assembling the College Training Section team, Adams had first reached to the Cornell campus to draw in Howes, who was indispensable in getting the program off the ground. In 1982, Howes vividly recalled that shortly after he had reported to the Navy, he was advised by a lieutenant (junior grade) about the Navy's approved way of writing letters. The first few that Howes sent to Adams for approval drew a sharp reaction: "Where in the hell did you learn to write letters like that?" Howes replied that he was just trying to do his letters in the proper Navy style. Adams straightened him out. "Forget the Navy way!" he said. "I brought you in to write to academic people. Use good, plain English!" And that's how all of the correspondence of the College Training Section was handled thereafter.[1]

George Winchester Stone, Jr., an associate professor of English on sabbatical leave from George Washington University, became interested in the V-12 project when he was told of it by his close friend, Lt. Dwight Taylor, who was also one of Adams's friends. Taylor was then working in the Officer Assignment Section of the Bureau of Naval Personnel. Upon Taylor's recommendation, Adams asked Stone to accept a commission as a lieutenant (junior grade). When he agreed, it was arranged for Stone to report to the College Training Section as soon as he could be put in uniform, without the formal officer orientation course. In March of 1943 there just wasn't time for such delays. Stone was needed immediately.[2]

Other officers with special skills were also directed to report to the College Training Section. Among them were Lt. Mode L. Stone, director

THE CTS IN ACTION

of instruction of the Florida Department of Education; Ens. Urban J. Peters Rushton, an instructor of English at the University of Virginia; Lt.(jg) John N. G. Finley, associate professor of history, University of Virginia; Lt. Arthur E. Marston, a Ph.D. and professor of mathematics; Lt.(jg) DeWitt Fisher, an associate professor of engineering at Stevens Institute of Technology; Lt. William V. Weber, associate professor of political science at Western Michigan College; Lt. Comdr. William K. Thompson, a Naval Academy graduate of the class of 1925 currently working in insurance; Lt. Wilber K. McKee, professor of English in the School of Education, New York University; Lt.(jg) Albert L. Demaree, professor of history at Dartmouth College; and a number of others.

These officers, who joined over a period of several months, had various duties at different times. Adams liked to move them around so they could become more flexible, but he made some of them responsible for particular areas of the program.

Howes, of course, was the *de facto* executive officer of the section. His first extra task was to write the initial version of the *V-12 Manual.*

G. W. Stone, Jr., was assigned to be the expert on the V-12 bulletins, and later was put on the NROTC desk. Mode Stone was involved with inspecting facilities and often traveled with the negotiating parties. At an early point, Rushton was responsible for coordination with the medical and dental schools. Finley was assigned the theological schools, which earned him the nickname of "Padre Jack." Marston handled the statistics and was in charge of seeing that the V-12 units received their approximate quotas of trainees each term. Thompson was assigned to the NROTC desk and midshipmen's schools, and later moved to the language and military government schools. McKee answered much of the correspondence written directly to the College Training Section as well as the letters about V-12 that citizens had sent to President Roosevelt. Weber was involved with the inspection of campus housing as a member of the negotiating parties, and in September 1943 was transferred to the Officer Assignment Section of BuPers, where he handled most of the V-12 officer assignments.

In addition to the specific responsibilities mentioned above, most officers helped handle the mountain of correspondence that reached the College Training Section. What did the correspondence cover? Everything possible! An examination of the files for the period before startup reveals an amazing degree of intelligence, tact, patience, and kindness but firmness in the prompt answers sent out from CTS. And they didn't use mimeographed form letters, either! Each inquiry brought an individually typed answer.

Young men and their parents wrote to request "all the information available" on the college program. High school principals, librarians,

THE CTS IN ACTION

and college armed services liaison officers did the same. The available information was promptly mailed out.

Teachers wrote to offer their services in the college program. (Answer: The Navy doesn't hire instructors. That's up to the colleges.) Other letters asked whether teachers in the program were entitled to exemption from the draft. (Answer: That decision is not within the Navy's jurisdiction.) College presidents solicited V-12 contracts for their colleges. (Answer: The Selection Committee will determine such things.) Textbook companies asked what texts would be required for the Navy V-12 courses. (Answer: That's up to the individual colleges.)

Parents wrote to request waivers for their "brilliant sons" from the strict physical requirements for eyesight, number of teeth, weight, and height. (Answer: No waivers will be given. There are thousands of other ready and eager young men who can qualify without waivers.) Parents also wrote to ask that the requirement that candidates be unmarried be waived for their sons, arguing that the lovely wives would be a great help to their husbands in the program. (Answer: No waiver.) Mothers wrote asking that their twin sons who had both qualified for V-12 not be given assignments that would separate them. (Answer: No promises, but we will see what we can do.)[3]

Most time-consuming of all were the hundreds of letters from congressmen and senators pleading for the same special treatment for their constituents that other citizens sought in direct correspondence with the Navy. Those requests, which sometimes bordered on demands, were all ticketed with pink slips marked "urgent priority." They were given the same basic answers that the CTS gave to similar letters from citizens. But the importance of the congressman always meant that a somewhat lengthier answer was necessary, and it usually had to be bucked up the chain of command for a captain or officer of higher rank to sign. It was then sent to the congressman with a carbon that he could send along to his constituent. Thus, such requests always took more time to answer and the constituent got his reply much later because of the protocol that had to be observed.[4]

Some congressmen were not easily discouraged. Prodded by his constituents, Congressman Lyndon B. Johnson requested repeatedly that the applications of Baylor University and Texas A & I College in Kingsville for V-12 be reconsidered. The Navy's answer was still no.

Senator David Walsh, chairman of the powerful Senate Naval Affairs Committee, made a number of requests on a variety of matters, but most were turned down. When, after urging that a second V-12 entrance test be given to a "bright young man" from Massachusetts who had failed his first one, he learned that Lieutenant Howes had drafted the negative reply, he called him directly to appeal the decision. When

THE CTS IN ACTION

Howes remained firm, Walsh warned, "I've been getting nothing but unfavorable replies from you. If I ever find that you're doing favors for other members of Congress that you're not doing for me, I'll have your job!"

Howes coolly replied, "Sir, if you find that I ever allowed an incompetent to become an officer in the U.S. Navy, someone ought to have my job — because I wouldn't want it myself."[5]

Many parents directed their requests to President Roosevelt, who sent their letters to Secretary of the Navy Knox. They were then sent down the chain of command to be answered at the College Training Section and then passed up the line for a signature by an admiral or Secretary Knox. Those requests, although they took infinitely more of the Navy's limited time, received the same basic answers as those given to letters sent directly to the College Training Section.

Other responsibilities handled by the officers assigned to the College Training Section involved such matters as recommending officers for assignment to V-12 units; inviting college presidents to the Columbia Conference on May 14 and 15; advising colleges of the expected arrival dates of negotiating parties; determining quotas for various schools and assigning the appropriate number of trainees to those schools; helping to secure scarce material priorities for the schools that needed to alter or add to their physical plants; answering questions about special uniform designations for V-12 trainees; helping determine trainee eligibility for interscholastic athletics; and expediting the delivery of bunks, mattresses, study tables, and lamps. These were just a few of the hundreds of subjects handled by College Training Section officers in the months immediately preceding July 1.

After July 1, new types of problems arose involving troubleshooting, guiding commanding officers in coping with unexpected problems, and trying to correct the few difficult situations that developed between unit officers and school officials.

The major task during the first six months of the program's actual operation, however, was to interpret Navy policy to the officers and school officials of the 131 undergraduate units and the graduate schools. Policies and their interpretations had to be uniform, reasonable, and authoritative. The primary method of dissemination was the V-12 Bulletin series. (See Chapter 15, "V-12 Bulletins."

The College Training Section officers, including Adams and Howes, traveled to the units frequently. Junior officers often went out with the negotiating parties, but Adams and Howes usually made their visits to handle special problems or to attend regional or naval district meetings of V-12 commanding officers.

To meet further needs for officers for the College Training Section,

THE CTS IN ACTION

Oberlin College Archives

Comdr. Arthur S. Adams being greeted by Oberlin College president Ernest H. Wilkins upon Adams's arrival for a conference with V-12 college presidents from Ohio, September 8, 1943. Adams, Howes, and other College Training Section officers frequently traveled to such meetings.

THE CTS IN ACTION

Adams still reached for old friends in whom he had confidence. In September of 1943, he sent to the far reaches of Canada to requisition the services of Jean Paul Mather, an assistant from his days at the Colorado School of Mines. Mather, a professor of economics and still a civilian, was in Canada's Northwest Territories trying to straighten out problems plaguing the Alaskan oil pipeline. His orders directed him to proceed to BuPers via the first available transportation, which was a complex proposition in that remote area.[6] He was given waivers on the eyesight requirement and the formality of officer orientation.

John W. Wight, a 1939 Cornell graduate with a major in English, was a sales representative of McGraw-Hill who had called upon Adams at Cornell. Wight was a college traveler whose job it was to seek manuscripts for new books and to bring his company's books to the attention of department heads. When V-12 and the Army Specialized Training Program were being readied, Wight was transferred to Washington by McGraw-Hill to call on Adams and his counterpart in the Army to see what textbooks the programs would be using.

In July of 1943, Wight applied for and received a Navy commission as ensign. He was immediately sent to Jacksonville, Florida, for Air Gunnery Officers School. Adams learned that he was in the Navy, however, and promptly had him reassigned to the College Training Section, where his familiarity with officials at dozens of colleges and universities would be very useful. He was made Rushton's understudy, and when Rushton was assigned to the fleet, Wight was made head of the V-12 medical and dental schools, even though he was just an ensign. His opposite number in the Army was a full colonel.

Henry F. Thoma, professor of English at Cornell University, was already in Washington, working as a civilian in the Armed Forces Institute. Thoma had been a student of Howes at Washington University and they had continued their acquaintanceship at Cornell. After they ran into each other in a Washington coffee shop in the fall of 1943, Howes recommended Thoma to Adams, who quickly arranged a commission as a lieutenant (junior grade) for Thoma.[7] Thoma came into the CTS directly, without an orientation course. He was given the assignment of rewriting the *V-12 Manual*, which took about two months.[8]

Adams received regular reports on the qualifications of new officers reporting to orientation schools at various locations, and he could pick those he wanted for his section. One was Lt. Phil B. Narmore, professor of mechanics and engineering drawing at Georgia Tech. Narmore had applied for a commission in order to get into the fighting Navy, and he was chagrined to find that he had been requisitioned by Adams. While regretting his time at the College Training Section, Narmore gave Adams high marks for the way the section was administered.[9]

THE CTS IN ACTION

Another officer brought in was Lt. Raymond B. Pinchbeck, who was dean of Richmond College at the University of Richmond.

With the new focus on problems in the V-12 units, when Adams needed replacements or additions to the College Training staff, he decided to look to unit officers who appeared to be doing good jobs. Among those he brought in were Lt. George W. Hulme, Jr., commanding officer at Howard College in Birmingham, Alabama, who had previously been a county superintendent of schools in Alabama; Lt. Ellis Hartford, a University of Kentucky professor of education, who had been commanding officer at Drew University; Lt. Lewis Adams, professor of economics at Washington & Lee University, who had been executive officer at Harvard; and Lt. Comdr. William S. Thomson, Jr., the commanding officer at Arkansas A & M.

Thomson was a Naval Academy graduate in the class of 1922. His roommate recalled him as being very easygoing and always conjuring up ideas to someday make a killing in the stock market.[10] When the class of 1922 graduated, the nation and the world were disarming their navies, so the Navy could only afford to commission and put on active duty a limited number of the class members. In June of 1922, Thomson chose to return to civilian life and spent the next twenty years working first for the Diamond Salt Company in Louisiana and then drilling for oil in Texas. He became quite successful and enjoyed a prosperous life.

He volunteered for naval duty in 1942 and received a commission in the Naval Reserve as a lieutenant commander. He was ordered to the NROTC unit at the University of Oklahoma on June 4, 1942, to become an associate professor of naval science and tactics. At the commencement of the V-12 program, he was assigned to Arkansas A & M as commanding officer.

Late in November of 1943, Lieutenant Commander Thomson was ordered to Washington to report to the College Training Section. Although it is doubtful that Adams or anyone else had tagged Thomson for higher duties at the College Training Section at that time, in less than six months from his November arrival he succeeded Arthur S. Adams as the officer-in-charge.

Thomson appeared to be an excellent officer for continuing a program already in existence, and that is exactly the role that Arthur Adams saw for him when Adams was moved upstairs to become officer-in-charge of the Administration Division, which had direct jurisdiction over the College Training Section. Adams replaced Capt. William W. Behrens.

For slightly more than a year, Thomson kept the CTS on an even keel. The program during that time did not call for great innovations or changes, but the procedures for winding it down were already in place and operating when he left at the end of June of 1945 to return to civilian life.

THE CTS IN ACTION

Page Thomson Steele

Lt. Comdr. William Sillers Thomson, Jr., officer-in-charge of the College Training Section from May 1944 to June 1945. Previously, Thomson had been commanding officer of the V-12 unit at Arkansas A & M.

The officers serving in the College Training Section agreed unanimously that the office was always a busy place. They worked six full days a week and had very little time for social get-togethers. In the second year of the program, the staff did participate in some farewell parties for men leaving the section en route to other duties or a return to civilian life. But the officers lived in various parts of Washington or its suburbs and were usually in car pools, so there was very little intra-section socializing, even directly after working hours. About the only semblance of socializing was provided by Commander and Mrs. Adams, who from time to time invited some officers to their house for dinner.[11]

When Adams was promoted to captain in May of 1944, the officers of the College Training Section held a cocktail party in his honor, with Howes and Thoma handling the arrangements.[12]

At the start of the College Training Section the enlisted staff consisted

THE CTS IN ACTION

of five WAVE yeomen. The WAVEs were credited as being "very diligent and efficient" by officers who were interviewed forty years later.

One of the WAVEs, Irma Jane Irwin, Yeoman Second Class, had been private secretary to the vice president of a publishing company. She joined CTS on July 18, 1943, as Adams's secretary. According to Howes, she was put in charge of supervising the distribution of the V-12 bulletins and organizing the handling of the College Training Section's correspondence, which at that time amounted to about 250 items per day. On March 7, 1944, Commander Adams recommended her for a commission in the WAVEs because of her excellent performance.

WAVE Muriel Schaack served as Lieutenant Howes's secretary.[13]

The office was a happy one by all accounts, with everyone getting along well and respecting the leadership provided by Adams, Thomson, and Howes. The lunch hours gave the officers a chance for a bit of camaraderie and intellectual discussion. Dr. J. P. Mather recalled with great relish the many luncheons when McKee, Wight, and Thoma would "have at each other" in a heated — but friendly — fashion.[14]

Cameras were frowned upon at the Navy's Arlington Annex, so apparently no photos exist of the staff that so wisely directed the V-12 program. The names of some officers and most of the enlisted personnel would have remained buried in voluminous Navy records were it not for the following bit of anonymously produced 1944 Christmastime doggerel, which apparently covered nearly everyone who was currently or had been in the section. Some forty years later none of the CTS officers interviewed could recall who the author was; those who had been transferred earlier had never seen the piece.

The next-to-last line indicates that the greeting came from "Administration," which was Arthur Adams's location at that time. His conspicuous absence from the ditty and his lifetime interest in music and the arts beg the question: Did Captain Adams write it?[15]

> A Christmas Ode to Administration
>
> (With apologies to Frank Sullivan for the mayhem
> committed upon his verse.)
>
> Christmas greeting to College Training, seat of
> unrestricted learning
> Best of luck from old BUSANDA* and the Midshipmen's
> School to Henry Thoma
> From IBM to old Doc Sterner, a gold punch card and
> mechanical turner
> Something borrowed and something blue for Muriel
> Schaack and Ginger, too
>
> * Bureau of Supplies and Accounts

THE CTS IN ACTION

To Colorado's Jean Paul Mather, less play and more
    work in the role of father
To Zlotek, Hayes, Smith and Knupp, the yeomen gone,
    may their luck keep up
For Irma Irwin and Wilma Wilson some nylon hose.
    And for Lillian Olson
A medical student age 28, and for Frances Las a
    higher rate
For Bill McKee and his right hand, Laakko, no more
    mail in the postman's socko
For Belva Mitchell, a captured ensign, and a billet
    in Springfield Mass. for Fenton
A cold snowball from Alaska's hills as love's sweet
    song to Dixie Mills
A wassail bowl for the Boston lady, known in BuPers
    as Smoky Deady
A trip back home to old St. Louis for little Miss
    Bode. And Whooey!
A muscular, oscular, strong Marine for the Sullivan
    family's sweet Norine
For Wisconsin's jolly blue-eyed Ruth a sweetie-pie
    for her Christmas tooth
A Gray's Anatomy for Johnny Wight until he's back in
    McGraw-Hill's bight
A joyous leave in Jersey green for IBM's chic Edie
    Keane
For Ellis Hartford an onerous billet with Valdo
    Weber prepared to fill it
FOR EXECUTIVE HOWES A MECHANICAL MAN TO GIVE
    SURCEASE FROM THE NEED TO PLAN
A Kant's Critique for Arthur Marston, A BOTTOMLESS
    WELL FOR COMMANDER THOMSON
A helm for Hulme on a new destroyer, for Helen Rose
    a new employer
For Lewie Adams of Harvard Square an annual trip
    with a prepaid fare
To Cambridge town. To Betty Kofel a first class
    rate in next week's raffle*
Let's not forget our good John Young, although he's
    out on the sea foam flung
On Narmore, on Weber, on Mode Stone and Lee
Up Rushton, up Bloomfield, up Al Demaree
Go Pinchbeck, go Matthews, go Win Stone and Brownie
Back to the prune leagues with Padre Jack Finley
Wander no more in this uniformed college
Secure in escape from our fountain of knowledge
Kris Kringle's kiss for The Training Activity
Fill up the cup on the day of nativity
A Happy New Year to all, from Administration
For this year and next year, and for all the duration.[16]

---

* "Raffle" refers to the weekly posting of lists of promotions
    for enlisted personnel.

CURRICULUM

THE WHOLE TONE of the academic side of the V-12 program had been set long before the Columbia Conference on May 14 and 15, 1943, but at that meeting the purpose was reiterated by Admiral Jacobs: "This is a *college* program. Its primary purpose is to give prospective naval officers the benefits of a college education in those areas most needed by the Navy."[1]

That was its main purpose as far as the Navy was concerned. The program was not intended to protect young men from the fighting, to save colleges from closing, or to achieve any of the other ends often ascribed to it by admirers and critics.

To facilitate transfers between any of its 131 schools, the Navy decreed that the V-12 program be placed on a year-round schedule of three terms of four months each, beginning on July 1, November 1, and March 1. It also planned for five and one-half full days of work each week to achieve its objectives in the most expeditious manner. Every V-12 student was required to carry a minimum of seventeen hours of academic work (plus physical training) for each term. The standard period of academic work was considered fifty minutes for lectures and recitations and two hours and fifty minutes for laboratory and drafting room periods.

The Navy's serious intent was perhaps most evident in the no-nonsense, no-deviation curriculum prescribed for all entering freshmen. For those who were destined to become deck officers, it contained four terms, and there was no room for electives. Curriculum I and Curriculum III (later termed 101 and 102) were required for all trainees (except premedical and predental) entering their freshman year. This included both Navy and Marine trainees.

The first two terms were prescribed as follows in V-12 Bulletins Nos. 1 and 2.

CURRICULUM

Curriculum I

	Periods per week*			
	First Term		Second Term	
Mathematical Analysis I or III,				
II or IV (1 or 3, 2 or 4)	5†	(5)	5†	(5)
English I–II (E1–2)	3	(3)	3	(3)
Historical Background of				
Present World War I–II (H1–2)	2	(2)	2	(2)
Physics I–II (PH1–2)	4	(6)	4	(6)
Engineering Drawing and				
Descriptive Geometry (D1–2)	2	(6)	2	(6)
Naval Organization I–II (N1–2)	1	(1)	1	(1)
	17	(23)	17	(23)
Physical Training				
(PT 1–2–3–4–5)	18	(9½)	17	(8½)
	35	(32½)	34	(31½)

* Figures in parentheses indicate contact hours per week in class and laboratory. Figures outside parentheses indicate the number of meetings per week in class and laboratory.

† Mathematical Analysis I and II — combination course in mathematical analysis for students entering with two or less units of mathematics. Mathematical Analysis III and IV — algebra, trigonometry, and analytical geometry; or analytical geometry and calculus for students entering with two and one-half or more units of mathematics.

Following up for the deck candidates in the third and fourth terms were more mandatory courses without an elective in the bunch!

Curriculum III

	Periods per week‡			
	First Term		Second Term	
Navigation and Nautical Astronomy,				
I, II (M8, 9)	3	(3)	3	(3)
Chemistry Ia–IIa, and Engineering				
Materials (C1a–2a and C6)	4	(6)	4	(6)
Elementary Heat Power (ME2)	3	(5)		
Electrical Engineering (A) — Elementary				
(EE2)			3	(5)
Calculus I, II and Analytical Mechanics I				
(M5, 6; A1)	5	(5)	5	(5)
Naval History and Elementary				
Strategy (N3)	3	(3)		
Psychology I–General (PS1)			3	(3)
	18	(22)	18	(22)
Physical Training (PT2–3–4)	17	(8½)	17	(8½)
	35	(30½)	35	(30½)

‡ Figures in parentheses indicate contact hours per week in class and laboratory. Figures outside parentheses indicate the number of meetings per week in class and laboratory.

CURRICULUM

The early outlines of the V-12 program had been largely shaped by the interaction of Dean Joseph Barker of Columbia University, who was serving as special assistant to the secretary of the Navy, and the Navy Advisory Educational Council, which had been set up in October of 1942 and utilized all of the members of the earlier committee on the V-1 program plus some new appointments. The Bureau of Naval Personnel had adopted all of the recommendations of that council, which was why the Navy's college program proved so acceptable to the colleges. The format of the Army Specialized Training Program, on the other hand, met with general opposition from the educational institutions.[2]

Admiral Jacobs realized that the educational content of the Navy college training program was vital to its success, so he left the planning to experts in the field. He asked his aide, Lt. Comdr. Milton C. Mumford, USNR, to find the right man to direct the curriculum portion of the program. Mumford contacted the head of the College Entrance Examination Board, John M. Stalnaker, who quickly suggested Dr. Alvin C. Eurich, professor of education at Stanford University, who was then working at the Office of Price Administration in Washington. Upon Mumford's recommendation, Admiral Jacobs selected Eurich to head the Standards and Curriculum Section of the Training Division and offered him a commission as a lieutenant commander.[3] The Standards and Curriculum Section was involved with supervision of the course content of every kind of training, not just V-12. The V-12 program occupied a major portion of its activities for the next few months, however. While the Office of Bureau Counsel was negotiating with the colleges and the College Training Section was working with the Officer Procurement Division on the numerous details of selecting the trainees, the Standards and Curriculum Section started work on the content of the educational part of the program.

The new V-12 students had diverse backgrounds. They ranged from young men just finishing high school to those who had completed seven semesters of undergraduate work in various majors. The College Training Section and the Standards and Curriculum Section reached an agreement on the terminology for differentiating these students. They were divided into the "regulars" and the "irregulars."

Raymond F. Howes explained the difficulty in finding a classification system in which one class did not seem to be superior to the other. For instance, if "A" and "B" were chosen, A would seem to have primacy; the use of numerical classification would have led to the same conclusion. It was felt that "regulars" and "irregulars" would not convey the presumption that one group was superior to the other.[4]

The regulars were those who had no college experience. They were required to take the standard curricula with no opportunity for elec-

CURRICULUM

tives. The irregulars were men who had college experience. They were to be given one or more V-12 semesters during which they would continue in whatever major they had already chosen. The irregulars, however, were expected to complete certain requirements set up for V-1s — specifically, a year of both math and science.[5]

One V-12 irregular later complained, "I wanted to take Chaucer but the Navy made me take physics. That was the price I had to pay to be in the V-12 Program."[6]

When Lt. Comdr. Alvin C. Eurich joined the V-12 program, he was given what he considered the "best of all possible instructions." Admirals Jacobs and Denfeld told him, "Al, we don't want a Navy curriculum; we want the best college education you can sell us. We'll take care of the Navy end of it but give these men a solid education."[7] With that direction, Eurich had a virtual free hand.

But Eurich was not without proffered assistance. Suggestions poured in from every quarter, not only from the Navy and the colleges, but also from textbook publishers and professional societies such as the Mathematical Society of America and the College Physics Society. The deans of engineering schools hurriedly assembled in Washington on March 18 to offer their contribution.[8]

Lieutenant Commander Eurich acknowledged that Dean Ivan Crawford of the University of Michigan College of Engineering was of great assistance to him in determining the curriculum requirements for the engineering specialties.[9]

With all of the consultations from professional societies, educators, and the Navy, Eurich and his assistants (Lt. Comdr. Frank Bowles, USNR; Lt. Comdr. A. J. Bartkey, USNR; and Lt. Comdr. Ray N. Faulkner, USNR) put together a list of suggested curricula which was adopted by the director of training and the chief of personnel.

As the academic planning moved ahead, the physical training portion of the V-12 program became quite an issue. Commander Gene Tunney, former heavyweight champion of the world, was in charge of the Physical Training Section of the Training Division of the Bureau. Not only was he totally opposed to drinking and smoking, he is remembered by the officers who dealt with him as a staunch advocate of calisthenics at every conceivable time. Furthermore, he was firmly opposed to having the V-12 trainees take part in intercollegiate athletics.[10] (See Chapter 33, "Intercollegiate Athletics.")

The physical training program was to take up nine and one-half hours per week during the first term and eight and one-half hours thereafter. It consisted of calisthenics for twenty minutes daily, six days a week; muster and inspection fifteen minutes daily, six days a week; conditioning (which included more calisthenics) and combative activi-

CURRICULUM

ties five hours weekly; and, during the first term, military drill, one hour weekly. For the second-term men, the military drill was dropped but the calisthenics and muster activities remained, and the five hours of conditioning and combative activities could be replaced by "maintenance activities," sports such as soccer, handball, and basketball for those who passed rigid minimums on the "strength tests" that were given every eight weeks.[11]

When the V-12 curricula are examined there appears to be a strange dichotomy. The irregulars were permitted to pursue their existing majors with very little interference, thus demonstrating that the Navy firmly believed in the virtues of a liberal arts education in preparing men to assume the responsibilities of officers. On the other hand, the regulars were given no choices and precious little exposure to the liberal arts as they pursued a difficult curriculum narrowly devoted to subjects considered more practical in equipping them for the duties of a naval officer. Theirs was really a pre-engineering curriculum.[12] The two widely differing college pathways were both planned to prepare the V-12s for their later duties as officers of the United States Navy.

In explaining this dichotomy, Dr. Alvin C. Eurich later said, "It would have placed an unreasonable demand upon the 'irregulars' . . . if we had required them to start over with the freshmen courses. This followed the Navy's policy of recognizing fully any college work that the student had completed."[13]

The Navy reached an early and popular agreement with the institutions regarding the eligibility of faculty to teach a course. That was to be determined solely by the institution, without prescription of criteria by the Navy. It was also agreed that the faculty teaching loads would be increased commensurate with the heavier demands of the accelerated program.[14] The institutions were also allowed to establish the content of the courses and to choose the textbooks as long as they conformed rather closely to current standards in the colleges and universities of the nation.

Bulletin No. 101, issued on November 1, 1943, contained the "Navy V-12 Curricula Schedules and Course Descriptions," replacing V-12 Bulletins Nos. 1 and 2. On page 2 of Bulletin No. 101, it was noted that "course descriptions were written with the aid of consultants who are specialists in the fields covered." A paragraph on "college credit" explained that each institution "shall determine whether or not credit toward a degree at that institution will be given for the completion of courses in the various curricula. Inasmuch as the content of most courses is practically equivalent to that of standard college courses in the same subjects, it is hoped that credit will be given quite generally."

The bulletin also stated that students could be dropped from the

CURRICULUM

program for failure to maintain adequate scholarship standards, for conduct requiring disciplinary action, or for failure to demonstrate satisfactory officer-like qualifications.

The schedules of V-12 curricula covered thirty-four pages in Bulletin No. 101, followed by two pages of minimum requirements to be completed in college by V-1 and V-7 transfers and all other students who had entered after completing some previous college work. Then followed fifty-five pages devoted to course descriptions.

In general, college and university administrators and faculty members were highly pleased by the Navy's approach to the College Training Program. The Navy's promise to keep hands off the instruction was well received. The Navy kept that promise, with only minor exceptions occasioned by an inordinate number of failures in midshipmen's school by the V-12s from a few colleges. [15]

The Navy's handling of curriculum matters established a fine starting point for July 1, 1943, and ensured the cooperation of faculty members throughout the life of the V-12 program.

9

OFFICERS FOR
THE UNITS

THE TRAINING DIVISION could not wait until school selection, contract negotiations, and all the details of the program were completed to start the search for the officers to operate the units. Although their procurement was strictly a function of the Office of Naval Officer Procurement, it was up to the Training Division to determine what it needed.

In January 1943, Training had decided that two officers would be sufficient to run each V-12 unit of six hundred trainees or less. Without knowing exactly how many units would be selected, Training asked the director of Naval Officer Procurement to find two hundred new officers who had the requisite qualifications. Later that number was increased to three hundred.[1]

These general specifications were set for the V-12 officers. They were to be between thirty-five and forty-five years of age; have a bachelor's degree, preferably in science or engineering; have experience in an executive or training capacity; and present a good military appearance.

According to the plan, those who qualified would be commissioned as lieutenants. In practice, those who met the qualifications but were in the lower end of the age range received the rank of lieutenant (junior grade) and became the executive officers. Older candidates were generally made commanding officers. The Navy did not wish to weaken its current commissioned strength to operate the new program, so at first it made no effort to find such officers within the commissioned establishment.

It should be noted that the twenty-seven NROTC schools were all assigned V-12 units. These NROTC units were already commanded by a regular Navy captain, who served as commanding officer of the V-12 unit, too. Officers in charge were still required for the new V-12 contingent, however.[2]

Information intended to attract officer candidates for the V-12 program was distributed in educational circles by direct letter and through pertinent publications.

OFFICERS FOR THE UNITS

It soon occurred to some college presidents that their schools might benefit by recommending to the Navy some eligible professors, who would soon be in oversupply in view of the rapidly declining enrollments. They forwarded such names — with recommendations — to the director of Naval Officer Procurement.[3]

The V-12 billet was recognized as an attractive proposition by many professors. They could serve their country, which was of great importance to them and to their communities. But they could also be assured of remaining in an academic environment and being able to have their families accompany them wherever they might be sent.

The suggested age range did not deter older men from applying. Perhaps the oldest applicant commissioned was Professor Lee Norvelle of Indiana University, who was in his fiftieth year when made a naval lieutenant.[4]

Most of the unit officers came from the faculties of colleges and universities. There were also a substantial number of deans, a few college presidents, and a few high school principals and county superintendents of schools.

Their academic backgrounds worked out exceptionally well, because they had little trouble relating to the problems and frustrations of the college officials. They were also understanding of and sympathetic to the trials and tribulations of the trainees. They realized that the trainees were carrying a much heavier load than the typical college student had borne prior to that time. This understanding was highly important to the success of the program.

To fill the increased quota of three hundred officers, some already commissioned officers with the requisite backgrounds were assigned from other duties, and a few over-age and previously retired regular Navy officers were ordered to V-12 units. Some of the latter worked out very well, but the group also produced some of the more serious problems because they could not all adapt to an academic environment. (See Chapter 28, "Navy-College Relations," and Chapter 29, "The Commanding Officers.")

When the newly procured officers reported for active duty, most were sent to the Naval Officer Orientation School at Columbia University, where they were given the same training provided for officers heading directly to general line duty. They were taught navigation, ordnance, and seamanship, all of which would be of minimal use in leading a V-12 unit. After a substantial chorus of complaints reached the Navy Department, the Training Division altered the orientation program to cover subjects that would be helpful in operating a V-12 unit, such as naval correspondence, orientation, and naval record keeping.

The aim of the College Training Section was to get the new command-

OFFICERS FOR THE UNITS

ing officers to the schools about thirty days before the start-up date of July 1. Where possible, the new commanding officers were ordered to attend the Columbia Conference held in New York City on May 14 and 15. There they learned the details of the program and received their first printed guide for operating their units. (See Chapter 14, "The Columbia Conference.")

Officers were assigned to the units in typical Navy fashion. They were asked to state their preferences, which in some cases were met exactly and in others totally ignored. The choices of officers who had been on active duty for some time were honored, as happened with Lt. John Guy. On the other hand, some of the newly commissioned, such as Lieutenant Norvelle, felt that the Navy was determined to give each new officer just the opposite of what he requested. Following his view of the procedure, Norvelle requested "anywhere but California" and was dutifully rewarded with an assignment to the College of the Pacific in Stockton, California. He noted that Lt. James Case had requested "California" but ended up assigned to Howard College in Birmingham, Alabama.[5]

In addition to the skippers and execs, the Navy ended up assigning some additional officers to most units to handle various other responsibilities. For instance, many colleges were not equipped to attend to the medical needs of so many trainees. Often the college physician or the local physician who served the college students had already joined the armed forces. In such cases, the Navy detailed a medical officer and sometimes a dental officer to care for the trainees in the unit.

A concentrated physical training program was also required of colleges, which had already seen their ranks of qualified athletic department personnel decimated by enlistments and the draft. Thus, in many colleges a Navy athletic officer was also detailed, along with several enlisted "athletic specialists," who may have been chief petty officers or first- or second-class athletic specialists. Most of those men had been coaches or college or professional athletes. A substantial number of the chief specialists were later commissioned and reassigned to other duty.

The matter of pay was important to everyone, so arrangements had to be made to include 131 units and seventy thousand men in the jurisdictions of existing pay offices, such as those found in large cities or nearby Navy bases, or in newly established disbursing offices. In nearly all instances the new offices were placed in charge of young WAVE officers who had just received their indoctrination training. Frequently, their assignments made them responsible for handling disbursing duties at anywhere from two to six V-12 units. Ens. Jane Rollman, for example, was assigned as disbursing officer for the units at Emory and Henry College in Virginia, Milligan College, Carson-New-

OFFICERS FOR THE UNITS

man College, and the University of the South in Tennessee; the four colleges spanned a distance of 250 miles.[6]

With the unit officers selected the V-12 program was ready to begin. Throughout the month of June the officers arrived at their posts; they found colleges in various stages of preparation to receive the trainees on July 1, 1943.

10

SELECTION
OF TRAINEES

A MAJORITY of the V-12 trainees for the start-up on July 1, 1943, had already been chosen. They were then in the Navy V-1 or V-7 or the Marine III(d) reserve programs and were enrolled in colleges and universities across the land.

Originally, these men had been promised that they could continue in college until graduation. Shortly thereafter the Navy men would be called to active duty to fill a slot in a reserve midshipmen's school, whereas the marines would go to boot camp before moving on to officer candidate school. But the reduction of the draft age to eighteen (from twenty) changed the ground rules for these reservists. Since the announcement of the V-12 program in December of 1942, they knew that they would be called to active duty in the summer of 1943 to complete whatever number of terms would be allotted to them by the Navy or Marines before being sent on to the advanced schools. But even if all of these reservists were brought to active duty, there would not be enough. It was finally decided in June of 1943 that seventy thousand men were needed for the V-12 program.

Besides the class III(d) reservists who were already in college, the Marine Corps had enlisted some seventeen-year-old high school seniors with the understanding that upon graduation they would continue their education by enrolling at an accredited college. The details of the Marine component of the V-12 program were announced by the Corps on March 24, 1943.

The V-1s and the Marine Corps reservists who were classified as freshmen or sophomores still had one more hurdle: a Navy "general intelligence qualifying examination" to be given on April 20, 1943. Those who passed went on to V-12, while the failures were given the opportunity to resign from the reserves or to be sent to general enlisted service at the end of their current college term. The failures were few.[1]

To fill the quota for the V-12 program other men were drawn from the V-5 aviation cadet program, from the trainees already on active duty on ships or at shore stations, and from the seventeen- to nineteen-year-old civilians who were (or soon would be) high school graduates or were already enrolled in colleges but had not enlisted in any reserve program.

SELECTION OF TRAINEES

The V-5 aviation cadet program had been building up rapidly and it soon became apparent to the Bureau of Aeronautics that more young men had been enlisted than could be trained at that time. BuAer had developed a reputation among the Navy establishment as always enlisting more than it needed in its program. But while the rate of airplane production was quite well scheduled, the number of pilot casualties in the Pacific was completely unknown, so the Bureau decided to err on the high side of personnel requirements, an altogether unsurprising decision. The V-12 program was used as a "holding pattern" that would deliver the aviation trainees to the BuAer program after two terms in the V-12.

The Navy had decided that many educationally qualified enlisted men already on active duty should be given an opportunity for a commission.[2] It was felt that their naval experience would be particularly useful in adapting to the role of officer. As first set up, the quota for fleet men was to be ten thousand in the first year of V-12, with one-third of them entering the program on July 1 and one-third each on November 1, 1943, and March 1, 1944. (See Chapter 18, "The 'Old Salts.' ")

The Marine Corps established a quota of one thousand enlisted men from active duty over the first year of V-12, with one-third reporting at the beginning of each term.[3] (See Chapter 20, "Marine V-12s.")

Minor additions to the V-12 program came from the U.S. Coast Guard, which was given an enlisted quota of 150 men for the first term and 125 for the second,[4] and from the Army Enlisted Reserve Corps students. The latter were enrolled in those colleges and universities where all of the male students were required to take ROTC training. At the time of their enlistment in the Reserve Officers Training Corps, they were given the opportunity to express a preference for another branch of the service. Those who had chosen the Navy or Marine Corps would be allowed to enter the V-12 program if they requested it when the members of the Enlisted Reserve Corps were called to active service.

Even with all of the enlisted components combined, there was still a substantial need for additional trainees, so plans were made early in 1943 to conduct a nationwide examination for seventeen- to nineteen-year-olds who would be graduated from high school no later than June of 1943 to find "the cream of the crop" in that age group. It was planned to give the examination in every high school in the continental United States. In addition, the exam was to be given at many colleges and universities to accommodate college students who were not in any reserve program. Many college students had left high school before graduation in order to complete as much college work as possible before entering the armed forces.[5]

The examination was set for April 2, 1943. More than 300,000 young men would take it.

11

THE NATIONWIDE
EXAMINATION

NOTICES of the April 2 qualification test for the Navy College Training Program were sent on March 2 to high schools and colleges across the land. The letter explained that "the purpose of the V-12 Program is to produce Naval Officers." The test was given prominent attention by the daily and weekly newspapers, high school and college papers, and the radio. Special radio announcements were prepared by the Navy Radio Section for use on the programs appealing to high school students, such as the "Jack Benny Show" (America's most popular radio program), the "Coca-Cola Spotlight Band," and the "Charlie McCarthy Show."[1]

In its February 20 official disclosure of the V-12 program details the Navy listed these qualifications for men taking the exam:

1. High school or preparatory school graduates who will have attained their seventeenth and not their twentieth birthday by July 1, 1943, or
2. High school or preparatory school seniors who will be graduated by July 1, 1943, in the same age bracket, or
3. Students who do not hold certificates of graduation from a secondary school but who are continuing their education in an accredited college or university in the same age bracket as mentioned above.[2]

In addition to the educational and age qualifications, the civilian candidates had to also meet the following requirements:

1. Be a male citizen of the United States,
2. Be morally and physically qualified, including a minimum visual acuity of 18/20,
3. Be unmarried and agree to remain unmarried until commissioning, unless sooner released by the Navy Department, and
4. Evidence potential officer qualifications, including appearance and scholarship records.

The preliminary application forms were distributed through local high schools and colleges. To gain admittance to the examination, each ap-

THE NATIONWIDE EXAMINATION

plicant was required to submit the form, properly filled out and certified by his high school principal or college administrator, who was directed not to approve those who were obviously below physical or educational standards. The Army was invited to participate in the test, but at the time of the announcement it was strictly a Navy examination. On March 8, however, the Army decided to join in the testing and to share the costs. Accordingly, on March 12, a letter went out to all high school principals and college presidents noting the Army's participation and pointing out that men through age twenty-one would now be permitted to take the exam, but that those twenty and twenty-one would be above the Navy's age range and thus eligible only for the Army.

This letter was followed up by a joint letter signed by Rear Adm. Randall Jacobs, Brig. Gen. M. G. White, and United States Commissioner of Education John W. Studebaker, asking that the widest possible publicity be given to the opportunity provided by the examination and noting that it would be at least six months before another test would be held. It was also explained that in subsequent tests, high school graduation would be required, so men who had skipped that formality in order to enter college earlier had only this chance to take the test.

The Navy had contracted with the College Entrance Examination Board (CEEB), of Princeton, New Jersey, to conduct the test. The CEEB, which had forty-three years of experience in testing college applicants, subcontracted with ten regional agencies to handle the mechanics.

On April 2, 1943, the examination was given to 315,952 young men across the continental United States.[3] The CEEB estimated that approximately 60 percent of the male students in the eligible age category took the examination.

This examination was a milestone in American education, the largest test of its kind and the first one ever offered to every male student, regardless of income level or educational background. It offered a doorway to a college education to thousands of young men who would otherwise have been unable to afford it. This is a fact gratefully recognized by many former V-12 trainees.[4]

At the start of the test the applicants could express a preference on the answer sheet for either the Army or the Navy. If they did not mark a preference or if they were twenty or twenty-one, they were put into the Army's category.

The two-hour examination was specially designed by the College Entrance Examination Board "to measure potentiality for college work rather than to rely exclusively upon extent of academic information."[5] The board thus recognized that a testing program that included the entire country had to be carefully designed to test only knowledge that

THE NATIONWIDE EXAMINATION

men of divergent backgrounds would have had relatively equal opportunities to acquire. "Accordingly, the test items selected were those relating to common experience but requiring clear thinking and practical judgment, placing the emphasis on aptitude rather than on special scholastic training."

The test included 150 multiple-choice questions in four principal categories: verbal, scientific, reading, and mathematical. The verbal section included sixty questions relating to word meaning, word usage, and general manipulation of verbal material.[6] The scientific section contained forty questions of "the common-sense physics type. The technical information required to answer them is not great, and for the most part intelligent scientific interest and alert observation would prove as valuable as academic training."[7]

The third section consisted of four paragraphs of about two hundred words each. Five questions followed each paragraph, and five answers were suggested to each question, the candidate being required to choose the best answer. "Here the candidate's ability to understand relatively difficult (but not technical) material was under investigation — an ability which is, of course, basic to college success." Three of the paragraphs dealt with economic and historical subject matter while the fourth was concerned with early experimentation on "spontaneous generation" of bacteria.[8]

The final section of the test covered mathematical material and was comprised of thirty questions. They were designed to test the candidate's facility with numbers, presupposing a background of elementary algebra and geometry.[9]

The tests were shipped from a central office in Chicago to the high schools and colleges as soon as the institution's order was received in the regional office. The packet included instructions for the supervisor to remove the manual accompanying the package and then place the sealed tests in the school's safe until the morning of the examination, when they were to be opened in the presence of all of the applicants.

On April 2 the test began at 9:00 A.M. sharp; the instructions were given in advance. The questions were contained in a booklet furnished to each applicant. He was supplied an answer sheet with blanks for his name, address, and date of birth, and a place to indicate his preference of service branch.

According to the CEEB, that examination was "the most extensive simultaneous testing project ever undertaken." Of the 315,952 men who took the examination, 117,295 expressed a preference for the Navy.[10]

The test ended promptly at 11:00 A.M. The booklets and answer sheets were collected and immediately sent to the regional test headquarters where the scoring was done.

THE NATIONWIDE EXAMINATION

The test went smoothly all across the nation, with only a few problems being reported to the Navy. At one small Illinois high school no one showed up to take it, so the principal shipped the papers back unopened. When the test didn't arrive in time to give it in one small Pennsylvania town, the principal sent all of his applicants to nearby Johnstown to take it. In another small town, the packet arrived on the afternoon of April 2, so the principal asked if a make-up date could be scheduled. Admiral Denfeld said it couldn't but noted that the next test would be given late in November.[11]

And at one Oklahoma high school, the principal confessed that he had lost both his supervisor's report sheet and the mailing label to affix to the return envelope, so he sent everything to the Navy Department in Washington, asked forgiveness for his carelessness, and expressed the hope that the papers would reach their proper destination. The Navy sent those answers to the regional agency handling Oklahoma, and at least one of the boys from that high school did enter the V-12 program.[12]

According to the CEEB, two hours was sufficient time for the vast majority of the applicants to complete all of the questions, and thus the test was scored strictly on the basis of the number of correct answers, without deducting for wrong answers as a penalty for guessing. Had the time been insufficient for the majority of the students, the CEEB indicated that it might have deducted for wrong answers. Each paper was scored twice, and a third time if the first two totals did not agree.

The CEEB noted that the Navy used a quota system "whereby from each state and each section of larger states would be selected a number of students proportional to the state population. Thus the 'critical' or minimum score for eligibility varied from state to state, ranging from 71 to 106." The 106 was New Hampshire and the 71 was in western Tennessee. Because of the variation in eligible scores from state to state and district to district, the Navy saw to it that all men who made a score of seventy-five or better, regardless of their districts, actually received consideration for the Navy program.

The regional offices then sent the record sheets of the men falling within the eligible range to the College Training Section in the Bureau of Naval Personnel.

In late April or early May those scoring above the minimum acceptable score received a letter from the nearest Office of Naval Officer Procurement telling them to report to that office at a stipulated time for an interview. Receipt of that letter marked an eventful day in the lives of the thousands of young men who were eventually selected for the program. But selection was not automatic; a winnowing process involving strict physical requirements that could not be waived and close scrutiny for academic excellence and officer-like qualities was still ahead.

12

INTERVIEW
AND PHYSICAL

A TYPICAL LETTER that went out in late April to a successful examination applicant directed the man to "appear at the above Office of Naval Officer Procurement at 10:00 A.M. on May 3 for interview. It is imperative that the appointment be kept inasmuch as failure to do so may result in forfeiture of your opportunity to make application."[1]

The applicant was notified that he must be physically qualified, as immediate rejection would result from failure to meet physical qualifications. One requirement was "that you must have minimum visual acuity of 18/20 each eye correctable to 20/20. It is suggested, therefore, that you do not strain your eyes before coming to the Procurement Office. If you do not meet this vision requirement or are not otherwise physically qualified, it is suggested that you do not go to the expense of making the trip to the Procurement Office." The applicant was advised to notify the office if he were unable or did not intend to apply for enlistment under the program.

He was also admonished that "it is absolutely essential that the following papers properly filled out are presented at the time of your appearance. If any of these papers are missing, or if they are not properly prepared, you will not be able to make application." The papers listed were (1) a birth certificate (also evidence of citizenship if not native born); (2) the consent of parents (required if the applicant would not be eighteen before May 1, 1943); (3) three letters of recommendation (including one from the high school principal, if the applicant was a high school student, or from a dean or armed services representative, if the applicant was a college student); (4) a high school transcript (also a college transcript, if the applicant was a college student); (5) a letter of approximately fifty words explaining why the applicant desired training in the Navy College Training Program; (6) two pictures, approximately two and one-half inches by two and one-half inches, one full face and one profile; and (7) Form NRB 24A, the application for enlistment.

The applicant was also advised that all of the travel expense was to be borne by him, and that he should be prepared to spend two days at the facility because it might take that long to complete the application,

INTERVIEW AND PHYSICAL

physical examination, and interviews. "Therefore, you should bring sufficient funds to pay for overnight accommodations if necessary."

In a final paragraph of information he was told that approximately one-half of the candidates who would be selected for the program would be placed on active duty in college on about July 1, 1943, and the other half on about November 1. No assurance could be given to an individual at the time of his enlistment that he would be ordered to active duty on a specific date.

When the candidate presented himself for the physical examination, he was in the company of many other applicants, all as frightened as he. It was a tough physical! Eyes were the cause of the most rejections, but overweight and such unexpected causes as "severe overbite" or "too many missing teeth" also resulted in disqualification. No waivers were granted. This remained a consistent policy of the College Training Program, despite many pleas from parents, senators, and congressmen for waivers of requirements in individual instances.

Although the original plan was to have the Selection Board interview the candidates, in most cases that did not occur. It will be recalled that the Selection Board consisted of a naval officer, an educator, and FDR's "good-common-sense civilian." The numbers probably dictated the abandonment of the personal interview by the Selection Board.[2]

As a consequence, the Selection Board had to rely on the record in the materials brought in by the student, including his transcript, and two interviews of the applicant by naval officers attached to the Procurement Office. Special attention was paid to evidence of his leadership in high school organizations.

The Selection Board reviewed each file and made its recommendation. The files of the College Training Section were later sprinkled with letters from board members who regarded that service as one of the most important things they had ever done.[3]

Sixteen thousand young men were selected for induction into V-12 as a result of this process. It was planned to call half to active duty on July 1 and the remainder on November 1.[4]

A number of men who later achieved high rank in the armed forces were selected for the V-12 program but resigned to accept appointments to one of the service academies. Their applications had been made earlier, but had not been acted upon at the time they were chosen for V-12. Among these was Stansfield Turner, who resigned as apprentice seaman, class V-12, to accept an appointment to the Naval Academy. He later became a full admiral and was director of the CIA in the Carter administration.[5] Jeremiah A. Denton, Jr., later rear admiral and U.S. senator from Alabama, spent just twelve days in V-12 at Millsaps College before his Annapolis appointment came through.[6]

INTERVIEW AND PHYSICAL

Another V-12 resigned from the Navy in June of 1943 to accept an appointment to the U.S. Military Academy at West Point. Considering his later rise to general in the U.S. Army, his service as White House chief of staff in the Nixon administration, his term as commanding general of the North Atlantic Treaty forces, and his four years as secretary of state in the first Reagan term, a question arises. How would Alexander M. Haig's success have been affected if he had stayed in the Navy as a V-12 and had later become Admiral Haig?[7]

Candidates selected by the board were notified promptly, usually within a week of their appearance for their interview and physical. The letter arrived from the director of Naval Officer Procurement at the location where the interview had taken place. "Subject: Acceptance in Class V-12."

The good news was presented in a mimeographed letter, which had only two bits of original input: the signature of the officer responsible for sending it and the name of the applicant, usually with only his initials. The good news read:

> 1. You are hereby notified that you have been selected for enlistment in Class V-12, U.S. Naval Reserve.
> 2. You are requested to report immediately for enlistment in this office or to the nearest main or semi-main Navy Recruitment Station if the travel is thereby reduced. . . . You *must* enlist before your eighteenth birthday.[8]

The applicant was also told to fill out the special application blank attached and give it to the recruiting officer effecting the enlistment. He was further advised that he would get orders to report for active duty at a college on or about July 1 or November 1. "If you do not receive active duty orders by July 1, 1943, you may assume that you will receive them on or about November 1, 1943."

The applicant then reported to either the Office of Naval Officer Procurement or the nearest listed recruiting station to be sworn in. When he left after that brief ceremony, he was given a letter of that date which said, "Gentlemen: This is to certify that the subject named man has this date been enlisted as an apprentice seaman in Class V-12 of the United States Naval Reserve." It was signed by an otherwise unidentified person with the words "by direction" under his signature.

As he returned home with that important piece of paper in his pocket, the new apprentice seaman in the U.S. Naval Reserve was facing a great opportunity. He would now wait anxiously to see if his orders would arrive during the month of June.

13

THE COLLEGES
PREPARE

BEFORE receiving a letter of intent, most of the colleges chosen for V-12 began in earnest to prepare for the July 1 start-up date. There was no time to lose. The expectation that good faith would prevail gave the colleges the courage to move ahead in preparing for the program. They were not disappointed.

Although there were inevitable arguments between the Navy and the schools over whether a necessary repair or improvement was an allowable commissioning expense or simply part of the college's deferred maintenance, the entire operation of shaping up all 131 schools to the Navy's standards came off surprisingly well.

There were major improvements to be made at some colleges. For instance, at Arizona State Teachers College it was necessary to order totally new kitchen equipment, and the Navy helped make priorities available for such materials, which were in critically short supply.

At Muhlenberg College, the dining room had to be enlarged to accommodate the V-12 unit. At Whitman College, dining space changes were still going on in Lyman Hall when the trainees arrived, so they were fed in the girls' dormitory until the remodeling was completed. Swarthmore College had originally asked for — and been granted — a quota of 450 V-12s, but when it learned that the Navy would not pay for the new dining room necessary to handle a unit of that size, it cut back its request to three hundred.

As mentioned previously, Marquette University found itself short of both housing and messing facilities and so purchased a nearby small hotel and leased another.

At the University of Louisville and the University of Oklahoma adequate housing was not available, so the universities began a crash program to build new dormitories, which could more fittingly be described as barracks. Louisville financed its new buildings, which included a mess hall, by a special fund drive that received contributions from the city, the university, and local business interests. This rush program brought a dedication visit by Rear Adm. Randall Jacobs, chief of the

THE COLLEGES PREPARE

Bureau of Naval Personnel, on July 21, 1943, three weeks after the program began.

Following the Navy's recommendation, the University of Louisville's new dorms had been constructed without interior doors, but it soon became evident that such an economy was not in the best interests of good scholarship. In September room doors were installed, with the Navy's consent.

Some schools that had seldom or never had a summer program needed window screens, especially for kitchen and dining facilities. Carroll College of Helena, Montana, had to install screens for the first time, and the University of Virginia had to add them to some of its 120-year-old dormitories.

A surprising number of the smaller V-12 colleges lacked swimming pools, which were important because a man would not be commissioned unless he could be classified as a swimmer. Colleges without pools had to arrange to use nearby facilities. Hampden-Sydney in Virginia contracted to use the pool in the State Women's College in nearby Farmville, a five-mile bus ride for the trainees. At Muhlenberg, the Jewish Community Center's pool was selected, and in it was installed one of the first underwater obstacle courses in the program. At a number of schools, including Carroll in Montana and Bates in Maine, a nearby YMCA pool was used. Municipal pools were used in many places. A nearby boys' club was utilized at Illinois Institute of Technology. Holy Cross used pools at two boys' clubs and a YMCA.

The Navy was especially tightfisted in the allocations it would approve for the weekly use of swimming pools owned by other organizations. Such fees had to be a component of the athletic expense allowable to each school. Most institutions using a pool belonging to another organization made arrangements to pay a certain amount per man per swim. At Carroll College, the YMCA charged the school twenty cents per man per swim, which caused the president of Carroll, Father Emmet J. Riley, to petition the YMCA board in May of 1944 to lower the rate to ten cents. Riley noted that the Navy had informed him that the twenty cent swimming fee was excessive and that the highest previous fee paid by a V-12 unit anywhere for use of a pool was twelve cents per man, which had later been renegotiated down to eight cents. [1]

At Arkansas A & M the trainees marched the three miles into Monticello to use the town's outdoor pool. One trainee recalled singing Christmas carols on the way to a December swim in that pool. [2]

In at least three schools, no adequate pool was available, so in warm weather the trainees used a lake or a dammed-up swimming hole in a nearby river or creek. That was the situation at Tufts College, Denison University, and St. Lawrence University.

THE COLLEGES PREPARE

At the University of Louisville the trainees swam at the Hotel Henry Clay. At Missouri Valley College, a swimming pool was hastily constructed in accordance with the school's promise in its bid to obtain a V-12 unit. At Mount St. Mary's College in Maryland a large outdoor pool was built. Doane College constructed an indoor pool due to the belief that when cutbacks were to be made in the program, schools without pools would be the first to be dropped.

Plumbing alterations were perhaps the most conspicuous changes dictated by the Navy program. In the many instances where the Navy took over girls' dormitories or sorority houses, the need for additional fixtures was obvious, but even in men's dormitories the doubling of peacetime quotas for room occupancy called for added toilets, urinals, and wash basins. In such cases, the Navy made the alteration an allowable commissioning expense.

Yale University balked at the idea of altering its historical stone housing units to double their capacity. The university felt that ripping into walls to provide additional plumbing would cause irreparable damage. The Navy was insistent. Finally Yale said that it would settle for only half its housing payment rate (per square foot) if it were allowed to keep its buildings as they were and leave their occupancy at prewar levels. According to Lt. Raymond F. Howes, Comdr. John Webb of Planning and Control was adamant: this was a Navy program and the Navy should control the decision. Yale said it would pull out of the V-12 program if the doubled capacity was a requirement.[3]

A hasty conference was held at BuPers. A "high Navy official" sided with Webb and asked, "Who is more important: Yale or the U.S. Navy?"

Howes spoke up: "In this case, Sir, Yale. We'd get a black eye if Yale pulled out of the program." Thus the decision was made in favor of Yale's position. Later Commander Webb unloaded on Howes, accusing him of "disloyalty" and "double-dealing."

Where the lighting in classrooms and dormitories was deficient, the Navy would not permit the necessary improvements to be considered a commissioning expense. It viewed such changes as a form of deferred maintenance, which was the school's responsibility.

In some institutions the gyms barely met minimum standards. At least one school, Emory University, had no showers available at the athletic facility, so the trainees had to return to their dormitories to shower after P.T. class, which made it difficult for them to arrive on time at the next class. It also presented problems in cleaning the heads as required by contract. They were in use nearly all the time![4]

Fire escapes were a most important consideration to the Navy, and improvements were required at a number of schools. Some of these improvements were minimal: at Milligan College, wooden ladders were

THE COLLEGES PREPARE

anchored to the outside walls at each end of the large, three-story dorm. In fire drills, however, trainees were never required to test the sturdiness of these makeshift arrangements, and the trainees did not volunteer to try them.

A commissioning expense allowed at all schools was the purchase of compartmentalized metal trays for the mess hall. The installation of cafeteria serving lines was also approved where students had previously been served at tables by waiters or waitresses.

To prepare for the academic demands, most schools found it necessary to convert some classroom space into mechanical drawing rooms, adding the desks and drawing equipment required for the engineering drawing course. The heavy concentration on science also led to the upgrading of physics and chemistry labs at many smaller schools. Central College in Missouri bought all of the laboratory equipment it needed from a defunct college in Des Moines.

The location and proper layout of offices for the Navy and Marine commanders and their staffs were also considered commissioning expenses.

Because of the great variety of different situations at the colleges, the Navy finally agreed to pay a lump sum per man for commissioning expenses. Nevertheless, there were quite a few disputes between colleges and the Navy as to whether various expenditures were allowable. The

The V-12 office at most schools looked much like this one at Doane College.

Doane College Archives

THE COLLEGES PREPARE

Navy had established a hard-and-fast rule requiring its permission in writing before a college made an expenditure for which it hoped to be reimbursed. If prior approval had not been obtained, the Navy was likely to disallow the expenditure.

The busiest man on any campus was invariably the college business manager. He was responsible not only for improvements and purchases, but for the increased staffing necessary in kitchens and maintenance areas. He also had to arrange for purchasing food and obtaining and safeguarding ration stamps for meat, coffee, canned goods, sugar, and butter.

On the academic side, the president and dean of the college also had their hands full. They needed qualified faculty members to teach the additional science and math courses, whereas the need for instruction in art, geology, and various other electives was much diminished. One solution was for professors of business, languages, and the arts to volunteer to teach science and math courses. Many recently retired faculty members also answered the call to help out. Every school, however, still had to do some recruiting to handle its increased load.[5]

Qualified teachers of the exact sciences were not easy to find. Their ranks had been severely diminished by the draft and enlistments, and they were now in great demand because of the Navy's concentration on math and science. The result was that the larger and more prestigious institutions lured some qualified professors from smaller institutions, and the smaller institutions made do with what they could find.

The competition for qualified instructors and the year-round teaching schedule led to increases in salaries, which were a matter of great concern to the presidents of small colleges. They feared that their postwar budgets would not be large enough to pay the inflated salaries authorized under the Navy program. Thus, they frequently balked at paying high salaries, even though they knew the Navy would pick up the current cost.[6]

The other problems facing the schools were mirrored in virtually every business in America — a shortage of adequate entry-level help. Young faculty men who joined the armed forces were frequently followed by their wives, who were one of the most important traditional sources of clerical help for colleges. But the V-12 program brought an unexpected bonus to the schools in the persons of the wives of officers and petty officers assigned to the units. They were soon working in virtually every V-12 school in the country.

In the smaller schools, the employment of a certified dietitian was a luxury that few schools could afford. Frequently the wife of the president or another official had served as the *de facto* dietitian, often with little or no training in the field. But traditional college fare, especially

THE COLLEGES PREPARE

where meals had been planned for girls, was often not sufficient to supply the energy needed for the rigorous physical training that took place in all of the V-12 units. In more than one school the trainees complained that they were not getting enough to eat. This often led to the employment of a qualified dietitian, and the Navy willingly stood the additional cost for such an employee.[7]

Specialized equipment such as study lamps, double-deck bunks, mattresses, and sheets was in short supply from civilian sources, so it was ordered out of Navy supply depots. As the first of July approached, the Navy sent out frantic messages for mattresses to be shipped via Railway Express in order to arrive at colleges in time. Sometimes they did, and sometimes they didn't!

As the deadline drew closer, every person officially connected with the 131 schools pitched in to get the campuses ready. At Muhlenberg, even the president was unloading food for the two days before the V-12s arrived.[8] It was a mammoth effort by everyone concerned and on July 1 the campuses were basically ready for the trainees.

14

THE COLUMBIA
CONFERENCE

As THE V-12 program began to take form, the desirability of a meeting between the Navy and officials of the 131 colleges and universities became apparent to all. Too many issues were still unsettled or not fully understood by all the concerned parties. Accordingly, near the end of April 1943, invitations went out for a conference to be held at Columbia University in New York City on Friday and Saturday, May 14 and 15.

The letters were signed by Rear Adm. Randall Jacobs, the chief of naval personnel. He invited the college presidents to the conference, explaining that he would attend "together with those officers of the Bureau who are responsible for the administration of the program, as well as most of the officers who will serve as Commanding Officers at the colleges and universities participating in the program." If it was not possible for the president to attend, then another college representative could be sent.[1] He also asked the colleges to submit a list of questions they wished to discuss at the meeting.

In his important speech at the conference, Admiral Jacobs noted that "the excellent attendance of naval officers associated with the Navy V-12 Program is no surprise; we in the Navy have ways of arranging such things. But it is gratifying that so many college presidents, deans, and other special representatives have been able and willing to find the time to come here and give us the benefit of their counsel." It was not surprising that attendance was good, for college representatives could not only have their many questions answered, but they hoped to meet the officers who would be commanding their units. In this they were disappointed, for the officers had not yet been assigned to specific schools.

In opening the conference in the McMillin Academic Theatre, Capt. Bruce Canaga, USN(Ret.), the director of training, noted that "the time for the actual inauguration of the V-12 Program is near at hand. The training of newly commissioned officers is nearly complete, and many of the V-12 students are already under orders. In two weeks the officers will report to the college campuses, and in six weeks the students will arrive. The time for solving problems with words is running short."

THE COLUMBIA CONFERENCE

Dean Joseph W. Barker, who was both a representative of the host school and the special assistant to Secretary Knox, was given the assignment of welcoming everyone to the meeting. In introducing him, Canaga pointed out that Barker had played an important role in shaping all of the recent Navy training programs. Barker himself noted that Secretary Knox had shown a keen interest in the development of the program and regretted that he could not be present.

Barker's brief message stressed the need for cooperation: "We are depending on you for the academic standards. We shall handle the naval discipline. You and the Commanding Officers who will be assigned to the V-12 units on your campuses will team together, each with responsibilities, but working cooperatively."

The tone for the entire V-12 program was set by Admiral Jacobs's speech, entitled "The V-12 Program — A Cooperative Venture in Education."

In his brief introduction of Jacobs, Captain Canaga said that the fact that Jacobs had given considerable time and effort to the formulation of V-12 policies and had kept in close touch with every phase of the procedure indicated how strongly he felt about the importance of "this great experiment in officer training." Canaga's statement was true. Both Jacobs and Admiral Denfeld, his assistant chief, took a great deal of interest in the V-12 program.

Jacobs outlined the development of the program and explained the philosophy that guided it. He noted that in the Navy's relations with colleges and students, it had followed three policies: (1) despite the need to move quickly, progress had been slow enough that every step could be given careful consideration; (2) the Navy had done its best to make no promises it could not keep; and (3) the Navy had tried to adapt its training requirements to the programs of the colleges to create as little disruption and confusion as possible.

The admiral stated that the program could have begun prior to July 1, but that the Navy had decided that it should start only after the most "thoughtful consideration both by the Navy and by leading educators of the country." He praised the Navy Advisory Educational Council for its effective assistance to the Bureau, and he similarly credited college administrators and professors who had been "untiring in aiding the Bureau to plan these courses and curricula."

Jacobs alluded at one point to a consideration that had guided the Bureau in developing the program. "In many ways, our program would be easier to administer if we did not feel bound by promises previously made to college students."[2] He was referring to the assurances given earlier to the V-1 and V-7 students that they would be allowed to complete their education before being called to active duty. He was also

THE COLUMBIA CONFERENCE

referring to the Navy's decision not to require advanced students to take the courses required of entering freshmen. In adopting that stance, the Navy had clearly given general academic considerations priority over technical courses that would have been of more immediate use for potential naval officers.

Jacobs also reassured the educators about the quality of the students who would be attending their schools under the program. He said,

> Every effort is being made to select the most intelligent students who also possess the necessary potential officer-like qualities for admission to our V-12 Program, so that the maximum time, energy, and money may be conserved by training men who will, in the end, measure up to officer qualifications for commission. Those students who are not successful in the college course will still be important additions to the enlisted complement of the fleet.

He also stressed that the colleges had "an important responsibility to offer education of highest quality to the students assigned them, and to help these students put forth their best efforts so the Navy will have a continuous reservoir of officer material to meet the needs of the service."

Jacobs then got to the heart of the matter: "This is a college program. Its primary purpose is to give prospective naval officers the benefits of college education in those areas most needed by the Navy."[3] He challenged the educators by noting that the Navy was not merely contracting for classroom, dormitory, and mess hall space and for a stipulated amount of instruction, but "for the highest teaching skill, the best judgment, and the soundest administration of which the colleges are capable. We desire our students to have the benefits of faculty counseling, of extracurricular activities — in short, the best undergraduate education the colleges can offer."

Jacobs also warned that in working out the relations between the academic and the military portions of the program, questions would arise on every campus that would tax the patience and ingenuity of the college administrators and the officers in charge. "I ask now that every effort be made by all parties concerned to solve such problems locally in a spirit of mutual confidence and full cooperation. The Bureau of Naval Personnel will be glad to offer suggestions, but at each college the final responsibility must rest on those immediately in charge."

The admiral emphasized that all phases of the V-12 program "are still open for discussion." His final words were noteworthy, both because they concisely stated the situation and because they prophesied the long-term effects of the V-12 program.

> Gentlemen, we are about to embark on an education program that will have important effects on American colleges, on the Navy, and most impor-

THE COLUMBIA CONFERENCE

tant of all, on the lives of thousands of this nation's finest young men. We must educate and train these men well, so that they may serve their country with distinction both in war and in peace. We must increase the temper of our education and our training. Everyone in this room and the hundreds of others whom we represent share the responsibility for the success or failure of this venture. I am confident that by pooling our resources of experience, judgment, and energy we shall start the program in the right way and carry it forward to a final achievement of which we all may be proud.

Jacobs emphasized his interest in the program by staying for the rest of the day and making himself available for questions.

Admiral Jacobs was followed by Capt. Cortlandt C. Baughman, USN, director of special activities in the Bureau of Naval Personnel. Baughman outlined the history of naval officer training since the passage by Congress of the Naval Reserve Act of 1938. He explained that the influence of the V-12 program would be felt in every community in the land by accepting young men who were then in college, just leaving high school, or already enlisted and scattered throughout the world. He noted that the course was designed for wartime and urged that trainees "be pushed to their utmost capacity and where possible given the benefit of broad educational courses. We are depending on you, who have taken over the job of preparing these boys for their role as officers."[4]

Next on the agenda came the man who was responsible for coordinating the development of the V-12 curricula, Lt. Comdr. Alvin C. Eurich, USNR, officer-in-charge of the Standards and Curriculum Section of the Training Division. To explain the curriculum, Eurich divided the trainees into three groups: (1) The V-1 and V-7 students who were already enlisted, but on inactive duty. This was the group Admiral Jacobs was referring to when he spoke of promises previously made. (2) Those who had just come into V-12 from college, but to whom the Navy had made no promises. (3) Students who were just beginning their college work as freshmen, either from high school or the fleet. Eurich noted that only the last group would be required to take the full prescribed curricula, but he indicated that men in the other two groups would be urged to include in their programs as many of those courses as possible.[5]

The remainder of Commander Eurich's remarks concerned the curricula for the third group, the "regulars." He explained how their carefully prescribed college training was based on the recommendations of the Navy Advisory Educational Council, the input of Dr. Joseph Barker, and the combined efforts of college administrators, subject specialists, and naval officers who viewed the curricula from the standpoint of practical applications to Navy problems.

THE COLUMBIA CONFERENCE

Commander Eurich anticipated one of the questions. Would deviations be permitted in the basic curricula? The answer was a definite no. He did not, however, rule out future changes resulting from the Navy's experience with the program.[6]

In conclusion, Eurich again stressed the Navy's emphasis on the college aspect of the program. "It can be said from the standpoint of both curricula and standards, the Navy is following the general policy of adapting, with the aid of college authorities, the best college practices generally in operation. The program calls for an intensification of effort which, I am sure, we are all willing and eager to give in obtaining one common purpose."

The early part of the conference dealt with academic matters, but the time came for Capt. William W. Behrens, USN, the officer-in-charge of the Administration Section of the Training Division, to speak about the day-to-day responsibilities of both the colleges and the naval officers assigned to the units. Behrens noted that the colleges were selected because their instructional facilities were known to be good, but he admitted that in recent weeks, in his office at least, the academic features of the program had been completely submerged by correspondence about dormitories and cafeterias.[7] He emphasized the need for sanitary galleys and dining halls and indicated that the Navy was ready to give reasonable aid to the colleges to bring facilities up to satisfactory standards.

Behrens also expressed the hope that the colleges would continue to provide normal extracurricular activities such as lectures and exhibits, and that V-12s would have opportunities to join musical clubs, fraternities, and other campus organizations, including intercollegiate athletic teams.

Behrens then reminded the unit commanding officers of their duties in maintaining satisfactory standards of housing, messing, and medical service. He told them that if the college did not supply an adequate staff for the physical training program, the officers themselves must do so. They were cautioned to stay in close touch with the academic progress of the trainees because it would be their responsibility, after receiving recommendations from college authorities, to order or recommend student transfers from one curriculum to another or from one college to another. In cases of academic failure, they would be responsible for dropping students from the program and assigning them to general duty.

Responsibility for discipline also rested with the naval officers, and they were admonished to see that proper decorum was maintained by the V-12s. The officers were expected to instruct V-12 students as soon as they arrived on campus concerning standards of conduct, including

THE COLUMBIA CONFERENCE

military bearing, wearing the uniform, and observance of naval customs.

Behrens further emphasized that

> V-12 students shall not be hampered in their studies by requirements to perform unessential military duties; on the other hand these students must not be permitted to do anything that would bring discredit on the uniform they wear.
>
> To be specific, there is no need for V-12 students to stand watch, to march to classes, or to take part in frequent military parades and reviews. Nor is it necessary that they be kept in bounds during particular portions of the day, or confined to quarters for definite study periods. On the other hand, they should answer reveille, take their morning calisthenics as a unit, march to meals, observe quiet hours in the dormitories during the evenings, stay in the vicinity of the college unless given official leave, and refrain from public drinking parties and other actions which would not be tolerated in other enlisted personnel.[8]

The final speaker for the Friday morning session was introduced by Captain Canaga as a man who was probably known to more of those in the audience than any other officer present, "because he is a respected educator as well as an able officer of the Navy." He was referring to Lt. Comdr. Arthur S. Adams, USN(Ret.), officer-in-charge of the College Training Unit of the Administration Section, whom Canaga described as "the one we all call on when we want the right answers, and he is here today to give the right answers to you."

Lieutenant Commander Adams first noted that every attendee should have three documents in hand: a copy of Admiral Jacobs's speech, a mimeographed copy of questions and answers, and an advance copy of the *Manual for the Operation of the V-12 Unit*.[9] He said that when the questions were solicited from the colleges, a total of 962 queries were received on 226 different subjects. They were carefully analyzed and segregated into classes that covered everything from curriculum and equipment to contracts and reimbursements.[10]

The answers, Adams stated, were written by the men who wrote the manuscript of the *Manual for the Operation of the V-12 Unit*, so he hoped there would be no inconsistency between the two documents. He again stressed that "one of the cardinal principles under which we work is the maintenance of our word."

Adams outlined the four principles upon which the program was founded, mentioning that they would provide a basis for solving future problems that would arise on every campus because they had not been dealt with by the materials provided at the conference. These four points were (1) to take maximum advantage of the academic resources already developed in the institutions; (2) to make maximum use of all

THE COLUMBIA CONFERENCE

of the institutions' experience and knowledge of educational procedure; (3) to avoid penalizing any institution; and (4) to expedite arrangements wherever possible.

To illustrate the third point, Adams said that they were much concerned in the Bureau by a number of letters in which the presidents used the phrase "taken over by the Navy." He stressed that "we're not taking over the institutions. Not at all. We want the institutions to help us do a piece of work. The institutions have offered so to do."[11]

Regarding the fourth principle, he noted that the Navy wanted to give everyone the most rapid service possible, but that in carrying out contract negotiations with so many schools it was not possible to get everything done as expeditiously as both sides desired.

Following Adams's talk the group adjourned for lunch. The afternoon session was devoted to fielding questions that could be answered with reference to the *Manual for the Operation of the V-12 Unit.* Adams asked that questions not covered by the manual be submitted in writing so the Bureau could give carefully considered answers, rather than trying to give off-the-cuff responses that might prove to be lacking in foresight. In handling the questions Adams was assisted by Admiral Jacobs, Dean Barker, and Lieutenant Commander Eurich.

One question that was asked in half a dozen different ways involved the delivery to the V-12 schools of the transcripts of the advanced college students. Originally, the Navy had stated that the transferred students would bring their transcripts with them when reporting. The college representatives pointed out that this would result in mass confusion in the early days of July as the schools tried to ascertain the proper placement of such advanced students and determine which of their credits would be recognized.[12] Several college representatives noted that the ordering and delivery of textbooks would be chaotic if the standings of advanced students had not been determined well in advance. Adams suggested that a list of transferring trainees be sent to each V-12 school about June 1 so the schools could write to the students' previous schools for transcripts. Objections were raised to that solution. Finally, after the conference, the Navy decided that the orders to active duty sent to all current college students who would be reporting to a different school would require the new trainees to immediately forward their transcripts to the new institution. This was undoubtedly the most important result from the question period.

At the end of the afternoon President Alan Valentine of the University of Rochester expressed the very great appreciation of all the college representatives present to Admiral Jacobs and the members of the Bureau of Naval Personnel for "the extremely courteous, sympathetic and understanding way in which this program has been presented."[13] Ob-

THE COLUMBIA CONFERENCE

viously, in the first day the Navy had accomplished its very important objective of getting the college-Navy relationship off to a good start.

The final session began on Saturday morning. It was devoted to the college contracts. The lead speaker was counsel for the Bureau of Naval Personnel, James A. Fowler, Jr. Fowler explained to the educators that the Navy already had considerable experience in developing similar contracts with ninety different institutions during the previous year. These were for the training of enlisted specialists such as electrician's mates and radio operators, and also in connection with the V-5 naval aviation program.[14] He noted the reasons for training at colleges instead of building new training stations: the savings of money, manpower, and material.

Fowler was careful to point out that the V-12 program was an entirely different situation from that which served as the basis for the Navy's 1942 negotiations with colleges. In the earlier period, the colleges were still enjoying good enrollments, so the addition of a Navy school that used messing facilities and space for housing and classes but did not utilize laboratories or regular academic courses taught by the school's faculty was of benefit primarily to the Navy. The schools had been awarded more lucrative payment terms then because they sometimes had to displace their own students and lose their tuition and fee payments. It was proper at that time for the Navy to keep the schools from suffering financially.

But now, in 1943, with the drafting of eighteen-year-olds, the colleges were emptying fast. The Navy was not ousting any of the schools' students, but was indeed providing a most beneficial service, helping to keep up enrollments and thereby employing existing faculty and college facilities.

In his usual straightforward style, Fowler noted that the administrators might have heard stories about some university getting a drill hall, a classroom building, or a new swimming pool from the Navy and suggested that possibly "some of you have some day-dream that that is going to happen to you at the present time." Bluntly, he said, "My suggestion to you is that you wake up." Fowler explained that the acute shortage of critical materials during the past six months had led to drastic restrictions on their use for construction at the V-12 schools or anywhere else.

After explaining the restrictions on commissioning expenses, Fowler outlined the composition and procedure of the negotiating parties that would soon arrive at each of the 131 schools to work out the details of the contract. He stressed that only six lawyers and six financial men would be conducting the negotiations for the entire country.

After copies of a sample contract, an explanatory memo, and some

THE COLUMBIA CONFERENCE

principles of contract were handed out to the audience, Fowler explained the uniform contract basis for V-12. He stressed the dedicated service of Robert B. Stewart, the controller of Purdue University, who was present at the session and later helped to answer questions on the subject. Stewart was chairman of the Joint Army and Navy Board for Training Unit Contracts.

Fowler noted that Stewart had recently drafted a set of principles of contract, which the Bureau of Naval Personnel had adopted just the previous week. Fowler summarized the three principles: (1) the purpose of this program is to serve the Army and the Navy; (2) to the extent that we use your facilities, you shall not be left in a worse position by reason of such use; and (3) to the extent that we use facilities, we are going to use them to capacity, concentrating our activities in the smallest amount of plant possible.[15]

On the basis of those principles, he explained, the Navy was not going to allocate its costs or payments on the basis of the institution's total operating costs. A number of factors enter into the cost of a typical college that are not essential or useful to the Navy in training the men or naval officers, Fowler said. He cited research and the large numbers of lightly used classrooms as two examples.

During his speech Fowler cautioned those administrators who considered themselves "shrewd businessmen" or "hard traders" that the Navy would have a vast amount of data from the 131 schools and that it was not going to agree to a higher amount in a contract with a particular school simply because it was up against a tough trader. He further warned that most of the rumors circulating were untrue, caused trouble, and wasted time, and he urged the college officials not to worry about what payments might be received by other schools dealing with the Army, Air Force, or Navy.

Throughout his talk Fowler detailed the rationale for the Navy's contract process. He noted that the Navy wanted only one prime contract with each college; the schools should subcontract with fraternities if their units were to be used for Navy housing.

In his final moments at the podium, Fowler urged everyone to exercise faith, patience, and cooperation. He stressed that such attributes were characteristic of military negotiations; most of the companies that were making tanks, planes, ships, guns, and other material for the Army and Navy had to proceed on faith and spend a lot of money before they had a definite contract or knew exactly how much they were going to be paid.

Fowler also noted that, although their facilities at the Navy Department were not the best and there was a lot of confusion there, the best way to get things done or questions answered was to directly contact

THE COLUMBIA CONFERENCE

the person most concerned about the matter. He strongly urged them not to use "some indirect method to get your problems or your situation discussed by us." In other words, don't use the political route to handle the problems!

Because of the extreme time pressure on the negotiation process, he urged that the colleges be prepared for the negotiating party and have all of their figures at hand. He also asked that they sign the contract promptly, noting that the contract could and would be amended from time to time to reflect actual costs, so the colleges should have no fear in signing it even if they were not 100 percent satisfied with it.

The final speaker of the day was Comdr. John C. Webb, USN. In introducing him, Captain Canaga noted that Webb had been on the committee that selected the V-12 schools, but that he was appearing at the conference as the officer-in-charge of the Finance Section of the Division of Planning and Control. Representatives from his office would be accompanying the lawyers from the Office of the Bureau Counsel in negotiating the contract with each school.

As a copy of "Material and Equipment Required by Naval Training Units, Navy College Training Program — Responsibility for Procurement of" was handed out to the college representatives, Webb asked that existing and available equipment and furniture at the university, whether for offices or trainee housing, be assigned to keep the procurement of additional equipment to a minimum. He again stressed the Navy's position on commissioning expenses: reimbursement within limits for alterations required by the Navy for the housing and subsistence of trainees would be granted only when there would be no residual values remaining for the school at the end of the program's life.[16]

Accompanying the handout was an enclosure providing "purely a rough guess at the moment" of the number of trainees and ship's personnel to be assigned to each school. On about June 1, he noted, each school would receive a list of the number of V-1 and V-7 students to be assigned there. They would be listed by major fields of study and by terms completed.

Webb mentioned the schools' responsibility to arrange laundry services at equitable prices for the personal wearing apparel and bedding of the students. The students would individually pay for this service. He also discussed the matter of medical and dental care. Then he delved into the very complicated matter of institutional costs, such as utilities that were not metered separately for the operation of galleys or messing facilities, and he explained the methods the Navy was proposing to use to assure an equitable distribution of costs between the Navy and the colleges. Like a number of previous speakers, Webb admitted that "we

THE COLUMBIA CONFERENCE

are in a real quandary" as to how to work out payment for instruction. Webb also concluded with the assurance to the colleges that "it is our endeavor to arrive at fair prices at the institution, both to yourself and to the Nation."

The question period took up the rest of the morning. Most queries were handled by Mr. Fowler and Commander Webb, but those dealing with priorities for materials and ration points for critical foodstuffs were answered by Lt. John L. Swasey. Questions on shipment by the Navy of equipment or material were covered by Lt. Bruce Buckmaster.

As far as most participants were concerned, the key question was asked near the end of the morning: what was the effective date of the contract, and would payments accrue from that date? Mr. Fowler noted that it was the Navy's intention to make the contract effective from July 1. With that deadline foremost in everyone's mind, the conference adjourned.

15

V-12 BULLETINS

ESTABLISHING WISE policies for the commencement and operation of V-12 was essential to the success of the program, but properly communicating those policies to 131 different schools all over the country was of equal importance.

The policies covered a wide range of subjects necessary to operate naval units in rented civilian quarters. A modicum of discipline kept the units functioning on a military basis, but most of the instruction was given by instructors who had no direct responsibility to the Navy. It was indeed a challenge!

The series of V-12 Bulletins was established by Rear Adm. Louis E. Denfeld on May 22, 1943.[1] At the very beginning the Bureau made it clear that the bulletins constituted the program's bible. On June 1, 1943, Admiral Jacobs spelled this out in a note that appeared on the inside front cover of Bulletin No. 4, the transcript of the "Conference on the Navy V-12 Program at Columbia University, May 14–15, 1943." The note said that

> These Bulletins will appear in printed form from time to time and will contain statements of policy and official information for the guidance of all concerned with the Program. Whenever a Bulletin appears in mimeographed form it shall be deemed to be of an interim nature, i.e., as soon as possible the subject matter of that Bulletin will be covered in a subsequent printed Bulletin.
>
> Each Bulletin will be numbered in sequence, and will include, at the end, a classified list of all earlier Bulletins in order that cross reference may be facilitated.
>
> It should be emphasized that all information and directives will be found in this series of Bulletins. Any letters or pamphlets which are not captioned "Navy V-12 Bulletin No. ___" shall be considered to have no official sanction.

But neither Randall Jacobs nor anyone else had the faintest idea of how many bulletins would be necessary to operate this gigantic program. No one knew how long the program would last or could foresee all of the problems that would arise, but even a wild guess of one hundred bulletins would probably have seemed outlandish in June of 1943. In fact, Bulletin No. 100 was distributed on October 7, 1943, and at least 376 V-12 Bulletins were issued before the program concluded.[2] One reason for the vast number was that they covered all of the programs under the

V-12 BULLETINS

V-12 title, not just the undergraduate program. Thus, the NROTC, medical, dental, theological, and pre-V-12 training courses were covered.

As policy in written form continued to spew forth, Jacobs's suggestion that mimeographed bulletins be deemed of "an interim nature" was soon forgotten. The material in the mimeographed bulletins was considered to be as reliable as material in printed bulletins unless it was rescinded or modified.

One helpful practice initiated at the start to quickly give recipients an idea of the subject matter of a bulletin was a set of symbols, A through L, that were usually placed immediately after the bulletin number. The letters stood for the following subjects: A, curriculum; B, training aids; C, administration; D, finance and contracts; E, procurement; F, physical training; G, medical and dental education; H, theological education; I, Marine Corps; J, Naval ROTC; K, general information on the entire program; and L, supplies and accounts.[3]

As the different classifications indicate, the bulletins did indeed cover everything! Numbers one and two dealt with curriculum, number seven with marking identifications on uniforms, number fifteen with fire safety, number sixteen with shoes, number thirty-two with the purchase of textbooks by the schools, number fifty-one with physical training, and number fifty-nine with chaplains' training.

There was no expert who could cover all of those subjects, so many of the bulletins emanated from other locations in the Bureau of Naval Personnel and in other parts of the Navy Department. Some came from Planning and Control, some from Curriculum and Standards, and others from the Bureau of Supplies and Accounts, the Bureau of Medicine and Surgery, and the Office of Naval Officer Procurement. Each of these offices dealt with the subject for which it was responsible. The bulletins were printed and distributed by the Public Information Office of the Bureau of Personnel.

Some bulletins of an urgent nature were disseminated promptly, but others, which contained controversial ideas or discussed subjects on which policy had not been firmly determined, were shuffled from office to office for input, revision, and approval. They were frequently sent back for redrafting or fundamental changes. This meant that the numbers of the bulletins were often out of order with the dates of issue; the numbers were usually assigned when the subject was first approved as appropriate for a V-12 Bulletin.[4] Thus, Bulletin No. 92, concerning the separation of trainees because of academic failure, was issued on September 21, 1943, while No. 96, covering separation because of failure to meet physical standards, had been printed and distributed on September 16, 1943. This inconsistency of dates and numbers was rather common.

V-12 BULLETINS

Like any series of policy decisions, the bulletins were not always understood in the same way by all of the recipients, who included the commanding officers of the V-12 units, the presidents of V-12 schools, the directors of training of the naval districts, other sections, divisions, and bureaus of the Navy, and many other commands. For instance, Bulletin No. 43, which stated the requirements for selecting trainees from various ships and stations around the world, received widespread dissemination as a Bureau of Naval Personnel circular letter.

Some of the bulletins were issued to amend, interpret, or supersede earlier ones, and these adjustments often led to requests for further interpretation.

Capt. Adams wisely designated several of his officers to become the experts on the content of the bulletins. Lt. George Winchester Stone, Jr., USNR, who in civilian life had been an associate professor of English at George Washington University, was selected as the coordinator and primary expert on bulletins dealing with the operation and administration of the central V-12 line officer program. To assist Stone on the subjects of premed and theology programs, Adams chose Lt.(jg) Urban J. Peters Rushton, USNR, and Lt. John N. G. Finley, USNR.

Stone was the man who could instantly respond to the question, "Isn't that already covered by some bulletin?"[5] When a commanding officer had a problem, he could call or write the Bureau and Stone would prepare the information for the reply. When a new situation arose in the V-12 section, Stone knew whether it had been dealt with as a policy matter before.

Stone was also directed by Adams to read all of the proposed bulletins, no matter where they originated, to see that they were clear and unambiguous. More than once he sent them back with suggestions for improving their clarity. In urgent situations, he often hand-carried the drafts to the officer responsible, waited while his questions were answered, and eventually brought the draft back to the College Training Section.[6]

Many of the bulletins dealt with subjects that did not directly affect the operation of a V-12 unit. For instance, the selection of trainees from the fleet, the assignment of premeds and predents to professional schools, and appointments to the Naval Academy were not really important to the day-to-day operations at any unit, but they were covered by V-12 Bulletins. Most of the bulletins, however, were directly related to the daily operation of the unit, and as such were a godsend to the commanding officers. Most of the commanding officers, it must be recalled, needed all possible help in carrying out their duties of command, since their backgrounds in the Navy were relatively meager.

Often bulletins were written in response to a problem that had arisen

V-12 BULLETINS

in one or several schools. An unacceptable practice discovered at one school might be stopped by the direct action of the director of training in that Naval District or by Washington. Since they did not know how widespread a problem may have become, however, the College Training Section needed to consider whether the subject should be covered by a bulletin to prevent comparable situations from arising elsewhere.

After ninety-nine bulletins had been issued, an index of bulletins was prepared (Bulletin No. 100, dated October 7, 1943), and it was helpfully cross-referenced so a commanding officer could quickly find all of the bulletins touching on a particular subject. To keep curriculum information current, there were frequent bulletins revising and coordinating material relating to the heart of the program, which was very important to the colleges and universities.

According to most of the former commanding and executive officers who were contacted in 1985 and 1986, the bulletins were very helpful, and they considered them to have been exceptionally well done.[7] They provided the basis for coordinating and disseminating information vital to the policies of the program.

16

QUOTAS AND
ORDERS

WHEN THE college presidents returned from the Columbia Conference, their respective campuses were already preparing feverishly for the July 1 start of the program. The presidents now had a clearer idea of the rules for the academic program and the ultimate Navy-college contract. They knew that the Navy negotiators would be firm but fair.

The colleges expected to receive more information about the composition of their V-12 student body before July 1. In the first week of June they received IBM print-outs that listed the students currently in college who would be assigned to their schools, along with information about their standings and majors.

The colleges also awaited the arrival of the V-12 commanding officers. Some schools had a longer wait because a number of the skippers were still in the orientation school at Columbia University. The orders for the officers had gone out in late May, directing them to report as soon as possible after June 1 or after the completion of their orientation course.[1] Some didn't reach their assigned duty stations until a few days before the start of the program.[2] Fortunately, in such cases one or more junior officers had arrived earlier and immediately started working with the colleges to get things ready.

The assignment of the seventy thousand V-12 undergraduates was an unprecedented undertaking. It was not a simple matter of preparing a few hundred orders for the movements of large contingents of men. These had to be individual orders directing a certain man to transport himself from one location (home, college, ship, or station) to a V-12 school, which might be in the same town or across the country.

The first set of figures to be determined with some finality was the quota to be assigned to each school. With the negotiating parties still on the road, it was often not known until near the end of June precisely how many trainees could be handled by some of the schools. Estimates had been given in the original letters of selection, but these were still being refined at quite a late date.[3]

QUOTAS AND ORDERS

A minor complication was the option given to V-7s who had only one term left to complete graduation requirements: they were allowed to remain on inactive duty for that term at their own expense. A surprising two thousand men took that option, probably reflecting many who were being ordered to colleges other than the ones they had been attending.[4]

Each trainee's name was transformed into an IBM "punch card," and the Navy then had the huge task of intelligently determining the destination of each man, writing his orders, and then mailing them soon enough for the man to report on time. It was not done as scientifically as might have been hoped, and there were some failures.

One transient officer, assigned to a few days' duty at the Bureau while awaiting orders, was given the task of making some trainee assignments. But he failed to grasp the importance of such crucial matters as assigning premedical students to schools providing premedical training. As a result, he put the cards into the pigeonholes assigned to various schools on the basis of his notion of a nice, even distribution. At the end of the first day, Lieutenant Howes discovered the officer's faulty process of assignment and instructed him again on the proper way to do it. He was soon transferred, however, and his work was subsequently done by an officer who properly understood the seriousness of the assignment process.[5]

For whatever reason, there were a few errors in the assignment of quotas, and these led to problems such as four hundred trainees arriving at Milligan College in Tennessee, which had a maximum capacity of three hundred. The surplus hundred had to be quartered in the gym and then reassigned to other schools over the next week.[6]

Since the V-12 program was oriented to the individual, it was planned that those who had advanced standing would continue the major they had previously been pursuing. One young chemical engineering student from the University of Iowa was ordered to Iowa State College, which at that time did not offer a degree in his chosen field. He reported this fact to the commanding officer at Iowa State when he checked in and asked to be transferred. The commanding officer didn't know where to send him, but the trainee was prepared. He said that the University of Wisconsin, a V-12 school, did offer that major. Within hours a transfer had been arranged and the trainee was on his way to Madison.[7]

There were some other foul-ups in the V-12 orders. On the first day of the program a number of liberal arts students reported to the University of Illinois, which was authorized only for engineering and premedical studies. They were immediately transferred to other schools, and in a few days the University of Illinois received some engineering specialists

QUOTAS AND ORDERS

David Nimick

Because Princeton University was not given an engineering quota in the V-12 program, approximately 115 Princeton engineering students were ordered to Cornell University, where they formed the Princeton Club and invited Princeton University President Harold W. Dodds to speak at a dinner on June 16, 1944. At the head table are (left to right): Apprentice Seaman Thomas Murphy, now chairman of ABC-TV; unidentified man; Dean S. L. Hollister of the engineering school of Cornell University; Capt. B. W. Chippendale, commanding officer of the Cornell V-12 unit; and President Dodds. The person speaking is unidentified.

from institutions such as Yale. This individual treatment of the trainee was one of the important strengths of the V-12 program.

The Navy had frequently expressed its intention that 80 percent of each school's V-12 student body be trainees with advanced college rank and only 20 percent be first-term freshmen. But that didn't always work out. At St. Ambrose College in Iowa more than 80 percent of the new student body was composed of beginning freshmen.

The Navy had made many tentative promises to the trainees and the schools about student assignment. Trainees who were already enrolled in a particular school would remain there, providing they were in a curriculum offered in that school under the V-12 program. But V-12 schools did not offer all of their civilian curricula under the program. For instance, Princeton University had an outstanding engineering school, but its V-12 assignment was basic, premed, and Marines. As a

QUOTAS AND ORDERS

result, over one hundred Princeton engineers in the V-1 and V-7 programs were sent to Cornell University.

College students in non-V-12 schools were told to expect assignment to a nearby school of comparable standing. Recent high school graduates were given three choices of schools with the understanding that an effort would be made by the Navy to honor their preferences. The fleet men who had been away from home were told that, if possible, they would be sent to a suitable school near their home towns.

While such promises were generally kept, it was not possible to keep them all. One problem was that the prestigious schools were overselected by the trainees, while few apparently opted for those of less reputation. A factor that may have caused some of the strange geographical assignments was the choice of a disproportionate number of Southern colleges, probably as a result of President Roosevelt's admonition to pick "good small colleges wherever situated" and pressure from long-term Southern members of Congress who held key spots on the Naval Affairs committees.

Whatever the reason, the geographic imbalance affected a number of schools. Newberry College in South Carolina received large numbers of transfer students from colleges in Illinois and Iowa. Of the three hundred men who finally remained at Milligan College in northeastern Tennessee, more than half came from considerable distances: sixty from downstate Illinois, eighty from Oklahoma, and smaller groups from Texas and California. At Mercer University in Macon, Georgia, eighty-seven Texans were included in that school's initial quota of 229 men.

Putting so many men on the public transport system to report on a single day caused great concern to the Navy. Fearing overcrowding, the Navy determined that half of those reporting to schools located in the Eighth Naval District (south-central United States) should report on July 2. Even so, many trainees reporting by rail to schools in Tennessee on July 1 spent the night sitting on suitcases in the coach aisles or standing up between cars.[8]

Six special trains were run from Grand Central Station in New York City on July 1 to handle the 1,450 New York City area trainees heading to thirteen eastern colleges.[9] The *New York Times* of July 2, 1943, reported that one young man showed up at Grand Central wrapped in blankets, suffering from a cold and a 101-degree fever. That was indicative of the determination of the average V-12 trainee.[10]

On July 1, the nation started a new venture. On July 16, Rear Adm. John Downes, commandant of the Ninth Naval District, stated that "from the point of view of American education the V-12 Program may be the most important step since the establishment of free public

QUOTAS AND ORDERS

schools. For the first time, on any large scale, men are allowed to go to college, not on the basis of social prestige or financial ability, but upon their own merit."[11]

Later in this speech to the assembled V-12s of Northwestern University, Admiral Downes succinctly explained their mission: "You have a single purpose, and that is to fit yourselves for the command of men."

17

REPORTING
FOR DUTY

ON JULY 1, 1943, seventy thousand men reported to 131 V-12 under-graduate schools in forty-three different states. They came from nearly every community in the country.

Their reasons for being in the V-12 program varied. Some were chiefly interested in furthering their education. Others regarded V-12 as a "safe harbor" — a place where they could avoid the shooting war for a time. Indeed, the charge that this was an important motivation was often made against the program by the envious parents of men who were in embattled parts of the world facing real danger. Years later a few other V-12s admitted such motives as, "I was basically a pacifist; that's why I wanted to get into the program." Others had no such thoughts when they joined but began to doubt the propriety of their being in college when they received word of the deaths of friends, neighbors, and classmates on the oceans and battlefronts of the world. Some carried vestiges of guilt more than forty years later.[1]

The overwhelming majority of the V-12 trainees, however, took the Navy at its word when it told them that this was the most important work they could be doing in the armed forces. The program was training them for the type of service in which their talents could best be used.

The Bureau of Naval Personnel frequently issued statements to assure the public that the V-12s were performing a key duty. It had to continually reassure the V-12s themselves to keep up their morale. (See Chapter 26, "Attrition," and Chapter 20, "Marine V-12s," for information on morale problems.)

The Navy's follow-through in increasing the number of men brought into V-12 from enlisted ranks, and particularly men from the war zones, emphasized the importance it placed on V-12. Finally, in mid-1944, it cut off civilian enrollment entirely. The realization that the Navy would bring key men back from the war fronts added to the general public perception that this was an important program. The Navy frequently said, "You can't fight a war with just enlisted men."

The fact that the V-12s were getting a higher education in pleasant

REPORTING FOR DUTY

surroundings helped them deal with the difficulties of their duties. Only those who were not in the program, or those who were in the program and did not try to succeed, could believe that it was a soft berth. There was constant pressure, and it continued for a comparatively long time.

For many officer candidates, reporting for duty on July 1 simply meant returning after an absence of a few weeks to the campus where they had spent most of their previous college life. Subsequently, however, they would not have the same degree of personal freedom, and how long they remained in college would be determined by the Navy. They were going on active duty after spending up to eighteen months on inactive duty. Of course, there were benefits. The Navy was now paying tuition, board, and room, plus fifty dollars a month.

Another sizable group of college men were transferring to a different school — perhaps even to the archrival of their chosen college. In other respects, however, their experience was similar to that of the first group — they were now in the Navy.

Nearly all of the 11,460 Marines reporting for active duty had come from college campuses. About 333 were active duty Marines, and a very few were Class III(d) reservists recruited directly from high school. Thus, many Marines also found themselves remaining on the same campus, but because there were only forty V-12 schools with Marine units, Marines were more likely to move to a different college than were Navy trainees.

The boys who entered the program just out of high school as a result of the nationwide examination simultaneously began two of the most abrupt and momentous changes that can be experienced by American men. They arrived at college and entered the armed forces — on the same day! For many, it also was the educational opportunity of a lifetime.

For the vast majority of aviation-bound V-5 enlistees, having to report to college was a great disappointment. Most saw it as an unwarranted and unwelcome delay in the pathway to their Navy wings. They wanted to get to the airplanes!

For most of the fleet men, July 1 brought a Christmas present that wrapped up many things they didn't believe possible: leave at home from forward areas, a chance to rise from the enlisted ranks to become an officer, and an opportunity for a college education, something that most had never dreamed of while growing up during the Great Depression. One fleet man exclaimed in 1986, "I won my lottery of a lifetime in the spring of 1943 in the Admiralty Islands!"[2]

Although most trainees were ordered to report on July 1, some arrived on June 30. They were usually accommodated, but several schools that had not previously housed a military unit told the early arrivals to come

REPORTING FOR DUTY

Oberlin College Archives

As soon as they stepped off the train at Oberlin, Ohio, the men reporting for the V-12 program came under the discipline of the Marine noncom. Here they are beginning to make their way to the campus.

back on the first, because that's when the college's contract with the Navy began. The early birds sought shelter at nearby hotels, and they were invariably the first to arrive on July 1. At Milligan College a pair who spent an eye-opening night (at least for seventeen-year-olds) at the local hotel reported at 0800* on Thursday, July 1, to turn in their orders. Milligan did not have preassigned rooms so they were instructed to go over to the large dormitory and select their own room. Being the

---

* Henceforth all times will be given the twenty-four-hour terminology used by the armed forces. It begins at midnight as 0000. All times later than 1200 (noon) may be reduced to familiar post-meridien (P.M.) readings by subtracting twelve hours. For example, 1525 is converted to 3:25 P.M. by subtracting 1200 and adding "P.M."

REPORTING FOR DUTY

first to arrive was a definite advantage, for they took the liberty of scouting the furniture supply in the entire dorm and then moving the choice pieces to their own room on the second floor.[3]

In most schools, rooms were assigned in advance, so the V-12s simply reported and were directed to their rooms. The first day was generally taken up by the check-in process. Trainees straggled in all during the day and night as trains and buses arrived.

Housing arrangements in the 131 schools varied substantially. Some V-12s were housed in conventional college dorms, including women's halls recently converted for male occupancy. Fraternity and sorority houses were taken over on many other campuses, forcing their civilian occupants to move to less desirable campus housing or to nearby off-campus homes.

Some trainees found themselves assigned to recently acquired hotels adjacent to the campus; others were put in newly constructed "dorms" that closely resembled barracks. At John Carroll in Cleveland some of the trainees were quartered in part of an orphanage next to the college. At another school the new dorms were still under construction and the trainees wound up in a varied assortment of temporary housing, including rooming houses and private homes, while awaiting the completion of the dorms. In some cases they had to wait more than six months.[5]

Eight hundred of the trainees reporting to Tulane University found togetherness in their housing in the school's gym, which had been partitioned to accommodate them. The same scheme had been used earlier at the University of Chicago and the University of Colorado to provide quarters for Navy enlisted men. Although the arrangement sounds substandard, Tulane students have noted that in the sultry New Orleans summer, those living in the gym had the coolest housing on campus.[6]

Having a place to sleep did not always mean the V-12 had something to sleep on. At North Dakota's Dickinson State Teachers College, the Navy mattresses had not arrived by opening day. Led by President Scott, college authorities scoured the campus and the town for spares, but during the whole first week some trainees still had to sleep on folded blankets.

Late on the first day a general orientation meeting was held, with the commanding officer presiding. He welcomed the men and told them what would be expected of them as naval officer trainees. The commanding officer, other officers, and chiefs described the routine to be followed in the upcoming days before classes began and also gave trainees an idea of what their daily schedules would be once academic sessions commenced. Most importantly, the officers specified the campus

REPORTING FOR DUTY

Among the first items on the agenda for the reporting V-12s was an orientation meeting. This one took place at Hobart College, Geneva, New York.

limits and announced the liberty hours. From that moment unlimited personal freedom ended for the V-12s.

At the orientation meeting the trainees were told in no uncertain terms that henceforth civilian terminology had to give way to Navy usage. The V-12 officers would not tolerate hearing about floors and walls — they were "decks" and "bulkheads." Windows were to be "ports," mops were "swabs," stairways were "ladders," halls were "passageways," restrooms were "heads," drinking fountains were "scuttlebutts," and the dorms usually became "ships."

The president and the dean of the college were usually present at that orientation meeting to add their welcomes and to outline the routine for registering for courses, procuring textbooks, and reporting for classes.

In addition to the verbal welcome by both the commanding officer and the college authorities, many schools also gave a welcoming letter to each V-12. Not infrequently, letters were sent by the college president or commanding officer to the parents of the men. At Illinois Institute of Technology the commanding officer, Lt. W. A. Hamilton, wrote parents "to congratulate you on the selection of your son for training in the Navy V-12 Program. He was chosen for this honor on the basis of out-

REPORTING FOR DUTY

standing aptitude and ability. You have every reason to be proud of him." The letter went on to state, "Your son is fortunate in having been assigned to the Illinois Institute of Technology, as this school is one of the outstanding schools of its kind in the country." He noted that the training would equip their son for service to his country and would be "invaluable to him in his career after the war." He urged parents to write their sons often, since they would need their encouragement and support more than ever. He concluded by writing, "the Navy is expecting great things from him. Let him know that you are, too."

At Minnesota's College of St. Thomas, the dean, Father Byrne, wrote all of the parents early in July. A month later Monsignor Vincent J. Flynn, president of St. Thomas, again wrote, assuring the parents that "this is a Christian College, and we feel a much greater obligation to any boy who comes here, whether he belongs to our faith or not. First of all, as Father Byrne has told you, we wish to give him an opportunity to practice his religion, whatever it may be. Secondly, we provide a chaplain who is ready to counsel any boy who comes to him. Thirdly, our faculty are trying to give your son whatever individual attention he needs in his classes." Such letters were certainly excellent for parent-Navy and parent-college relations.

A key aspect of the orientation process was the complete physical examination administered to each trainee. These exams began on the first day and continued until all men had been checked. They were conducted by the medical officer and his staff of pharmacist's mates.

The results suggest that the exam's thoroughness varied from school to school. At some schools the medical officer reported that 100 percent of the V-12s were physically qualified, while at others a surprisingly high number of trainees were found to be unqualified. The men, it may be recalled, had been examined just a couple of months earlier. At Central Michigan College of Education the medical officer noted that "many . . . were rejected at this station."[7] In all, fifteen hundred trainees were rejected nationwide.

Rejection because of the physical exam led to return to inactive duty to await further assignment to other Navy duty; a discharge, if the individual clearly lacked the physical qualifications for general service in the Navy; or return to inactive duty so that correctable conditions could be handled through civilian health care and the V-12 could be called up on November 1.

The basic examination included checking the eyes, blood pressure, pulse (before and after exercise), heart, and lungs, along with weight, height, chest, and girth measurements. It also included a Kahn blood test and urinalysis, and the trainees were required to go through various calisthenics to determine whether they had any skeletal or mus-

Newly outfitted V-12s at Muhlenberg try on their jumpers for the first time.

REPORTING FOR DUTY

cular defects.[8] At many schools the standard inoculations for tetanus, typhoid, and smallpox were given at the same time as the initial physical exams, but in other colleges they were saved for later in July.

During the first four days of the V-12 program at all of the schools, there was much waiting in line — to take physicals, to register for courses, to draw books, and to pick up the clothing issue. Although registration and the issuing of books differed little from civilian practice, the distribution of Navy and Marine Corps clothing, sheets, blankets, and towels was a highly complicated process at most of the new Navy facilities.

Imagine a typical V-12 unit of three hundred trainees, more than 90 percent of whom were coming from civilian life. They needed to be fully equipped with GI clothing, but the Navy had little information about the sizes necessary to outfit them. Accordingly, it had to estimate appropriate quantities and sizes for everything from jumpers to shoes. Only with blankets, sheets, pillows, and towels was it freed from that uncertainty.

Shoes provided the biggest headaches for the new V-12 units. Seldom was a qualified person available to fit them. In V-12 Bulletin No. 16, the Navy had advised the commanding officers that most of the shoes were coming from the factories of the Florsheim Company, and that therefore they should call upon the local Florsheim dealer to obtain some qualified assistance.

As in most military organizations, it was convenient to organize activities alphabetically, so those whose names began with letters early in the alphabet had little trouble getting clothing and shoes of the proper size. When the latter part of the alphabet was reached, however, the sizes needed had frequently run out. One trainee recalls making at least three liberties in sailor whites and brown civilian wing-tip shoes, and such an occurrence was not unique at the beginning of the nationwide program.

Another common problem was that some items were not received on time. At the University of Kansas, belts failed to arrive, so on the first liberty two enterprising trainees hopped into the car one had stashed on the far end of town (against regulations) when he reported for duty. They drove the thirty-five miles to the Olathe Naval Air Station and bought all the standard white web belts in its "small stores." The twenty-five-cent belts sold like hot cakes at one dollar each when the entrepreneurs returned to Lawrence.[9]

At the University of Illinois the commanding officer decided to delay the wearing of uniforms until all of the men had received a complete issue, so it was nearly the middle of July before the unit all suddenly appeared in summer whites.

REPORTING FOR DUTY

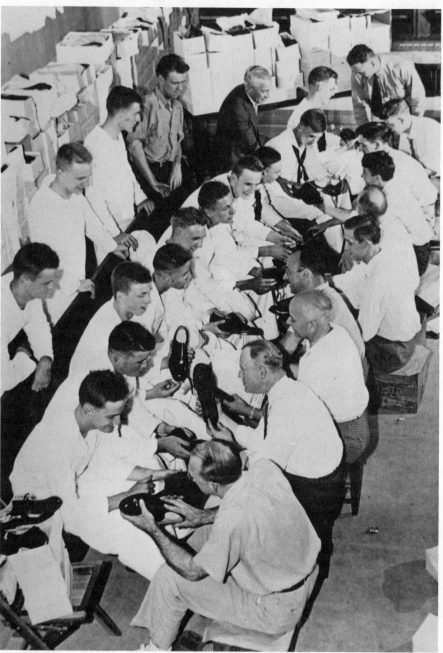

Muhlenberg College Archives

Fitting of shoes was a major task in equipping the V-12s, as this photo at Muhlenberg College shows. Often the men doing the fitting were brought in from local shoe stores.

REPORTING FOR DUTY

Towels were often in short supply, and once again those near the end of the alphabet were the ones left out. In a few schools it was weeks before enough arrived to supply every man. Some trainees used their undershirts for towels for the first week, or at least until they could find towels at a nearby store.

Despite the foul-ups at most schools, the uniform allotments arrived when they should at some. At Hobart College in Geneva, New York, all the men had drawn their requirements on the first day, so that unit may have been the first to be completely uniformed.[10]

Villanova University Archives

Because uniforms of the proper size often ran out before the end of the alphabet, some new V-12s marched in formation in civilian clothes during the first few days, as shown by this group at Villanova College.

The next order of business after issuing the uniforms was to stencil them. The uniforms belonged to the Navy and would have to be turned in at midshipmen's schools or other future assignments, so the Navy held every man accountable for everything issued to him. From hats to jumpers, all had to be identified with the man's assigned number. A stencil was provided for each man, and ink and brushes were made available in each dorm. After the ritual had taken place, all of the newly marked gear had to be exposed to the air while the ink dried. The chiefs

REPORTING FOR DUTY

James G. Schneider

Stenciling of clothes was a big job in a room with four occupants because the ink had to be exposed to the air to dry. Newly stenciled clothes were hung in every conceivable place. These two trainees at Milligan College appear to be all in from the arduous task.

and "old salts" gave the new "boots" instructions on the proper way to wear uniforms and tie neckerchiefs.

After receiving, stenciling, and learning how to wear their uniforms, the V-12s faced another problem, which existed in virtually every unit: getting adequate laundry service. Previously, the commercial laundries of college towns had not done much business with the student body because so many students mailed their dirty clothes home to their mothers in a laundry case.[11] Furthermore, civilian students never had the pressure of a daily Navy inspection to ensure that their clothing was in tiptop condition. Thus, the volume of laundry increased dramatically when the V-12s arrived on campus.

Invariably, local laundries tried their best to cope, but the huge new demand and the chronic shortage of adequate help made their lot a tough one. Getting the laundry done also became a major problem for the trainees and commanding officers at most V-12 units. It must be remembered that this occurred before the day of coin-operated laundries.

REPORTING FOR DUTY

In most towns three- or four-day service was considered very good. It was usually picked up by the cleaner from a V-12 drop-off point, although in very small towns like Oberlin, Ohio, the trainees took it right to the laundry. At the University of Dubuque the Presbyterian school enlisted ecumenical support by contracting with the nuns at a local convent to take on the laundry chore.

It is no wonder that many trainees — particularly old salts — took to doing their own in wash basins in the heads. Some trainees also received help with washing and ironing from their steady girl friends. Many a set of sailor whites was washed in girls' dorms.

In the summertime the white uniforms presented special laundry problems. Just two or three days after the program started, the commanding officer at Mount St. Mary's College called Lieutenant Howes at CTS with such a problem. At the end of June, thanks to special help from Howes, the C.O. had been able to send a truck to pick up the white uniforms when they hadn't arrived. This time the C.O. reported that since there was no auditorium large enough to hold the entire unit, he had held the orientation meeting outdoors. "Now nobody here knows how to get grass stains out of white duck pants," he lamented.[12]

Other types of stains also showed up in that sticky summer weather. At Milligan College the officer of the deck (O.O.D.) logged at noon on July 17, 1943, "All students returning from physics lecture hall and naval organization classes have varnish stains on their clothes."[13] That incident may have hastened the decision to make dungarees the Milligan uniform of the day during the summer. The college's isolated location and the fact that there were no civilian students enrolled made that an easy choice. But very few other units were allowed to have dungarees as the uniform of the day. At Howard College in the steel-producing city of Birmingham there was always a lot of soot in the air, which led to continued requests by the trainees and a steady flow of editorials in the student newspaper to authorize dungarees as the summer uniform of the day. Those pleas apparently met with no success.

The peak of the summer heat did bring a slight relaxation in the uniform of the day at some units. The jumper was omitted, so the basic uniform was white pants and tee shirt (or "skivvie shirt" in Navy jargon).

V-12 skippers looked for various ways to appear "regular Navy." There was an old Navy tradition of airing bedding on a regular basis. For many V-12s, that meant taking the blankets out every week and spreading them on nearby lawns, bushes, or fences for a number of hours.

Registration for classes was held sometime during the first three or four days of July. As soon as the trainees were registered, they were given book lists and then proceeded to the campus bookstore or what-

REPORTING FOR DUTY

James G. Schneider

Bedding was aired once a week at most of the V-12 units, in accordance with Navy tradition. Every available surface was used at Milligan College.

REPORTING FOR DUTY

ever room was temporarily used for the distribution of textbooks. The colleges provided the texts, billing the Navy for them.

By Monday or Tuesday, July 5 and 6, classes had begun for most of the seventy thousand undergraduate V-12s. At last the program was in operation, and future naval officers were beginning the work to which they had been assigned. At the first naval organization class, the trainees learned such necessary things as how to salute and to recognize the various ranks.

Although each commanding officer was allowed to set his own unit's schedule, the typical V-12 unit heard reveille between 0530 and 0600 six days a week. At most units reveille was sounded with a bugle, in spite of a dearth of talented buglers. Some units amplified reveille over a public address system. At others a shrill referee's whistle and pound-

The most unpopular man in any military unit — the bugler. He started the day for the V-12 trainees.

REPORTING FOR DUTY

James G. Schneider

The old salt in charge of section seven at Milligan College gives the men the orders for the day and all the latest dope.

After receiving the orders for the day these men at Milligan College march off to chow.

James G. Schneider

REPORTING FOR DUTY

ing on room doors brought on the new day. At Union College, they used the heating plant's steam whistle!

After reveille, the V-12s had five or ten minutes to assemble at the appropriate place for calisthenics. In many units, this was in front of the building in the street, which was perhaps blocked off. In some schools, however, such as Emory and Henry in Virginia, there was a half mile of double time down to the athletic field, where the entire unit took calisthenics, following a leader on an elevated wooden platform.

Some units did calisthenics rain or shine, whereas others canceled them when it rained. At Central Michigan College, a trainee wrote in an article for the alumni magazine, "I doubt if even the drought of '35 brought forth so many fervent prayers for rain."[14]

At a typical V-12 unit, the trainees had thirty minutes after returning from calisthenics to get themselves and their rooms ready for morning inspection. At the 0700 muster they were inspected by their student platoon leader and given the day's orders before marching off to the mess hall for "morning chow." Trainees also marched to noon and evening meals.

After breakfast they returned to their rooms independently to get books for their 0800 classes. In most schools they walked to class, but in some overly "GI" units the "regulars" were required to march to class, since they were all on basically the same schedule.[15]

The quality of food served to V-12s varied from unit to unit. Every kitchen should have started out with first-class ingredients, even though only about one dollar per day was allocated to feeding a V-12. But what came out to the serving line was often the subject of intense debate by the trainees.

At Duke University, the Thursday noon meal was invariably hamburgers, long a favorite of teen-aged boys. But these hamburgers didn't measure up to expectations and were rejected by scores of trainees, who suggested that the hamburger had been provided by "old Dobbin." The homemade buns and the locally grown onions were excellent, however, so it was "onion sandwiches" at all the tables. That, of course, made for a most fragrant atmosphere in the Thursday afternoon physics lab.

The *Manual for the Operation of a Navy V-12 Unit* (V-12 Bulletin No. 22) made the commanding officer responsible for the quality of food. He delegated that daily responsibility to the medical officer and the O.O.D. At most schools, meals were served on a tight schedule, so the O.O.D. also had the duty of checking how much time was required to serve the unit.

At one college the chief petty officer serving as O.O.D. wrote the following in the unit's log on July 13, 1943: "1205 Dinner served. Menu: One meat ball with gravy, spoonful creamed cabbage, jello with fruit,

REPORTING FOR DUTY

Marine trainees at the University of Washington believed in getting a full meal.

bread and butter, milk and coffee, ice cream. Several boys not liking cabbage had little to eat. The whole meal was inadequate."[16]

The next day the athletic officer serving as O.O.D. wrote "1200 — Chow. Meal too light for men working hard. 1250. Chow completed as to lines — fifty minutes." Several similar protests about quantity appeared in the following days, but within a week the commanding officer's complaints to the college had been heard and acted upon. The log entries for meals began to include such comments as "Good chow, plenty," and "Chow: excellent meal, plenty for all." Generally, the V-12 meals ranged from adequate to good.

At Bucknell University the serving of the 500,000th meal on June 1, 1944, was marked by a photograph of the recipient and his tray. He was promised that his tray would be gold plated and presented to him later, but that never happened.[17] The memorable 500,000th meal? Hot dogs!

For most trainees classes were finished by 1600 and the time until evening chow formation was theirs to do with as they pleased. Depending upon the location of the school and the proximity to stores, many units granted liberty within a restricted area, but in others the men were confined to the campus except for special nights of the week. In more isolated schools, there was no weekday liberty at all.

REPORTING FOR DUTY

Muhlenberg College Archives

Navy V-12 trainees at Muhlenberg College "chow down."

From the evening meal until taps, which varied at different schools from 2200 to 2400, trainees were expected to spend most of their time studying. At many units, procedures were changed over the course of the V-12 program to allow those doing adequate academic work to take liberty, but those who were failing in one or more subjects were usually required to spend their evenings studying.

Two orientation matters taken up later during July were the importance of every trainee's signing up for National Service Life Insurance and the purchase of U.S. War Bonds. Technically, the trainees could make voluntary decisions on these matters, but they were told that it would be in everyone's best interests if the entire unit signed up for both.

Pressure to produce such a result was put on the commanding officers, who dutifully passed it on to the ship's company and the trainees. Many units did achieve 100 percent on the life insurance, which entailed a deduction of slightly more than six dollars per month.

All of the trainees were reminded how fortunate they were to be in the V-12 program, and that their minimum bond allotment should be $6.25 per month, which would purchase a twenty-five-dollar War Bond every three months. Only trainees who were supporting impoverished,

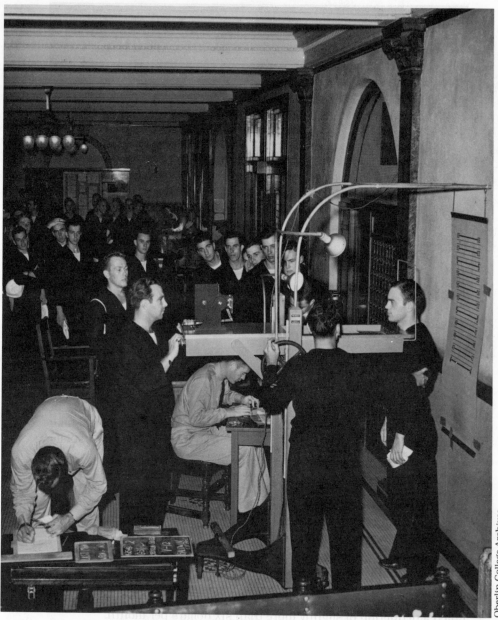

Oberlin College Archives

One of the anxiously awaited Navy visits was that of the official photo identification unit, which took the pictures and assembled the information for
official ID cards and dog tags. Often liberty beyond the local area was not
granted until the official ID cards had arrived.

REPORTING FOR DUTY

Oberlin College Archives

At the beginning of V-12, most of the trainee officers for the battalion, companies, and sections (or platoons) were chosen from among the "old salts" or "old leathernecks" to take advantage of their experience. Later, other V-12s were given opportunities to lead. This group of V-12 officers at Oberlin College shows the arm bands generally worn by such leaders.

widowed mothers were able to avoid making a "voluntary" commitment.

In some V-12 units, more than 90 percent of the trainees bought bonds, a handful of units were 100 percent, and only a few slipped below 80 percent. The commandant of the naval district almost always rewarded the high-percentage units with pennants for their bond support.

Other matters of considerable importance in the orientation process had to await the arrival of the traveling Navy units that handled such tasks. Navy roentgenology units, for example, were scheduled to take the chest x-rays of each man. Another important traveling group took photographs for official Navy ID cards. Until those photos had been taken and the ID cards made up and sent back to the units, commanding officers were reluctant to allow V-12s to go outside the immediate locality on liberty. A paper or cardboard liberty pass with no official Navy

REPORTING FOR DUTY

identification card might not be satisfactory to curious shore patrolmen some distance from the unit. At the University of Rochester, the delayed delivery of ID cards and dog tags held up approval of distant liberty destinations for more than two months. The boys from Brooklyn did not appreciate that.

Early in the orientation process, platoon and company leaders were appointed from among the trainees, with the C.O. usually delegating the selection chore to chief specialists (A), who were the leading petty officers of the unit. The petty officers nearly always selected men from the fleet to fill leadership positions, which was one of the great benefits of including enlisted men in the V-12 program. Their experience from boot camp and subsequent duty gave them the basic military knowledge totally lacking in most of the V-12s coming from other sources. The help of the fleet men was incalculable in teaching the new trainees the rudiments of military drill.

The "old salts" appreciated the recognition accorded them and moved into their jobs with great relish, promising the chiefs that they would get the "boots" squared away quickly. Their task was made easier by the boots' eagerness to learn all they could in as short a time as possible. They wanted to look as though they belonged to the regular Navy. Soon the new trainees settled in and their regimented life fell into place.

18

THE
"OLD SALTS"

ARTHUR ADAMS'S insistence that men from the enlisted ranks be included in V-12 was one of the most important ingredients in the program. As Lieutenant Howes and others noted, Adams was determined to ensure that there was input from the fleet.[1]

During the first year the program called for ten thousand men from the fleet. The Office of Naval Procurement divided this total into quotas for every major naval establishment and provided that all qualified men would be able to apply. The opportunity was available to men stationed in the United States, at sea, or overseas.

Bureau of Naval Personnel Circular Letter No. 14-43, dated February 9, 1943, established the following requirements for application by enlisted men for the V-12 program:

1. Be on active duty.
2. Be a male citizen of the United States.
3. Be morally and physically qualified for a commissioned rank; have a minimum visual acuity of 18/20 in each eye.
4. Have, at minimum, a high school diploma with a "creditable scholarship rating" and, at maximum, three years of college.
5. Be between their seventeenth and twenty-third birthdays on the date the application is submitted.
6. Be unmarried and agree to remain unmarried until commissioned.
7. Be recommended by their commanding officer.
8. Have passed a general classification test with a grade of eighty-five or higher.
9. Sign a statement that they are willing to accept a change in rating to apprentice seaman immediately prior to enrollment in the college to which they are assigned.[2]

The recommendation of the commanding officer was the most important single factor in selecting candidates for training.[3]

THE "OLD SALTS"

The commanding officers who recommended their best men for V-12 made a most unselfish decision. Since the C.O.'s own fitness report depended upon the performance of the men under him, he was handicapping his own unit by sending his most outstanding men back to the States. Few replacements would be as experienced and capable as those who were transferred.

Lt.(jg) Richard B. Eaton was in a fighter direction detachment on an island in the southwest Pacific in the spring of 1944 when his commanding officer recommended their best radar man for V-12. At that time, radar was so new that there was great difficulty in supplying trained men to meet the technical needs of the many radar units scattered around the Pacific, so the loss of that operator was keenly felt by the entire unit.[4] This was true in many other detachments and ships, where the petty officers recommended were truly the best and brightest men available.

Another man selected from the fleet was the leading quartermaster on an LST that was shuttling between Naples and Anzio during the spring of 1944. One morning, as the man was working in the chart room, the executive officer came in and said, "Get your things together. You have to be off the ship by noon. You are going home."

The quartermaster replied, "Now that's one hell of a trick to play on me!" After five minutes of explaining, the exec convinced the man of his good fortune. He was off the ship in three hours and helped cast off one of the lines as the LST pulled away from the pier. He later recalled, "My closest friends were standing on the bow waving good-bye. As excited as I was about going home, I wept as I watched my friends and my ship leave."[5]

On a mine sweeper in the Atlantic, the skipper could have had only the noblest of motives to recommend his chief quartermaster, Morris Mitchell, for V-12. Mitchell was so impressed with his skipper's description of the opportunity for a wonderful education at Swarthmore College that he named that school as his first preference. The Navy granted it.[6]

While most of the commanding officers were conscientious about recommending their best men, there were some complaints that the personal prejudices of commanding officers may have been influential. One Jewish trainee reported that he had applied at three different stations for the V-12 program. Despite his unquestioned qualifications, he was not recommended by any of the commanding officers. Upon receiving a fourth rejection, he went to see the Protestant chaplain on the base and discussed with him the possibility that an anti-Jewish bias was keeping him from being recommended. The chaplain looked at his qualifications and apparently agreed with the enlisted man's assessment of

THE "OLD SALTS"

the problem. He discussed the matter with the commanding officer, and as a result the trainee was selected for V-12. The V-12 reported in 1986 that he had encountered absolutely no anti-Jewish bias in the V-12 program itself.[7]

Giving up the rate, privileges, and pay of a petty officer in the United States Navy meant a considerable sacrifice for all who followed the enlisted route to V-12. Relinquishing the comparative freedom that went along with being a chief petty officer in the hope of eventually receiving an ensign's stripe reflected the trainee's great determination to secure a college education.

When the final selection had been made of the men who were to be transferred to V-12 from a certain naval unit, they were divided into thirds. The first group consisted of men approaching age twenty-three, who might be overage if they waited for the contingent four months later. The other two groups were also based on age, with the youngest men, aged eighteen or even seventeen, being called last.

CWO Debs Sutro Darling took an interest in getting Ralph Johnson of Nashville, Tennessee, an eighteen-year-old storekeeper striker at the Pearl Harbor Freight Depot, into the first contingent. Because of Johnson's age, it appeared that he would be assigned to the group heading to the college training program in the fall or later, but he was anxious to get started on the officer training. Darling's plea for Johnson was effective, however, and the lieutenant commander at Pearl who was scheduling the men to V-12 agreed in mid-May to put Johnson into the first vacancy if there were any cancellations from the southwest Pacific. One came up, so the eighteen-year-old was soon on his way to the west coast V-12 staging area at the San Diego Naval Training Station.[8] There he became part of a group of about two thousand men who watched the bulletin board to see who got V-12 orders each day. As they waited, the Navy checked to ensure that each man was up to date on his inoculations and had a full sea bag of the uniforms he was supposed to have. Most of the men in that group were twenty to twenty-two and a half years old. When an age count was made, Johnson recalled, there were only one seventeen-year-old and four eighteen-year-olds among the two thousand.

Many trainees noted that the presence on campus of the beribboned fleet men, including quite a number who had been at Pearl Harbor on December 7, was good for morale. One V-12 said that "Even the officers had a different, more respectful attitude towards 'the old salts' with all their decorations and service stripes."[9]

Many of the enlisted men selected for V-12 had earned medals or other decorations for their prior service, but the awards were slow in catching up to them. When they did arrive, the commanding officer invariably

THE "OLD SALTS"

presented them during a weekly or monthly Saturday afternoon inspection.

Not all of the officers were impressed by the old salts, however. The athletic officer at Trinity College, a lieutenant (jg), apparently did not like the fleet men who came to that school. He allegedly told one of them, "You don't belong here — I'm going to see that you go back to sea duty." Subsequently, he did his best to carry out that threat. First, he told the men from the fleet that they were not to wear their service ribbons when in V-12. One trainee who had come from more than a year in the Armed Guard in the Atlantic showed up at inspection wearing his ribbons. The officer told him he was out of uniform and not to do it again. The

Lt. George C. Decker, commander of the V-12 unit at Texas Christian University, presented the Air Medal to trainee David E. Hibbard for his part in raids on Tarawa and Wake islands prior to his assignment to V-12.

THE "OLD SALTS"

fleet man replied, "Sir, the Chief of Naval Operations has authorized me to wear these ribbons and I will continue to do so until he orders me not to." That stumped the officer but hardened his bias against the old salts.

At another inspection, the lieutenant said to a fleet man he had just passed, "What did you say?" "I didn't say anything, SIR!" Snapped the officer, "That's ten demerits for 'silent contempt'!" which was enough to give the man the one hundred demerits necessary for expulsion from the unit. On another occasion the officer took out his penknife to dig dust out of an inlaid panel in the hundred-year-old door to the room occupied by two enlisted men in order to find something to fail them on during the daily room inspection.[10]

Fortunately, such attitudes were rare. Most V-12 officers did everything they could to accommodate the old salts.

This accommodating attitude was not always reciprocated by the fleet men. As one nonfleet trainee recalled, the fleet men "bent the daylights out of Navy Regs, and were good at doing it without getting caught." He also noted that some "held the reserve officers in open contempt."[11]

The military experience of the old salts sometimes helped keep the new officers and CPOs from getting too officious. At Dartmouth a CPO called down a former radio man with three years of experience with Navy regulations with this reprimand: "——, I went through your dresser today and it was a mess!" The old salt shot back, "No one opens an enlisted man's locker in his absence. The next time you do that I'll haul you up to the captain!" The CPO did it again, so the sailor filed a report with the executive officer. The officer did a bit of fancy footwork to keep the chief from a disciplinary hearing called a captain's mast, and the CPO never again went through a V-12's dresser.[12]

The democratic selection of the enlisted men was one of the strengths of the V-12 program, but it was also one of its major weaknesses. Frequently the best men in a unit or ship were those who had a practical working knowledge of their jobs and the Navy in general, but that did not necessarily mean they had the academic background to handle the V-12 courses. As indicated in the chapters "Academic Load" and "Attrition," the enlisted men usually had to work much harder than the men just out of high school to succeed. On campus after campus their determination to master the work was an inspiration to their fellow trainees, the unit officers, and the faculty.

Those enlisted men who entered the program after a gap of several years in their formal education had their work cut out for them. One old salt recalled, "I entered V-12 from active duty, four years out of high school, to compete with sharp, well-prepared eighteen-year-olds in the battle of my life for survival." He did survive, earning his commission

THE "OLD SALTS"

through the deck curriculum and midshipmen's school. After the war he returned to college for two degrees.[13]

Although the overwhelming majority of the enlisted men were imbued with that kind of determination to succeed, a few men took the V-12 opportunity solely because it was a chance to get home leave. Their only penalty when they eventually bilged out and were returned to their former ratings was the loss in the difference of pay for the number of months they were in V-12. It was a credit to the wisdom of their commanding officers that very few of the men took that kind of advantage of the program.

The Navy soon recognized the problem of the inadequate educational backgrounds of many men from the fleet and took a number of steps to remedy it, most of which are detailed in the chapter titled "Attrition." One key measure was to change the freshman math and physics requirements, adding a no-credit course to provide the necessary back-

As the V-12 program moved along more men were called back from duty at sea or overseas to fill the openings in the program. This contingent at Colorado College in 1944 shows that they were a sizable group. Note that, unlike earlier V-12s, nearly all of these trainees are wearing service ribbons.

THE "OLD SALTS"

ground for the men to complete those tough courses over three terms instead of two. Learning from the experience of the first contingents, the Navy also set additional qualifications for the recruitment of enlisted men in subsequent terms, requiring applicants to have successfully completed high school algebra and plane geometry.

In addition to setting up a better selection procedure, the Navy established six-week pre-V-12 schools at various places, including Asbury Park and Princeton University. These schools gave the men preliminary work in math and science so they could successfully compete with their civilian counterparts coming directly from high school or college. The first pre-V-12 course started at Asbury Park on May 24, 1944, to prepare men for the July 1 quota.[14]

The new selection process and the pre-V-12 schools largely remedied the deficiencies of the former plan, and numerous commanding officers and professors noted that the academic quality of the enlisted men coming into the program later was much better than in the early terms.

At the end of the war at a number of schools the question was asked how the V-12 program could have been improved. In several places the answer was to bring all of the men in from enlisted service instead of civilian life. This was a tribute to the old salts, who were the leavening that made the program rise to the expectations of the men who designed it. Without their contribution, the program would have been substantially less successful in turning out mature young men qualified to become naval officers.

19

THE
"FLY BOYS"

THE MEN who enlisted in the Navy V-5 aviation cadet program had one thing on their minds: to win those wings of Navy gold. For them, the fastest way to that goal was the most desirable.

Traditionally, Navy officers had been college graduates, but early in the build-up of the aviation arm the educational requirement for aviation cadets was reduced to two years of college. In April of 1942, because such a large number of flyers were projected as necessary for winning the war, the college requirement was dropped entirely to permit the enlistment of high school graduates.[1]

Lowering the educational requirements had its desired effect: enlistments in V-5 ran very high. Soon the Bureau of Aeronautics had more future flyers than it could train. The advent of the V-12 program gave BuAer a "holding tank" similar to those provided later by the Pre-Midshipmen's School at Asbury Park for deck candidates and the orderly programs at naval hospitals for the medical and dental school freshmen awaiting the start of their classes.

The Navy explained that the diversion into the V-12 program was to give the officer candidate the advantages of some of the educational background previously required and always regarded as desirable. Unfortunately, the V-12(a)s, as they were designated after admittance to the V-12 program, did not see it that way. They regarded their time in V-12 as an unnecessary and undesirable interruption of their progress.

One reason for the surplus of aviation candidates was that air casualties had been much lighter than originally estimated. After a major battle, however, the leaders of BuAer would frequently speed up aviation training to start the lengthy process of replacing recent casualties.

In February 1944, the initial contingent of V-12(a)s completed their two-term requirement. Their classification was changed back to V-5. Training facilities for all members of such a large group were not immediately available, however, so many were sent to what was called "tarmac duty." "Tarmacs" were described by one trainee as "a bunch of flunkies on the line, fueling aircraft, spinning props, and things like that."[2] But at least the fly boys were around airplanes, which made them happier than they were in classrooms on college campuses.

V-12(a)s (now V-5s) fortunate enough to go directly into the aviation progression, either directly from V-12 or after a short period of tarmac duty, headed for a flight preparatory school such as the one at Murray State Teachers College in Kentucky.[3] In moving, they traded their traditional swabbie clothes for the natty uniforms of aviation cadets. They were paid the princely sum of seventy-five dollars a month, and the Navy began paying for their National Service Life Insurance. Flight prep took four months and covered training in aerodynamics, theory of flight, and the study of engines. It also involved a very strenuous physical fitness program.

The next move was to pre-flight school, another four-month program of arduous physical training and further study of the things an aviation cadet needed to know before being allowed in a plane. Successful completion of pre-flight led to primary flight school for another four months (using old Stearman trainers), and subsequently to either Single-Engine School at Corpus Christi, Texas, or Multi-Engine School at Pensacola. These schools lasted up to a year, but trainees were commissioned sometime after the first six months.

After commissioning, there was post-flight school, in which trainees received special training in handling the aircraft and running special missions. For the single-engine men it included carrier landings and takeoffs.

This was the progression when everything worked as planned, but it seldom did. Scheduling problems always handicapped the program.

In June of 1944 came what has been described by numerous cadets as "the great purge." The Navy informed the men then in flight prep schools around the country that only half of them could be expected to successfully complete the program, and that the Navy wanted as many as possible to choose other programs to avoid the unhappy necessity of "washing out" many cadets who were basically qualified.

The purge was a great shock to all of the men in the program. Of the two hundred-plus at the flight prep school at Murray, ninety-two indicated they would withdraw from pilot training. Twenty-two chose to go to midshipmen's school, for which they were qualified by having at least two years of college training; another twenty-two decided to return to V-12; twenty-five wanted to go to aviation machinist's mate school; seventeen opted for the civilian discharge that had also been offered; two former petty officers chose to return to their previous rating; three picked general duty as seamen second class; and one selected gunnery school.

Those who remained in the pilot training program, assuming they

THE "FLY BOYS"

WHAT NOW LITTLE MAN

THE EVENTFUL DAY OF JUNE 17, 1944 BROUGHT DILEMMA INTO THE CADETS LIFE.

FROM NAVY DEPT.

MANY WISH TO GO ON TO PRE~FLIGHT

DON'T JUST STAND THERE, DO PUSH-UPS!

SOME WANT MID-SHIPMAN SCHOOL & A COMMISSION

LST. NAVY

"THE SPOTLIGHT IS ON THE AERIAL GUNNERS"

OTHERS WANT AAM SCHOOL.

WE LOSE MORE DARN GUNNERS THIS WAY.

SOME WILL RETURN TO OLD RATE

I AINT BIN EATIN SALT TABLETS FUR NUTTIN.

A FEW WANT CIVILIAN LIFE.

SOLWID CHARWHACTUR

A FEW TALK ABOUT JOINING THE LUFTWAFFE, BUT WE HEAR THEIR PROGRAM IS "CLOSING" SOON.

BY JECMEN

From the *TaleWind*, Murray, Kentucky, flight prep school; courtesy Burton L. Mann

Although the V-5 cadets at Murray flight prep school were dismayed at the "big purge" of June 1944, cartoonist Emil M. Jecmen could still find a little humor in the situation. Illustrated are the choices the Navy gave to the disappointed V-5s.

THE "FLY BOYS"

successfully passed each of the schools, were in single- or multi-engine schools when the war ended in August of 1945. Thus, it appears that no former V-12(a) trainee went into combat as a pilot in World War II.

Of those purge victims who returned to V-12 schools, a few were sent to the one to which they had originally been assigned. The V-12(a)s who were in V-12 in the spring of 1944 were told via V-12 Bulletin No. 213, dated April 26, 1944, that they would remain in the V-12 program for "a minimum of three terms." That was a major disappointment for most of them.

A second big "purge" came on September 15, 1944, when the Bureau of Aeronautics finally admitted it had more men than it needed in the V-5 pipeline. The eighteen thousand V-12(a)s then in the V-12 program were told that only half of them would be chosen for pilot training. The other half could choose another route by the end of their second term. Many selected NROTC.[4]

A few of the men who were diverted from flight training by one of the purges but were eventually commissioned at midshipmen's schools or through the V-12 or NROTC programs became regular Navy after the war and eventually earned their Navy wings as commissioned officers.

The Navy tried to deliver on its enlistment-time commitments to the V-5s, but due to the happy circumstance of minimum casualties in the Pacific it was impossible to keep all of those promises. For most V-12(a)s, the program was one long, frustrating experience. But they were given choices all along the way, a wise Navy policy that softened the blows. Those choices often provided opportunities that led aviation-minded lads into lifetime careers in other fields.

20

MARINE V-12s

FROM the first announcement of the program the Marines had been an important part of the V-12. But it was not until March 24, 1943, that the commandant of the Marine Corps explained the details of the leathernecks' program in a press release.

Historically, most of the Marine Corps's officers have been college educated. Since the Corps does not have its own military academy, it has relied heavily upon civilian colleges and universities to provide the academic training for its officers, even though a few are also commissioned from the graduates of the Naval Academy and from the enlisted ranks. In 1943, officer training in the Marine Corps involved boot camp for the candidate, followed by officer candidates' class (OCC).[1]

Most of the marines called into the V-12 program on July 1, 1943, were college men who had enlisted in the Marine Reserve, Class III(d), but a small number came from the enlisted ranks and a few came directly out of high school, having signed up for that segment of the III(d) plan. None apparently came to the Marine V-12 as a result of the nationwide examinations.[2]

In line with the Marine Corps's reputation for toughness and the belief that athletes would best fit their needs, the Marines enrolled a large number of college football players, although they did not slight those who were active in other sports. It was commonly recognized on college campuses that most of the "jocks" were enlisting in the Marines, and many coaches actively encouraged their players to sign up.

Another factor that directed men to the Marine Corps instead of the Navy was the latter's insistence that its officer candidates have a strong mathematics background. If a college man didn't have such a background and didn't want to take the necessary courses, he tended to enlist in the Marines, which originally had no such requirement.

By early April, when enlistment in the III(d) program at the high school level had ceased, the Marines had 12,149 men qualified for the V-12 program. The Navy at that time was prepared to place only 11,500 marines in the program, so there was an excess of 649.[3] Inactive duty

MARINE V-12s

Marine Corps reservists who were freshmen or sophomores, like the enlistees in the Navy's V-1 program, were required to take an annual examination to test their progress in the academic world. The marines and V-1s took the test on April 20, 1943, at colleges throughout the nation. As a result of that test, the Marines dropped enough men with low scores to cut the Marine V-12s to 11,460. Those who were dropped from the III(d) program could go on general duty with the Marine Corps (i.e., boot camp) or be discharged, which would subject them to the draft.

Marine Corps V-12 detachments were established at 40 of the 131 Navy V-12 schools. No detachments were installed at schools that were not involved with the Navy V-12 program. Of the forty schools, twenty-five had only the basic Marine curriculum, two had the engineering curriculum only, and thirteen had both basic and engineering.

Basic Curriculum Only

Arizona State Teachers	Muhlenberg
Arkansas A & M	North Carolina
Bowling Green State	North Texas Agricultural
Colgate	Oberlin
College of the Pacific	Occidental
Colorado College	Pennsylvania State
Denison	Princeton
Emory	Redlands
Franklin and Marshall	Southwestern Louisiana
Gustavus Adolphus	Southwestern University (Texas)
Louisiana Tech	Southern California
Miami (Ohio)	Western Michigan
Millsaps	

Engineering Only
University of Colorado
Georgia Tech

Basic and Engineering
Bucknell
California
Cornell
Dartmouth
Duke
Michigan
Northwestern
Notre Dame
Purdue
Rochester
University of Washington
Villanova
Yale

MARINE V-12s

During the second term of the V-12 program it became apparent that the combination of Marine plans to add relatively few men to the program, the high academic attrition rate at several schools, and the large number of marines scheduled to graduate from the program in February would leave quite a few units with smaller than desirable complements. The problem called for consolidation of the Marine units. Thus, effective February 28, 1944, six units were disbanded and their remaining students in good standing were sent to other Marine Corps V-12 detachments, generally to units closer geographically to the boot camp at Parris Island, South Carolina.[4] In October of 1944, a similar need for consolidation caused the Marine Corps to drop twenty schools,[5] leaving just fourteen in the program. The Georgia Tech unit disbanded at the end of February 1945 and the Oberlin detachment was discontinued a year later. The final twelve continued to the last day of the V-12 program, June 30, 1946.[6]

The leadership of the nationwide Marine V-12 program was vested in Thurston J. Davies, who was then on leave of absence as president of Colorado College. The Marine Corps, like the Navy, saw the advantages of putting an educator in charge of its V-12 program. It had selected a man who knew what was expected of a marine. Davies had served in the Corps in World War I; he was wounded twice and cited for heroism. He received the Silver Star and the Croix de Guerre. He volunteered again in 1943, reporting as a major on February 24 and being promoted to lieutenant colonel on March 5, 1944.[7] He returned to Colorado College in 1945.

Lt. Col. Martin S. Rahiser, USMC, a 1925 Naval Academy graduate, was the officer-in-charge of the military operation of the Marine units. In that capacity he made formal visits to each of the forty detachments.[8]

In each Marine unit there was just one commissioned officer, whose title was "Officer-in-Charge of the Marine V-12 Detachment." He was never the highest ranking officer in the entire V-12 unit unless the commanding officer was absent or had been transferred and his replacement had not yet come aboard. This occurred at Dartmouth College in September of 1943 when Comdr. William Francis Bullis, USNR, was transferred to BuPers for further assignment and the highest ranking V-12 officer was Major John Howland, USMCR.

On March 9, 1943, the director of the Division of Plans and Policies had recommended to the commandant of the Marine Corps (CMC) that officers assigned to operate the program have college backgrounds and, preferably, be graduates. He also urged that a special two-week orientation course be given at Quantico, Virginia, for the officers-in-charge, beginning about May 22. Both recommendations were approved by the CMC.[9] According to Jack T. Lytle, Marine officer-in-charge at Arkansas

MARINE V-12s

Lt. Col. Thurston J. Davies, USMCR, was the officer-in-charge of the Marine V-12 program. In civilian life he was president of Colorado College.

MARINE V-12s

A & M, a key point at the Quantico course was "Get along with the Navy."[10]

Many of the officers chosen for V-12 units were combat veterans, and some had been invalided home with extensive injuries. Such circumstances gained them instant respect from the V-12s.

Serving under the officer-in-charge there was usually a warrant officer, frequently a Marine gunner, who acted as officer-in-charge in the absence of the commissioned officer. Several sergeants, corporals, and perhaps a private first class completed the Marine enlisted complement. As might be expected, and as the Marine Corps insisted, these noncoms gave the trainees much more exacting military training than was provided by their counterparts in the Navy program. The officers knew what they were training the men for and were as rough as possible to properly prepare them.

The physical fitness program for marines was planned with the twin goals of sharpening their physical condition and teaching them the skills necessary for survival in combat. The great emphasis was put on leadership. They still took the same "strength tests" as the sailors, but were in separate classes and had an entirely different PT program, clearly a much more rigorous one.

Marines at Louisiana Tech illustrate the emphasis on hand-to-hand combat in the physical training program designed for the leatherneck V-12s.

MARINE V-12s

Marines at Colgate are given a demonstration on how to disarm an opponent wielding a knife.

MARINE V-12s

The leathernecks' schedule was divided into four areas, each of which was taught for six weeks: combative sports, group sports, gymnastics, and swimming. In addition to those basics the marines had swimming, games, and guerrilla exercises once a week. [11]

In combative sports the trainees were taught the fundamentals of boxing, judo, and wrestling, with emphasis on hand-to-hand fighting. Sometimes the noncoms got carried away with the combative sports program. At Duke University on September 23, 1943, two marines ended up in the hospital as a result of the judo class. [12]

In the group sports area, they were taught and played various games, but special importance was placed on teaching and conditioning. The gymnastics area consisted of coordination drills on the various pieces of apparatus. The time spent in the swimming area emphasized "the various skills necessary to make a man competent under any conditions in the water." [13] The man was required to swim at least half a mile, using various strokes; to swim twenty-five yards under water with and without clothing; to learn the elements of life saving and jump from a high platform in the proper manner; and to use his trousers as water wings after inflating them.

The Marine V-12 academic curriculum was generally not as rigorous

Marines at Colgate University study map reading.

MARINE V-12s

as that of the Navy V-12, especially for men who entered the program with no previous college training. Their basic course was the same as the Navy V-12s' for the first two terms, but in the third and fourth the Marines were exempted from calculus and allowed to take various electives. They did have some additional requirements, such as map reading. Special instruction was given to the marines in weapons, and their instructors tried to prepare them for boot camp.

The Marine engineering curriculum, however, was exactly equivalent to the Navy program, with six terms for the engineering generalists and eight for the specialists. The basic Marine course leading to officer candidates' class was limited to four terms; those who had advanced college standing, as in the Navy program, would finish in less time.

For marine graduates of the basic curriculum in the V-12 program, the route to a commission as a second lieutenant entailed boot camp at Parris Island, South Carolina, if the V-12 had not previously gone through basic training. After successfully completing the eight-week boot camp, the marine went to officer candidates' class (OCC) at Quantico Marine Base in Virginia or to the candidates' detachment at Camp Lejeune, North Carolina, where the marines were held until there were openings in OCC at Quantico. The OCC course was normally scheduled

It wasn't enough for a marine to strip and reassemble a rifle — he had to learn to do it blindfolded, as shown at Colgate University.

for twelve weeks, but it was speeded up several times to accommodate the Corps's immediate need for second lieutenants. After they completed OCC and were commissioned, the new second lieutenants started in the twelve-week reserve officers' class.[14]

The Marine Corps was continually plagued by the imbalance between the large number of OCC candidates and its limited capacity to train them. The disparity became apparent during the first term of the V-12 program. Twenty-four hundred men were scheduled to finish their allotted time in V-12 at the end of October, but OCC capacity was only three hundred new second lieutenants per month. This meant that even with a 10 percent attrition rate, it would take up to seven months to process all of the men.

The Corps knew that the surplus could not be allowed to back up the OCC supply line for longer than four months, because by the end of February another large contingent would graduate from V-12 and be ready for OCC. On the other hand, there would be a terrible effect on morale if the Corps decided to "wash out" large numbers of candidates during the winter of 1943–1944. So the Marine brass proposed, and the Navy leadership agreed, that only sixteen hundred marines be taken from the V-12 program on November 1, leaving the other eight hundred in college for an additional term. The marines remaining in college were those who needed only one more term to complete their degree requirements; when that group was fully assigned, the youngest marines would be held back to complete the quota of eight hundred.[15]

The surplus candidate problem was thus delayed, but the strategy resulted in a more difficult situation just four months later. Approximately thirty-two hundred more marines were scheduled to complete their portion of the V-12 program on February 28. It was decided to retain half that number — 1,620 — for an additional trimester in V-12. Continual delays of this sort wreaked havoc on marine morale.

The flexibility of the V-12 program was proven again when the Navy noted that there was an urgent need for reserve midshipman candidates in the Navy. Any marine who was to be held over for an additional term starting in March 1944 was given the option of resigning from the Marine Corps and enlisting in the Navy officer candidate program. A joint letter dated February 9, 1944, from the commandant of the Marine Corps and the chief of naval personnel announced this plan to the commanding officers of Navy V-12 units that had marine detachments.[16]

A surprising 613 Marine trainees accepted the offer. They were discharged and immediately enlisted in the Navy V-12 program to go on to midshipmen's school. Because of the glut developing at midshipmen's schools, most were shipped to the newly established pre-midshipmen's school at Asbury Park, New Jersey, where they were kept busy while awaiting openings in future classes at the reserve midshipmen's schools. The marines were assured that if a man failed to make the grade in midshipmen's school, he could apply for reinstatement in the Marine Corps and, if accepted, would be discharged from the Navy.

For the Marine V-12s who were sent on to Parris Island for boot training and then became eligible for OCC (later in 1944 the name was changed to "platoon commanders' school"), the back-up was most discouraging. They were sent to a giant holding area at Camp Lejeune, North Carolina, where their unit was known as "candidates' detachment," where they were organized into companies of two hundred. The companies were assembled by age, with the oldest marines being put in the company which would be called first for the next available class at Quantico. Those in the youngest group faced the possibility of up to thirty-six weeks in candidates' detachment. In the words of one candidate, the busy-work there consisted of "rigorous training, much of it sleeping in fox holes dug freshly each night in the mosquito-ridden swamps of coastal North Carolina and practicing landings from the little PCs then in vogue."[17]

After about six weeks of that routine, three of the youngest marines decided they'd had enough. They requested permission to resign as officer candidates and be transferred to general duty as privates first class. This caused great consternation in the Marine Corps. A lieutenant drove out to the swamp and ordered them back to headquarters, where after showering and donning clean uniforms they were ushered before Maj. Gen. John Marston, the commandant of Camp Lejeune. His question: "Why do you want to be transferred to general duty?" They told him their reasons, but the officers of the Marine Corps still didn't understand them. Two naval psychiatrists were sent down from Washington to examine the men. Shortly afterwards all three were assigned to general duty. Two were ordered to a rifle company of the Second Battalion of the Twenty-Ninth Regiment, and they were on Guadalcanal within three months.

As a result of the heavy officer casualties in the Marianas campaign and on Peleliu in the southwest Pacific, a second officer candidates' class was later established at Camp Lejeune. This class, a speeded-up version lasting only three weeks instead of the normal twelve weeks at Quantico,[18] took care of part of the continuing backlog.

The scheduling of marines out of V-12 was very uncertain. The slowdown of February 1944 was followed a few months later by an acceleration. On June 30, 1944, a total of sixteen hundred men had been scheduled to finish the V-12 program and move on to boot camp and OCC, but the stepped-up war in the Pacific brought higher casualties

MARINE V-12s

and more demands for junior officers. Thus, three hundred additional trainees were taken from the colleges on July 1, 1944, for a total increment of nineteen hundred.[19] Similarly, on November 1, the scheduled figure of 1,800 V-12 graduates was increased to 2,125.

At the other end of the pipeline, 480 marines had been brought into V-12 from the enlisted ranks on November 1, 1943, while 323 came aboard in March of 1944. The commandant had approved the entrance of one thousand marines into V-12 during fiscal year 1945, which started on July 1, 1944. On that date approximately 333 men entered the program, but five hundred were added in November and again in March for a total of 1,333.[20] In July 1945 the fiscal year authorization was increased to six hundred men each term, but the contingents for the last two terms were dropped when the war ended in August.

The enlisted marines who were brought into the program were far different from those in the Marine Reserve, Class III(d), who comprised the bulk of the first contingent on July 1, 1943. The new marines were battle-tested veterans of the Pacific campaigns, not just college men with an aptitude for athletics. Some of those veteran marines gave up the stripes of quartermaster sergeants and staff sergeants to have a chance for a college education. The Marine Corps was obviously looking ahead for some regular officers to serve in the postwar force.[21]

In the first V-12 term starting on July 1, 1943, there were 11,460 marines in the program, but by the time the war ended in August of 1945 the Marine complement had dropped to 1,902. The Marine V-12 complements on other dates: November 1, 1943 — 10,965; March 1, 1944 — 5,495; July 1, 1944 — 3,653; November 1, 1944 — 1,858; March 1, 1945 — 1,808; July 1, 1945 — 1,874; December 31, 1945 — 1,251; March 31, 1946 — 683.[22]

The V-12 program, both Navy and Marine, always had to contend with a morale problem that arose from the sense of urgency to get out to the "real war." This attitude was most pronounced in the Marine Corps, which is probably not surprising in view of the Marines' reputation as a fighting force and the macho image of the individual marines.

The problem became especially acute at some schools during the first term. Impatience caused many marines to decide to purposely flunk out. As at most schools, trainees failing one or more courses were called in for an interview with both school authorities and the V-12 education officer.

Marines stationed at Georgia Tech who were called for such a meeting were asked why they were not doing better. When they answered that they wanted to be "fighting marines," and this was the only acceptable way for them to get to the war, the education officer said that he fully

MARINE V-12s

understood their reasoning and complimented them for being of that mind.[23]

By the end of October, forty-five marines had failed academically at Georgia Tech and fifty-nine at nearby Emory University, most of them deliberately. Early in November they were put on a San Diego-bound train, heading for boot camp.[24] Dr. Eugene B. Sledge, author of *With the Old Breed at Peleliu and Okinawa*, who was one of those "Dago people," recalled that Capt. Donald Payzant, the officer-in-charge of marines at Georgia Tech, gave them a pep talk before they left campus, calling them "the best men and the best marines in the detachment." They left in high spirits.[25]

As explained by Sledge, the marines who were leaving V-12 felt called to a higher duty and acted on that belief. After boot camp, some of them may have regretted their decision. Sledge himself noted that if he had been sent to boot camp before V-12, he might have become a Phi Beta Kappa in V-12.

In most Marine V-12 units, the academic failure rate during the first term was quite similar to the rate for Navy V-12s, but in at least nine detachments the rate exceeded 15 percent and in some, such as Emory, Millsaps, and the University of California, it approached or exceeded 25 percent.[26]

Finally, however, the frequency of such academic failures brought official recognition by the Marine Corps of the real reasons for them. V-12 Bulletin No. 93, dated September 21, 1943, established a procedure for channeling requests for "transfer to general duty," thereby avoiding further deliberate academic failure. But no requests under this procedure were to be approved before November 1.

The marines who opted out of the program during the first term "to get to the war" soon had their wishes fulfilled. They fought in many of the campaigns in the southwestern and western Pacific. Casualties to former Marine V-12s were heavy in a number of operations, including Peleliu, Iwo Jima, and Okinawa.

Large numbers of those who stayed with the program and received commissions first got into combat on Okinawa, but some of the early V-12 graduates first saw battle in the same campaigns as those who had deliberately dropped out. Some early V-12 graduates served along-side a few of the officers-in-charge of detachments, who were sent overseas after their detachments were disbanded. Said Capt. Jack Doyle, formerly of Redlands, "They [V-12s] were excellent officers!"[27]

In the fall of 1943 the roster of schools with Marine V-12 detachments was almost identical to the list of schools with leading football teams. Included were Notre Dame (ranked number one in college football), Michigan, Purdue, Northwestern, Western Michigan, College of the Pa-

MARINE V-12s

cific, Southwestern University, Colorado College, Duke, Georgia Tech, Southern California, University of Washington, and such previously obscure football schools as Southwestern Louisiana Institute and Arkansas A & M. (See Chapter 33, "Intercollegiate Athletics.")

A cardinal requirement of the Navy V-12 program, and its predecessors the V-1 and V-7 programs, was that enlistees not be married and agree to remain unmarried until commissioned or released by the Navy Department. This had not been stipulated for the Marine Class III(d) enlistees, however, so when V-12 began a number of Marine V-12s were already married. This came to the attention of the Navy and Marine Corps in the first term. In early August, Marine Corps headquarters directed that further marriages were prohibited unless they had been approved in advance. Those presently married were allowed to remain in the program.[28]

Theoretically, the married marines were required to live in the barracks except on weekends, but evidence indicates that marine officers-in-charge did not enforce that policy strictly.[29]

At Denison University three marines were already married. The wife of one of the married marines, Pvt. Harold Van Tongeren, was scheduled to give birth in Holland, Michigan, early in August. On the weekend when the baby was expected, the marine asked for an out-of-area liberty pass from Comdr. Maurice Van Cleeve, USN(Ret.), and stated the reason for his request. Snapped Van Cleeve, "Denied!" As the downhearted marine was leaving the office, Van Cleeve said, "Oh, go ahead — granted." The baby did not arrive that weekend but was born shortly thereafter, and soon the baby and his mother joined Private Van Tongeren at Denison.[30]

A considerable number of V-12 marines were recalled to active duty in 1950. They suffered severe casualties in the fighting near the Chosin Reservoir in Korea. Some V-12 marines provided quality leadership for the Corps for nearly forty years. A surprising number of V-12s remained on active duty after World War II. The following V-12s reached the ranks indicated before retiring in the late 1970s or early 1980s:

George R. Brier	Brigadier General
Edward J. Bronars*	Lieutenant General
Paul Graham	Brigadier General
Harold A. Hatch	Lieutenant General
Joseph Koler, Jr.	Major General
Kenneth McLennan	General
Noah C. New	Major General
Arthur J. Poillon	Major General
Adolph G. Schwenk	Major General
Philip D. Shutler	Lieutenant General

MARINE V-12s

William L. Smith	Brigadier General
Harvey Spielman	Brigadier General
Hal W. Vincent †	Major General
LaVerne E. Weber	Lieutenant General (Army)
Edward A. Wilcox	Major General
Herbert L. Wilkerson	Major General

* Was in the Navy V-12
† Actually a V-5 attached to a V-12 unit

The Marine Corps received a full measure of service and leadership from its V-12 graduates.

21

COAST GUARD
V-12s

FROM the time of the first announcement of the V-12 program on December 17, 1942, the Coast Guard and the Marines had been included as integral parts of the Navy's plan. Whether the Coast Guard really needed additional officers or simply wanted to be considered a fully equal service is hard to determine some forty-three years later. Whatever the reason, the Coast Guard's part was carefully limited from the beginning. On June 5, 1943, Comdr. W. B. Tucker, USN, of the Procurement Office, established in a letter to the commandant of the U.S. Coast Guard that the Coast Guard's quota for the July 1 term would be 150 V-12s — a small number, even considering the relative sizes of the Navy and the Coast Guard.[1]

The Coast Guard had no equivalent to the V-1, V-7, or V-5 programs and so could not draw officer candidates from such sources. Neither did it participate in any meaningful way in the nationwide examination of April 2. It was true that Navy applicants successful in the examination could request assignment to the Coast Guard or the Marines, but it appears that those services never intended to use that source to fill their quotas.

The Coast Guard decided to allot its entire quota to enlisted men already on active duty with the Coast Guard. The first term allocation of 150 was divided as follows:

Arizona State Teachers College	9
College of the Holy Cross	6
Duke University	19
Harvard University	11
Northwestern University	8
Tufts College	7
Tulane University	7
University of Michigan	8
University of New Mexico	4
University of North Carolina	20
University of Pennsylvania	12
University of Redlands	6
University of South Carolina	4
Yale University	29

COAST GUARD V-12s

Later there were minor revisions in this allocation, but essentially it was maintained.[2]

About two-thirds of the total Coast Guard input was called July 1 and the other part on November 1. By the end of 1943 there were 274 Coast Guard V-12s.[3]

The Coast Guard apprentice seamen seem to have been of the same caliber as the Navy trainees chosen from the active duty enlisted men. They were assigned directly to a specific V-12 unit and placed under the naval officers in charge. No Coast Guard personnel, either officers or enlisted, were detailed to assist in the program.

In the first quarterly muster roll reported by the Navy commanding officers on September 30, 1943, the Coast Guard men were simply interfiled in the Navy lists. This did not satisfy the commandant of the Coast Guard, however, who requested that a separate muster roll of Coast Guard trainees be sent to him quarterly from each V-12 unit. This was done on December 31 at all units having Coast Guard quotas, and some also filed amended returns for the September 30 muster report.[4]

Before the second term had been completed, the Coast Guard decided that it did not need the V-12 program. Again, it is difficult to determine whether it had no need for additional officers or whether it just didn't wish to put up with the administrative problems caused by 274 of its men being assigned to Navy units.

Navy V-12 Bulletin No. 188, dated February 19, 1944, gave each Coast Guard V-12 two choices: (1) receive a discharge from the Coast Guard and then re-enlist in the Navy to continue as a Navy V-12; or (2) leave the V-12 program and return to his former rating at an assigned Coast Guard duty station. Those set on a Coast Guard career could realistically only choose the latter, whereas men who were looking forward to that officer's stripe and the educational benefits remained in V-12. This approach provided a graceful, face-saving way out for men who were having difficulty with their studies. They only needed to assert a desire to remain in the Coast Guard and did not have to admit failure.

Between early March and May, the Coast Guard program self-destructed. Investigations at several schools showed that about 80 percent of the trainees opted to continue in the V-12 program and the other 20 percent returned to the Coast Guard at their former ratings.[5]

Except for the extra quarterly report required for its trainees, the Coast Guard's participation had caused no problems, and its disappearance in early 1944 went virtually unnoticed except by the 274 men who had been Coast Guard V-12s.

22

NEGRO V-12s

IN MID-1942 the Navy finally opened every enlisted rating to blacks. Until then they had been given only two Navy choices: steward's mates or seabees (construction battalion). The possibility of black officers had not been seriously addressed.[1] Thus, with the announcement of the April 2, 1943, V-12 examination, the question arose: "Is the program open to Negroes?" It was asked by Dr. Mordecai Johnson, the president of Washington, D.C.'s Howard University, one of the nation's leading black institutions, in a letter to the Navy in late March.[2]

But Secretary of the Navy Frank Knox's reply of March 30 was quite ambiguous, so on April 1 Dr. Johnson fired back a request for clarification. He wrote, "My specific question to you on behalf of Howard University and on behalf of the students who are preparing to take these examinations, is whether the Navy now has a policy which will admit a Negro student to the real possibility of becoming an officer in the Navy and whether these examinations in reality do as a matter of fact offer such a Negro student a first step toward this end."[3]

Finally, on April 3, the day after the nationwide examination, Secretary Knox made this unequivocal statement in reply: "the Navy College Training Program admits all students selected for this program, including Negroes, to the possibility of becoming officers in the Navy and the examinations offer the first step toward this end."

This was the first public statement that blacks were eligible, but the decision had already been made in March when the ten regional directors and the College Entrance Examination Board director, Dr. John M. Stalnaker, were in Washington to get final instructions for the examination. They asked the Navy if Negroes would be allowed to take the test. Lt. Comdr. Alvin C. Eurich, USNR, director of the Curriculum and Standards Section, went to see Rear Adm. Randall Jacobs, chief of personnel.[4] Jacobs told him it was an interesting question and should be studied. Eurich protested that they had been studying it for months and that the point of decision had been reached. Jacobs told him to send him a memo on it. Eurich returned to his office, typed up the memo, and put a red sticker on it to denote "urgent." Jacobs passed the memo to Secretary Knox, who in turn sent it to the White House.

NEGRO V-12s

The memo came back promptly with these words penned on the side: "Of course Negroes will be tested! F. D. R." Thus, the decision was made at the highest level of góvernment.

As the exchange between the Navy Department and Dr. Mordecai Johnson illustrated, however, this monumental decision by President Roosevelt was not made public. It was only after Dr. Johnson's persistence that the word was passed around that blacks were to be considered.

The question of whether the Navy would carry through on its promise remained. The possibility of a commission as a naval officer was heady stuff for a white seventeen-year-old high school senior. To blacks, the opportunity must have seemed impossible — there wasn't even one black officer in the U.S. Navy at that time! But the black students who applied for the V-12 program proceeded with the attitude that they had nothing to lose by applying.

Unfortunately for historical research, the race of an applicant was not noted on the V-12 application blank, so the College Training Section was apparently unaware of how many black V-12s were actually accepted. It did not know who they were or where they were. In some cases its first definite knowledge came on the July 1 starting date, when one or more blacks, in accordance with orders, reported to colleges in the deep South, where the mixture of the races in educational institutions was then prohibited by state law.[5] In answer to urgent calls from the commanding officers of those units, the College Training Section again demonstrated its marvelous adaptability. Dr. Raymond F. Howes, Commander Adams's right-hand man, recalled, "We had just gotten out V-12 Bulletin No. 5, which authorized each commanding officer to transfer up to 5 percent of his complement to another unit for 'valid academic reasons.' So we directed them to use that authority." That took care of the immediate crisis.

How many Negroes were actually in V-12 units that first term? That is unknown, but in a memo to Secretary Knox on September 29, 1943, Assistant Secretary of the Navy Adlai E. Stevenson wrote, "I feel very emphatically that we should commission a few Negroes. We now have more than sixty thousand already in the Navy and are accepting twelve thousand per month. Obviously, this cannot go on indefinitely without making some officers or trying to explain why we don't. Moreover, there are twelve Negroes in the V-12 Program and the first will be eligible for a commission in March 1944."[6]

But an internal Navy Department memo issued a year later on September 20, 1944, indicated that a maximum of nine blacks could have been in the V-12 program at the time of Stevenson's message to Secretary Knox. Thus, it is clear that the Navy was not sure of how many

NEGRO V-12s

Negroes were in the program in the first year. The memo itself indicated in its last sentence that "since no separate records are kept for Negroes, this summary may be incomplete."[7]

The summary included in the September 20 memo stated that at that date two Negroes had been appointed to commissioned rank after completing V-12 and that another one was presently in a reserve midshipmen's school.[8] It continued, "In addition to the three who have completed their training in V-12 there are thirty-seven Negroes now in the Navy college program and five of the original forty-five have been separated." The thirty-seven still in the program had entered it in classes as follows:

Classes Entering

July 1, 1943	2
November 1, 1943	4
March 1, 1944	6
July 1, 1944	25
	37

Of those thirty-seven, the memo said, "Eighteen had expressed a preference to become deck officers, eight engineering, two supply, five premedical and four are in dental school." It also noted that of the twenty-five blacks who entered the V-12 program on July 1, 1944, seventeen were enlisted men from the ranks and eight were civilians who had come by the examination route.

In March of 1944 the Navy commissioned twelve Negroes as ensigns and one as a warrant officer at the Great Lakes Naval Training Station. These were the first black officers in the history of the U.S. Navy.[9] None, however, was a V-12.

By June 1, 1945, there were thirty-six male and two female black officers in the Navy. There were also thirty-six men in the V-12 program and three in the supply corps school at the Harvard Graduate School of Business Administration.

In the fall of 1943 the Negro Newspaper Publishers Association asked the secretary of the Navy if there were any racial barrier to blacks' entering the V-12 program. Instead of replying that there were already Negroes in V-12, the secretary simply answered that there were no racial barriers.[10] Later that fall, Bureau of Naval Personnel Circular Letter No. 269-43, issued December 15, 1943, stated that the V-12 was open to all men without discrimination on account of race. But no publicity had been given to the presence of Negroes already in the V-12 program.

The caption of the photo in *Life* magazine of April 24, 1944, showing the first twelve black ensigns commissioned by the Navy failed to mention anything about the V-12s coming up through the program. Earlier

NEGRO V-12s

in April, a mother in Seattle had written Secretary Knox asking if there was "a program for Negro boys like the V-12 Program you have inaugurated for white boys." She noted that her son would be seventeen in August and that he was "more interested in the air division of the Navy or Marines than in seafaring."[11]

The reply came on May 12, 1944, after Secretary Knox's death, from a lieutenant commander in the Officer Procurement Division. He advised the mother that "the V-12 Program is open to Negroes" but added that quotas for this training had been filled and it was not known when another qualifying examination would be given. Again the Navy had an opportunity to state unequivocally that Negroes were already in the program, but it failed to do so. The letter added that "as yet no provision has been made for the acceptance of Negroes in the Naval Aviation Cadet Program."

The figures available from isolated memos and even *The Negro in the Navy* volume of the administrative history of the Navy in World War II written in the fall of 1945 do not indicate exactly how many blacks actually entered the V-12 program or how many successfully completed it. But making allowances for those already commissioned, those who washed out of the program, and those known to be in it on June 1, 1945, it is unlikely that the total number for the three years of V-12 exceeded seventy-five.

The few blacks who did enter the program found life in V-12 to be about the same as their white colleagues did. It was a tough program and they had to give it their best to succeed. One black V-12 said, "I had to work like crazy just to survive!" But the opportunity was there, and it could lead to the highest levels of the Navy.

When Samuel L. Gravely, Jr., received his orders to the V-12 program in October 1943, he was on Navy duty at the section base in San Diego. Having passed the V-12 test, Gravely had been recommended for the program by his commanding officer.[12] Gravely's orders sent him to the University of Southern California in downtown Los Angeles, where he began registration and spent the night. The next morning he was directed to report to the administration officer, who advised him that he was to be transferred to the V-12 unit at UCLA. The reason for the transfer was not explained.

Having already completed some college, Gravely spent only two semesters in the V-12 unit at UCLA. On July 1, 1944, he reported to the pre-midshipmen's school in Asbury Park, New Jersey, and a month later was transferred to the reserve midshipmen's school at Columbia University, where he received his ensign's stripe on December 14, 1944.

Ensign Gravely was released to inactive duty in 1946, but was recalled by the Navy in 1949 as assistant officer-in-charge of the Navy Recruiting

NEGRO V-12s

Station and Officer Procurement Office in Washington, D.C. Thereafter Gravely transferred to the regular Navy and had a variety of assignments, including Korean War duty. In 1962 he received command of the U.S.S. *Falgout,* a destroyer escort. Lieutenant Commander Gravely thus became the first black to command a Navy warship.

After several other seagoing commands he advanced in 1971 to rear admiral; again, he was the first black to achieve such a rank. In 1976 he became Vice Admiral Gravely. He served as commandant of the Eleventh Naval District, commander of the Third Fleet for two years, and director of the Defense Communications Agency for his final two years before retiring from the Navy in 1980.

Carl T. Rowan, nationally syndicated columnist and former U.S. ambassador to Finland, was another of the pioneer black V-12s.[13] On November 1, 1943, Rowan reported to the V-12 unit at Washburn College, Topeka, Kansas, where he apparently was the only black in the unit. On July 1, 1944, he was transferred to Oberlin College, where he roomed with two other blacks, Samuel Leonard Dean, Jr., and Alonzo James Fairbanks. Oberlin College, which had a long history of equal opportunity regardless of race, provided a hospitable environment for these pioneer V-12s.

On October 27, 1944, Rowan completed V-12 and was transferred to the midshipmen's school at Fort Schuyler, New York, where he received his ensign's commission four months later. He returned to Oberlin after the war to earn his bachelor's degree.

Dr. Horace B. Edwards, another black V-12, recalled that social life was nearly nonexistent for him during the term he spent at Union College in the summer and fall of 1944. He was transferred at the end of October to Denison University, but he remained there only a few days before being assigned to Oberlin College, where he moved into the room just left by Carl T. Rowan. His roommates were Samuel L. Dean, Jr., and Alonzo J. Fairbanks. At Oberlin he found a much happier environment.[14] After two semesters there he was transferred to the NROTC unit at Marquette, where he obtained his degree and commission. In 1986 he was president of the ARCO Pipeline Company in Independence, Kansas.

Samuel L. Dean, Jr., was transferred to the midshipmen's school at Notre Dame on February 28, 1945, and was commissioned four months later. He later graduated from law school and lived in Washington, D.C.[15]

Alonzo J. Fairbanks, who came into V-12 after passing the March 1944 nationwide examination, finished his Navy work in the NROTC unit at the University of Wisconsin at Madison, where he was located when the wartime program ended. He received his bachelor's degree in

NEGRO V-12s

1948, but he declined the commission offered at the conclusion of his peacetime NROTC training. He later earned a master's degree and a Ph.D. in biophysics and taught physics for several years at the American University in Beirut. In 1986 he was on the staff of the Inter-Varsity Christian Fellowship at the University of Minnesota, working primarily with international students.[16]

When James E. Ward and Arthur "Pete" Wilson entered the Princeton University V-12 unit in July of 1945, some of the faculty members expressed disapproval and a few alumni voices were raised in protest to the commanding officer, Capt. F. G. Richards, USN, and to the officer-in-charge of V-12, Lt. John A. Guy, USNR. The protestors clearly implied that they would ask Secretary of the Navy James V. Forrestal, a Princeton alumnus, to transfer the men in question to another V-12 school if Captain Richards did not initiate such a move himself.[17]

Wilson, Ward, and Lieutenant Guy all recalled that Captain Richards summoned the two trainees to his office and apprised them of the objections raised by the faculty and alums. Richards told the two trainees that he would be glad to transfer them to another school if that was what they wished, but if they wanted to stay at Princeton he would back their decision. Both Wilson and Ward had been happy with their situation at Princeton and hadn't known any problem existed until the captain advised them, so they decided to stay.

Captain Richards said, "Fine! Now if anyone attempts to go over my head to transfer you, I'll recommend to the Navy Department that the Princeton V-12 Unit be closed." After that stand was communicated to the objectors, the problem ceased to exist.

Ward and Wilson were discharged when the V-12 program closed in June 1946. Both enrolled in the peacetime NROTC program at Princeton. Upon his graduation in the fall of 1947, Ward was commissioned an ensign in the U.S. Naval Reserve. Years later, when he was participating in a Black Awareness Seminar at Princeton, Ward was identified by the *Princeton Alumni Magazine* as "one of the first three black graduates of the University."[18]

Ward graduated from Seton Hall Law School and served as personnel administrator of Research Cottrell, Inc., in Bound Brook, New Jersey. He later became a hearing officer for the Texas Railroad Commission, the state agency that regulates pipeline companies.

Wilson played on the Princeton varsity basketball team both as a V-12 and as a civilian. He remained in the NROTC unit at Princeton during the postwar period, but after his marriage between his junior and senior years, he was not allowed to continue because the requirement that trainees not be married carried over into NROTC. He continued to take the naval courses, however, and after his graduation from Prince-

Princeton University Archives

V-12 trainees James E. Ward and Arthur "Pete" Wilson talk over the V-12 program at Princeton.

NEGRO V-12s

ton in 1948 he took the officer qualification test in Chicago and received his commission as an ensign in the U.S. Naval Reserve shortly thereafter. After many years of service as U.S. marshal for the Eastern District of Illinois, Wilson retired. In 1986 he was an investigator for the Illinois Department of Children and Family Services.[19]

In 1986, Dr. R. Fred Sessions, the former commanding officer at Illinois Institute of Technology, remembered designating one of the two blacks in the unit as a platoon leader. He recalled that at the school's Navy Ball at the Stevens Hotel the black platoon leader was the only trainee to bring his date over to meet the skipper and his wife.[20]

The two black V-12s at IIT were William Jenkins and Frank A. Crossley. On June 23, 1945, Crossley completed the chemical engineering course at IIT and was awarded his B.S. He was commissioned four months later at Columbia Midshipmen's School and then served aboard the U.S.S. *Storm King* (APA 171) in the Pacific.[21]

Crossley was the subject of two columns in the *Chicago Defender*, a weekly (now a daily) serving the black community. The columns were written by S. I. Hayakawa, a professor of English at Illinois Institute of Technology and later U.S. senator from California. Hayakawa's first column appeared early in 1945, when Crossley was the only black among five hundred V-12s at IIT. On August 17, 1946, after Crossley returned to inactive duty, Hayakawa interviewed him again for an account of the experience of being one of fewer than forty black officers in the U.S. Navy.

On the troop transport to which he had been assigned, Ensign Crossley was the only black among thirty-five officers. Under his command were thirty-six men, all white. Columnist Hayakawa asked him, "Did your men show any resentment over being commanded by a Negro officer?" "No," said Crossley. "Well, didn't they even notice that you were Negro?" "Yes," Crossley said, "When they first saw me, they looked surprised — the way the boys at Illinois Tech look at you when they find that you are going to be their English teacher. After they got over their surprise, they acted towards me just as they do to other officers."

Stopped on that approach, Hayakawa tried again. "How about your brother officers? Did they treat you right? Did any of them try to cold-shoulder you?"

"No," said Crossley. "They treated me just as another officer. The men asked me the same kinds of questions they ask other officers. The officers talked to me no differently from the way they talked to each other."

Hayakawa summed up Crossley's experience in this manner: "So Frank Crossley has come home from his Navy service with no dramatic stories of injustice, of fights against prejudice, of indignities nobly borne, of triumphs over discrimination. Yet his uneventful and un-

NEGRO V-12s

triumphant tale is itself a triumph. His kind of uneventful, peaceful integration in joint work with other men is the kind of thing that we hope for all over America."

After the war, Crossley returned to IIT to earn his master's degree in metallurgical engineering in 1947 and his Ph.D. in the same specialty in 1950. He was employed as an instructor at IIT, then served fourteen years as senior scientist at the Illinois Institute of Technology Research Institute. He became a senior member of the Research Lab at Lockheed Missiles and Space Company for the following eight years and then managed the Department of Productibility and Standards at Lockheed Missiles for four more. In 1986 he was a consulting engineer to Lockheed Missiles.

At Swarthmore College, a Quaker school with a long tradition of equal opportunity, it took the V-12 to bring about racial integration. The Navy apparently sent three black V-12s to Swarthmore.[22] One of these men was Norman T. Matlock from Akron, Ohio.

DePauw University at Greencastle, Indiana, was another V-12 school that had some black trainees. One was Jesse T. Holmes, who was ultimately commissioned. Another was Robert L. Randolph, who came to DePauw on November 1, 1943, from East St. Louis (Illinois) High School after passing the nationwide examination on April 2, 1943. He was commissioned an ensign in 1945. After the war he returned to DePauw to get his A.B. degree in 1948.[23] Randolph was recalled to the Navy in 1950; he left as a lieutenant (junior grade). He earned an M.S. at the University of Illinois in 1954 and a Ph.D. at Illinois in 1958. He served in various educational positions, including executive vice president of Chicago State University and president of Westfield (Massachusetts) College. He then became vice chancellor of the Massachusetts state college system, and later president of Alabama State University. He also served in the 1960s as deputy executive director of the U.S. Equal Employment Opportunity Commission and as deputy associate director of the Job Corps.

Besides the schools already mentioned, other V-12 units that had black trainees at one time or another include Dartmouth College (Fritz Alexander), the University of Notre Dame (Carl Coggins and Alexander Poindexter), Miami University, and Purdue. It appears that Purdue had the only blacks in the Marine V-12 program. There were least nine.[24]

Other black V-12s who successfully made it through the program and received their commissions are mentioned in the 1951 book, *The Integration of the Negro into the U.S. Navy*, by Dennis D. Nelson.[25] Nelson did not identify their V-12 colleges. They included Theodore Chambers, Elmer Garrett, John W. Lee, John McIntosh, William Morgan, Joseph Pierce, and James E. Saunders. Nelson noted that "on March 15, 1947,

NEGRO V-12s

Ens. John W. Lee, a former V-12 graduate . . . , was transferred into the Regular Navy — the first Negro officer in history so selected."[26]

Despite the lack of complete information on the numbers of black V-12s, it appears that their success rate in the V-12 program was very good. Their postwar achievements are considerably above average. Five of those mentioned above have been listed in *Who's Who in America*. When this is considered in comparison to the estimated total of less than seventy-five black V-12s, it appears that in terms of percentages, their postwar achievement was considerably above average.

For its time, the V-12 program's decision to include blacks was an exceptionally bold step. The educators in command of the program believed in seeking the men best qualified to become naval officers, and Comdr. Arthur Stanton Adams had the authority to back that decision.

How did the V-12 program affect the black V-12s? Vice Admiral Gravely said, "The V-12 Program was for me a turning point in my life. It gave me an opportunity to compete on an equal footing with people I had never competed with before. It gave me an opportunity to prove to myself that I could succeed if I tried."[27]

The V-12 program was the first step in the integration of the officer corps of the United States Navy. It admitted black trainees to the officer training route a full nine months before the United States commissioned its first black naval officer. It was a pioneering effort, established by the decision of the president of the United States and carried out faithfully by the officers in charge of the V-12 program. As such, it deserves landmark recognition.

When this is considered in comparison to the estimated total of less

23

PATHWAYS
BEYOND V-12

FOR the irregular V-12s, those with advanced college standing when the
program began, opportunities and pathways were limited by the majors
they were already pursuing and by the number of terms they were to be
allowed in the program. Trainees with a business or economics major,
for example, might be directed into the supply officer route, going to
supply school at the Harvard School of Business for either the four-
month program, which was comparable to midshipmen's school, or the
twelve-month program, during which the trainee had midshipman status for the first four months and became a commissioned officer for the
last eight. Those admitted to the twelve-month program were getting
the Navy version of the advanced course of the Harvard School of Business; the program trained many future leaders of the American business community.

Irregulars who were already in a premedical, predental, pretheological, or engineering curriculum continued toward those goals. Irregulars
with other majors usually moved into the deck officer route and were
admitted to a reserve midshipmen's school when they had completed
their allotted number of terms in the V-12 program. At the end of each
term, however, the program turned out so many men eligible for midshipmen's schools that the schools could not immediately absorb them
all.

A pre-midshipmen's school was first set up at Norfolk, Virginia, but
it was moved in the spring of 1944 to two adjacent resort hotels on the
boardwalk at Asbury Park, New Jersey.[1] It was primarily a holding area
to keep the V-12 graduates busy and in good physical shape while awaiting openings at the midshipmen's schools.

The regulars, those entering the V-12 program as beginning freshmen, were given the Navy screening test during the second term of their
V-12 experience. Test results were of key importance in determining
future pathways in the program and beyond. The screening tests resulted in these possibilities for the regulars:

PATHWAYS BEYOND V-12

1. Engineering. A general engineering course in the V-12 program was set up for six terms, including those already completed. The specialty engineers were given a total of eight terms to complete electrical engineering, chemical engineering, etc. The engineering graduates were expected to go through midshipmen's school, but special two-month courses was set up for civil engineering grads at Camp Perry, Virginia, and Camp Endicott, Davisville, Rhode Island.

2. Supply. The supply officer route sent trainees to several V-12 units that were designated supply specialties starting March 1, 1944. These led to the four-month or twelve-month courses at Harvard, as mentioned earlier.

3. Deck. Those who were not directed elsewhere continued in the V-12 specified curriculum for four terms and were then sent to midshipmen's school, or to pre-midshipmen's school if the midshipmen's schools were full.

4. Naval Reserve Officers Training Corps. The NROTC program was originally set up to supplement the production of naval officers by the U.S. Naval Academy; the commissions could be obtained in the regular Navy. At the start of the war, twenty-seven institutions had NROTC units; the students were enlisted in the Navy but remained on inactive status. They were not paid and generally wore their uniforms only once a week, when they had marching drill.

NROTC students were called to active duty on July 1, 1943, and at that time they technically became part of the V-12 program and received the pay and other benefits of V-12s. But their curricula continued as before and included many courses not offered to or required of the basic V-12 trainee, such as ordnance, seamanship, and foreign language. The plan was for students to simultaneously receive the degree of bachelor of science in naval science and commissions as ensigns without having to attend a reserve midshipmen's school.

When a critical need for junior officers arose in preparation for the landings in Europe and the stepped-up fighting in the Pacific, the Navy decided to call up the junior class of the NROTC. Thus, both seniors and juniors were commissioned in February of 1944, the juniors at the end of just six terms.

At the start of the V-12 program, it had been determined that additions to the NROTC program after July 1, 1943, would come exclusively through the V-12 program. Thus, the screening test given in November of 1943 led to V-12s being assigned to become the new sophomore class in the NROTC, replacing in March the seniors who graduated in Feb-

PATHWAYS BEYOND V-12

ruary. The sudden February call-up of the junior class meant that twice as many vacancies occurred in the NROTC, so 500 additional irregulars were taken into the program at the start of March, and interviews were held early in the March term of 1944 with hundreds of regulars in the standard deck curriculum. Those regulars who were seriously thinking about making the Navy a career were steered toward NROTC. The war-time NROTC program entailed a total of seven terms.[2]

The V-12(a)s, who were originally enlisted as V-5s to pursue the flight training program, had simply been diverted into V-12 for what was scheduled to be two terms. During the second term of 1943, some additional pilot trainees were needed, so a quota was given to each V-12 school. Traveling teams from the Bureau of Aeronautics went around to interview candidates who wanted to switch from straight V-12 to V-12(a) with the intention of moving on to flight training. Those who wished to take advantage of that opportunity greatly outnumbered the slots available, so the traveling boards had no trouble filling the openings.

The aviation pathway was a most difficult one for all who came into the program as V-12(a)s or who converted to that route as a result of the opportunities offered in late 1943. The aviation program was an on-again, off-again affair that continually encouraged and then dashed the hopes of the aviation-minded men. The main reason for this erratic performance was the good news that casualties in the Pacific had been much lighter than the Bureau of Aeronautics had feared.

When quotas for the aviation pathway were being reduced, the V-12(a)s were given several opportunities to switch to the deck pathway. In September of 1944, when it was decided that only about half of the qualified V-12(a)s would be accepted for flight training, all V-12(a)s who had entered on November 1, 1944, were given the opportunity to switch to the upper-level deck programs. Those who entered on March 1, 1944, were automatically transferred to V-12 and given the same options as any other V-12.[3]

Those who entered V-12 from the enlisted or examination routes were originally given an opportunity to express a preference for premedical, predental, pretheological, or engineering training. If no preference was expressed or the Navy did not see fit to grant it, the trainee became a regular deck candidate.[4]

After the screening test was given and the results were made available to the Navy officers, the trainees were not arbitrarily switched to what-ever routes the officers felt were most appropriate for their talents. They were given a chance to apply for the specialty of their choice. They were judged on aptitude (shown by the screening test), past academic perfor-mance, and desire by one or more naval officers and often a faculty

PATHWAYS BEYOND V-12

member from the requested specialty. If a transfer of specialty or college was recommended, it was made at the beginning of the next term.

The premedical and predental curricula were identical, entailing five terms for those starting as beginning freshmen on July 1, 1943. All of the premeds, whether regular or irregular, when entering their fifth term, were asked to apply to medical or dental schools and to list their first three choices, one of which had to be in the naval district where the trainee was then located.

The medical and dental schools had set up their own separate committees of the deans of all of the medical and dental schools in each naval district. The district training officer served as a consultant to each committee to judge the officer-like qualities of the candidates. The committees classified all of the applicants from that district mainly by their academic performance. They were listed as A, B, or C, with a number next to each letter giving them a ranking within each group. A man rated A-1 would be better than one listed A-6. The deans then proceeded to fill the quotas for each school.

Often the end of the undergraduate V-12 term did not coincide with the beginning of the medical school freshman terms, which usually only began once a year, traditionally in the fall. If the accepted trainee finished his V-12 program before medical school began, he would be sent to a naval hospital for orderly duty until the start of the medical program. Some trainees stayed in the naval hospitals for nearly nine months.

Premeds and predents who were not selected for a medical or dental school were not just dropped from the program. The Navy offered them the opportunity to go to a reserve midshipmen's school, which could lead to a commission as a deck officer. This again showed the wonderful flexibility of the V-12 program.

The Navy's concern for the individual choices of the men and for their success, along with its flexibility in assignments, made the V-12 program one that has been favorably remembered by nearly all of the men involved in it.

24

PHYSICAL TRAINING

ALTHOUGH there were some exceptions, such as the athletes who signed up for the Marine III(d) program, most of the V-12s reporting from civilian life were not, at least in the Navy's view, in top physical condition. In fact, most were far from it. Although the Navy purposely kept military training to a minimum in the V-12 program, it clearly planned to bring the trainees up to a much higher standard of physical fitness. The Navy referred to the process as "physical hardening."

In connection with its aviation program and the officer orientation and midshipmen's schools, the Navy had for some time been using a series of prescribed courses to achieve its physical fitness goals. It measured progress by standard tests. According to an article in the *Dartmouth Alumni Magazine*, the Navy had decided that its personnel, both officers and enlisted, must be prepared

> for long periods of standing, climbing, swimming, moving quickly, and enduring physical strain. Accordingly, in its physical training the Navy endeavors to develop strength, muscular endurance, agility, flexibility, and a certain amount of speed. The concomitants of these are mental alertness, efficiency, initiative, and competitive spirit. The main objective is not to develop the specialized skill of the expert but to bring each individual to the highest level of all-around fitness.[1]

The man in charge of the Physical Training Section of the Training Division of the Bureau of Naval Personnel was Comdr. James Joseph (Gene) Tunney, the former heavyweight boxing champion of the world. The Navy had brought this sports celebrity on board in 1940 to develop and carry out its physical fitness program. Those who came in contact with Tunney in the Navy agree that he favored calisthenics at every conceivable time of the day. He also strongly opposed smoking, drinking, and intercollegiate athletics.[2]

When the V-12 program was being organized, the Navy's physical training program was already well established, so it was simply a matter of adapting it to the new officer training program. It was decided that the trainees would have an hour a day of physical training in classes for five days a week, and on a sixth day there would be military drill, which

PHYSICAL TRAINING

would be credited to the physical training requirement. In addition, twenty minutes of early morning calisthenics and running six days a week were a standard part of the program.

The commanding officer of each unit was responsible for carrying out the program. The assignment was given to a commissioned officer designated as the athletic officer. The program was actually operated by petty officers designated specialists (A), with the "A" standing for athletic.

The college's athletic department was expected to furnish as many instructors as possible for the PT program. At most schools other than major universities, however, nearly all of the instruction was provided by the Navy. Most physical education departments had been decimated by enlistments in programs such as the Navy chief specialist (A) and its counterparts in the other services. Whether or not civilian instructors were involved, the V-12 physical training was controlled by the designated Navy officer.

Comdr. James Joseph (Gene) Tunney, USNR, officer-in-charge of the Physical Training Section of the Training Division of the Bureau of Naval Personnel, receiving a letter of commendation from Vice Adm. Randall Jacobs, chief of naval personnel.

National Archives

PHYSICAL TRAINING

The specialists (A) had been recruited nationwide from among coaches, athletic directors, and professional athletes to conduct physical training programs at a variety of Navy activities. Some former college athletes were also secured for the programs, even if their current line of work was not directly related to physical fitness. Most were high school and college coaches, but the ranks of the specialists (A) included many well-known names, such as George McAfee, highly regarded halfback of the Chicago Bears. The majority of the men recruited for this program became chief petty officers, but those who had been assistant coaches were often made specialists (A) first class or specialists (A) second class. Some were also commissioned as ensigns.

The specialists (A) received their training at the Norfolk Naval Station. Before V-12 began, a two-week orientation class was held at the Bainbridge Naval Training Station near Baltimore for those being assigned to V-12. Commander Tunney liked the way the physical training program was being operated at Bainbridge and decided it should be the pattern for the V-12 program. About five hundred specialists took the two-week course. For the final days, Commander Tunney arrived and gave the specialists (A) some advice on handling the V-12s: "Make them work!"[3] With those words firmly in mind, the five hundred specialists were sent off to meet their charges in the 131 V-12 units.

The calisthenics were held just after reveille, which occurred between 0530 and 0600. Depending upon how scattered the housing units were and their distance from the athletic field, the exercises were held either in front of the dorms or on the athletic or drill fields. At schools where the only suitable place for the exercises was the athletic field, trainees had to double-time to and from the field, where a specialist (A) directed the men from a high platform. These exercises were scheduled rain or shine in many V-12 schools. In others, however, calisthenics were canceled when there was a downpour. Indeed, V-12s were quoted in a number of campus newspapers as praying for rain more fervently than the farmers did in the Dust Bowl during the 1930s![4] But even when the hated exercises were called off because of inclement weather, the trainees were not allowed an extra twenty minutes of sleep. Often a "field day" was declared to get some extra cleaning done in their rooms.

At some schools where the gym or field house was large enough to accommodate all of the trainees, calisthenics were moved indoors during cold weather. In other units, trainees had to wear raincoats, peacoats, watch caps, and knitted woolen gloves to stay warm outside.

In some northern schools, early morning exercises were suspended temporarily by flu epidemics. The commanding officer at Alma College in Michigan got specific approval from the College Training Section of

PHYSICAL TRAINING

Marine Corps Historical Section

Reveille brought the V-12s out for calisthenics, even in cold weather, as the above shot of University of Washington Marines clearly shows. Some could not keep their eyes open or their mouths closed at that early hour.

In many V-12 units the chief specialist leading calisthenics performed on a platform like this one at Central Missouri State Teachers College.

Central Missouri State University Archives

PHYSICAL TRAINING

his decision to discontinue the exercises during the most severe part of the winter.[5]

The exercises usually started off with the jumping jack, which was the easiest exercise, and therefore the favorite of most V-12s. The others consisted of deep knee bends, squat jumps, squat thrusts, touching the toes, and various other bending and trunk-twisting measures.

The chiefs were always on hand to make sure that the men did not "goof off" during calisthenics. This was deemed especially necessary in the wintertime when the event was held in comparative darkness. One trainee recalled with distaste that the C.O. was usually "lurking in the bushes" to see if he could catch anyone not performing.[6]

At units with Marine detachments the leathernecks sometimes had their own early morning program, which at times resembled field maneuvers and lasted the whole hour from five to six.[7]

The hour of physical training class was set up in many different ways. At some large schools with ample facilities, all the PT classes were scheduled to meet at one specified hour during the good weather of the summer and fall. When winter began, their classes were scheduled at different hours of the day in the school's gym.

The Marines had an entirely different physical fitness program, which stressed combative activities. (See Chapter 20, "Marine V-12s.")

For the first term every Navy V-12 trainee was involved in the basic training program. The first eight weeks were devoted to general conditioning, involving a great deal of calisthenics and much cross-country running. Much of this running was double-time with the intervals of single-time (marching) becoming further apart as the physical condition of the men improved. Usually part of the running took the men off campus, so the chiefs designated one man to be in charge, who led at the front of the platoon. Two and a half to three miles was the running distance considered sufficient for inclusion in the hour's class.

In many schools the prescribed route was only one to one and a half miles long, so it had to be traversed twice. In nearly every place where such a situation prevailed, a few trainees decided that running the route once was easier than doing it twice. At an appropriate spot away from campus and the chief's watchful eye, they would dive into some bushes, rest until the group returned, and then unobtrusively rejoin it. They got away with this maneuver at most schools, but at one college (and probably several more) a chief apparently noticed the diminished numbers as the group passed through the campus at the end of the first lap, so he ordered it to halt and then called the class roll.[8] There is no record of the punishment meted out to the goldbricks, but in keeping with the Navy's disciplinary tradition of making an example of the "wise guys," it is a good bet that the absentees spent more than a few weekends on campus.

PHYSICAL TRAINING

The two to three miles of running usually ended with a trip through the unit's obstacle course. All obstacle courses were different, but every chief specialist aimed to make his the most difficult one in the naval district. It was a competition in toughness. Sometimes they glamorized it a bit by calling it a "commando course." At Gonzaga they called it "the fracture farm."

Climbing over and under barriers, wriggling under low-strung barbed wire, scaling walls, climbing ropes, using a rope to swing across large puddles or small streams, climbing cargo nets, and traversing sizable distances hand over hand on overhead parallel bars were a few of the more common ingredients in V-12 obstacle courses. One school had three obstacle courses!

The second eight weeks of the basic course involved more combative and competitive conditioning activities, such as boxing, wrestling, and hand-to-hand simulated combat.

The basic course included swimming. The Navy, as could be expected, needed to make adequate swimmers of its officers, so early in the program it required a swimming test to judge the ability of each man. He was classified as a "nonswimmer" until he could enter the water feet first from the height of five feet and swim fifty yards. Generally, about 10 percent of the V-12s were put into the "nonswimmer" category at the start of the program.

The Navy classified "swimmers" into three classes. A third-class swimmer was one who passed the bare minimum to escape the "nonswimmer" label. A second-class swimmer could enter the water from a height of ten feet and remain afloat for ten minutes while swimming one hundred yards using each of three strokes for a minimum distance of twenty-five yards each.

To be classified as a first-class swimmer the man had to remove his trousers in the water and inflate them by tying knots in the bottoms of the legs and blowing air into them from under water. They would then support the man in the water, much like the water wings of the 1930s. He also had to swim 220 yards using any strokes he desired. He had to be able to disengage himself from the grip of a man of his own size while maneuvering to get the man into a carrying position, and then tow him twenty-five yards. Finally, he had to swim underwater twenty-five yards, breaking the surface only twice during the distance.

In the basic physical training course, one day a week was devoted to swimming for everyone, while the "nonswimmers" were required to put in three days a week in the pool. This was not recreational swimming; the chiefs worked the men very hard, providing an additional incentive for them to pass the swimmer's test and escape that three-day-a-week harassment.

At the end of the first sixteen-week term, the trainees had a chance

PHYSICAL TRAINING

Erling Lagerholm

After a couple of miles of double time, the V-12s started the obstacle course at Muhlenberg College.

Every obstacle course was a bit different. At Worcester Polytechnic, the trainees were required to traverse this span hand over hand.

Erling Lagerholm

PHYSICAL TRAINING

This wall had to be scaled at Milligan College.

On the Milligan College obstacle course, more than one pair of shorts got snagged on this low-strung barbed wire.

PHYSICAL TRAINING

Shipboard evacuation technique was taught at all of the schools by having the trainees jump into the pool in uniform, strip off their pants, tie the legs, blow air into the legs, and use them as water wings. This scene at the University of Dubuque was repeated in all of the schools.

PHYSICAL TRAINING

Climbing out of the pool fully clothed and wringing wet and then scaling the cargo net was another essential in learning to be rescued after an abandon-ship procedure.

PHYSICAL TRAINING

to go into a "maintenance" program, which consisted of competitive sports, including basketball, touch football, and softball. For many men it was the first introduction to more exotic sports such as handball, soccer, lacrosse, and squash. The maintenance program was clearly more enjoyable than the basic.

How did the Navy determine who was eligible for the maintenance program? By a diabolical device officially known as the "Navy Standard Physical Fitness Test" but popularly known as the "strength test." It was given to all trainees on the eighth and sixteenth weeks of each term. It was a five-item motor fitness test that consisted of sit-ups, push-ups, pull-ups, squat jumps, and squat thrusts. The sit-ups, push-ups, and pull-ups had to be done in the manner the Navy specified. Any cycle done incorrectly would not be counted.

The first three exercises were fairly well known to American high school and college men, but most were not introduced to squat jumps and squat thrusts until they entered Navy life. The squat jumps were described as follows:

> The subject stands in a comfortable position with heel of left foot even with toes of right foot. The hands are then interlocked with palms down and held on top of the head. From this position the subject drops to right heel and immediately springs with both feet to an upright position, interchanging feet and dropping to the left heel. This exercise is continued until exhaustion occurs. [9]

The squat thrust was the only exercise done against time. This was a one-minute performance in which the man started in an upright standing position. Then he bent his hips and knees to a squatting position and placed his hands on the floor either between, in front of, or outside his knees. He then thrust his legs in an extended position backward so that the body assumed the push-up position. The man then returned his legs to the squat position and stood erect to complete the cycle. It was necessary to come to a straight standing position with the chest up, but the Navy noted that "a slight, total body lean is permissible." [10]

The Navy's scoring system for each event gave one or more points for each time the required exercise was performed, but the scoring worked something like a reverse geometric progression, at least for sit-ups. To achieve a 90 percent score the trainee had to do one hundred sit-ups, but to achieve a 100 percent mark it was necessary to do 205. One hundred and five more sit-ups for a mere 10 percent addition to the score!

The strength tests were done throughout the V-12 schools during the early weeks of the term to measure the physical condition of all the men entering the program for the first time. In the first V-12 term the eight-week tests were actually given in the first few weeks of September of

PHYSICAL TRAINING

Webb Institute of Naval Architecture Archives

The hated strength test was especially difficult at Webb Institute, where the trainees doing squat thrusts had to perform them on a brick pavement. Other trainees counted how many were completed in one minute.

1943 and the sixteen-week tests were administered near the end of October.

V-12 Bulletin No. 51, issued July 23, 1943, set the standard that apprentice seamen with the lowest 30 percent of all the scores for the unit were to be considered as "falling below the established standards" and were to be "reassigned to the basic training program until they meet requirements." Thus, no matter how well they performed in those tests, the lowest 30 percent were destined to return to the basic program. The possibility of escaping from basic was a powerful incentive to all of the V-12s to try harder on the next round of tests. A later V-12 Bulletin set the standard for avoiding a repeat of the basic program at a score of fifty. This permitted 95 percent or more to move into the maintenance program.

Sharp improvements in V-12 strength test scores are indicated by those reported from St. Ambrose College in Davenport, Iowa. The entering July 1943 average score was forty-seven points, which by the September test had risen to fifty-five points. By the end of October St. Ambrose's average had climbed to fifty-seven.

The St. Ambrose *Sea Breez* reported that a memorandum from Ninth

PHYSICAL TRAINING

Naval District headquarters stated that the district average in July was 45.7, which by October had risen to 59.3. The highest V-12 score in the Ninth Naval District was 71.4 (Peru State Teachers) and the lowest 52.2. The *Sea Breez* noted with chagrin that "Of 48 schools in this District, only eight schools had a lower October average than St. Ambrose!"

By the summer of 1944 the *Sea Breez* announced that Company Three had placed first in the most recent strength test "with a staggering average of 70.1. Second Company gained second place with 68.4 and Company One trailed with 67.8."

St. Ambrose trainee Johnny Longsdorf was generally the leader of his unit, scoring 81.8 in September and 95.0 in June. In the June 1944 test second and third places scored 89.0 and 88.0, respectively. It was noted that of the St. Ambrose trainees "only ten men could top 80.0, but a large number went over the 70.0 mark."

School newspapers took great pride in the strength test feats of their trainees. At the University of California, for instance, *The Spyglass* of May 13, 1944, proudly noted that Marine Private Philip H. Skarin had racked up a 93.2 score in the strength test. He scored 100 percent in sit-ups (205 sit-ups), push-ups (89), and squat jumps (127), while scoring forty-three out of a possible forty-eight squat thrusts for an 87 percent score and twenty-two out of a possible thirty-seven chin-ups for a 79 percent score in that category. Lt.(jg) C. L. Hepler, the athletic officer, said he believed that Skarin had set a national record. As noted earlier, a St. Ambrose trainee scored a 95.0 a month later, in June.

Often the leading company in strength tests was given a special liberty as a reward for its achievement, which was probably the best incentive that could be made available to the V-12s.

The athletic officer in a unit kept a card file recording the scores of each man in successive strength tests. Most trainees felt it behooved them to show continual improvement, so once a man had achieved enough in a test to remain out of the basic course, he tended not to overdo it so that it would be easier to improve the next time the test was given.

That kind of foresight was also used in other phases of the physical training program, especially in the boxing classes. Usually a trainee was paired off with someone about the same size. Most partners reached a mutual understanding: "You don't hurt me and I don't hurt you." But the chiefs understood this and were always ordering the men to "mix it up" and "throw some real punches!"[11]

The toughness of the physical training leadership varied a great deal from campus to campus and depended upon both the orders of the

PHYSICAL TRAINING

athletic officer and the zeal of the individual chiefs. At some schools the program was exceedingly tough.

Especially in the Southern climes where the humidity and temperature remained high for months at a time in the summer, cases of heat exhaustion were fairly common. Dr. Rufus C. Harris, president of Tulane University, received a number of complaints from parents and others, so he enlisted the medical officer's support to curb the excesses of the program during summer months.[12]

Many other complaints also reached BuPers, and finally, on September 14, 1943, V-12 Bulletin No. 86 made it clear that the physical conditioning program was planned to be one of gradual achievement and not a crash program. Commanding officers were instructed to make it less rigorous, but few V-12s remember that happening. Perhaps the cooler weather of the fall and the improving condition of the men coincided with the appearance of the Bulletin, so that any possible slackening of the standards went unnoticed.

One curious aspect of the program pertained to the issue of physical training uniforms, including shorts, swimsuits, and sweat suits. Instead of furnishing them along with the rest of the uniforms, the Navy decided to charge each trainee for this clothing. The total cost was just over three dollars. But for that money the trainees got superb quality. The sweat suits lasted some V-12s for up to ten years.

The Navy had a standard list of physical training equipment for each V-12 unit, the quantities depending upon the number of trainees. For Carroll College, in Montana, with 270 V-12s, the list was as follows:[13]

Boxing gloves	45 sets
Footballs	12
Medicine balls	12
Basketballs	30
Softballs	72
Softball bats	36
Softball masks	12
Catcher's mitts (softball)	12
Fielder's gloves (softball)	36
Pairs punching bag gloves	36
Volleyballs	18
Volleyball nets	9
Soccer balls	9
Skipping ropes	30
Fast inflated punching bags	6
Handballs	18
Punching bag platforms	6
Swivels	8
Electric pencils (a wood-burning type of tool)	3

PHYSICAL TRAINING

In addition to these items, six more could be ordered if the unit wanted them. They were:

Heavy punching bags	6
Slip covers for mats (5' x 10')	32
Overall mat covers (22' x 22')	4
5' x 10' two-inch thick mats	8
5' x 10' three-inch mats	8
Jumping standards (for high jump)	1

This equipment was designated for physical training classes and did not include such nonessentials as uniforms or equipment for intercollegiate athletics, which remained strictly the school's obligation.

One result of the rigorous physical training was that the trainees needed bigger meals. In more than one unit the trainees complained that they were not getting enough to eat. That was usually taken care of in just a few days.

In most units, one chief petty officer was unofficially singled out for unflattering recognition by the trainees for his diligence in applying the physical hardening process. Usually the eager-beaver chief got his comeuppance when the trainees put on skits for "happy hours" or, at some schools, in elaborate musical reviews. The chief could easily be recognized as a ridiculous character. In Southern Methodist's "V-12 Varieties," for example, Chief Sandig became "Chief Sandtic."

Every unit had its stories about the chiefs. In one unit, a chief specialist put a trainee in charge of calisthenics and told him to work the men hard until he got back. Then he forgot and didn't return until forty-five minutes later when the V-12s were in a state of exhaustion. Of course, the chief then chewed them out for being "in such lousy condition."

Other chiefs were known to hold fingernail inspections and then give ten-minute lectures about dirty fingernails. Some held skivvie inspections, too. They always seemed ready to surprise the trainees and chew them out if possible.

In spite of the complaints at the time and a few unhappy recollections of those classes, the PT program did achieve its goal of significantly improving the physical condition of the men. Most trainees of that first period freely acknowledged in later years that they had never before — and never again — been in such good physical shape. They were indoctrinated into the benefits of physical conditioning long before that practice became a national interest in the 1970s and later.

One trainee recalled some forty-three years later that "the physical education program was excellent. I was relatively weak and poor in

PHYSICAL TRAINING

The rope climb required of all trainees aided the "physical hardening process."

sports and the V-12 Program toughened me up immeasurably and gave me a new interest in sports." Another trainee with a long memory, while admitting that the physical training was "outstanding," said, "The use of football coaches as chief athletic specialists was inspired as we all wanted to go back after commissioning to receive salutes."

A casual look at the V-12s returning for reunions some forty years after the program indicates that the habits developed during the program have provided a lifetime of benefits to the individuals. A study of the health histories of the V-12s might well produce a medical stamp of approval for that arduous but beneficial physical conditioning that they all hated so much.

25

ACADEMIC LOAD

THE V-12 academic load was a much heavier one than students carried in a normal civilian program, and the rigorous physical training program was very demanding as well. In addition, countless snatches of time were spent carrying out the various facets of military discipline, including the trainees' mustering for and marching to chow and taking responsibility for the tidiness of their persons, rooms, and personal effects.

The forced schedule of reveille, study hours, and lights out also placed a burden upon the V-12 trainee that was not felt by his civilian counterpart. In a February 1945 article in *Northwest Science*, Ronald V. Sires, assistant professor of history at Whitman College, questioned why it was necessary "to force people to rise at 6:00 A.M. or thereabouts." He wrote, "I have watched otherwise healthy young men week in and week out in a depressing state of fatigue and wondered why it was necessary to have it so."[1]

Professor Sires's observation was shared by instructors in all 131 V-12 schools. Those whose classes followed breakfast, lunch, or the trainees' hour of physical training found that up to half of the men dozed off at some time during the hour.[2]

The trainees still vividly recall the strain they were under. One of them wrote, "The academic standards were not relaxed. If anything, they were more severely enforced. In my case, there was very little social life. I was stretched to maintain the academic load with the physical fitness and Navy training programs."[3]

Dean Karl S. Pister of the College of Engineering of the University of California (Berkeley) remembered it this way from his trainee days: "Looking backwards in time, I would have to say that academic standards at that time were rigorous and that no special concessions were made because the majority of students on campus were in military programs." He was referring to the University of California campus.[4]

Academically the V-12s were neatly divided into two groups by ground rules set up at the time of the first announcement of the program in December of 1942. Basically, those who were already in college would be allowed to pursue their majors; only minimal requirements would be

ACADEMIC LOAD

added by the V-12 program. They were given the name of "irregulars." The comparative difficulty of the academic load for an irregular V-12 was determined by his major, which he had chosen himself. Thus, he was not faced with surprises or courses outside of the scope of his general interest and capabilities.

The second group was comprised of men who were entering college for the first time. They were called the "regulars." At the time of the original V-12 announcement the prescribed curriculum for the regulars had not been determined. The Standards and Curriculum Section, with input from professional societies, deans of various colleges and universities, and the Navy Advisory Educational Council, soon established that curriculum and announced it on March 31, 1943. This report eventually became V-12 Bulletin No. 1. The beginning curriculum was totally prescribed, heavy on math and science, and allowed no deviation. Thus the regulars clearly had a tough schedule. They had no option of pursuing something more to their liking.

The men involved in the regular program were (1) the recent high school graduates who came into the program from civilian life as a result of the April 2 examination; (2) the V-12(a)s, who wanted to fly and were generally not interested in attending college at that time; and (3) the men from the fleet, many of whom had never expected to pursue

Drew University Archives

ACADEMIC LOAD

a program of higher education and so had not taken a college preparatory course in high school. While a few of the old salts did have a college
prep background from high school, they had usually been away from
academic work for a year or more, which added to their burden.

As was noted in Chapter 18 ("The 'Old Salts' "), the selection of the
first three contingents from the enlisted ranks was flawed by not properly qualifying the applicants. The original method brought into the
program a number of bright men who were totally unsuited — either
by education or temperament — for academic work at the V-12 college
level. Within a week or two after the scholastic work began in July of
1943, the problems of inadequate educational background began to
appear. The first tests that were given in another few weeks provided
proof of the difficulties.

One thing that must be remembered is that many of the teachers
were not giving instruction in their usual subjects, even at schools with
great reputations. Professors of geography were teaching physics, and
art teachers were involved with engineering drawing. Even with such
shifts, even at the large schools, some additional faculty members had
to be hired from outside the institution.

This scene of V-12s at Hobart College illustrates that every available space was
used in teaching the engineering drawing classes. (Note the flypaper streamer
hanging down in the middle of the photo.)

Hobart and William Smith College Archives

ACADEMIC LOAD

While the major schools were able to attract the cream of the available talent, the smaller, less prestigious schools were not so fortunate. There the dean had to settle for the best he could find among the ranks of recent graduates, older graduates who had not taught in many years, and high school teachers.

Thus, inevitably, in certain courses some schools were providing inferior instruction for the V-12s.[5] Since most of the new instructors were hired to teach math and science to the regulars, the poorest teaching was more common in some of those difficult courses. The combination of some inadequate educational backgrounds, inferior teaching, and the inherent difficulty of the regular curriculum worked together in most schools to produce major problems.

The results of the first tests inescapably indicated that if something wasn't done — and soon — a sizable proportion of the V-12 regulars would soon be on the way to boot camp or to the restoration of their former enlisted rating, a process referred to as "academic attrition." At Oberlin College a report dated August 24, 1943, indicated that 31 percent of the sailors and 48 percent of the marines were failing one or more courses. A full one-fourth of the men were failing two or three courses.[6]

Many colleges realized almost simultaneously that trainees having difficulties would need tutoring. Dean Steve Lacy of Milligan College believes his school was the first to bring the pressing need for formal tutoring classes to the attention of the College Training Section. Milligan had quickly set up such a program and invited the CTS to send some officers (preferably college deans in uniform) to visit the school to evaluate the program. This was done early in August of 1943. Shortly thereafter, the Navy gave its blessing to such "refresher courses," setting forth details in V-12 Bulletin No. 67, issued on August 25, 1943.[7]

Several weeks after Bulletin No. 67 was issued, Dean J. C. Peebles of Illinois Institute of Technology wrote to his counterpart at George Williams College, which was a subcontractor in the Navy V-12 program operating under IIT. The freshman V-12s assigned to IIT were housed and taught at George Williams College nearby on the south side of Chicago. Dean Peebles wrote:

> It has recently come to my attention that certain "refresher" classes in Physics have been organized during the last few weeks at George Williams College. My information is that about forty students are receiving additional instruction. These students have been divided into sections of five men each and instructors have been secured from among graduate students in Physics at the University of Chicago.
>
> I am advised that these classes were organized at the request of the students, and that a fee of forty cents per lesson was charged each student in order to remunerate the special instructors.

ACADEMIC LOAD

In general, the Navy, I believe, will have no objection if an individual student, acting purely on his own initiative, makes arrangement for some tutorial assistance. However, when as many as forty men ask for such help, I believe this is something which should have the attention of the institution. "Refresher" classes should be organized when as large a group as this is involved, and the responsibility should be on the institution and not on the student.[8]

Dean Peebles cited Navy V-12 Bulletin No. 67 and acknowledged the Navy's willingness to pay for such instruction as a part of the program. He then stated, "The Navy objects to any courses . . . for which the students are charged a fee."

During the early months of the program, some professors, particularly at the schools with high admissions standards, decided to reevaluate their role in teaching the V-12s. In the past, many of them had sought to challenge and weed out the inadequately prepared, but now

Sailors, marines, and a civilian discuss a physics lab experiment at Oberlin College, illustrating that most of the V-12s had classes with civilian students.

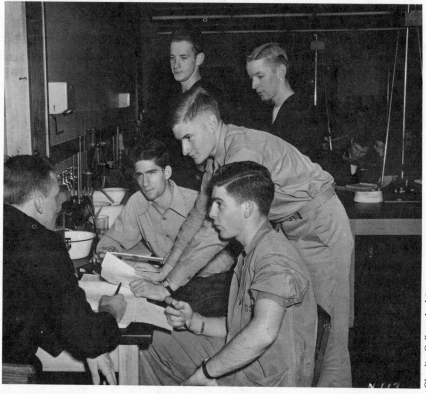

Oberlin College Archives

ACADEMIC LOAD

it appeared to them that their goal had changed and as a result, some of their teaching methods needed to be revised. Instead of flunking students, they recognized the need to help them succeed in order to become commissioned officers. Washing out a salvageable trainee did not help the war effort.

What motivated the trainees? The most powerful force was their desire to become commissioned officers in the United States Navy. The old salts saw this great opportunity most clearly and thus were prepared to sacrifice the most for it. The aviation students knew that they needed to stay in for the two terms in order to get on with their goal of flying, so they could put up with the inconvenience for that relatively short period of time. For the regular V-12s who came as a result of the high school examination, this was an opportunity that was almost too good to be true. These young V-12s were the group that had been most thoroughly screened and were presumably the best prepared to handle the program academically. Most were from the top halves of their high school classes and were highly motivated.

Second in importance to the will to succeed was the ever-present threat (except for the fleet men) of boot camp. Although they made light of it with their songs, such as "When the Roll Is Called at Bainbridge I'll Be There," for most of the nonfleet men that was a fate to be avoided at all costs.

The threat of being restricted to campus because of academic defi-

Marines and sailors set out at Villanova on a civil engineering class.

Villanova University Archives

ACADEMIC LOAD

ciencies was used universally to spur the trainees — irregulars as well as regulars — on to better classroom performance. Although at some schools the commanding officer and college authorities euphemistically referred to the posted names as the "academically weak" list, the list still denoted restricted men, and most V-12s tried their utmost to avoid being restricted. This was particularly true of trainees at men's colleges that were quite remote from civilian contact, particularly contact with young women. Restriction was a hated, but effective, procedure.

Early in the program there was a general perception among trainees that failure in one course meant separation from the program. But, in fact, one failure did not automatically mean boot camp. The first V-12 Bulletin to treat academic separations was No. 92, issued on September 21, 1943.

The efforts of the Navy and the colleges to provide additional instruction were important in keeping many of the men in the program. Still, an alarming number of men wound up failing courses. When they did not automatically go to boot camp, but were put on academic probation, they realized that one failure did not mean an automatic ticket to Bainbridge or to Great Lakes. On all campuses, this knowledge created a great sense of relief.

The Marine Corps had an even more tolerant attitude toward course failures. At Duke University in 1944, even marines failing two courses were retained in the program if there was evidence that improvement was being made and that the trainees were good officer material.[9]

At the second Navy-college conference on the Navy V-12 program held at Columbia University on May 12 and 13, 1944, Capt. Arthur S. Adams told of an encounter he had had with a V-12 at a western college. It was during the free time in the day, and Adams was wandering around the dorm when he came upon a young sailor. "What was your work in the V-12 Program like during the term just passed?" he asked. Replied the sailor, "Oh, I averaged about a B, Sir." Adams said, "That's good," patted him on the back, and turned to go. As Adams related it, "Then with the utmost respect he laid his hand lightly on my arm and said, 'Pardon me, Sir, you don't seem to realize that for me a grade of B is *damned good.*'"

Adams told his Columbia Conference audience, "It is that spirit of reaching forward, of extending oneself, that I think has characterized the students in the V-12 Program. If it is true, as I am sure you will agree it is, that we only grow by stretching, there are thousands of young men who, contrary to the Biblical statement, have added many cubits to their stature."[10]

One of the most interesting aspects of the difficult curriculum for the regulars was that it brought together the very youngest group of V-12s

ACADEMIC LOAD

Iowa State University Archives

V-12s in this math class at Iowa State College gave their undivided attention to their professor.

with the oldest group. Most of the fleet men were freshmen, so they were thrown in with the seventeen-year-olds who had come directly out of high school college preparatory courses. The irregulars, the college men with advanced standing, were taking higher level courses and thus were not in a position to give much help to the fleet men.

The older men had learned from their seagoing experiences to seek help wherever it could be found, so they were not shy about asking for help from the high school boys. The young men were flattered by this recognition from the old salts and readily responded to it. They in turn felt closer to the older men and eagerly welcomed the Navy tips that were freely offered in a sort of *quid pro quo* arrangement. The result was that the younger men were helped to mature and the older ones were helped to succeed in the academic program. It was a mutually beneficial association.

Trainees from practically every V-12 school have remarked about the willingness of trainees to help others. Many a trainee went down the hall during study hours and poked his head in room after room until he got a positive answer to his query, "Were any of you guys able to work problems number fourteen and fifteen in Analyt?"

ACADEMIC LOAD

What did the faculty members think of the academic qualifications of the V-12 students? An article in the *Dartmouth Alumni Magazine* of March 1944 ("Teaching Navy Trainees") noted that "many of the [V-12] students are handicapped by their schooling." Professor Arthur Dewing, the author of the article, mentioned the previous overseas service of many of the older trainees and added, "Many are likely to have had to work in shops or factories, less often offices, and sometimes on fishing boats or farms. Most feel more natural with tools, motors, radios, or machinery than books."

When asked more than forty years later about the academic abilities of V-12s, most faculty members from all institutions could still easily distinguish between the regulars and the irregulars on the basis of the courses they were enrolled in. Generally, the professors thought the irregulars were equal to the civilian students they were replacing.

The Navy's policy of leaving men entering V-12 from the V-1 or V-7 programs in the schools where they were currently enrolled created a solid core of irregulars at the school, sometimes equaling 40 percent of the V-12 enrollment. Thus, many of the irregulars were the same students the professors had taught as civilians in another course the previous term.

Regarding the regulars, it was difficult for most professors in the 1980s to distinguish between the V-12s who had come from the fleet and those who had arrived directly from high school. But all of the faculty members recalled quite vividly that a number of their students in the regular curriculum had problems because of their inadequate educational backgrounds.[11]

When asked how the V-12s compared to their previous students, the professors' answers seemed to depend upon how selective the schools were regarding admissions standards. Professors at some schools with rigorous admittance standards, such as Dartmouth, felt that the V-12s as a whole were not as good scholastically as the men they had taught before. On the other hand, Professor A. R. Sweezey of Williams College wrote in *The Williams Record* (p. 2) on May 9, 1945,

> I have found as many bright students among the V-12s as among the pre-war students, and they are just as bright. Both groups have had their fair share of those at the other end of the scale; but, again, the proportion is no greater in the V-12 Unit and the dumbest are certainly no dumber — in fact, I think that would probably be impossible — than they were in my big sophomore economics course before the war. Not only do the V-12s compare favorably as to intellectual ability with our pre-war students, they are, it seems to me, more serious, more mature in outlook, and more active in their interest in college. This is evident, not only in class, where I find a generally more vigorous, alert atmosphere, but also in outside activities.

ACADEMIC LOAD

Teachers from the small state and private schools with relatively easy admittance standards regarded the V-12s as "among the best students we have ever had on the campus."[12] Schools with admission standards in the middle ground found the V-12s to be about equal to the school's previous civilian students.

Many V-12 schools gave entering V-12 freshmen the same screening tests they gave to their civilian students so they could make a valid comparison. At Ursinus College, the results showed that the school had been able to maintain its academic standards of incoming freshmen, even though 40 percent of them came through the Navy program. The college, which routinely gave tests prepared by the American Council on Education, reported that its 1943 freshmen ranked eleventh in the group of 241 colleges and universities that used the test; in 1944 they ranked tenth out of 282 colleges using the test.[13]

At Baldwin-Wallace College a study made at the end of the first term indicated that the entering V-12 freshmen were "significantly better prepared intellectually for college work" than the average college freshman.[14]

An interesting sidelight of the academic program was how the honor codes were handled at the relatively few schools where they had been in place when the V-12 program began. The codes generally stated that a student's work, whether a term paper or an examination, must be his own and be done under honorable conditions. Evidence of cribbing, copying, or other forms of cheating were grounds for expulsion from the institution. In many schools, such as the University of Virginia, the control of the entire honor system had been delegated to the students. Being selected as a member of the Honor Committee was one of the highest forms of campus recognition.

For civilian students who had matriculated because they wanted to attend a particular school, the honor system was an important facet of the school's life. The system was always emphasized in interviews with prospective students and in promotional literature, and it was part of the obligation of students attending that institution.

But for the sailor or marine being sent to the school the situation was entirely different. In some cases he had never heard of the institution before being ordered there. Naturally he knew nothing about its honor code. His "honor code" was probably an unwritten one derived from his experiences in the military, high school, or another college that lacked an honor code. For the average V-12, then, the honor code system that was explained to him when he arrived was a totally new experience. Expecting hundreds of men to immediately and totally comply with such a code called for a "Pollyanna" faith in the inherent goodness of man.

ACADEMIC LOAD

The basic premise that each man should do his own work was consistent with Navy regulations. The sticky part of most honor systems was the requirement that the student turn in any violation he observed, which was at variance with American boys' hesitancy to become "squealers."

For various reasons, the honor codes were suspended for the duration of the war at Yale and several other schools. But at Rice Institute, Trinity College, the University of North Carolina, the University of Virginia, Williams College, the University of the South, California Institute of Technology, Webb Institute, and other schools, they remained intact.

The most intense debate on the honor code took place at the University of Virginia, where nearly twelve months elapsed from the time of arrival of the V-12s until the honor code's place in V-12 was finally settled.

During the first few months the role of the honor system was the subject of some private debate. The debate came to a head on December 10, 1943, when a campus poll was taken to determine if the honor code should be applied only to academic matters or carried over to other phases of university life as well. Specifically, the question was "Shall the university's Honor Code cover the Navy's mustering system?" Would a false muster, or failure to report a false muster, be a violation that had to be reported to the Honor Committee? [15] If it was determined that the honor code covered false mustering, and if the committee found such charges against a man to be valid, it was bound to order expulsion of the student, which meant an automatic end to his life as a V-12 and, thus, his chance to become an officer in the U.S. Navy.

According to *College Topics*, the campus newspaper, 761 students voted in the December 10 poll. By a ratio of fourteen to one, they voted to keep the mustering system out of the honor code! [16] The paper reported that University of Virginia medical students overwhelmingly voted with the majority, and that even the undergraduate civilian students, who were not subject to the mustering system, were opposed to putting it into the honor code. Accordingly, the Honor Committee ruled that false musters were not included.

But the matter had not been finally settled. Six months later an open letter sent to the Honor Committee and published in *College Topics* called for a reevaluation of that decision, pointing out that "the exclusion of certain lies from the Honor System is not compatible with the Honor Code and must not be tolerated." [17] The letter was signed by thirty-nine prominent students, some of them V-12s. A week later another eighty-four students added their names to it, and some faculty members also chimed in. Some members of the Honor Committee made their support of the idea public as well. [18]

ACADEMIC LOAD

Then, on June 13, 1944, another vote was held, this time just among V-12s and NROTCs. It was overwhelmingly in favor of restoring the one-hundred-year-old honor code to its former coverage of all phases of student life. The subject was finally settled![19]

Why the change in attitude among the trainees? Part of the reason is that those who were not able to handle the academic work and those who were not serious about it had long since departed, leaving the conscientious and more capable students still in the program. They recognized the benefits of an honor code and felt they could live up to even the false mustering situation. No V-12s were ever dismissed from the University of Virginia for false musters, although a few were expelled for other offenses against the honor code.[20]

The College Training Section recognized early that required study hours were going to be necessary for the success of the program. It was a heavy schedule and the trainee's time had to be allocated effectively. Still, the Navy allowed individual commanding officers to establish the proper study hours on each campus. Some skippers went overboard and set up a very burdensome schedule, while others were at the opposite end of the spectrum. At Westminster College, a change of command in the spring of 1944 brought the first required study hours.

The time for taps and lights out was left to the commanding officer. The time varied from school to school between 2200 and 2400. Reveille, also at the C.O.'s discretion, was between 0530 and 0600.

The hours between lights out and reveille left a minimum time for sleeping. In fact, sleep was always in short supply at the V-12 units. One reason was that most station regulations prohibited trainees from being in their bunks at any time during the normal class day, which meant they were allowed to occupy the bunk only after 1630 in most schools. They could not use the study hours to sleep, either.

The rigidity of the lights out regulation varied from unit to unit. Some schools made absolutely no exceptions, while others permitted rooms to keep the lights on for an extra hour or more by special permission. Some units set up late-hour study rooms so that those cramming for exams or finishing term papers had the time and place to work, albeit at the expense of their limited sleep time. In some schools the mess hall was set up as a study room in the late evening hours. After official lights out the heads often became crowded with V-12s studying for tests. It was not unknown for trainees to resort to the use of flashlights under their blankets when cramming for tests.

The duty officer was always watchful for violations of the lights out policy, which could lead to demerits and restriction on the weekend. The moral: don't get caught studying late without permission.

It can be seen, then, that the academic program was a source of

ACADEMIC LOAD

constant pressure. There was never enough time! The serious student had to use part of his weekends to catch up on both his sleep and his studying. The less serious student, who wouldn't let anything cut into his liberty time, often paid for that decision in his academic performance.

How did the V-12s stand up under this constant pressure? The next chapter deals with attrition.

26

ATTRITION

ACADEMIC failures are, unfortunately, a part of college life, and the difficulty of V-12 assured that they would occur in that program. The structure of the V-12 program provided the trainees with exceptional motivation to succeed, but at the same time the war provided some men with strong motivation to withdraw from the program through academic failure.

Why would a man want to deliberately flunk out and forgo such a fine opportunity to advance himself both educationally and militarily? First, an academic failure did not adversely affect his service record, whereas misconduct of various types could. Thus, those wishing to get out of the program found the academic process to be the easiest way. Second, a few of the men who came into the program from overseas were motivated primarily by the prospect of home leave; they were never seriously interested in the program. Third, a few enlisted men claimed they were sent to the program against their wishes.[1] There were also those who grew impatient about getting into the "real war." The V-12(a)s enlisted to become flyers and saw the V-12 program as an unnecessary interruption.

Comprising the largest group of academic failures were those men who had had inadequate preparation in high school or had completed their formal education four or five years before and as a result had rusty academic skills. Some average or below-average students simply could not handle the difficult science and mathematics classes. Finally, some trainees could not stand the constant pressure — they gave up.

The first term brought the highest number of separations for academic reasons. Those who wanted to get out of the program were able to leave, and some who had inadequate educational backgrounds were separated. Those who were not able to handle the stress of the program were also terminated.

The second term also saw a number of separations due to inadequate backgrounds and inability to master the work. Many who left in the second term had been placed on probation at the end of the first term to give them another chance. In the third and fourth terms, there were generally substantially fewer losses. Many regulars were transferred at

ATTRITION

Muhlenberg College Archives

Whether off to boot camp or midshipmen's school, these Muhlenberg V-12s believed in living it up as they pulled out of the Allentown station.

the end of the second term because some of the smaller schools did not have either the faculty or the laboratory equipment to teach the upper-level science courses. Some third- and fourth-term attrition resulted from transfers from weaker schools to those that were more scholastically demanding.[2] The number of failures diminished for the balance of the V-12 program to levels comparable to the civilian rate, approximately 8 percent of the trainees per trimester.[3]

The report of Navy V-12 academic attrition, detailed in the *U.S. Naval Administration in World War II, Bureau of Naval Personnel, Training Activity, The College Training Program*, Volume IV, page 122, showed that during the first term 3,673 men (about 6 percent) were separated from the program. They were divided into the following categories:

Causes	Number of Cases	Percentage
Inadequate preparation	508	13.82
Low mentality	1558	42.40
Lack of application	1202	32.73
Lack of officer-like qualifications	321	8.76
Emotional instability	24	0.66
Physical illness	60	1.63
	3673	100.00

ATTRITION

These causes, of course, represent the judgments of the school authorities and the commanding officer, as reported by the commanding officer to the College Training Section in accordance with Navy V-12 Bulletin No. 87, issued October 5, 1943.

The Navy's study of first-term academic failure[4] showed that of those who flunked out, 28.57 percent had failed mathematics, 24.89 percent had failed physics, 10.14 percent had failed history, 9.20 percent had failed chemistry, 9.13 percent had failed English, and 6.04 percent had failed engineering drawing.

A comparison of the grade point averages of Navy V-12, Marine V-12, and civilian students was made at Duke University. In the second term, November 1943 to February 1944, the undergraduate civilian men achieved a grade point average of 1.0920. (In this system, a 3.0 is an A, 2.0 is a B, 1.0 is a C, and a D is 0.) The Navy students (including NROTC) averaged .9025 and the Marine trainees trailed at .6763.[5] This poor Marine showing may have been related to the low morale prevalent in many Marine V-12 detachments during the first term. (See Chapter 20, "Marine V-12s.")

Whether because more pressure was applied by the Navy and Marine officers or because most poor students had dropped out earlier, there was a dramatic turnaround in the March to June 1944 term. The civilian students' average declined to .8220, which may reflect an increase in the number of seventeen-year-olds as more upperclassmen were called by Selective Service. The Navy students scored 1.0611 and the marines became the top group with 1.0744. In the next period, the marines remained at the top of the list with 1.1054, the Navy followed with 1.0636, and the civilians trailed slightly at 1.0033. The marines left the Duke campus at the end of October 1944 but the Navy students continued to outperform the civilian students by a sizable margin until at least June of 1945.

Marine Corps attrition at Duke during the first term was 18 percent. At other units, figures also show that during the first term rates of Marine Corps academic failure were very high, in the area of 25 percent or even higher in some units.

Although grade point averages varied widely throughout the V-12 program, in many institutions the V-12s were the leading group. This was not always true, however. At Dartmouth College the civilian students, who were still being very carefully selected, consistently outperformed the V-12s.[6]

As noted earlier, failing one course was not sufficient to terminate a Navy V-12, but failure in two major courses was usually followed by dismissal from the program. When it became apparent that the trainee was in some danger of being terminated, he was called before the academic committee of the institution or the V-12 educational officer, who

ATTRITION

in the smaller schools was the executive officer. The interview was a last-ditch attempt to find out if the trainee's problems could be resolved in the hope that the Navy's already substantial investment in his education could be preserved.

The final recommendation for dismissal came from the institution to the commanding officer, who passed it to BuPers along with his evaluation of the reasons for the recommendation. It normally took about two weeks for BuPers to return its approval, so a trainee who knew he was being dismissed usually had a nonproductive period. According to Capt. Grant Brown, V-12 administrator in the Ninth Naval District and later district training officer, there was no record of the College Training Section's ever turning down the commanding officer's recommendation for separation.[7]

At many schools a letter was sent by either the commanding officer or the dean to the parents of the trainee, explaining what was occurring. In at least one instance, such a notification led a distraught mother to spend an entire morning trying to persuade a commanding officer that termination would destroy her son's future and pleading that he be given an additional chance.[8]

Although those who were obviously anxious to leave the program were dismissed as soon as their desire became evident to school and Navy officials, trainees who were making serious efforts were usually allowed to complete the term, even though it may have been apparent that separation was inevitable.

A main concern of most trainees was keeping their physical condition up to the rigid standards of the V-12 program. Their chief worry was deterioration of eyesight, which is a common problem among college students who do an inordinate amount of reading. In the V-12 program, a trainee who could no longer correctly read the eye charts could be dismissed from the program.[9] Trainees who felt themselves in danger of failing the next eye test took ingenious steps to get around that problem. Some memorized the eye charts frontwards and backwards and were ready for an eye exam at any time. A trainee at Princeton, who may have had deficient eyesight when he entered the program, had one of the first sets of contact lenses and made it through several terms of the program before the deception was discovered by the examining officer. At other schools, trainees who considered themselves in danger from the eye standards scheduled (at their own expense) regular appointments with optometrists, who were then in the early stages of developing remedial exercises for the eye. The office of Day and Day in Raleigh, North Carolina, had a number of regular patients from the Duke University V-12 unit.[10]

Some trainees who contracted serious illnesses such as rheumatic

ATTRITION

fever and polio were necessarily discharged from the Navy. A polio epidemic in the Los Angeles area caught up with several V-12s at Occidental College.

Trainees requiring major operations were usually sent to the nearest naval hospital for the procedure, although emergency situations such as appendicitis were taken care of at the closest civilian hospital. Usually, trainees who had serious surgery remained in the program, but they frequently had to drop out of the current term and pick up an additional term to make up for it.

Those who successfully completed their V-12 academic requirements and maintained their physical eligibility could pursue a variety of diversified and interesting pathways to commissions in the U.S. Naval Reserve or the U.S. Marine Corps Reserve — provided, of course, that they did not run afoul of disciplinary requirements.

27

DISCIPLINE

WHEN the V-12 program was introduced to the public, the Navy Department emphasized that "the educational training will be carried on while the men are on active duty, in uniform, receiving pay, and under general military discipline." The mention of discipline was no doubt intended to ward off criticism by those who thought the V-12 program was an unnecessary wartime boondoggle.

Military discipline covers a lot of ground. It entails (1) the inherent discipline resulting from men being bound by Navy regulations and the station regulations of their unit; (2) active ongoing-training discipline, which requires the men to be at certain places at certain times and to behave in certain ways; and (3) retaliatory discipline, which makes the men regret that they did not conform as expected to the other two types.

At all V-12 units there was a one-hour drilling period each week during the first term. Thereafter the drilling proceeded in connection with the unit inspections, which were held at the pleasure of the commanding officer and were therefore usually called "Captain's Inspections." At some schools they occurred every Saturday, while at others they varied from twice a month to once a month. Any time a visiting dignitary such as a Navy captain, governor, U.S. senator, or congressman appeared, the commanding officers were ready to hold a review of the entire unit.

Politicians appeared regularly at some units. At Southwestern University in Georgetown, Texas, Congressman Lyndon Baines Johnson addressed the students nearly every term, and each address usually called for an inspection. At one inspection in September of 1943, the special guests were Lt. Robert Taylor, the well-known movie actor, and Comdr. Jack Dempsey, USCGR, former world heavyweight boxing champion, who were in the area making a special war bond tour.[1]

Except for the sailors and marines in boot camp, the V-12s were probably subjected to more of the "chicken" type of regulations than any other servicemen — and for a much longer period than the men in boot camp. Every day there was an inspection for uniform tidiness and cleanliness. Daily room inspections also kept trainees on their toes.

Such commonplace events as eating an ice cream cone while walking down the street, not having his hat "squared," or holding a girl's hand

An inspecting officer at Hobart College instructs a trainee on the proper wearing of the neckerchief.

Room inspection was held daily, with a "white glove" inspection often scheduled for Saturdays. This inspection was at Colgate University.

DISCIPLINE

Marines stand at attention at Princeton while a Navy officer completes room inspection.

Marines at the University of Washington polish up the windows, both inside and out, getting ready for the Saturday morning room inspection.

DISCIPLINE

James G. Schneider

A Milligan College trainee walks off demerits by marching up and down a hill with a fully loaded sea bag.

could result in demerits for a trainee. One trainee at Harvard received five demerits for "conduct unbecoming an apprentice seaman." His offense: a lady crossing the street glanced up at Eliot House and saw the trainee looking out the window clad only in his skivvies.[2] Too many demerits could mean extra duty, such as drilling for one to three additional hours after everyone else had gone on Saturday liberty, or loss of liberty for the entire weekend. Fortunately, not too many demerits were handed out away from the campus.

Trainees, of course, were quick to learn how to avoid demerits. Showing up for a captain's inspection without being in proper uniform was a sure way to acquire demerits or perhaps be deprived of liberty for the weekend. In the wintertime those inspections meant wearing the blue flat hat, peacoat, and knitted gloves. One Tufts trainee who had lost his gloves was resigned to showing his bare hands at inspection when a roommate suggested, "Why don't you take off your socks and put them on your hands? Keep your pants down over your shoes and maybe the skipper won't notice." He took the suggestion, and the skipper did not notice.

At the Saturday inspection at one Marine detachment, the gunnery sergeant instructed a trainee battalion commander, "If you see any un-

DISCIPLINE

fastened buttons, jerk them off and hand them back to the owner."
Seeing an unfastened blouse pocket, the trainee reluctantly yanked the
button. It didn't give. He tried it again and again, without success. By
that time the sergeant was steaming. He pushed away the battalion
commander and gave the button a mighty pull. Again and again he
tried, but the button held fast. By this time all of the men were laugh-
ing. Grudgingly, the sergeant moved on. He didn't want to break up the
entire inspection.[3]

The V-12s were generally on their good behavior at all times. There
were exceptions. Some marines got into trouble in one town where a
liquor store closed earlier than they thought it should. It took exceptional measures by some college officials and the promise of full restitution to the store owner to keep the men in the program and out of a
court-martial.

On most campuses where there were marines, the marine officer-in-
charge was placed in charge of discipline for the entire unit. A trainee
at the University of Rochester remembers the nightly "perimeter pa-
trols" instituted by Capt. H. W. Coulter, Jr., USMC, to keep the trainees
without liberty cards from sneaking off campus. Coulter was remembered by the same trainee for busting the entire V-12 unit out of their
sacks on several nights and having Sergeant Botti drill them — par-
tially at double-time — for an hour or two because of some infraction of
the rules by an unknown perpetrator. Botti inferred that they would be
drilling all night unless somebody confessed. As far as can be determined, no one ever confessed, but eventually the men were allowed to
return to their bunks. However, calisthenics came awfully early that
next morning and the classes seemed especially long that day.[4]

A few days later, *The Company,* the student paper, had a little one-
inch box at the top of page six. It read, "Thanks, Sgt. Botti! Sailors and
Marines alike echoed that on Wednesday night (not so he could hear it
though). Sleep is getting precious with increased daily assignments."[5]

At units where there were no marines, either the executive officer or
the athletic officer usually ended up with the disciplinary chores. Of
course, the buck stopped at the commanding officer's desk, so when a
captain's mast (hearing for minor infractions) or a separation from the
unit was recommended, the C.O. had to make the final decision.

Most of the disciplinary problems at V-12 units were very minor, involving such problems as a man getting back from liberty half an hour
late, failing to appear for watch duty at the appointed time, or being
insubordinate to a chief athletic specialist. The last-mentioned was
something nearly every trainee contemplated but few actually carried
out. One sailor at Berea College believed that their universal hatred of a
particular chief petty officer was the catalyst that bound the trainees
into an effective unit.[6]

DISCIPLINE

Depending on the severity of the offense for which they were restricted or the proclivity of the trainees on that campus for leaving without permission when under weekend restrictions, the restricted trainees may have been required to report to the duty officer or to muster every four hours during the weekend, including the normal sleeping hours.

When the Navy brought in nearly three hundred new officers from civilian life and placed more than one hundred of them in charge of

An invitation to see the executive officer was not usually considered good news. This Ohio Wesleyan trainee seems to be prepared for a disciplinary session with the exec.

DISCIPLINE

V-12 units, it was inevitable that some would be "eager beavers" who took their military discipline duties far more seriously than was warranted. They were the kind who would threaten court-martials if a trainee was even slightly derelict in his duty or was impertinent when being taken to task for his infraction.

At Louisiana Tech, a trainee on one occasion reported for a noontime telephone watch about ten minutes late. The lieutenant was not pleased, presumably because he was inconvenienced for a luncheon appointment. He told the V-12 he would have him court-martialed. Wiser heads prevailed, however, and the trainee was finally given a captain's mast, the lowest form of trial under the Navy judicial system. The trainee ended up being restricted to the campus for two weekends, but that didn't turn out to be a major problem for him since his girl friend also attended Louisiana Tech.[7]

By and large the discipline at V-12 units was rather evenhanded, with the punishments usually fitting the infractions. Sometimes, in fact, punishments were milder than they might have been at another naval station, primarily because of the Navy's desire to protect the large investment it had already made in the education and training of the V-12s.

At Central College in Missouri, one trainee and his girl decided it was time for him to meet her folks, who lived some sixty miles away. Unfortunately, on the weekend selected he found himself restricted to the campus for academic reasons. He thought he had covered his tracks well and left to visit the girl's home. But a special muster during his absence tripped him up. He was destined to return to his former enlisted rating when the athletic officer interceded on his behalf and he was finally let off by being restricted to the campus for two months.[8]

Some unusual disciplinary cases also came the skipper's way. At one Southern college, a very polite, well-mannered V-12 had attended an evening church service at a nearby town and had walked a young lady home. By his account, and hers, too, nothing out of the ordinary happened. But they were met at the door by her father, who insisted that all kinds of dire happenings must have occurred on the way home and demanded that the trainee, who had just met the girl, marry her!

The V-12 excused himself and headed back to the school. The next day the father called the commanding officer to demand that this man who had "defiled" his daughter marry her. The commanding officer talked to the college president, who recalled that the same man had made the same charge against a civilian student at the college just a year earlier, so the C.O. decided to ignore the complaint.

But the father was persistent and kept contacting the sailor, insisting that he "do right" and marry the girl. The trainee had no intention of

DISCIPLINE

marrying her, first, because he barely knew her, and, second, because it would mean expulsion from the V-12 program. The commanding officer talked to the trainee and assured him that he did not have to marry the girl. The harassment by the father continued and finally the trainee asked the commanding officer to transfer him to boot camp so he could get out of the situation. The commanding officer refused, saying he was not concerned about the situation and the trainee shouldn't be either. The trainee was insistent, but the C.O. was firm.

Later that day, the V-12 went AWOL into the nearby town and placed a call to the commanding officer, saying, "This is Apprentice Seaman ———, sir. I am AWOL. Now you will have to send me to boot camp." The C.O. told him to get back on station and nothing would be done. He refused to return immediately, however, so when he finally came back, the commanding officer felt he had no alternative but to transfer him to Great Lakes the following day.[9]

As a matter of record, there were few serious charges made against V-12s. Most were handled by dismissing the men from the program. But in at least two units, the commanding officers did have major problems with members of ship's company, involving conversion of Navy funds and falsification of records.[10]

Probably the most common disciplinary problem at the V-12 units was taking unofficial liberty. As one trainee described it, V-12 units were "military encampments without fences," which led to a substantial number of surreptitious departures without proper authority. But most of the trainees had the good sense to be careful and get back within a reasonable time, so their absences were not usually discovered.

Most of the first-year men were too scared of the consequences to use that method for a few hours in town, but the old salts sometimes took their chances. So did the irregulars who had been civilian students on that campus and therefore knew all of the nooks and crannies thereabouts.

In addition to requiring strict adherence to the rigid schedule, the V-12 program involved all trainees with some military responsibilities. They marched to chow three times a day, unless their mess hall was in the same building where they were quartered. For limited periods at a few schools, such as Princeton, the regulars had to march to their first morning class, too.

All took their turns standing watch duty.[11] Sometimes it was an active fire watch, which required the man on duty to constantly patrol the buildings assigned. At other times, it was more a security watch, especially in larger cities. In such cases, the men were frequently seated at a table that had a commanding view of the building entrances to bar strangers from entering and require trainees to check in and out. It was

DISCIPLINE

this type of watch that first turned in the alarm one night when the Princeton gym caught fire during the early morning hours.

Capt. J. K. Richards was commanding officer of the Columbia V-12 unit, the Webb Institute of Naval Architecture V-12 unit, and the Naval Reserve Midshipmen's School at Columbia. He liked to do things in the traditional way. When the V-12 on watch reported to him in his office in a dormitory at 1600 every day, he was required to say, "Sir, the time is reported to be 1600. The galley fires are out and all prisoners are ashore." The challenge to the V-12s was to keep a straight face when they made their reports.[12]

On weekends, when the dormitories were sometimes almost deserted by trainees on liberty, the watch section probably performed its most useful work in protecting the building and trainee possessions from sneak thieves, who would have had as little trouble getting into the area without proper clearance as trainees appeared to have in leaving it.

The commanding officers were frequently directed through V-12 Bulletins to reduce the emphasis on the military and disciplinary side of the program. From the beginning, the College Training Section had declared that academics was the most important part of the program.[13]

Despite the pettiness sometimes directed toward the trainees, most of them got used to the process and weren't unduly perturbed by it. In fact, some trainees derived a lifelong benefit from it. Said one former V-12, "The Navy training and discipline I've used every day of my life. Sayings like 'a taut ship is a happy ship' and 'respect and consistency are more important than being popular because if your men respect you the rest will come' I've utilized daily in my career."[14]

Venereal disease was a topic given some importance in V-12, as well as the rest of the Navy. The VD films were shown regularly at whatever location could handle large numbers of viewers. One former trainee recalled the ludicrous situation of marching in cadence in the evening to see a VD film shown in the chapel.[15]

V-12 Bulletin No. 95, dated October 14, 1943, established strict rules for V-12s who acquired a venereal disease. Those who contracted syphilis would be eliminated from the program, immediately transferred to V-6 (general enlisted duty), sent to a naval hospital for treatment, and then sent on to boot camp or elsewhere. Gonorrhea or chancroidal infections were to be reported immediately so treatment could begin, but those diseases did not result in separation from V-12.

Bulletin No. 95, however, noted in section 5 that "Concealment of venereal infection by a trainee is a very serious offense and warrants not only immediate separation from the V-12 Program but additional punishment."

The bulletin also reminded the commanding officer of his responsi-

DISCIPLINE

bilities for the education of his unit in this area, but ever mindful of Navy-college relations, it cautioned him that "the film 'Sex Hygiene' should not be shown if the academic authorities object. The conspicuous display in dormitories and other housing units of the usual placard warning against venereal infection is not appropriate."

As the program moved along it became apparent that some of the men selected did not possess the officer-like qualities which the Navy felt were essential for success in the commissioned role.

At midshipmen's schools, although the Training Division had charge of education, the final decision on whether to commission a man was made by the officers of the Office of Naval Officer Procurement (ONOP). They were finding too many candidates "whose officer-like qualities left much to be desired." Such candidates would have been dropped in times of less urgent need, but some had been allowed to continue in the program and were eventually commissioned.[16]

Finally, however, in July of 1944, the ONOP decided to end situations in which a few men would be washed out at the last moment because of their lack of officer-like qualities after many months of V-12 work and three and one-half months of midshipmen's school training. Clearly, the fault for such situations lay in the selection of the men in the first place by the Office of Naval Officer Procurement, and in V-12 unit officers' not detecting the deficiencies and acting on them sooner.

Recognizing the waste to both the men and the Navy involved in bringing trainees who were not considered qualified to the final decision on commissioning, the Bureau of Naval Personnel issued Navy V-12 Bulletin No. 241 on July 18, 1944. It urged all V-12 unit commanders to carefully examine "on a continuing basis" the officer-like qualities of every man in their commands. They were further directed "to recommend promptly to the Bureau of Naval Personnel the elimination from training of all students who are unsatisfactory or borderline *in any respect.*" The Navy did not wish to provide additional training unnecessarily. It also wanted top quality officers. As a result of Bulletin No. 241, in nearly every unit some men were dismissed from the program for reasons other than discipline and academic failure.

One University of Illinois trainee had a terrible decision to make on October 1, 1944. As a loyal St. Louis Browns fan he wanted to go to St. Louis to see his heroes clinch their one and only American League pennant. The Navy, however, felt that he should use that afternoon to make up a swimming deficiency. The trainee decided on St. Louis, where he saw his Browns whip the Yankees 5 to 2. Unfortunately for the trainee, the Navy felt that he had demonstrated "unofficer-like qualities," so he was on his way to Great Lakes the next day.[17]

On March 1, 1945, V-12 Bulletin No. 291 told the commanding offi-

DISCIPLINE

cers they would soon get some help in establishing the standards for judging "unofficer-like qualities." They would be sent a list of every one of their former trainees who had been separated from any of the midshipmen's schools for any reason except physical disqualification. The list would indicate whether the separation was for academic reasons, unsatisfactory officer-like qualities, or disciplinary action. They were also given a listing of the class ranking of their successful candidates.

V-12s who ended up at boot camp often reported that they were combined in selected companies with V-12s who had washed out at other schools. Such companies were nearly always the leaders in their boot camp classes. In fact, most trainees who were sent to boot camp after a substantial period in the program found it much easier than V-12.

Men dismissed from the V-12 program, whether for academic, disciplinary, or unofficer-like reasons, still proved to have substantial attributes that the Navy could use in various enlisted ratings. Thus, after boot camp, most ended up in an enlisted school and came out rated men, holding responsible positions in the Navy.[18]

A number of men who washed out for academic reasons acknowledged in later years that they just did not have the maturity at that time to take advantage of the opportunity that was offered, but a high percentage of them eventually went back to college after the war, and some ended up getting advanced degrees and working on the faculties of distinguished colleges and universities. They proved that there was life and hope for a young man, even after washing out of the V-12 program.

28

NAVY-COLLEGE
RELATIONS

FROM the first day of the program, the Navy was highly conscious of the need for a positive relationship with the schools. It drilled the importance of this matter into the officers during the V-12 orientation course, and the V-12 Bulletins later added reinforcement.

The first Columbia Conference was the Navy's attempt to achieve broad recognition of the benefits to both parties of the close cooperation needed to successfully implement the program. When the college presidents left the meeting, it appeared that the effort to lay the foundation for a good working relationship had been successful. The negotiating parties were time and again told to be fair and reasonable in their dealings with the schools. They were not to compromise on major points, but they were to leave the institutions feeling good about the Navy relationship.

To impress the second-level college authorities with the broad objectives of the program, a two-week orientation course for deans and V-12 liaison officers was set up for the late summer and early fall of 1943. In the letter of invitation, Rear Adm. Louis E. Denfeld said that the purpose was to promote "a wider understanding of the Navy itself, its operation and its mission. It is believed that such a course will be of considerable value to the Navy and to those who are responsible for counseling V-12 students."[1]

The course was held at the Naval Reserve Midshipmen's School at Columbia University in four identical sessions, each lasting thirteen days. The first one began on Tuesday, August 17, and the last on Friday, October 1. They did not take time off for Saturday or Sunday. To secure good attendance the Navy agreed to pay transportation to and from New York City, furnish weekday lunches, and arrange transportation to the activities, including those at Quantico Marine Base. At Quantico, those attending would be fed and housed at the expense of the Navy.

It was an impressive course. The top brass from Washington was rolled out for this program, and other speakers were brought in from

NAVY-COLLEGE RELATIONS

the fleet. Among them was Vice Adm. J. S. McCain, one of the outstanding leaders of the Pacific war. On the first day the luncheon speaker was Admiral Denfeld.

This thirteen-day review of the Navy and its major activities was so comprehensive that on the first morning all of the men attending were required to take an oath not to divulge confidential or secret material covered during the course. Dean Joseph Barker led off the first morning, extending greetings from both Columbia University and Secretary of the Navy Knox. Also covered on the first day was an outline of the course and of the history of the Navy. The second and third days were devoted to instruction on ships of the Navy, antisubmarine tactics, ship design, damage control, ordnance, and gunnery. On the fourth day there was a trip to the Brooklyn Navy Yard, which included inspection of ships and a visit to two Navy enlisted schools.

The fifth day covered naval aviation, which was followed on the sixth day with discussions of communications, naval intelligence, logistics, and surgery in combat. The following day the attendees visited the Navy school at Fort Schuyler, the Women's Reserve Training School at Hunter College, and the Visual Aids Training Center.

On the eighth day some stars of BuPers spoke. The first was Capt. J. L. Reynolds, who discussed the recreation and welfare program, followed by Capt. Bruce L. Canaga, who covered the Training Division. Types of training programs were then presented by Capt. William W. Behrens, and the training of enlisted men was handled by Capt. J. P. Womble. Following luncheon with a guest of honor from the fleet, Lt. Comdr. W. K. Thompson spoke on officer training at midshipmen's schools. The session finished with Lt. Comdr. Alvin C. Eurich explaining curricula and standards.

On the ninth day Comdr. Arthur S. Adams spent two hours covering the administration of the V-12 program. He was followed by James A. Fowler, Jr., counsel for the Bureau, who covered Navy contracts. In the afternoon the men heard about the curriculum of midshipmen's schools and then toured the Columbia Midshipmen's School. The tenth day was devoted to Navy research, officer procurement, civil engineering, and the seabees.

The eleventh morning was spent on the Marine Corps. Covered were organization, mission, amphibious operations, training programs, officer procurement, the relation of the Marine Corps to the V-12 program, and the Marine Corps schools. Among the speakers was Maj. Thurston J. Davies, the officer-in-charge of the Marine V-12 program, who was on leave of absence as president of Colorado College.

Even though only forty of the 131 V-12 units had a Marine contingent, in the afternoon the entire group departed for Quantico Marine

NAVY-COLLEGE RELATIONS

Barracks. They stayed there for the final two days while inspecting and observing activities, including the officer candidates' class, the reserve officers' course, field problems and training methods, and general activities. Quarters and messing were arranged to give the deans a good view of the daily routine and living conditions at Quantico.

At the second Columbia Conference, held May 12 and 13, 1944, Davies referred to this overnight visit of the deans, noting that "if you have never heard forty college executives snore at the same time you haven't had a liberal education."[2]

Inevitably, the dean's departure for the orientation was covered in the college newspaper and upon his return he was interviewed about the course. Usually he addressed the faculty and administrators, describing the marvelous things he had seen. The Navy got very good press from the orientation course.

On most campuses, particularly among the smaller schools, the V-12 officers were welcomed wholeheartedly. After all, here were brother educators in uniform sent to the school to do a very important job. Often they were added to faculty committees and given formal standing as faculty members, even though their teaching load was limited to naval orientation and naval correspondence. In the twenty-seven schools with NROTC, some officers, from the commanding officer down, had already been accorded faculty rank as professors and associate professors of naval science. The warm reception and inclusion in the faculty ranks of the new officers inevitably led to excellent Navy-college relations.

At some schools, however, the initial reaction of faculty members was to consider the V-12 as strictly a Navy training school, and not as a real college program, even though that was the goal clearly enunciated by Adm. Randall Jacobs at the Columbia Conference.[3] Furthermore, Dartmouth and some other schools did not at first give trainees the standing of full college students. In all cases, however, recognition and full credit were eventually given for courses taken in V-12.

The academic problems of some trainees surfaced as soon as the first round of tests had been completed in July or early August of 1943. This brought about the first instances of close cooperation between Navy education officers (or executive officers) and the deans and various department heads. On many campuses an academic committee was established with at least one Navy officer serving on it.[4] The intention was to help retain as many students as possible, which led to various plans for tutoring. The Navy had made an investment in these men because it needed them as officers, so most faculty members saw it as their duty to help them succeed if the trainees had the necessary ability.

At some universities with extremely high standards, however, the projected failures of many trainees brought about a crisis in Navy-col-

NAVY-COLLEGE RELATIONS

lege relations. At the University of Virginia, the commanding officer directed an open letter to all faculty members in August, pleading for special consideration for the twenty men from enlisted ranks who were having a difficult time after being away from academic work for so long. It appeared that this Navy intrusion into faculty prerogatives was not well received by some of the faculty members. The Navy followed with a telegram from Washington directing that no trainee be dismissed for academic reasons until the end of the term.[5]

Due to the arrangement of the V-12 contract, the Navy and the colleges had many potential points of conflict. For example, the sanitary condition of the food service was under the jurisdiction of the medical officer, who made daily inspections and then reported his findings to the commanding officer. If unsatisfactory practices were observed, the Navy was obliged to bring them to the attention of the college and ask that corrective action be taken. An occasional case of food poisoning would sometimes bring letters from parents or even U.S. senators complaining about the messing conditions at a particular unit.[6] This generally required a response from both the Navy and the institution.

The V-12 units were unique in that they were very much in public view, unlike most of the military units in the country, which were on closed bases. Thus, parents were not hesitant to bring up their sons' complaints, being far less intimidated by the V-12 program than by the regular military system.

Inadequate maintenance and janitorial service of buildings, hallways, and toilet facilities of the dormitories were other points of conflict, as was failure to furnish heat and hot water.[7] Such physical problems were usually correctable with minimum difficulty, however, and caused no lasting damage to Navy-college relations. It was when the Navy chose to exercise oversight in the field of college administration or teaching that the serious conflicts arose.

One extreme example occurred at Northwestern University, where the commanding officer, Capt. Smith D. A. Cobb, USN(Ret.), made some remarks to President Franklyn Bliss Snyder that Snyder considered derogatory toward the university's registration procedures.[8] Snyder wrote the commanding officer that he and the dean were extremely interested in what Cobb had to say, and asked him to put his remarks in writing. Cobb did so, holding back very little

The C.O.'s letter of September 13, 1943, noted that under V-12 regulations students with advanced standing were to be allowed to take courses in pursuit of their major studies; they were required to take only those subjects they had agreed to take upon entering V-1 and V-7. He complained that at Northwestern such students "were given no choice in the courses they were registered in. This violation of the rights

NAVY-COLLEGE RELATIONS

of the students was accomplished by the deliberate creation on the part of those in charge of the registration, of the absolutely false impression that the Navy was forcing the students to take the courses that the University representatives were registering the students in." Cobb accused them of "illegally intimidating" the men into taking such courses, and remonstrated that "registration was administered so poorly that I was unable to get copies of the registration of the students, and the class lists until very nearly one month after classes started." Cobb concluded by questioning the value of some of the courses set up by the university purportedly to help the trainees in their future Navy and Marine Corps duties.

President Snyder referred Cobb's letter to Dean Homer B. Vanderblue and Professor G. Donald Hudson, the V-12 coordinator. In a letter of September 15, 1943, they refuted virtually everything that the captain had charged, on a paragraph by paragraph basis. They said that Cobb was incorrect in stating that the advanced students had to take only those subjects they had agreed to take when entering V-1 and V-7. They referred to Navy V-12 Bulletin No. 22, which on page 12a listed the core subjects that all such students were required to take if they had not already completed them. They noted that "it is not administratively or educationally possible with six hundred new men with varied backgrounds, and in many instances, with up-to-date transcripts unavailable until after July 1, to offer every course normally in the University curriculum." Vanderblue and Hudson categorically stated that Cobb's charges of "deliberate creation" of an "absolutely false impression" and of "illegal intimidation" were untrue and without foundation. They also noted that the captain had received substantially all the class lists by the middle of the third week of the term and that he had a duplicate of every student's schedule of classes and hours as soon as he asked for it.

President Snyder wrote Captain Cobb on September 15 enclosing the letter from Vanderblue and Hudson and noting that he concurred in both their statements of fact and their conclusions. A copy of the letter was sent to Capt. O. F. Heslar, district training officer for the Ninth Naval District.

On the Northwestern campus, then, the lines of battle had clearly been drawn. The removal of Captain Cobb by the Navy was the inevitable outcome. (See Chapter 29, "The Commanding Officers.")

When problems of instructional quality arose on some campuses, the Navy did not hesitate to take corrective action where it felt such was necessary. At a number of small colleges the Navy had to prod the school's administration to spend the money to hire competent instructors, emphasizing that the Navy would pick up the additional expense.

NAVY-COLLEGE RELATIONS

Of course, finding competent instructors was not easy in the war years, especially in schools located some distance from major educational centers.

At one small Midwestern institution, the high failure rate in midshipmen's schools of the school's former trainees required that the Navy do something. The V-12s at that unit were not being adequately prepared for their advanced training, to the detriment of both the individuals and the Navy. District V-12 administrator Grant H. Brown visited the school to recommend corrective measures. He recalls that when he presented the facts and figures to back up the charges, the administration of the school was extremely cooperative and did make the necessary changes in course content and faculty.[9]

While "official" Navy-college relations depended upon the interaction between college officials and the Navy officers on board (and their superiors in the naval district and in Washington), the trainees themselves also influenced the campuses. At many schools the authorities and parts of the local populace feared the worst when it was announced that sailors and marines would be sent to their campuses. Marines were feared the most, at least by parents of daughters.[10] The perceived dangers to the school's standards that caused the trustees of Gustavus Adolphus to withdraw their invitation for a unit and then reverse themselves just forty-eight hours later has already been mentioned.

Were these fears justified? Hardly! After five months of the program, Maj. M. V. O'Connell, editor of *The Headquarters Bulletin* of the Marine Corps, asked the various Marine detachments to obtain evaluations from campus leaders, including the president, dean of students, football coach, and others. All were glad to testify to the good conduct of the marines, even though they sometimes criticized the selection process and some marines' lack of application to the educational opportunity that had been given them. But even the librarians had only good things to say about the conduct of the marines on the V-12 campuses.[11]

Looking at all 131 schools, it can be fairly stated that the relations between the Navy and the colleges were excellent. That units were operated in a cooperative spirit between the Navy and the institution was indicated by the special certificates awarded by most schools to trainees who were not ready for graduation but had successfully completed their V-12 work at the school and were being transferred to their next step in the process, usually midshipmen's schools.[12]

When the program was completed, it was apparent that the Navy had achieved its objective of being favorably remembered by the schools that had undergraduate V-12 units. In a masterstroke of public relations, at the final graduation of V-12s from each school the Navy presented a scroll commending the school for its cooperation.

NAVY-COLLEGE RELATIONS

This
MARK OF COMMENDATION
is awarded
by the
NAVY DEPARTMENT
to
EMORY & HENRY
COLLEGE
For effective co-operation
with the U.S. Navy
in the training of officer candidates
under the Navy V-12 Program
1 JULY 1943
31 OCTOBER 1945

James Forrestal
Secretary of the Navy

Later the Navy sent to each school a bronze plaque that again expressed the Navy's appreciation and gave the school a more lasting token of that esteem.

This
MARK OF COMMENDATION
is awarded to
GONZAGA UNIVERSITY
For effective cooperation
in training Naval personnel
during World War II
Navy V-12 Unit
Navy V-5 Unit

James Forrestal
Secretary of the Navy

At many end-of-term graduations, the colleges invited high-ranking Navy officials to give the commencement address. Frequently they also awarded the speaker an honorary degree. Secretary of the Navy Frank Knox appeared at several schools, and his special assistant for educational matters, Dean Joseph Barker of Columbia University, spoke at many commencement exercises. Rear Adm. Randall Jacobs and Rear Adm. Louis E. Denfeld were honored regularly. The commandant of the Marine Corps, Gen. Alexander Vandegrift, appeared at Princeton and Virginia.

Of all of the available Navy speakers, Capt. Arthur S. Adams was the most in demand. His commencement appearances included schools such as Emory and Henry, Newberry, Muhlenberg, and Duke. Comdr. William S. Thomson also made a number of appearances on the commencement circuit, including Newberry and Trinity.

NAVY-COLLEGE RELATIONS

Muhlenberg College Archives

Appearing overjoyed with his visitors, who were receiving honorary degrees at the Muhlenberg commencement on October 25, 1943, is President Levering Tyson (middle). His honorees were (left to right): Capt. Bruce L. Canaga, director of training, Bureau of Naval Personnel; Rear Adm. Louis E. Denfeld, assistant chief of naval personnel; Capt. Edgar W. Davis, chief of chaplains in the *Fourth Naval District*; and Dr. D. Luke Biemesderfer, president of the Millersville State Teachers College in Pennsylvania.

After James V. Forrestal became secretary of the Navy, his first public address was at his *alma mater,* Princeton, where he was the commencement speaker in June of 1944. His second appearance was somewhat surprising: he gave the commencement address and received an honorary degree at Swarthmore College. That the civilian head of one of the largest military organizations in the world should be the honored speaker at the Quaker school illustrates the extent to which Navy-college cooperation had developed in World War II.

Typical of the feelings the V-12 schools expressed toward the Navy were these words from the report of the college treasurer (for the academic year 1944–1945) to the board of directors of Ursinus College:

> Our contract with the Navy has been terminated and the final bills have been submitted in accordance with its terms. Our experience with the Navy has, on the whole, been very pleasant. We were not required to go to much additional expense to handle the program. We were always treated with con-

NAVY-COLLEGE RELATIONS

sideration and fairness, while the financial advantage to our College of the V-12 Program during the past few years has been almost immeasurable.[13]

The report of President N. E. McClure of Ursinus at the same time noted that

> participation of the College in the Navy College Training Program has been a source of satisfaction to us all. It has enabled the College (1) to make a direct and important contribution to the war effort, (2) to carry on the work of higher education in those areas in which Ursinus is best able to serve, namely, in the liberal arts, and (3) to make maximum use of our instructional and housing facilities.[14]

At Gustavus Adolphus College, where in April of 1943 the directors had reversed themselves twice within forty-eight hours on whether they wanted a V-12 unit on their campus, the enthusiasm for the V-12 program was clear when the Navy departed in October of 1945. In his report to the president and board of directors on November 14, V-12 coordinator O. G. Winfield said, "As one looks back . . . on this experiment in cooperation, one . . . is happy because it has been possible for us to serve our country in its educational effort . . . [and] because of the vision and insight of the Naval Bureau as to their educational philosophy. The Navy knew what it wanted . . . and . . . it has been generally recognized that the purposes were realized."[15]

And what did the Navy officers think of the college authorities during the V-12 program? In response to a question asking for an evaluation of the job done by the college, Meldrim F. Burrill, commanding officer at Illinois State Normal University, replied, "ISNU did an outstanding job! The President, instructors, and Regents not only lived up to the Navy V-12 contract but went above and beyond in their individual efforts to contribute to the success of the program."[16]

Lieutenant Commander Burrill's comments were echoed by the officers at nearly all of the other colleges and universities involved. Capt. James L. Holloway, Jr., while director of training in the Bureau of Naval Personnel in the middle of 1944, said, "The effectuation of the V-12 Program is one of the outstanding accomplishments in training in this war, which reflects enormous credit upon the colleges who have participated in such an open-handed and intelligent manner."[17] Comdr. Grant H. Brown, director of training of the Ninth Naval District, in 1945 stated that the operation of the Navy V-12 program was "enormously successful and cooperation at the colleges exceeded any expectations."[18]

When the planning for the V-12 program began, the Navy was concerned that its program differ from the Army S.A.T.C. program of World War I, which was remembered with distaste by the colleges involved. The planners determined to do everything in their power to avoid such

NAVY-COLLEGE RELATIONS

an unhappy situation. By putting its program into the hands of educators and by constantly striving to be fair in all of its dealings with the institutions, the Navy succeeded beyond its expectations in establishing and continuing an excellent relationship with virtually every school involved in the program. As the president of Southwestern Louisiana Institute put it, "The V-12 Program should be remembered as one of the most successful government-college joint ventures."[19]

29

THE COMMANDING
OFFICERS

WITH A military background that often was limited to the six-week V-12 orientation course at Columbia University, the commanding officer of a V-12 unit assumed a responsibility that bordered on awesome.

He was in charge of the whole operation of a military unit, often located hundreds of miles from headquarters or another naval station where he might find guidance. Although he could telephone for help with major problems, the Navy discouraged unnecessary use of the long-distance system, so he was very much on his own. He had to rely on his own resources and those of his junior officers, with some help on Navy regulations and protocol from the experienced enlisted men assigned to him as ship's company.

One of the major burdens for the new commanding officer was handling military discipline for anywhere from two hundred to eight hundred young men, 90 percent of whom were newer to the Navy than he was. Fortunately, serious problems involving the military justice system were rare in V-12 units.

For trainees violating station regulations or other matters of good order, the commanding officers' most frequent punishment was a weekend of restriction to the campus. More serious infractions of Navy or station regulations could be handled by a captain's mast. Offenses involving cheating or lying were usually punished by dismissal from the program, which meant either transfer to boot camp or, for those who had entered from the enlisted ranks and would be resuming their former ratings, to a naval station.

The commanding officer had to set a fine example. He had to look military and he had to be military. He had to be circumspect in every way. He was the first commanding officer that most of the men had ever seen, and as such, he formed the trainee's opinions of what a naval officer should or should not be. He was generally the reviewing officer at the Saturday inspections, and he was the one who gave out the Purple Hearts and other medals and commendations that had been earned by some of the enlisted men in their service prior to V-12.

THE COMMANDING OFFICERS

James G. Schneider

Lt. Royal F. Sessions, skipper at Milligan College, set a fine example of how a commanding officer should look and act.

THE COMMANDING OFFICERS

The C.O. also had to handle various types of local ceremonies that required a naval officer, such as burials of naval personnel originally from that area or of their own V-12s. Lt. George W. Hulme, Jr., the commanding officer at Howard College in Birmingham, Alabama, recalled that he once had to accompany the hearse carrying a Howard V-12's body to his home in Macon, Georgia. The Navy had only a pickup truck, which didn't seem appropriate, and the college's one auto had threadbare tires. The tires from the Navy's truck were put on the college's car, which permitted Hulme to adequately represent the Navy at the burial.[1]

The skipper had to digest the continuing flow of V-12 Bulletins and act on their directives. For a while those bulletins came out at the rate of one a day. If the directives were unclear, he needed to interpret the instructions, or perhaps call the district training officer at the naval district headquarters for help.

He also had to be conversant with Navy regulations. Again he could turn to the district training officer for help in determining their proper application.

The commanding officer was also responsible for directing the ship's company, and the ship's company was ordinarily one of his greatest assets in running the V-12 unit. For newly commissioned officers it was a comfort to be able to rely on the enlisted personnel, all of whom had been in the Navy longer than he had. If he were fortunate enough to have a chief yeoman or a yeoman first class in his ship's company, he usually received a great deal of assistance from him. At Gonzaga University Yeoman First Class Pat Cohen was so able and so highly regarded by both the commanding officer and the trainees that he was usually referred to around campus, and even in the college newspaper, as "the junior exec."[2]

Especially fortunate were the commanding officers who had a disbursing officer stationed at their unit. In the more outlying areas a disbursing officer, usually a young WAVE officer, would cover three or four V-12 schools. But at her home base the skipper could turn over to her all of the many chores involving uniforms and supplies. Otherwise, the commanding officer or exec had to oversee that part of the necessary business of every V-12 unit.

Lt.(jg) Jane E. Rollman was the disbursing officer who covered the V-12 units at Milligan College, where she was stationed; at Emory and Henry College in Virginia; and at Carson-Newman College and the University of the South in Tennessee. Later, her office was moved to Sewanee (University of the South), and the Vanderbilt University Medical School's V-12s were added to her assignment, extending the breadth of her territory to more than three hundred miles. Fortunately, the Navy

THE COMMANDING OFFICERS

Doane College Archives

Typical of the ship's company at a smaller V-12 unit was the one at Doane College, which included the commissioned officers, the chief athletic specialists, and the other enlisted personnel.

allowed trainees at those outlying units to be paid by check, so the cash payday had to be handled by the disbursing officer and her assistants on the home base only.[3] At the other schools arrangements were usually made for a check-cashing service for the trainees, which was provided by either a local bank or the college itself.

At one unit, a WAVE storekeeper was called in one day by the commanding officer, who said he understood that she had been dating one of the trainees, and if that were true he thought she should stop. Of course, nothing in Navy regulations prohibited such dates, but to the skipper it seemed inappropriate. The young lady protested, "But, Sir, if I can't date trainees, whom can I date? There are no young men in town and all the officers are married!" The C.O. laughed and said, "I guess you're right! Forget I ever said that."[4]

The commanding officer's first duty was to work up standing or station orders for the V-12 unit. Among other things, these defined the boundaries of the campus beyond which a trainee could not go without having an official liberty pass or leave papers in his possession. The standing orders also covered the daily routine, smoking regulations, and the demerit system that was in effect at all V-12 units.

THE COMMANDING OFFICERS

Demerits were assigned for various minor infractions, such as smoking or eating in unauthorized locations, failure to salute an officer, general disrespect, not having the hat squared away, and other evidence of being "out of uniform." Trainees were required to keep their demerit cards with them at all times so that an officer or petty officer could enter an infraction on the card at the time it occurred.

The demerit system was handled in two ways, the more usual one being that a person who received twenty-five demerits in one week received no liberty for that week. An accumulation of a much larger number of demerits could mean expulsion from the program. The other way of using the demerit system was to enlist peer pressure by granting a special liberty to the companies that had the fewest total demerits in a month's time.

Once the standing orders were prepared and published, the C.O. had to concentrate on the rest of his responsibilities for the unit: health and sanitation, physical training, satisfactory messing, satisfactory lighting conditions in the classrooms and quarters, uniform outfitting, and procedures for receiving and transferring men.

He also had to oversee the institution's performance in providing the services for which it had contracted with the Navy, yet he had to do so without seeming to direct those services. This often required great diplomacy. Working with the college authorities was, however, the easiest part of the job for most commanding officers. The majority had come from academia, and thus possessed the experience and wisdom to carry out oversight responsibilities without giving offense. Commanding officers with other backgrounds, on the other hand, found that relations with the college could be the most difficult part of the job. Indeed, problems in this area led to the downfall of commanding officers at a number of institutions.

The Office of Naval Officer Procurement had tried to find three hundred men with academic experience to fill the officer slots at most of the V-12 schools. (The larger universities, and especially those with NROTC units, were usually commanded by a regular Navy officer or a regular officer who had been retired and then called back to active service.) When the procurement effort fell short of the goal, a search was made among officers presently serving to find some with the requisite backgrounds. The shortage that remained was made up primarily by assigning officers who had been retired for various reasons and had been called to active service at the commencement of the war, or even the year before.

Although the majority of those officers served most satisfactorily,[5] a number did not. In fact, most of the commanding officer problems that arose in the V-12 program involved formerly retired U.S. Navy officers.

THE COMMANDING OFFICERS

They were not accustomed to working with educators. Lacking such experience, they tried to operate their units as naval stations, in which the commanding officer's word was the law and went unchallenged. That viewpoint inevitably came into conflict with the authority — both actual and perceived — of the college president. He, too, had grown accustomed to making unchallenged judgments and receiving unswerving obedience. The typical college president of the early 1940s was something of a monarch.

When the Navy commanding officer and the college president clashed, the regular Navy man was often unwilling to retreat, reasoning that V-12 was a Navy program, and the Navy should be supreme in cases of conflict. But since the college presidents had so many important contacts, and since they could wield the threat of removing the V-12 unit from the campus, they almost always prevailed when compromise became impossible.

At large units such as Dartmouth, Northwestern, and Yale, the presidents demanded that the Navy transfer the commanding officers.[6] The Dartmouth College problem was perhaps the earliest one to surface. An unofficial request was sent to the Navy by the president of the college, and it was supplemented by some informal communications from junior officers who had friends in the Bureau and by the parents of some of the trainees.

President Ernest M. Hopkins of Dartmouth had a long-standing friendship with Secretary of the Navy Frank Knox. The subject of the C.O.'s transfer may have been broached during Knox's visit to Hanover early in August of 1943. The gist of the complaints against Comdr. William F. Bullis, USN (Ret.), was that he was treating the trainees just as he had handled the prep school or high school graduates who had attended his private school, the Bullis School, which prepared applicants for potential appointments to the Naval Academy.

By all accounts the complaints against Bullis were accurate.[7] V-12s at Dartmouth College were required to stand deck watches, which even took precedence over class attendance. They were forced to comply with a burdensome check-out and check-in procedure to visit the college library in the evening, and even when they complied, their maximum time at the library was limited to two hours. As a consequence, the library was not used very much. Weekend restrictions were considered excessive by both trainees and faculty. Even when they were allowed weekend liberty, the V-12s had to return by six o'clock Sunday, which severely limited any out-of-area travel.

As a result of such regulations, unit morale sank to a very low level. But according to Dr. William V. Weber, who was then a lieutenant serving as the College Training Section's representative in the Officer As-

THE COMMANDING OFFICERS

signment Detail at BuPers, transfers such as the one requested by President Hopkins were not made solely upon the basis of a complaint. They had to be investigated before action would be taken.[8] Several officers were assigned to visit Dartmouth early in September; they included Weber and Lt. Raymond F. Howes, Arthur Adams's right-hand man. When they returned to Washington, Howes recommended that Bullis be reassigned, and he promptly was.[9]

The transfer of Bullis left the Marine officer-in-charge at Dartmouth as the senior officer present. Thus, Maj. John Howland, USMCR, a wounded veteran of Guadalcanal, was the acting commanding officer at Dartmouth at the time of the quarterly muster roll of September 30, 1943. As far as can be determined, this is the only time a Marine officer served as C.O. of a V-12 unit, except in an acting capacity when the Navy officer commanding was away on leave or on Navy business.

The removal at Dartmouth was not unique. At Northwestern University, Capt. Smith D. A. Cobb, USN(Ret.), was transferred following university president Snyder's request, as detailed in Chapter 28.[10] At Yale University, too, the commanding officer was transferred after requests by university authorities. The main problems were apparently his rather abrasive attitude toward Yale's procedures and some objections to his personal life.[11]

It was not just at the large schools that dissatisfaction with the commanding officer arose. At Gustavus Adolphus College in Minnesota some complaints reached the Bureau requesting the transfer of Comdr. Jesse Smith, USN(Ret.). The requests, however, originated from sources other than the college president.[12] Smith had apparently been assigned to Gustavus Adolphus in error. The Navy had intended to retire him to the inactive duty list, but he was instead ordered to head the unit at the Minnesota school. He was ill and longed for his Florida home. He would gaze at the bright winter sunshine in St. Peter, Minnesota, and wistfully ask, "How can the sun shine so brightly and have so little pep?"[13]

An investigation was made, with Lt. Comdr. William S. Thomson, who was later to become the officer-in-charge of the College Training Section, and Lt. Grant H. Brown, assistant district training officer of the Ninth Naval District, visiting the campus in November 1943. Lieutenant Weber also paid a call at Gustavus Adolphus. By the end of December, Smith had been permanently retired to Florida.[14]

There were also some reserve commanding officers who did not find favor with the college authorities. Oberlin College formally requested the transfer of both its commanding officer and the Marine officer-in-charge. Lt. Mode L. Stone, USNR, from the College Training Section, was sent to investigate. When Stone had been on campus long enough

THE COMMANDING OFFICERS

to size up the situation, he called Washington from the president's office and added his approval to the college's request.[15] A few weeks later Stone was assigned to Oberlin as officer-in-charge until the replacement commanding officer arrived.

At the College of the Pacific, Comdr. Burton E. Rokes, USN, was a regular Navy three-striper who had come up from the ranks. He despised Naval Academy graduates, college professors, the College of the Pacific's president, and everything having to do with colleges. Thus, he was not terribly well suited for his role in the V-12 program.[16] The president of the college, Dr. Tully Knowles, called in the executive officer, Lt. Lee Norvelle, USNR, and informed him that the college would request that the C.O. be transferred and that Norvelle be appointed as commanding officer in his place. Norvelle adamantly protested that he would have no part in such an arrangement and that if the college succeeded in transferring Rokes, he would also request a transfer so as not to be put in the embarrassing position of cooperating with the removal effort. Thus rebuffed, President Knowles abandoned the request, but he avoided most further contact with the C.O. by having another officer of the college stand in for him in such matters.

Just as Commander Rokes was frustrated by his forced involvement in a program he did not like, at least one college president disliked the program. Dr. Charles E. Burns, president of Milligan College, strongly opposed having a military unit on the campus. He was against it from the start, but the board of trustees, faced with the certain prospect of having to close the school due to the loss of male students, saw the V-12 unit as the institution's salvation. Milligan decided not to operate a civilian program, so it became the only school in the country to devote all of its resources to the V-12 program. For two years Milligan was exclusively a Navy V-12 school, and it inevitably became more like a military station than any of the other 131 schools.

The frustrations of constantly having to deal with the military and seeing his campus completely occupied by the Navy were finally too much for Burns. One day in March of 1944 he walked into the office of the commanding officer, Lt. R. Fred Sessions, USNR, and said, "The Navy wants to run this school, so go ahead! Here are the keys! I have resigned!" With that, he turned on his heel and walked out.[17]

Sessions immediately went over to Dean Steve Lacy's office and gave him the keys. The C.O. had no intention of "running the school." He was keenly aware of the strict line the Navy had drawn between responsibility for academic training and responsibility for the military portion of the V-12 program. Lacy provided the interim authority until the board of trustees selected a new president, Dr. Virgil Elliott, who had already become familiar with the Navy while serving as a civilian chap-

THE COMMANDING OFFICERS

lain to a Navy unit in Pennsylvania. He arrived on campus in June of 1944 and from then until the unit closed a year later Navy-college relations at Milligan were excellent.[18]

At Arkansas A & M, President Marvin Bankston had provided what was described as "uninspired leadership." He frequently boasted that he had "never been away from the county."[19] A variety of problems arose at A & M, some starting before the program got under way. Late in June 1943, most of the food ration stamps at A & M mysteriously disappeared, and without those ration points, certain essential kinds of food could not be procured to feed the sailors and marines. A special board of investigation was dispatched from the Eighth Naval District in New Orleans, and when it found no Navy involvement in the disappearance it recommended that another supply of ration stamps be furnished so that the program could get under way. Otherwise, chaos would have resulted when the V-12s arrived on July 1.

Another problem pertained to A & M's buildings and furnishings. Most of the buildings were new, having been built by Works Progress Administration (WPA) funds and labor in the Great Depression. But the lounge that the school had agreed to provide for the trainees did not have a stick of furniture in it or any recreational equipment for them to use.

Comdr. William S. Thomson and his officers decided to use the gate receipts from the A & M football team to fund a new student government association, which could then allocate part of the money to provide the furniture and recreational equipment for the lounge.

To start the student government organization, the V-12 students "volunteered" to contribute ten dollars as an activity fee, which purchased stationery, transportation for the football team, and other vital materials needed before the fund was augmented by the gate receipts from the team's well-attended games in Memphis. (See Chapter 33, "Intercollegiate Athletics.") First Lt. Jack Lytle believes it was "the best financed student council in the nation."[20] The Navy officers had a lawyer in Monticello draw up papers to incorporate the group as the "Athletic Council at Arkansas A & M College." Membership would include some civilian students along with Marine and Navy representatives. The articles of incorporation also provided that upon the dissolution of the V-12 unit, the remaining funds were to be donated to Navy Relief.

This incensed President Bankston and Business Manager C. C. Smith, who immediately protested to the Navy. An investigating board of a captain and several commanders flew out to look into the matter. They finished their investigation with a report that the arrangement was entirely proper and that the charges brought by Bankston and Smith should be disregarded. Within two weeks, the commanding offi-

THE COMMANDING OFFICERS

cer of the unit, Lt. Comdr. William S. Thomson, was transferred to the College Training Section in Washington. Obviously the action he had taken favorably impressed the officers of the CTS.

Problems of the sort described were rare exceptions in the V-12 program. At nearly all of the schools the relations could be described as ranging from satisfactory to excellent. In some schools, at the termination of the program, the commanding officers were awarded honorary degrees.[21] At the University of Washington and at Tulane University, the harmony was such that the commanding officers were offered (and accepted) key positions with the universities after retiring from the Navy.[22]

When the College Training Section wished to recommend a particular commanding officer for a unit, it so advised the Officer Assignment Section. Some of the men chosen were exceptionally well suited to their schools. The school that had perhaps been the most apprehensive of all about the V-12 program was Swarthmore College. As a Quaker school with a pacifist tradition, it had given overwhelming support to the conscientious objectors (to military service) among its students and alumni. Swarthmore was concerned about whether there should even be a military unit on its campus. Indeed, just a few months before it acquired the unit President John Nason issued a statement on "college wartime policy." He declared on December 14, 1942, that Swarthmore could make a more significant contribution to the world by developing an extensive program aimed at postwar reconstruction and rehabilitation than it could make by training men in uniform for purposes of war. He proudly noted that unlike many small colleges that were "seeking frantically to find some form of military service which they can render" in order to keep alive, Swarthmore preferred in general not to train men in uniform.[23]

When the Navy Department sent to Swarthmore as commanding officer a lieutenant who just a few months earlier had been dean of students at the University of Kansas City, the faculty wondered, "What kind of a naval officer do you get out of a former dean?"[24] But the Navy had chosen well. Lt. Glenn G. Bartle's calm manner soon allayed the fears of the school officials, both faculty and administration. In fact, the faculty invited Bartle and his executive officer to attend all of the faculty meetings. Although not Quakers, Bartle and his wife attended some services at the Friends Meeting House, and he even rose to speak on at least one occasion.[25] At the close of the V-12 program at Swarthmore, besides making the pleasant remarks customary at such formal ceremonies, President Nason held a reception in his home for the Bartles. It might have been a very different twenty-eight-month relationship if the Navy had sent Swarthmore one of its retired Navy officers. Credit

THE COMMANDING OFFICERS

for not making such an inappropriate decision must be given to those running the program.

Although the typical trainee had more contact with the executive officer than the C.O., the morale of a V-12 unit depended to a great extent upon the C.O.'s personality. If he could balance Navy strictness with fairness and temper it with common sense, chances were the unit would be a happy one. But a leader who did things strictly by the book did not get much respect from the college administration, the faculty, or the trainees themselves. After all, more than 90 percent of the V-12s had not undergone the obedience orientation of boot camp, and they had to be persuaded of the essential fairness of the commanding officer to accord him respect beyond the obedience required.

The Navy had wisely chosen as V-12 officers men who had academic experience. Most had advanced degrees, and the time and associations required to earn them provided an excellent background for their Navy positions. The considerable number of county superintendents of schools who became V-12 officers also had recent experience working closely with students. Thus, they too could relate to trainee problems in a helpful way and were well suited to their posts.

In some units, one man served as commanding officer from start to finish. Obviously, both the Navy and the institution must have been satisfied with the way he handled the job. In many schools, there was only one change of top leadership, but in quite a surprising number there were three or more commanding officers during the program.

According to Dr. William V. Weber, V-12 officers were not transferred solely to broaden their experience. They were transferred to other naval duty to meet the urgent needs of the service or as a result of a request filed by the College Training Section, the officer himself, or the institution.[26] Sometimes the changes were hard to understand, such as when the commanding officers from Emory and Henry in Virginia and St. Ambrose College in Iowa switched places.

As the war and the program moved along, the number of trainees was steadily reduced because of the declining need for additional officer candidates. This led to the transfer of some officers out of the V-12 program. Other transfers resulted from the need for officers for impending naval campaigns. Such officers were often located in searches of V-12 units and other naval stations to find surplus officers.

At the larger V-12 units the duties of the commanding officer were mostly administrative, so he had relatively little direct contact with the individual trainees. Daily contacts with trainees were mostly the responsibility of the personnel officer, the education officer, or the athletic officer. Problems with the trainees usually came to the executive officer or the officer assigned to handle discipline.

THE COMMANDING OFFICERS

But in the smaller V-12 units, which predominated, it was possible for the skipper to take a personal interest in his trainees. At many units he went down to the depot to see his men off to their new assignments. At most units there were only three officers on board at any time, the third one usually being in charge of athletics.[27]

As educators, the officers were able to follow their natural inclination to watch the progress of the students. Even forty-three years later some commanding officers recalled with great pleasure a few of the outstanding trainees who served under them. They were most impressed by the fleet men, who often came to V-12 with inadequate academic preparation. Many of those men had a strong will to succeed and so made the most of their splendid opportunity. The determination with which they tackled their studies was an inspiration, even to those experienced educators.

Lt. Russell Seibert, USNR, first executive officer and later command-

Many commanding officers took a personal interest in their men. Here Lt. George C. Decker of Texas Christian University went down to the Fort Worth depot to see some of his V-12s off for midshipmen's school.

Mrs. George C. Decker

THE COMMANDING OFFICERS

ing officer at Baldwin-Wallace College, still recalls "the best student I ever saw," a trainee (and Pearl Harbor survivor) from the enlisted ranks who provided great leadership for the unit and later became a college president.[28] Lt. Charles P. McCurdy, the second commanding officer at Gustavus Adolphus, also had no difficulty in identifying his most outstanding trainee.[29]

The role of the V-12 commanding officer was not an easy one, but for those who had the right temperament and background, it assumed reasonable proportions. There were also some nice benefits that went with the position. In many smaller communities, the commanding officers and their junior officers were welcomed into the town as celebrities. They were given complimentary memberships in local clubs and were sought-after guests at social functions. Lt. Maxwell Kelso of Central Michigan College recalled that since Mt. Pleasant was in the midst of Michigan's oil-producing area, many well-traveled people with money had come into the town, resulting in a very busy social life. Lieutenant and Mrs. Kelso often invited the nearby Alma College C.O. and his wife to join them for special occasions.[30]

Dr. Russell Seibert pointed out another facet of the position that both surprised and delighted the commanding officers: the high degree of autonomy they enjoyed. They were not used to that in academia.[31]

Upon reflection some forty years later, most C.O.s revealed that they were extremely conscious of their twenty-four-hour-a-day responsibilities and put in long hours at the unit six or even seven days a week. They worked hard and served conscientiously. For nearly all of them it was a very satisfying experience. The war had not left them behind.

30

THE DISTRICT
TRAINING OFFICERS

WHEN a V-12 commanding officer came up against a knotty problem that he and his staff could not resolve, he frequently sought the advice of a fellow V-12 skipper at a nearby school. If that didn't help, the commanding officer's next stop was the District Training Office located at the headquarters of the naval district. In the smaller naval districts, he might talk to the district training officer or his assistant, but in the larger districts a V-12 administrator was frequently the first line of contact. If the problems presented by a unit were too difficult for the Training Office to handle alone, it had ready access to the College Training Section in Washington.

At the start of the V-12 program, the position of district training officer was a comparatively new one, such positions having been added in each of the districts in late 1942. The officers had more to do than oversee the V-12 units — they were responsible for monitoring all other training activities in the district, except aviation.

Frequently the man selected as district training officer was a regular Navy officer who had been retired and then recalled to active duty. Such a person was Lt. Comdr. Scott G. Lamb, USN(Ret.), who had been a classmate of Arthur S. Adams in the Naval Academy class of 1919. When he became the training officer of the Fourth Naval District, which had its headquarters in Philadelphia, the position brought him a spot promotion to lieutenant commander, to allow him to deal more effectively with the commanders and captains who usually headed the training schools.

In the Ninth Naval District at Great Lakes, Capt. O. F. Heslar, USNR, had been a long-time reservist, serving his initial active duty in World War I. He named as his V-12 administrative officer Lt. Grant H. Brown, USNR, who in civilian life had been manager of the American Book Company office in Chicago.

Although far from the oceans, the Ninth Naval District trained about 33 percent of the Navy personnel during World War II and built nearly that percentage of naval vessels, including many LSTs and some de-

stroyers and submarines. With forty-eight V-12 units, the district training officer had a lot of ground to cover, so the inspections were put in
charge of Lieutenant Brown. The District Training Office scheduled a
visit to each unit at least once every four months.

At the beginning of the planning for the V-12 program, officers were
sent from the headquarters of the naval districts to make the initial
inspections of the colleges applying for V-12 units. They checked to
determine which schools could adequately meet the Navy's standards
for messing, housing, and education. Colleges that had already proven
their friendship for the Navy by installing schools in radio, cooking and
baking, diesel, or others were looked upon most favorably.

The Training Office was subjected to a great deal of political and other
pressure to select certain schools. Special connections to the Navy also
had to be considered. Both Secretary of the Navy Frank Knox and his
wife, for instance, were graduates and Knox was a trustee of Alma College in the middle of lower Michigan, so that had to be taken into account. At the University of Louisville, President Raymond Kent had
been on the important Navy Advisory Educational Council that provided
the civilian input into the shaping of the V-12 program. President Kent
died of a heart attack on the train on his way home from one of the
Council meetings in February 1943, so perhaps extra efforts were made
to select his school. Other schools that furnished officials to important
Navy committees may also have received an advantage of some kind.

When the schools had been selected for the program, a representative
of the District Training Office and a medical officer usually joined the
negotiating party when it entered the district. Later, when the program
went into operation on July 1, the regulations called for the inspection
of each unit once a term by a representative of the District Training
Office. These representatives checked such things as sanitation, house-
keeping, the quality of the food, and, when reasons existed to investigate it, the quality of instruction. The inspection report was a fourteen-
page form that even covered such matters as whether the housing units
had proper cross-ventilation, which was an important consideration in
the hot summers before air conditioning.

The district training officer was also a troubleshooter for Commander
Adams and the College Training Section. If there were complaints about
excessively strict administration of a unit, the district training officer's
representative would usually accompany the man sent out from BuPers.
Evidence of a "loose ship" also brought a prompt inspection and sometimes led to a recommendation for a transfer of the commanding officer.
This occurred at Westminster College, where no study hours had been
established and no serious effort had been made for a uniform "lights
out" policy. When Lt. Donald E. Field, formerly the executive officer at

THE DISTRICT TRAINING OFFICERS

Gustavus Adolphus, was transferred to Westminster as commanding officer in May of 1944, he immediately instituted the lights out and compulsory study hall features. He noted that "almost every school in the Ninth Naval District has adhered to a much more rigorous schedule" than Westminster.[1]

When emergencies such as the fire at the main dorm and administrative office of a unit at Illinois State Normal University occurred, the District Training Office was the first organization notified. Another type of emergency occurred at a state teachers college in North Dakota, where a considerable number of trainees decided they would all refuse to study in order to deliberately flunk out. The situation had all the earmarks of a low-grade mutiny, so Lieutenant Brown of the District Training Office was dispatched to the school. He was told to take whatever steps were necessary to end the situation, even to the point of recommending the withdrawal of the unit from that school. After he got the attention of the trainees and their officers by explaining the seriousness of such concerted action and the possible consequences to the individual trainees, the threat evaporated.[2]

Morale building was an important part of the assignment of the inspecting officer from the District Training Office. In many units after the departure of an inspecting officer, the commanding officer proudly boasted to the trainees directly or through the school newspaper that Lieutenant Commander so-and-so had said, "This is one of the best units in the naval district, if not in the United States." Boosting pride in the organization was always a challenge for the commanding officer, and help of this sort made his job somewhat easier.

One way the District Training Office kept in close touch with the commanding officers and their problems was to call them in to the district headquarters at least once a year for a V-12 conference. This gave the C.O.s a chance to tackle common problems and to learn Washington's thinking on the directions the program was going to take. The conferences also benefited the district training officer, who could deliver the College Training Section's new directives, get instant reactions, and avoid the problem of misinterpretation. Sometimes the conferences involved a brief cruise on a Navy ship.[3]

Many district training officers developed a periodical to send to the V-12 units to disseminate information on directives from Washington and to provide a medium for exchange of information among the various units. Capt. Newton L. Nichols, USN, director of training in the First Naval District, distributed the "District V-12 Memorandum."[4]

All the evidence suggests, then, that the district training officers and the unit commanding officers had a mutually helpful relationship. This is evident in the remarks of Lt. J. L. Bostwick, commanding officer of the Whitman College V-12 unit:

THE DISTRICT TRAINING OFFICERS

In the opinion of this command, the conferences of the V-12 Commanding Officers of the Thirteenth Naval District were most worthwhile and enlightening, as was the five day tour of "sea duty" aboard the U.S.S. CASABLANCA. The special indoctrination session for the Executive Officers of the V-12 units in this district was equally beneficial.

The tour of duty under the direction of Captain A. W. Sears, District Training Officer, and his staff, has been consistently pleasant. They have exhibited, in every respect, a sincere feeling of understanding and patience with a group of officers who came into the service with only a vague knowledge of the many problems to be encountered and with little or no Naval experience to combat these difficulties.

The task was made simpler, and in many instances, enjoyable, by this spirit of cooperation and patience.[5]

The District Training Offices were yet another reason why the V-12 program was carried out so smoothly and evenhandedly.

31

THE TRAINEE
AND THE COLLEGE

As NOTED BEFORE, the democratic selection processes brought men into V-12 from every region, state, and nearly every community in the country. Upperclassmen in schools with V-12 units were assigned where they were already enrolled, but if their school had not been selected for a V-12 unit, the Navy sent them to nearby schools.

The Navy considered the choices expressed by the boys from high school and the fleet, but there just weren't enough schools with the right specialties and in the right places to accommodate everyone. Thus, on July 1, 1943, V-12s had to be distributed over an unexpectedly wide area. Hundreds of men from Texas were sent to Georgia. Californians were sent to Texas, Montana, Nebraska, and North Dakota. Iowans were sent to South Carolina, Oklahomans to Tennessee, and big-city men to schools in rural areas. Seven V-12s directly out of high school in a northern Illinois county ended up at five different schools stretching from Tennessee to Vermont. Many Southern students were sent to the University of Idaho (Southern Branch) at Pocatello.

One result of this geographical distribution was what a number of former V-12s have described as "culture shock." The term was used in trainee questionnaires by a farm boy from Illinois who ended up in Tennessee and two Californians who went to Texas and Indiana.[1]

This wide dispersal turned out to be one of the unexpected strengths of the program. It resulted in nearly incessant state rivalries which brought rude comments from newly arrived trainees about the desirability of the state where they ended up. Those states were defended by their residents, who made counterclaims in the same coarse terms about the livability of the states whence the detractors had come. The upshot was that V-12s got to know men from all sections of the country. They roomed with them, ate with them, studied with them, and made liberties with them. The boys from outside the area got acquainted with the local girls and found that they were pretty much like those who had been left behind. A state school like Southwestern Louisiana Institute in Lafayette could boast that its trainees came from forty-three states,

237

THE TRAINEE AND THE COLLEGE

the District of Columbia, Puerto Rico, and Mexico. Provincialism at that school was definitely diminished!

The same process occurred at the denominational colleges, where previously students of a faith other than that of the sponsoring church had been rarely seen. While the eleven Roman Catholic colleges in the V-12 program had always had some Protestant students, there were relatively few unless the school was located in or near a large city. Since the V-12s were assigned without regard to their religion, however, vast numbers of non-Catholics were sent to Catholic schools. Similarly, Baptist schools such as Mercer University, Howard College, and the University of Redlands soon had more Roman Catholics enrolled in their courses than had probably ever visited the campus before. No longer could Catholic schools require attendance at daily mass, nor could Protestant schools insist upon attendance at chapel if there was any significant religious content to the program. In some schools, the name was changed to "convocation" and the religious content was supposedly removed, although that has been disputed by many V-12s. At Oberlin College the Tuesday chapel was required and the Thursday chapel was optional; presumably there was substantial religious content to the Thursday meeting.

Chapel attendance by V-12s was required in a few schools, where it was called "convocation," but in many schools it was an optional campus activity. Attendance was usually good, as this photograph at Union College indicates.

Union College Archives

THE TRAINEE AND THE COLLEGE

Besides the cultural and religious shocks, there was also a "weather shock." It occurred when Californians were sent to North Dakota and Montana, Northerners were ordered to Mississippi, Louisiana, and Texas at the height of the summer, and Southerners were sent to face the winters of Idaho and New Hampshire. In 1986, a Hanover, New Hampshire, physician vividly recalled a conversation he heard while trudging through the snow behind two Dartmouth V-12s on a twenty-below afternoon in February of 1944. Judging from their accents, the boys were from well below the Mason-Dixon line.

First trainee: It sure is cold, don't you think?

Second trainee: Yes, it is! *Did you know* there are *some* people who live here the year round?

First trainee: That's hard to believe. I'd think it would affect them.

Second trainee: As a matter of fact, did you ever notice the look on some of the natives?[2]

Trainees from the North who were sent to the South soon had their first taste of black-eyed peas, greens, grits, and sweet potato pie. At some schools the grits could be expected once a day, which occasionally brought some rude comments from trainees who had not yet become acclimated.

The faculties and administrations of the schools that received a great influx of students from other areas of the country and other religious backgrounds were fearful of the changes that might develop at their institutions. It was upsetting enough to have a military program on campus and, at least at the top-rated schools, to have doubts about the quality of the incoming students. Those concerns led to an understandable worry about the success of the program. Such apprehensions occurred among both the trainees and the colleges.

After the first tests, the doubts turned into despair in the faculties at many schools. Could the program be made to succeed without seriously compromising the educational standards of the school?

Most faculty members were determined to make the program successful. They were all working long hours, and many were teaching unfamiliar subjects, so the preparation time was often much longer than normal. In addition, some were teaching the special remedial classes and doing the formal tutoring described in Chapter 25, "Academic Load."

An example of the concern of the professors occurred at Duke University. Dr. John L. Gergen, chairman of the mathematics department, found in his calculus class a distressing lack of background among the students who had just transferred from a small Southern school. Their analytical geometry courses under curriculums 101 and 102 should have prepared them adequately for calculus, but apparently they hadn't.

THE TRAINEE AND THE COLLEGE

After the first test Gergen asked the transfer trainees to stay after class for a few minutes. He said, "Obviously you didn't learn much about analytical geometry at your last college. Most of you will be shipping out to Great Lakes if we don't do something about that. I will be in this classroom from 5:00 to 6:00 every afternoon Monday through Friday from now until we have the problem solved. Come in if you like. It's not mandatory." All of the students he addressed came in every day for several weeks. Finally, one by one, they dropped out of the special session because at last the proverbial light had been turned on for them. All succeeded in passing calculus. This was an example of faculty concern above and beyond the call of duty. No one knew about the extra class except those who were involved in it. No one paid for it, and no report was made to the Navy about it. It was this kind of extra help that made the V-12 program succeed.[3]

The faculty-student relations are remembered fondly by nearly all of the V-12 students. Students at Hampden-Sydney College remembered especially Dr. W. T. Williams, who allowed the students to use his living room as a substitute for a USO. There they could sit, talk, drink Cokes, or place off-campus phone calls. Professors at many schools invited small groups of trainees to their homes for dinner, despite the current food rationing.

Some professors understood better than others what motivated the trainees. For instance, a professor of engineering drawing at Gustavus Adolphus was late for class one morning because his car had broken down. The class had left after the usual waiting time. When he arrived and found an empty classroom, he thought a minute and then headed to the local tavern, where he found all of the V-12s assembled. The class was held there, with "the topic unassigned, but mutually of value."[4]

At Yale University the school's system of collegiate housing provided a master of each college who lived in the unit with his family and served *in loco parentis.* Once a week, an invitation was sent to a certain number of the men in the unit to come to the master's quarters after 2100 on Thursday to enjoy refreshments and talk. Soft drinks and beer were usually available.

Dean of students Norman Buck and his wife, Polly, were determined to make Yale men out of all the trainees who had come to their college unit from the four corners of the country. It was not enough that the trainees attend college at Yale University — they wanted the trainees to become part of the school. At the end of each Thursday evening social hour, Dean Buck passed out the little grey Yale song books, sat down at the piano, and led the group in singing the traditional Yale songs.[5] Not surprisingly, a high percentage of those men returned to Yale after the war to complete their education.

THE TRAINEE AND THE COLLEGE

At some other Ivy League colleges, trainees who had something less than the customary background for students of that school soon perceived that they were not really welcome; rather, they were tolerated as a temporary wartime sacrifice on the part of the school and its civilian students. The trainees who sensed such a lukewarm reception felt that it was not limited to the students but carried over to a substantial number of faculty members. Certainly most faculty members were as cordial as they could possibly be, but others seemed only to tolerate the new students with the "inadequate" credentials.

An editorial in the Williams College newspaper on May 2, 1945, praised most of the faculty members for their excellent efforts and attitude. But it also raised questions about "the attitude which a few [faculty members] have adopted toward Navy men. It is the attitude expressed by the phrase, 'You're getting paid to be taught,' and is accompanied by a hostile bearing toward the V-12ers. It is an outlook which is unfriendly to the extent that it prevents several students per class from grasping enough of the subject to pass the course. In other words it is an attitude which definitely curbs the teaching abilities of the faculty member who accepts it."[6]

At a number of colleges, some individual professors were cited by V-12s as vindictive and "determined that we could not enjoy ourselves on the weekend, because he gave impossible tests on Thursday and when we flunked we were restricted for the weekend."[7]

At all of the schools, the faculty did appreciate several things about the V-12 trainees: (1) they were unfailingly respectful, usually adding "sir" to their questions, and (2) they did not cut class. Their attendance was excellent because the penalty for cutting was so great.

The courtesy of the V-12s was also noticed in other areas of the colleges. For example, early in the second term the clerical personnel in the registrar's office at the University of California were asked their impression of the V-12 trainees. They noted the special courtesy of the sailors and marines.[8]

How well the V-12s and the college authorities got along depended to a certain extent upon how liberal the college was with regard to campus social life. At Colgate University, for the traditional end-of-term dinner held by the Marine detachment in the student union dining room and attended by the Marine officer-in-charge, the Navy commanding officer, and Colgate president Everett Case beer was served to all.

And then there were the socially conservative schools. The *Manual for the Operation of All Navy V-12 Units* (V-12 Bulletin No. 22, issued June 18, 1943) asked the commanding officers to try to work out compromises with those college authorities on such things as times and places for smoking.[9] It was recognized at all schools that most of the

THE TRAINEE AND THE COLLEGE

trainees were not on campus of their own volition, so the rules were often liberalized.

A prime example was Kentucky's Berea College. The president of Berea made a trip to Washington to discuss various matters, and he took time to explain to Lt. Raymond F. Howes that he would like to relax the campus rules to allow social dancing but feared the reaction of his trustees. He broadly hinted that if the Navy were to recommend such a course of action as good for morale, he thought the trustees would find it palatable. A suitable letter was sent to the president, and social dancing was soon introduced on the Berea campus.[10]

Louisiana Tech was another school that allowed dancing for the first time — provided the boys and girls were at least six inches apart.[11]

At some colleges, however, there was to be no relaxation. At Mercer University and Milligan College, the old rules prevailed. At Milligan it was especially onerous because there were no civilian students on the campus — it was 100 percent Navy. President Charles E. Burns, a minister of the Christian Church, nevertheless told the trainee delegation seeking permission for a dance in the school gym, "Gentlemen, there never has been a dance at Milligan College and there never will be a dance at Milligan College."[12] As a consequence of such restrictions, the trainees departed on the weekends, seeking their social life elsewhere.

At Carson-Newman College the strictness led trainees to avoid campus events and resulted in a perceptible strain in the relations between the trainees and the civilian students. It took several terms for the rift to heal. Similarly, at the University of Redlands, the unbending attitude of the administration led to an undeclared war, which was fought primarily by the marines. Some of the ways the marines struck back at the leadership of that strict Baptist school are detailed in Chapter 34, "Humor, High Jinks, and 'They Shouldn't Have.' "

But as is always the case, the real faculty-student relationships depended upon the individuals involved. One former trainee at Newberry College in South Carolina referred to a professor there as the best teacher he ever had, and his academic career included undergraduate work at a major state university and three years of law school. A highly successful tax lawyer in Washington, D.C., stated that "three of the professors I had at Idaho State were among the best teachers I've ever known." Later in his educational career he had attended the Harvard Business School and the Harvard Law School. A trainee from Iowa State said that he had consulted with one of his V-12 professors on every major business decision he had made during the rest of the professor's life. A prominent American editor stated that one of the best teachers he ever had was an English professor at Emory and Henry College. Other trainees referred to individual professors with such comments as

THE TRAINEE AND THE COLLEGE

"She kept me from going to Great Lakes" and "I came back to this reunion just to see Mr. ——." Most of the faculty members were indeed giving more than a full measure, and they were appreciated by the V-12s.

Every V-12 school had to bring in new faculty members. At Dartmouth College, the new appointments included the third woman ever to be a member of the school's faculty. She was hired to teach engineering drawing.[13]

At some schools, particularly the smaller ones, the quality of the newly hired instructors was very uneven. Some of the poorer ones left a very unfavorable impression — and some academic scars — upon the V-12s. At a few schools the commanding officer or the district director of training had to get involved to insist that the college hire better-qualified persons to teach one or more subjects.

The faculty members worked long and hard to keep up with this program, which continued year round, unlike the regular academic program. Yet there was no complaint. Even after forty years they recall that, since it was wartime, they were expected to work harder, and they did.[14] In 1980, Dr. Ivor Jones, professor emeritus of English at Milligan College, wrote of the V-12 days, "I dearly loved teaching you boys; I sincerely appreciate your sacrifice to keep us a safe and free people; and I am inordinately proud of the men you are. Thank you for all of these things."[15]

The real effect of the V-12 educational experience can be seen by noting how many thousands of the V-12 trainees went into education. The ranks are filled with hundreds if not thousands of college professors of everything from computer science to English and history, and there are college and university deans and presidents by the score. School teachers, coaches, and superintendents of schools also abound. Many chose education as a lifetime career because of the inspiration provided by teachers in the V-12 program. Their influence was well stated by Dr. Stanley J. Idzerda, a Pearl Harbor survivor, trainee at Baldwin-Wallace College, and later professor at Cornell, Yale, and Michigan State, dean at Wesleyan University, dean of the honors college at Michigan State University, and president of the College of St. Benedict:

> One of the most important aspects of my V-12 experience was meeting, and being taught by the faculty at Baldwin-Wallace College. They were an extraordinary crowd: modest in demeanor, gentle Christian scholars, devoted to the life of the mind, and earnest teachers. My memory for most persons is not good, but I remember at least twenty persons on the faculty and staff at Baldwin-Wallace then, and I owe to them and their efforts much of whatever inspiration or achievements I can claim as an academician. Indeed, I think I left the Navy and entered the GI Bill program for grad school with a fixed

THE TRAINEE AND THE COLLEGE

image in my mind: someday I would be a scholar and a teacher like the persons I knew as faculty at Baldwin-Wallace, and maybe even teach in a place like that. I've never regretted that ambition, for they were timeless models.[16]

Although V-12 was difficult and demanding, the overall impression the program left with the trainees was excellent. Arthur Adams would be proud of the vast contribution the V-12 program has made to the teaching profession.

32

CAMPUS LIFE

THE arrival of the V-12s on 131 campuses across the nation was greeted with widespread approval from the people involved with the institutions, including faculty, administrators, employees, and suppliers. The V-12 program meant job security and a chance to help in the war effort. But the most enthusiastic welcome everywhere was given by the girls, who looked to the male students for some or all of their social life. In the coeducational schools, those girls were students themselves. In the men's schools, they included the girls living in the area and those attending nearby girls' schools or nurses' training programs connected with local hospitals.

At many schools, parents, faculty members, deans of girls, and housemothers warned the girls about the sailors and marines who would be arriving on the campus, but it is doubtful that those warnings were given much heed.

At some colleges the civilian part of the student body stayed on a traditional semester plan rather than converting to the Navy's accelerated trimester program. At those schools, the girls did not arrive until September, which usually meant a long, dry summer for the men. Under the headline "Dull Summer," the 1945 Duke University yearbook, the *Chanticleer*, expressed it this way: "With the return of the women, Duke, the Navy V-12 training base, became once again Duke, the university."[1]

In the American high school and college life of the early 1940s, when young men and young women got together someone inevitably suggested having a dance. So it was when the V-12s arrived on campus. Many schools had "get acquainted" dances to which all students, civilians and V-12s, were invited. At many schools these were very successful and marked the opening of an active social season that continued for the life of the V-12 unit.

At other schools, much to their chagrin, the girls found that many of the trainees were not what they had been warned about; in fact, they were nearly the opposite. There were not aggressive and would line the walls of the dance floor like wallflowers themselves. The dissatisfaction with the dances that resulted was often taken up by the college news-

CAMPUS LIFE

paper. To resolve the problem, some schools set up a dating bureau, sometimes through the student government association and sometimes through a newly organized independent organization. At some schools, voluntary dancing classes were provided during the trainees' free time. Very few V-12s had the good fortune of those stationed at Harvard, where a social hostess in each housing unit would, upon request, arrange blind dates for the trainees living in that house.

Invitations came readily to the V-12 unit from nearby girls' schools, particularly the "sister schools" of all-male colleges. Other girls' schools, coed schools without military units, and nursing schools also sent frequent invitations to the V-12 units.

Not all V-12 colleges permitted dancing on the campus. In fact, there were strict prohibitions against it at some schools, and in at least one college a coed was expelled for dancing with a marine at the campus soda fountain. Although the same couple danced together frequently in town, the coed knew it was forbidden to dance on the campus and protested, but the marine dragged her out on the floor. A few days later her termination notice was given. Because the marine was in the V-12 unit, the college was powerless to discipline him. The marine made the unfairness of the situation known to the commanding officer, who took it up with the college president. The expulsion was subsequently reduced to a ten-day suspension.[2]

Several other schools, such as the University of Redlands in California, had their first on-campus social dancing as a direct result of the V-12 unit.[3] But other colleges, such as Mercer University, Milligan College, and Carson-Newman College, retained their prohibitions. The trainees at such schools spent most of their liberties in nearby towns or more distant towns that had been especially hospitable.

By and large the V-12s were a church-going lot. Their attendance at voluntary chapel services on the campus and services in the local churches and synagogues was excellent. Some V-12s even held prayer meetings in their dorm rooms.

The Navy's policy in regard to V-12 participation in normal college activities had from the very beginning been one of full support, provided the activities did not interfere with the students' V-12 requirements. At the National Inter-Fraternity Conference annual meeting in New York in November of 1942, even before the V-12 program had been formally announced, the Navy made it clear that it would permit its college training program students to join fraternities if it did not interfere with their duties.[4]

Fraternity houses at V-12 schools had been pressed into service for other uses by the time the V-12s arrived on campus. Sometimes they were used to house the V-12s themselves, as at the University of Wash-

CAMPUS LIFE

V-12s served as acolytes at the daily mass at Marquette University.

Marquette University Archives

CAMPUS LIFE

ington and Wabash College. In other cases they provided lodging for coeds displaced from dorms assigned to the V-12 program, as at College of the Pacific and DePauw University. And at some schools, the fraternities were used to house any male civilians who needed housing, whether or not they belonged to the fraternity.

Despite the loss of houses, most fraternities attempted to continue some form of activity during the V-12 years. At a few colleges, the fraternities looked upon the V-12s as "transients" who were not up to the standards they were accustomed to, so they made no effort to pledge Navy or Marine V-12s. But at most of the schools with fraternities, the V-12s became the mainstay of the chapters during the wartime years.

The active fraternities often had only a room on campus assigned for their meetings, but they competed as a group in intramural sports and held their own dances, picnics, and cabin parties. It was a very brief fraternity experience for many V-12s, and some new initiates dropped from sight and never again made contact with their national headquarters. But most of the fraternity men continued their association with

At many schools, the V-12s provided a good portion of the fraternity membership, as this 1945 shot of the ATO chapter at Duke University indicates.

The Palm of Alpha Tau Omega

their groups after the war, and those who received further education often participated fully in fraternity life in the postwar years.

On many V-12 campuses, fraternity members who had transferred to colleges that lacked local chapters organized themselves — mainly for social purposes — into clubs that met weekly. At Westminster College they called themselves "The Stray Greeks."

Intercollegiate athletics provided a major focus for campus life at many schools. (See Chapter 33, "Intercollegiate Athletics.") To help spur on their college teams, many V-12s served as cheerleaders.

In most schools the V-12s were in the thick of campus politics. This was particularly true in the smaller schools, where the V-12s frequently dominated the political scene. At the larger institutions they formed strong but relatively unpredictable blocs. Many V-12s were elected president of student government associations, head of the schools' social committees, or to such positions as the board of student publications or the honor code committee.

In at least one instance, however, the V-12s and NROTCs were specifically ordered to stay out of a major campus controversy. In late 1944 the trustees of the University of South Carolina proposed that after the war the university should be moved to a new, uncongested location at the outskirts of Columbia. Dishonoring Robert E. Lee would not have generated any greater controversy! Alumni, faculty, and students all joined in the fray. Mass meetings were scheduled to direct the protest. Faced with that explosive situation, the commanding officer specifically ordered the Navy men not to attend any meetings to oppose the trustees' plan.[5]

At colleges that kept their civilian students on the traditional semester plan, there was sometimes no real opportunity for the V-12s to occupy positions of leadership in campus organizations. Because the V-12s' presence on the campus did not coincide with the traditional office-holding periods, they were almost never elected to office in such organizations as the interfraternity council. In fact, in most two-semester campuses, the V-12s weren't even a part of the student government! At first, except for their welcome participation on the intercollegiate athletic teams, they were not even considered a real part of the college. The University of Richmond, for instance, kept all its civilians on a separate schedule, so there was no intermixing of civilians and V-12s in classes. The instructors and civilian students both referred to the "V-12 school" as something totally separate. At the end of the fourth term of the V-12 program, the Richmond *Collegian* admitted that at first the V-12s had been "resented" by the rest of the students. The article went on to note, however, that as time went on the V-12s from the original group had contributed a great deal to college life at Rich-

CAMPUS LIFE

mond and "kept many activities going." It acknowledged that there were now "full bonds of comradeship" between civilians and V-12s and wished the departing V-12s good luck.[6]

When the V-12s arrived on the 131 campuses, they found that many of the student newspapers had ceased publishing, as a result either of the usual summer hiatus of college papers or of an earlier decision to suspend publication for the duration of the war. At such schools, there was no way of communicating about current and future events. On the large campuses the daily newspaper had usually folded because it was impossible to maintain the staff or secure the paper and the printing services necessary to publish the paper so frequently. The major schools had opted for a smaller edition, usually once a week, such as the *Bulletin* that replaced the *Crimson Daily* at Harvard University. The *Daily Trojan* at the University of Southern California came out three times a week. But at the smaller colleges, particularly those where the civilian students remained on the semester plan, there was no newspaper at all, and publication would not resume until the return of the coeds in September. In some schools, however, the weekly paper had been continued and gave good coverage to the advent of the V-12 program.

In most colleges where no paper would be published until September, the V-12s themselves took steps to start a newspaper. In many cases it was typed by volunteers with marginal skills, had small pages, and was run off on a mimeograph machine of dubious quality. Usually the V-12s gave a nautical name to their newborn publication, such as the *Masthead*, the *Scuttlebutt*, the *Periscope*, the *Sea Breez*, or for the first issue at Arkansas A & M, the *What Zit*. The paper was renamed the *Link* when the second issue went to press.

Those mimeographed newspapers usually had stories about the officers and chief specialists (A) of the unit, the number of trainees on board, and lots of coverage of intramural and intercollegiate sports. The editors frequently chided the trainees for not making the most of their wonderful opportunity, called for the sailors and marines to show "some real school spirit," and urged them to take part in extracurricular activities. Later, reports of trainees who had gone either to boot camp or to midshipmen's schools were printed to help boost the incentive for succeeding in the program. Speculation on leaves, liberties, restrictions, and the future of the V-12 program also took up considerable space. The fillers were the typical college jokes that had been run in papers for the previous twenty years, sometimes altered into nautical versions.

The presence of the Navy put some constraints on the traditional freedom of the collegiate press. While the academic side of the program could be criticized, a V-12 chided the Navy at his peril.[7]

CAMPUS LIFE

In larger schools with NROTC units, where an existing staff was firmly in control of the student paper, V-12s were invited to join the staffs. Usually they served as reporters because the top spots were already taken. In the smaller schools where the trainees dominated the student body, the major positions were filled by V-12s. Those who had previous journalistic experience soon found themselves occupying an editor's chair.[8] Most V-12s who volunteered were put to work.

All the papers, large or small, faced the problem of finding a cooperative printer, sufficient stocks of newsprint, and the time to get the newspaper written, edited, and published. Because of the shortage of the zinc necessary for photographic reproduction, photos were rare. If the school did not provide some funding, the papers had modest to severe economic problems.

In a few schools where V-12s felt that their interests were not being given enough space in the student newspaper, the trainees started their own competitive paper. Such was the case at Alma College, where the trainees started the *Scuttlebutt* in competition with the *Almanian*, the regular college paper. At some colleges, the two publications existed separately for a while and then the Navy publication was incorporated into the existing paper as either an insert or a special page. This was done at Howard College in Alabama, where the *Scuttlebutt* became a part of the *Crimson*.

Thanks to the interest and perseverance of those hardy journalists, whether Navy, Marine, or civilian, the week-by-week story of the V-12 units has been well preserved. Unfortunately, many of the papers were mimeographed on poor-quality paper and are now crumbling at an alarming rate. A few years from now, there will be little left to recount the V-12 story on many campuses. At schools where this is occurring, steps should be taken to preserve what is still available.

The yearbooks were another means of preserving the story of the V-12 units. Unfortunately, some schools were not able to publish yearbooks because of shortages of help, materials, finances, or a suitable printer. The story of V-12 on those campuses is less complete because the yearbooks are missing.

On the other hand, some universities published yearbooks that were exceptional pieces of college journalism. Foremost among them is the 1944 *Rotunda* of Southern Methodist University, whose front and back covers featured a full-color wrap-around photo showing girls, civilian men, and V-12s in a typical campus scene. Forty years later those covers have retained remarkable quality.

Yearbooks were often the province of the coeds, who were on campus long enough to see such time-consuming projects through to fruition. While V-12s were welcomed to help with most of those publications,

CAMPUS LIFE

and indeed took a sizable proportion of the pictures, credit for the existence of such records in coeducational schools goes mainly to the women students.

The men's schools also had some outstanding yearbooks. They were often edited by the NROTC trainees, who may have been on campus before V-12 started and who stayed on campus longer than the average V-12 regular. Rensselaer Polytechnic Institute published two excellent issues of the *Transit.*

Other campus activities included frequent musical revues, many of them with original music written by V-12s and other students. Often the theme was a spoof on the Navy program, its officers, and its trainees. Names of such shows included "This Ain't the Navy," "V-12 Varieties," and "You Cur, Sir."

The "All-Navy Show" at Indiana State Teachers in June of 1944 featured a cast of more than fifty, including this snappy all-V-12 chorus line and pit orchestra.

Martin Photograph Collection, Indiana State University

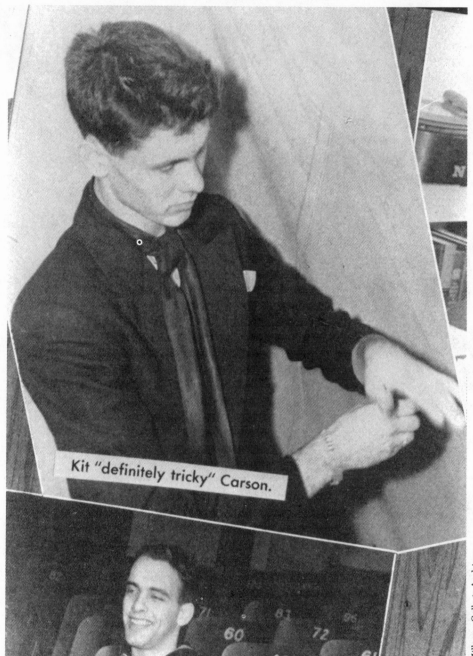

Kit "definitely tricky" Carson.

Johnny Carson performed magic tricks for fellow V-12s at Millsaps College.

CAMPUS LIFE

Some future entertainment stars appeared in those early V-12 shows. At Millsaps College in Jackson, Mississippi, magician "Kit" Carson, whose first name was John and who hailed from Norfolk, Nebraska, mystified his audiences with sleight-of-hand tricks. At the University of Idaho (Southern Branch) at Pocatello, the student body enjoyed the piano music of Louis Weertz, now known as Roger Williams.

V-12s turned out in good number for the marching bands at every school big enough to have one. The first appearance of the bands made a striking show with the civilians in normal band uniforms, the Navy trainees in white sailor hats, and the marines in their summer uniforms.

Every campus had its excellent V-12 dance band, many of which had unique names, such as the "Nautical Knaves," the "Solid Mac's," the "4.0 Sky Birds," and the "V-12 Thirteen." The bands played such good music that they were in demand for appearances elsewhere on the weekends, which often provided some unofficial income for the band members. In a number of schools the band played once or twice a week during evening chow.

V-12 dance bands were created on nearly every campus; in quality they sometimes rivaled the leading big bands of the 1940s. This group was at Dickinson State Teachers College.

Dickinson State College Archives

There wasn't much spare time in the V-12 program but these marines at the University of Washington occasionally grabbed fifteen minutes for a quick jam session.

CAMPUS LIFE

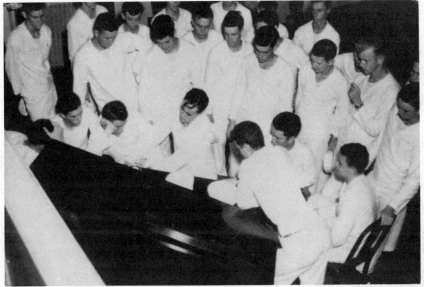

Robert Webber

Singing around the piano or during intermission at dances was a favorite pastime at nearly every unit. This shot was taken at Peru State Teachers College.

Singing was a big part of the V-12 experience. Many units not only sang when marching, they also gathered around the piano at the USOs, faculty homes, and campus hangouts to sing such numbers as "A Man Without a Woman" and "The Great Ship Titanic." At the bars they resorted to such memorable ditties as "I Used to Work in Chicago" and "Roll Me Over, in the Clover."

V-12s took a major interest in serious choral music, too, and many V-12 or college glee clubs traveled some distance to perform for churches and service clubs. In the spring of 1946, the glee club at Southwestern University in Texas made half a dozen road appearances.

Fraternities, sororities, churches, and various campus groups held frequent dances, but usually the big social affair of any trimester was the naval ball, military ball, or quarterdeck hop sponsored by the V-12 unit. Normally a V-12 queen was chosen from among many contestants. At the larger schools name bands were booked, including Woody Herman, Les Brown, Bobby Sherwood, Artie Shaw, Sammy Kaye, Tony Pastor, Art Kassel, and Elliot Lawrence.

An event of nationwide notice was the appearance of big bands such as Les Brown and Tony Pastor on campuses for broadcasts of "Coca-Cola Spotlight Band." The Mutual Broadcasting System had a weekly broadcast featuring the Marine Corps called "The Halls of Montezuma."

CAMPUS LIFE

The Navy Ball was a traditional high point in each term during the V-12 program, as shown by this photo at Hobart College.

CAMPUS LIFE

Two marines mix it up in a boxing match at the University of Washington. Matches like this one were often held as part of "smokers" or "happy hours."

Early in 1944 one program was devoted to Marine V-12 units in various parts of the nation.

Traditional campus events continued at most schools during the V-12 program. The Winter Carnival at Dartmouth remained one of the important events of the year. At the Bates College competition in snow carving, new talent was evident in the depictions of V-12s performing various activities. At Worcester Polytechnic Institute the age-old rivalry between the freshmen and sophomores continued as before, with such events as the "rope pull" and the "paddle rush." At the University of Louisville, Kentucky Derby Day was the big event and V-12s were glad to join in. At one point, *Life* magazine devoted its feature "Life Goes to a Party" to visits to a number of V-12 campuses such as Williams College in Massachusetts and the University of Texas.

At nearly every unit the V-12s put on happy hours or smokers, which featured boxing matches, skits, musical performances, and every form of entertainment the V-12s could produce. These activities were usually open to the rest of the campus, which produced a nice public relations benefit for the unit.

Every campus had a soda shop, malt shop, or other student hangout that served as the number-one gathering spot. That was the place to

CAMPUS LIFE

meet a girl for a Coke, just as in civilian days. In some of these hang-outs, such as Bowling Green State University's Falcon's Nest, dancing was allowed on Sundays for the first time.

Perhaps the most interesting campus event of all occurred at Swarthmore College in late 1943, when the Chinese navy moved in with the V-12s. Forty-nine Chinese naval officers were assigned to Swarthmore to improve their English before going on to other schools for advanced naval courses. Instead of quartering the Chinese by themselves, the Navy moved them into rooms with V-12s in order to make their English improvement a full-time project. They were put on the same schedule as V-12s for everything except classes. They answered reveille, took calisthenics, marched to chow, participated in physical training classes, and honored the study hours and lights out schedule. During their six months at Swarthmore the Chinese got along well with everyone. Special friendships developed between them and the V-12s. The V-12s thought they were great guys, but a little strange in one respect: the Chinese genuinely liked calisthenics and P.T.!

In the engineering schools most of the able-bodied men had been drafted, so there were comparatively few civilians in those programs, which lasted for six or eight terms under the V-12. Thus, V-12s came to dominate the engineering publications and the various engineering fraternities and clubs.

At all of the V-12 units the chiefs, officers, and school coaches organized a very active intramural program. The competition was spirited and of high quality, particularly at colleges that had discontinued some or all of the intercollegiate athletic program. Extra liberty was frequently given to the winning teams.

Tournaments were held with amazing frequency at schools such as St. Lawrence University. In July and August 1943, swimming and track tournaments were organized, and in September and October a round-robin football tournament was held. At a number of the units the officers joined in pick-up volleyball games and took part in the unit tournaments. At Central Michigan the doubles crown in tennis was taken by the skipper and the exec.

At most schools, men who were performing academic work with a C average or better were not required to adhere to study hours. They could visit the library, the campus hangout, or the coeds in the lounges of their dorms or sorority houses. The V-12 program provided a switch from the typical campus situation in which the girls had to be in their housing units at a specified time: now it was the men who had deadlines. Professor Richard Mahard of Denison University noted that every faculty member knew better than to be near the pathway leading from the upper campus where the girls lived to the lower campus where the V-12s were quartered anytime near to 2200, because the V-12s would

CAMPUS LIFE

Competitions in athletics and inspections between dorms and companies were undertaken constantly in the V-12 program, as this shot at Colgate University attests. The banners were usually awarded at the end of the term as part of a farewell to some colleagues who were departing for boot camp or midshipmen's school. Some thoughtful person placed two bottles of Utica Club Beer in front of each man attending this banquet.

come flying down the pathway and nothing could stop them from getting to their muster on time.[9]

Along with the pleasures of campus life came some responsibilities in addition to those expected by the V-12 authorities. When local emergencies of various kinds came up, the V-12s provided the manpower to cope with them. Volunteer parties of V-12s formed at a number of units in agricultural areas to help save crops that otherwise would have rotted in the fields because there was no one to pick them. In upstate New York, V-12s at Colgate and Cornell loaded into trucks on summer Saturdays to go out and pick beans. At Middlebury, Vermont, part of the apple crop was brought in by V-12 and civilian volunteers on weekend duty. At the North Dakota State Teachers Colleges some V-12s volunteered to help with the wheat harvest, which meant a legal payment of up to seventy-five cents per hour (by special ruling of the Ninth Naval District) and the opportunity for some great farm dinners.

When the freeze warning went out to the orange growers around Red-

CAMPUS LIFE

lands, California, an appeal was sent to the V-12s at the University of Redlands to set out the smudge pots to ward off the cold. Although it was billed as volunteer duty, one trainee said, "Voluntary, my foot!"[10]

Fire was another calamity that brought out V-12 volunteers. At Mount St. Mary's College in upstate Maryland the unit's kitchen went up in flames on the night of November 7, 1944, and the V-12s were forced to move to the gym. No classes were held the next day; every man turned out to clean up the mess. A field kitchen from a nearby Army camp served the meals.

At Princeton University on May 24, 1944, an early morning fire in the gymnasium was discovered by a V-12 trainee on watch in Little Hall. He sounded the alarm and the V-12s aided the local firemen, but the gym was a total loss.

At Durham, North Carolina, a Liggett & Myers tobacco warehouse caught fire on a Saturday night in the summer of 1944, and V-12s — in whites — turned out to help man the hoses. As a result, the Duke laundry was presented with a monumental cleaning job.

At Berea, Ohio, a blaze on October 5, 1943 destroyed nearly a block of the main business district. V-12s from Baldwin-Wallace manned the hoses and then patrolled the area during the night to prevent looting.

Near Carson-Newman College, a July 1943 fire at a zinc mine brought V-12 volunteers, but as soon as the word was passed that the fire was approaching a cache of dynamite, they backed off.

Fire struck the roof of Fell Hall, the main V-12 dormitory at Illinois State Normal University, on the morning of November 9, 1943. The nearby classrooms were immediately emptied. C. O. Meldrim Burrill calmly phoned the District Training Office from his office in Fell Hall to report the problem and to state that he already had it under control — the trainees were moving out furniture to set up temporary housing in the gym. The fire was soon put out, and two days later the V-12s moved back to the dorm.

At Hartford, Connecticut, a flash fire struck the main tent of the Ringling Brothers, Barnum & Bailey Circus during an afternoon performance on July 6, 1944. Several V-12s at the show immediately reported to the police and were put to work helping evacuate the crowd and assisting in removing some of the victims. They worked from 1500 to 0100 the next morning, without letup. The fire took 163 lives, mostly women and children, and injured more than two hundred. Four Trinity College V-12s received Navy commendations for their work.[11]

When the Ohio River flooded in the spring of 1944, the trainees at Bethany College in West Virginia volunteered to help the families living along the river move their possessions to higher ground. But when the flood waters had subsided a few days later and the civilian authorities

CAMPUS LIFE

called on the commanding officer for more V-12 assistance, the C.O. drew the line. The V-12s were available to help in true emergencies, but their basic academic work was more important than the nonemergency work of moving people back to their homes.

Campus life involved fun, creativity, and responsibility, and V-12 participation was excellent in all three.

33

INTERCOLLEGIATE
ATHLETICS

COMDR. James Joseph "Gene" Tunney adamantly opposed intercollegiate athletics for the V-12 trainees. On the other hand, Adm. Randall Jacobs indicated in a speech at the Columbia Conference of May 14 and 15, 1943, that V-12 was "a college program" and that the trainees would be allowed to participate in college activities as long as they didn't interfere with their studies. Most of the officers in the College Training Section and nearly all of those assigned to the V-12 units came from educational positions and backed the view prevailing at the 131 V-12 schools that competition should be permitted. The stage was set at the Bureau of Naval Personnel for quite a contest to determine whether in fact the trainees would be allowed to participate.[1]

Commander Tunney was a favorite of President Franklin D. Roosevelt and was occasionally invited to lunch at the White House. When he returned to the Bureau from such meetings, he frequently noted that "the President likes what I'm doing."[2] Thus, the prestige of the White House had been thrown onto his side of the fray, although probably not with Roosevelt's blessing.

After protracted deliberation, the decision was finally officially announced by the secretary of the Navy. He said that intercollegiate athletics would be permitted, subject to eligibility rules. Those rules, which were issued later, stated that first-term freshmen would not be allowed to participate.[3] Another restriction, in addition to the ruling that athletics not interfere with the basic mission of the V-12 program, was that the intercollegiate athletic program could not take the trainees away from their units for more than seventy-two hours at a time. V-12 Bulletin No. 86, dated September 14, 1943, reduced time away from the unit to forty-eight hours, including travel time. In spite of the restriction, the decision to allow V-12 participation was welcomed by most of the colleges and universities. Commander Tunney, who had suffered a major defeat in the matter, was sent by Admiral Jacobs to make a study of the physical training opportunities in Australia, an assignment that kept him away from BuPers for a long time.[4]

INTERCOLLEGIATE ATHLETICS

Because of declining enrollments of male students prior to the start of V-12, approximately three hundred colleges had already decided in 1942 and 1943 to discontinue intercollegiate athletics for the duration of the war.[5] In a few colleges, such as Southwestern Louisiana Institute, the decision was changed after a V-12 unit had been secured, but others, including John Carroll University in Cleveland, held to their original decisions.

With a few notable exceptions, such as the 1944–1945 national champion DePaul University basketball squad, colleges with only civilian enrollments did not offer much athletic competition during the war years. But exceptionally strong teams came out of military camps and stations, where any amateur or professional athlete was allowed to compete. Thus, service teams such as Great Lakes, Randolph Field, March Field, El Toro, Camp Grant, and Iowa Pre-Flight became the powerhouses of the nation. The V-12 schools provided a fine quality of competition, both among themselves and against military base teams.

One great problem for the V-12 teams was lack of time for practice. The coaches had to get the equivalent of three hours of practice finished in one or one and a half hours on the field. This took a great deal of concentration from both the players and the coaches.

In football, nearly every school that had a Marine unit produced an outstanding 1943 team. Some colleges or universities that had never before been noted for this sport achieved amazing records.

A real Cinderella team was Arkansas A & M at Monticello. In earlier years, A & M had played a regular varsity athletic schedule. Since the Arkansas National Guard had been activated and sent to the Aleutians shortly after Pearl Harbor, however, very few athletic young men were left in Arkansas colleges. To continue its program, Arkansas A & M permitted a semiprofessional group known as "the Wandering Boll Weevils" to travel under its name. The Weevils toured the Southwest burlesquing football and playing for laughs: running the wrong way on football fields; giving the other team the ball when they should have been on defense; and wearing weird uniforms such as top hats and tails. The Wandering Boll Weevils folded at the end of 1942, taking the school's football equipment and leaving behind a number of outstanding bills.[6]

In the summer of 1943, Lt.(jg) Homer Cole, a trainer of the Chicago Bears in civilian life but then the athletic officer of the A & M unit, was approached by V-12s about having a team. Many of the marine trainees had starred in football at Southwestern Conference schools. It was pointed out to the men that the school did not even own a football, let alone uniforms and other equipment, so the matter was dropped.[7]

Lieutenant Cole subsequently noted that the University of Arkansas

INTERCOLLEGIATE ATHLETICS

at Fayetteville had an open date on its early October schedule, so he wrote the athletic director offering to play a "practice game" on that date if the university could furnish them uniforms. The university was pleased to fill the date and told A & M to send a list of sizes needed. A & M practice began on Monday of the week of the game without proper equipment. Some players wore tennis shoes and others went barefoot for those few practices.[8] No one was more surprised than the University of Arkansas when it lost 20 to 12 at the hands of the ill-equipped Arkansas A & M squad.

At about the same time, because of disobedience of orders, the Navy decided that the powerful Naval Air Technical Training Command (NATTC) team at Memphis should no longer be allowed to compete in football. The NATTC already had its schedule arranged for that year and the next; it had marvelous equipment and stadium dates in Memphis's Crump Stadium. A high officer at the NATTC read about A & M's surprising victory over Arkansas, and called Lt. Comdr. William S. Thomson, the C.O. at A & M, suggesting that he come over to talk about their equipment. On Monday, Thomson, Cole, and Lt. George W. Greene, the executive officer and assistant football coach, traveled to Memphis and came home with a truckload of football equipment and a two-year schedule for the team. Practice began in earnest, and the new Boll Weevils of Arkansas A & M established a marvelous record of seven wins, one loss to a team with many marines at Southwestern University (Texas), and one 20 to 20 tie with Southwestern Louisiana Institute. Near the end of the season A & M downed unbeaten Keesler Field, 19 to 7. Keesler was such a powerhouse that in two of its games it had given up only one first down.

At Southwestern Louisiana the marines provided the nucleus for an outstanding football team that put together an undefeated season of four wins, one tie, and no losses, downing the powerful Fort Benning, Randolph Field, and Southwestern University teams. The tie was with Arkansas A & M. The standouts were quarterback Alvin Dark, who later starred in professional baseball, and guard Weldon Humble, who was later elected to the Pro Football Hall of Fame. When neither Arkansas A & M nor Southwestern Louisiana Institute received a bowl bid for January 1, 1944, some promoters in Houston put together the "first annual Oil Bowl." On a rain-drenched field, the SLI Bulldogs beat A & M 24 to 7.[9]

Notre Dame, led by V-12 Marine quarterback Angelo Bertelli, became the Associated Press's top national team, winning nine games before the final game against Great Lakes. (Bertelli had by then been transferred to Parris Island for recruit training.) In the last twenty-five seconds, the powerful Great Lakes squad scored on a pass to win 19 to 14.

INTERCOLLEGIATE ATHLETICS

At the University of Michigan, the team consisted mainly of V-12s, who included such stars as Marine Elroy "Crazylegs" Hirsch, formerly of the University of Wisconsin, and fullback Bill Daley, a Navy transfer from Minnesota. Michigan shared the Big Ten championship with Purdue, which had leathernecks and sailors from most of the Big Ten schools on its first and second teams. The AP ranked Michigan, with a record of eight wins and one loss, third in the nation behind Great Lakes. Purdue, the only major undefeated and untied college team playing a full schedule of nine games, earned the fifth spot, after Navy.

At Evanston, Illinois, Marine reservists from the University of Minnesota were important in establishing one of the best seasons Northwestern University ever had. The Wildcats had six wins and two losses and were ranked ninth nationally by the Associated Press.

At Southwestern University in Texas the talent supplied by Marine reservists from the University of Texas and other schools brought the Pirates a record of ten wins, one loss, and one tie in 1943. Included was a win over the Longhorns of Texas. Southwestern received bids to the Sun Bowl in El Paso for two years running. Despite the loss of its Marine V-12s, Texas had enough power to finish first in the Southwestern Conference in 1943. Its only loss was to Southwestern. Texas Christian took the crown in 1944 with a record of seven wins and no losses.

In the Rocky Mountains, Colorado College's team swept away all opposition, thanks to its V-12 sailors and marines.

On the West Coast, the University of Washington team, which included many marines, had a difficult time lining up a schedule, since most of its traditional opponents did not field football teams in 1943. Thus, it produced only four wins (and no losses), but its convincing 27 to 7 win over powerful March Field earned it a trip to the Rose Bowl.

The College of the Pacific in Stockton, coached by eighty-one-year-old Amos Alonzo Stagg, won seven games and lost only to March Field and the University of Southern California.[10] Southern Cal had a record of seven wins and two losses, including a 35 to 0 loss to March Field. The team, which included a number of marines, topped Washington in the 1944 Rose Bowl. Wartime travel restrictions kept the Rose Bowl from including a nationally ranked team from another conference.

The 1943 Duke team, which won eight games and lost only to Navy (14 to 13), took the Southern Conference crown and was ranked seventh nationally by the Associated Press. The 1944 Blue Devils went to the Sugar Bowl, where they beat the University of Alabama, 29 to 26. Georgia Tech captured the Southeastern Conference championship in both 1943 and 1944 and won a bid to the Sugar Bowl in 1944 and the Orange Bowl in 1945.

In 1943, Oberlin College had its best season ever, winning seven

INTERCOLLEGIATE ATHLETICS

games with one tie. The tie, a scoreless affair with DePauw University, occurred in the first game. DePauw also had an outstanding team, running up 206 points against its opponents in six games while allowing them only 6 points. Franklin and Marshall College had a record of eight wins and one loss and was considered for some of the lesser bowl games. Rochester had a record of six and one, the same as Dartmouth.[11]

Of course, not all V-12 teams were successful — not even those with marines! According to Redlands trainees, its 1943 football team, although laden with talent transferred there by the Marines, was the most scored-upon squad in the country. They blamed that upon the coach's unique "Y" formation. The quarterback often got sacked before he could get rid of the ball. Perhaps that's why the "Y" formation never caught on![12]

The 1943 All-American selections were overwhelmingly V-12, as were many of the all-conference and all-state teams in places where the V-12 was well represented. Of the twenty-five players chosen for various first-team All-American squads, thirteen were Marine V-12s.[13]

One practice that developed among a few coaches was promptly nipped in the bud by the College Training Section. V-12 Bulletin No. 5 permitted the commanding officers to transfer up to 5 percent of their

These Marine football players from Oberlin College do not seem at all concerned about the next day's game with the University of Rochester in October 1945. Their lack of concern was apparently warranted — they won the game 27 to 12.

Jack Kinkopf

INTERCOLLEGIATE ATHLETICS

trainees to other units "for valid academic reasons." Early in the first term, Lt. Raymond F. Howes was visiting Northwestern University's head football coach Lynn "Pappy" Waldorf when a huge young man in Navy uniform appeared at the door and said to Waldorf, "I am the new guard from Wisconsin, traded for a halfback." Lieutenant Howes said that when the man apparently noticed his uniform for the first time, he hastened to cover up by adding, "I am a V-12 transfer, Sir, for valid academic reasons." When Lieutenant Howes returned to Washington, this misinterpretation of the rules in V-12 Bulletin No. 5 was promptly set straight.[14]

In basketball, V-12s were tremendously important to the success of their schools. One outstanding team was Bowling Green State University, which went to the National Invitational Tournament (NIT) two years in a row, losing in the first round in 1944 but going all the way to the finals in 1945, where it lost to the champion DePaul University. Muhlenberg was another V-12 college that made it to the NIT that first year.

Western Michigan College of Education in Kalamazoo achieved recognition when its 1943 football team lost only to Michigan and Great Lakes. Its 1943–1944 basketball squad was rated fourth in the nation, with a fifteen and four record. It beat Notre Dame, Northwestern, and Michigan (twice), its only collegiate loss coming at the hands of Temple.

The University of Oklahoma team, dubbed "the round ball runts" because their average height was five feet nine and one-half inches, shared the Big Six (now Big Eight) championship with Iowa State, another V-12 school. Marquette was ranked eighth nationally at the end of the 1943–1944 season.

In some schools that had previously been anything but name performers in the athletic world, the V-12 program brought intercollegiate basketball to the highest point in the school's history. At Milligan College a surprisingly strong basketball team was put together by Ens. Gordon Wellborn through the skillful use of some all-state high school players from Oklahoma and Illinois. This team compiled a sixteen and one record during the early part of the season, including back-to-back victories over Duke and the University of North Carolina on their own floors. Milligan was ranked nationally for several weeks.

The Gonzaga University 1943–1944 cagers beat the University of Washington three games out of four and compiled a twenty-one and two record, which earned them recognition as the "Champions of the Northwest" and a national college ranking of thirteenth.

All across the nation many other V-12 schools produced exceptional records, for there was an abundance of talent in the trainee ranks and the men were in excellent physical condition.

INTERCOLLEGIATE ATHLETICS

Gonzaga University Archives

Basketball played an important role in V-12 intercollegiate athletics. The Gonzaga University quintet above was recognized as the "Champions of the Northwest." They compiled a twenty-one and two record, which included three wins in four games with the University of Washington.

Other sports also benefited from the V-12 program. V-12 schools won conference championships and state recognition in track, swimming, soccer, wrestling, and baseball. V-12s even brought a national track title to MIT, a school not generally noted for athletics. Four MIT V-12s took the National A.A.U. indoor two-mile relay championship in Madison Square Garden in 1945.[15]

The 1944 Western Michigan baseball team inflicted back-to-back end-of-the-season defeats upon the University of Michigan, which was the Big Ten champion and had previously been undefeated. Quality collegiate competition for baseball teams was sometimes unavailable, how-

INTERCOLLEGIATE ATHLETICS

Although there were still civilians at Doane College, most of the baseball team was made up of V-12s, as the uniforms indicated.

ever. The 1944 baseball team at Bowling Green State University turned in a spectacular twenty and three record, but some of the wins occurred in summer-league play against such teams as the Toledo Red Cabs and Toledo AutoLites. Arkansas A & M played a semipro schedule in the summer of 1944.

In remote areas, the difficulty of finding competition and in arranging travel during wartime was formidable. In baseball, some nearby V-12 units played each other so often that the season seemed like a miniature world series. Milligan and Carson-Newman Colleges in eastern Tennessee had that kind of relationship in 1944, facing each other seven times during the season.

Unfortunately for the coaches, the end of the V-12 terms did not coincide with the completion of the football and basketball schedules. Transfers from a V-12 unit to midshipmen's school, Parris Island, or another V-12 school had ominous results for most of the successful teams. The Bowling Green State University basketball team that made it to the NIT in March of 1944 had lost three of its regulars due to Navy and Marine transfers at the end of February. Thus handicapped, it dropped its opening game to the defending champs, St. John's of Brooklyn. Football teams that won their first four games sometimes lost

INTERCOLLEGIATE ATHLETICS

their last four because of extensive transfers on October 31. Half of Penn State's 1943 squad, seventeen men, was transferred at the end of October.

At some schools football players who had been regulars on one team found themselves transferred to an opponent scheduled to play the original team just a week later. This happened to a University of Pittsburgh fullback who was called to active duty at Penn State on November 1 and then helped his new team beat his old one 14 to 0 just three weeks later. Tackle Ted Hapanowicz faced the University of North Carolina twice in 1943: once with Penn State's Nittany Lions and, after a November 1 transfer, once with the University of Pennsylvania.[16] Such transfers of players had occurred for years in professional sports, but this was a first in collegiate athletics because all eligibility waiting periods had been waived for the duration.

Intercollegiate sports were credited in some schools for "helping bring the various elements of the campus together."[17] Everywhere they provided a most welcome relief from the drudgery of five and a half days of hard academic work and weekend restrictions because of low grades. Most observers of the V-12 era agree that intercollegiate athletics were very beneficial to campus morale.

Player brilliance on the football fields often transferred to the battle-fields. According to Col. John Gunn, USMC(Ret.), who has built up extensive files about Marine football, the marines who played V-12 football were awarded a total of two Navy Crosses, seven Silver Stars, three Bronze Stars, and various other decorations for heroism and valor in the Battles of Iwo Jima and Okinawa.[18]

34

HUMOR, HIGH JINKS, AND "THEY SHOULDN'T HAVE"

No ONE ever accused the V-12s of not having a sense of humor, although some college authorities and Navy officers wished it had been on a somewhat higher plane. Often it was expressed as good, plain American humor. Some offerings were very refined, whereas others were on the coarse side. Unfortunately for history's sake, the more sophisticated humor has mostly been forgotten, whereas the low-grade examples are well remembered, in part because of their shock effect. For example, one of the most common phrases used in all of the V-12 units when there was a factual dispute involved this challenge: "If that isn't so, I'll kiss your —— on the quarterdeck, and give you twenty minutes to assemble the crowd." This was taken to be a figure of speech in most places, but at one Southern school it was made the condition of a serious bet. The crowd was duly assembled to watch what one witness described as the loser's placing "his orbicularis oris muscles in the state of contraction upon the gluteus maximus" of the winner.[1]

Besides being men of their word, V-12s were also men of action. One trainee at a small school had a strong aversion to bathing, and in the summertime it became a real burden to be downwind of him. The trainees called him "Bathless Joe," after Al Capp's comic strip figure of that era. Finally, his roommates and classmates could take it no longer and bodily took him into the shower. He did not seem to benefit from the lesson, for it had to be repeated a month later.

In the middle of July 1943 Commander Horner of the Union College unit addressed the new V-12s at one of the three "chapels" held each week. His message was "You are disgracing your uniform." He told them they were expected to behave like officers and gentlemen and to be a credit to the Navy. "Why," he said, "the other day I saw a V-12 coming

HUMOR, HIGH JINKS

back to campus with his hat on the back of his head while eating an ice cream cone, and then, instead of walking around the chain he jumped over it — but he didn't make it! I could go along without getting too upset with his hat not squared and eating the ice cream cone, and even trying to jump over the chain, but I cannot abide a man who cannot clear three feet!"[2]

Although they got along very well on nearly all the campuses, at Trinity College there was continual competition involving pranks and practical jokes between the "old salts" and the "college boys." Some of the traditional college stunts such as "short-sheeting" the bunks of the old salts brought swift retaliation to the suspected perpetrators. In one of the more innovative examples, a fleet man triple-stitched closed one arm of a trainee's sweat shirt and one leg of his sweat pants. That was enough to thwart the trainee in the last seconds before calisthenics the next morning, so he had to appear in the freezing weather in just his trunks and skivvy shirt.[3]

Nearly every school had its share of schemes for trainees to sneak out during study hours to take in a movie or visit the local beer hall. Sometimes they even left after bed check for a late date. At Milligan College, trainees going to town to see a movie had to jump from the window to a fire escape and silently move through the campus to the main road, where they were met by a taxi. A back-up scheme was arranged with the theater's projectionist so that if a trainee friend called from the college to say that a bed check was expected, a certain signal was put on the screen, which promptly emptied the theater of V-12s, who madly hailed taxis and dashed back to the campus.[4]

In the summer of 1945, when the war had ended and security had been relaxed, a V-12 living in the gym at Tulane felt he frequently had good reason to absent himself for the night. But one unfilled bunk among eight hundred filled bunks would be noticed, so he hired a civilian student to sleep in his sack. The going rate for such substitute service was five dollars a night, which was a lot of money in those days. The civilian enjoyed it, too, since he reported that the gym, with its constant breeze, was the coolest place on the whole Tulane campus.[5]

Getting caught on an AWOL trip to town could mean dismissal from the program, but more often it meant one or more weekends of restriction to the campus. Some schools had an especially rigorous procedure, the trainees being required to report to the officer of the deck or the guard on duty every two hours for thirty-two consecutive hours.

Some marines at the University of Rochester held one last "rounder" (using nonapproved liquid spirits) before they were moved out of a fraternity house to another housing unit. Several disputes ensued during the evening and in the process a number of pieces of furniture in the

HUMOR, HIGH JINKS

lounge were thoroughly wrecked. Early in the morning, wiser heads saw the potential problems that could result from breaking up furniture leased by the U.S. Navy, so a diligent task force set about repairing the chairs and tables. Yankee ingenuity took over. They rounded up all the chewing gum they could find and then sent runners out for more, using it to restore the furniture to an appearance of normality. They finished just before the final inspection of the house, and everything looked fine when the sailors moved in. The first time they sat down, the chairs collapsed, and the Navy blamed the sailors and punished them. No one could understand how the sailors could do so much damage after those rough marines had left the house in good shape.[6]

The *Rochester Alumni-Alumnae Review*, in an article entitled "Fraternity Houses in Good Shape Now," said that when the houses were turned back to the fraternities on November 1, 1944, they were found to be in good shape, adding that "some damage done earlier to one house had been satisfactorily repaired."

At Iowa State College a bunch of trainees living in Friley Hall got in the habit of listening to a WHO (Des Moines) program at 0745 that featured such classic children's fare as "dressing races." The hosts, Uncle Stan and Cowboy Ken, had a "magic eye" and could tell whether the boys or the girls won the race on any particular day. One day they announced a big premium offer: for sending in a certain number of box tops from Coco Wheats cereal, the children could receive a genuine "Hortense, the Happy Little Honey-Bee."[7] Hortense was a paper honey-bee attached to a wooden base that had a rubber band around it. Whirling Hortense through the air by means of a string created a buzzing sound that was guaranteed to delight small children. On the way to analytical geometry class that morning, several of the V-12s decided that every red-blooded V-12 should have his very own Hortense, the Happy Little Honey-Bee, so they decided to write to Uncle Stan and Cowboy Ken.

The letter was written and then signed by seventy-six men. It mentioned that the Navy boys in Ames were big fans of the program but they couldn't join in the dressing contest because the commanding officer made them get up too early. Worst of all, they didn't get to eat Coco Wheats for breakfast so couldn't get any box tops to send in. They asked if a special dispensation would be possible so they could get some honeybees without the box tops.

A couple of days later Uncle Stan read the letter on the air. He sent the trainees a nice reply and forwarded their request to the Little Crow Milling Company, Inc., in Warsaw, Indiana. Two days later the V-12s received a letter from C. L. Maish, the president of the company, who wrote,

HUMOR, HIGH JINKS

Uncle Stan seldom gets mail from kids over ten years of age, but maybe the Navy is taking them younger than we imagined. If "Hortense, the Happy Little Honey-Bee" is the only thing that will make you boys happy, we are willing to do our part. In the box you will receive there are seventy-six bees, one for each of the children in your group.

Never mind trying to get the Navy to serve Coco Wheats. If they did, your commanding officer would keep all the boxtops and get all the nice things we give away anyway.

Yours for winning the war after you are through playing with the bees.

The excitement ran high on the Iowa State campus! The student paper featured the story every day. Finally the bees arrived. But so did the impostors — V-12s claiming they had signed the letter and were entitled to a Hortense. There was only one thing for the organizers to do: they made each applicant sign his name and then compared it to the signature on their copy of the letter, thus putting Hortense only into deserving hands.

Sometimes humor was unintentional. One Sunday at Miami University in Ohio some V-12s were at a girls' dorm visiting with newly arrived coeds. After a while a sailor asked a freshman, "Miss, where's the head?" "Oh," came the prompt reply, "She's out of town."[8]

At Union College the V-12s were scheduled to parade on Armistice Day night, November 11, 1943. It turned out to be bitterly cold when the men assembled at about 1630 on upper State Street, the prime residential area of Schenectady. They were freezing in the cold for more than an hour; the parade still hadn't started, and darkness had fallen. One by one the V-12s found it necessary to slip out of ranks to relieve themselves, so they used the only available places: the lawns of the large homes on upper State Street. Finally the parade was held, with no major foul-ups.

When the trainees assembled for calisthenics at 0545 the next morning, the athletic officer was apoplectic! He chewed them out royally, like the captain in *Mr. Roberts.* "You have embarrassed the United States Navy!" he shouted. "You have disgraced your uniform! You have brought shame to the Union V-12 Unit!"

The men were puzzled, because they thought they had performed quite well in the parade. Then he told them what the problem was. "You peed all over those people's yards. Nothing will grow there for a hundred years! I'm going to make you sorry for that — ten laps!"[9]

The Navy V-12 trainees had a number of subgroups within their ranks, so nicknames were used frequently. The V-12(a)s were called "fly boys" and "airdales," while they in turn referred to the regulars by such prejudicial names as "deck apes." And between the sailors and the marines, of course, there was a constant rivalry over practically everything.

HUMOR, HIGH JINKS

The most common names in use were "swabbies" or "swab jockeys" for the sailors and "bellhops" or "gyrenes" for the marines.

When two marines at Dartmouth were visited in their room by three especially obnoxious sailors, they soon got fed up, took matters into their own hands, and threw the offending men out of a second-story window into a deep snow bank. Fortunately, there were no serious injuries, but the matter was duly reported. The marines were called up before the commanding officer. The Marine officer-in-charge, Major Howland, intervened in the hearing, asking that the men, since they were marines, be remanded to him for punishment. The C.O. agreed, so the major took the offenders to his office. When he heard their story, he howled with laughter and said the sailors got what they deserved. The major ordered the two marines to serve as his enlisted aides during their free time for the next week. Both reported that they had a most enjoyable time.[10]

At one college there was a newly hired professor who made little effort to maintain decorum in the classroom. He taught a first-year math course, which met immediately after lunch. One trainee started sleeping during most of the lectures, which naturally offended his colleagues. For the sailor's own benefit it was decided to wake him so that he could keep up with the class. He was awakened by the traditional "hotfoot," which involved wedging a "farmer match" in between the sole and upper part of his shoe, matchhead first. Lighting the bottom of the matchstick soon ignited the matchhead, which "aroused" the sleeper, to put it mildly.

When the drowsy V-12 continued to sleep day after day despite continual "hotfeet," his fellow trainees decided that sterner measures where called for. One of them brought in a can of lighter fluid and applied the liquid all around the sole of the sleeper's shoe. When it was ignited, the flames shot up all around the sleeper's foot. Rudely awakened, he jumped two feet in the air. The professor chided, "Boys, you shouldn't really do that."[11]

True to tradition, the bugler was not a very popular member of the V-12 unit, at least at 0545! He was frequently the object of some devilment. At Trinity College one bitterly cold winter morning, he was awakened, as customary, by the janitor pounding on his door and announcing the time. The bugler found a note hanging from the top bunk: "Your bugle is on the window ledge." So it was. But during the night one of the fleet men had filled it with water and left it out to freeze solid. Not a note was sounded. The bugler had to go door to door doing his own pounding to wake up the rest of the trainees.

Another time the same bugler was awakened by the janitor's call, "Wake up, it's 0545!" He stumbled out of his bunk, grabbed the bugle,

HUMOR, HIGH JINKS

went outside, and proceeded to blow reveille. But there was one trouble: it hadn't been the janitor who had awakened him, and it wasn't 0545. It was 0230. The bugler was restricted for waking the whole campus at such an unearthly hour.[12]

On August 12, 1944, the V-12s at a Southern college who were walking off demerits during the early part of a Saturday liberty had to seek refuge off the drill field when they were buzzed by a Piper Cub, which did spins and loops and acted like a dive bomber. The V-12 trainee who rented the plane at a nearby airport was never discovered at the time, but he confessed it at a V-12 reunion nearly forty years later.[13]

At Yale, on V-J night, the commanding officer unwisely decided that the V-12s could not be allowed to roam the town with the rest of the happy populace, so they were restricted to their quarters. A never-ending parade of people and vehicles came down the street outside one of the housing units. The temptation was too much! The marines placed a spotter on the roof to signal when an open convertible came down the street. Wastebaskets had already been filled with water, and when the signal was given the contents were pitched out the open window in the head, time and again making direct hits on the convertibles and their occupants. But such was the mood of the time and place that even those who were drenched laughed it off. The festivity continued for hours.[14]

A clever ruse was pulled off at the University of Michigan on an occasion when only the marines had been invited to a sorority house dance. Some sailors were resentful, so late that afternoon one of them prevailed upon a girlfriend to write a bogus letter and deliver it to the sergeant on duty. It read, "Dear Marines, Due to University regulations, we are changing our party to a picnic. It will be held at the Island at 7:30. Wear old clothes, as games will be played. Jean Demo, Pi Phi Co-Chairman."

In hopeful anticipation, the marines went to the picnic spot some distance from the campus. At the appropriate time the sailors started calling the sorority house inquiring how the dance was going. Although mystified as to the whereabouts of the marines, the girls faked it, telling the sailors, "Just great!" After the girls were more than an hour overdue, the marines realized they had been taken, and they were not happy about it. But the leathernecks finally got to the sorority house, where they danced for the final hour of liberty. They swore revenge upon the sailors, but not that night. According to *The Michigan Daily* report of the incident, by morning muster the tension in the atmosphere had been detected by the officers, and one of the orders of the day was "No rioting."[15]

In another incident, a University of Kansas V-12 had smashed his Plymouth convertible into a taxi on the main street of Lawrence. To make matters worse, the cab had spun around, its trunk had flown

HUMOR, HIGH JINKS

open, and the loose spare tire had catapulted through a nearby bank window, setting off the burglar alarm. Trainees were forbidden to have cars, and the trainee thought he would soon be at Great Lakes.

Fortunately, the garage where the V-12 sometimes stored his car was just a half-block away. Benefiting from his Navy training in fast thinking, the V-12 ran to get the owner, who quickly brought the wrecker and hauled the damaged car back to the garage.

As luck would have it, the cab driver had often been hired by the V-12 to take him to the far side of town, where the illegal auto was sometimes stashed. When the police arrived, the guilty vehicle was nowhere in sight, and both the cabbie and the trainee agreed that whoever hit the taxi had "taken off like a bat out of hell."[16] It was reported that the cab driver subsequently received wonderful tips whenever he had that particular passenger.

The marines at the University of Redlands, a conservative Baptist school, had a running dispute with the school's administration. One bone of contention was the school's expectation that all V-12s show up for chapel. Since chapel at Redlands was definitely a religious service, the Navy could not enforce attendance. The marines became sensitive about the frequent criticism of their poor attendance record, so it became a ritual for those returning from weekend visits to the gin mills to stop by the front yards of the president and the dean of students to give them several lusty verses of "Onward, Christian Soldiers."[17] They would also carefully gather up every liquor bottle they could find, and the night before the trash pickup they would divide the collection equally between the garbage cans of the dean and the president.

The marines' most spectacular performance at Redlands came on New Year's Eve in 1943 when they were restricted to the campus because of previous wrongdoing. They had orders to muster every hour, on the hour, until midnight. It must be noted that the strict social rules at Redlands then prohibited social dancing anywhere on the campus. Presumably that ban covered the chapel steps on New Year's Eve.

In the words of one of those who was present,

Denied an official opportunity to celebrate the advent of 1944, the Redlands Marines pulled out all the stops. For starters, they wired the tower of Memorial Chapel with loudspeakers connected to a record player, then passed the word to key coeds. That evening, between hourly musters, there was a gala dance on the steps of the University's holy of holies.

Glenn Miller's "Jersey Bounce" could be heard all over Redlands and halfway to Colton. There was a particularly melancholy recording of "Wait For Me, Mary" that reduced even the sober ones to tears. Alas, "demon rum" was there, too: valiant coeds provided a steady stream of beer and more devilish concoctions. Hand-holding was rampant. At the eleven o'clock muster, there were three stone-sober Marines; two dozen or so semi-sobers. The rest were three-sheets-to-the-wind-and-listing-heavily-to-starboard. The coeds, to their

HUMOR, HIGH JINKS

credit, had departed by this time — matters were getting out of hand. There was no midnight muster. Chaos had taken over.

Someone finally turned off the record player and pulled the wires after midnight; all of Redlands was surely aroused [including UR's President Elam J. Anderson], but no gendarmes appeared.[18]

Within two months the University of Redlands had decided that it would permit dances on the campus, provided they were held in the Commons, which had been leased to the Navy. The Redlands board of trustees reasoned that the Navy had exclusive use of the building, so that it was not technically part of the campus. The military ball was held in the Commons on Saturday, February 19. The student body was jubilant.[19]

35

LIBERTY
AND LEAVE

LIBERTY and leave were very important to every man in the service, and nowhere was that truer than in the V-12 program. These respites from constant pressure were what kept the men going.

Where did the V-12s go on their liberty? That depended upon where they started from. At many large schools, such as Duke University and the University of North Carolina, they often stayed on campus because there was more going on at the school than anywhere else. At some other large universities, such as Northwestern, UCLA, and Washington, trainees had the best of all possible worlds. The coeds and campus activities were numerous, the nearby water gave them opportunities for recreation, and they had access to big cities that offered myriad ways to spend a liberty.

This was not true at every large school, however. One trainee at Columbia reported that "campus social life was zilch," but New York offered more varied opportunities for spending a weekend than any other city in the country.

At the isolated men's schools, weekends provided the opportunity to search for female companionship. At Williams College in northwestern Massachusetts the trainees dispersed into the nearby Berkshire Mountains. At Hampden-Sydney in Virginia, trainees usually traveled to nearby Farmville to see girls at the State Teachers College. The V-12s at the University of the South at Sewanee headed for Chattanooga or anywhere else to get off "that blankety-blank mountain." The smaller coeducational schools, on the other hand, came alive during the weekends, so there had to be rather important enticements for men to travel elsewhere.

Travel on liberty was limited by several factors: (1) the normal liberty territory was strictly defined in the station orders; (2) the time allowed was very limited, to about thirty hours at the typical V-12 unit; and (3) most trainees had to operate on very limited funds.

The travel radius was often set at forty or fifty miles from the V-12 unit, but depending upon the school's location, it may have extended

LIBERTY AND LEAVE

to seventy-five or even one hundred miles. Travel beyond that limit could not be done on the simple cardboard liberty pass that was issued to the trainee just before he left and was taken back by the officer on duty when the trainee returned. Loss of the liberty card meant demerits, and probably restriction for the following weekend.

Trainees who wished to travel beyond the limit needed to give a special reason. Visiting home was usually sufficient. Traveling to see a girlfriend may or may not have been sufficient, depending upon the whims of the chief athletic specialist who was in charge of considering such requests at most schools. If a chief did not grant many out-of-area liberties for such reasons, allegedly visiting the home of another V-12 who lived outside the area was a convenient excuse.

With limited spending money, the typical V-12 used a lot of liberty time just hanging around the business district, at least until the USO opened for the evening. These eight sailors in downtown Cape Girardeau, Missouri, are on liberty from Southeast Missouri State Teachers College.

Anzell Lee

LIBERTY AND LEAVE

The shore patrol regularly worked the trains and bus stations. They usually checked the liberty or leave papers of any man in service to see whether he was on an authorized absence or AWOL. A cardboard liberty pass that set forty miles as the limit of a man's travel would not help him if he was found by the shore patrol one hundred miles away. He needed a specially signed authorization to travel beyond the normal limit.

The trainees of Bethany College in the panhandle of West Virginia had an especially difficult time when they left their Fifth Naval District. They only had to go a few miles east or west and they were in the Fourth or Ninth Naval District. The trip to Pittsburgh or across the Ohio River to Ohio could bring them face to face with a shore patrol who didn't

Payday was the most important day of the month for V-12s. Note these trainees at Ohio Wesleyan putting their right index fingerprint on the pay receipt before the WAVE officer pays out the money. At some units payday was held twice a month.

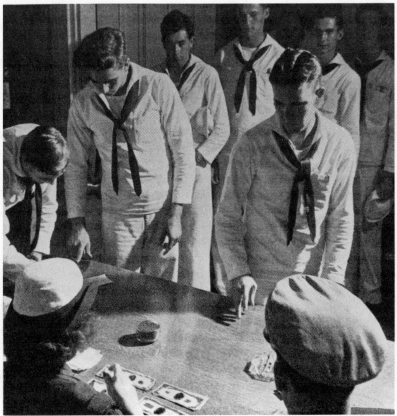

Ohio Wesleyan University Archives

LIBERTY AND LEAVE

understand what men from the Fifth Naval District were doing in their district with just liberty passes.

Lack of cash also restricted the trainees' liberty travels, and sometimes influenced their local destinations as well. It will be recalled that the trainees were paid fifty dollars per month. But, as noted in Chapter 17, "Reporting for Duty," two big deductions were usually taken off the top for National Service Life Insurance and War Bonds. Those totaled nearly thirteen dollars. Then there was the laundry expense, which could easily be six to eight dollars a month. The cost was higher in the summer, when whites were the uniform of the day. (V-12s who attended all-male schools were often allowed to wear dungarees during the week, which reduced their laundry bills somewhat.)

Then there were the normal school expenses such as fountain pens, ink, pencils, notebooks, and other school items not supplied by the Navy. After paying for soft drinks, cigarettes, small stores purchases, telephone calls, and "malt shop" dates on campus, most V-12s had somewhat less than thirty dollars left for the whole month before they

Trainees from Iowa State College climb aboard the Fort Dodge, Des Moines and Southern interurban on their way to liberty in Des Moines.

Iowa State University Archives

LIBERTY AND LEAVE

even set foot off the campus. They didn't have a lot left for transportation, movies, beer, and restaurant meals, which is why the USOs and invitations to dances at girls' schools were so popular.

At the hour when liberty terminated, each platoon leader was required to muster his men. Sometimes men covered for a roommate who was late in returning. In the darkness of an outside muster at 2200 on a Sunday night, one man's "yo" sounded pretty much like another's. Things became a bit obvious, however, when a name was called and five "yos" were heard.[1]

Longer shore leaves — beyond seventy-two hours — were generally limited to the periods between terms, but the traditional Christmas vacation was worked into the schedule of nearly every V-12 college. Students gladly attended classes on Thanksgiving Day and even some Saturday afternoons in order to get a head start on the Yuletide vacation.

Because of the delays in getting classes started in July of 1943, the time available for leave between the first and the second terms had been

Although trains served many of the V-12s heading out of town, these sailors at Southeast Missouri piled onto the local bus to begin their leave.

Anzell Lee

LIBERTY AND LEAVE

Ohio Wesleyan University Archives

A frequently used method of transportation for the V-12s, particularly when they weren't going far, was hitchhiking. It wasn't difficult in the war years, when nearly every car would stop for a serviceman. This hopeful V-12 is on liberty from Ohio Wesleyan.

minimal. Most units had, at best, a seventy-two hour liberty. So most V-12s were looking ahead to a Christmas leave of a week or ten days, as had always been the rule at colleges in civilian days. Plans were made in nearly every unit toward that end.

But their hopes were dashed. To reduce the expected overload on the nation's transportation facilities over the Christmas holidays, early in

LIBERTY AND LEAVE

November orders came from Washington that only 10 percent of any naval establishment could use public transportation on official leave during the Christmas holidays. Others granted leave had to provide proof of their alternate transportation plans, which usually involved private automobiles. Hitchhiking was not considered an approved alternate plan because of the possibility that the hitchhiker would switch to public transportation facilities. Ordinarily, a man applying for Christmas leave with alternative transportation had to provide an exact itinerary, the name of the driver of the car, and even the license number of the vehicle.[2]

At units where more than half of the men came from distant areas, it appeared that the Christmas leave had evaporated. This brought a rash of appeals from V-12 skippers, who pointed out to the College Training Section that the institutions had already set their schedules. Both faculty members and civilian students had made plans to depart, so it would be impossible to continue the educational program over the holidays. Fifty or 60 percent of the V-12s would be left with nothing to do, which would produce a terrible morale problem. Couldn't an exception be made?

Again the College Training Section went to bat for its trainees. Commander Adams had the friends and the persuasive powers to have an exception made. V-12 Bulletin No. 144, sent by telegram on November 17, 1943, said, "BECAUSE OF SPECIAL CONDITIONS INVOLVING RELATIONS WITH FACULTY AND CIVILIAN STUDENTS NAVY V-12 STUDENTS ARE EXEMPTED FROM PROVISIONS OF LETTER . . . 30 OCTOBER RESTRICTING TRAVEL OF NAVAL PERSONNEL DURING CHRISTMAS HOLIDAYS. COMMANDING OFFICERS SHOULD HOWEVER MAKE EVERY EFFORT TO RELIEVE STRAIN ON TRANSPORTATION FACILITIES."

Air travel was out for any trainee, since it was so limited that only officers, government officials, or civilians in a necessary assignment could obtain the priority needed for a plane reservation. Only an emergency leave was sufficient to get that kind of priority, and even that was not always possible if space were not available.

During Christmastime of 1943, the railroads threw into operation every piece of ancient equipment that would run. Pullman cars were used as day coaches, night and day. Nevertheless, buses and trains were packed as servicemen and civilians alike sat on suitcases in the aisles. At times, conductors couldn't even get through coaches. As long as the train was moving, however, the men made progress toward their home leave.

For Californians assigned to V-12 schools in other parts of the country, the seven or ten days authorized for leave made it nearly impossible

LIBERTY AND LEAVE

to return home. Such a trip would have meant four or five days on the train, with only a few left for the visit. At Illinois Tech and no doubt some other schools, too, trainees traveling more than five hundred miles from the unit were dismissed a day earlier than the rest of the men so they could get a head start. They could leave at 1700 on the twenty-third instead of the same time on Christmas Eve.

The time was still not sufficient for everyone to get home. Those who had to stay were often invited to spend Christmas with the family of one of their buddies, or faculty members invited them to come over for Christmas Day.

The other V-12 leaves were set for the breaks between terms, which allowed men being transferred to other units or to midshipmen's schools to complete their travel. All leaves and liberties were eagerly anticipated from the time a man returned from his previous one. They served a necessary purpose — as the pressure-relief valves of the V-12 program.

36

V-12 AND
THE PUBLIC

BECAUSE of the broad geographic distribution of the trainees, the V-12 program affected nearly every community of any size in the country. President Roosevelt's edict required that all regions be represented, which was a great help for the program's public image. It also helped that people could see that the men going into the program were among the most promising in their communities, whether they came out of high school or college or were brought back from other duty in the Navy or Marines.

The democratic selection process also impressed the public. Many trainees came from families that otherwise could not have sent their boys to college. Of course, the wide distribution created problems as well. Every community had many young men fighting in the far corners of the earth, and the parents of those servicemen were understandably dubious about the wisdom of allowing other men from the same town to go to college while all the fighting was going on. Such a position was especially easy to arrive at for a mother living in a college town with a V-12 unit. Every day she could see young sailors and marines carrying books to class, walking down the street with girls, and having fun on Saturday nights and Sundays while her boy was fighting for democracy in some hellhole. Quite a number of those upset mothers fired off letters to their congressmen, the newspapers, and even President Roosevelt.

The Navy, with great patience, answered all of the complaining letters, pointing out the greater responsibility the men would have when they completed their training. The answers unfailingly noted that the Navy felt so strongly about the importance of this program that it had brought many of its best men back from overseas to train them for their future responsibilities.[1] Whether the answers ever allayed a mother's anger is doubtful.

One woman in Johnson City, Tennessee, reported to the commanding officer of Milligan College the secret marriage of a Milligan V-12. The trainee had made the mistake of visiting his wife in the hospital, where she had just delivered their first-born. Within a few days he was on his

V-12 AND THE PUBLIC

way to Great Lakes for violating his pledge not to marry while in the V-12 program. The commanding officers did not go out of their way to uncover secret marriages, but when proof was delivered to them, they had to take action.[2]

As always, a few congressmen pandered to the critics with speeches on the floor of the House. An editorial ("The V-12 in Congress") in the January 28, 1944, issue of *The Campus,* the University of Rochester weekly, began, "The V-12 Program has been taking it on the chin these past few days — by Congressional discussion, by radio commentators, by armchair diplomats, by men who win wars and lose them."[3] But the speeches apparently led nowhere — the congressmen merely satisfied a few of their constituents.

A B'nai B'rith chapter in Oregon wrote to the Navy Department asking, "Can we put a star on our service flag for a boy who is in a V-12 Unit at a college?" A veteran's organization in the South reported a heated debate among members about whether a V-12 was really on active duty in the Navy and could therefore wear "the ruptured duck" when discharged.[4] The College Training Section answered both of these inquiries in the affirmative, pointing out the important role the trainees would have as officers in the expanding Navy.[5]

The trainees themselves often joked that "V-12" stood for "victory in twelve years or we fight," and at most units they sang this song, to the tune of "My Bonnie Lies Over the Ocean":

> Take down your service flag, Mother.
> Your boy is safe in V-12.
> He'll never get hurt by a slide rule.
> He'll always stay happy and well.

But in more than one region, this derogatory view of V-12 was thrown up to the trainees time and again by civilians. Another common gibe was, "Join the V-12: release a WAVE for active duty." At Bloomsburg State Teachers the commanding officer of the unit finally had to complain to the local chief of police about "a rough element in town" that was harassing the trainees whenever they went on liberty. The C.O. stated that his men had avoided one or more brawls by exercising great restraint, but that he could not expect his men to keep ignoring this type of harassment. In a few days, the chief reported that he had talked to the "ringleaders" and he thought there would be no more trouble.[6]

Most communities with a V-12 unit took genuine pride in having the unit there. Many of those towns were far removed from regular military bases, and they liked having their own military unit. This was not true everywhere, however. At Monticello, Arkansas, the location of the Ar-

V-12 AND THE PUBLIC

Robert Webber

V-12s at Peru State Teachers practice marching on an unpaved street in Peru.

kansas A & M unit, most of the young men in town had been called up with the National Guard early in 1942 and were serving in the Aleutian Islands. As a result, there was a general resentment against the sailors and marines going to college in that community.[7] These feelings were soon perceived by the V-12s, so they usually left Monticello on liberty and went to more hospitable towns. One such was the city of Pine Bluff forty-eight miles away, which was fondly remembered by many A & M V-12s.

But nearly everywhere else, the townspeople located near V-12 schools were extremely cooperative. In Newberry, South Carolina, the mayor and the town council took an ad in the college paper at the start of each term to welcome the new trainees, and at the end of the term another ad listed the transferees by name, showed where they were going, and wished them well. The town also put on an annual "watermelon cut" for the V-12s.

Although the V-12 units in the larger cities tended to get swallowed up in the complexities of metropolitan life, in the smaller towns they brought new interest and excitement to the rather drab wartime scene.

V-12 AND THE PUBLIC

Martin Photograph Collection. Indiana State University Archives

V-12s from Indiana State Teachers College parade in downtown Terre Haute.

V-12 AND THE PUBLIC

The trainees could spark up any parade, whether it be for Labor Day, Armistice Day, Memorial Day, or the Fourth of July. If there was to be a war bond rally, the V-12 band was always there, and sometimes a select platoon put on a demonstration of close-order drill.

V-12 athletic teams gave some small colleges athletic recognition they had never known before, and the towns proudly enjoyed sharing in the new attention to their area. Major college opponents and winning teams brought out the fans and were good for the college's box office receipts.

As Mrs. David Taylor of Johnson City, Tennessee, so aptly put it at a V-12 reunion in 1985, "The V-12 Unit made a great contribution to our community by bringing happiness to all of us."[8] In return the community did all it could to make life easier for the trainees. In many areas they organized committees to provide entertainment for the V-12s, which often led to the establishment of an official United Service Organization (USO) center. In Granville, Ohio, at Denison University, the USO was established under the auspices of a local committee in a storefront operated by the Salvation Army. In Hamilton, New York, at Colgate, the local committee had a magnificent Victorian house supplied by the village government. In Johnson City, Tennessee, at Milligan, the sponsoring group was given use of the American Legion's hut. Local laws in Johnson City prohibited movies, dancing, and even the playing of juke boxes on Sundays in places of public accommodation, but the USO was apparently exempt from such ordinances, so the Milligan V-12s made it their social headquarters. They even danced on Sundays!

The songs played on the juke boxes at those USOs were not changed very often, but they usually included a fine selection of the best big band music of the day and thoroughly pleased both the sailors and the girls. More than forty years later they could still sing, hum, and whistle most of those classics, such as Tommy Dorsey's "Boogie Woogie," Benny Goodman's "String of Pearls," Glenn Miller's "In the Mood," Margaret Whiting's "My Ideal," and some relatively obscure numbers such as Tony Pastor's "Paradiddle Joe" and the Johnnie Mercer-Jo Stafford rendition of "Conversation While Dancing."[9]

The National Society of the USO did more than just give out charters and supply a bit of know-how. It also contributed monthly financial support to each USO. At Hamilton, New York, for instance, the local center received twelve $250 checks a year from the national organization.

The hostesses at the USOs had to be approved by a committee and were governed by firm rules of conduct, which prohibited the hostess from allowing herself to be monopolized by any particular serviceman and from leaving the USO in the company of any serviceman. Naturally, it was not long before some hostesses had special boyfriends, which

V-12 AND THE PUBLIC

often meant that the hostess would not appear at the USO so she could spend more time with her favorite V-12. Many of those USO friendships led to postwar marriages.

In small towns, country clubs often invited the V-12s to use their facilities. Elks Clubs and other fraternal groups provided space for dances and invited the trainees to stop in at any time. American Legion and VFW posts did likewise. Service clubs invited the unit officers to speak and had trainee musical groups perform at their meetings throughout the year.

But no welcome was quite as warm as that offered by churches. No trainee could leave after a church service without receiving at least one or two invitations for dinner, and the women who offered the second and third invitations and were turned down usually tried to line up alternate dates for the following weekend. This also gave the women of the town a chance to look over the young men to see whether it would be safe for their daughters to go out with them.

Many churches wrote letters to parents assuring them that their boys were regularly attending church. A large Methodist church in one V-12 town included this offer: "If there's anything we can do for your boy or

The woman on the right is a five-hundred-hour volunteer at the USO at Hamilton, New York, serving the unit at Colgate University. USOs were popular with all of the V-12s.

Colgate University Archives

V-12 AND THE PUBLIC

you, please let us know." The mother of one trainee wrote back saying, "Yes, there is. I am coming for my son's eighteenth birthday. Will you please find me a place to stay with kitchen privileges so I can fix him his birthday dinner?" The church complied, and the trainee and his room-mates were able to get special liberty to celebrate his eighteenth birthday with a home-cooked meal, even though he was eight hundred miles from home.[10]

Even in the larger cities, mothers' clubs did their best to provide for the needs of the trainees. In Milwaukee, a Navy mothers' club made bathrobes for the Marquette V-12s, and at Tulane University and Swarthmore College women's groups provided free alteration services for uniforms.[11]

In smaller towns far distant from military bases, children took a special delight in watching the marching men. They often walked along with them and tried to engage the men in conversation. Two eight-year-old girls in Middletown, Connecticut, frequently marched along with the men as the girls cut across the Wesleyan campus on their way to school. Forty-two years later, one of the girls remembered that her "favorite sailor" claimed his name was "Robinson Crusoe" and always

Catching up on the Sunday comics at the Hamilton, New York, USO are three V-12 trainees. The familiar Coca-Cola machine is in the background.

Colgate University Archives

Children loved the marching V-12s. Here the band at the College of St. Thomas is just marching to a practice, but the children cannot stay away.

College of St. Thomas Archives

V-12 AND THE PUBLIC

chatted with her as they marched along. A year later when she tried to make conversation with a newly arrived marching trainee, he reached in his pocket and flipped her a dime, saying, "Sister, give me a call when you're sixteen." She thought that that wasn't a very bright suggestion — how could she call him if she didn't even know his name?[12]

Probably no one in town loved the V-12s as much as the canines. One, two, or half a dozen dogs could be seen loping along with the V-12s almost every day. And the dogs were faithful, too! They always waited for the trainees to come out of the mess hall, where they were frequently rewarded with appetizing scraps saved from the garbage can. The dogs also loved the weekly inspections and would gather on the athletic field at the appropriate time. In fact, President Arthur C. Willard of the University of Illinois classified every review of the unit in terms of the number of dogs that showed up. There were, for example, "three-dog inspections."[13]

At a number of units an official — or at least, semiofficial — canine mascot was adopted. In this realm, the marines took the lead. At Muhlenberg there was "Rusty Gizmo," at Rochester just plain "Gizmo," and at Princeton the favorite was "Red Dog." At Central Michigan, "Sadie," the sailors' mascot, was officially adopted by the C.O.'s family when the unit closed.

Most communities began their relationship with the V-12 units in a very upbeat mood. The trainees caught that feeling and responded in kind. They were, by and large, a most responsible group of young men: respectful, polite, and well disciplined. That is why, more than forty years later, the men of the V-12 units are still favorably remembered by the citizens of the communities where they trained. The men have that same fondness for the towns and, as a V-12 expressed it at a 1985 reunion, for "those dear people."[14]

37

CHANGES IN
THE PROGRAM

ONCE in place, the V-12 program rolled along smoothly. The control of policy was firmly centralized in the College Training Section, but the implementation of policy was about as decentralized as a military organization could be.

On November 1, 1943, 13,927 men entered the Navy V-12 program. Approximately 3,333 entered as the second part of the enlisted quota for the year, 125 enlisted men came from the Coast Guard, and the rest were civilians who had passed the April 2 examination or enlisted in the V-5 program. At the same time, 480 marines entered the program.[1] On November 1 there were 52,079 men in the Navy V-12 and 8,120 in the Marine V-12.[2]

By March 1944 the Marine V-12 had been cut nearly in half, even though 1,620 marines were kept on board for an additional term. Approximately 1,600 had been sent to boot camp and officer candidates' school, and 613 had opted out of the Marine Corps to immediately reenlist in the Navy and were sent to midshipmen's or pre-midshipmen's schools. Only 323 enlisted marines were brought into the program on March 1, whereas a fairly sizable number had left the V-12 program via academic attrition or their own application to leave V-12 for general duty, as had been authorized by V-12 Bulletin No. 93, issued September 21, 1943. The Marine Corps V-12s totaled 5,495 on March 1, 1944.[3]

The Navy V-12 program received 18,946 trainees on March 1. They were enlisted men or successful civilian applicants from the November 9, 1943, nationwide examination. The Navy V-12 complement was 55,366 on March 1.[4]

In May of 1944, in accordance with the policy of frequently shifting personnel, the Bureau of Naval Personnel made Comdr. Arthur S. Adams officer-in-charge of the Administration Division, which had been headed by Capt. William W. Behrens, USN, when it was designated the Administration Section.[5] This was the position to which the College Training Section had always reported. At the same time, on May 1,

CHANGES IN THE PROGRAM

1944, "College Training Section" became the proper name for what had previously been called the College Training Unit of the Administration Section. Thus, both the unit and the Administration Section were upgraded in the Navy nomenclature and organization chart.[6]

To make dealings with higher-ranking officers easier, it had been traditional to make the officer-in-charge of the Administration unit a captain. Thus, Capt. James L. Holloway, Jr., director of training, recommended a spot promotion for Commander Adams and he received it in May, to rank as captain as of May 3, 1944. Thus, Adams had been promoted from lieutenant (junior grade) in 1941, when he was recalled by the Navy, to captain in 1944 — quite a phenomenal rise! Several officers have pointed out that his classmates were simply trying to bring "Beany" up to their rank.[7] It was easy to do when an officer had the capabilities of Adams.

In choosing his successor for officer-in-charge of the College Training Section, Adams decided upon Lt. Comdr. William S. Thomson, USNR, who was a 1922 noncommissioned graduate of the Naval Academy. He had not seen active service until he applied for a commission in the Naval Reserve in 1942. Nevertheless, his education at the Naval Academy was probably considered a key requirement for the job. He had also spent a pre-V-12 year in officer training at the NROTC unit at the University of Oklahoma, and he was the first C.O. of the V-12 unit at Arkansas A & M, which included both sailors and marines. Furthermore, Thomson had served under Adams in the College Training Section for nearly six months, and Adams was apparently pleased with the way he handled his assignments.

Several of the officers stationed in the College Training Section believed that Thomson was chosen because he had such an even disposition and would continue to faithfully carry out the program as Adams had established it. Two men who were closely associated with him during the V-12 program described him as "absolutely unflappable."[8] Nothing could disturb Thomson. He had a level-headed approach to every problem that developed. He was not an educator, but had spent most of his post-Naval Academy life drilling for oil in Texas.

Adams knew that Thomson would need the help of Lt. Raymond F. Howes, who had been Adams's right-hand man, so Howes was left in place as the *de facto* executive officer. Thomson and Howes worked together closely, meeting each morning to map out the day's program.[9]

Thomson was not expected to change much, and he didn't. He capably guided the College Training Section for fourteen months, at which time he was released from active duty and returned to his first love, the oil business he had left in Texas.

Succeeding Thomson on July 1, 1945, was Lt. Raymond F. Howes,

CHANGES IN THE PROGRAM

who received a spot promotion to lieutenant commander.[10] Howes was in charge of the College Training Section for the rest of its existence, and was promoted to full commander in November of 1945 when he agreed to stay on for the final eight months of the program. He oversaw the winding down of the V-12 program and the phasing in of the new postwar NROTC program.

The final civilian additions to the V-12 program were made on July 1, 1944, as a result of the qualifying examination taken on March 15, 1944. The College Training Section and Officer Procurement Division decided jointly that all additional trainees would come from the fleet.[11]

In July of 1944, the total addition to V-12 was 18,832, with approximately 6,000 from Navy enlisted sources, 4,800 from the nationwide examination of March 15, 7,700 in the aviation program, and 340 marines. This brought the total V-12 enrollment to 61,906, including 58,253 apprentice seamen and 3,653 privates.[12]

Six hundred and seventy-one civilians from the March 15 nationwide examination could not be accommodated in the July quota, so they were finally called to active duty in November 1944, along with 172 fleet men. A large contingent of regular deck candidates who had entered the program on its first day had completed their V-12 training in October and were off to midshipmen's schools or Pre-Midshipmen's School at Asbury Park, New Jersey. Since many trainees left and relatively few entered the program, the November 1944 total dropped significantly to 42,309.[13] It was the first major cut in the Navy program.

On November 1, the Marines brought 529 enlisted men to V-12, but since a large contingent of four-termers had completed their work in October, the Marine Corps V-12 contingent dropped to 1,858.[14]

The Navy did not add new trainees in March of 1945 because it was looking forward to moving many V-12s to NROTC in July 1945. The Marine Corps, however, added six hundred men to its V-12 total, keeping it nearly steady at 1,808. The Navy V-12 total on March 1 was 30,181.[15]

The transition to NROTC had to be postponed until the fall, but the Navy still added more V-12s on July 1, 1945. Two thousand enlisted men became V-12s, and 4,225 new V-5 recruits were sent to V-12 units for a projected three-term educational program. The V-5 curriculum was identical to that of the regular V-12s in the first two terms and similar for the third term, but the V-5s kept a separate identity. The Navy V-12 complement on July 1 was 22,523.[16]

The Marines ordered 585 seasoned men to V-12 in July 1945, bringing the Marine V-12 enrollment to 1,874.[17]

It was projected that five hundred marines would be added to the program on November 1, 1945, and another five hundred on March 1,

CHANGES IN THE PROGRAM

1946, but those plans were cancelled when the war ended. No Navy additions had been planned beyond July 1, 1945, since the program already had all the officer candidates the Navy thought it would need. On November 1, 1945, there were 14,772 Navy V-12s, and on December 31, there were 1,251 Marine V-12s. On March 1, 1946, the Navy had 3,890 men remaining in V-12; Marine V-12s had dwindled to only 683 on March 31, 1946. At Colorado College there were only twenty-three Marine V-12s on March 31, 1946.[18]

Undergraduate V-12 Enrollment

Terms Beginning

	7/1/43	11/1/43	3/1/44	7/1/44	11/1/44	3/1/45	7/1/45	11/1/45	3/1/46
Navy	57,327	52,079	55,366	58,253	42,309	30,181	22,523	14,772	3,890
Marine	11,460	8,120*	5,495	3,653	1,858	1,808	1,874	1,251	683
Total	68,787	63,044	60,861	61,906	44,167	31,989	24,397	16,023	4,573

* Total taken from muster rolls — the number of Marines on 11/1/43 listed in NavAdm (10,965) is in error.

Sources: *U.S. Naval Administration in World War II, Bureau of Naval Personnel, Training Activity, Volume IV, The College Training Program*, and Muster Rolls for V-12 units, National Archives.

The V-12 program had been so well established that it really almost ran itself, except during the transition periods between terms. During 1944, after the program had been running for several terms, the officers in the College Training Section had what can best be described as some "slow days." Once a new term had started, there was not much to do. Soon, however, it was again time to make decisions about quotas and transfers for the following term, so life resumed the same breakneck pace.

As the V-12 program "graduated" more of its trainees and brought in fewer men than left the program, the Navy had to decide whether to eliminate some units or to reduce quotas proportionately over the entire 131 units. The Navy chose the latter course. This pleased the schools, because when the 25 percent cut came in November of 1944, the war was still going strong, and the men who would be returning to campuses as veterans were still in the armed forces. Every school needed a continuing income from the Navy. The Navy gave the schools the option of dropping the program at any time, but none accepted the offer until after VE day. The Navy was always proud of that fact.[19]

The ranks of Marine V-12s were diminished greatly over the course of

CHANGES IN THE PROGRAM

The termination of the V-12 program on a campus meant that the coeds could once again occupy the choice dorms at the school. These coeds at Ohio Wesleyan can hardly wait to remove the sign and take over.

the program, mainly because Marine casualties had been much lighter than feared, so it was not necessary to replace most of the V-12 "graduates." Thus, the consolidation of the forty Marine V-12 units into a smaller number began on February 28, 1944. The Navy, however, had always considered the Marine component a part of the V-12 quota guaranteed to a school, so when a Marine detachment left a college more Navy V-12 trainees were ordered there to take their places. This was another example of the flexibility of the V-12 plan.

When the V-12 reductions on a campus grew to be substantial, train-

CHANGES IN THE PROGRAM

ees were moved between dorms as the schools and the Navy consolidated them into fewer and perhaps better-equipped residence halls. This freed some of the more desirable space for civilian students, who had earlier been forced to take whatever housing was available.

In the winter of 1944–1945, when the engineering V-12s at Duke University were required to move from the East Campus, which they shared with Duke's coeds, to the all-male West Campus, the engineers went out in style. They had a gala weekend, complete with dancing and a torchlight parade.[20]

In the spring of 1946, the pressure of returning veterans was great at every college in the country. Housing was at a premium. To oblige the University of Washington, the Navy brought a "barracks ship" into Portage Bay at the edge of the campus and moved all the V-12s there for the balance of that final term. No longer were all of the V-12s dry-land sailors![21]

As the time came to close some units, the negotiating teams again took to the road and determined which equipment and materials would be Navy surplus and could be sold to the colleges. Bids were also accepted from other civilian agencies and persons. Lt. Maurice Burkholder, the commanding officer at Oberlin College, recalled that the Navy dentist assigned to the unit was able to purchase all of the dental equipment for fifteen hundred dollars.[22] The actual execution of the bidding process for the surplus equipment was put into the hands of the commanding officer of the unit after the negotiating team had established minimum prices.

The negotiating teams, which included a lawyer, finance officer, and training officer, also had to work with the institutions to establish the payment the Navy should make for wear and tear on the facilities. This involved such matters as new flooring in dining rooms, resurfacing of tennis courts worn out by marching feet, and the conversion of Navy cafeteria-style mess halls to dining rooms for civilian use. The partitioning in the offices used by the Navy also had to be removed. Again, the colleges found the Navy team to be fair. The Navy was probably less determined to protect Navy dollars than it had been at the onset of the program.

The V-12 program began to be phased out in June of 1945, when six units were discontinued.[23] At that time, the members of the negotiating teams, who were all reserve officers, were getting the "short-timer's attitude" that became prevalent throughout the armed forces. The war with Germany was over and great progress was being made against Japan, although at least another year of bloody fighting was anticipated by most observers.

By the time the second group of V-12 units was discontinued at the

CHANGES IN THE PROGRAM

end of October 1945, the two atomic bombs had been dropped and the war had ended. By this time everyone had the "short-timer's attitude," including the V-12s. Getting released to inactive duty was of the utmost importance to officers on the negotiating teams, so they were amenable to any reasonable suggestions that would help to avoid lengthy delays in closing the units.

From an historical point of view, V-12 Bulletin No. 298, dated April 11, 1945, was unfortunate. It directed the commanding officers of all V-12 units except Dartmouth, upon deactivation of the station, to dispose of all of the records according to the "Field Records Disposal Schedule." This was done so thoroughly at most units that very little material exists today on the military side of the V-12 picture except what remains in the files of the presidents of the colleges. Some of the schools followed the directive and destroyed most of their records, too.[24]

Seventy more units were discontinued on October 31, 1945. The Oberlin College unit closed on February 28, 1946, but the Muhlenberg unit was reactivated at the same time, so there was a total of fifty-four original V-12 units to close on June 30, 1946. Forty-two of these units, plus ten newly selected schools, continued to offer Navy officer training under the peacetime NROTC program.

The bold wartime educational experiment had done its job, producing the officers necessary for the Navy's needs. The abrupt ending of World War II could not in any way diminish the program's success.

38

V-12 AND POSTWAR OFFICER TRAINING

As THE WAR appeared to be winding down in early 1945, the Navy felt it had enough pilots in training or in combat areas to meet its requirements for the rest of the war, but it took a serious look at its postwar needs. The war in the Pacific had clearly established the aircraft carrier as the Navy's number-one capital ship, so a continuing flow of aviators would be required.

Since the Navy knew that most of the fliers who were then in the combat areas would be leaving as soon as possible after the war's end, it decided to train a substantial number of young men while the aviation training schools were still in place. Pilot training would take eighteen to twenty months after trainees finished their V-12 involvement, so it was time to get moving on those postwar needs.

Accordingly, in the spring of 1945 the Navy began a strenuous recruitment drive for men for the V-5 aviation program. Although they were enlisted and classified as V-5s, these men were sent for three terms of college education to various V-12 schools.

In the earlier days of V-12, the V-5s had been changed to V-12(a)s and included in the muster rolls of the V-12 program. The only real difference with the 1945 enlistees was that they vehemently claimed — as they still do today — that they were not V-12s, but V-5s. Some of the earlier V-12(a)s felt the same way.

Even before the stepped-up recruiting of aviation cadets began, the Navy had begun planning for its future need for line officers. Obviously the postwar Navy would need to be several times larger than the prewar one, and thus it would require many more officers than could be provided by the Naval Academy and the prewar NROTC units that existed at twenty-seven colleges and universities. Although a number of junior officers would probably stay in the Navy to meet the immediate officer needs, the service had to think of the future supply. Enlarging the Naval Academy was considered and eventually ruled out, so it was decided to expand the NROTC program.

V-12 AND POSTWAR OFFICER TRAINING

On November 22, 1944, Capt. Arthur S. Adams testified before the Senate Naval Affairs Committee that the V-12 program was gradually being terminated and plans were being made to transfer enough V-12s to NROTC to bring that total to 23,700 men by July 1, 1945, providing Congress authorized the expansion to 24,000. Some senators objected to having such a high limit in peacetime, however, and suggested that the Navy develop a provision to restrict the new authorization to the war emergency period.[1]

Early in 1945 Congress passed and the president signed the NROTC Expansion Bill (HR 621), which provided that 24,000 NROTC men could be under training at a time; the previous law had limited the number to 7,200. The bill also required, however, that one year after the war the 24,000 officer candidates would be reduced to 14,000.[2]

A special committee appointed by the secretary of the Navy and composed of civilian educators and senior officers of the Bureau of Naval Personnel began selecting colleges and universities for the new NROTC units. Vice Adm. Randall Jacobs, who was then still chief of naval personnel, estimated that about twenty-three additional NROTC schools would be selected.[3] The actual number turned out to be twenty-five.

Students had been transferring into NROTC from V-12 during most of V-12's existence, and the number of transfers was stepped up on March 1, 1945. Most of the men were expected to be transferred on July 1 and November 1. All V-12s were to be transferred to NROTC except those in a specialty program such as engineering, aerology, physics, presupply, pretheological, premedical, and predental. The Marine V-12 units would continue to be separate, as before.[4] Again, V-12 students who desired flight training had the option of applying for transfer to class V-5 on or before July 1, 1945.

Deck candidates in V-12 who had six terms of college (both Navy and civilian) on July 1 became eligible for immediate transfer to a midshipmen's school. Those who had completed five terms of college on July 1 would be transferred to the NROTC for three additional terms, and those who had completed four terms would be transferred for four additional terms. A portion of the latter group was transferred to NROTC on March 1. It was planned that other V-12 students then in their first or second term would be transferred to NROTC on July 1. No new Navy students were to be added to the V-12 program on March 1, 1945.

The original plan to transfer most V-12 trainees into the expanded NROTC was to become effective on July 1, 1945. Congress did not make the appropriations in time to permit that, so the expansion date was moved up to the fall. Even though the funding had still not passed Congress, the Navy decided to proceed with its plan for the new units. In March 1945, the selection board took off on a fast cross-country jaunt to visit the schools proposed for new NROTC units.

V-12 AND POSTWAR OFFICER TRAINING

Secretary of the Navy James V. Forrestal announced the selection of the twenty-five new schools on May 1, 1945.[5] They were: Alabama Polytechnic Institute, Case School of Applied Science (later replaced on the list by Ohio State University), Columbia University, Cornell University, Dartmouth College, Illinois Institute of Technology, Iowa State College, Miami University, Oregon State College, Pennsylvania State College, Princeton University, Purdue University, Stanford University, University of Idaho, University of Illinois, University of Kansas, University of Louisville, University of Mississippi, University of Missouri, University of Nebraska, University of Notre Dame, University of Rochester, University of Utah, University of Wisconsin, Vanderbilt University, and Villanova College.

Most of the new NROTC units started up on November 1, 1945, but colleges that were on the traditional semester plan began their NROTC participation at the start of the fall term in September.

Everything seemed to be starting well that fall, but Congress still had not made the needed appropriations for the expanded NROTC program. The war was over, and Congress had suddenly become very conscious of its need to curb the wartime military spending. Since it lacked proper funding, in December of 1945 the Navy sent formal notices to the schools involved that all V-12 and NROTC units would be terminated on February 28, 1946.[6] In retrospect, this seems to have been a game of "chicken" between the Navy and the Congress. The pressure that immediately resulted from this potential disruption of the colleges was soon felt by congressmen, who quickly passed an emergency appropriations bill to keep the college programs operating through June 30, 1946.[7]

The first plan proposed for the postwar expansion of NROTC called for converting the Naval Academy program into a two-year course for candidates who had already completed their sophomore year at civilian colleges. This plan, which would double the Academy's annual output of ensigns, was called the Jacobs-Barker Plan, after its authors, Vice Adm. Randall Jacobs and Dean Joseph W. Barker of the Columbia Engineering School. Both had been intimately involved in the V-12 program.[8]

Secretary of the Navy Forrestal did not approve the Jacobs-Barker Plan. Instead, he convened a board to study the problem and recommend the best way for the Navy to proceed. Any new plan had to be authorized by Congress, however, so even if the board's recommendations were approved by the Navy, other hurdles remained. The board was headed by Rear Adm. James L. Holloway, Jr., USN, who, it will be recalled, was a classmate of Arthur Adams in the Naval Academy's class of 1919. The board included both civilian educators and naval officers. The following civilians accepted the appointment: Dr. Henry T. Heald,

V-12 AND POSTWAR OFFICER TRAINING

president of the Illinois Institute of Technology; Dr. James P. Baxter, president of Williams College; and Dr. Arthur S. Adams, who had been retired by the Navy and was serving as provost of Cornell University. Admiral Holloway later said, "Those three people were intellectuals in the finest sense of the word."[9]

The four uniformed members of the Holloway Board were captains who were described by Holloway as "hard chargers." They were Charles D. Wheelock of the Navy Construction Corps, Academy class of 1921; John P. W. Vest, a naval aviator and a graduate of the class of 1922; Felix L. Johnson of the class of 1920; and Stuart H. ("Slim") Ingersoll of the class of 1921, who was then the commandant of the Naval Academy. Ingersoll was described by Holloway as "an old carrier pilot and, of course, he was in there pitching for the Academy."

Comdr. Charles K. Duncan and Comdr. Douglas M. Swift were made the two recorders for the board. At the end of the Holloway Board's work, it was unanimously decided that Duncan and Swift should be listed as members to reward them for their excellent work.[10]

In accordance with Navy protocol, the board's proposal became known as "the Holloway Plan," in deference to its senior member. But Admiral Holloway himself often said and finally wrote, in a September 1980 article entitled "A Gentlemen's Agreement" in the Naval Institute *Proceedings*, that

> The key man in working this out was my classmate "Beanie" Adams. He'd had a great deal of experience in the V-7 and V-12 officer training programs early in the war, and he was the one who developed the techniques that were involved in the NROTC Program. Then, after the plan was approved, he was in charge of its implementation. He selected the schools and his office evolved the method and organized the system of selecting and screening the candidates, who had to be accepted by both the Navy and the school. "Beanie" Adams was the real architect of "The Holloway Plan." It just had to have a flag officer's name on it to make it Navy.[11]

As one of its first decisions, the Holloway Board unanimously rejected the proposal of turning the Academy into a two-year finishing school for candidates who had received two years of college elsewhere. The college representatives felt strongly that a four-year experience at one school was more important, and the Navy men agreed.

The board then developed its own recommendation, which was eventually passed into law by Congress. The young men who were accepted into the NROTC program would receive four years of tuition and fees, along with fifty dollars a month pay. Those who finished the program would be obliged to spend a certain period on active duty, which would assure the Navy of a supply of junior officers to supplement the Academy's graduates. After that required service period, some of the officers

V-12 AND POSTWAR OFFICER TRAINING

would decide to make the Navy a career while others would be returned to inactive duty.

Holloway wrote that the major problem that divided the board related to the training of aviators. Captain Vest, who represented the aviation community, wanted to send the midshipmen into flight training at the end of their sophomore year. Then, when they had received their wings and spent two or three years in the fleet, they would return to finish their last years of college as officers. Vest backed this up with some data indicating that it was easier to train aviators at age eighteen than at twenty-one or twenty-two.

According to Holloway,

> Beanie Adams was thoroughly opposed to this idea, and he and Johnny [Vest] locked horns. They were men of strong conviction and it was a sight to behold their eyes flash across the table. In the end, I helped Johnny push the thing through because he wouldn't budge an inch and that was the only way I could get unanimity. I told Beanie, "This will work itself out" and it did. After a few years the aviation community decided that it would rather train newly-minted ensigns than sophomores out of college.

The Holloway Board also recommended that the NROTC program and the Naval Academy produce exactly the same number of new ensigns so there would be complete fairness and neither group would become dominant.

The board reached a unanimous decision, which was soon adopted by the secretary of the Navy and recommended to Congress. Congress, however, was extremely dilatory in this matter, perhaps as a result of Army views. The Army was afraid that the Navy plans were too generous to the trainees and would attract the best candidates to the naval service, leaving the other services with men of lesser quality.

The House testimony on the Holloway Plan was taken in early April 1946. The Navy called Captain Adams back to active duty from Ithaca so that he could appear before the committee in the uniform of a naval captain. Comdr. Raymond Howes and Adams's Naval Academy classmate, Capt. William G. ("Bud") Fisher, who was director of training, masterminded the scheduling of witnesses and the contact with various congressmen. Howes wrote Adams on May 12 to suggest that he ask President Edmund E. Day of Cornell to contact the other NROTC school presidents to lend their active support to the measure "without any perceptible pressure from the Navy," and this was done.[12]

When, in July of 1946, the House had still not acted on the bill, Admiral Holloway visited Carl Vinson, the powerful chairman of the House Naval Affairs Committee, at his Georgia farm. Holloway pointed out that colleges were starting in less than two months and that unless

V-12 AND POSTWAR OFFICER TRAINING

the legislation were enacted promptly the NROTC program could not start up in the fall. As a result, there would be a break between the wartime and postwar NROTC programs.

Vinson responded by calling his aide to put the bill on the House calendar for the following week. It was passed by an overwhelming vote and sent to the White House. President Truman also displayed some reluctance; perhaps he, too, was influenced by the Army's concern. Eventually, however, he was persuaded that the plan was in the best interests of the nation, so he signed the bill into law in the middle of August.

The Holloway Plan, founded upon the experience of the V-12 program, formed an excellent basis for meeting half of the Navy's officer requirements for many decades.

39

WINDING DOWN

THE winding down of the V-12 program was in the planning stage long before the war was over in Europe. Everything pointed to a total victory in Europe in 1945, but no one knew when it would occur, nor did anyone know how long the war with Japan would last. Vast distances of the Pacific would still have to be traversed to bring the fighting to the Japanese homeland.

Nevertheless, the Bureau of Naval Personnel determined that it had in the V-12 pipeline nearly all of the officers it would need to complete the war. With that in mind, it started to plan changing the V-12 program into what would eventually be the postwar NROTC program. The framework to accomplish this transfer was provided by congressional passage in February of 1945 of the bill to enlarge the NROTC.

According to V-12 Bulletin No. 314, issued June 12, 1945, the V-12s with five terms or less would be moved into the NROTC program. V-12s who already had six terms in the engineering, physics, or meteorology programs would stay in the V-12 program until graduation.

A few V-12 men who had advanced standing were assigned to some of the new NROTC schools, where they remained in their sailor uniforms. Thus, some of the new schools were technically V-12 schools, although they were not a part of the original 131.[1]

As mentioned previously, in the summer of 1945 the Bureau of Aeronautics recruited a large contingent of V-5s and sent them to V-12 schools to receive some college training, as had always been traditional in the air arm until the emergency of the previous three years. This kept the fliers busy while the aviation training schools were being cleared of the men who had come through the V-12 program as V-12(a)s.

At some schools in the term beginning July 1, 1945, there were only fifteen or twenty true V-12s, the rest of the men being V-5s. In many schools the NROTCs, V-12s, and V-5s were all lumped together in the muster roll. As a result, figures for 1945 and 1946 in the Appendix on the number of men classified as V-12s are not always accurate.

Shortly before the war ended, a point system was announced by the armed forces to provide for the orderly discharge of the older men in all

WINDING DOWN

branches of the service.[2] Immediately after the war with Japan ended, the point system was revised to start the return to civilian life of all men and women in service who wanted to get out.[3] The magic number of points needed for discharge was set separately for enlisted men, male officers, enlisted women, and female officers. As the demobilization process moved along, the point requirements were continually reduced. The Navy promised that the entire task would be accomplished by September 1, 1946.[4]

The point system meant that many of the old salts who had come into the V-12 program with between six months and three years of prior service could be discharged very early. They were faced with a decision:

Victory in Europe was a memorable day for V-12s, for it meant that they could only be sent to one area of the war in the future — the Pacific. On every V-12 campus a memorial service was held.

Harvard University Archives

WINDING DOWN

to stay with the program to get the rest of their allotted education, or to leave the military and become civilians again. Most, but not all, opted for the latter choice.

The Navy decided to stop the active duty professional training of medical, dental, and theological students at the end of the terms that began prior to November 1, 1945, according to V-12 Bulletins No. 322, 325, and 327, dated September 1, 15, and 24, 1945. The affected men, who were both the graduate students and the undergraduate trainees pursuing such studies, would be released to inactive duty (regardless of points) provided they stipulated that they would continue as civilians the training they were pursuing in V-12, and upon its completion would accept a reserve commission. Otherwise they would be sent to V-6, general duty, until they qualified for separation under the point system.

A factor that influenced the decision of other men on whether to stay in the V-12 units for the rest of their allocated time was the GI Bill of Rights, which Congress had worded so that it would only provide educational benefits to men who had at least ninety days of "general service" in the armed forces. Serving in a V-12 unit was not considered "general service." To make themselves eligible for the educational benefits, the men who entered V-12 directly from civilian life had to go to boot camp and then on to other general duty. V-12s who were otherwise academically sound suddenly began to fail courses in order to be dismissed. Until November 2, 1945, there were only four grounds for separating students from the V-12 program, as set forth in Navy V-12 Bulletin No. 241, dated July 18, 1944: (a) physical, (b) academic, (c) aptitude, and (d) disciplinary. Realistically facing the facts, a new V-12 Bulletin, No. 334, dated November 2, 1945, added another category: "(e) own request."

The bulletin directed each trainee who desired separation at his own request to so state in writing in an official letter to the chief of naval personnel via his commanding officer. The commanding officer was required to forward three copies of the letter to the Bureau of Naval Personnel with an appropriate endorsement. As soon as the approval returned from the Bureau, the commanding officer would take immediate steps to detach the trainee and to notify the college authorities of his action.

On January 9, 1946, Navy V-12 Bulletin No. 344 authorized the release of V-12s who had acquired sufficient points. The Navy did not want men to continue in the program unless they would agree to remain in the service until the program ended. Those who wished to continue were required to sign the following statement: "I agree to remain on active duty in the NROTC-V-12 Program until approximately 1 July 1946, regardless of my eligibility for demobilization, and further

WINDING DOWN

agree to accept a commission in the U.S. Naval Reserve if offered." Men who signed the statement who would have sufficient points for release from active duty as officers or enlisted men before completing NROTC or V-12 training were promised that they would be commissioned but not ordered to active duty as officers unless they so requested or unless there was a need for their services.

Bulletin No. 344 also gave men the opportunity to transfer to the regular Navy, but it noted that no such request could be promulgated until the officer had been on active duty for at least six months in a commissioned status. Therefore, graduating students who had an interest in the regular Navy were "urged to take advantage of this six months active duty, during which time they may make their final decision as to their choice of career."

The commanding officer was directed to separate from the program and to transfer to general enlisted duty at the end of the current term (February 1946) all men who would not sign the statement. By taking these steps, the Navy had stabilized the V-12 program until it was terminated on June 30, 1946.

Earlier, on August 24, 1945, the Navy Department had announced it was shutting down admissions to the remaining reserve midshipmen's schools, effective immediately.[5] V-12s who completed their college work by October 31, 1945, thus had no midshipmen's schools available, so the Navy ordered them to selected naval stations, where they were commissioned and then released to inactive duty unless they requested active service.[6]

In February of 1946, all of the eight-term engineering V-12s who had started as freshmen in July of 1943 had completed their requirements. There were about twenty-five hundred of them. They were commissioned upon graduation from their V-12 schools and assembled at Camp Elliott in Davisville, Rhode Island. On about April 1, they were put aboard four cruisers, which plied up and down the Atlantic Coast for three months while the newly commissioned ensigns, wearing sailor suits, received their equivalent of midshipmen's school. They would don their officers' uniforms when they made liberty in ports such as Charleston, Boston, Bermuda, and New York.[7] Some of those who participated in that program described it as "a great experience," whereas it convinced others that they did not wish to make the Navy a career.[8]

When their shakedown cruise was completed in late June, the new ensigns were released to inactive duty, except for those who requested that they be kept on active duty because they were considering transfer to the regular Navy.[9]

The June 1946 graduates from engineering or other V-12 courses were also commissioned upon completion and then released to inactive duty unless they agreed to serve for at least six more months.

WINDING DOWN

Former V-12s in the NROTC program who had not completed their college work on June 30, 1946, had already been given the choice of remaining in the program or being discharged.[10] Since they had decided to stay in the program until completion, they were expected to enroll in the civilian NROTC starting in September. Many did, and they received their commissions in 1947 or early 1948. Some then went on active duty, and others did not. The choice was theirs.

The college training program that had started boldly in July of 1943 disappeared with very little notice on June 30, 1946. But it had served its purpose. The Navy's decision to operate the program until June 30 was intended primarily to provide for orderly transfer to the peacetime NROTC program, but it resulted in a great benefit for the remaining V-12s themselves. It was a final embodiment of the principle of treating the trainees as individuals. When the V-12 program ended, nearly all of the men who had ever been in it were singing its praises.[11]

40

THE KOREAN WAR

WHEN the Korean War began on June 25, 1950, many V-12s had finished college and had been working at their civilian jobs for some time. Others were just finishing professional school. Most of the men were married, and some had already started families.

A surprising number of V-12s had stayed on active duty and eventually transferred to the regular Navy. Others, although they were on inactive duty, had stayed in the active Naval Reserve, meeting once a week at reserve units around the country. When President Truman announced on June 27 that the United States forces would come to the aid of the Republic of Korea (South Korea), most of the reservists began to watch their mailboxes with some concern. In September and October many of them received orders to report to a specified naval station, usually for refresher training before joining the fleet or being assigned to duty elsewhere. Although figures on how many V-12 reservists were recalled are not readily available, it appears from a sampling of more than one thousand questionnaires from V-12s that about 22 percent of those who were commissioned after V-12 were returned to active duty in the Korean War.[1]

The United States Marine Corps also called back many reserve officers, a large proportion of whom were trained in the V-12 program. Marine Corps officers assigned to Korea suffered heavy casualties after the Chinese forces swept south from the Yalu River in November of 1950.[2]

At the time the men were ordered to active duty, no promise or estimate of how long that duty would last was given. It would, of course, depend upon the course of the war. As it turned out, most served two years or just a few months short of that.

While probably none of the recalled officers was pleased about having his life disrupted a second time, most recognized that their training was intended to cover such an eventuality. One trainee's comment probably reflected the thoughts of many: "The V-12 Program helped me get a college education. The two years in Korea probably evened things out."[3]

Since the Navy did not know how long the involvement would last, it had to prepare for the worst. It decided to renew the V-12 planning so that an educational training program could be reactivated for officer candidates if the war proved to be a long one.

Capt. Grant H. Brown, USNR, was recalled to active duty in Washington and given the assignment of updating the college training plans. He had finished World War II as the district director of training for the Ninth Naval District and had written a District Training Office summary that had been included in the *U.S. Naval Administration in World War II* series. Because of important business commitments, Brown attempted to have his orders canceled. The Navy finally worked out an agreement that he could return to inactive duty as soon as he had finished modernizing the plans.[4]

Brown recalled, "Our sessions were very hush-hush — we met in a very secluded room which we called 'The Black Hole of Calcutta.' On the basis of previous experience, colleges were designated and quotas assigned. To the best of my knowledge and belief those quotas were never revealed." The source of the personnel: college students.[5] When everything was ready to begin if it should become necessary, Brown was allowed to return to Chicago and inactive duty.

Fortunately, the peace talks that began in 1951, although they dragged on for several more years, did avoid the escalation of the war and thereby eliminated the need to reactivate the College Training Program. But if it had been required, the Navy was ready.

41

V-12 OFFICERS
AFTER
WORLD WAR II

THE MEN who accepted commissions in the U.S. Naval Reserve specifically to serve in the College Training Program, like those who were drawn into it after serving as commissioned officers elsewhere, came to the program because they had records of success in their previous work, most often in education. In their postwar careers, they also achieved significant success.

The officers who ran the individual units were divided into two main classes: the retired regular Navy officers who had been called back and the educators who were called in for the first time. When the former regulars again returned to retired status, most went back to what they had been doing before. If they had been in education or manufacturing, they returned to those fields; those who were fully retired resumed their retirement. At least two retired regulars, however, assumed major positions in the universities where they had served as commanding officers. Capt. Forrest U. Lake became the dean of admissions and special assistant to the president at Tulane University, and Capt. Eric Barr became director of summer schools at the University of Washington.

Most of the educators among the V-12 unit officers went back to education. Often they changed schools, sometimes through contacts made in the Navy. For instance, the first commanding officer at Peru State Teachers College, Lt. R. B. Lowe, returned to Peru as dean of men after the war ended. Later he served as governor of American Samoa and governor of Guam.

Lt. John A. Guy, who had been V-12 administrative officer at Princeton, became dean of students at Illinois Wesleyan University because the Navy associate who had been dean of students before entering the Navy decided to remain to teach navigation at the Naval Academy. He recommended Guy for the job as dean. After a few years in that position, Guy joined State Farm Insurance Company, where he served for many years as director of training.

Lt. Charles P. McCurdy, commanding officer at Gustavus Adolphus,

V-12 OFFICERS AFTER WORLD WAR II

returned after the war to William and Mary, but he eventually became executive secretary of the Association of American Universities in Washington. His office was in the same building as Arthur Adams's and Raymond Howes's when they were with the American Council on Education. Now retired, McCurdy lives in Arlington, Virginia.[1]

Lt. Comdr. Glenn Bartle, skipper at Swarthmore, became the founding president of Harpur College, which later evolved into the State University of New York at Binghamton.[2]

At the Bureau of Naval Personnel, officers from the Counsel's Office and the Finance Section of Planning and Control generally went back to the practices and firms they had left to go to Washington to serve in their specialties. James Alexander Fowler, Jr., counsel of the Bureau of Naval Personnel, returned in November 1944 to his New York law firm, Cahill, Gordon, and Reindel, where he was a partner until retirement. He also served a term as president of the Harvard Law School Alumni Association. Fowler died in November of 1985 at the age of eighty-eight.

Gerard Swope, who went to the Bureau Counsel's Office in December of 1942 as a civilian, was later commissioned a lieutenant commander. He succeeded Fowler as counsel of the Bureau when the latter returned to his New York practice. After the war Swope went back to the General Electric Company, where he became international counsel. He was also chairman of the Woods Hole Marine Laboratories for twenty years. He died in 1979.

W. Glasgow Reynolds, following his Navy service, returned to the E. I. DuPont Company in Wilmington, serving as chief counsel to the Advertising, Public Relations, and Central Research Departments until his retirement in 1971, when he went into private practice with a Wilmington law firm. He died in January of 1987.

R. Dean Pine returned to the Dixie Cup Company and served for many years as general counsel of the American Can Company before retiring to Kintnersville, Pennsylvania.

Francis X. Reilly, Jr., practiced law in Worcester, Massachusetts, after the war. In 1953 he joined Wilson and Company in Chicago as treasurer and corporate attorney. He later was vice president of LTV Corporation, B. F. Goodrich Company, and Katy Industries. For the eight years before he retired in 1984 he was vice president and general counsel of Rollins, Burdick, and Hunter, a leading Chicago insurance firm. He lives in Barrington, Illinois.

John F. Meck, Jr., was elected treasurer of Dartmouth College upon his return from the service and later added vice president to his title. He died at a comparatively young age.

Lt. Comdr. F. Vinton Lawrence, Jr., returned to the investment bank-

V-12 OFFICERS AFTER WORLD WAR II

Raymond F. Howes

Arthur S. Adams received a Legion of Merit in 1945 for his work in organizing and directing the Navy V-12 program. From 1953 to 1955 he was chairman of the Reserve Forces Policy Board. In the above scene President Eisenhower's secretary of defense, Charles Wilson, recognized Adams for his service as chairman of the Reserve Forces Policy Board.

ing firm of Scudder, Stevens, and Clark in New York and later became managing partner.

In recognition of his World War II service Capt. Arthur Stanton Adams was awarded the Legion of Merit.[3] He returned to Cornell University in 1945, where he was named provost. In 1948, Adams was elected president of the University of New Hampshire. During his brief tenure there, he was also elected chairman of the American Council on Education, which a short time later asked him to become its president and chief executive officer. Adams served as president of ACE from 1951 to 1961, and was often in the news on educational matters. From 1953 to 1955 he was chairman of the Reserve Forces Policy Board. Adams retired to Durham, New Hampshire, in 1961. During his lifetime he received twenty-eight honorary degrees, at least fifteen of which came from V-12 schools.[4]

During his retirement Dr. Adams stayed active, serving as president of the Salzburg Seminar in American Studies for the years 1961 to 1965. From 1961 to 1967 he was a member and then chairman of the

V-12 OFFICERS AFTER WORLD WAR II

U.S. Coast Guard Academy Advisory Committee. In the late 1960s and 1970s, Adams was a consultant to the University of New Hampshire and the New England Center for Continuing Education. The Adams Residential Tower in Durham is named in his honor.

Arthur Stanton Adams died on November 18, 1980, at the age of eighty-four. He was buried with full military honors in Arlington National Cemetery.

Comdr. Raymond F. Howes, who was with the College Training Section from beginning to end, rejoined Cornell University and was soon named secretary of the university. When Adams became president of the American Council on Education, he asked Howes to again join him, so Howes spent the next eleven years in Washington. In 1962, Howes moved to California, where he became assistant to the chancellor of the University of California (Riverside). His retirement home was in Riverside, where he died on February 28, 1986.

After the war ended in Europe, the good-natured Comdr. William S. Thomson, the second officer-in-charge of the College Training Section, was champing at the bit to get back to his oil interests in Texas, which had been put in a caretaker status while he and his partner, Herbert Williams, were in the service. The partnership of Williams and Thomson enjoyed great success over the next few years, but it dissolved when they disagreed on whether to drill in a field that held great promise but had been already tried by many major firms with negative results. Thomson's optimistic nature led him to try that field by himself, but the results were unsatisfactory. The high cost of the project reduced his lifestyle to a rather modest level for the remainder of his life. He died in 1977.[5]

Lt. Comdr. William K. Thompson, who had been in charge of midshipmen's schools and NROTC at the College Training Section, was an inveterate poker player and died while enjoying his favorite pastime. He was a victim of the LaSalle Hotel fire in Chicago on June 5, 1946.

Dr. George Winchester Stone, Jr., resumed teaching English at George Washington University, becoming a full professor in 1947. In 1955 he became professor of English at New York University and then dean of the Graduate School of Arts and Sciences from 1964 to 1971, when he was appointed dean of libraries at NYU. He was elected president of the Modern Language Association of America in 1967. Dr. Stone lives in Bethesda, Maryland, where he continues his research at the Folger Library. He is the author of numerous books and is coauthor (with George M. Kahrl) of *David Garrick: A Critical Biography.*

Dr. Jean Paul Mather returned to the Colorado School of Mines as a professor of economics but later rejoined Adams for two years when the latter was president of the American Council on Education. Mather was

V-12 OFFICERS AFTER WORLD WAR II

elected provost of the University of Massachusetts in 1953, succeeding to the presidency a short time later and serving from 1954 to 1960. Arthur Adams gave the inaugural address at Mather's installation at the University of Massachusetts. Mather retired to Pittsfield, Massachusetts.

Lt. John W. Wight resumed his relationship with McGraw-Hill Publishing Company and after various positions of increasing responsibility became executive vice president of the firm. He now lives near Savannah, Georgia.

Lt. George W. Hulme returned to Alabama and later became president of the First National Bank of Alexander City. He is retired in Alexander City.

Dr. William Valdo Webber, who was in the College Training Section in the vital start-up phase and then moved to the Officer Assignment Section of BuPers, returned to Western Michigan University at Kalamazoo, where he was professor of political science and active in civic affairs. He served a term in the Michigan legislature before retiring to Bradenton, Florida.

Lt. Phil Narmore moved back to Atlanta where he became executive dean at Georgia Tech. He retired in the Atlanta area.

Lt. Urban Joseph Peters Rushton was assistant dean of the College of Arts and Sciences and taught history at the University of Virginia after the war. He died in 1949 at age thirty-four.

Lt. Wilber McKee took up his position as professor of English at New York University and continued there until his death in the 1960s.

Immediately after the war William S. Thomson invited Lewis K. Adams to join him in the oil business. Adams spent a week in Houston looking over the situation but decided to return to Washington & Lee University, where he became dean of the School of Business. He died in 1971.[6]

Lt. Albert L. Demaree returned to Dartmouth College, where he was professor of history.

Lt. Raymond B. Pinchbeck returned to his position as the dean of Richmond College at the University of Richmond.

Lt. Mode L. Stone returned to Florida as professor of school administration at Florida State University. He later became dean of the School of Education. He died in 1979.

The University of Kentucky reclaimed Lt. Ellis F. Hartford, who became director of the university schools of the School of Education. He wrote a book, *What I Did in the War.*

The head of the Standards and Curriculum Section, Dr. Alvin C. Eurich, returned to Stanford University, where he became vice president. He was also acting president in 1948. He was the first chancellor

V-12 OFFICERS AFTER WORLD WAR II

of the State University of New York system and later became a vice president of the Ford Foundation. He lives in New York City, where he is president of the Academy for Educational Development. Eurich's assistant in Standards and Curriculum was Lt. Comdr. Frank H. Bowles, who later became director of the College Entrance Examination Board.

The head of the Marine V-12 program, Thurston J. Davies, USMCR, resumed his position as president of Colorado College. He retired from Colorado in 1948 and later became the executive director of the Town Hall, Inc., in New York City.

All of the Marine V-12 officers-in-charge who have been located are retired except for Capt. Paul Moore, Jr., USMCR, who had been ordered to the University of Washington after service on Guadalcanal. In 1986, he had been serving as the Episcopal Bishop of New York for fifteen years.

The officers who had such important parts in the success of the V-12 program were accustomed to winning. They came to Washington or to their individual units with the intention of putting things together in the right way. And they did. In later life they enjoyed much success in various fields, but they should also be recognized for the important contributions they made to the V-12 program.

42

DID THE
NAVY ACHIEVE
ITS GOALS?

ALTHOUGH at the first Columbia Conference Rear Adm. Randall Jacobs referred to V-12 as "a college program," both Jacobs and the College Training Section consistently emphasized that the basic purpose of the program was to provide officers for the Navy. This was explicitly stated to the Joint Army and Navy Board for Training Unit Contracts by Chairman Robert B. Stewart at various meetings in the summer of 1943. The negotiating teams worked and the program was run in accordance with that principle.

The Navy knew how many ships and planes were to be built and when they would be delivered. It knew how many officers it needed. When the V-12 graduates were commissioned, there were billets for all of them. They weren't obliged to wait for assignments.

The production of those new officers required a great deal of careful planning over a considerable time period. V-12 was being planned before the lowering of the draft age became official in November of 1942. Everyone knew that eighteen-year-olds would soon be drafted, and the Navy recognized that it had to protect its supply of future officers.

It must be remembered that until the two atomic bombs were dropped on Japan in early August of 1945, no one knew how long the war would last. The distances involved were so great and the fortified areas to be taken so numerous that leaders had to plan for a long war.

When the V-12 program opened on July 1, 1943, Secretary of the Navy Knox had just delivered an address in San Diego in which he said the Navy was planning for another three or four years of fighting.[1] At a press conference a few weeks later, Knox asserted that "our best naval and military brains are now planning for battles which may have to be fought in 1949." Vice Adm. Frederick J. Horne added that the fleet expansion program was not scheduled for completion until that year.[2]

In view of the probabilities, could the Navy bet that the war would be short? Obviously not.

To provide facilities for training future officers, the Navy could not

DID THE NAVY ACHIEVE ITS GOALS?

use existing naval stations — they were all in peak use because of the Navy's rapid expansion. It could have built a special training camp at some new location, but the time, materials, and labor necessary to erect such training facilities were in very short supply. The Navy recognized that most college campuses would be, at best, only half filled because of the draft of eighteen-year-olds.

The colleges themselves had been offering their facilities to the armed forces since January of 1942, when the representatives of one thousand schools assembled in Baltimore. Six months later a representative group of colleges met again and lamented the fact that the armed forces had not accepted their offer. Following that meeting, the American Council on Education worked closely with both the Army and the Navy to create plans for using college facilities.

By placing their training programs in existing colleges that had housing and messing facilities, trained faculties, and scientific equipment, the Army and the Navy made the only logical decision.

The Fiscal Section of the Division of Planning and Control of the Bureau of Naval Personnel estimated that creating the facilities for the V-12 program in a naval station would have taken a capital investment of $97,500,000 to accommodate 71,412 men. It would have required an annual operating outlay of $7,712,496.

In contrast, the Navy found far more satisfactory facilities in the V-12 institutions and saved money, too. The Navy spent approximately $4 million on commissioning expenses, but only $849,338 of it was paid for alterations and equipment at the institutions. The Navy paid the colleges an annual rental of $5,244,497 and the annual operating costs amounted to $8,715,119, for a total yearly outlay of just under $14 million.

The Fiscal Section concluded that the Navy's use of the colleges saved it more than $81 million over a two-year period. It also noted that such use conserved a huge amount of materials and a large segment of manpower at a time when there were critical shortages of both.[3]

The extensive utilization of existing educational facilities was one of the reasons why the United States and its allies were victorious over its enemies, according to V-12 coordinator Grant H. Brown:

We now know that the Axis Powers [Germany, Italy, and Japan], in assessing their chances of success in a war with the United States, took full cognizance of our productive capacity to outproduce them many fold in all of the instruments of war. They reasoned that, caught by the impact of a full scale war, we could not — in time — train the personnel to use the equipment we could produce. Here was where they miscalculated. They figured on our industrial might but they forgot our educational resources.

One of the great lessons we should have learned from World War II is

DID THE NAVY ACHIEVE ITS GOALS?

that our educational institutions are a vital part of our national defense program.[4]

In considering the approaches of the Army's ASTP and the Navy's V-12 programs, Raymond F. Howes felt that the Army "demeaned" the colleges by regimenting them, whereas the Navy organized the schools' creative abilities. That, he affirmed, is why the Navy's college program is so favorably remembered.[5]

According to *U.S. Naval Administration in World War II, Bureau of Naval Personnel Training Activity, Volume IV, The College Training Program*, "more than 50,000 officer candidates" had been delivered to the Navy and Marine Corps by the V-12 program by the end of the war. Thousands more came after that date, but exact figures are not readily available. At least once, in 1946, the total was estimated to be in excess of sixty thousand officers.

Many of the first V-12 graduates who went to midshipmen's schools in November 1943 soon found themselves in the amphibious force. A substantial number headed to Normandy on D-Day, and some V-12s were killed in those landings. The victory over Germany on May 9, 1945, allowed the nation and its allies to concentrate on the defeat of Japan. The vast distances in the Pacific and the numerous enemy strongholds made a long war seem very probable. The culmination would be the invasion of Japan, which was eventually planned to begin on about November 1, 1945, as "Operation Olympic." How long would victory over Japan take? No one knew.

On May 16, 1945, Williams College president Dr. James Baxter was interviewed in the student newspaper. Dr. Baxter, who was described as "one of the foremost naval historians of our time," was a member of the Holloway Board planning for the postwar NROTC program. In answer to the question "How long do you think the war will last against Japan?" Baxter declared, "I will be surprised if the war takes less than a year and disappointed if it takes two years."

Professor of history Newhall of Williams said it was "conceivable that the war will end in a year," but that he really couldn't judge it.[6]

As these men were being interviewed, the bloody campaign on Okinawa and the kamikaze attacks against the Navy were continuing. Many V-12 trainees who had come into the program with some college background, the irregulars, were already with the Fifth Fleet off Okinawa, and they suffered their share of casualties. There were even a few V-12 regulars on duty off Okinawa. These were the men who came in directly from high school in July of 1943 and finished their V-12 requirements in October of 1944. If they were assigned immediately to a midshipmen's school without the waiting period at pre-midshipmen's

DID THE NAVY ACHIEVE ITS GOALS?

school, they were commissioned about the first of March. Some of those new ensigns received orders directly to ships of the Fifth Fleet.[7]

Other regulars were in various schools or en route to the fleet when the war against Japan ended. Many of them had orders that would have put them in the first assault against the Japanese mainland under the Operation Olympic plan. The fortunate early termination of the war made most V-12s who were en route to the Pacific or were already there firm believers in the wisdom of President Harry Truman's decision to drop the atomic bomb.[8]

In planning for a long war, the Bureau of Naval Personnel had placed enough qualified men in the V-12 program to ensure that the officers would be ready when the ships and planes were available. The fact that the war ended abruptly, long before most observers thought possible, cannot in any way diminish the accomplishments of the program or of the V-12 trainees themselves.

Attending the second Columbia Conference, May 12–13, 1944, were (left to right) Lt. Col. Thurston J. Davies, USMCR, officer-in-charge of the Marine Corps V-12 program; Capt. James L. Holloway, Jr., USN, director of training, Bureau of Naval Personnel; Capt. J. K. Richards, USN, commanding officer of the Columbia Midshipmen's School and V-12 units at Columbia University and Webb Institute of Naval Architecture; Vice Adm. Randall Jacobs, USN, chief of naval personnel; and Capt. Arthur S. Adams, officer-in-charge of the Field Administration Division, Bureau of Naval Personnel, formerly officer-in-charge of the College Training Section.

New York Times

DID THE NAVY ACHIEVE ITS GOALS?

Vice Adm. Randall Jacobs, the chief of naval personnel, addressed this subject at the second Columbia Conference held in New York City on May 12 and 13, 1944, three weeks before the invasion of France by the Allies and nearly fifteen months before the end of the war.

> The end of the war may well find in every V-12 Unit an overwhelming majority of men who have been called back to college after combat service. But if, as we all pray, the war ends at such an early date that many V-12 trainees have never seen a ship, let no one impugn their patriotism. They are serving the Navy where the Navy has ordered them to serve. They are serving where the Navy needs them most. The Navy is not keeping them from combat to protect them from danger; it is keeping them in college to man ships which will later join the fleet.[9]

In the same speech, Jacobs said, "The Navy cannot fight a war with enlisted men alone, and officers must continually be trained both for the fleet, and, in smaller numbers, for specialized duty in hospitals, navy yards, and other shore establishments."

The V-12 program was established to train tens of thousands of officers for the Navy and Marine Corps. The Navy accomplished what it set out to do. What more could be asked of a program?

43

BENEFITS TO
V-12 COLLEGES

THE COLLEGES offered their facilities to the armed forces immediately after Pearl Harbor, but more than eighteen months passed before the Navy used them in the V-12 program. Thereafter, however, there was a very warm relationship between the Navy and the colleges.

How necessary was the V-12 program to the survival of the colleges and universities of the United States? Many large, heavily endowed schools had no major worries, but even they would have had to reduce their faculties because of the diminished number of students had it not been for the Army and Navy programs. The state-supported schools would also have survived, but legislatures would undoubtedly have sharply reduced their appropriations, which could have forced the schools to cut costs and faculties in line with enrollments.

It was the small, lightly endowed schools that faced disaster. They did not have the resources to continue without a paying student body. Inevitably they would have had to dismiss a substantial portion of their teaching staffs. The issue of whether the schools would be able to survive at all was debated vigorously on many campuses.

The fierce competition for military units required that colleges use all the political influence they could muster. On April 14, 1943, Father Emmet J. Riley, the president of Carroll College in Helena, Montana, sent the following wire to his friend and political ally in efforts to get a V-12 contract, Postmaster General Frank Walker: "THE PROBABILITY IS THAT MONTANA'S ONLY CATHOLIC COLLEGE FOR MEN WILL BE FORCED TO CLOSE ITS DOORS UNLESS CALLED UPON TO SERVE IN THE TRAINING OF NAVY MEN UNDER THE COLLEGE TRAINING PROGRAM."[1] Many other small colleges felt the same pressure, but not all of them put their fears into writing.

Schools that landed V-12 contracts received many benefits. Being selected for V-12 increased the prestige of any college. For major schools, it was a nice compliment. For smaller schools, the recognition that they were considered qualified by the Navy would reflect favorably upon them for many years. Selection for V-12 also meant that the insti-

BENEFITS TO V-12 COLLEGES

tution's facilities would be kept in use and in good repair. Their faculties and administrative personnel would be fully employed — indeed, every school had to search for additional teachers to handle the academic load necessitated by the V-12 unit. Just a few months earlier, the schools had been considering cutting back their faculties or even closing for the duration.

Schools involved in V-12 also had the great satisfaction of knowing that they were helping to win the war. In 1986, this satisfaction was recalled by the Reverend Arthur L. Dussault, S. J., who had been acting dean and moderator of athletics at Gonzaga University during the V-12 days: "The V-12 and V-5 together put us near the front line of the war effort. We needed no longer to stand by and watch the awfulness and splendor [of war] unleash themselves. We could do something."[2]

The schools selected for V-12 contracts sometimes gained the most national attention they had ever received. In some cases, this recognition resulted from the exceptional performance of athletic teams dominated and led by V-12 men. It also arose from the fact that students came from all over the nation and the colleges ceased to be purely local institutions. The introduction of trainees from distant areas also provided the schools with a certain number of future students for the postwar period.

When the units disbanded in 1945 or 1946, the colleges had a chance to buy surplus equipment, which would be most helpful in handling the deluge of students every school experienced in the postwar years. Equipment would be in short supply between 1946 and 1948, so the schools took full advantage of the offer to buy chairs, study tables, lamps, blankets, bunks, and mattresses at very low prices. This gave them an advantage over schools that did not have such an opportunity.

The new housing that some schools had acquired to land the V-12 contracts also put them in good standing in the postwar period. It is doubtful, for example, that Marquette University ever regretted buying or leasing those small hotels near the campus or that the University of Louisville or the University of Oklahoma were ever sorry that they had constructed new dormitories.

The program also helped bring the colleges and the communities closer together. In some towns there were excellent relations between the two groups before the war, but in the typical college town there was often antipathy between the townspeople and the college people.[3]

From the standpoint of the educational institutions involved in it, then, the V-12 program was a huge success. This assessment was reported in many ways at many institutions to many boards of trustees. The Navy had accomplished its abiding goal: it was to be well remembered by the colleges. The colleges had profited by maintaining financial soundness and contributing to the victory over the Axis powers.[4]

44

IMPACT ON
HIGHER EDUCATION

DID THE V-12 program have any lasting effects upon higher education?

The accelerated year-round schedule of the V-12 program was not a popular one. After the war, nearly every school reverted to the traditional two-semester plan, which pleased both the faculty and the students. Students who wanted to complete their education in the shortest time possible could and did make use of the broadened postwar summer school sessions. Dr. Martin G. Abegg, president of Bradley University and a V-12 trainee at the University of Illinois, believes that V-12 demonstrated the practicality of year-round education "and could very well have established the productive possibilities of summer program offerings."[1]

Arthur Adams did not favor the accelerated schedule for postwar education. On January 16, 1947, in an essay prepared for a radio broadcast on the Columbia Broadcasting System's feature "In My Opinion," Adams answered the question, "Should American education adopt the military intensive methods of instruction?" He replied with a firm no, but he did not approve of students' spending their summer holiday in idleness. "The student," he wrote, "can best employ this time getting a job and engaging in practical work within the subject he has studied. By so doing he broadens his over-all understanding of the subject; and of even more value, increases his ability to evaluate himself. He comes to be sure of what he knows and of what he can do."[2]

One of the most important effects of the V-12 program was that it opened the V-12 colleges to students from a much broader economic spectrum. Once that breakthrough had occurred in wartime, the schools could not revert to the mixture of students typical before the war. Even the Ivy League schools took many more students from less prosperous economic backgrounds than they had in their prewar years. State teachers colleges and the small nonsectarian schools also registered students from a wider range of economic backgrounds.

The GI Bill of Rights gave students from diverse backgrounds the chance to matriculate at any school they desired, but as a practical

IMPACT ON HIGHER EDUCATION

matter the huge numbers of postwar applicants caused the highly selective schools to revert to their stringent admissions policies. In response to pressure from legislatures and parents, state schools frequently reacted to the flood of applications to their institutions by limiting the number of out-of-state enrollments. Understandably, the religious schools again gave preference to applicants from their own denominations.

Although many V-12 students chose to attend schools closer to home than those they had attended in the program, some returned to their V-12 college — because they had had particularly good experiences there or because they had left behind young women in whom they were interested.[3]

Thus, the nationwide experiment in distributing students to colleges without regard to wealth, religion, or home location had some short-term influence on higher education, although it varied widely in visibility and intensity.

In 1986, the question of the long-range influence of the Navy V-12 program upon higher education was put to several educators who had been intimately involved with V-12. Two college presidents, Bill Lillard of Oklahoma's Central State University (a V-12 trainee at Milligan College) and Robert L. Poorman of Lincoln Land Community College, Springfield, Illinois (a trainee at Ohio Wesleyan University), noted that an unusually high percentage of V-12 trainees pursued careers in higher education. Obviously, the men who chose such careers had been impressed by their contacts with their professors. The V-12 teachers' willingness to make extraordinary efforts to help the trainees succeed and the excellent job done by educators who served as commanding officers in many of the units may have contributed to this career orientation.[4]

Poorman pointed out that the careers of the V-12s who became academicians undoubtedly perpetuated the influence of Navy leadership training. This may have resulted in their setting higher goals for the students they have taught throughout the years.

Another benefit of V-12 was pointed out by Dr. Martin G. Abegg, who noted that the large number of V-12s who turned to teaching after the war "provided a bridge for that period of time when faculty would have been in short supply because of the interruption in college education through the draft and enlistments."

According to Dr. James H. Zumberge, president of the University of Southern California and a former Marine V-12 at Duke University, the Navy's decision to allow college students already enrolled to continue in their courses of study was a wise one. As he put it, "leadership qualities can be best developed in a person who has a heavy dose of liberal arts."[5]

IMPACT ON HIGHER EDUCATION

Dr. John E. Corbally, former president of the University of Illinois and former V-12 at the University of Washington, agrees with Zumberge's observation:

> One key outcome of the Navy V-12 Program and similar programs conducted by the Armed Forces during World War II was the recognition that a college education was an important tool on behalf of national purposes. While toward the end of the war, the V-12 Program stressed support of engineering and scientific curricula, at the outset there were no limits placed upon the degree purposes of V-12 candidates. Thus, the officer corps of the Navy was enriched with individuals with liberal arts degrees, with degrees in education, with degrees in business, as well as with degrees in engineering and the sciences. This recognition of the importance of an officer corps with broad educational backgrounds has had important influence upon the service academies, upon R.O.T.C. Programs, and upon the general viewpoint of our citizenry toward appropriate educational backgrounds for military officers.[6]

What has been V-12's most important influence on higher education? It provided a great deal of educational leadership in the forty years following the end of the program, which was a period of great expansion of higher education in the United States. The effect of such strong leadership will continue to benefit the nation for many years to come.

45

TRAINEE BENEFITS

FOR THE trainees, the V-12 program offered many great benefits other than prestige, higher pay, greater responsibilities, and the innate satisfaction of becoming a naval officer. One of these benefits was discipline. The V-12s were taught not only how to take orders, but how to give them. In most units, platoon responsibilities were passed around, which gave most of the trainees their first real taste of military leadership. If they succeeded in the V-12 program, they eventually received more leadership training on their way to their commissions, but the V-12 experience provided the base of self-confidence upon which they built.

The trainees were forced to develop a great deal of self-discipline. They had to learn to cope with demanding assignments and to allocate their very limited time. Of course, most college students must learn to allocate time as a part of their maturing process, but the V-12s had to learn very quickly. They didn't have four years in which to mature — if they didn't learn in the first 120 days of their V-12 experience, they might be leaving for boot camp.

The V-12s had to handle stress. Pressure was always present. Most of those who learned how to cope with pressure succeeded, but those who could not handle it failed. Severe psychiatric problems occurred at a number of schools. They were uncommon, but they did happen. At one school a trainee who set extremely high goals for himself became depressed and tried to throw himself under the wheels of the local train. At another school a trainee reacted to the stress by carrying his mattress out to the drill field in the middle of the night, hoisting it to the top of the instructor's platform, and sleeping there to be sure he would be on time for calisthenics at 0600. It appeared to be a sleepwalking episode, but the trainee was sent to a naval hospital that day.

The educational rewards of the V-12 program were impressive. The program gave those who were just a term or two away from graduation the chance to finish their degree requirements. In a number of schools some trainees took on an inordinate academic load to complete their requirements and graduate during the time allocated to their schooling

TRAINEE BENEFITS

by the Navy.[1] Eventually, the College Training Section put an end to that practice because it put too much stress upon individual men.

Entering V-12 permitted those who were already in premed, engineering, or other specialties to continue in their chosen fields as long as they continued to meet the stiff requirements.

Men who started college as members of a V-12 unit and opted for an engineering curriculum received fine undergraduate training at the best engineering schools in the nation. The training lasted six or eight terms, depending upon the specialty they were allowed to pursue. At the end of the war, these engineers could move on to graduate school or directly to industry or professional engineering firms. They had received an excellent education, which gave them the tools they needed for their life's work.

Many men admitted to the NROTC program from V-12 earned bachelor of naval science degrees that enabled them to enter graduate school immediately after the war. Others were usually only one term away from a degree.

Those who pursued the aviation pathway, despite their aversion to V-12, weren't really hurt by it. The program gave many their first taste of a college education. That experience led thousands of them back to campuses after the war to complete their work for degrees.

The regulars, the first-term freshmen who were in the deck officer program, received four terms of education, which was heavily oriented toward science and math. They acquired a fine background for engineering or other specialties using math and science. If English or history was their interest, however, V-12 gave them little direct academic help other than providing transferable credits so they could claim junior status in their postwar educational pursuits. As a result, they could earn their undergraduate degrees in the standard eight terms.

If a regular trainee decided to seek his B.A. in political science, for example, he had no credits toward his major's requirements when he arrived at his postwar school. The next two years had to be devoted largely to his major and the college's requisites in such fields as foreign language and philosophy. Thus, if he decided to finish his degree in the minimum time, it was at the expense of electives in the liberal arts.

Although regulars in certain fields received little direct help toward their educational goals, their V-12 experience gave them invaluable indirect educational benefits. It taught them how to study. Passing calculus and physics showed them that they could successfully compete academically with nearly anyone.

The greatest benefit to the young men fortunate enough to fall into the right age group and to have the correct physical, mental, and educational qualifications for admittance to the V-12 program was the *op-*

TRAINEE BENEFITS

portunity. The program provided thousands of young men who never could have afforded it the chance to attend college.

One particularly interesting example was a student in New England whose parents were opposed to his going to college. His father felt he should go to work. Since the boy was only seventeen, he needed to persuade his parents to sign the form approving his enlistment into V-12. That the boy was going into the Navy apparently made the situation somewhat more palatable to the father. The young man eventually earned a Ph.D. and pursued a career in education.

Another who made the most of the opportunity was a young man attending Cornell as a civilian. His widowed mother was scrimping to pay the tuition while he held a part-time job to earn enough for his room and meals, which consisted mostly of peanut-butter-and-jelly sandwiches. Admittance to the V-12 program relieved his mother of a tremendous burden, and he gained fifteen pounds in the first two months. He ultimately devoted his life to teaching and research.

The most outstanding opportunity — for its time — was that given to the few blacks who were admitted to V-12. As Vice Adm. Samuel L. Gravely said, "The V-12 Program was for me a turning point in my life. It gave me an opportunity to compete on an equal footing with people I had never competed with before. It gave me an opportunity to prove to myself that I could succeed if I tried."[2]

The V-12 program changed tens of thousands of lives by giving those intelligent men a chance for a college education. That opportunity was the factor most appreciated by the V-12s. Typical was the comment of one national leader, who said in 1986, "It [V-12] was the making of me!"

Although most trainees were very enthusiastic about V-12, a handful found fault with the program. Sometimes their complaints concerned the quality of the educational facilities provided by the schools they attended, and such complaints were sometimes justified. In other instances their complaints concerned, not the incompetence of particular faculty members, but the appearance of poor faculty attitudes toward the V-12s and resentment of the V-12 presence on the campus. These attitudes were seen by the complainers as attempts to compel V-12s to remain on the campus for the weekend by failing them in tests given late in the week.

But probably the most common objection was to officers and chiefs who were overly concerned with their own importance and decided to run too strict a "ship." One trainee at a small midwestern college wrote, "It's quite ungrateful of me but I didn't like the Navy. People of modest talent in positions of major responsibility. A 'make work mentality.' "

Those who entered the V-12 late in the program had another basis for dissatisfaction. Said one trainee who entered in November of 1944,

TRAINEE BENEFITS

"By the time I joined the program it had lost its purpose and had become too bureaucratic to have much *esprit*. We were anticipating the end of the war and Navigation II was both difficult and prospectively useless."

Many of the upperclassmen who were in V-12 for only one term did not see the program as anything more than an extension of their civilian education, and some felt it was unimportant in their lives.

A few of the trainees who had serious objections to the program did not want to be in the armed forces at all. One described it as "a voluntary enlistment" in that it was preferable to the Army or prison. Another trainee, who admitted that he was a lifelong pacifist, could find very little merit in the entire program.

But the overwhelming majority — perhaps 98 percent — concluded that the program ranged from good to outstanding. How did these trainees evaluate the program? Here are a few examples.

An architect said, "The V-12 worked very well for myself and others for whom a military career was the farthest thing from our minds when we enrolled in the fall of 1941. The V-12 Program preserved the faculty at many sites and prepared young men for a long war. From a short-range viewpoint, the V-12 Program had little point, but long-range it was a masterstroke that should be emulated even now in some kind of reincarnation. I have no doubt that the nation was strengthened after World War II as a result of it."

A professor of engineering said, "I really appreciated that the Navy was interested in your education. Everything else was put in second place. V-12 did a good job of turning college men, mostly dilettantes, into serious, hard-working persons."

A federal judge noted, "I would surely give the Navy V-12 Program a 4.0."

The head of a large corporation said, "The V-12 Program gave me an invaluable basis for later life. This program, including midshipmen's school, provided at a young age experiences that would have taken years to develop. I, of course, am talking about the fundamentals of leadership [management] coupled with the sensible application of discipline. The program proved training and its subsequent application can be condensed from a time standpoint and that the only limit on attainment is the individual."

The dean of engineering of a major university said, "I regard it as one of the best investments that our country ever made."

A Marine trainee noted, "The V-12 Program managed to stockpile potential leadership resources, continued to develop these resources and feed them into the active units as needed. This program was one of the real innovations in manpower developments."

TRAINEE BENEFITS

A recently retired vice president of a major corporation commented, "It was a remarkable program! It has had the highest return of any investment the United States has ever made."

A university professor said, "V-12 was a superb program in all aspects!!"

A manufacturer called V-12 "an extraordinarily wise and effective enterprise which was responsible for the early training of a great number of future leaders. It is impossible to give the Navy V-12 Program too much credit for whatever happened to me in later life."

A high-ranking regular Navy officer who came up through the V-12 ranks called it "brilliantly conceived and executed."

Another high-ranking Navy officer who came through V-12 noted, "To this day [1986], I've seen no academic program that was tougher, no school discipline more rigid, no program with such high attrition, nor any body of men who have contributed more to our country in leadership, military, industrial, and academic."

Another professor of engineering called the V-12 program "surprisingly far-sighted." He added, "Probably the circumstances could never occur again. It must have been expensive in the short-term but the investment is still paying off."

Another V-12 reported, "the extra pressure of the program put me in a mood to spend my life studying and writing — which I have done."

Other V-12s commented on the educational opportunity the program provided — how it broadened the trainee's experience and outlook and forced him to mature rapidly. One trainee commented, "The intense training under V-12, the excellent and understanding officers, and the high level of the Franklin and Marshall faculty gave me an educational base I have valued all these subsequent years."

A successful executive with an energy firm wrote, "I came from a family which had little appreciation for education, little money, little world outlook. At the College of the Pacific I had my first intellectual stimulation. Whereas I had almost flunked English in high school, I got an 'A' in my first semester in V-12. I can say unreservedly that my experience in the V-12 Program was a major influence in my life in intellectual growth, physical ability, and leadership development."

The chairman of a major manufacturing firm said, "I will always be appreciative of the opportunity the V-12 Program offered me. The experience taught me discipline, which I believe is the true basis of any success in life."

A professor of mechanical engineering in a major university noted, "I regard V-12 as a key experience in my life. It gave me a direction which I have followed ever since. It was great for me and good for the country to have had the program. Had the war continued in the Pacific, we surely would have been key participants."

TRAINEE BENEFITS

A lifelong educator offered this observation: "I was a career Navy man [with five years' service] when I entered the V-12 Program. What it did for me was to introduce me to the whole universe of intellectual and cultural life which is our heritage, and I found that with the new universe before me which was so fulfilling, I was ready to reach out to a different career than I had foreseen. Originally that had been to become a chief electrician's mate, and perhaps make warrant officer someday."

Another successful trainee said, "I would not trade my V-12 training and education for anything."

A school official noted that the V-12 program set him on a course where he could gain knowledge and stature in education and subsequently "give back in good measure all that I received and . . . contribute in many other ways to my country. I am forever grateful!"

That feeling was echoed by another V-12 with Midwestern roots: "V-12 was the most fortunate thing to ever happen to me. I will always be grateful to the U.S. Navy."

A professor of engineering wrote, "By expanding my contact base, the V-12 Program changed my life. The impact of the V-12 education led me to pursue graduate study, a very unlikely possibility otherwise. My subsequent career has produced far more in benefits to society than would probably have occurred without V-12."

Another trainee spoke of the practical role of V-12: "It was invaluable to me. It led to my service as a radar officer, and as such I think I was more valuable to the Navy than if I had gone to combat at age eighteen."

Another benefit of the program was noted by another man: "The most valuable aspect of my V-12 education was learning to study hard and strive for excellence."

A communicator noted that "V-12 fostered a fraternal feeling that provided a base for compassion all through [my] life."

A prominent Southern clergyman stated, "It provided me with real training in discipline, self reliance, and working under authority."

A Midwestern attorney noted that it "was a reasonably caring, instant-maturity program. It took young men and taught them responsibility."

A utility executive mentioned how he grew up: "My V-12 school was academically poor, but I matured, knew it was up to me."

A prominent banker offered this observation about the V-12 program: "The responsibilities thrust upon young men at that time were greater than we would ever experience in business. It was broadening and maturing."

A widely known educator recalled, "The Navy helped me 'grow up.' I was only nineteen years of age when I reported aboard the USS Hale (DD642) as Torpedo Officer. When the Executive Officer looked at my personnel records, he exclaimed, 'My Gawd, never tell your age, Mister!'

TRAINEE BENEFITS

Then, he ordered me to grow a mustache, which, fortunately, I could do. All the NCOs and men under me were older than I was. Soon, we were out to sea, and I was standing OD watches. Our ship was in the thick of it in battles with the Japanese. Only on a Destroyer during a war would a young fellow such as myself get such responsibility."

Many V-12s were commissioned at age nineteen, and a few of the early candidates for midshipmen's school were held up until they became nineteen. This experience thrust heavy responsibility upon very young men.

AND WHEN DID YOU GET YOUR COMMISSION?

Ralph E. Ricketts: appeared in *The Gangway*, Pre-Midshipmen's School, Asbury Park, January 1945

It is clear that most of the V-12s thought very highly of the program and were grateful for the benefits they received. Indeed, several regretted that such a fine experience is not available to today's young people, and specifically to their own children. They pointed out that V-12 entailed much more than the NROTC programs and scholarships offered today. It was full time, and it required total dedication. They felt that V-12 shaped their lives for the better.

What did the V-12s think of their fellow trainees? How did they regard their intellectual capacity? The answers to these questions depend somewhat upon the individual trainee's own educational background. A professor of psychology offered this observation: "As a graduate of one

TRAINEE BENEFITS

of the best high schools in the country, I found nothing exceptional about the intellect of V-12ers at my school."

His opinion is at variance with the overwhelming majority of trainees. Here are some other recollections of fellow V-12s.

The president of a large food concern said, "I never saw a more top-notch group of students."

The dean of an engineering school noted, "The quality of students was generally very good."

Some other observations: "Our group was talented, motivated, and ambitious. I have little doubt that the average V-12 was intellectually and physically well above the national average.

"This was probably the most outstanding group of people I have ever been associated with."

The head of a Midwestern distribution firm noted that V-12s were "bright, energetic, and as lively a group of young men as I can imagine. Any study of the V-12 Program should take into account that the selection process . . . made it a certainty that the group would do very well in civilian life.

"The memorable part of the program . . . was the splendid quality of the participants, whether from public high school, the fleet, prep school, or college, and whether from the south or north, rich or poor, etc. It was an honor and a pleasure to be part of the group."

A former trainee from Cornell University observed, "Fleet and non-fleet men mixed with no problem — usually roommates helping each other with naval or academic shortcomings. Having the same clothes, pay, quarters, etc., made for ease of association and friendships not seen previously in Ivy League schools."

A common thread through many of the comments was an expression of the patriotism that motivated the V-12s. One described the situation this way: "We had purpose; we had meaning; and we would lay down our lives for our country."

A Northern trainee who was sent to a small college in the South recalled his V-12 comrades in these terms: "V-12 gave me a total experience at being part of a very special group, a group of intelligent young men who were healthy in both body and mind. . . . Never since . . . have I worked with a group of people all of whom were strong, stable, well-balanced in mind."

The program provided a lifetime of encouragement for most of the men who were in it. Sometimes a humorous experience provided the spark. A trainee from Cornell vividly recalls a stubby chief athletic specialist of French-Canadian extraction shouting encouragement to a heavy trainee on the obstacle course who was hand-walking along the parallel bars, facing a plunge into the mud puddle below if he should

TRAINEE BENEFITS

falter. "You can do eet, fat boy!" the specialist shouted. The trainee who reported this incident said he always recalls it when he is faced with an extremely difficult problem. "I remember, 'You can do eet, fat boy!' and I *always* can!"

The V-12 program produced a generation of leaders in every area of American life. Probably more ended up in education than in any other field, which seems to indicate that the relentless pressures of the program did not discourage them.

V-12 also graduated a great number of engineers. In the late 1940s and early 1950s, the engineering profession probably contained a larger proportion of former V-12s than any other profession, including medicine. At the University of Washington at one point after the war, seven of thirty-five faculty members in the School of Engineering had been educated in the V-12 program.

Many physicians, surgeons, and dentists also received a substantial portion of their training in the V-12 program. V-12s have abounded in law and government service at the federal, state, and local levels. They occupy many important judicial positions, from the local level to state supreme courts and U.S. courts of appeal. Basic research, religion, journalism, the fine arts, entertainment, athletics — all received outstanding contributors from the program. Many of the brightest stars in business and finance owe part of their education to the Navy's College Training Program. The most surprising result of all is the number of V-12s who rose to the highest ranks of the Navy and Marine Corps.

There is hardly any facet of American life that has not been influenced significantly by the V-12 program. The trainees were transformed into a generation of leaders, some of whom are listed in the next chapter.

46

V-12s LATER

THE V-12 program produced leaders in nearly every field of endeavor and in every sizable community in the nation. Although lawyers, educators, and engineers apparently comprise the largest groups of former V-12s, the fields of medicine, dentistry, business, industry, advertising, journalism, publishing, sports, the fine arts, show business, politics, and government service are all well represented.

Surprisingly many V-12s also rose to the top of the Navy and the Marine Corps. Regardless of their induction paths, most Navy reservists in World War II felt that after the war the Navy would revert to the closed club that it had been before the war, when an Annapolis class ring was necessary if an officer hoped to aspire to higher echelons. Had it not been for this popular (if mistaken) belief, it is likely that even more V-12s would have elected to try the regular Navy.

But the Navy kept its postwar promise to judge its naval officers by merit and not origin.[1] The V-12 background was sufficient to start many officers up the ladder to success. At least eighteen trainees eventually rose to the rank of vice or rear admiral in the regular Navy or Coast Guard without attending the Naval Academy, and at least three more attained those ranks in the Naval Reserve. An additional seventeen V-12s who were appointed to the Academy during or after their V-12 service made flag rank.

At least fifteen V-12s rose to the highest levels of the U.S. Marine Corps. This is not as surprising as the later success in the Navy of sailor V-12s because the Marine Corps had traditionally obtained most of its officers from among college graduates across the country. Only a small percentage had come via the Naval Academy. At least two Marine generals started out as Navy trainees, and at least one admiral entered the program as a marine.

The most unusual military success story of a Marine V-12 is that of LaVerne E. Weber, who was in the unit at Louisiana Tech and was subsequently commissioned in the Marine Corps. After the war, when he returned to civilian life, he joined the Oklahoma National Guard. The unit was called to active duty in the Korean War, and after completing several more years of service Weber decided to transfer to the regular

V-12s LATER

Army. He retired on June 30, 1984, as a lieutenant general in the Army.

Lt. Gen. Robert J. Baer, U.S. Army, was a V-12 at Westminster College, and Lt. Gen. Hillman Dickinson, U.S. Army, was a V-12 at MIT, when they were appointed to West Point.

V-12s Who Reached Flag Rank in the U.S. Navy
(without Naval Academy)

	V-12 Unit(s)	Rank
Robert L. Baker	Louisiana Tech	Rear Admiral
Robert H. Blount	Rensselaer	Rear Admiral
Kent J. Carroll	St. Ambrose	Vice Admiral
Earl B. Fowler	Georgia Tech	Vice Admiral
James H. Foxgrover	Western Michigan	Rear Admiral
Samuel L. Gravely, Jr.	UCLA	Vice Admiral
Eugene A. Grinstead	North Carolina	Vice Admiral
Kenneth G. Haynes	North Texas Agricultural	Rear Admiral
Thomas J. Hughes	Harvard	Rear Admiral
Wayne E. Meyer	Kansas	Rear Admiral
A. J. Monger	UCLA	Rear Admiral
Gordon R. Nagler	Duke	Vice Admiral
James R. Sanderson	Washington, Willamette	Vice Admiral
George D. Selfridge	Muhlenburg	Rear Admiral (DC)
Charles P. Tesh	North Carolina	Rear Admiral
William Thompson	Wabash	Rear Admiral
Thomas T. Wetmore III	Yale	Rear Admiral, USCG
Almon C. Wilson	Union	Rear Admiral (MC)

V-12s Who Reached Flag Rank in the Naval Reserve

	V-12 Unit(s)	Rank
Thomas A. Kamm	Wabash	Rear Admiral, USNR
Richard Lyon †	Yale	Rear Admiral, USNR
Charles H. Mayfield *	Southwestern Louisiana	Rear Admiral, USNR

V-12s Who Reached Flag Rank in the U.S. Navy
(after appointment to the Naval Academy)

	V-12 Unit(s)	Rank
Thomas J. Allshouse	Stevens	Rear Admiral
John C. Barrow	Berea	Rear Admiral
Frank W. Corley, Jr.	Richmond	Rear Admiral
Kenneth M. Carr	Louisville	Vice Admiral

V-12s LATER

	V-12 Unit(s)	Rank
William F. Clifford, Jr.	Holy Cross	Rear Admiral
Tyler E. Dedman	Kansas	Rear Admiral
Jeremiah A. Denton, Jr.	Millsaps	Rear Admiral
Paul J. Early	Union	Rear Admiral
Robert H. Gormley	Texas	Rear Admiral
Donald P. Harvey	Doane	Rear Admiral
John S. Kern	Louisville	Rear Admiral
Robert B. McClinton	Williams	Rear Admiral
Edward J. Otth, Jr.	Northwestern	Rear Admiral
William D. Robertson	South Carolina	Rear Admiral
Robert S. Smith	Northwestern	Rear Admiral
Edward F. Welch, Jr.	MIT	Rear Admiral
Donald B. Whitmire	North Carolina	Rear Admiral

V-12s Who Reached Field Rank in the U.S. Marine Corps

	V-12 Unit(s)	Rank
George R. Brier	South Carolina	Brigadier General
Edward J. Bronars	Illinois State	Lieutenant General
Paul Graham	Franklin and Marshall	Brigadier General
Harold A. Hatch	Northwestern, Oberlin	Lieutenant General
Joseph Koler, Jr.	College of the Pacific	Major General
Kenneth McLennan	Arizona State Teachers, Southwestern Louisiana	General
Noah C. New	Bethany	Major General
Arthur J. Poillon	Princeton	Major General
Adolph G. Schwenk	Dartmouth	Major General
Philip D. Shutler	Union	Lieutenant General
William Smith	North Carolina	Brigadier General
Harvey Spielman	Denison	Brigadier General
Hal W. Vincent ‡	Western Michigan, Colgate	Major General
Edward A. Wilcox *	Occidental	Major General
Herbert L. Wilkerson	Idaho (Southern Branch)	Major General

* = Deceased
† = First reserve officer recalled as deputy chief of Navy Reserve
‡ = Actually a V-5 attached to a V-12 unit

The names of some V-12 trainees are recognized by nearly every informed citizen of their age group, but only a few would ever associate their names with the Navy or Marine College Training Programs. These well-known former trainees (both Navy and Marine) include:

V-12s LATER

V-12 Trainee	V-12 Unit(s)	Position(s) (past or present)
Brock Adams	Washington	Senator from Washington, U.S. secretary of transportation
George H. Allen	Alma	Professional football coach
Howard H. Baker, Jr.	University of the South, Tulane	Senate majority leader, White House chief of staff
Angelo Bertelli	Notre Dame	Football great, Heisman Trophy winner
Johnny Carson	Millsaps	TV personality
Louis J. Cioffi	Muhlenberg	ABC-TV News bureau chief, United Nations
Jackie Cooper	Notre Dame	Actor, producer, director
Alvin Dark	Southwestern Louisiana	Major League baseball player, manager
Jeremiah A. Denton, Jr.	Millsaps	Senator from Alabama
Daniel J. Evans	Washington	Senator from Washington, governor of Washington
Harry R. Haldeman	Redlands	Presidential assistant, White House chief of staff
Elroy Hirsch	Michigan	Football great; athletic director, University of Wisconsin
Robert F. Kennedy*	Harvard, Bates	U.S. attorney general, senator, presidential candidate
Bowie Kuhn	Franklin and Marshall	Commissioner of baseball
Melvin Laird	St. Mary's	Secretary of defense
John U. Lemmon III	Harvard	Actor
Charles McC. Mathias, Jr.	Yale	Senator from Maryland
James A. McClure	Idaho (Southern Branch)	Senator from Idaho
J. William Middendorf II	Harvard, Holy Cross	Ambassador to European Community; secretary of Navy
Daniel P. Moynihan	Middlebury, Tufts	Senator from New York
Robert C. Pierpoint	California Tech	CBS-TV News national security correspondent
Albert L. Rosen	University of Miami	Major league baseball player; president, San Francisco Giants
Carl T. Rowan	Washburn, Oberlin	Syndicated columnist, ambassador to Finland

V-12s LATER

V-12 Trainee	V-12 Unit(s)	Position(s) (past or present)
Pierre Salinger	North Dakota State Teachers (Dickinson)	ABC-TV News chief foreign correspondent; presidential press secretary; senator from California
Thomas G. Wicker	North Carolina	Syndicated columnist
Roger Williams (Louis Weertz)	Idaho (Southern Branch)	Musician

Equally important are the following former Navy and Marine V-12s whose names are not household words across America, but whose past and present positions in business, industry, education, the arts, the judiciary, the professions, finance, and government service place them among the nation's top leaders.[2]

Martin G. Abegg	Illinois	President, Bradley University
Kenneth ("Bud") Adams	Kansas	President, Houston Oilers
Robert McCormick Adams	MIT	Secretary, Smithsonian Institution
Vernon R. Alden	Brown	President, Ohio University
Joseph H. Anderer	Stevens Tech	President, Revlon
Roy A. Anderson	Kansas State Teachers	Chairman, Lockheed Corporation
Hans H. Angermueller	Harvard	Vice chairman, Citicorp
Herbert K. Anspach	Oberlin	President, Whirlpool Corporation
Charles F. Baird	Dartmouth, Middlebury	Undersecretary of the Navy; chairman, INCO
Ray W. Ballmer	New Mexico	President, Rio Algom
Norman Barker, Jr.	Dartmouth	Chairman, First Interstate Bank, California
Thomas D. Barrow	Texas	Chairman, Kennecott Corporation
Raymond C. Baumhart	Northwestern	President, Loyola University (Chicago)

* = Deceased
† = First reserve officer recalled as deputy chief of Navy Reserve
‡ = Actually a V-5 attached to a V-12 unit

V-12s LATER

V-12 Trainee	V-12 Unit(s)	Position(s) (past or present)
Stephen D. Bechtel, Jr.	Colorado	Chairman, Bechtel Group
Wallace B. Behnke, Jr.	Northwestern	Vice chairman, Commonwealth Edison
Francis X. Bellotti	Tufts	Attorney general of Massachusetts
Paul Berg	Penn State	Nobel Prize in chemistry, 1980
Michael A. Bilandic	Notre Dame	Mayor of Chicago
Baruch S. Blumberg	Union	Nobel Prize in medicine, 1976
Howard Boozer	Howard	Executive director, South Carolina Commission on Higher Education
William B. Boyd	South Carolina	President, University of Oregon
Robert H. Boykin	Park	President, Federal Reserve Bank of Dallas
Lewis McA. Branscomb	Duke	Vice president and chief scientist, IBM
Balfour Brickner	Holy Cross	Rabbi, Stephen Wise Congregation, New York City
Clarence J. Brown*	Duke	Congressman from Ohio
William L. Brown	Newberry	Chairman, First National Bank (Boston)
James L. Buckley	Yale	Justice, U.S.Court of Appeals; senator from New York
Willard C. Butcher	Middlebury	Chairman, Chase Manhattan Bank
Owen B. Butler	Dartmouth	Chairman, Procter & Gamble
Will M. Caldwell	Western Michigan	Executive vice president, Ford Motor Company
Silas S. Cathcart	Notre Dame	Chairman, Illinois Tool Works
E. Otis Charles	Trinity	Dean, Episcopal Divinity School, Cambridge, Mass.
Warren M. Christopher	Redlands	Deputy U.S. secretary of state
David R. Clare	MIT	President, Johnson & Johnson
Hal Cooper	Michigan	TV director
John E. Corbally	Washington	President, University of Illinois
Edmund T. Cranch	Cornell	President, Worcester Polytechnic Institute; president, Wang Institute
Fenwick J. Crane	Michigan	Chairman, Family Life Insurance

V-12s LATER

V-12 Trainee	V-12 Unit(s)	Position(s) (past or present)
William E. C. Dearden	Ursinus	Chairman, Hershey Foods
William L. Dickinson	Mississippi College	Congressman from Alabama
Robert N. Dolph	Michigan	President, Exxon International
Myron DuBain ⌐	California	President, Fireman's Fund Corporation
Richard J. Durrell	Gustavus Adolphus	Publisher, People magazine
Horace B. Edwards	Union, Oberlin	President, ARCO Pipeline Company
Huntley A. Elebash	Georgia Tech	Episcopal bishop, Eastern Carolina
Chalmers "Bump" Elliott	Purdue	Athletic director, University of Iowa
Peter R. Elliott	Park	Executive director, Pro Football Hall of Fame
John N. Erlenborn	Indiana State, Notre Dame	Congressman from Illinois
James L. Everett III	North Carolina, Penn State	Chairman, Philadelphia Electric
John H. Filer	DePauw	Chairman, Aetna Insurance
Robert H. Finch	Occidental	Lieutenant governor of California; secretary of U.S. Department of Health, Education, and Welfare
Edward S. Finkelstein	Harvard	Chairman, R. H. Macy
James F. Fitzgerald	Baldwin-Wallace	President, Milwaukee Bucks basketball team
William H. Folwell	Georgia Tech	Episcopal bishop, Central Florida
Robert R. Frederick	DePauw	Chairman, RCA
Clarence L. French, Jr.	Columbia	Chairman, National Steel and Shipbuilding Corporation; chairman of the board, Webb Institute of Naval Architecture

* = Deceased
† = First reserve officer recalled as deputy chief of Navy Reserve
‡ = Actually a V-5 attached to a V-12 unit

V-12s LATER

V-12 Trainee	V-12 Unit(s)	Position(s) (past or present)
William D. Fugazy	Cornell	Chairman, Fugazy International
Robert A. Fuhrman	Michigan	Chairman, Lockheed Missiles
Alan C. Furth	California	President, Southern Pacific Company
Robert L. Gale	Gustavus Adolphus	President, Association of Governing Boards of Universities and Colleges
Hoyt D. Gardner	Westminster	President, American Medical Association
Joel Goldberg	Dartmouth	Chairman, Rich's
Oscar M. Gossett	Stevens Tech	Chairman, Saatchi & Saatchi Compton Worldwide
Thomas C. Graham	Louisville	Vice chairman, U.S. Steel
Joseph Granville	Missouri Valley	Stock market advisor
Ellis T. Gravette	North Dakota State Teachers (Minot)	Chairman, Bowery Savings Bank
Duncan M. Gray, Jr.	Tulane	Episcopal bishop, Mississippi
Russell H. Green Jr.	Texas	President, Signal Oil
Frank J. Guarini	Dartmouth	Congressman from New Jersey
Louis T. Hagopian	Alma	Chairman, N.W. Ayer
Arthur G. Hansen	Purdue	President, Purdue University
Herbert E. Harris, II	Missouri Valley	Congressman from Virginia
Robert C. Hart	Milligan, Louisville	President, Tennessee Eastman
Arthur Hauspurg	Columbia	Chairman, Consolidated Edison
Phillip Hawley	California	Chairman, Carter Hawley Hale
James D. Head	Washburn	Editor, *Parade* Magazine
Ernest Henderson III	Harvard	President, Sheraton Hotels
Karl G. Henize	Denison	Astronaut
James McN. Hester	Princeton	President, New York University
Richard S. Hickok	Muhlenberg	Chairman, Main Hurdman
Ralph P. Hofstad	Gustavus Adolphus	President, Land O'Lakes
Leonard W. Huck	DePauw	President, Valley National Bank of Arizona
Harry R. Hughes	Mount St. Mary's	Governor of Maryland

V-12s LATER

V-12 Trainee	V-12 Unit(s)	Position(s) (past or present)
J. Lawrence Hughes	Colgate	Chairman, Wm. Morrow & Company
Gene M. Hummel	Miami (Ohio), Dartmouth	Member, presiding bishopric, Reorganized Church of Latter Day Saints
Henry J. Hyde	Duke	Congressman from Illinois
William F. Hyland	Pennsylvania	Attorney general of New Jersey
Robert P. Jensen	Iowa State	Chairman, Tiger International
William S. Kanaga	Kansas	Chairman, Arthur Young & Company
Howard C. Kauffmann, Jr.	Oklahoma	President, Exxon
Howard H. Kehrl	Illinois Tech	Vice chairman, General Motors
Victor K. Kiam II	Yale	President, Remington Products
Richard D. Kilpatrick	Richmond	President, Connecticut General Insurance
Edward J. King	Brown	Governor of Massachusetts
Samuel M. Kinney	Penn State	President, Union Camp Corporation
Charles G. Kiskaddon, Jr.	Columbia	President, Alcoa Steamship Company
Jack F. Kofoed	Middlebury	President, Binney & Smith
John S. Lalley	Villanova	Chairman, PHH Group
Donald E. Lasater	Southeast Missouri	Chairman, Mercantile Bancorporation
Gerald D. Laubach	Mount St. Mary's	President, Pfizer
Lawrence E. Lindars	Dartmouth	Vice chairman, C. R. Bard
C. Edward Little	Duke	President, Mutual Broadcasting System
Barton H. Lippincott	Yale	Chairman, J. B. Lippincott
Lewis Lowenstein	Cornell	President, Supermarkets General Corporation
Thomas A. Luken	Bowling Green	Congressman from Ohio
Aleck MacD. Mackinnon	Cornell	President, Ciba-Geigy Corporation
Clifford B. Maines	Central College	President, Safeco Corporation
Roland F. Marston	DePauw	Chairman, State Farm Insurance

* = Deceased
† = First reserve officer recalled as deputy chief of Navy Reserve
‡ = Actually a V-5 attached to a V-12 unit

V-12s LATER

V-12 Trainee	V-12 Unit(s)	Position(s) (past or present)
Thomas J. McCollow	Dartmouth	Chairman, (Milwaukee) Journal Company
Clarence J. McConville	Miami (Ohio)	President, Title Insurance Company of Minnesota; president, American Land Title Association
R. Gordon McGovern	Williams, Holy Cross	Chairman, Campbell Soup
John J. McHale	Central Michigan	President, Montreal Expos
J. Donald McNamara	Dartmouth	President, the Interpublic Group of Companies
Robert E. Mercer	Yale	Chairman, Goodyear
Harry A. Merlo	Southwestern Louisiana	Chairman, Louisiana-Pacific Corporation
Reuben F. Mettler	California Institute of Technology	Chairman, TRW; chairman of the board of trustees, California Institute of Technology
Franklyn W. Meyer	Cornell	Co-inventor, freeze-dried coffee process
Harold T. Miller	Franklin and Marshall	Chairman, Houghton Mifflin
Thomas J. Moore, Jr.	Princeton	Chairman, Virginia Electric & Power
William S. Moorhead	Yale	Congressman from Pennsylvania
Robert B. Morgan	North Carolina	Senator from North Carolina
Richard M. Morrow	John Carroll	Chairman, AMOCO
Clint Murchison *	Duke	Texas investor
Robert J. Newhouse, Jr.	Princeton	Chairman, Marsh & McLennan
Edward N. Ney	Williams	Chairman, Young & Rubicam
Richard McKay Oster	Central College	Chairman, United Vintners
A. E. Pearson	Southern California	Chairman, PepsiCo
John E. Pearson	Gustavus Adolphus	Chairman, Northwestern National Life
David Samuel Peckinpah	Southwestern Louisiana	Motion picture director
Donald E. Petersen	Washington	Chairman, Ford Motor Company
James R. Petersen	St. Thomas	President, Parker Pen Company

V-12s LATER

V-12 Trainee	V-12 Unit(s)	Position(s) (past or present)
Walter R. Peterson	Dartmouth	Governor of New Hampshire
Harold A. Poling	Emory and Henry	President, Ford Motor Company
Avery D. Post	Ohio Wesleyan	President, United Church of Christ
David S. Potter	Yale	Undersecretary of the Navy
Edmund T. Pratt, Jr.	Duke	Chairman, Pfizer
William J. Pruyn	Harvard	Chairman, Eastern Gas and Fuel Associates
Carl Ragsdale	Denison	Carl Ragsdale Associates; Academy Award for best documentary film, 1966
Robert L. Randolph	DePauw	President, Alabama State University
Roland C. Raustenstraus	Colorado	President, University of Colorado
Donald G. Raymer	Michigan	President, Central Illinois Public Service
Ralph Regula	John Carroll	Congressman from Ohio
Robert L. Remke*	Northwestern	Chairman, RJR Foods
John B. Rhodes, Jr.	Cornell	Vice chairman, Booz, Allen & Hamilton
Clayton Rich	Swarthmore	Dean, Stanford University Medical College
Richard M. Ringoen	Dubuque	Chairman, Ball Corporation
Charles C. Roberts	DePauw	Vice chairman, DeKalb Corporation
John F. Robinson	Franklin and Marshall	President, Reliance Insurance Company
Frederick J. Ross, Jr.	MIT	President, Carborundum Company
Leo J. Ryan*	Bates	Congressman from California
Kenneth G. Ryder	Harvard	President, Northeastern University
Ronald E. Samples	Notre Dame	Chairman, Consolidated Coal
Robert M. Schaeberle	Dartmouth	Chairman, Nabisco

* = Deceased
† = First reserve officer recalled as deputy chief of Navy Reserve
‡ = Actually a V-5 attached to a V-12 unit

V-12s LATER

V-12 Trainee	*V-12 Unit(s)*	*Position(s) (past or present)*
Donald A. Schaefer	Colgate	President, Prentice-Hall
Herbert S. Schlosser	Princeton	President, National Broadcasting Company
John A. Schneider	Notre Dame	President, Warner-Amex Satellite Entertainment Corporation
Marshall Schober	MIT	President, Latrobe Steel
Erwin E. Schulze	DePauw	President, CECO Industries
Wallace M. Scott, Jr.	North Dakota State Teachers (Dickinson), University of Minnesota, Berea	Chairman, MSL Industries
Gordon M. Sears	Emory	Chairman, T. J. Ross Associates
Sheldon J. Segal	Dartmouth	Director of Population Sciences, Rockefeller Foundation; United Nations World Population Award, 1984
John S. R. Shad	Southern California	Chairman, Securities & Exchange Commission
Frank J. Shakespeare	Holy Cross	Vice chairman, RKO-General; ambassador to Portugal
William C. Sherman	Louisville	Ambassador to the Security Council of the United Nations
James F. Short, Jr.	Denison	Professor of sociology, Washington State University; president, American Sociological Association
Phillip R. Shriver	Yale	President, Miami University
Charles E. Silberman	Cornell	Author *(Crisis in Black and White)*
Robert D. W. Simms	Milligan	Chief justice, Oklahoma Supreme Court
L. Edwin Smart	Harvard	Chairman, Hilton International
Craig R. Smith	Case Institute	Chairman, Warner & Swasey
Richard M. Smith	Bloomsburg, Ohio Wesleyan	Vice chairman, Bethlehem Steel
William Reece Smith, Jr.	Georgia Tech	President, American Bar Association
William S. Sneath	Williams	Chairman, Union Carbide
Edson W. Spencer	Northwestern, Michigan	Chairman, Honeywell

V-12s LATER

V-12 Trainee	V-12 Unit(s)	Position(s) (past or present)
Malcolm T. Stamper	Richmond, Georgia Tech	President, Boeing Company
Marvin L. Stone	Emory and Henry	Editor, *US News and World Report*
John Strohmeyer	Muhlenberg	Editor, *Bethlehem Globe Times*; Pulitzer Prize for editorial writing, 1972
Dwight L. Stuart	Washington	President, Carnation Company
William Styron	Duke	Author *(The Confessions of Nat Turner)*, Pulitzer Prize for fiction, 1968
John F. Sullivan, Jr.	Washington	Chairman, Bath Iron Works
Glen Tetley	Franklin and Marshall	Award-winning choreographer
Hank Thompson	Southern Methodist, Texas	Country and Western entertainer
Keith L. Turley	Arizona State Teachers	Chairman, Arizona Public Service Company
Richard F. VanderVeen	University of the South	Congressman from Michigan
Blair Vedder	Colgate	President, Needham International
Hicks B. Waldron	Minnesota	Chairman, Avon Products
Leland J. Walker	Iowa State	President, American Society of Civil Engineers
Hans W. Wanders	Yale	Chairman, Wachovia Corporation
Charles H. Watts II	Brown	President, Bucknell College
William H. Webster	Williams	Director, Federal Bureau of Investigation
William W. Weide	Marquette	President, Fleetwood Enterprises
John L. Weinberg	Princeton	Chairman, Goldman Sachs
William G. Weinhauer	Trinity	Episcopal bishop, Western North Carolina
John J. Wildgen	Kansas	President, American Academy of Family Physicians
Richard D. Wood	DePauw	Chairman, Eli Lilly

* = Deceased
† = First reserve officer recalled as deputy chief of Navy Reserve
‡ = Actually a V-5 attached to a V-12 unit

V-12s LATER

V-12 Trainee	V-12 Unit(s)	Position(s) (past or present)
John F. Yardley	Iowa State	President, McDonnell Douglas Astronautics
W. T. Ylvisaker	Stevens Tech	Chairman, Gould
George P. Young	Denison, Kansas	Superintendent of schools, St. Paul, Minnesota
Richard W. Young	Dartmouth	President, Houghton Mifflin
John W. Zick	Northwestern, Denison	Cochairman, Price Waterhouse
James H. Zumberge	Duke	President, University of Southern California

In regard to the corporate affiliations shown above, it must be noted that only major U.S. businesses have been listed, and only the top two or three officers of those companies have been considered for inclusion on these pages. Literally hundreds of former V-12 trainees are executive vice presidents, senior vice presidents, and vice presidents with special areas of expertise who have top responsibilities in those and many other national businesses. Space limitations make it impossible to list all of those men, but adding their names would give overwhelming evidence of the types of leaders turned out by the program.

In addition to those listed, at least fifteen other V-12s are college and university presidents, and hundreds of ex-trainees are deans, professors, and coaches in colleges throughout the land. Many V-12s also serve as high school principals, teachers, and coaches.

Across the nation, hundreds of former V-12s are widely known in their own states. They have headed state bar, banking, savings and loan, dental, medical, and accountancy associations. Dozens of federal and state judges and legislators have made their mark on states and communities. There are too many to list in this chapter, but many of them are noted on the pages for each college in the appendix.

Then there are the thousands of V-12s who are known mainly in their own communities as professional and business men. These are the men who help run the school boards, hospitals, YMCAs, and United Way organizations, and lead the chambers of commerce and the Rotary, Kiwanis, Lions, and Exchange clubs. They represent the leadership provided to all of America as a by-product of the V-12 program.

Over the past forty years one of the best known V-12s has been Frank Thurlow Pulver, the irrepressible ensign of *Mister Roberts*.[3] Although author Thomas Heggen never specifically affirmed that Pulver was a V-12, most men who were in the program have no doubt of it. Each unit had at least one Frank Pulver.

V-12 Jackie Cooper portrayed Ensign Pulver on the stage in the na-

V-12s LATER

tional touring company in 1949, and V-12 Jack Lemmon won an Oscar for best supporting actor for playing him in the Warner Brothers movie *Mr. Roberts.* Undoubtedly both Cooper and Lemmon had known Pulver in their units.

In a questionnaire, hundreds of former V-12s were asked how the program helped them in later life. A frequent response was "It thrust heavy responsibility upon me at an early age, and taught me to make a decision." V-12s have been making important decisions all across America ever since, and America is the better for it.

47

THE MELODY
LINGERS ON

"THE Song is Ended (But the Melody Lingers On)" was Irving Berlin's 1927 hit.[1] In his August 1944 report to the chief of naval personnel, Bureau Counsel James A. Fowler, Jr., used this title to describe the V-12 negotiating process. He hoped that the colleges' favorable recollection of the Navy's College Training Program would linger on. Indeed, that was one of the major goals of the Bureau and of Mr. Fowler's office.[2]

The V-12 program ended more than forty years ago. Has the melody lingered on? On those 131 campuses there is little tangible evidence of it. At some schools, the bronze Navy plaque given after the end of the program is mounted on a prominent wall in a place of honor. At others it is lost among the many other awards received by the college. In a few it is gathering dust in a storeroom assigned to college archives. The certificates signed by Secretary of the Navy Forrestal have met similar fates. Some are in places of honor, but some remain unframed and others probably can't be found.

Is there anything else to remind the casual campus visitor of the Navy V-12 program? In a few colleges the company and platoon flags are exhibited in glass cases. Photo displays appear here and there in campus museums. But not much else can be seen at most of the V-12 schools.

But there are exceptions. In the Trinity College chapel there is a carved pew end given by the trainees who finished their V-12 work in October 1944. John Paul Jones, the father of the American Navy, stands astride the top of the pew end; the U.S.S. *Constitution*, under full sail, adorns the main panel. Symbolically, the V-12s included the motto, "We have not yet begun to fight."

In the chapel of the University of the South (Sewanee), the platoon flags and a list of all of the trainees are displayed in a corner of the chapel, and in the narthex is a stained glass window showing the V-12 unit marching.

At Bloomsburg State University a two-story brick building opposite

THE MELODY LINGERS ON

Trinity College Archives

This carved pew end depicting John Paul Jones was presented by the departing trainees to Trinity College in October 1944 in appreciation of the school's efforts on their behalf.

THE MELODY LINGERS ON

the library is identified in large letters as "NAVY HALL." That's where the trainees took many of their classes and where the V-12 headquarters was located.

Is there any evidence — tangible or otherwise — of the V-12 program elsewhere in the nation? Very little. Even in the Navy Department Library, there are fewer than half a dozen V-12 entries in the entire card catalogue.

But every year, in a few places in the country, the V-12 program is vividly recalled and brought back to life by former trainees holding reunions. It hasn't happened at every V-12 school, but it has occurred at enough units to keep the memory of the program alive.

Holding a V-12 reunion is not an easy task, for most V-12 schools have current addresses only for those trainees who received their degrees in the program or returned to do so after the war. But the lack of addresses is not the schools' fault. Very few V-12s made an effort to keep in touch. (Former V-12s who have not kept in touch with their schools but who would be interested in a reunion should contact their alumni office.)

Some V-12s and a few very energetic college alumni directors have made noteworthy efforts to maintain contact between the schools and the V-12s. The struggles to locate addresses have renewed some longstanding friendships between the V-12s themselves. The ultimate result has been the V-12 unit reunions. At other schools, V-12 gettogethers have become a distinct part of the class reunions for those war years.

Some of the schools that have had V-12 reunions on campus are: Alma College, Arkansas A & M, Bates College, Berea College, Bethany College, College of the Pacific, Denison University, Franklin and Marshall College, Illinois State Normal, Iowa State College, Louisiana Polytechnic Institute, Milligan College, Millsaps College, Minot State Teachers College, Park College, Southeast Missouri State Teachers College, Southwestern Louisiana Institute, Union College, University of Idaho (Southern Branch), University of Illinois, University of Redlands, University of Washington, Western Michigan College, and Worcester Polytechnic Institute.

What do they do at V-12 reunions? Visit the campus, locate their old rooms, have lunch or dinner with college officials from the V-12 era, and invite former hostesses from the local USOs for dinner and dancing. They spend the rest of their time visiting, remembering, and regaling their shipmates and wives with stories from the V-12 days, which seem to get better with age.

The enthusiasm of the trainees who meet at reunions is impossible to overstate. V-12 was such an important part of their lives that they

THE MELODY LINGERS ON

James G. Schneider

At the Milligan College Reunion, the welcome was set at the edge of the campus.

Former trainees (and wives) review the Milligan campus they left forty years ago.

James G. Schneider

THE MELODY LINGERS ON

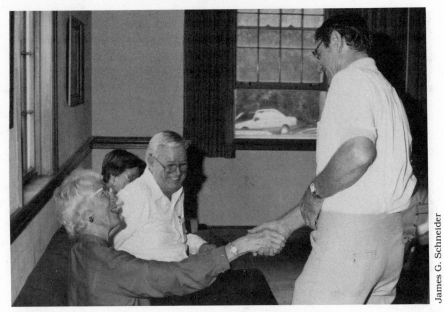

James G. Schneider

Trainees stop to visit with Dr. Ivor Jones, their English professor.

Four Milligan trainees speculate on whether they could run up the steps from the athletic field in double time as they did forty years earlier.

James G. Schneider

THE MELODY LINGERS ON

Lots of reminiscing goes on at a V-12 reunion. These trainees talk over old times at the 1985 Milligan V-12 reunion.

Like other V-12 reunions, this one at Milligan College in 1985 closed with everyone singing the Navy hymn, *Eternal Father, Strong to Save.*

THE MELODY LINGERS ON

are unwilling to let it disappear. Some of the best friendships they ever had date back to the V-12 days.

As a group, the Marine V-12s have been most diligent about their own reunions. That special effort undoubtedly results from the noted *esprit de corps* of the Marine Corps. Marines from the College of the Pacific have held many reunions, most of them in San Francisco. Louisiana Tech marines have had six gatherings and received nationwide Associated Press coverage of the fortieth anniversary meeting in 1983.

While Gonzaga has not had a reunion on campus, there have been many annual assemblies of Zag V-12 trainees who live in the San Francisco area.

The numerical record for V-12 meetings is undoubtedly held by a small group of trainees who lived in Birch Hall at Iowa State College. Calling themselves the "Birch Hold Gang," they have met annually for thirty-eight years. Their first meetings were held in various Midwestern cities, and the twenty-fifth anniversary in 1968 was celebrated on campus in Ames. In recent years, their reunions have been held at a cottage owned by a former trainee at Iowa's Clear Lake. Two of the trainees have perfect attendance. During the annual gathering they place collect calls to any missing members. Calls have been made to France, Sweden, Switzerland, and Norway.[3]

At a number of the reunions, trainee contributions have provided some tangible evidence of the unit's existence on campus, such as V-12 scholarship funds at Milligan and Union colleges and a flagpole with a V-12 designation at Bethany College. Perhaps other such efforts will provide future students with a reminder of that World War II training plan.

The V-12 program was planned to produce officers for the U.S. Marine Corps and for the largest navy the world has ever seen. Although the war slammed to a halt in August of 1945, by the time the V-12 program terminated on June 30, 1946, it had delivered more than sixty thousand men who subsequently became Navy or Marine Corps officers. If the conflict had lasted longer, the war records of many V-12s would undoubtedly have been more significant, and the results of the program would have been evident for all to see. But the war did not linger, so the trainees quietly scattered to nearly every community in the nation to pursue their further education, start their careers, and contribute their share to the betterment of America.

Unfortunately, people who have chronicled the achievements of former V-12s did not know of their association with the program. Now that such a connection has been made, the results clearly speak for themselves: the V-12 program turned out to be a design for leadership.

Both the trainees and the nation should give credit to the civilian

THE MELODY LINGERS ON

educators, the naval officers, and the 131 colleges and universities involved in planning, organizing, and carrying out the V-12 program. Their production of a generation of patriots and leaders is one of the best things that has ever happened to the United States of America.

APPENDIX:
A GLIMPSE INTO
THE 131 V-12 SCHOOLS

THIS appendix includes a page for each of the 131 V-12 undergraduate units. The purpose is to provide a glimpse of each of the institutions during those war years. It is not possible to give a detailed picture of a V-12 unit in one page, but it is hoped that readers will gain some appreciation of the school's contribution to the overall success of the V-12 program. It is also expected that the V-12 trainees who served at the school will find some familiar references and will recognize the scenes in the photographs.

Instead of skipping around the country in alphabetical order, the units are presented in the format the Navy used, by naval districts and then by states alphabetically within each district. The map of the United States on page 367 identifies the districts; each district begins with a map showing the locations of the schools.

The information on each page has been assembled from many sources, including yearbooks, student newspapers, alumni magazines, official reports of both the college and the Navy, and interviews with and letters from trainees, officers, faculty members, and administrators. It includes a list of a few of the men who achieved some postwar prominence, who engaged in particularly interesting occupations, or who were otherwise representative of the V-12s from the unit. V-12s are now of retirement age, and many have taken early retirement. The positions indicated were held at some time, but not necessarily at the time of retirement or at the time the manuscript was completed.

Some of those listed are deceased. Where this is known by the author, it is indicated by an asterisk (*).

Because of their size, institutions with large units turned out more highly prominent individuals than can be listed. No attempt has been made to list every successful V-12; only a representative sample is intended.

Many of the trainees were stationed at two or more schools. Because

APPENDIX

of space considerations, the V-12s are ordinarily listed only once, usually in either the smallest of their schools or in the one first attended.

Tracing men after forty years would never be an easy task, but the application of the "right to privacy" statutes by some alumni offices has made it extremely difficult to locate men today. While trying to trace one of my V-12 shipmates from Korean duty days, for example, I stopped at the alumni office of the major university he had attended. I suspected I would not be able to get his address, so I just asked if he was alive. The young woman found his name but noted that they did not have a current address — mail had been returned from the one they had used. I asked if she could give me the name of the town where he formerly lived. "Oh, no," she said, "the privacy law won't allow that." "You mean to say you can't even give me a *bad* address?" "That's right."

Upon publication, additional V-12s will undoubtedly be brought to the author's attention. If an especially prominent V-12 has been overlooked in these school listings, it was not by design. It may have been because his biographical information in various reference works did not indicate his participation in the V-12 program or even service in the Navy. He may have ignored a request for confirmation of his V-12 participation, or it may have been a simple oversight by the author. The reader's indulgence is requested.

Where such information is available, reunions of V-12 units have been mentioned. V-12s who want information about such gatherings should contact the alumni office of their school.

The numbers used for the charts of V-12s are taken from quarterly Navy muster rolls from each V-12 unit at the end of March, June, September, and December. Those muster rolls arrive at a figure by showing the number already on board, reporting, and transferring during the period. Thus, because of subsequent transfers out of units, in all cases more trainees reported to a school in July of 1943 than were present at the end of September. This accounts for discrepancies between the figures quoted in the text and those shown in the chart. At a few units the Navy reports were incomplete or have been lost; in such cases figures supplied by the institutions have been used.

Some muster roll totals include NROTC trainees and therefore overstate the separate V-12 numbers. Such totals are indicated by the symbol (#).

In July 1945, 4,225 V-5 recruits were sent to V-12 units. While they remained classified as V-5s, they were invariably included in the V-12 unit muster rolls for that term and later terms, resulting in inaccurate V-12 figures. But, as mentioned in Chapter 37, "Changes in the Program," the V-5s took the same basic curriculum as V-12s, so there is no real reason to be concerned with this discrepancy.

APPENDIX

Commanding officers or Marine officers-in-charge were not usually changed at the beginning of an academic term, but lacking exact dates I have chosen to show the transfers of command as occurring at the start of trimesters. The reader should be aware that the actual transfers could have occurred several months earlier or later than the date given. Many commanding officers were promoted during the time of their service, but no attempt has been made to indicate their rise to higher rank.

A key problem in properly representing each school has been to obtain a picture showing V-12s in a recognizable campus scene. Many institutions simply have no original photographs of their V-12 unit. Thus, some of the pictures have of necessity been made from photographs that originally appeared in yearbooks or alumni magazines.

A few of the photos are of poor quality, but they are the best I could find. Any readers who have better original pictures of trainees on a particular campus could gladden the heart of the school's archivist by sending those photos (or photographic quality copies) to the school.

UNITED STATES NAVAL DISTRICTS
1943

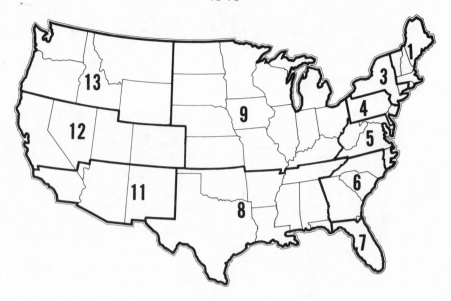

*Second and Tenth Naval Districts were outside
the continental United States.

First Naval District
Maine
1. Bates College

Massachusetts
2. College of the Holy Cross
3. Harvard University
4. Massachusetts Institute of Technology
5. Tufts College
6. Williams College
7. Worcester Polytechnic Institute

New Hampshire
8. Dartmouth College

Rhode Island
9. Brown University

Vermont
10. Middlebury College

Bates College Lewiston, Maine

The most memorable event for most Bates College V-12s was the two-day cruise from Portland to Camden and back on the *APC 94*. Cruising the Atlantic in winter made many men seasick. Trainees also remembered the weekly march to the Auburn YMCA for swimming class.

During the winter carnival of 1943–1944, the *APC 94* was sculpted in snow by Parker Hall V-12s and a V-12 leaning against a bar was created by the sailors of the "New Dorm." Next to the V-12 snowman was a sign that said, "Victory in 12 years or we fight."

The Quality Shop, George Ross Ice Cream Parlour, Sam's Italian Sandwiches, and Peterson's Bakery were patronized by the sailors. For the daring, there was the Blue Goose, an off-limits bar.

During the second year of operation, Navy smokers became a popular campus event. They started out being just for V-12s, but then turned coed.

The Bates unit had its first reunion in 1984, with forty-seven V-12s attending.

Some Bates V-12s: Winslow W. Bennett, chairman, Gold Run Mining Company, Vancouver, B.C.; Capt. Alan B. Crabtree, USN; Dexter Foss, vice president, Bankers Trust Company of New York; Capt. Clifford Gates, USN(MC); Joseph Houghteling, chairman, California Parks Commission; Robert F. Kennedy,* U.S. senator and attorney general; Donald Richter, attorney, Hartford, Conn., and trustee, Bates College; Leo Joseph Ryan,* congressman from California murdered by the followers of Jim Jones in Guyana; Louis Scolnick, Maine Supreme Court justice; Watson Sims, world news editor, Associated Press; and Davis P. Thurber, chairman, Bank of New Hampshire Corporation.

	1943		1944			1945	
	Jul.-Oct.	Nov.-Feb.	Mar.-Jun.	Jul.-Oct.	Nov.-Feb.	Mar.-Jun.	Jul.-Oct.
Navy	286	285	272	285	204	136	109
C.O.	Lt. John C. Cass						

College of the Holy Cross Worcester, Massachusetts

Robert U. Parish

V-12s arriving at this hundred-year-old Catholic men's school found the NROTC and a flight training school already in place. The V-12s were quartered in college dormitories and fed in commodious Kimball Hall. One of the changes at Holy Cross was the elimination of the required morning mass, but the Navy adjusted its schedule so that the period from 0700 to 0740 was free, thereby allowing Catholics to attend mass. A service was provided for non-Catholics at the same time; it was probably the first time Protestant services had been conducted at Holy Cross.

The V-12s carried on the athletic traditions of the Crusaders by fielding strong teams in all of the major sports. Swimming classes used the pools at the YMCA and two private clubs.

Although the high academic standards required extra effort from most of the trainees, they still had time for organizations like the Ski Club and the Yacht Club. A Naval ball was held each term. On weekends the Worcester USO was a popular spot, while Cosgrove's, the Eden, and Johnny Hines' were frequented by V-12s with a few dollars in their pockets.

The Tomahawk reported on weekly campus events, but the trainees started up their own *Beacon* and joined with the NROTCs in putting out the bimonthly *Cross and Anchor*. The Navy yearbook, *The Crest*, appeared in 1945 and 1946.

Distinguished campus visitors included Senator David Walsh, chairman of the Senate Naval Affairs Committee, who gave the commencement address in February of 1944, and Rear Adm. Robert Theobald, the commandant of the First Naval District, who reviewed the Holy Cross V-12s on Fitton Field just two months after they arrived on campus.

Some Holy Cross V-12s: Rabbi Balfour Brickner, Steven Wise Congregation, New York City; Rear Adm. William F. Clifford, Jr., USN; Judge John J. Gibbons, United States Court of Appeals, Third Circuit; Dr. Frank H. Healy, Jr., president, Lever Research; John J. Kearney, Jr., secretary, Long Island Lighting Company; J. William Middendorf II, secretary of the Navy and U.S. ambassador to European Community; Capt. James A. Mulligan, USN, prisoner of war in North Viet Nam and author (*The Hanoi Commitment*); and Frank Shakespeare, vice chairman, RKO-General, and ambassador to Portugal.

	1943		1944			1945			1946
	Jul.-Oct.	Nov.-Feb.	Mar.-Jun.	Jul.-Oct.	Nov.-Feb.	Mar.-Jun.	Jul.-Oct.	Nov.-Feb.	Mar.-Jun.
Navy	476	468	423	392	223	133	18	NA	102
C.O.	Capt. Guy Davis					Capt. F. C. Sachse			Capt. E. P. Hylant

NA = Not Available

Harvard University Cambridge, Massachusetts

Harvard University Archives

Henry M. Shine, Jr.

This 350-year-old school was swarming with servicemen when the V-12s arrived in July of 1943. The seven hundred trainees joined a total of seven thousand military men on campus plus another two thousand civilians. The total exceeded the peacetime enrollment by about one thousand.

The V-12s were housed and fed in Eliot and Kirkland houses. They formed the nucleus of the athletic teams and filled many important positions in other student activities.

When the V-12s arrived, the *Daily Crimson* had been discontinued and was replaced by the *Harvard Service News*, a semiweekly. The yearbook, the Harvard *Album*, gave some coverage to the V-12s. Classes were attended by Radcliffe College girls, who, while not officially enrolled, were considered "co-instructees." An unusual feature of the Harvard V-12 was the organization of "Tuckey's Terrors," a shore patrol squad that covered the Cambridge area.

Highlights of the V-12 tour: Winston Churchill's surprise visit to receive an honorary degree on Labor Day 1943, Gen. George Patton's appearance in June of 1945, and the honorary degree for Admiral Ernest King, chief of naval operations.

Some Harvard V-12s: Hans H. Angermueller, vice chairman, Citicorp; Dr. William A. Cox, chief of cardiovascular surgery, Brooke Army Medical Center; Dr. Robert P. Davis, professor of medical science, Brown University; Edward S. Finkelstein, chairman, R. H. Macy and Company; Drew Harrison, vice president, John Wanamaker and Company; Ernest Henderson III, president, Sheraton Corporation of America; Rear Adm. Thomas J. Hughes, USN; Cornelius F. Keating, senior vice president, CBS/Records Group; Herbert Keppler, publisher, *Modern Photography;* John U. Lemmon III, actor; Robert Marcus, president, Alumax; Lawrence I. Marks, executive vice president, Culbro Corporation; William J. Pruyn, chairman, Eastern Gas and Fuel Association; Dr. Kenneth G. Ryder, president, Northeastern University; Dr. Henry M. Shine, Jr., executive vice president, California Bankers Association; Dr. Lewis Slack, associate director, American Institute of Physics; L. Edwin Smart, chairman, Hilton International Company; Morton S. Waldfogel, chairman, Allied Plywood; and Judge Robert J. Ward, United States District Court, Southern District of New York.

	1943		1944		1945		
	Jul.-Oct.	Nov.-Feb.	Mar.-Jun.	Jul.-Oct.	Nov.-Feb.	Mar.-Jun.	Jul.-Oct.
Navy	728	783	718	691	391	221	2
C.O.	Capt. G. N. Barker			Capt. C. H. J. Keppler			

Massachusetts Institute Of Technology Cambridge, Massachusetts

The 910 V-12s reporting to MIT in the first term were mostly engineers, with a few specialists majoring in aerology, physics, and mathematics. They were quartered in the Graduate House, which had formerly accommodated slightly more than four hundred graduate students. A new mess hall, which later became the Campus Room, was installed in the building.

The academic standards of MIT were maintained. Of the 1,751 trainees who entered, 482 completed the degree requirements and 732 were returned to general duty or sent to boot camp (the rest were transferred to midshipmen's schools or to other V-12 or NROTC units). Although intercollegiate athletics had always been of minor importance at MIT, competition was maintained in ten sports during the V-12 period.

A V-12 Welfare Committee was formed to further the social lives of the trainees. It sponsored a number of dances, including the V-12 Anniversary Dance in July of 1944. Frequent Friday-night smokers were held in the mess hall.

Campus events were reported weekly by the *Tech*. The *Technique*, the yearbook, appeared in all three years of the V-12 program.

Some MIT V-12s: Dr. Robert M. Adams, secretary, Smithsonian Institution; William F. Blitzer, president, Lightolier; Dr. William F. Brace, chairman, department of earth and planetary sciences, MIT; David R. Clare, president, Johnson and Johnson; Lt. Gen. Hillman Dickinson, U.S. Army; Jack H. Frailey, director, MIT Student Financial Services; Theodore P.

MIT Museum

Heuchling, vice president, Arthur D. Little; Dr. R. Duncan Luce, chairman of the psychology department and Victor S. Thomas Professor of Psychology, Harvard University; Frederick J. Ross, Jr., president, Carborundum Company; Marshall Schober, president, Latrobe Steel Company; Dr. Joseph F. Shea, senior vice president for engineering, Raytheon Company; Roger P. Sonnabend, chairman, Sonesta International Hotels Corporation; Harold Thorkilsen, president, Ocean Spray Cranberries; James L. Waters, founder, Waters Associates; Rear Adm. Edward F. Welch, Jr., USN; and John W. L. White, chairman, Consumers Water Company.

	1943		1944			1945			1946
	Jul.-Oct.	Nov.-Feb.	Mar.-Jun.	Jul.-Oct.	Nov.-Feb.	Mar.-Jun.	Jul.-Oct.	Nov.-Feb.	Mar.-Jun.
Navy	910	853	854	855	761	699	418	235	34
C.O.	Capt. C. S. Joyce			Capt. R. H. Blair				Capt. W. H. Buracker	

Tufts College Medford, Massachusetts
(Now Tufts University)

Norman Peacor

The 792 V-12s reporting to Tufts were quartered in the Delta Upsilon fraternity house, Richardson, Stratton, and Wilson houses, and Dean, East, West, Fletcher, and Paige halls. The mess hall was located in Curtis, and the food service was provided by Seilers, a well-known Boston catering firm. By most accounts it was excellent chow! The V-12 offices and sick bay occupied the Theta Delta Chi fraternity house.

Tufts provided an excellent gymnasium, but since it had no pool, swimming classes were held at Mystic Lakes at the Medford Boat Club.

The *Tufts Weekly* continued throughout the war years, while other papers fell by the wayside. At the end of the V-12 program, a 104-page Navy yearbook, the *Shakedown*, was issued. It covered the final classes and the history of the Navy V-12 program.

One occasion recalled by all the V-12s was the big football game with Harvard in November of 1943. The entire unit marched from Medford through Somerville to Cambridge and then to Harvard Stadium, where the Tufts and Harvard V-12 and NROTC units tried their best to outdo each other in military performance. The football game was a memorable one,

with the Jumbos winning thirteen to seven over an "informal" Harvard team. (Harvard had officially given up football for that season.) Tufts beat an official Harvard team seven to six in 1945.

The Tufts V-12s were well represented on the athletic teams and in other activities. In addition, the trainees gave their all to happy hours, parties, and dances on the Tufts campus, and spent a good deal of liberty time with the girls at adjacent Jackson College.

Some Tufts V-12s: Dr. Philip Barkan, professor of mechanical engineering, Stanford University; Francis X. Bellotti, attorney general of Massachusetts; James F. Mulligan, vice president and secretary, Lukens; C. Norman Peacor, executive vice president and chief actuary, Massachusetts Mutual Life Insurance Company; David B. Preston, executive director, American Waterworks Association; Malcolm K. Shepard, president, Miller Printing Equipment Company; and S. Rayburn Watkins, president, Associated Industries of Kentucky and recipient of Key Award of American Society of Association Executives.

	1943		1944			1945			1946
	Jul.-Oct.	Nov.-Feb.	Mar.-Jun.	Jul.-Oct.	Nov.-Feb.	Mar.-Jun.	Jul.-Oct.	Nov.-Feb.	Mar.-Jun.
Navy	819	879	739	679	457	228	87	35	18
C.O.	Capt. P. B. Haines							Capt. D. V. Gladding	

Williams College Williamstown, Massachusetts

When the 440 V-12s arrived at Williams on July 1, 1943, they found that campus life was nearly nonexistent. The board of trustees had voted to drop intercollegiate athletics after July 1 for an indefinite period and the yearbook and the *Williams Record* were both discontinued for the duration.

Perhaps these factors contributed to a feeling on the part of many V-12s that some civilian students and a few faculty members resented the Navy's presence on the Williams campus. A highly visible animosity existed between the V-12s and the civilian students for a good part of the unit's stay, but early in October of 1945, a joint Navy-civilian weekend house party — the first in two years — was a huge success and left everyone feeling that unity had returned.

The V-12s started their own paper, the *Blinker,* which appeared weekly until November 1944, when its staff was instrumental in the revival of the *Williams Record* after an eighteen-month lapse.

The Williams happy hours, directed by C.Sp(A) Frank Scott, occurred about every two months. They were eagerly anticipated and much talked about afterwards. Comedians, bands, boxers, magicians, and spoofs on the commanding officers — those happy hours had it all. They became so popular that two shows were required — one for the trainees and one the next night for the general public, with proceeds from the second performance going to the Williamstown Boys' Club.

Weekend house parties were the main social event at Williams. Williams was a men's college; dates for the

Williamsiana Collection, Williams College

men came from most of the women's schools in New England.

Like the newspaper, intercollegiate athletics were eventually revived. Fifty-four men turned out for the baseball team in 1945. Still, because of the distances and scarcity of opponents, they were only able to schedule five games.

Some Williams V-12s: Dr. Richard F. Fenno, Jr., Distinguished University Professor of Political Science, University of Rochester; Rear Adm. Robert B. McClinton, USN; R. Gordon McGovern, president, Campbell Soup Company; Edward N. Ney, chairman, Young and Rubicam; Frederick H. Sacksteder, foreign service officer, U.S. State Department; William S. Sneath, chairman, Union Carbide Corporation; and William H. Webster, director, Federal Bureau of Investigation.

	1943		1944			1945	
	Jul.-Oct.	Nov.-Feb.	Mar.-Jun.	Jul.-Oct.	Nov.-Feb.	Mar.-Jun.	Jul.-Oct.
Navy	440	400	393	504	367	239	185
C.O.	Lcdr. H. C. Walters					Lt. R. M. Bateman	

Worcester Polytechnic Institute Worcester, Massachusetts

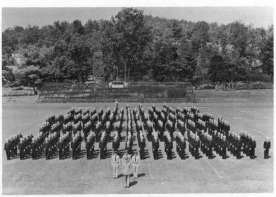

WPI Archives

Erling Lagerholm

An all-engineering unit, the Worcester Polytechnic Institute V-12s were quartered in Sanford Riley and Stratton halls. Some were reservists from WPI; many others came from other engineering schools that did not have V-12 units, such as Lafayette College and General Motors Institute.

Although a regular Navy captain was the commanding officer of both WPI and the unit across town at Holy Cross, the officer-in-charge was Lt.(jg) Albert J. Schwieger, USNR, who had been a Worcester Poly professor just a few months before and later became head of the department of economics, government, and business. This was apparently the only case of such a home-school assignment in the V-12 program.

The *Peddler*, the WPI yearbook, reported that many of the traditional class competitions continued despite the military presence on campus. The sophomore-freshman rope pull, interclass track and swimming meets, interclass football and soccer games, and such events as the "paddle rush"

and the "tech carnival" continued as in prewar days.

WPI fielded teams in most sports, and the trainees carried on many of the regular campus activities. At least seven V-12s have served as alumni trustees on the WPI board of trustees.

Some WPI V-12s: Roy Baharian, group vice president, Diamond International; John Lott Brown, president, University of South Florida; William G. Daly, president, General Plastics; Walter A. Densmore, senior vice president, Norton Company; Joseph W. Gibson, Jr., senior technical specialist, E. I. DuPont Company and winner of an Olney Medal, awarded by the American Association of Textile Chemists and Colorists for outstanding achievement in textile chemistry; Dr. Stuart D. Kearney II, president, Kearney and Son, manufacturer of customized golf clubs; John C. Metzger, Jr., group vice president, photosystems and electronic products, E. I. DuPont Company; and Albert F. Myers, group vice president, Lear Siegler.

	1943		1944			1945			1946
	Jul.-Oct.	Nov.-Feb.	Mar.-Jun.	Jul.-Oct.	Nov.-Feb.	Mar.-Jun.	Jul.-Oct.	Nov.-Feb.	Mar.-Jun.
Navy	322	315	310	310	283	249	165	232	15
C.O.	Capt. Guy E. Davis					Capt. F. C. Sachse		Capt. E. P. Hylant	

Dartmouth College Hanover, New Hampshire

Dartmouth College Archives

Dartmouth College, with two thousand Navy and Marine trainees on July 1, 1943, was the largest unit in the nation. The sailors occupied all of the dorms west of Main Street; the marines were quartered in Topliff, New Hampshire, and South Fayerweather halls. The mess halls were in Freshman Commons and Thayer; sick bay occupied the first two floors of South Massachusetts Hall.

In August of 1943 the new V-12s were successively reviewed by Secretary of the Navy Frank Knox, Undersecretary of the Navy James V. Forrestal, and New Hampshire gover-

nor Robert O. Blood. Discipline was unduly strict for the first two and one-half months, but a change in command at that time brought about a more reasonable approach.

The 1944 *Aegis,* the yearbook, gave an exceptionally detailed report of the life of the V-12s at Dartmouth. The *Daily Dartmouth* had suspended publication for the duration; the *Dartmouth Log* was the weekly replacement, concentrating on campus and local news.

The trainees took part in a variety of college activities, from the Dartmouth Outing Club to the Dartmouth Play-

	1943		1944			1945			1946
	Jul.-Oct.	Nov.-Feb.	Mar.-Jun.	Jul.-Oct.	Nov.-Feb.	Mar.-Jun.	Jul.-Oct.	Nov.-Feb.	Mar.-Jun.
Navy	1337	1412	1614	1557	1125	862	# 627	# 799	529
C.O.	@	Capt. Damon B. Cummings							
Marines	622	401	242	178	182	161	146	118	68
O-in-C	Maj. John Howland				Maj. James J. Anderson			Capt. Anthony A. Akstin	

\# Includes NROTC   @ Cdr. William F. Bullis, Maj. John Howland

Dartmouth College

ers. The college provided wonderful recreational facilities, including the Robinson Hall Rec Center for "stags" and the Hostess House for V-12s who had dates or whose parents were visiting them. A weekly dance for a single V-12 company was given in the trophy room of the gym. The campuswide dance each term was the Quarterdeck Hop.

The 1943 football squad, dominated by V-12s, had a six-and-one record, losing only to Pennsylvania, seven to six.

Some Dartmouth V-12s: Norman Barker, Jr., chairman, First Interstate Bank of California; Owen B. Butler, chairman, Procter and Gamble Company; Harry T. Carter, general counsel, U.S. Information Service; Dr. John H. Copenhaver, Jr., professor of biology, Dartmouth College; Judge William B. Enright, U.S. Court for the Southern District of California; Joel Goldberg, chairman, Rich's; Frank J. Guarini, congressman from New Jersey; Holman Head, executive vice president, Alabama State Chamber of Commerce; Lawrence E. Lindars, vice chairman, C. R. Bard; Thomas J. McCollow, chairman, the (Milwaukee) Journal Company; J. Donald McNamara, president, the Interpublic Group of Companies; Gilbert O'Day Robert, chairman, Albany (New York) Savings Bank; Dr. Walter R. Peterson, governor of New Hampshire; Robert M. Schaeberle, chairman, Nabisco; Maj. Gen. Adolph G. Schwenk, USMC; Dr. Sheldon J. Segal, officer, Rockefeller Foundation, and recipient of United Nations' World Population Award, 1984; Dr. Walter A. Snickenberger, vice president for student affairs, Southern Methodist University; Ronald I. Spiers, U.S. undersecretary of state; Dr. Wilcomb E. Washburn, director, Office of American Studies, the Smithsonian Institution; and Richard W. Young, president, Houghton Mifflin Company.

Brown University Providence, Rhode Island

When the V-12s arrived at this 179-year-old men's school, they found it already oriented somewhat to Navy ways because of the NROTC unit. Trainees had the opportunity to take field trips to the many nearby naval stations and to take some one-day cruises on small coastal craft, an experience unavailable in many V-12 units.

The 1943 Brown *Herald-Record* was a merger of the Brown *Daily Herald* and the Pembroke *Record*. It was agreed that a Pembroke College girl would be editor in chief, to ensure continuity. V-12s were welcomed to the staff of the new *Brunavian* magazine, which had been started just prior to V-12 by the NROTC. This bimonthly and *Liber Brunensis*, the yearbook, gave excellent coverage to the V-12 unit.

Brown participated in most varsity sports, with the 1943 and 1944 football teams enjoying successful seasons. The intercompany sports schedule was intensive. It featured ten different competitions, including rope climbing and an obstacle course competition. When cold weather began, the chiefs even set up an obstacle course in the gym. The excellent strength test scores reflected the concentration on conditioning.

The Ship's Service Board was organized to coordinate planning for social functions and to put on dances and other entertainments financed by profits from the soft drink machines. The "Scuttlebutt" show in early 1944 depended upon V-12 participation.

The hurricane that roared up the coast in September of 1944 was one of the most remembered events. Trees were felled on the campus, and as the water ran deep in the Providence streets, many V-12s went out in the early hours to survey the scene.

Some Brown V-12s: Dr. Vernon R. Alden, president, Ohio University; Charles H. Doebler IV, director of admissions, Brown University; Roger W. Frost, president, Frost Manufacturing Company; Edward J. King, governor of Massachusetts; William J. Roach, professor of journalism and communications, University of North Florida; Melvin E. Sinn, foreign service officer, U.S. Department of State; and Dr. Charles H. Watts, president, Bucknell College.

	1943		1944			1945			1946
	Jul.-Oct.	Nov.-Feb.	Mar.-Jun.	Jul.-Oct.	Nov.-Feb.	Mar.-Jun.	Jul.-Oct.	Nov.-Feb.	Mar.-Jun.
Navy	424	472	491	386	232	149	76	46	25
C.O.	Capt. H. M. Briggs			Capt. E. A. Lofquist			Capt. C. G. Gesen		Capt. F. D. McCorkle

Middlebury College   Middlebury, Vermont

Middlebury College Special Collections

The trainees who reported to Middlebury were quartered in Hepburn and Gifford halls. They soon dubbed themselves the "Otter Creek Fleet." Nearly 60 percent of the V-12s were freshmen, which put heavy demands on the faculty for instruction in math and physics.

After only two reviews, the V-12 unit was inspected by Secretary of the Navy Frank Knox on August 6, 1943. He addressed the trainees, urging that "Every moment of time you have in training for these tasks is immensely valuable, and I pray and beseech you to make the most of it."

The first military ball was held on September 2. Starting in June of 1944 a Naval weekend or Naval day culminated the social life at the end of each term.

V-12s were recruited to help the local apple growers harvest their crop in 1943. That fall they were also reviewed by Rear Adm. Robert A. Theobald, USN, commandant of the First Naval District, and by Vermont governor William A. Wills. The *Middlebury*
Campus reported at regular intervals on the tensions between the civilian and Navy students. The former protested that the V-12s lacked school spirit and did not take part in many activities, and the sailors countered that they were not really welcomed to those activities.

The Middlebury Winter Carnival was covered by *Life* magazine in 1945.

Some Middlebury V-12s: Robert M. Ajemian, Washington bureau chief, *Time* magazine; Charles F. Baird, chairman, INCO, and former undersecretary of the Navy; Willard C. Butcher, chairman, Chase Manhattan Bank; Richard Kinneman, coach, Arlington Heights (Ill.) High School, elected to Illinois Basketball Coaches Hall of Fame, 1978; Jack F. Kofoed, chairman, Binney and Smith Company; Daniel Patrick Moynihan, U.S. senator from New York; Francis J. Palamara, executive vice president, ARA Services; and Frederick C. Weiss, Jr., senior vice president and sales manager, Knight-Ridder Newspapers.

	1943		1944			1945	
	Jul.-Oct.	Nov.-Feb.	Mar.-Jun.	Jul.-Oct.	Nov.-Feb.	Mar.-Jun.	Jul.-Oct.
Navy	479	457	452	432	298	224	183
C.O.	Lt. Edward M. Clark		Lcdr. C. L. Alderman				Lt. L. F. Lybarger

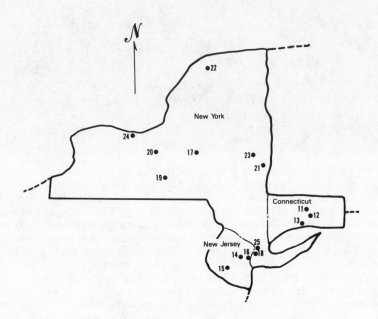

Third Naval District

Connecticut

11. Trinity College
12. Wesleyan University
13. Yale University

New Jersey

14. Drew University
15. Princeton University
16. Stevens Institute of Technology

New York

17. Colgate University
18. Columbia University
19. Cornell University
20. Hobart College
21. Rensselaer Polytechnic Institute
22. St. Lawrence University
23. Union College
24. University of Rochester
25. Webb Institute of Naval Architecture

Trinity College Hartford, Connecticut

Perhaps the best known V-12 at Trinity College was the canine mascot, "4.0." When Hartford's papers referred to him as "HO" after he marched ahead of the V-12s in a parade in Hartford, Prof. Henry A. Perkins wrote a strong letter to the editors pointing out their blunder and listing the attributes of the mascot. He mentioned that, in the classroom, he was "quiet, orderly, and discreet; in fact his conduct is quite human, including going to sleep if the lecture bores him."

The 410 V-12s arriving on July 1, 1943, found that of twenty organizations, only six were still active. The yearbook was suspended for the duration, and the *Trinity Tripod* was struggling to keep its weekly schedule. Unfortunately, the *Tripod* only lasted until 1944.

The all-Navy basketball squad in 1943–44 had a season that ranked among the best in the school's history, and the 1944 track team was undefeated in four meets.

The V-12s held six Sports Nights, which featured boxing and wrestling matches. They also put on four dramatic productions, including a version of "Julius Caesar" that portrayed Navy life at Trinity College.

The V-12s were quartered in the college dormitories and took their meals in Cook dining hall. The contingent leaving for midshipmen's schools in October of 1944 presented to the chapel a hand-carved pew end topped with a bust of John Paul Jones. On the pew end was a V-12 version of Jones's famous words: "We have not yet begun to fight."

Prominent campus visitors were Governor Raymond E. Baldwin and Rear Adm. Randall Jacobs, chief of personnel.

Some Trinity V-12s: Robert H. Allen, vice president, ITT Corporation; the Right Reverend Edgar Otis Charles, dean, Episcopal Divinity School, Cambridge, Mass.; John J. J. Jones, New York Supreme Court justice; Dr. Peter E. Stokes, chief of the division of psychobiology, New York Hospital–Cornell Medical Center, New York City; and the Right Reverend William G. Weinhauer, Episcopal bishop of Western North Carolina.

	1943		1944			1945	
	Jul.-Oct.	Nov.-Feb.	Mar.-Jun.	Jul.-Oct.	Nov.-Feb.	Mar.-Jun.	Jul.-Oct.
Navy	395	397	341	360	232	135	135
C.O.	Lt. Ives Atherton			Lt. F. E. Mueller			Lt. V. J. Conroy

Wesleyan University Middletown, Connecticut

When the Wesleyan V-12s arrived in July of 1943, they found part of the campus already occupied by a Navy Flight Preparatory School. The V-12s were housed in North College and spent some of their time drilling on Andrus Field.

The Southern New England Telephone Company thoughtfully provided a "Handbook for Navy V-12 Trainees at Wesleyan University," a little blue book that could fit in a jumper pocket. It contained maps of the business district and campus as well as information about demerits and other vital matters.

Wesleyan's president, Dr. Victor L. Butterfield, was adept at tapping the Bureau of Naval Personnel for commencement speakers. On February 23, 1945, Comdr. William S. Thomson, then head of the V-12 program, spoke in the company of Governor Raymond E. Baldwin of Connecticut.

Four months later the graduation address was given by Capt. Edward R. Durgin, USN, assistant director of training.

Variety shows featuring purely mythical characters like "Lieutenant Splurge," smokers to welcome new trainees, and plenty of dances kept the Wesleyan V-12s busy. The show by Glenn Miller and his 418th Army Air Corps band in September of 1943 was one of the highlights of the Wesleyan V-12 program. Another was the Abe Lyman Orchestra's appearance in the Coca-Cola Spotlight Band series in July of 1944.

Some Wesleyan V-12s: David R. Baldwin, U.S. assistant secretary of commerce; Lloyd W. Elston, senior vice president, Cadbury Schweppes; Seth S. Faison, chairman, Brooklyn Academy of Music; and Dr. Kenneth E. Mortenson, dean of engineering, Rensselaer Polytechnic Institute.

	1943		1944			1945	
	Jul.-Oct.	Nov.-Feb.	Mar.-Jun.	Jul.-Oct.	Nov.-Feb.	Mar.-Jun.	Jul.-Oct.
Navy	134	NA	146	327	252	210	NA
C.O.	Lt. Lyle L. Morris		Lt. Henry C. Herge				

NA = Not available

Yale University   New Haven, Connecticut

Yale University Archives

Yale's wholehearted welcome to the trainees made it unique among the Ivy League schools. Its traditional system of dividing the living units into "colleges" where the trainees both lived and ate meant they didn't have to march to chow. Branford, Davenport, Pierson, and Saybrook colleges housed the V-12s. Marines and sailors shared the same houses.

The master's house was the center of activity, and the master and his wife did their best to make "Yale men" out of trainees. V-12s were invited to the master's house for weeknight song fests, which included lots of conversation, beer, and other refreshments. Girlfriends visiting on weekends could occupy a guest room in the master's house.

The "fellows of the college," who were faculty members selected by the master, were frequent guests at dinner, which gave V-12s a better chance to know their instructors.

Some other V-12 recollections: the late-night civilian radios and noise followed at 0600 by the bugler; the taunts (and pop bottles) sent back and forth between V-12s and Army Air Corps trainees; and Good Humor bars being hoisted up in shoes that had been lowered to the street vendors.

Some Yale V-12s: Judge James L. Buckley, U.S. Court of Appeals, District of Columbia, and former U.S. senator from New York; James F. Cobey, Jr., president, United Illuminating Company; John H. Field, vice president for strategic planning,

	1943		1944			1945			1946
	Jul.-Oct.	Nov.-Feb.	Mar.-Jun.	Jul.-Oct.	Nov.-Feb.	Mar.-Jun.	Jul.-Oct.	Nov.-Feb.	Mar.-Jun.
Navy	1079	NA	NA	NA	NA	NA	NA	NA	NA
C.O.	Capt. C. C. Gill					Cdr. H. O'D. Hunter		Capt. P. E. Pendleton	
Marines	298	241	143	91	121	156	161	135	54
O-in-C	Maj. Thomas J. Cross				@	Capt. John J. Smith			2 · 3

NA = Not available   @ Capt. Robert L. Raclin   2. Capt. C. O. J. Grussendorf   3. Capt. D. W. Banks

Yale University

Union Carbide Corporation; James J. Harford, executive director, American Institute of Aeronautics and Astronautics; Townsend W. Hoopes, president, Association of American Publishers, and former undersecretary of the U.S. Air Force; Victor K. Kiam II, president, Remington Products; Barton H. Lippincott, chairman, J.B. Lippincott; Rear Adm. Richard Lyon, USNR, first reserve officer recalled to active duty as deputy chief of Navy Reserve; Charles M. Mathias, Jr., senator from Maryland; Walter J. McNerney, president, Blue Cross/Blue Shield of Illinois; Robert E. Mercer, chairman, Goodyear Tire and Rubber Company; William S. Moorhead, congressman from Pennsylvania; David S. Potter, vice president, General Motors Corporation, and undersecretary of the Navy; Bruce M. Rockwell, chairman, Colorado National Bank, Denver; Dr. Philip R. Shriver, president, Miami University; John W. Wall, president, Rhode Island Hospital Trust National Bank; Hans W. Wanders, chairman, Wachovia Corporation; and Rear Adm. Thomas T. Wetmore III, U.S. Coast Guard.

Drew University Madison, New Jersey

Drew University had given up hopes of landing a V-12 unit, but on June 7, 1943, it was officially notified that it had been selected. Feverish preparations during the next three weeks brought Drew to full readiness to receive the 192 men assigned there. The previously planned summer session was canceled. The V-12s were quartered and fed in Hoyt-Bowne Hall, which had formerly housed the divinity students of Drew Theolcgical School. At first, the trainees were served their meals at tables for four, but the arrival of the cafeteria equipment in September thereafter sent them through chow lines like other V-12s.

On July 1, 1943, for the first time, coeds were admitted to Drew "for the duration," and Drew continued to admit women after the war. Between the V-12s and the coeds, the enrollment at Brothers College was higher than it had ever been. Another interesting change was that, although Drew was a Methodist school, more Roman Catholics than Methodists were enrolled.

Drew fielded an excellent basketball team, with a fourteen-and-three record in 1943–1944. One of its losses (43 to 42) was to nationally ranked St. Joseph's of Philadelphia. Drew played the last three minutes of the game with only four men because the rest of the team had fouled out. It was the best basketball squad in the history of the Circuit Riders. They outscored their opposition 1,042 to 652 and averaged 61.3 points a game.

The *Drew Acorn* reported weekly

Dr. H. Simester   Drew University Archives

events on campus. The *Oak Leaves*, the school's yearbook, came out on schedule.

Some Drew V-12s: Walter Bullwinkel, vice president of operations, Thomson Company, Thomson, Ga.; John Cimaglia, vice president, New York Life Insurance Company; Comdr. Milton Gassow, USN(Ret.), senior vice president, McGraw-Hill; Ely N. Gonick, senior vice president of technology, International Paper Company; John O. Hedden, vice president, Kidder, Peabody; the Reverend Harry L. Norlander, Presbyterian missionary; and Dr. Arthur H. Schomp, vice president, Merrill Lynch.

	1943		1944			1945		
	Jul.-Oct.	Nov.-Feb.	Mar.-Jun.	Jul.-Oct.	Nov.-Feb.	Mar.-Jun.	Jul.-Oct.
Navy	192	190	185	196	190	125	116
C.O.	Lt. Ellis F. Hartford	Lt. E. O. Olson		Lt. Alfred Busselle			

Princeton University Princeton, New Jersey

Princeton University Archives

At the start of V-12 at Princeton, the military comprised 75 percent of the two thousand students on campus. The unit had strict discipline, which required that the V-12 regulars march to classes. They had a constant companion during their marching — "Red Dog," the faithful Irish setter mascot of the unit.

Many Navy dignitaries paid official visits to the Princeton campus, including Secretary of the Navy James V. Forrestal, a Princeton alumnus, and Lt. Gen. Alexander A. Vandegrift, commandant of the U.S. Marine Corps.

On liberty or leave, most V-12s rode "the Rattler," the connecting train to the main line of the Pennsylvania Railroad.

The most spectacular event during V-12: the fire that destroyed the Princeton gymnasium in the early morning of May 24, 1944. The 1945 *Bric-A-Brac* said, "Few who saw it will ever forget the spectacle of that great Gothic bastion filled with flames, which poured from the tower as from a chimney." The alarm had been turned in by the V-12 on watch in Little Hall.

Some Princeton V-12s: Dr. Frederick G. Hammitt, professor of nuclear

	1943		1944			1945			1946
	Jul.-Oct.	Nov.-Feb.	Mar.-Jun.	Jul.-Oct.	Nov.-Feb.	Mar.-Jun.	Jul.-Oct.	Nov.-Feb.	Mar.-Jun.
Navy	405	446	NA	NA	276	176	NA	NA	# 403
C.O.	Capt. G. E. Sage		Capt. Roy Dudley		Capt. F. G. Richards				
Marines	241	199	139	97	157	155	147	116	78
O-in-C	Capt. Ralph Powell			Capt. Irving B. Hayes			Capt. Joe A. Gayle		@

Includes NROTC   @ Capt. Robert L. Gillis   NA = Not available

Princeton University

engineering, University of Michigan; Dr. James M. Hester, president, New York University; Stephen K. Kurtz, principal, Phillips Exeter Academy; William M. Miller, executive vice president, Elizabeth Arden; Thomas J. Moore, Jr., chairman, Virginia Electric and Power Company; Robert J. Newhouse, Jr., vice chairman, Marsh and McLennan Companies; Steven E. Nightingale, treasurer, Union Carbide Corporation; Thomas R. Pellett, senior vice president and chief financial offi-cer, Pet; Gen. Arthur J. Poillon, USMC; Dr. Thomas A. Pond, executive vice president and acting president, State University of New York at Stony Brook; Fred C. Poppe, president, Poppe-Tyson, New York City; Herbert S. Schlosser, president, National Broadcasting Company; Dr. Gabriel F. Tucker, Jr., president, American Laryngological Association; and John L. Weinberg, chairman, Goldman, Sachs.

Stevens Institute of Technology   Hoboken, New Jersey

The 513 V-12s reporting to this all-male engineering school on the banks of the Hudson River could at least see the bright lights of Manhattan, even if their grades didn't always permit them to visit.

Stevens fielded teams in most sports, and the V-12s provided most of the manpower. Trainees took part in the Glee Club, Yacht Club, and Navy band. Stevens also had its share of dances, including the Sophomore Hop, the Harvest Moon Ball, and a prom. It was noted in the *Stute*, the campus newspaper, that prom tickets had to be purchased in advance and that no refund would be made "except to Navy men who are restricted."

The Stevens Date Bureau lined up men to attend weekend dances at Montclair State Teachers College and other nearby schools.

If campus entertainment was at low ebb, V-12s sometimes sought comfort at Bill Gallagher's Tavern, formerly called the Stute Shop.

Adm. Harry E. Yarnell, former commander of the United States Asiatic Fleet, reviewed the Stevens unit in October of 1944.

Some Stevens V-12s: Rear Adm. Thomas J. Allshouse, USN; Joseph H. Anderer, president, Revlon; Dr. Robert F. Cotellessa, professor of electrical engineering and computer science, and provost, Stevens Institute of Technology; Dr. Richard A. Easterlin, professor of economics, University of Pennsylvania (Pittsburgh); Oscar M. Gossett, chairman, Saatchi and Saatchi Compton Worldwide; Dr. Robin B. Gray, Regents' Professor and associate director of aerospace engineering, Georgia Institute of Technology; Earl W. Mallick, vice president for public affairs, U.S. Steel; Wallace Markert, Jr., vice president for research and development, Babcock and Wilcox Company; and W. T. Ylvisaker, chairman, Gould.

	1943		1944			1945			1946
	Jul.-Oct.	Nov.-Feb.	Mar.-Jun.	Jul.-Oct.	Nov.-Feb.	Mar.-Jun.	Jul.-Oct.	Nov.-Feb.	Mar.-Jun.
Navy	510	511	498	509	308	263	203	369	268
C.O.	Lt. R. E. Boyles						Lcdr. J. A. Permenter		

Colgate University   Hamilton, New York

Colgate University Archives

Colgate's fraternity houses were used to quarter the Marine and Navy V-12s who arrived there July 1, 1943. Sixteen months later the V-12s were moved into the university dormitories just vacated by the departing V-5s. At all times, they were fed at the Student Union dining hall, which was an excellent operation.

The yearbook was suspended for the duration, but the *Maroon* came out weekly, as scheduled. The monthly Colgate magazine, formerly known as the *Colgate Banter*, became the *Colgate-Navy Banter*; in 1945 it reverted to the old title.

The 1943 football team had a good season with a five, three, and one record. The basketball squads in the first two V-12 years turned in records of eleven and five and twelve and four, among the best in Colgate's history. The 1943–1944 hockey team went four and two; opportunities for intercollegiate games were limited.

The Colgate Co-op was the on-campus soda fountain and general student center. For most of the time, half of the V-12s on liberty were restricted to a five-mile limit and the other half faced a fifty-mile limit. This put considerable pressure on the recreational facilities in Hamilton, so the USO was opened on November 13, 1943, and became the trainees' focal point on weekends. Girls came from Utica, Rome, and other nearby towns for weekly USO dances at the Student

	1943		1944			1945			1946
	Jul.-Oct.	Nov.-Feb.	Mar.-Jun.	Jul.-Oct.	Nov.-Feb.	Mar.-Jun.	Jul.-Oct.	Nov.-Feb.	Mar.-Jun.
Navy	213	253	280	278	227	190	137	154	122
C.O.	Lcdr. Omar C. Held						@	Lcdr. R. G. Rishel	
Marines	193	166	111	81	92	118	128	88	58
O-in-C	Capt. Leonard M. Foley			Capt. Grenville Clark, Jr.			Capt. Robert F. O'Brien	Capt. Andrew M. Zimmer	

@ Lcdr. E. J. Aylstock

Colgate University

Union. The Marine unit organized a successful stage show during the first term, and other trainee variety shows were undertaken during later terms. V-12s also participated in the University Theatre for more serious drama.

Highlights of the V-12 stay were the appearances of Secretary of the Navy Frank Knox, and the Coca-Cola Spotlight Band program featuring Shep Fields and his orchestra.

Nearly one-third of the 736 sailors and 402 marines who went through V-12 at Colgate returned after the war to obtain their bachelor's degrees.

Some Colgate V-12s: Robert F. Ehinger, vice president and secretary, Western Electric Company; James L. Hoagland, president, Graybar Electric Company; J. Lawrence Hughes, president, William Morrow and Company; Robert E. Rhodes, editor, Corpus Christi *Caller;* Thomas F. Richardson, chairman, Union Trust Company, Stamford, Conn.; Donald A. Schaefer, president, Prentice-Hall; Robert S. Taylor, art critic and book columnist, *Boston Globe;* Blair Vedder, chairman, Needham International; and Dr. Charles E. Weaver, director of the School of Geophysical Sciences, Georgia Institute of Technology.

Columbia University New York, New York

National Archives

The 549 V-12s reporting to Columbia University were quartered in Hartley and Livingston halls and faced what was reputed to be the toughest discipline of any unit in the country. The commanding officer was Capt. J. K. Richards, who was later promoted to commodore. He was also the skipper of the Columbia Midshipmen's School (formerly the *Prairie State*), and he apparently expected the V-12s to maintain the same standards of conduct and discipline as the midshipmen. When they didn't, they came to regret it. At least the Columbia V-12s did not have any fears about meeting the discipline standards at midshipmen's schools, whether at Columbia or elsewhere.

The academic side of the program at Columbia was just as tough, so the survivors were among the fittest V-12s produced.

The *Spectator* ceased to be a daily during the war, and for a while it came out only weekly. The Columbia version of "happy hour" was called "the Varsity Show."

The demands of the Columbia V-12 program kept many athletes from reporting for the intercollegiate teams, so the school's record was generally undistinguished.

Social life on campus was reported as "zilch," but with Manhattan's hot spots and USO activities readily at hand, the trainees didn't really care.

Some Columbia V-12s: Clarence L. French, Jr., chairman, National Steel and Ship Building Corporation, and chairman of the Webb Institute of Naval Architecture; Dr. Robert L. Graves, professor, Graduate School of Business, University of Chicago; Arthur Hauspurg, chairman, Consolidated Edison Company; Dr. Wilmot N. Hess, director, National Center for Atmospheric Research; Dr. Sheldon E. Isakoff, director of engineering research and development, DuPont Company; Ralph D. Ketcham, senior vice president of the Lighting Business Group, General Electric; Edwin A. Kiernan, Jr., senior vice president, general counsel, and secretary, the Interpublic Group of Companies; Charles G. Kiskaddon, Jr., president, Alcoa Steamship Company; Dr. James L. Lubkin, professor of civil engineering, Michigan State University; Dr. Joseph D. Matarazzo, professor and department head, University of Oregon Health Sciences; and Warren L. Serenbetz, chairman of the executive committee and CEO, Interpool Limited.

	1943		1944			1945				1946
	Jul.-Oct.	Nov.-Feb.	Mar.-Jun.	Jul.-Oct.	Nov.-Feb.	Mar.-Jun.	Jul.-Oct.	Nov.-Feb.	Mar.-Jun.
Navy	549	561	536	475	421	281	# 366	# 321	# 216
C.O.	Capt. J. K. Richards						Capt. T. F. Wellings		

Includes NROTC

Cornell University Ithaca, New York

In the fall of 1943 the Cornell campus was aswarm with military uniforms. There were Army programs, Navy officer programs (including diesel school and general service school), and 1,642 V-12s, including 330 marines. Nearly three-fourths of the V-12s were engineering students; the rest were premeds and basics. In March of 1944, the general service school was phased out and replaced by a new midshipmen's school.

The V-12s were quartered in twenty-one fraternity houses, five small residences, and a section of Baker dormitory. They stood twenty-four-hour watch duty, which meant that each man missed two or three classes a month. Trainees were fed in the mess hall built earlier to accommodate all of the Navy personnel on campus.

Academic life at Cornell was very demanding, but there was still time for a bit of social life and other campus activities. The USO in Barnes Hall had weekday dances between 1900 and 2000, and the V-12s met coeds in some unusual ways, such as picking beans to meet the emergency needs of the farmers in Cortland County. The 425 V-12s who volunteered for the Saturday bean harvest joined nearly one hundred coeds to bring in the $200,000 crop.

Cornell participated in all major sports and had a full program of intra-

	1943		1944			1945			1946
	Jul.-Oct.	Nov.-Feb.	Mar.-Jun.	Jul.-Oct.	Nov.-Feb.	Mar.-Jun.	Jul.-Oct.	Nov.-Feb.	Mar.-Jun.
Navy	1320	1443	1379	1383	1063	904	617	# 868	# 432
C.O.	Capt. D. W. Chippendale								
Marines	291	222	177	121	148	129	139	105	49
O-in-C	Capt. William J. Dumas				Maj. Wilson Stradley		Maj. William E. Sperling III		

Includes NROTC

Cornell University

murals. The *Cornellian*, the yearbook, was published each year and gave an excellent account of campus life.

Some Cornell V-12s: Dr. James F. Carley, professor of chemical engineering, University of Colorado; Dr. Edmund T. Cranch, president, Worcester Polytechnic Institute, and president, Wang Institute; George B. Dessart, Jr., vice president, CBS Broadcasting Group; Harold F. Faught, group vice president, Emerson Electric Company; William D. Fugazy, chairman, Fugazy International; Horace R. Johnson, president, Watkins-Johnson Company; Dr. Louis Lowenstein, president, Supermarkets General Corporation, and professor of law, Columbia University; Francis H. Ludington, Jr., chairman, Chase Bag Company; Aleck M. Mackinnon, president, Ciba-Geigy Corporation; Franklyn W. Meyer, general manager, International Division, General Foods, and co-inventor, freeze-dried coffee process; Thomas S. Murphy, chairman, ABC-TV; John B. Rhodes, Jr., vice chairman, Booz, Allen and Hamil-

ton; Charles E. Silberman, author (*Crisis in Black and White*); Dr. William C. Stewart, professor of statistics, Temple University; and Sanford M. Whittwell, executive vice president, National Distillers and Chemical Corporation.

Hobart College   Geneva, New York

The 393 V-12s reporting to this Episcopal men's school on the shores of thirty-five-mile-long Seneca Lake were glad to find that it was adjacent to a sister school, William Smith College. The V-12s were quartered in Hobart's Medbery Hall and in Geneva, Comstock, and Miller halls, which had formerly housed William Smith students.

Campus life included "happy hours," which involved skits, concerts, boxing, and guest speakers, and "religious exercises," which were conducted each Friday evening in the college chapel. The athletic teams consisted almost entirely of V-12s. In the first season, the basketball squad had a very respectable ten-and-seven record against tough competition. Two of the losses were to Cornell University.

The *Herald* was the Hobart weekly; the *Echo,* the yearbook, appeared only in a very slim version in 1944. The V-12s, however, published their own pictorial record of the unit (under the name *All Hands*) from its beginning until October of 1944.

Newsweek's August 2, 1943, story told the nation about the Hobart unit, citing it as a typical example of what the Navy and colleges had arranged in the nationwide V-12 program. Tommy Dorsey and his orchestra appeared on November 8, 1943, in the Hobart gym as part of the Coca-Cola Spotlight Band program, which was carried by 160 stations around the country. One of the memorable occasions of that first winter was the "defense of Miller Hall with snowballs at twenty feet." The casualties, as reported by *All Hands,* were "seven windows and one weekend."

Some Hobart V-12s: Dr. Allen E. Dumont, Jules Leonard Whitehill Professor of Surgery, New York University School of Medicine, and editor, *Lymphology;* James G. MacDonald, chairman, Teachers Insurance and Annuity Association; Richard Sassenberg, inventor, and president, Piclear; Joseph R. Spector, vice president and general counsel, UMC Industries; and Michael D. Stashower, senior vice president for finance, Perkin-Elmer Corporation.

	1943		1944		1945		
	Jul.-Oct.	Nov.-Feb.	Mar.-Jun.	Jul.-Oct.	Nov.-Feb.	Mar.-Jun.	Jul.-Oct.
Navy	397	385	394	379	275	165	148
C.O.	Lt. Daniel L. Evans						Lt. Angus B. Rothwell

Rensselaer Polytechnic Institute   Troy, New York

When the 620 V-12 engineering candidates arrived at this school on July 1, 1943, it was already home to the only NROTC unit in New York State. The friendly rivalry between the V-12s and the NROTCs was a fact of life on this campus during the entire V-12 program.

The V-12s were quartered in the Freshman Quadrangle. Russell Sage Dining Hall became their mess hall.

The list of activities on the RPI campus rivaled that of any V-12 school in the country. The governing body, the Rensselaer Union, planned student activities, supported the athletic program, and provided most of the entertainment on campus. The all-V-12 Blue Jackets dance band was in great demand; it even drew crowds to rehearsals. The full sports schedule included football, basketball, swimming, lacrosse, boxing, soccer, skiing, winter track, and cross-country.

The high scholastic standards at RPI resulted in many trainees making the restricted list, which was quaintly referred to as "the academically weak list."

The *Rensselaer Polytechnic* changed from a weekly to a biweekly and kept up with the many campus activities. The *Transit* was the yearbook that reviewed the year's activities. The 1947 volume covered the history of the V-12 program at RPI.

One of the high spots for the unit was the presentation of the Navy Cross to Capt. Charles R. Stephan, USN, the executive officer of the unit.

Some Rensselaer V-12s: Robert L. Bartlett, vice president, Shopsmith; Edward J. Blanch, chairman, Ford of Europe; Rear Adm. Robert H. Blount, USN; Dr. Robert H. Conn, assistant secretary of the Navy; Fred Heller, president, Lightolier; Stanley L. Krugman, executive vice president, Jacobs Engineer Group; Leonard B. Mackey, vice president and general patent counsel, ITT; Dr. Morris Ojalvo, professor of civil engineering, Ohio State Univeristy; Devere W. Ryckman, president, REACT, St. Louis; and Dr. Stanley Weiss, vice president of engineering, Lockheed Corporation, and chief engineer and associate administrator, NASA.

Capt. C. R. Stephan, USN(Ret.)

	1943		1944			1945		1946	
	Jul.-Oct.	Nov.-Feb.	Mar.-Jun.	Jul.-Oct.	Nov.-Feb.	Mar.-Jun.	Jul.-Oct.	Nov.-Feb.	Mar.-Jun.
Navy	565	561	468	489	443	347	204	311	125
C.O.	Capt. M. C. Bowman							Capt. M. T. Farrar	

St. Lawrence University Canton, New York

St. Lawrence University Archives

A surprising number of the first V-12s to arrive at St. Lawrence came from New York City and Chicago, so the upstate New York campus became the setting for a "battle of the big cities," just as in other parts of the country large contingents from the North and South fought the Civil War again.

The V-12s were housed and fed in the Men's Residence, now known as Sykes Hall. The V-12 office was also there. The sick bay occupied the Florence Lee Cottage, formerly a residence for freshman women.

Although the manpower was available and the college was willing, intercollegiate sports had a hard time at St. Lawrence due to wartime travel restrictions and the distances to potential competitors. A very extensive intramural program was started, however; it held the attention of students and even townspeople. Swimming and track meets between the four companies started just after the V-12s arrived, and they were followed by a round-robin football tournament in September and October. St. Lawrence had no swimming pool, so the Navy swimming tests and classes were held at the "Sand Banks," a swimming hole in the Grasse River just east of the campus.

The townspeople of Canton welcomed the V-12s with a July 31 dance put on by the mayor's committee on entertainment. It was held in Brewer Fieldhouse, and the *Canton Plaindealer* termed it "a huge success."

Some St. Lawrence V-12s: Milton F. Fillius, Jr., chairman, Vita-Pakt Citrus Products Company; Stewart F. Halpine, U.S. Information Agency; Capt. Charles Richelieu, USN; and John G. Wick, president, Merchants Mutual Insurance Company, Buffalo.

	1943		1944			1945	
	Jul.-Oct.	Nov.-Feb.	Mar.-Jun.	Jul.-Oct.	Nov.-Feb.	Mar.-Jun.	Jul.-Oct.
Navy	347	349	328	317	209	142	125
C.O.	Lt. D. H. Moyer						

Union College   Schenectady, New York

Union College Alumni Office

The 482 V-12s reporting to Union were quartered in North and South Colleges and six on-campus fraternity houses. They were fed in the new mess hall, which had all the charm of a typical military-style mess hall. It had been added to the Hale House dining room, replacing the former courtyard. But the food was good!

The V-12 office was in Silliman Hall and sick bay was in the Kappa Alpha fraternity house.

The V-12 day at Union started at 0545, when reveille was sounded by the college's steam whistle. According to the editor of the alumni magazine, the whistle could be heard as far away as Albany.

Union V-12s took part in all of the campus activities and became the mainstays of the band and glee club. In their free moments trainees gathered around the Scuttlebutt, a soda bar in Washburn Hall. But studies were not neglected: at the end of the first term, sixty-nine of the V-12s were on the dean's list.

Football was reluctantly dropped for the 1943 season after the coach and men trying out for the team found that the necessary practice time just wasn't available. In 1945, when the no football decision was made in the spring, the student paper, the *Concordiensis,* assailed the student council for not presenting the question directly to the students.

One of the most memorable occasions for the Union V-12 unit was the 1943 Armistice Day parade. (See Chapter 34, "Humor, High Jinks, and 'They Shouldn't Have,' " for further details.)

The Union V-12s have had several successful reunions.

Some Union College V-12s: Robert

	1943		1944			1945			1946
	Jul.-Oct.	Nov.-Feb.	Mar.-Jun.	Jul.-Oct.	Nov.-Feb.	Mar.-Jun.	Jul.-Oct.	Nov.-Feb.	Mar.-Jun.
Navy	482	504	465	NA	NA	NA	NA	NA	NA
C.O.	Lcdr. Maurice L. Horner			Lt. F. B. Andreen				@	Lcdr. Oliver Evans

NA = Not available   @ Lt. Gordon J. Longley

Union College

E. Bischoff, manager, international marketing, General Electric; Dr. Baruch S. Blumberg, Nobel laureate in physiology, 1976; Robert A. Boyar, insurance broker to Broadway shows and stars; Capt. R. P. Chrisler, USN; Harrison E. Demgen, director, alumni affairs, Union College; Terrence E. Devine, president, Fugazy International Travel Headquarters, Albany; Rear Adm. Paul J. Early, USN; Dr. Horace B. Edwards, president, ARCO Pipeline Company; Capt. William C. Olin, USN; Eric J. Schmertz, dean, Hofstra University Law School; Lt. Gen. Philip D. Shutler, USMC; Judge Robert J. Sise, chief administrative judge, State of New York; Dr. Weston E. Vivian, congressman from Michigan; Dr. James Vollmer, senior vice president, RCA; and Rear Adm. Almon C. Wilson, USN(MC), deputy surgeon general, U.S. Navy.

Union College Alumni Office

University of Rochester Rochester, New York

University of Rochester Archives

The 370 marines and 433 sailors assigned to the University of Rochester took over all of the housing on the men's campus, known as the River Campus. They were quartered in fraternity houses, Crosby Hall, Burton Hall, Alumni Gymnasium, and Stadium Dormitory. The mess hall was in Todd Union.

The female contingent of the University of Rochester was located on the Prince Street campus, about three miles away. The girls remained on the traditional semester schedule. At the first get-acquainted mixer when they returned in September of 1943, the

coeds and V-12s found they had little in common, which resulted in animosity instead of good feelings. It took a studied effort by both groups to heal that rift in the ensuing months.

Rochester fielded a winning football team, with a six-and-one record. The basketball team was of the same caliber, finishing the 1943–1944 season with eleven wins and four losses. Top bands visited the campus. Fred Waring offered a "victory salute" to V-12s on August 19, 1943, and Tony Pastor and his band followed a few months later.

The student weekly, the *Campus*,

	1943		1944			1945			1946
	Jul.-Oct.	Nov.-Feb.	Mar.-Jun.	Jul.-Oct.	Nov.-Feb.	Mar.-Jun.	Jul.-Oct.	Nov.-Feb.	Mar.-Jun.
Navy	430	490	528	640	480	381	293	# 345	# 216
C.O.	Lcdr. William M. Neill					Capt. George C. Towner			
Marines	362	246	170	109					
O-in-C	Capt. Herbert W. Coulter, Jr.		@						

Included NROTC   @ Warrant Officer Roman J. Szumigala

University of Rochester

gave excellent coverage to the V-12 unit, including feature stories about the marines' mascot, "Gizmo," and V-12s volunteering for harvesting chores in the fields surrounding Rochester.

The commanding officer set up and taught part of a special pre-midshipman's course for the last half of the third term to give the V-12s heading for midshipmen's schools more preparation for what they would encounter. They received work in naval ordnance, navigation, construction, handling stowage, small boats, and proper naval terminology. The May 1944 commencement speaker and honorary degree recipient was Dr. Joseph W. Barker, dean of engineering at Columbia University and special assistant to the secretary of the Navy on educational matters.

Some Rochester V-12s: Earle Coleman, archivist, Princeton University; Dr. Robert L. Love, academic dean, Alfred State College, State University of New York; Dr. Edward A. Mason, vice president for research, AMOCO Corporation; Dr. William Rabinowitz, professor of educational psychology, Pennsylvania State University; Dr. Benedict M. Reynolds, professor of surgery, New York Medical College; Rupert B. Southard, Jr., chief, National Mapping Division, U.S. Geological Survey; Donald E. Vincent, university librarian, University of New Hampshire; and Evan Whallon, conductor/music director, San Francisco Opera.

Webb Institute of Naval Architecture New York, New York
(Now in Glen Cove, New York)

Norman A. Hamlin

Webb Institute had the smallest V-12 unit in the country. With between sixty-five and seventy trainees, it was about half the size of the next largest unit. But the camaraderie that resulted from this small size gave Webb a school spirit rivaled by none.

The Webb V-12s were quartered and fed in the main building of the Institute. The unit was under the command of Capt. J. K. Richards, the commanding officer of the Columbia Midshipmen's School, but it had its own officer-in-charge and a chief specialist (A) to put the men through their paces in the physical training program. Despite the small enrollment, Webb's Spiders gamely fielded teams in basketball, baseball, tennis, and track.

The school paper, the *Binnacle,* produced special graduation numbers at the appropriate times to serve as yearbooks. Campus activities included the honor and governing councils, the student organization, and the glee club. Social life was not neglected —

the unit sponsored Christmas dances, senior proms, and ring dances. Off campus they frequented a place known as Hubbe's, and the picnics at Tibbett's Brook are well remembered by the Webb trainees.

The commencement speaker in June 1945 was Ralph A. Bard, undersecretary of the Navy.

Some Webb V-12s: Thomas H. Bond, professor of electrical engineering, Webb Institute; Dr. John P. Breslin, professor and director of Davidson Laboratory, Stevens Institute of Technology; Dr. James A. Fay, professor of mechanical engineering, Massachusetts Institute of Technology; Jack G. Gilmore,* project engineer, Polaris submarine, and master bird carver; Dr. Norman Hamlin, professor of naval architecture, Webb Institute; John J. Nachtsheim, chief naval architect, U.S. Bureau of Ships, and president of the Society of Naval Architects and Marine Engineers; and Dr. David M. Young, Jr., professor of mathematics, University of Texas (Austin).

	1943		1944			1945			1946
	Jul.-Oct.	Nov.-Feb.	Mar.-Jun.	Jul.-Oct.	Nov.-Feb.	Mar.-Jun.	Jul.-Oct.	Nov.-Feb.	Mar.-Jun.
Navy	68	66	68	67	68	68	49	42	17
C.O.	Capt. J. K. Richards						Capt. T. F. Wellings		

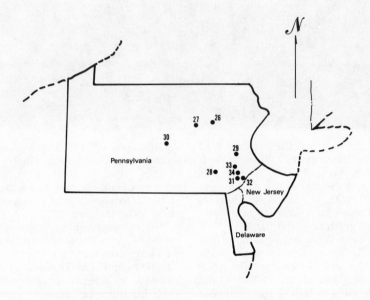

Fourth Naval District

Pennsylvania

26. Bloomsburg State Teachers College
27. Bucknell University
28. Franklin & Marshall College
29. Muhlenberg College
30. Pennsylvania State College
31. Swarthmore College
32. University of Pennsylvania
33. Ursinus College
34. Villanova College

Bloomsburg State Teachers College   Bloomsburg, Pennsylvania
(Now Bloomsburg University of Pennsylvania)

When the 175 V-12s arrived at this campus on the hill at the east end of Bloomsburg's Main Street, they learned to their disappointment that the coeds were still on the semester system. It was only a matter of a few months before the college coordinated everything with the Navy trimester schedule, so the girls came back by November 1, 1943.

Football had been suspended for the duration by the college board, but the V-12s still tried to see if a football team could find some intercollegiate competition. Despite their efforts, the team did not materialize until 1944. Bloomsburg was not about to let the annual Homecoming Day go by the boards in 1943, however, so two Navy squads were trained by the officers and chiefs and did battle on Saturday, October 16, during a heavy rainfall. The Reds ground out a six-to-zero victory over the Whites.

The 1943–1944 basketball squad turned in a creditable eleven-and-three record, and the wrestling, soccer, track, swimming, and baseball teams competed on a limited intercol-legiate schedule.

The Bell Telephone Company of Pennsylvania gave a Christmas party for all of the V-12s on December 17, 1943, replete with lots of girls, food, and dancing. In the spring of 1944 a canteen was put into operation; its profits provided the funds necessary for the publication of the *Obiter* yearbook.

The *Maroon and Gold*, the campus weekly, covered all the college activities. The Navy office was housed in the "new" junior high school, which became unofficially known as "Navy Hall." To show its appreciation for the V-12 program, the Bloomsburg board of trustees officially designated that building Navy Hall after the war.

Some Bloomsburg V-12s: Dr. Barnes W. McCormick, professor of aerospace engineering, Pennsylvania State University; Donald R. Riley, aerospace research engineer, NASA; Richard M. Smith, vice chairman, Bethlehem Steel Corporation; and Joseph Stulb, vice president and treasurer, Stulb Paint and Chemical Company, Philadelphia.

	1943		1944			1945	
	Jul.-Oct.	Nov.-Feb.	Mar.-Jun.	Jul.-Oct.	Nov.-Feb.	Mar.-Jun.	Jul.-Oct.
Navy	163	NA	NA	NA	165	NA	NA
C.O.	Lt. W. D. Greulich		Lt. Lloyd P. Jordan		Lt. Russell J. Ferguson		

NA = Not available

Bucknell University Lewisburg, Pennsylvania

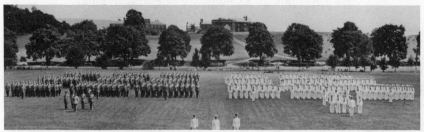

The sailors and marines arriving at Bucknell for the V-12 program were quartered in university dormitories and fed in a former fraternity house that had been acquired by the university and remodeled into a mess hall. The first few weeks at this ninety-seven-year-old Baptist institution were hectic. The marines did not receive uniforms for three weeks. Nevertheless, campus social life started promptly on July 9 with dances at three different locations on campus.

The Bisons gave a good account of themselves in athletics during the V-12 years; they had a five-and-three record in football in 1943. That winter, the basketball team upset Penn State and the highly regarded Muhlenberg Mules, who went on to the National Invitational Tournament. The newly acquired university bus was busy five nights a week hauling V-12s to the YMCA swimming pool in nearby Milton.

The *Bucknellian* reported on campus events weekly. *L'Agenda*, the year-book, gave the summary of the year.

Interesting events on the Bucknell campus were the attention given to the 500,000th meal served in the mess hall, the appearance of Louis Prima and his band in the Coca-Cola Spotlight Band Program in Davis Gymnasium on June 3, 1944, and Rear Adm. Randall Jacobs's appearance as commencement speaker in October of 1943.

Some Bucknell V-12s: Leon C. Holt, Jr., vice chairman, Air Products and Chemicals; Dr. Charles L. Hosler, Jr., vice president for research and dean of the graduate school, Pennsylvania State University; Richard L. Moore, vice president for public affairs, W. R. Grace and Company; Corwin L. Rickard, executive vice president, General Atomic Company; Wendell I. Smith, vice president, Bucknell University; and Dr. William J. Williams, professor and chairman of the department of medicine, State University of New York at Syracuse.

	1943		1944			1945			1946
	Jul.-Oct.	Nov.-Feb.	Mar.-Jun.	Jul.-Oct.	Nov.-Feb.	Mar.-Jun.	Jul.-Oct.	Nov.-Feb.	Mar.-Jun.
Navy	306	NA	NA	NA	NA	NA	NA	338	5
C.O.	Lcdr. J. E. Fleming					Lt. O. E. Dunckel			Capt. W. T. McGarry
Marines	285	194	135	94					
O-in-C	Capt. Paul M. Miller		1st Lt. J. P. Franceski						

NA = Not available

Franklin and Marshall College   Lancaster, Pennsylvania

When the V-12s arrived at this 156-year-old men's school, they found that they faced high academic standards. The Navy recognized this and assigned an extraordinarily high percentage of premedical and predental V-12s to the unit. The mess hall was located in the Academy Building, as was the V-12 office. The top two floors were used for housing, as were two other dorms and four fraternity houses.

The Marine detachment helped assure a splendid intercollegiate athletic program for the F and M Diplomats. The 1943 football team went undefeated until its final game, when it dropped the annual Thanksgiving Day Classic to Bucknell, twenty-one to thirteen, before an overflow crowd of ten thousand.

The *Student Weekly* not only reported on activities at F and M, it even sponsored some of the dances, including a formal at the end of the second term. V-12s took a leading part in the glee club and the Green Room Club, the theatrical organization.

A rigorous intramural program was operated during the life of the V-12 unit. Morning calisthenics were discontinued on January 1, 1944, because of the inclement winter weather, but time was added to the daily physical training classes to compensate. To the delight of the V-12s, however, morning calisthenics remained discontinued until March of 1945. That

Archives and Special Collections, Franklin and Marshall College

was probably the longest period any V-12 unit went without the hated early-morning exercises.

Some F and M V-12s: Robert J. Donough, vice chairman, Norstar Bancorp; Brig. Gen. Paul Graham, USMC; Bowie Kuhn, commissioner of baseball; Harold T. Miller, chairman, Houghton Mifflin Company; John F. Robinson, president, Reliance Insurance Company; Dr. Irving H. Sandler, author on contemporary American art, and professor of art history, State University of New York; Edwin W. Snider, secretary, National Geographic Society; Dr. Melvin Spira, professor and head of the division of plastic surgery, Baylor College of Medicine; and Glen Tetley, award-winning choreographer.

	1943		1944			1945	
	Jul.-Oct.	Nov.-Feb.	Mar.-Jun.	Jul.-Oct.	Nov.-Feb.	Mar.-Jun.	Jul.-Oct.
Navy	316	410	394	428	335	222	194
C.O.	Lcdr. A. R. Pierson, Jr.	Lcdr. Clark Olney			Lt. Lloyd P. Jordan		Lt. W. C. Darrah
Marines	212	170	130	85			
O-in-C	1st Lt. Earl B. Dane, Jr.			W.O. Thomas R. Rowell			

Muhlenberg College   Allentown, Pennsylvania

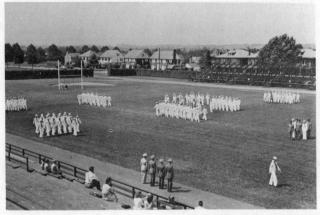

Muhlenberg College Archives

The Muhlenberg V-12 unit was unique in a number of ways: it was the only unit to be discontinued (June 30, 1945) and then reactivated (March 1, 1946). Its Muhlenberg Mules basketball team finished the 1943–1944 season with a twenty-and-three record, the 1944–1945 year with a twenty-four-and-four record, and it was invited both years to the National Invitational Tournament in Madison Square Garden. It had an unrivaled parade of important Navy figures speaking at its commencements.

Credit for the last-mentioned achievement goes to energetic college president Levering Tyson, who secured the following V-12 dignitaries and awarded them honorary LL.D. degrees in commencements from October 1943 to a year later: Capt. Bruce Canaga, USN(Ret.), BuPers director of training; Rear Adm. Louis E. Denfeld, USN, assistant chief of naval personnel; Dr. Joseph W. Barker, special assistant to Secretary Knox; Capt. Arthur S. Adams, USN(Ret.), first officer-in-charge of the V-12 program; and Capt. James L. Holloway, Jr., USN, BuPers director of training.

The first underwater obstacle course in a V-12 unit was installed in the pool used by the V-12s at the Jewish Community Center. "Rusty Gizmo," the Irish setter mascot of the unit, was officially "discharged" by Lieutenant Commander Abel in June 1946.

Some Muhlenberg V-12s: Louis J. Cioffi, ABC-TV News bureau chief at the United Nations; Robert E. Gralley,

	1943		1944			1945			1946
	Jul.-Oct.	Nov.-Feb.	Mar.-Jun.	Jul.-Oct.	Nov.-Feb.	Mar.-Jun.	Jul.-Oct.	Nov.-Feb.	Mar.-Jun.
Navy	253	315	296	344	277	193	Unit deactivated, replaced by Navy Academic Refresher Unit 7/45 to 2/46		150
C.O.	Cdr. H. P. Lowenstein	Lcdr. Frederick L. Douthit			Lt. W. D. Greulich	@			Lcdr. T. T. Abel
Marines	195	149	120	81					
O-in-C	1st Lt. R. Dawson	Capt. Michael W. Sceisi							

@ Lt. R. H. Light   NA = Not available

Muhlenberg College

vice president and secretary, MONY Financial Services; Dr. Robert W. Haigh, professor, Colgate Darden Graduate School of Business Administration, University of Virginia; Richard S. Hickok, chairman, Main Hurdman (CPAs); Dr. George D. Selfridge, retired rear admiral and now dean of the Dental School, Washington University, St. Louis; and John Strohmeyer, editor, Bethlehem *Globe-Times*, winner of the Pulitzer Prize for editorial writing, 1972.

Pennsylvania State College State College, Pennsylvania
(Now Pennsylvania State University)

Normally, six hundred V-12s were considered a sizable unit, but there were so many military personnel already on the Penn State campus that little notice was taken of the arrival of the V-12 unit, which was the last military body to make its appearance. In fact, although they were full-time academic students, the V-12s were not even listed in the student directories.

The sailors and marines were quartered in fraternity houses and fed in McAllister Hall. The V-12s were on the trimester schedule, but the rest of the campus remained on the traditional semesters, which hampered full trainee participation in campus organizations. Athletics was one area that was supported mainly by the V-12s. One hundred and fifty men turned out for the 1943 football team, and V-12s became the key players. They were also big participants in basketball, track, baseball, soccer, and swimming. One Marine V-12 won five letters in nine months at Penn State.

The *Daily Collegian* became the weekly *Collegian* in the summer of 1943. In 1944 a "Ship Ahoy" column about and for V-12s became a regular feature of the paper. The yearbook, *LAVIE*, was published in each of the V-12 years.

The Navy and Marine V-12s found plenty of opportunity for social life.

Pennsylvania State University Alumni Association

They participated in such events as a V-12 weekend in June of 1944 and a ship's ball nearly every term. In September of 1944, the fourth-term men held a farewell dinner-dance at a local hotel.

In the fall of 1945, an NROTC unit was awarded to Penn State.

Some Penn State V-12s: Capt. William Abomitis, Jr.,* USN; Dr. Paul Berg, professor of biochemistry, Stanford University, and recipient of Nobel

	1943		1944			1945			1946
	Jul.-Oct.	Nov.-Feb.	Mar.-Jun.	Jul.-Oct.	Nov.-Feb.	Mar.-Jun.	Jul.-Oct.	Nov.-Feb.	Mar.-Jun.
Navy	297	378	343	415	360	245	202	# 285	# 193
C.O.	@	Cdr. Walter S. Gabel		Lt. Trusdell Wisner			Capt. W. T. McGarry		
Marines	291	219	187	124					
O-in-C	Capt. Samuel Whittle, Jr.								

Includes NROTC @ Lcdr. John H. Smith

Pennsylvania State College

Prize in chemistry, 1980; James L. Everett III, chairman, Philadelphia Electric Company; Samuel M. Kinney, Jr., president, Union Camp Corporation; Frank H. Lehr, president, Frank H. Lehr Associates, East Orange, N.J., and chairman, New Jersey Natural Resources Commission; Richard Little III, publisher, *Scranton Tribune;* Capt. Roger M. Netherland,* USN, killed in action in Vietnam; Willard R. Powell, senior vice president, UMC Industries; Dr. Seymour Schuster, professor of mathematics, Carleton College; and Dr. Johannes Weertman, Walter P. Murphy Professor of Material Sciences, Northwestern University.

Swarthmore College   Swarthmore, Pennsylvania

Friends Historical Library.
Swarthmore College

This Quaker college had to wrestle with its principles in considering whether to allow a military unit on its campus. Patriotism and economic pressures eventually brought forth a positive response. After several months of mutual skepticism and suspicion, the military and civilian parts of the student body came together for the benefit of everyone, and most especially for Swarthmore. Thereafter, their relationship was warm and friendly, and their eventual parting was regretted by both sides.

The V-12s were quartered and fed in Wharton dormitory. They took part in intercollegiate athletics and after the first few months took leading roles in everything from the student council and Little Theatre Club to the *Phoenix*, the weekly publication, and the *Halcyon*, the yearbook. The trainees also published their own paper, the *Scuttlebutt.*

During naval open houses, held once a term, civilians were invited to tour the V-12 quarters. The Navy band and the Navy chorus added their talents to many campus events.

Swarthmore V-12s had the unique experience of welcoming to the campus and rooming with forty-nine Chinese naval officers, who came to the college to take instruction in English before moving on to technical schools. During their seven-month stay the Chinese made many friends on the Swarthmore campus.

The other major event was the appearance at the June 1944 commencement of Secretary of the Navy James V. Forrestal, who had occupied that office for only a month.

Some Swarthmore College V-12s: Dr. George A. Heise, professor of psychology, Indiana University; Arthur R. Littleton, attorney, Philadelphia; Robert W. Mannel, traffic manager, *Chicago Tribune;* A. W. Martin, consulting engineer, Wayne, Pa.; Frank D. Register, president, National Association of Retail Grocers; Dr. Clayton Rich, dean, Stanford University Medical College; and Dr. Milton A. Wohl, chairman, department of orthopedic surgery, Albert Einstein Medical Center, Philadelphia.

	1943		1944			1945			1946
	Jul.-Oct.	Nov.-Feb.	Mar.-Jun.	Jul.-Oct.	Nov.-Feb.	Mar.-Jun.	Jul.-Oct.	Nov.-Feb.	Mar.-Jun.
Navy	291	281	261	279	244	201	167	238	181
C.O.	Lt. Glenn G. Bartle					Lt. David R. Reveley			

University of Pennsylvania Philadelphia, Pennsylvania

The 784 V-12s who arrived at the University of Pennsylvania for the first term were quartered in university men's dorms and fed in the Houston Hall mess. The six hundred Navy Flight Prep School cadets and the NROTCs also ate in Houston.

As always, athletics played a big part in campus life at the University of Pennsylvania. The 1943 Red and Blue football team defeated Princeton, Yale, and Dartmouth in the first three games and finished with an outstanding record. The 1944–1945 basketball team captured the Intercollegiate League crown for the first time since 1937.

The Society of the Alumni treated the V-12s to a smoker with a lavish buffet supper at the Union League Club in March of 1944.

The V-12s made it possible to continue the annual Mask and Wig Club productions, the fifty-sixth and fifty-seventh in an unbroken string. "Red Points and Blue" was the title of the 1944 production, which gave four performances to capacity audiences. The 1945 show, "Hep to the Beat," also played to full houses.

The daily *Pennsylvania Bulletin* had been replaced by the *Pennsylvanian*, which covered news of the campus and all of the military units. No yearbook appeared until 1946.

Some University of Pennsylvania V-12s: Ralph W. Detra, president, Avco Research Labs; Martin Friedman, director, Walker Art Center, Minneapolis; Dr. Harry J. Gray, professor of electrical engineering and computer and information sciences, the Moore School of Electrical Engineering, University of Pennsylvania; William F. Hyland, attorney general of New Jersey; Dr. George A. Russell, chancellor, University of Missouri at Kansas City; Henry P. Sullivan, senior vice president and general counsel, Consolidated Natural Gas Company; and Dr. Edward H. Whitmore, chairman, department of mathematics, Central Michigan University.

University of Pennsylvania Archives

	1943		1944			1945			1946
	Jul.-Oct.	Nov.-Feb.	Mar.-Jun.	Jul.-Oct.	Nov.-Feb.	Mar.-Jun.	Jul.-Oct.	Nov.-Feb.	Mar.-Jun.
Navy	605	706	579	582	343	195	104	72	49
C.O.	Capt. L. M. Stevens							Capt. F. R. Dodge	

Ursinus College   Collegeville, Pennsylvania

Although it was one of the smallest in the country, the V-12 unit at Ursinus College was greatly appreciated by the faculty and administration, as indicated in the annual reports to the board of trustees. The two hundred men were housed in Brodbeck, Freeland, Derr, and Stine halls at the start of the program, but eight months later were consolidated in Brodbeck and Curtis halls. Approximately half of the trainees were premeds, the other half being mostly trainees in basic. There were also a few prechaplain sailors — the school is affiliated with the Evangelical and Reformed Church.

A full social schedule was maintained. There was a Navy ball each term: Elliot Lawrence and his orchestra played for the final Navy ball in October of 1945. The trainees took part in all of the campus activities and pro-

vided the main support for the athletic teams. The commanding officer, Lt. George D. Miner, USNR, and the exec, Lt.(jg) Edward F. Heffernan, USNR, were the coaches for all of the intercollegiate teams, which made Ursinus unique among V-12 schools. Miner was the skipper for the entire life of the unit, and Heffernan served for most of it.

At the end of the V-12 program, the college held a farewell dinner for all of the trainees. Summing up the Ursinus experience was this toast offered by one of the trainees:

We have learned to know why Ursinus College enjoys the privilege of standing among the top colleges and universities in this country. We were absorbed on the athletic

	1943		1944			1945	
	Jul.-Oct.	Nov.-Feb.	Mar.-Jun.	Jul.-Oct.	Nov.-Feb.	Mar.-Jun.	Jul.-Oct.
Navy	196	168	NA	331	208	160	NA
C.O.	Lt. George D. Miner						

NA = Not available

Ursinus College

teams, the debating and dramatic clubs, on the campus and in the classrooms. Indelibly stamped upon every one of us is something of the tradition and greatness of Ursinus. Our hope is that the faculty and the staff of Ursinus College may prosper as they deserve and that some small recompense shall be theirs for the large measure of good done for all of us.

Some Ursinus V-12s: William E. C. Dearden, chairman, Hershey Foods Corporation; Walter W. Hauser, vice president for manufacturing, Hershey Chocolate Company; Dr. John Patrick Kelly, professor of elementary education, University of Nevada, Reno; Ernest C. Miller, president, AMACON, a division of American Management Association; and Dr. William L. Nobles, president, Mississippi College.

Villanova College   Villanova, Pennsylvania
(Now Villanova University)

Villanova University Archives

When six hundred V-12 trainees reported to this hundred-year-old Catholic men's school on July 1, 1943, the college was ready. Most of the four hundred Navy men were quartered in Fedigan and Mendel halls, with some overflow going to Alumni Hall. Alumni Hall also housed some of the two hundred Marine V-12s, the rest being located in Austin Hall. The sick bay was placed in a newly acquired house next to O'Dwyer Hall.

At the start of the program the V-12s made up approximately three-fourths of the student body. The number of resident students was larger than ever before.

A recreation center was set up by a group of private citizens on Lancaster Pike, near the edge of the campus. The leader of the project was Mrs. LaDow, the owner of the drugstore next door, who donated the use of what had formerly been her storeroom. She persuaded customers and friends to provide the financial support needed to make this spot available to the V-12s.

The unit had a very extensive schedule of intramurals, and the school competed in intercollegiate football,

	1943		1944			1945			1946
	Jul.-Oct.	Nov.-Feb.	Mar.-Jun.	Jul.-Oct.	Nov.-Feb.	Mar.-Jun.	Jul.-Oct.	Nov.-Feb.	Mar.-Jun.
Navy	377	415	428	445	287	196	144	#252	#162
C.O.	Cdr. E. J. Milner		Lcdr. Edward Hannah					Capt. T. C. Thomas	
Marines	193	173	141	95	111	123	104	81	57
O-in-C	Capt. Robert L. Morgan						Capt. Roger S. Toussaint		Capt. John L. Bricker

Includes NROTC

Villanova College

basketball, baseball, and track. The 1944 football Wildcats had a five-and-three record, including a win over Princeton.

Social life was not neglected. Unit dances featured orchestras led by such well-known musicians as Bobby Sherwood and Elliot Lawrence. Les Brown's orchestra made a "Coca-Cola Spotlight Band" appearance in the Villanova Field House on April 29, 1944. The V-12 drum and bugle corps of thirty-two men helped the trainees keep step in all of the inspections and many of the drill sessions.

The September 1945 *Leatherneck*, magazine of the U.S. Marine Corps, featured Villanova and Princeton marines in a major article.

Some Villanova V-12s: the Reverend C. Dendy Garrett, senior minister, Grace United Methodist Church, Des Moines, Iowa; John S. Lalley, chairman, PHH Group; John Thomas McDonnell, vice president, Gulf Oil Exploration and Production Company; Allen Franklin Rhodes, president, Anglo Energy, and president, American Society of Mechanical Engineers; and Dr. Alan Schneider, professor of engineering sciences, University of California at San Diego.

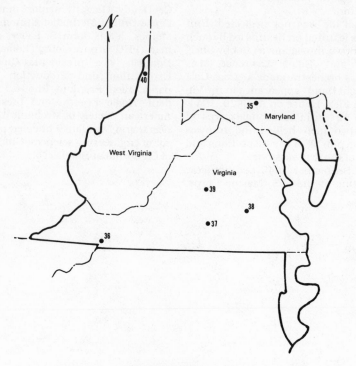

Fifth Naval District

Maryland

   35. Mount St. Mary's College

Virginia

   36. Emory and Henry College
   37. Hampden-Sydney College
   38. University of Richmond
   39. University of Virginia

West Virginia

   40. Bethany College

Mount St. Mary's College Emmitsburg, Maryland

The V-12s reporting to this 135-year-old Roman Catholic men's school were quartered in DuBois Hall. McCaffrey served as the mess hall.

The 1943–1944 basketball team won the Mason-Dixon Conference championship. Members of the college community, however, were angry and disappointed when Catholic University from the same league was invited to represent the section in the National Invitational Tournament.

The *Mountain Echo,* the student paper, reported many interesting events in the lives of the V-12s: the completion of the huge (150 by 140 feet) outdoor swimming pool constructed by the college to serve the V-12 program; the tragic drowning of a V-12 trainee; the V-12 bugler who did reveille in ragtime and received a "whopping restriction" for it; the impressive scene of three hundred blue jackets in formation on Echo Field for a military mass; and the chief who swore at the men lined up in front of the seminary as he shouted that they must end their use of "crude language."

The most remembered event on the Mount was the fire that destroyed the kitchens of the mess hall on November 7, 1944. The V-12s helped fight the fire and then moved to the gymnasium for the remainder of the night. Breakfast was served behind the Junior Building with the help of a field kitchen borrowed from nearby Camp Ritchie. Classes were suspended for the day so the V-12s could help clean up the fire-damaged premises.

Some Mount St. Mary V-12s: Louis

Mount St. Mary's College Special Collections

Fleck, chairman, Red Bull Inns of America; Dr. Jerome K. Holloway, professor, Naval War College; Harry R. Hughes, governor of Maryland; John Spalding Lalley, chairman, PHH Group; Dr. Gerald D. Laubach, president, Pfizer; Judge Joseph L. McGlynn, Jr., U.S. District Court of Eastern Pennsylvania; and Jeremiah P. Shea, chairman, Bank of Delaware.

	1943		1944			1945	
	Jul.-Oct.	Nov.-Feb.	Mar.-Jun.	Jul.-Oct.	Nov.-Feb.	Mar.-Jun.	Jul.-Oct.
Navy	200	212	214	202	192	115	101
C.O.	Lt. Roderic D. Matthews	Lt. M. S. Lee	Acting C.O. Lt.(jg) R. J. Richards	Lt. Roderic D. Matthews		Lt.(jg) W. G. Pyles	

Emory and Henry College Emory, Virginia

Emory and Henry College, a Methodist institution, lived up to its reputation for excellence by turning out many V-12 premeds who eventually became medical doctors. The tough standards brought many weekend restrictions for poor grades. The *White Topper*, the campus newspaper, challenged the practice in an editorial entitled "Educational Policy? Is It Flunking or Training?"

On weekends the buses to Bristol were filled, but there were still lots of campus social events: dances, box lunches with 340 girls from Sullins College, and a yearbook snapshot contest that offered an expenses-paid date with the queen of the nearby all-girl Virginia Intermont College.

Capt. Arthur S. Adams, USN, the head of the national V-12 program, was the commencement speaker on June 19, 1944.

The three dormitories housing the V-12s were named the Saratoga, the Yorktown, and the Lexington. The unit marched in the Labor Day parade at Bristol and was awarded a banner for being the top unit in war bond purchases in the Fifth Naval District.

Some Emory and Henry V-12s: Judge Robert F. Chapman, U.S. Court of Appeals, Fourth Circuit; John M. Hudgins, Jr., president, Hop-In Food Stores, Roanoke; Harold A. Poling, president, Ford Motor Company; Dr. J. M. Reynolds, professor of dentistry, Medical College of Georgia; John F. Ryan, vice president, ITT; Marvin L. Stone, editor, *U.S. News and World Report*; and Victor G. Wagner,* engineer and president, Water Pollution Control Federation.

	1943		1944			1945	
	Jul.-Oct.	Nov.-Feb.	Mar.-Jun.	Jul.-Oct.	Nov.-Feb.	Mar.-Jun.	Jul.-Oct.
Navy	291	273	293	274	205	147	120
C.O.	Lt. William A. Shimer		Lt. M. S. Lee	Lt. Arthur E. Jensen			Lcdr. A. K. Burt

Hampden-Sydney College Hampden-Sydney, Virginia

Hampden-Sydney college sent its first students off to war in the American Revolution, so it was not surprising to find a V-12 unit in this Presbyterian men's college in 1943.

Fore 'N Aft was the weekly mimeographed paper. The *Kaleidoscope* yearbook (1944 only) provided an overall picture of wartime campus life.

For the June 1944 commencement address, President E. G. Gammon secured Capt. Arthur S. Adams, who organized the nationwide V-12 program. The fine cooperation and respect between the Navy and the college was evidenced by the awarding of an honorary Doctor of Science degree to Lt. George F. Howe, commanding officer during the entire existence of the unit, at the June 1945 commencement.

Social life revolved around the schedule of the State Teachers College at Farmville, where hundreds of coeds were in residence from September to May. Trainees looked forward to the bus trips to use the STC's swimming pool. Six dances were held at HSC with music by the student dance band.

Dr. W. T. Williams very generously opened his home to the V-12s. They spent many off-duty hours relaxing there and made many off-campus phone calls on the Williamses' phone.

Some Hampden-Sydney V-12s: Boyd C. Bartlett, senior vice president, Deere and Company; Dr. William R. Biddington, dean, West Virginia University School of Dentistry, and president, American Association of Dental Schools; Henry W. Brockenbrough, senior vice president and trust officer, United Virginia Bank, Richmond; Louis A. Graham, corporate research and development manager, American Viscose Division, FMC Corporation; Dr. Thomas O. Hall, Jr., professor and chairman of the department of philosophy and religious studies, Virginia Commonwealth University; and Dr. Wayburn S. Jeeter, professor of microbiology and director of the laboratory, cellular immunology, University of Arizona.

	1943		1944			1945	
	Jul.-Oct.	Nov.-Feb.	Mar.-Jun.	Jul.-Oct.	Nov.-Feb.	Mar.-Jun.	Jul.-Oct.
Navy	238	213	227	239	195	109	111**
C.O.	Lt. George F. Howe						

** All V-5s

University of Richmond   Richmond, Virginia

The V-12s reporting to the University of Richmond found themselves on the new trimester schedule, while the civilian students remained on the traditional two-semester plan. The V-12s were treated by other students and faculty as though they were in a separate school. When the civilians returned in the fall, there was some resentment of the V-12s, and the two groups got acquainted very slowly. Eventually the V-12s were invited into all campus organizations except the student government, which remained geared to the two-semester year.

The V-12s found their outlet in the football team, which turned out to be one of the best in the school's history. The 1943 Spiders lost only one game (to Duke) and finished as the Virginia state champs. The basketball team that season also had an excellent year and was acclaimed the "Big Six" title holder. Those winning teams helped bring the two student bodies together.

Near the end of the fourth term, on October 20, 1944, the *Richmond Collegian* gave full credit to the V-12s "of the original group" for the success of many continuing campus activities.

Although Richmond was a Baptist school, it did not prohibit dancing. The campus canteen was opened on Friday, October 6, 1943, with the Westhampton College (University of Richmond's women's campus) girls in attendance and a floor show at 2230. The excellent V-12 band played for tea dances and other events at Westhampton. The Midwinter Dance at Westhampton had to be postponed, however, when the V-12 unit was quarantined for three weeks after forty-four trainees contracted the mumps in November of 1944.

On October 19, 1945, the *Collegian* gave this farewell tribute to the V-12s: "They have been a welcome addition to college life."

Some Richmond V-12s: Bernard S. Browning, chairman, General Business Services; Rear Adm. Frank W. Corley, Jr., USN; Robert D. Kilpatrick, president, Connecticut General Insurance; Willard C. Osburn, director of communications, the Medical Society of Virginia; and Malcolm T. Stamper, president, Boeing Company.

	1943		1944			1945	
	Jul.-Oct.	Nov.-Feb.	Mar.-Jun.	Jul.-Oct.	Nov.-Feb.	Mar.-Jun.	Jul.-Oct.
Navy	362	386	362	343	241	156	121
C.O.	Lt. J. H. Neville						Lt. Thomas Stritch

University of Virginia Charlottesville, Virginia

The V-12s assigned to "Mr. Jefferson's University" were quartered in the Halls, the Ranges, and the Lawns. Window screens had to be made for some of the nearly one-hundred-year-old dorms. The men were fed in the University Commons. This was the first regular session of the university to be held in the summer in over one hundred years.

The high academic standards of the university made it especially difficult for men who had been away from college or had never attended before. In August 1943, the commanding officer wrote an open letter to the faculty members asking that special consideration be given to the fleet men, who were diligently applying themselves but through "rustiness" were having some difficulties in coping with the stringent requirements. The Bureau of Personnel followed with a telegram on September 5, 1943, instructing that no separations should be made at that time for academic reason.

The weekly *College Topics* reported campus life in full detail. The biggest problem faced by the university and the V-12s was the long-running controversy over the operation of the 101-year-old Virginia honor system, which was entirely student-run and had the power of expulsion. (See Chapter 25, "Academic Load.")

The social life at the University of Virginia was excellent. The V-12 dances often featured the music by the "Goldbrix," the V-12 dance band. Smokers were held fairly regularly. Distinguished visitors to the campus included Secretary of the Treasury

University of Virginia Archives

Henry Morgenthau and Gen. Alexander A. Vandegrift, commandant of the Marine Corps. Bands playing on the campus included Bobby Sherwood, Jack Teagarden, and Gene Krupa. The *Corks and Curls,* the yearbook published by the fraternities and organizations of the university, gave excellent coverage of the V-12 program.

Some University of Virginia V-12s: Dr. Richard M. Brandt, dean, School of Education, University of Virginia; George M. Coleman, Peace Corps director in Brazil and international public health specialist; Roger D. Fraley, senior vice president, Dean, Witter, Reynolds Company, Denver; Jesse T. Hudson, Jr., chief financial officer, senior vice president, Reynolds Metals Company; Dr. O. L. Miller, Jr., professor of biology, University of Virginia; Jonathan W. Old, Jr., president, Liggett Group; M. Lee Payne, chairman, United Virginia Bank, Norfolk; and Robert I. Stewart, senior vice president, Torchmark Corporation.

	1943		1944		1945			1946	
	Jul.-Oct.	Nov.-Feb.	Mar.-Jun.	Jul.-Oct.	Nov.-Feb.	Mar.-Jun.	Jul.-Oct.	Nov.-Feb.	Mar.-Jun.
Navy	577	576	527	540	477	417	423	542	270
C.O.	Capt. E. M. Williams							Capt. S. H. Hurt	

Bethany College Bethany, West Virginia

Bethany College Archives

Basic, premedical, and predental V-12s were sent to this 103-year-old liberal arts college, the only school in West Virginia selected for the V-12 program. The program turned out an amazing number of future physicians and dentists.

The V-12s represented twenty-eight states and the District of Columbia. They were quartered in Phillips and Cochran halls; the mess hall was located in the basement of Phillips. Discipline was extremely tough for the first few months, but then it eased up a bit. Campus life revolved around the Beehive, the soda fountain and campus hangout that had been unceremoniously uprooted from the basement of Phillips to make way for the V-12 contingent. The Beehive was moved to the Masonic Temple Building, occupying the basement and first floor.

The student social committee was diligent in planning some activity for every weekend. The V-12s formed a very popular dance band, which played for a number of the affairs. Dances included a military ball and a New Year's Eve Ball, which was held in Phillips and featured a buffet supper at 2300.

The theater group at Bethany was active all the time, as were the students interested in journalism. For a small school, they put out many publications. The mimeographed *Tell*, which came out weekly, reported on campus activities. The *Bethanian* was a general-interest monthly magazine, the *Bison* was a humor and features magazine that appeared from time to time, and the *Bethany Log* was the yearbook that recorded the whole scene.

V-12s remember touring the Weirton Steel Plant, moving families out of flood waters in the spring of 1945, and V-12 reunions in 1965 and 1983.

Some Bethany V-12s: Dr. Warren J. Brown, fellow of the American Academy of Family Physicians, Largo, Florida; Eugene Miller, vice president, U.S. Gypsum Company; Maj. Gen. Noah C. New, USMC; Dr. Arnold Schrier, professor of history, University of Cincinnati; and Dr. Kyle Swisher, professor of cardiology, University of Maryland Medical School.

	1943		1944			1945	
	Jul.-Oct.	Nov.-Feb.	Mar.-Jun.	Jul.-Oct.	Nov.-Feb.	Mar.-Jun.	Jul.-Oct.
Navy	309	303	311	305	199	147	131
C.O.	Lt.(jg) Daniel Z. Gibson	Lt. Sherman D. Henderson		Lt. Gordon J. Longley			

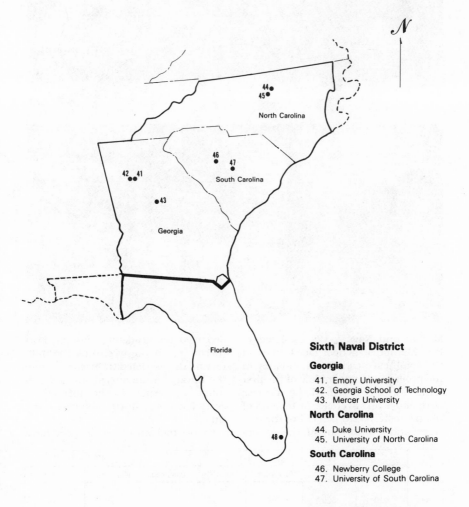

Sixth Naval District

Georgia

41. Emory University
42. Georgia School of Technology
43. Mercer University

North Carolina

44. Duke University
45. University of North Carolina

South Carolina

46. Newberry College
47. University of South Carolina

Seventh Naval District

Florida

48. University of Miami

Emory University Atlanta, Georgia

Marine and Navy V-12s assigned to this Methodist school faced some of the toughest academic standards in the program. In the middle of the first term, only one-fourth of the trainees were above a D average. At the end of the trimester, 32.6 percent of the marines and 16 percent of the sailors departed for academic reasons. Furthermore, on the weekends the military made restricted trainees march to the library in the afternoons and evenings and report to the duty officer every few hours during the rest of the time.

Emory had one of the most complete

	1943		1944			1945	
	Jul.-Oct.	Nov.-Feb.	Mar.-Jun.	Jul.-Oct.	Nov.-Feb.	Mar.-Jun.	Jul.-Oct.
Navy	419	529	388	605	390	229	153
C.O.	Capt. J. V. Babcock						Capt. Robert Strite
Marines	195	109					
O-in-C	2nd Lt. P. R. Stanley						

intramural programs, but it did not engage in interscholastic sports, with the exception of swimming.

But life was not all dull: lots of dances were sponsored by the student council, the fraternities, the Emory School of Nursing, and Agnes Scott College, Emory's sister institution, with more than four hundred young women. The orchestras of Les Brown and Artie Shaw played for some of those dances, and actress Jane Withers turned up at one.

Other events of interest: the January 8, 1944, head-on train wreck just a few hundred yards from the campus; two marines being seriously scalded in the showers due to faulty plumbing; and the suspension of classes for two days in December of 1943 due to "cat fever" ("flu" to civilians), which sent ninety-five trainees to the hospital or a temporary sick bay in Alabama Hall.

Some Emory V-12s: Dr. Edward E. David, science advisor to President Nixon and president, Exxon Research and Engineering Company; Dr. Robert F. Durden, chairman and professor, department of history, Duke University; H. Carey Hanlin, president, Provident Life and Accident Insurance Company, Chattanooga; Frank C. Jones, attorney, and president, State Bar of Georgia; William L. Matheson, New York lawyer and chairman of the board, Michigan Resources Company; Judge James C. Paine, U.S. Court for the Southern District of Florida; Gordon M. Sears, chairman, T. J. Ross and Associates, New York City; and Wallace O. Westfeldt, senior producer, NBC News, New York City.

Georgia School of Technology Atlanta, Georgia
(Now Georgia Institute of Technology)

With more than nineteen hundred servicemen, the all-male Georgia Tech campus in 1943 looked like a military base. Besides Navy and Marine V-12s, Tech had a Naval ROTC unit and a large ASTP contingent. After most of the ASTPs were withdrawn in March of 1944, the military enrollment dropped to one thousand.

As in prewar days, sports played a big part in Tech life. The "Rambling Wreck" took the Southeastern Conference football crown in 1943 and 1944, and each team went to a bowl game. On January 1, 1944, Tech topped Tulsa twenty to eighteen in the Sugar Bowl. Later, the game ball was auctioned off by actress Jane Withers for $5 million in war bonds. Tech again faced Tulsa in the 1945 Orange Bowl game, but lost twenty-six to twelve.

The 1943–1944 basketball squad dropped only two games and the 1944 track team captured the Southeastern Conference crown.

The Georgia Tech Marine drill team was so exceptional that Capt. J. V. Babcock, USN, the commanding officer, issued a commendation to be placed in the files of all fifty-three marines who put on the exhibition at the Tech-Carolina game on October 7, 1944.

V-12s took leading roles in publishing the *Blueprint,* the Tech yearbook, and they also dominated the *Technique,* the weekly newspaper. Social life was not ignored — dances fea-

	1943		1944			1945			1946
	Jul.-Oct.	Nov.-Feb.	Mar.-Jun.	Jul.-Oct.	Nov.-Feb.	Mar.-Jun.	Jul.-Oct.	Nov.-Feb.	Mar.-Jun.
Navy	586	726	717	710	595	459	334	381	444
C.O.	Capt. J. V. Babcock					Capt. Robert Strite			
Marines	192	125	111	86	78				
O-in-C	@	Capt. Donald G. Payzant			2				

@ 2nd Lt. George W. Holmes III   2. Capt. Derrol E. Huddleson

Georgia School of Technology

tured such bands as Sammy Kaye and Les Brown.

Some Georgia Tech V-12s: Joseph H. Anderer, chairman, Warren Corporation, Stafford Springs, Conn.; Capt. Robert G. Beuchler, USN; Dr. Charles B. Cliett, professor and chairman, department of aeronautical engineering, Mississippi State University; the Right Reverend Huntley A. Elebash, Episcopal bishop of East Carolina; the Right Reverend William H. Folwell, Episcopal bishop of Central Florida; Vice Adm. Earl B. Fowler, USN; George B. Hills, Jr., senior vice president, Stone Container Corporation; Dr. William B. Jones, professor of electrical engineering, Texas A and M; Dr. James E. Sellers, David Rice Professor of Ethics, Rice University; Kendall G. Shaw, artist; Dr. Eugene B. Sledge, professor of biology, University of Montevallo, and author (*With the Old Breed at Peleliu and Okinawa*); and William Reece Smith, Jr., attorney, and president, American Bar Association.

Mercer University Macon, Georgia

Howard Purcell

On July 1, 1943, Mercer University, a Baptist institution, was invaded by 229 Navy trainees, including sixty-seven Texans. In the second year, many of the new trainees came from Georgia and southern Illinois, which made for some interesting North-South rivalry. And, of course, fleet men came to the Mercer campus with each new term.

How well did these massive changes work out? Just fine! The 1945 *Cauldron*, the Mercer yearbook, was dedicated to the officers and men of the naval V-12 unit with these words: "We feel a peculiar pride in dedicating this book to the Navy for all it has contributed to our life in the past two years. Transformations have come about through constructive changes brought by the Navy along with many men who have been outstanding students and leaders. The V-12s here at Mercer personify the characteristics of discipline, honor, leadership and valor attributable to Naval tradition."

The V-12s were all housed in Sher-wood Hall, which became known as the "USS Lexington Barracks." They took part wholeheartedly in all of the campus activities from publications to athletics. But dancing, card playing, and the like were not permitted on the Mercer campus, so the V-12s looked elsewhere for much of their social life.

The Mercer unit had good continuity — the same commanding officer and the same executive officer remained there during the entire V-12 program. This was the only college that had that experience.

Some Mercer V-12s: Dr. Hubert H. Blakey, psychiatrist, Alexandria, Va.; Bryant A. Meeks, Pittsburgh Steelers football player and realtor and management consultant, Sarasota; Rear Adm. William O. Miller, USN, judge advocate general of the Navy; Dr. Sanford A. Mullen, pathologist, and president, Florida Medical Association; Judge Harold Barefoot Sanders, Jr., U.S. District Court for Northern Texas; and Preston C. Williams, Jr., president, Southern Frozen Foods Company.

| | 1943 | | 1944 | | | 1945 | |
	Jul.-Oct.	Nov.-Feb.	Mar.-Jun.	Jul.-Oct.	Nov.-Feb.	Mar.-Jun.	Jul.-Oct.
Navy	220	218	221	184	201	117	112
C.O.	Lt. Robert G. Matheson						

Duke University Durham, North Carolina

James G. Schneider

Duke University had one of the largest V-12 units. It consisted of basics, engineers, premeds, predents, pretheologicals, NROTCs, and marines — a total of sixteen hundred at the beginning. An Army Finance School of more than one hundred officers was also on the campus, so the V-12s had many opportunities to practice their saluting.

The V-12 engineers were quartered in Southgate Hall on the East Campus, where the Engineering School was located. The other residents of the East Campus were the Duke coeds.

The rest of the V-12s lived on the West Campus, where the union, chapel, library, gym, stadium, and other athletic facilities were located. The Duke University Hospital was at-

	1943		1944			1945			1946
	Jul.-Oct.	Nov.-Feb.	Mar.-Jun.	Jul.-Oct.	Nov.-Feb.	Mar.-Jun.	Jul.-Oct.	Nov.-Feb.	Mar.-Jun.
Navy	806	952	1004	1012	670	261	104	279	280
C.O.	Capt. A. T. Clay			Capt. C. P. McFeaters			Capt. A. M. Kowalzak, Jr.		
Marines	578	368	321	187					
O-in-C	Maj. Walter G. Cooper			@					

@ Warrant Officer Joseph E. Blanchard

tached to the West Campus, and the student nurses lived there, too.

In football the 1943 Blue Devils lost only one game, a fourteen-to-thirteen squeaker against the fourth-ranked Naval Academy team. Duke took the Southern Conference championship that year and ended the season ranked seventh nationally. The 1944 squad went to the 1945 Sugar Bowl, where it beat the University of Alabama, twenty-nine to twenty-six.

The *Chronicle* reported weekly on campus events, which included dances, picnics, lectures, and meetings of all kinds. When Les Brown and his Band of Renown visited in the summer of 1944, the V-12 president of the student body escorted Doris Day around the campus. The *Chanticleer* gave a fine yearbook view of Duke in wartime.

The Goody Shop was an off-campus hangout that was popular with the V-12s. The Union soda fountain, called the Dope Shop, supplied their in-bounds needs.

Some Duke V-12s: Lewis M. Branscomb, chief scientist and vice president, IBM Corporation; Clarence J. Brown, congressman from Ohio; Wil-

liam J. Ferren, vice president, Moody's Investors Service; Joseph M. DiMona, author (with H. R. Haldeman, *The Ends of Power*); John W. Hartman, international president of the Young Presidents Organization; Henry J. Hyde, congressman from Illinois; John S. Lanahan, president, the Greenbrier Hotel; Dr. Karl J. Lange, vice president, George Washington University; C. Edward Little, president, Mutual Broadcasting System; Dr. Phillip K. Lundeberg, curator of naval history, Smithsonian Institution; Harris H. Mullen, founder and publisher, *Florida Travel* magazine; Clint Murchison,* Texas investor; Vice Adm. Gordon R. Nagler, USN; Henry R. Nolte, Jr., vice president and general counsel, Ford Motor Company; Edmund T. Pratt, Jr., chairman, Pfizer; Walter L. Ross, vice president, Mattel; Col. John B. Sims, USMC; Capt. Henry L. Stanfield, USN; William Styron, author (Pulitzer Prize in 1968 for *The Confessions of Nat Turner*); T. Murray Toomey, international lawyer, Washington, D.C.; and Dr. James H. Zumberge, president, University of Southern California.

University of North Carolina Chapel Hill, North Carolina

The 796 sailors and 312 marines who arrived at the oldest state university represented thirty-seven states and the District of Columbia. They were quartered in twelve fraternity houses and seven older dormitories; the newer and better dorms were already occupied by the two thousand V-5 cadets at the Navy Pre-Flight School. The V-12s were fed at Swain Hall, which was generally called "Swine Hall." The first two terms of the V-12 program involved no watches, no compulsory study hours, and no bed checks, but beginning in the spring of 1944 the discipline was tightened up.

The Tar Heel athletic teams consisted mainly of V-12s; there were thirty-seven marines on the 1943 football squad. The *Tar Heel* became a weekly publication. The yearbook, the *Yackety-Yack*, appeared on schedule. During the first sixteen months university civilians remained on a quarterly schedule while the trainees were on the Navy's trimester schedule, but in November of 1944 the entire campus went on the Navy's schedule.

	1943		1944			1945			1946
	Jul.-Oct.	Nov.-Feb.	Mar.-Jun.	Jul.-Oct.	Nov.-Feb.	Mar.-Jun.	Jul.-Oct.	Nov.-Feb.	Mar.-Jun.
Navy	796	905	961	829	417	234	93	NA	NA
C.O.	Capt. W. S. Popham			@	Capt. E. E. Hazlett, Jr.			Capt. D. W. Loomis	
Marines	298	212	189	133	147	161	144	107	89
O-in-C	Capt. James W. Marshall					Capt. Preston S. Marchant			Capt. R. E. Brown

NA = Not available   @ Capt. W. T. Mallison

University of North Carolina

In January of 1944 a new canteen for V-12s, the Scuttlebutt, was opened in a building added to the Book Exchange. Profits from the Scuttlebutt supported dances and parties for the entire V-12 unit (including NROTCs) as well as separate parties for the V-12s and NROTCs.

The trainees were reviewed by Lord Halifax, the British ambassador, and in February of 1944, Rear Adm. Randall Jacobs, chief of personnel, was the commencement speaker.

Some North Carolina V-12s: Vice Adm. Eugene A. Grinstead, USN; Carrell S. McNulty, Jr., president, NB Instruments; Edward M. Mead, publisher, the *Erie Times* (Pennsylvania); Robert B. Morgan, senator from North Carolina; Brig. Gen. William L. Smith, USMC; Rear Adm. Charles P. Tesh, USN; Dr. James N. Waggoner, medical director, the Garrett Corporation, and president, Aerospace Medical Association; Judge Harry W. Wellford, U.S. Court of Appeals, Sixth Circuit; Rear Adm. Donald B. Whitmire, USN; Thomas G. Wicker, nationally syndicated columnist of the *New York Times;* and Donald S. Willard, executive vice president, Teachers Insurance and Annuity Association of America.

Newberry College   Newberry, South Carolina

Nichols' Studio, Newberry, South Carolina

The V-12s were warmly welcomed to Newberry College by school officials, fellow students, and local citizens. In fact, the city council of Newberry took out full-page ads of welcome in the *Indian*, the student newspaper. At the end of the program the city council's ad thanked the departing V-12s and even listed where they were going.

In the first contingent of 325 V-12s, 122 came from Illinois and 21 each came from Iowa's Grinnell and Luther colleges.

The Lutheran Synod of South Carolina provided funds for the rental of first-run films, purchased Ping-Pong tables, and provided pennants for the platoons. Local citizens raised thirty-six hundred dollars to build and equip a recreation building, the "Zack Shack." Every summer there was a huge "watermelon cut" for the V-12s and other students. Dances, "happy hours," and campus barbecues added to the social life.

The 1944 *Newberrian*, the yearbook, was issued in February and was dedicated to the Navy. Thereafter during the V-12 existence on campus, the *Newberrian* came out every two terms, which, considering the difficulties of printing during wartime, was a considerable achievement.

Commencement addresses were given by the first two officers-in-charge of the nationwide V-12 program: Comdr. Arthur S. Adams in February 1944 and Lt. Comdr. William S. Thomson in October 1944.

Some Newberry V-12s: William L. Brown, chairman, First National Bank of Boston; Dr. Peter Hackes, NBC television, Washington, D.C.; Dr. Allen Hodges, program director for mental health, region eight, U.S. Department of Health, Education and Welfare; and C. W. Korndoerfer, chairman, Korndoerfer Construction Company, Racine, Wis.

	1943		1944			1945	
	Jul.-Oct.	Nov.-Feb.	Mar.-Jun.	Jul.-Oct.	Nov.-Feb.	Mar.-Jun.	Jul.-Oct.
Navy	320	280	309	287	239	164	145
C.O.	Lt. Leroy W. Farinholt			Lt. Arden O. French			Lt. C. B. Ford

@ Lt. C. B. Ford

University of South Carolina Columbia, South Carolina

When the V-12 program started at the University of South Carolina, the Naval Flight Preparatory School (V-5) with about 650 men and the CAA–War Training Service with a quota of 120 were already on campus. The Naval ROTC program had been in existence since 1940 and went on active duty when the V-12 program began.

Summertime dances were held on the bricks at the top of the horseshoe in front of the new library. That library is now the McKissick Museum, named for university president James R. McKissick, who died suddenly on September 3, 1944. A V-12 was one of the pallbearers when McKissick was buried on the campus in front of the Carolineana Library.

V-12s took part in all campus activities. The 1943 Carolina-Clemson football game was a thirty-three-to-six triumph for USC. The 1943–1944 basketball team, made up entirely of Navy personnel, compiled a thirteen-and-two record, but Navy authorities vetoed the acceptance of an invitation to the Southern Conference Tournament at Chapel Hill, so Carolina passed up a great opportunity to capture the Southern crown.

When the trustees of the university voted in December of 1944 to move the campus to another location at the outskirts of Columbia after the war, the student body and alumni were in an uproar. The Navy didn't want to get involved, so an order was issued prohibiting V-12s from attending any meetings concerning the controversy. Eventually it was decided not to move the campus.

Some South Carolina V-12s: Brig. Gen. George R. Brier, USMC; Dr. William B. Boyd, president, University of Oregon; Dr. Billy F. Bryant, professor of mathematics, Vanderbilt University; Capt. Roger Carlquist, USN; Dr. James W. Fisher, chairman, department of pharmacology, Tulane University Medical School; Leon S. Goodall, chairman, Carolina Continental Insurance Company; Dr. Kenneth G. Picha, dean, School of Engineering, University of Massachusetts; and Rear Adm. William D. Robertson, Jr., USN.

1944 *Garnet and Black* yearbook. Courtesy of McKissick Museum, University of South Carolina

	1943		1944			1945			1946
	Jul.-Oct.	Nov.-Feb.	Mar.-Jun.	Jul.-Oct.	Nov.-Feb.	Mar.-Jun.	Jul.-Oct.	Nov.-Feb.	Mar.-Jun.
Navy	586	631	611	731	543	425	52	34	18
C.O.	Capt. R. C. Needham					Capt. M. G. Kennedy			

University of Miami   Coral Gables, Florida

The 290 men assigned to the V-12 unit at the University of Miami were envied by their friends. Imagine being ordered to a place where the palm trees sway and the moon beams brightly! But the chiefs decided to mix a little work with all the fun and frivolity, so they organized a tough physical training program and then a boxing tournament in which all of the V-12s were invited to participate. It was an invitation that could not be turned down. There were 142 separate bouts in the tournament.

Too far from other schools to find much intercollegiate competition, the V-12s at the University of Miami entered teams in various leagues formed by naval units in the area. They were in softball, touch football, basketball, and even tennis and boxing. A water show was put on at the Venetian Pool, a Coral Gables showplace where the Miami swimming classes were held. An interdorm league provided intramural competition for the Miami V-12s.

The V-12s were housed in Santander, DeCastro, LeJeune, and Stohn.

Trainees took part fully in school activities, holding many class offices and the leadership in the Miami Student Association. They organized their own marching and swing bands and worked on the publications, the weekly *Hurricane* and the annual *Ibis.*

The V-12 "happy hours" featured skits put on by each dorm, the winners of the competition receiving special liberties and awards of ice cream and cake at the campus "Slop Shop."

Capt. James L. Holloway, Jr., USN, director of training, was the commencement speaker on June 23, 1944.

Some U of M V-12s: Dr. Henry W. Blackburn, Jr., professor and director, division of epidemiology, University of Minnesota Medical School; Dr. Robert A. Butler, professor and chairman of the department of behavioral sciences, University of Chicago; Norman M. Giller, architect, Miami Beach, and professor, University of Miami; Jerome W. O'Connor, chairman, WCIU-TV, Chicago; and Albert L. Rosen, president, San Francisco Giants baseball club.

	1943		1944			1945	
	Jul.-Oct.	Nov.-Feb.	Mar.-Jun.	Jul.-Oct.	Nov.-Feb.	Mar.-Jun.	Jul.-Oct.
Navy	271	274	252	245	200	126	109
C.O.	Lt. Mode L. Stone	Lt.(jg) Leon N. Henderson			Lt.(jg) E. G. Raburn		

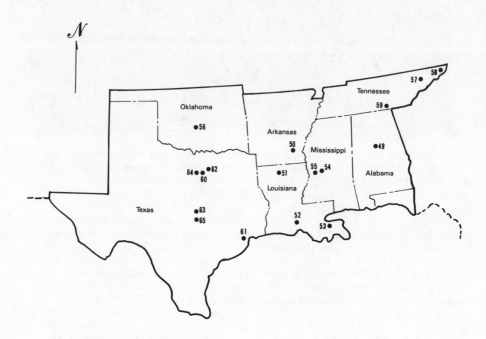

Eighth Naval District

Alabama

49. Howard College

Arkansas

50. Arkansas A & M College

Louisiana

51. Louisiana Polytechnic Institute
52. Southwestern Louisiana Institute
53. Tulane University

Mississippi

54. Millsaps College
55. Mississippi College

Oklahoma

56. University of Oklahoma

Tennessee

57. Carson Newman College
58. Milligan College
59. University of the South

Texas

60. North Texas Agricultural College
61. Rice Institute
62. Southern Methodist University
63. Southwestern University
64. Texas Christian University
65. University of Texas

Howard College   Birmingham, Alabama
(Now Samford University)

The V-12 unit of this Baptist college was secured almost single-handedly by the college president, Maj. Harwell Davis, who told the 1943 Alabama State Baptist Convention that "the College would be unable to operate unless it secured some program training men in the service of our country." The V-12s were quartered in Renfroe and Smith halls, which had formerly been girls' dormitories. The coeds were then assigned to two vacated fraternity houses and another building purchased by the college for a girls' dormitory. These three buildings were quickly christened "Ration," "Duration," and "Inflation."

Samford University Library

The Navy Social Committee sponsored semiannual smokers and boxing matches and the Midshipmen's Ball held every trimester. These represented quite a change for a Baptist college!

The Howard *Crimson* continued as the school newspaper, but there were few V-12s on the staff. In August of 1943 the Navy men started the *Scuttlebutt*, which carried all of the Navy news, interviews, and humor. It was inserted as a part of the *Crimson*. An editorial in the *Scuttlebutt* of April 12, 1945, urged that dungarees be substituted for the weekday summer uniform because whites were so quickly soiled from the coal and iron ore dust permeating the Birmingham atmosphere. But whites remained the summer uniform.

In 1946 the *Entre Nous* yearbook contained a letter from President Davis complimenting the departed V-12s: "We salute them all with admi-

ration touched with affection and express the hope that the recollections of their service at Howard College may be as pleasant as the recollections Howard College will have of them."

Some Howard V-12s: Dr. William T. Alderson, director, Margaret Woodbury Strong Museum, Rochester, New York; Dr. Howard Boozer, executive director, South Carolina Commission on Higher Education; John M. Bradley, president, Resources Management Service (forestry management), Birmingham; James B. Davis, real estate broker and chairman, Eastern Health Systems, Birmingham; William S. Pritchard, Jr., attorney, and president, University of Alabama Law School Foundation; Ben L. Summerford, artist and chairman of the art department, American University; George P. Taylor, director of West African operations of the Peace Corps, and professor of law, University of Alabama School of Law; and Dr. Charles B. Vail, president, Winthrop College.

	1943		1944			1945	
	Jul.-Oct.	Nov.-Feb.	Mar.-Jun.	Jul.-Oct.	Nov.-Feb.	Mar.-Jun.	Jul.-Oct.
Navy	228	221	230	205	196	127	118
C.O.	Lt. George W. Hulme, Jr.			Lt. Arthur S. Postle			Lt. C. A. Schade

Arkansas A & M College Monticello, Arkansas
(Now University of Arkansas at Monticello)

Fred McClory

About two hundred marines and an equal number of sailors arrived at A & M. The marines were quartered in Harris Hall and the sailors took over Horsfall. Their first commanding officer was Lt. Comdr. William S. Thomson, USNR, who a few months later was ordered to Washington for duty with the College Training Section. By May of 1944 he was in charge of the entire V-12 program.

The monumental happening at A & M was the "Cinderella of the Southwest" football team, which is described in Chapter 33, "Intercollegiate Athletics." It ended up with a seven, one, and one record, its only loss coming from Southwestern University,

seven to zero. The tie was with Southwestern Louisiana Institute. The first annual Oil Bowl was organized in Houston for January 1, 1944, to match SLI and A & M. SLI won in a rain-soaked game, twenty-four to seven.

The student council fund was first developed by "voluntary contributions" of ten dollars from each of the V-12s, plus the proceeds from the Coca-Cola machines. When the gate receipts from the A & M football games in Memphis began rolling in, it became the best-funded student council in the United States. Organized as the Athletic Council of Arkansas A & M, it purchased furniture and recreational

	1943	1944				1945	
	Jul.-Oct.	Nov.-Feb.	Mar.-Jun.	Jul.-Oct.	Nov.-Feb.	Mar.-Jun.	Jul.-Oct.
Navy	191	226	243	299	288	204	153
C.O.	Lcdr. William S. Thomson	Lt. C. G. Browne		Lt. George W. Greene			
Marines	204	176	137	99			
O-in-C	Capt. Jack T. Lytle						

Arkansas A & M College

George C. Scheu

equipment for the bare student lounge in Royer Hall, and it sponsored all the dances and parties of the school.

The V-12s organized a student newspaper dubbed the *Link* to signify the bond between the Navy and the college. *The Log of the U.S.S. Arkam* was the annual put together by the V-12s to record Navy life at A & M. The receipt for the advance purchase of the *Log* was required for admission to the show, "Half Hitches." Another entertainment extravaganza was an all-marine show called "You Cur, Sir."

Some A & M V-12s: Herbert W. Beattie, Jr., concert artist, professor of music, Hofstra University; Sterling Cockrill, Jr., majority leader and speaker of the house, Arkansas General Assembly; Capt. Ernest E. Connelley, USN; Dr. Jess B. Covington, chairman, department of journalism, University of Arkansas (Fayetteville); Tom E. Dean, assistant football coach, Southern Methodist University; Kenneth E. Edwards, vice president for marketing, Culligan International; Edgar A. Holloway, vice president for finance, the Clorox Company; Fred McClory, vice president, Donovan Engineering, Chicago; Dr. Lester E. McGonigle, state medical director, Blue Shield of Wyoming; and Dr. Robert G. F. Spitze, professor of agricultural economics, University of Illinois.

Louisiana Polytechnic Institute Ruston, Louisiana
(Now Louisiana Tech University)

Roy E. Baxter

When V-12s reported to this school in the hills of northern Louisiana, they found modern buildings built during the administration of Governor Huey P. Long. They also found friendly people and some nice campus traditions, including a Wednesday-night supper sing.

Strong competition developed between the Navy and Marines. The company winning the monthly review got special liberty privileges and was honored at a candlelight dance with music furnished by the Tech Collegians.

Tech Talk kept a weekly campus record. The Tech Marines contributed a seven-minute segment to the nation-wide "Halls of Montezuma" broadcast on Mutual Radio in early 1944. Another interesting event was the seven-mile march by a detachment of marines and sailors to Camp Ruston, a German prisoner of war camp, for a softball game. Tech beat the Army guards, who then fed them at the camp mess and gave them a ride back to the campus.

Tech V-12s fondly recall the Ruston

	1943		1944			1945	
	Jul.-Oct.	Nov.-Feb.	Mar.-Jun.	Jul.-Oct.	Nov.-Feb.	Mar.-Jun.	Jul.-Oct.
Navy	279	355	330	438	358	210	159
C.O.	Cdr. G. W. Moyers		Lcdr. E. J. Aylstock		Lt. Fred C. Blanchard		
Marines	289	229	171	90			
O-in-C	Capt. Shelton H. Short, Jr.			W.O. Bermon E. Anderson			

Louisiana Polytechnic Institute

Roy E. Baxter

USO, the picnics in the meadow near the school, and campus activities such as the YMCA, debating, dramatics, and sports. After the program closed Tech sent each of the trainees a V-12 picture booklet as a remembrance of their times at Ruston.

Some Louisiana Tech V-12s: James B. Armor, president, Thrift Drug Company; Rear Adm. Robert L. Baker, USN(MC), selected in 1973 as clinical admiral; Roy E. Baxter, vice president, U.S. Brass Corporation; M. L. Borchelt, vice chairman, Central and Southwest Corporation; Cloyce K. Box, guard, Detroit Lions, chairman, OKC Corporation, and chairman of the board, West Texas State University; Col. Harold L. Davis, USMCR, head basketball coach, University of Texas (El Paso); William A. Kistler, Jr., chairman, Hughes Tool Company; Fred N. McCain, athletic director, North Texas State University; Dr. Stephen L. McDonald, professor of economics, University of Texas (Austin); William J. Noonan, senior vice president, Merrill Lynch; William J. Raggio, attorney and Nevada state senator, Reno; William E. Ridgeway, president, Mancos Petroleum Company; Dr. Terry Triffett, associate dean of engineering (research), University of Arizona; and Lt. Gen. LaVerne E. Weber, United States Army.

Southwestern Louisiana Institute   Lafayette, Louisiana
(Now University of Southwestern Louisiana)

The marines and sailors ordered to the V-12 unit at Southwestern Louisiana Institute were quartered in the dorms near the stadium, and some of the sailors were in the stadium itself. They all ate at the mess hall in commodious Allen Dining Hall.

A friendly campus, SLI and its students had some kind of entertainment, dance, or party every weekend. The unit marched in war bond parades in Lafayette and put on a boxing show where ten thousand dollars' worth of bonds were sold.

The Marine unit "adopted" a small Lafayette boy, outfitted him in a miniature uniform, promoted him from private to gunnery sergeant, and even let "Sergeant Max" march the men to chow.

The most exciting days of the V-12 unit centered about the football team of 1943, which had acquired talent from many of the football powers of the South and Southwest. The squad went four, zero, and one, the tie being a game played at Memphis in rain, mud, and fog against Arkansas A & M. The two teams met again in the 1944 Oil Bowl at Houston, and again played in a driving rain, but this time the SLI Bulldogs topped the Boll Weevils twenty-four to seven. All but three of the SLI squad were marines. The team turned over forty thousand dollars from gate proceeds to relief agencies.

	1943	1944			1945		
	Jul.-Oct.	Nov.-Feb.	Mar.-Jun.	Jul.-Oct.	Nov.-Feb.	Mar.-Jun.	Jul.-Oct.
Navy	310	399	352	418	373	273	142
C.O.	Cdr. William O. Baldwin	Lcdr. H. F. Taggart			Lt. Ben R. Miller		
Marines	285	232	207	139			
O-in-C	Capt. Reed F. Taylor						

Southwestern Louisiana Institute

SLI's president gave a farewell dinner each term to honor those heading to other stations. The commencement address in June of 1944 was given by Dr. Joseph W. Barker, special assistant to the secretary of the Navy. V-12 reunions were held in 1983 and 1985.

Some SLI V-12s: Dr. Bernard J. Bienvenu, professor of business administration and head of the department of management, University of Southwestern Louisiana; Alvin Dark, player, coach, and manager in major league baseball; Capt. Warren P. Decker, USNR, and investment banker; J. J. ("Jay") Hebert, professional golfer; Weldon Humble, guard on Cleveland Browns professional football team; Rear Adm. Charles H. Mayfield,* USNR, senior vice president, First National Bank of Commerce, New Orleans; Harry A. Merlo, chairman, Louisiana-Pacific Corporation; Fletcher B. Moore, director of electronics and control lab, Marshall Space Flight Center, NASA; David ("Sam") Peckinpah, motion picture director; William S. Pollard, Jr., professor of civil and urban engineering, University of Colorado (Denver); and Wilkes C. Robinson, president, Gulf Coast and Great Plains Legal Foundation, Kansas City.

Tulane University   New Orleans, Louisiana

The Tulane V-12 unit was the second largest in the Eighth Naval District. When the trainees arrived on campus on July 1, 1943, an observer noted that it looked like an "outdoor Union Station" with hundreds of men in lines, some sitting on suitcases and others hurrying from one location to another.

Eight hundred and sixty-seven V-12s found togetherness in the Tulane gymnasium; the rest of the unit was quartered in the Athletic Dorm, the Music and Drama Dorm, and three small units of Sophie Newcomb College: Warren House, Richardson House, and Doris Hall. The men in the Newcomb dorms ate at the Warren House mess hall, and the rest were fed in Bruff Commons. The V-12 office was located in the Tilton Law Building.

With the gym otherwise occupied, all of the home basketball games were played in other locations off campus. Tulane maintained its sports record by fielding teams in all major sports. The trainees took swimming classes in the outdoor pool at nearby Audubon Park.

The Student Center was the focal point of V-12 social life. It had fine facilities for recreation, and on Friday afternoons the girls from Newcomb College came over for the weekly "student stomps." The weekly *Hullabaloo* reported on campus activities. The *Jambalaya* was the yearbook.

The women of the Newcomb Alumni Association provided free alterations and repairs for Navy uniforms; in just a few months they altered more than six thousand garments. Fleet Adm. Chester W. Nimitz was the speaker at the final Tulane function attended by V-12s, a memorial convocation to honor the university's war dead.

Some Tulane V-12s: Capt. Elgin C. Cowart, Jr., USN(MC), director, Armed Forces Institute of Pathology; the Right Reverend Duncan Montgomery Gray, bishop of the Episcopal Diocese of Mississippi; Griff C. Lee, vice president, J. Ray McDermott and Company, and member, advisory board, Tulane College of Engineering; Dr. James V. McConnell, professor of psychology, University of Michigan; and Dr. J. Chester McKee, vice president for research and graduate dean, Mississippi State University.

	1943		1944			1945			1946
	Jul.-Oct.	Nov.-Feb.	Mar.-Jun.	Jul.-Oct.	Nov.-Feb.	Mar.-Jun.	Jul.-Oct.	Nov.-Feb.	Mar.-Jun.
Navy	850	962	949	877	600	382	196	271	103
C.O.	Capt. Forrest U. Lake							Capt. Harry D. Power	

Millsaps College Jackson, Mississippi

The 184 marines ordered to Millsaps on July 1, 1943, were quartered in Founders Hall; the 196 sailors took up residence in Burton, Whitworth, and Galloway halls. The V-12 mess hall was in Galloway, while the unit headquarters was located in Whitworth.

Like many other units, the Millsaps V-12s put on some excellent variety shows featuring everything from musicians to magicians. The student paper, *Purple and White*, diligently reported all of the activities of the unit, and the yearbook, *Bobashela*, gave an excellent report of the unit's years.

There was no football in 1943. The Purple and White basketball squad competed in a six-team service league, which included the V-12 unit at Mississippi College. Most of the Millsaps V-12s took part in the extensive intramural competition held on a continuous basis at the college.

Social life was not neglected. A number of dances were held each term, some of them formals in the Victory Room of the Hotel Heidelberg in downtown Jackson. The Christmas Hop on December 17, 1943, was one such formal. Other social activities included barbecues and picnics.

The Millsaps V-12s have had reunions on campus in 1968 and 1984, and in Fredericksburg, Texas, in 1986.

Some Millsaps V-12s: Richard M. Allen, special assistant attorney general, state of Mississippi; Robert E. Bolen, mayor of Fort Worth; Johnny Carson, "Tonight Show"; John Christmas, vice president for enrollment, Millsaps College; Chief Judge Charles Clark, U.S. Court of Appeals, Fifth Circuit; Harper Davis, athletic director and head coach, Millsaps College; Rear Adm. Jeremiah A. Denton, Jr., USN, also U.S. senator from Alabama; Dr. S. Duncan Heron, Jr., professor of geology, Duke University; and B.J. Pevehouse, president, Adobe Resources, Midland, Texas.

	1943		1944		1945		
	Jul.-Oct.	Nov.-Feb.	Mar.-Jun.	Jul.-Oct.	Nov.-Feb.	Mar.-Jun.	Jul.-Oct.
Navy	181	270	377	343	223	136	116
C.O.	Lt. C. L. Alderman		Lt. E. S. Gard		Lt. Harold G. Leffler		
Marines	177	108					
O-in-C	Capt. Loyce E. Biles						

Mississippi College Clinton, Mississippi

The V-12s reported to this 117-year-old Southern Baptist school in one of the hottest summers on record. They were quartered in Chrestman and Alumni halls. The V-12 office was also located in Chrestman.

Some of the best coverage of any V-12 unit was given by the *Watch*, the mimeographed weekly paper that appeared initially on August 11, 1943. It was recognized by the Eighth Naval District as the first V-12 publication in the district. The trainees also put out two excellent Navy annuals, called the *Pelorus*, which were loaded with photographs of the unit and its activities.

In addition, there was the college's annual, the *Tribesman*, which also gave good coverage of the V-12 unit.

Dancing was not allowed on campus, and by some accounts not in the town of Clinton, either. For social life, V-12s headed off campus to Jackson and sometimes to Vicksburg. The commanding officer gave a Tuesday night liberty in August of 1943 so V-12s could attend a USO dance in Jackson. He explained to the Eighth Naval District that this was an "attempt to revive the very bad recreational situation here." V-12 variety shows were held on August 6 and 27, and about once a month thereafter. They featured their snappy dance band, the 4.0 Skybirds. Unit dances were held nearly every month in the Victory Room of the Heidelberg Hotel in Jackson.

The unit was 100 percent in purchasing war bonds and National Service Life Insurance.

V-12s took part in many campus activities and were elected class officers and president of the student body. The athletic program was devoted mostly to intramurals — only the basketball, softball, and boxing teams had competition in service leagues.

Some Mississippi College V-12s: William L. Dickinson, congressman from Alabama; Robert W. Hirsch, majority leader, South Dakota senate; Charles R. Johnson, area news editor, Milwaukee *Journal*, and author (*The Green Bay Packers — Pro Football's Pioneer Team*); Raymond Maginn, controller, Central Illinois Light Company; and Dr. Joseph L. Peyser, dean of faculties, Indiana University (South Bend).

	1943		1944			1945	
	Jul.-Oct.	Nov.-Feb.	Mar.-Jun.	Jul.-Oct.	Nov.-Feb.	Mar.-Jun.	Jul.-Oct.
Navy	335	296	326	283	240	139	122
C.O.	Lt. A. K. Burt			Lt. B. C. Watts			

University of Oklahoma Norman, Oklahoma

When the first four hundred V-12s arrived at Norman, they were temporarily housed in fraternity houses and a variety of other places while awaiting the completion of the new student housing — or barracks — south of the stadium. Some trainees stayed in temporary housing for more than six months. The war dormitory project was the largest construction project at OU up to that time. It included seven two-story housing units, a mess hall, and an administration building. The new Navy dorms were designated Cleveland, Lincoln, Jefferson, Washington Irving, Worcester, and Sequoyah houses.

V-12s participated in all phases of student life, held many class offices, and furnished a good deal of the manpower that led OU to Big Six championships in football in 1943 and 1944. The basketball team, known as the "Roundball Runts" because their average height was five feet nine and one-half inches, brought OU a tie for the Big Six crown in 1943–1944.

June Week was the year's big occasion for the V-12s, following the traditions of the Naval Academy. A regimental review in Owen Stadium and a farewell ball brought out the entire regiment. The music was furnished by Johnny Long and his orchestra.

The *Sooner*, the yearbook, gave wide coverage to the V-12s and their unit activities.

An all-engineering unit, the Oklahoma V-12s had their own airplane to tear down and reassemble. They also took part in writing and editing the *Sooner Shamrock*, a well-regarded engineering magazine.

Some OU V-12s: Mack S. Burks, president, Heritage Concrete Products; Frank W. Cole, president, Saxony Industries; Gordon D. Goering, senior vice president, Phillips Petroleum Company; Earl E. James, Jr., engineering chief, Fluid Dynamics Laboratory, Convair; Norman McDermott Hulings, Jr., president, ONEOK Energy Companies; Howard C. Kauffmann, Jr., president, Exxon; and Dr. R. Wayne Robinson, professor of agricultural economics, University of Wisconsin (Madison).

	1943		1944			1945			1946
	Jul.-Oct.	Nov.-Feb.	Mar.-Jun.	Jul.-Oct.	Nov.-Feb.	Mar.-Jun.	Jul.-Oct.	Nov.-Feb.	Mar.-Jun.
Navy	# 664	# 685	# 672	# 632	# 596	# 494	154	71	33
C.O.	Capt. J. F. Donelson						Capt. E. W. Armentrout, Jr.		

Includes NROTC

Carson-Newman College   Jefferson City, Tennessee

Carson-Newman College Archives

The 527 V-12s who passed through Carson-Newman College were housed in Sara Swann Home and Blanc-Davis Hall, formerly girls' dormitories.

Under Coach Sam ("Frosty") Holt, the Carson-Newman gridiron teams lost only one game in two seasons — to Vanderbilt, by a score of twelve to six. Coach Holt regarded the 1943 squad as one of the best he ever coached. The basketball teams also enjoyed successful years.

During the first two trimesters the rigid social rules of this Baptist school led to some friction between the civilian and Navy students, but by the third trimester, problems seem to have been resolved and a good spirit prevailed thereafter. With the no-dance rule in effect on campus, many V-12s made Knoxville their liberty headquarters.

The *Orange and Blue*, the student paper, carried some Navy news, but the trainees also published a mimeographed paper, the *Periscope*. Lamented a trainee columnist for the *Orange and Blue:* "Why couldn't the College have been built on level ground? These mountains are terrific on the leg muscles and lungs." The yearbook, the *Appalachian*, was published in 1944 and 1946 and featured the V-12 influence on the Carson-Newman campus.

The July 1943 fire in the nearby zinc mine brought trainees rushing to assist, but they backed off when they were told that some dynamite might explode at any time.

	1943		1944			1945
	Jul.-Oct.	Nov.-Feb.	Mar.-Jun.	Jul.-Oct.	Nov.-Feb.	Mar.-Jun.
Navy	251	207	230	232	196	127
C.O.	Lt. Arthur S. Postle			Lt. Victor H. Kelley		

Carson-Newman College

Some Carson-Newman V-12s: Oscar G. Brockett, Waggener Professor of Fine Arts and former dean of fine arts, University of Texas; Billy F. Bryant, professor of mathematics, Vanderbilt University; Thomas E. Carpenter, senior vice president, United Methodist Publishing House, Nashville; Ralph D. Creasman, chairman, Lionel D. Edie and Company, New York; William E. Forbis, vice president for sales, Procter and Gamble; Harold Hicks, Sr., powerline contractor, Morristown, Tennessee; and Jim E. Larue, head football coach, University of Arizona.

Milligan College   Milligan College, Tennessee

James G. Schneider

R. F. Sessions

Milligan College was the only school in the United States that turned over its entire campus and schedule to the V-12 program. There were no civilian students at Milligan. It was, in reality, a military base, as the Council on Abandoned Military Posts recognized by awarding the school a plaque in 1980. As a result of its exclusivity and isolation, the Milligan C.O. permitted dungarees to become the uniform of the day in the warmer months.

Affiliated with the Christian Church, Milligan's principles prohibited dancing on campus, so the USO set up by the citizens of nearby Johnson City became the social headquarters for the trainees. Unit dances were also held at the Hotel John Sevier. The campus ban on social dancing gave way (for the only time in Milligan history) for the final party of the V-12 unit held in the Cheek Hall gymnasium on Friday, June 15, 1945.

An extremely rigorous physical program and an infusion of talent resulted in above-average Milligan teams. The 1943–1944 basketball squad had an excellent season (twenty-two wins and two losses) and received national attention when it whipped Duke and North Carolina on successive nights on their home courts.

Since Milligan had no ongoing student body, there were no organiza-

	1943		1944		1945	
	Jul.-Oct.	Nov.-Feb.	Mar.-Jun.	Jul.-Oct.	Nov.-Feb.	Mar.-Jun.
Navy	288	293	315	285	199	131
C.O.	Lt. R. F. Sessions				Lt. Russell Griffin	@

@ Lt. Gordon R. Wellborn

tions in existence when the V-12s arrived. They formed their own glee club, band, and international relations club. Friday night "happy hours" in the gym brought out the trainees' talents in skits and music. They started their own newspaper, the *Masthead*, which was published on an irregular basis.

V-12 reunions held in 1980 and 1985 brought seventy and fifty-six trainees, respectively, back to Johnson City and Milligan.

Some Milligan V-12s: James S. Dunn, attorney, and mayor, Coral Gables, Florida; Robert F. Etheridge, vice president for student affairs, Miami University; Jackie D. Fouts, assistant football coach, Cornell University; William B. Gordon, Cleveland radio and television personality; Robert C. Hart, president, Tennessee Eastman Company; Billy J. Lillard, president, Central State University, Edmond, Oklahoma; Wendell W. Ogg, nuclear radiation physicist and director of the International Atomic Energy Agency's Radiological Protection Groups in South Korea, Iran, and several South American nations; Dr. Ralph M. Peters, graduate dean, Tennessee Tech University; Dr. David K. Rowe, president, Tennessee State Dental Association; Robert D. W. Simms, chief justice, Oklahoma Supreme Court; Duard B. Walker, athletic director, Milligan College; and Navy captains Charles McCall, David I. Draz, and Jack L. Wilson.

University of the South   Sewanee, Tennessee

The V-12s ordered to the University of the South probably had qualms about the school's isolated location, but the large number of V-12s who returned after the war indicated that they found it an excellent institution. The V-12s were quartered in the Sewanee Inn and Johnson, Cannon, and Hoffman halls. The mess hall was located in Magnolia.

The Navy officers cooperated in maintaining many of Sewanee's traditions, including the honor system and regular chapel. The noon mess was arranged to come immediately after the chapel service ended, so trainees attending chapel were excused from noontime musters at their dormitories. As a result, chapel attendance was excellent.

The *Sewanee Purple* reported the campus visits of Navy brass, including Rear Adm. Randall Jacobs, chief of personnel, who was the commencement speaker in June of 1944. Jacobs was joined by Rear Adm. A. C. Bennett, commandant of the Eighth Naval District, and Capt. Harry D. Power, director of training for the Eighth. At the June 1945 commencement the speaker and honorary degree recipient was Capt. Arthur S. Adams, original officer-in-charge of the V-12 program.

The *Gown and Anchor,* the yearbook, was published in both 1944 and 1945.

A limited intercollegiate athletic schedule was maintained, and the V-12 program provided most of the manpower. Dances were held on the campus several times a term. Many of the dates came from Chattanooga, Nashville, and Ward-Belmont College.

After the V-12s departed a stained glass window commemorating their stay on the campus was placed in the narthex of All Saints Chapel.

Some Sewanee V-12s: Howard H. Baker, Jr., majority leader, U.S. Senate and White House chief of staff; Col. Elmer D. Davies, Jr., USMCR, and circuit judge, Franklin, Tennessee; Dr. James F. Govan, university librarian, University of North Carolina; Dr. Paul S. Moorhead, geneticist, University of Pennsylvania School of Medicine; Dr. William R. Nummy, director, pharmaceutical research, Merrell Dow Labs, Dow Chemical Company; Dr. E. Rex Pinson, Jr., executive vice president for central research, Pfizer; Luther J. Strange, assistant professor, University of Florida School of Building Construction; and Richard F. VanderVeen, congressman from Michigan.

	1943		1944			1945	
	Jul.-Oct.	Nov.-Feb.	Mar.-Jun.	Jul.-Oct.	Nov.-Feb.	Mar.-Jun.	Jul.-Oct.
Navy	296	285	296	296	224	119	117
C.O.	Lt. D. M. Alexander	Lt. John G. Cornwell					Lt. Russell M. Robinson

North Texas Agricultural College   Arlington, Texas
(Now the University of Texas at Arlington)

Pete Stout

A total of 317 V-12s — nearly equally divided between marines and sailors — arrived at NTAC on July 1, 1943. They were quartered in Davis Hall and Arlington Dormitory. The V-12 office and sick bay were also located in Davis.

The NTAC V-12s established a 100 percent record in signing up for National Service Life Insurance and a 99.4 percent record in war bond deductions. They also made frequent donations of blood at the Fort Worth Blood Bank.

The V-12s dominated the football squads. Fifty-two of the fifty-three men on the 1943 team and fifty-three of sixty men on the 1944 team were V-12s. In the first basketball season all of the traveling squad members were V-12s, and in 1944–1945 approximately half were V-12s.

The big social event each term was the farewell dance to honor those who were heading to other stations. The marines had a short tour at NTAC, leaving in February of 1944 for the University of North Carolina, Texas Christian, Southwestern University, and Arkansas A & M.

The *Short Horn* was the weekly student paper and the *Junior Aggie* was the yearbook. A total of 894 sailors and marines were stationed in the V-12 unit during the twenty-eight months of its existence.

Some NTAC V-12s: William M. Brooks, attorney, Lancaster, Texas;

	1943		1944			1945	
	Jul.-Oct.	Nov.-Feb.	Mar.-Jun.	Jul.-Oct.	Nov.-Feb.	Mar.-Jun.	Jul.-Oct.
Navy	163	208	278	261	198	98	93
C.O.	Lcdr. M. V. Lewis		Lt. Robert S. Via				Lt. Paul E. Richards
Marines	156	99					
O-in-C	1st Lt. Eber B. Philips						

North Texas Agricultural College

Vernon L. Gladwin, home builder and land developer, Fort Worth; Frank Rogers, personal manager, Floyd Cramer (recording artist); Rear Adm. Kenneth G. Haynes, USN; Gene Smyers, senior vice president, Alexander and Alexander Insurance Services, Fort Worth; and Pete Stout, back, Washington Redskins professional football, and rancher.

Rice Institute Houston, Texas
(Now William Marsh Rice University)

The 342 engineering V-12s at Rice were quartered in East, West, and South dormitories, along with the NROTC trainees.

The honor code was the cause of major controversy between the Navy and the institute. The latter threatened to pull out of the V-12 program if it couldn't maintain honor code standards. The resulting compromise allowed the Rice Honor Council to function with only one change: if a violation by a V-12 was reported to the Council and found to be valid, it recommended expulsion from the school but sent its report to the commanding officer for action. If he agreed, the trainee was separated from both the school and the program, but if the C.O. did not find sufficient evidence to warrant removing the trainee from the program, he transferred him to another V-12 school.

V-12s took part in all of the campus activities and formed a widely acclaimed Navy glee club. Although nearly all of the football players from the 1942 team enlisted in the Marine V-12 program and were sent to Southwestern Louisiana Institute, Rice still conducted a full intercollegiate athletic program. More than half of the players were V-12s, and the football coach reported that he had never had a harder working bunch.

There was no swimming pool at Rice so trainees used the Houston YMCA for classes and tests. On Sunday mornings the Houston Tennis and Swimming Club's pool was available for recreational use.

Rice University Archives

The Rice V-12s took part in the mammoth postwar parade in downtown Houston for Fleet Admiral William F. Halsey, Jr.

Some Rice V-12s: William M. Boren, vice chairman, Big Three Industries; Dr. Alan J. Chapman, professor of mechanical engineering, Rice University; John L. Cox, independent oil producer, and trustee, Rice University; and William C. Milstead, chairman, Austin Industries.

	1943		1944			1945			1946
	Jul.-Oct.	Nov.-Feb.	Mar.-Jun.	Jul.-Oct.	Nov.-Feb.	Mar.-Jun.	Jul.-Oct.	Nov.-Feb.	Mar.-Jun.
Navy	346	298	336	281	196	150	NA	NA	65
C.O.	Cdr. C. A. Whiteford	Capt. D. D. Dupre		Cdr. V. F. Rathbun				Capt. J. E. Cooper	

NA = Not available

Southern Methodist University Dallas, Texas

When the V-12s arrived at SMU they took over the former girls' dormitories, Snider and Virginia halls. A year later, a reshuffling sent them to Atkins Hall and the coeds returned to Snider and Virginia.

One of the streetcar lines ended at SMU, so the trolley was the usual form of transportation to and from downtown Dallas. The tea dances held at least one afternoon a week gave V-12s a good chance to get acquainted with the coeds.

The 1944 *Rotunda* may have been the finest yearbook in the country; it featured a full-color photo that extended from the front around to the back of the cover. It showed a typical campus scene with students, including V-12s, on the lawn in front of impressive Dallas Hall.

The "V-12 Varieties" show drew rave reviews as a result of the musical talents of the sailors and a spoof of the unit's officers.

Vice Adm. Randall Jacobs, chief of personnel, was the commencement speaker in 1945. His June 25 visit coincided with the excellent extensive review of V-12's two years at SMU in the special V-12 commemorative issue of the student newspaper, the *Campus.*

Some SMU V-12s: Dr. Durward A. Baggett, physician, and president, Texas Academy of Family Physicians; Dr. James L. Brewbaker, professor of horticulture and genetics, University of Hawaii; Charles L. Callings, president, Raley's Supermarkets, Sacramento, Calif.; Dr. Kenneth Foree III, ophthalmologist, Dallas; Dr. Jack W. Harkey, dean of undergraduate engi-

neering, Southern Methodist University; Dr. Ross E. McKinney, N.T. Veach Professor of Environmental Engineering, University of Kansas; Philip S. Sizer, senior vice president, Otis Engineering, Dallas; Alan H. Snyder, vice president, Robco, and president, Eye Bank Association of America; and Henry ("Hank") Thompson, country-and-western entertainer.

Sara Marie Lee

	1943		1944			1945			1946
	Jul.-Oct.	Nov.-Feb.	Mar.-Jun.	Jul.-Oct.	Nov.-Feb.	Mar.-Jun.	Jul.-Oct.	Nov.-Feb.	Mar.-Jun.
Navy	199	207	189	205	214	162	155	171	109
C.O.	Lt. Oscar Y. Gamel		Lt. Hugh B. Wood					Lt. V. A. Folsom	2, 3

2. Lt. Elmer C. Rieck   3. Lcdr. Carl R. Reng

Southwestern University Georgetown, Texas

Southwestern University

As a result of the persistent personal interest of Congressman Lyndon B. Johnson, Southwestern University was one of the first V-12 schools selected, the announcement coming on February 28, 1943. LBJ subsequently addressed the V-12s nearly every trimester. Another highlight was an inspection on August 27, 1943, by LBJ, Lt. Comdr. Jack Dempsey, USCG, and movie actor Lt. Robert Taylor (see photos).

The contingent of marines at Southwestern contained football stars from all over the Southwest, which made this Methodist school a powerhouse that lost only one game during the 1943 season. It advanced to the Sun Bowl in El Paso on New Year's Day, 1944, where it whipped the University of New Mexico, seven to zero. The 1944 squad was also picked for the Sun Bowl. This time it was an international contest, with SU defeating the University of Mexico thirty-five to zero.

V-12s took part in all phases of campus life and held many class offices. The "Pirate Tavern" was the campus hangout.

Fleet Adm. Chester W. Nimitz, USN, was the commencement speaker in June 1946, at the close of the Southwestern University V-12 unit.

Some Southwestern University

	1943		1944			1945			1946
	Jul.-Oct.	Nov.-Feb.	Mar.-Jun.	Jul.-Oct.	Nov.-Feb.	Mar.-Jun.	Jul.-Oct.	Nov.-Feb.	Mar.-Jun.
Navy	197	248	263	276	237	180	166	311	309
C.O.	Cdr. M. A. Heffernan			Lt. L. H. Schnell			@	Lt. George F. Howe	
Marines	178	141	93	74					
O-in-C	1st Lt. John J. Fitzgerald								

@ Lt. C. C. Dunsmoor

Southwestern University

V-12s: H. K. Allen, vice chairman, Export-Import Bank of the United States; Joseph W. Baumgardner, independent oil producer; George Bean, aerospace engineer, Martin-Marietta; Dr. Roger M. Busfield, Jr., president, Arkansas Hospital Association; Jack M. Denson, district manager, American Petrofina Company; Charles R. Groux, staff vice president, RCA; James W. Harrison, executive director, Southwestern New Mexico Council of Governments; Martin James Heffernan, director of public affairs, National Football League; Dr. Jack P. Hudnall, founding president, Bristol Community College, Fall River, Massachusetts; Walter M. Merchant, president, American College of Musicians; William F. Roden, independent oil producer; and Dr. David K. Switzer, professor of pastoral care and counseling, Perkins School of Theology, Southern Methodist University.

Texas Christian University Fort Worth, Texas

W. D. Smith Commercial Photography, Fort Worth (courtesy Mrs. George C. Decker)

While many colleges saw their student bodies dwindle in 1943, the combination of the V-12 unit and the already present V-5 group gave Texas Christian University its largest enrollment ever — 2,390. But the V-12 unit was one of the smallest in the country, with 242 trainees at its peak. Some of the V-12s fondly remembered the high ratio of women to men on the campus; some recalled it as being five to one and others claimed it was about eleven to one.

The Horned Frogs fielded teams in most intercollegiate sports and the 1944 gridiron squad landed a 1945 Cotton Bowl assignment.

The V-12s were quartered in Clark Hall during their entire time in Fort Worth.

Near the end of the V-12 unit's existence, the commanding officer told the social chairman that there was ap-proximately nine hundred dollars in the Navy Rec Fund (from the profits on the pay telephones) and instructed him that anything left over when the unit closed would be sent to Navy Relief. The unit's social program ended with one of the grandest dinner-dances ever held at the Blackstone Hotel in Fort Worth. There was only $7.42 to be forwarded to Navy Relief.

Representative of the friendliness of this Disciples of Christ university was the excellent coverage of the V-12 unit provided by the *Horned Frog*, the annual, and the *Skiff*, a weekly.

Some TCU V-12s: Ransom ("Randy") Jackson, Chicago Cubs professional baseball player; the Reverend Alla Winston Robertson, military chaplain for twenty-eight years and recipient of the Bronze Star in Vietnam; and Dr. Albert D. Sellstrom, professor of languages, University of Texas at Austin.

	1943		1944			1945	
	Jul.-Oct.	Nov.-Feb.	Mar.-Jun.	Jul.-Oct.	Nov.-Feb.	Mar.-Jun.	Jul.-Oct.
Navy	227	214	222	215	203	119	122
C.O.	Lt. George C. Decker						Lt. C. M. Schmidt

University of Texas   Austin, Texas

University of Texas at Austin Archives

The University of Texas had the largest V-12 unit in the Eighth Naval District. With NROTC and a large Pre-Flight School, the Navy dominated the school.

The 1943 football team, strongly augmented by V-12s, captured the Southwest Conference crown and went to the 1944 Cotton Bowl, where it held topflight Randolph Field to a seven-to-seven tie. The 1944 baseball and track squads also took the Southwest Conference championships.

Life magazine (May 28, 1945) gave extensive coverage to "Pickup Weekend" in its "*Life* Goes to a Party" series. The weekend was intended to counteract the traditional letdown suffered by students following the Roundup week of the Texas Relays. The male-female roles were reversed, so the girls ran the races and the men campaigned for election as male sweetheart. A V-12 won the coveted honor in 1945.

In the winter of 1943–1944, a remarkably heavy snowfall resulted in many snowmen joining the V-12 unit.

Some Texas V-12s: Dr. Malcolm D. Abel, president, Texas Independent Producers and Royalty Owners Association; Thomas D. Barrow, chairman, Kennecott Copper Corporation; Dr. Benjamin B. Ewing, professor of engineering and director of the Institute for Environmental Studies, University of Illinois; Rear Adm. Robert H. Gormley, USN; Russell H. Green, Jr., president, Signal Oil Company; Joe A. Moss, vice president, secretary, and general counsel, American Petrofina; William D. Phillips, professor and chairman of the chemistry department, Washington University; Calvin D. Sholtess, president, Hughes Tool Division, Hughes Tool Company; Dr. John D. Sudbury, vice president, Conoco Coal Development Company; and John F. Watkins, senior vice president, Earle M. Jorgensen Company.

	1943		1944			1945			1946
	Jul.-Oct.	Nov.-Feb.	Mar.-Jun.	Jul.-Oct.	Nov.-Feb.	Mar.-Jun.	Jul.-Oct.	Nov.-Feb.	Mar.-Jun.
Navy	874	946	801	957	787	554	309	144	46
C.O.	Capt. John J. London		Cdr. D. J. Friedell	Capt. R. J. Valentine				Capt. M. Y. McGown	

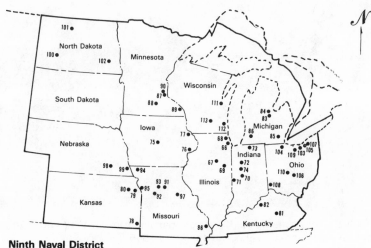

Ninth Naval District

Illinois

66. Illinois Institute of Technology
67. Illinois State Normal University
68. Northwestern University
69. University of Illinois

Indiana

70. DePauw University
71. Indiana State Teachers College
72. Purdue University
73. University of Notre Dame
74. Wabash College

Iowa

75. Iowa State A & M College
76. St. Ambrose College
77. University of Dubuque

Kansas

78. Kansas State Teachers College
79. University of Kansas
80. Municipal University (Washburn)

Kentucky

81. Berea College
82. University of Louisville

Michigan

83. Alma College
84. Central Michigan College of Education
85. University of Michigan
86. Western Michigan College of Education

Minnesota

87. College of St. Thomas
88. Gustavus Adolphus College
89. St. Mary's College
90. University of Minnesota

Missouri

91. Central College
92. Central Missouri State Teachers College
93. Missouri Valley College
94. Northwest Missouri State Teachers College
95. Park College
96. Southeast Missouri State Teachers College
97. Westminster College

Nebraska

98. Doane College
99. Peru State Teachers College

North Dakota

100. State Teachers College, Dickinson
101. State Teachers College, Minot
102. State Teachers College, Valley City

Ohio

103. Baldwin-Wallace College
104. Bowling Green State University
105. Case School of Applied Science
106. Denison University
107. John Carroll University
108. Miami University
109. Oberlin College
110. Ohio Wesleyan University

Wisconsin

111. Lawrence College
112. Marquette University
113. University of Wisconsin

Illinois Institute of Technology   Chicago, Illinois
(And George Williams College)

IIT Archives

The V-12 arrangement at IIT was unique: it was the only school in the country to sublet a substantial part of its Navy contract to another accredited institution. The Navy awarded IIT a quota of 690 engineers, 300 of whom were to be quartered at George Williams College, about two miles from IIT on Chicago's South Side.

The freshmen and some sophomores were officially enrolled as Tech students but were assigned to George Williams College, where they slept, ate, and attended classes in U-shaped Dole Hall. They went to the IIT campus for lab courses; and some even had to travel to Chicago's West Side for a night class at the old Lewis Institute building. The men traveled independently on Chicago's streetcars, buses, and elevated trains. (Men in uniform rode free at all times.) The Williams participation in V-12 ended in February 1945.

At the IIT campus near the shore of Lake Michigan, the trainees were housed in fraternity houses and residences, designated Quarters One through Seven. Chicago's "el" trains rattled north and south all through the day and night just a block from the quarters.

The award-winning *Technology News* reported on campus events weekly, and the *Integral*, the yearbook, gave good V-12 coverage. The 1943 Navy Ball, held in the grand ballroom of the Stevens Hotel, featured the music of Woody Herman and his orchestra.

The 1943–1944 IIT basketball squad operated on a two-team system of play, putting an entirely fresh five in at the beginning of each quarter. It

	1943		1944			1945			1946
	Jul.-Oct.	Nov.-Feb.	Mar.-Jun.	Jul.-Oct.	Nov.-Feb.	Mar.-Jun.	Jul.-Oct.	Nov.-Feb.	Mar.-Jun.
Navy	686	678	691	667	519	430	288	# 367	# 192
C.O.	Lt. W. A. Hamilton				Lt. R. F. Sessions		Capt. Donald McGregor		

Includes NROTC

Illinois Institute of Technology

Robert G. Walsh

John P. Houston

worked, bringing Illinois Tech fifteen victories in a row for a sixteen-and-two season, the best in the school's history. One of the losses was to George Williams College, where Tech V-12s were members of the team. This was a unique situation in intercollegiate athletics: officially enrolled Tech students played on both sides!

Some IIT V-12s: Dr. James J. Brophy, vice president for research, University of Utah; Dr. Frank A. Crossley, consultant in engineering, Lockheed Missiles and Space Company; Warren A. Furst, vice president and secretary, Katy Industries; Alan J. Grant, executive vice president, Aero Jet General Corporation; Don E. Helbling, vice president, Natural Gas Pipeline Company of America; Howard H. Kehrl, vice chairman, General Motors; Chief Judge Frank H. McFadden, U.S. Court for the Northern District of Alabama, and now chairman, Blount Energy Resources Corporation; and Robert G. Walsh, president, Dearborn Electric Company, Chicago.

Illinois State Normal University Normal, Illinois
(Now Illinois State University)

Camera Craft Studio, Normal, Illinois

In July of 1943 most of the ISNU V-12s settled into Fell Hall, which also housed the mess hall and the V-12 office. The rest of the men were in Smith Hall.

On November 9, 1943, the alarm sounded: Fell Hall was on fire! While the firemen were fighting the blaze in the attic and on the roof, Lieutenant Burrill, still in his Fell Hall office, called the district training officer to report it. At the same time the trainees were removing their beds and other furniture to McCormick Gym, where a temporary barracks was set up. The blaze was confined to the roof and attic, with little harm to the rest of the building other than water damage. The mess hall was back in operation in less than a day and the trainees moved back in three days. Only half a day of classes was missed.

The 1943–1944 basketball team won the conference championship.

The Navy formal each term was the great social event on campus. Both the *Index*, the yearbook, and the *Vidette*, the campus newspaper, gave excellent coverage to the V-12 unit.

The V-12 unit held a twenty-fifth anniversary reunion in 1970.

Some ISNU V-12s: Lt. Gen. Edward J. Bronars, USMC, president, Navy Relief Society; D. W. Cather, director of public works, Miami, Fla.; Stanley P. Hutchison, chairman, Washington National Life Insurance Company; Donald A. Prince, vice president, Rand McNally and Company; Donald G. Tennant, chairman, Don Tennant Advertising; Marvin J. Tepperman, vice president, Hyatt Corporation; Navy captains Daniel D. Ruebsamen and James S. Williams; and Dr. Edward H. Whitmore, chairman, department of mathematics, Central Michigan University.

	1943		1944			1945
	Jul.-Oct.	Nov.-Feb.	Mar.-Jun.	Jul.-Oct.	Nov.-Feb.	Mar.-Jun.
Navy	252	239	242	242	196	141
C.O.	Lt. Meldrim F. Burrill					

Northwestern University Evanston, Illinois

The Northwestern V-12s and NROTC took over the north quadrangles, which consisted of seventeen fraternity houses and five dorms. They were located right on the shore of Lake Michigan, which was great in the summer, but not in the winter!

Since Northwestern was near Great Lakes Naval Training Station, a parade of top Navy brass came to the campus. Rear Adm. John Downes (commandant of the Ninth Naval District) spoke to trainees just two weeks after the program began. Fleet Adm. Ernest J. King reviewed and addressed the trainees in October of 1944. Fleet Adm. Chester C. Nimitz was there at the end of the program in June of 1946.

The Navy Ball held in January of 1944 at Chicago's Stevens Hotel featured the music of Johnny Long and a drop-in performance by Duke Ellington. A year later the V-12s and their dates danced to the music of Frankie Masters and his band in the Gold Room of the Congress Hotel in downtown Chicago.

The football squad of 1943, augmented by V-12s, turned in a fine six-and-two season, even toppling Great Lakes, which was the only team to defeat the number-one-ranked Notre Dame. The Wildcats were nationally rated number nine.

When the Marine detachment was disbanded in February of 1944, a Navy

pre-supply school curriculum was established in its place.

Some Northwestern V-12s: the Reverend Raymond C. Baumhart, S.J., President, Loyola University (Chicago); Wallace B. Behnke, Jr., vice chairman, Commonwealth Edison Company; J. Armin Bierbaum, president, U.S. Ethanol Corporation; Francis K. Iverson, chairman, Neucor Corporation; Rear Adm. Edward J. Otth, Jr., USN; Robert L. Remke,* chairman, R. J. R. Foods; Emil Reutzel, editor, *Norfolk* (Neb.) *Daily News*; Rear Adm. Robert S. Smith, USN; Edson W. Spencer, chairman, Honeywell; Frank P. Wendt, chairman, John Nuveen and Company; Arthur R. Whale, patent counsel, Ely Lilly Company, and president, American Patent Law Association; and John W. Zick, chairman, Price Waterhouse.

	1943		1944			1945			1946
	Jul.-Oct.	Nov.-Feb.	Mar.-Jun.	Jul.-Oct.	Nov.-Feb.	Mar.-Jun.	Jul.-Oct.	Nov.-Feb.	Mar.-Jun.
Navy	626	670	872	834	596	422	248	91	33
C.O.	@	Capt. A. D. Denney		Capt. R. A. Hall		Capt. C. J. Stuart			
Marines	286	238							
O-in-C	Capt. B. E. Hamrick								

@ Capt. S.D.A. Cobb

University of Illinois Urbana, Illinois

University of Illinois Archives

The 450 V-12s who arrived at the University of Illinois found a major military contingent already there. It included one thousand ASTP soldiers (with more on the way) and another one thousand sailors in the Navy Diesel and Signal schools.

The V-12s were housed in Busey, Evans, and Illini halls and were fed in the converted former ice skating rink. Most of the V-12s were engineers, but there were twenty-five premeds in the first term.

If an Illini V-12 didn't know the name of his commanding officer during the first two months, it was hardly his fault. There were four changes in that post within eight weeks, all of them occasioned by the skippers' being ordered to duty at other stations.

The V-12s provided a large number of musicians for the Illini Marching Band, and they also had their own V-12 dance band. The Navy V-12 Spring Formal was one of the big campus events.

The University of Illinois V-12s held autumn reunions in 1972, 1977, and 1982. The next meeting is scheduled for 1987.

Some U of I V-12s: Dr. Martin G. Abegg, president, Bradley University, Dr. James W. Bayne, professor of mechanical engineering, University of Illinois; Dr. Robert M. Boynton, professor of psychology, University of California at San Diego; Dr. Charles H. Braden, Regents Professor of Physics, Georgia Institute of Technology; Dr. James C. Bresee, senior scientist, U.S. Department of Energy; Dr. Roger W. Burtness, associate professor of electrical engineering, University of Illinois; Dr. Max M. Mortland, professor of crop and soil sciences, Michigan State University; Richard J. Piersol, vice president for original equipment, B.F. Goodrich Corporation; Dr. Leigh M. Roberts, professor of psychiatry, University of Wisconsin Medical School; and Henry M. Willis, director of information services, Sandia National Laboratories.

	1943		1944			1945			1946
	Jul.-Oct.	Nov.-Feb.	Mar.-Jun.	Jul.-Oct.	Nov.-Feb.	Mar.-Jun.	Jul.-Oct.	Nov.-Feb.	Mar.-Jun.
Navy	442	417	418	420	321	306	314	415	245
C.O.	@	Lt. R. I. Damon			Lcdr. J. H. Todd		Lt. Arthur Blake	Capt. L. R. Lampman	

@ Four commanding officers in eight weeks

DePauw University   Greencastle, Indiana

The 383 V-12s who arrived at Greencastle joined 600 V-5s in the Navy Flight Preparatory School. The V-12s, 150 of whom were premeds, were quartered in Lucy Rowland and Rector halls, both formerly girls' dormitories.

Tough academic standards, exciting athletic teams, and a full social life kept the V-12s busy. The old "U" shop of DePauw was converted into the "Barn" to serve as a campus hangout. Greencastle USO centers moved from place to place but provided some activity on most weekends. The DePauw Little Theatre kept an active schedule, and the student radio guild put on a weekly show, "Our Navy's Men," that featured the military experiences of individual DePauw V-12s who came from the fleet.

The 1943 football team was nothing short of sensational. It won five, lost none, and tied one, scoring 206 points to its opponents' 6. The zero-to-zero tie with Oberlin came in the opening game of the season. The 1944 football Tigers had a change of direction at term break, losing the first five games and then winning the last six. The 1943–1944 basketball team took the Indiana collegiate championship with a twelve-and-six record, whereas the

1944–1945 Tigers put together a ten-and-eight season that included one-point victories over both Indiana and Purdue. The track and tennis teams of 1944 topped the state.

The *Mirage,* the yearbook, and the *DePauw,* the thrice weekly paper, provided an excellent record of the DePauw V-12 unit.

Some DePauw V-12s: Dr. Cole Blasier, professor of political science, University of Pittsburgh; Robert E. Bublitz, executive assistant to the chairman, Chase Manhattan Bank; John H. Filer, chairman, Aetna Insurance; Robert R. Frederick, president, RCA; William F. ("Bill") Hayes, actor ("Days of Our Lives") and singer (gold record for "Ballad of Davey Crockett"); Leonard W. Huck, president, Valley National Bank of Arizona; Roland F. Marston, chairman, State Farm Insurance Company; Dr. Edward H. Polley, professor of anatomy, University of Illinois Medical School; Dr. Robert L. Randolph, president, Alabama State University; Charles C. Roberts, vice chairman, DeKalb Corporation; Erwin E. Schulze, president, CECO Industries; and Richard D. Wood, chairman, Eli Lilly, and trustee, DePauw University.

	1943		1944		1945		
	Jul.-Oct.	Nov.-Feb.	Mar.-Jun.	Jul.-Oct.	Nov.-Feb.	Mar.-Jun.	Jul.-Oct.
Navy	339	399	377	590	389	246	227
C.O.	Lcdr. W. B. Dortch				Lt. J. M. Hanna		Lt. F. H. Addington

Indiana State Teachers College   Terre Haute, Indiana
(Now Indiana State University)

Of the 380 men who reported to Indiana State on July 1, 1943, nearly two-thirds were freshmen. A Navy Flight Preparatory School already existed on the campus. Trainees were quartered in Residence Hall. The Administration Building housed the V-12 office and the sick bay was in Science Hall.

The V-12s found a hospitable campus with many activities. The Sycamore Players put on regular productions in the Sycamore Theatre, and many V-12s took starring and supporting roles. V-12s also put on their own variety shows, an outstanding example being the "All-Navy Show" on June 13, 1944, which featured a cast of more than fifty V-12s (see photo in Chapter 32, "Campus Life." The popular dance band made up of V-12s was called the Sycamore Swingsters.

V-12s spent a lot of time at the USO located in the YMCA. Jan Garber and his orchestra appeared on campus in September of 1943 for the Coca-Cola "Victory Parade of Spotlight Bands," a nationwide radio broadcast. Dances for V-12s were held at the barracks,

	1943		1944			1945	
	Jul.-Oct.	Nov.-Feb.	Mar.-Jun.	Jul.-Oct.	Nov.-Feb.	Mar.-Jun.	Jul.-Oct.
Navy	366	314	383	339	232	172	156
C.O.	Lt. M. J. Galbraith		Lt. E. J. Erickson			Lt. V. H. Kelley	

Indiana State Teachers College

and all-campus dances took place in other locations. The mezzanine of the college bookstore was taken over for a Navy lounge.

The *Indiana Statesman* was an excellent campus paper and reported all of the achievements of the hard-fighting Indiana State athletic teams. The first year's basketball team, with only one player who was not a V-12, averaged over fifty points a game while rolling to a seventeen-and-four record. The 1944–1945 version of the "Fightin' Sycamores" again won seventeen games and dropped only six. The strong 1944 tennis squad whipped Indiana University and tied Purdue.

The yearbook, the *Sycamore*, gave a splendid picture of the V-12 years.

Some Indiana State V-12s: Herbert C. Anderson, architect, Houston; William Calhoon, president, Farm and Home Life Insurance; John Erlenborn, congressman from Illinois; Walter Gerard, animal nutritionist, Peet's Feeds, Council Bluffs, Iowa; William G. Osborn, chairman, Germania Federal Savings and Loan Association, Alton, Ill.; Gene Paitson, owner, Paitson Tru-Value Hardware, Terre Haute; George Roesch, Jr., public schools principal, Evansville, Ind.; and George Schuerman, plant manager, Kyanize Paint Company, Springfield, Ill.

Purdue University West Lafayette, Indiana

John P. Houston

In mid-1943 Purdue was a military campus, with nearly four thousand men in uniform and only twenty-eight hundred civilians. The V-12 contingent of 1,263 was one of the largest units in the country; two-thirds were sailors and one-third were marines. They were quartered in Carey Hall and various fraternity houses. Those living in Carey ate in the mess hall there, while the others boarded at the Purdue Memorial Union.

The 1943 Purdue football team, composed almost entirely of V-12s, was the talk of the nation. With nine wins and no losses, it was the only major college team to complete the season undefeated and untied. One of its victories was over the powerful Great Lakes Naval Training Station, which was ranked second in the nation. Purdue settled for a co-Big Ten championship with Michigan and number five ranking in the nation.

Social life on the Purdue campus flourished. There were frequent dances at the Union and many organizational parties. The USO near the campus had dances every Wednesday at 1900 as well as on weekends. The engineering organizations were dominated by V-12 trainees.

The *Debris,* the yearbook, gave excellent historical coverage to the V-12 unit, and the *Exponent,* a thrice weekly student paper, covered current events.

Some Purdue V-12s: Chalmers

	1943		1944			1945			1946
	Jul.-Oct.	Nov.-Feb.	Mar.-Jun.	Jul.-Oct.	Nov.-Feb.	Mar.-Jun.	Jul.-Oct.	Nov.-Feb.	Mar.-Jun.
Navy	816	898	891	1005	658	512	361	# 452	NA
C.O.	Cdr. H. J. Bartley							Capt. J. R. Hamley	
Marines	429	349	292	187	181	146	141	96	38
O-in-C	Capt. Everett W. Whipple			@	Maj. Ernest W. Jones			Capt. Henry J. Woessner II	

NA = Not available   # Includes NROTC   @ Capt. John J. Smith

Purdue University

"Bump" Elliott, athletic director, University of Iowa; Anthony S. Greene, chairman, Barber-Greene Company; Dr. Richard H. Haase, professor of statistics, Drexel University; Dr. Arthur G. Hansen, president, Purdue University; James C. Holzwarth, director of programs and plans, General Motors Research Labs; Charles C. Johnson, Jr., Assistant Surgeon General, U.S. Public Health Service; Milton C. Lowenstein, author (*What's Your Game Plan?*); Dr. Donald R. Matthews, professor of political science, University of Washington; Dr. Gerald Nadler, professor and chairman of the department of industrial and systems engineering, University of Southern California; Walter R. Pavelchek, director, American Institute of Chemical Engineers; Herbert J. Rowe, associate administrator, NASA; Virgil G. Trice, Jr., chemical engineer, U.S. Department of Energy; and Robert W. Weeks, vice president and general counsel, Deere and Company.

University of Notre Dame Notre Dame, Indiana

When the Navy and Marine V-12s arrived at the University of Notre Dame, there were twelve hundred men attending the U.S. Naval Reserve Midshipmen's School on the campus. The sailors occupied Alumni and Dillon halls and the marines were quartered in Zahm and Cavanaugh halls.

To most Americans at that time, Notre Dame and quality football were synonymous, and the V-12 era was no exception. With a heavy concentration of V-12s, the 1943 squad was the outstanding collegiate team of the nation, turning in a nine-and-one record, which included victories over the powerful Army, Navy, and Iowa Seahawks teams. The Irish's bid for an undefeated and untied season was lost in the last twenty-five seconds of the final

	1943		1944			1945			1946
	Jul.-Oct.	Nov.-Feb.	Mar.-Jun.	Jul.-Oct.	Nov.-Feb.	Mar.-Jun.	Jul.-Oct.	Nov.-Feb.	Mar.-Jun.
Navy	904	1098	1197	1238	829	434	133	106	102
C.O.	@	Capt. J. R. Barry							
Marines	654	456	315	165					
O-in-C	Capt. John W. Finney			2					

@ Capt. H. P. Burnett   2. Maj. Ernest W. Jones

University of Notre Dame

game, when the outstanding Great Lakes Navy team scored to win nineteen to fourteen. The 1944 football team had only five returning lettermen, but again it posted a terrific season, losing only to Navy and the great Army team.

The daily masses at Notre Dame were moved from early morning to late afternoon. They were held in each of the V-12 halls at 1700 and 1845. (The later mass was for football players and others who could not attend at the earlier time.) The Servicemen's Center in South Bend and the many campus dances gave the Notre Dame V-12s an active social life.

Some Notre Dame V-12s: Angelo Bertelli, All-American quarterback, Heisman Trophy winner, president, Bertelli's Liquors, Clifton, N.J.; Michael A. Bilandic, mayor of Chicago; Silas S. Cathcart, chairman, Illinois Tool Works; Jackie Cooper, actor, director, producer; Claire V. Hansen, president, Duff and Phelps; James Kraus, president, Handy and Harman Auto Group, Martinsburg Division; William E. Love, chairman, Equitable Savings and Loan Association, Portland, Oregon, and president, National Association of State Racing Commissioners; Dr. James H. Meyer, chancellor, University of California at Davis; Ronald E. Samples, chairman, Consolidated Coal Company; John A. Schneider, president, CBS-TV Network, and president, Warner Amex Satellite Entertainment Corporation; and William Voll, president, Sibley Machine and Foundry Corporation, South Bend.

Wabash College Crawfordsville, Indiana

The three hundred V-12s who arrived at this 110-year-old men's college in July 1943 were quartered in two dorms and six fraternity houses and fed in a new mess hall just installed in a previously abandoned old science building, Peck Hall. Kingery Hall held the sick bay.

The *Wabash*, the yearbook, was discontinued for the years 1944 and 1945, but the *Bachelor* appeared each Friday during the school year until 1944, when it came out fortnightly. Early in 1945, however, it too was dropped because of the lack of personnel and time to publish it. While it existed, the *Bachelor* gave nearly undivided attention to the V-12s, who comprised about 90 percent of the student body.

Besides a rugged intramural program Wabash carried on intercollegiate athletics in both football and basketball, with the 1944 Little Giants, an all-V-12 team, compiling a football record of three wins, one loss, and two ties.

Smokers were held on a regular basis, sometimes at the Crawfordsville Sportsman's Club. They included boxing and a variety of entertainment and ended with community singing, occasionally led by the skipper.

There were some dances on campus, but the Crawfordsville USO was the main center of social life for most V-12s. Some trainees took weekend trips to DePauw and other coed schools.

Some Wabash V-12s: Dr. Richard E. Chapin, director of libraries and professor of journalism, Michigan State University; Dr. Edward H. Fleming, Jr., senior scientist, Lawrence Livermore National Laboratories; Capt. Kenneth A. Horn, USN; Capt. Lee F. Ison, USN; Rear Adm. Thomas A. Kamm, USNR, deputy director, U.S. Naval Reserve; Capt. George G. Ryon, USN; and Rear Adm. William Thompson, USN(Ret.), president, U.S. Navy Memorial Foundation, Washington, D.C.

	1943		1944			1945	
	Jul.-Oct.	Nov.-Feb.	Mar.-Jun.	Jul.-Oct.	Nov.-Feb.	Mar.-Jun.	Jul.-Oct.
Navy	283	281	277	265	193	122	115
C.O.	Lt. Harold G. Leffler			Lt. James H. Case, Jr.			Lt. L. D. Gilboy, Jr.

Iowa State College Ames, Iowa
(Now Iowa State University)

The ISC V-12s were all engineering students. They were first quartered in Roberts, Birch, Lyon, and Welch halls, which had formerly been used by women students. In November 1944, after the other Navy enlisted schools were discontinued, the V-12s moved into Friley Hall. The Memorial Union housed the Navy mess hall.

Two V-12s were elected student body president during the three years of the program, and other trainees were active in nearly every type of organization on campus. In sports the Iowa State Cyclones relied heavily upon the V-12s. In basketball the 1943–1944 team went thirteen and three, but it had a nine-and-one record in the conference, which meant it shared the Big Six championship with the University of Oklahoma. In 1944–1945 it had a ten-and-six record, but that was good enough for the Big Six crown.

A Navy ball was held every term to honor those who were graduating from the program after eight terms in engineering. The Coca-Cola Spotlight Band program took place at the Iowa State Great Hall on February 13, 1945; it was the show's second such appearance at Ames during the Navy's tenure there. ISC's own Navy Swing Band performed for many campus dances.

In November 1945 the Navy affirmed its appreciation of ISC and the quality of its programs by establishing one of the new NROTC units on campus.

Some ISC V-12s: John F. Cota, president, Michigan/Wisconsin Pipeline Company; Dr. Richard S. Eckaus, professor of economics, Massachusetts Institute of Technology; Robert P. Jen-

Robert W. Jordan (from *The Iowa Engineer*, September 1945)

sen, chairman, Tiger International; Rocco Lo Chiano, executive vice president, ENRON Corporation; Dr. Robert N. Maddox, Leonard F. Sheerar professor of chemical engineering, Oklahoma State University; Dr. Robert M. Stewart, Jr., professor of computer science and engineering, Iowa State University; Dr. Gerald L. Thompson, professor of applied mathematics and operations research, Carnegie-Mellon University; Capt. Chandler L. von Schrader, USN; Leland J. Walker, president, American Society of Civil Engineers; Daniel J. Watkins, engineer, and chairman, Chamber of Commerce of Greater Kansas City; and John F. Yardley, president, McDonnell Douglas Astronautics Company.

| | 1943 | | 1944 | | | 1945 | | 1946 | |
	Jul.-Oct.	Nov.-Feb.	Mar.-Jun.	Jul.-Oct.	Nov.-Feb.	Mar.-Jun.	Jul.-Oct.	Nov.-Feb.	Mar.-Jun.
Navy	767	795	718	878	636	537	563	# 814	# 217
C.O.	Cdr. A. F. Duernberger			Lcdr. C. W. Myers				Capt. R. B. Devin	

Includes NROTC

St. Ambrose College Davenport, Iowa

Like many schools, St. Ambrose College had a world of new experiences with its V-12 unit. Previously, nearly all of its students had been Catholic, but of the 296 trainees the college received, only 20 percent were Catholic. An overwhelming proportion of the V-12s came from the state of Iowa or nearby sections of Illinois.

The college had expected 60 freshman V-12s, but 178 arrived. As a result, many first-year classes were overcrowded, but academic standards were strictly maintained. At one time in the spring of 1944, 166 of the 284 trainees were on the academically restricted list.

To make room for the V-12s, St. Ambrose moved faculty and civilian students out of Davis and Ambrose halls. It already had a unit of sixty V-5s on campus when the V-12s arrived.

To replace the discontinued *Ambrosian News*, the V-12s started their own mimeographed weekly, the *Sea Breez*, in September of 1943, and it continued until October 13, 1945, just before the unit disbanded.

The Davenport USO, American Legion, Masonic orders, and other civic groups staged lots of dances, parties, open houses, and concerts for the V-12s. They held their own dances, too, and gave one specifically for the departing commanding officer in August of 1945. They thought so highly of him that they chipped in to present him a set of *Lee's Lieutenants* and a gold watch band, even though the practice was against naval regulations. The ladies of the First Presbyterian Church made free clothing alterations and repairs for the V-12s.

Some St. Ambrose V-12s: Vice Adm. Kent J. Carroll, USN; Keith A. Foiles, senior vice president, Harcourt Brace Jovanovich; Dr. Dwight C. McGoon, Stuart W. Harrington Professor of Surgery, Mayo Medical School; Kenneth F. Thompson, executive vice president, Sperry Rand Corporation; the Reverend Dr. Norman Ullestad, senior pastor, Grace Lutheran Church, Des Moines, Iowa.

	1943		1944			1945	
	Jul.-Oct.	Nov.-Feb.	Mar.-Jun.	Jul.-Oct.	Nov.-Feb.	Mar.-Jun.	Jul.-Oct.
Navy	286	266	288	230	217	157	145
C.O.	Lt. Clifford S. Blackburn			Lt. A. K. Burt			Lt. Arthur E. Jensen

University of Dubuque   Dubuque, Iowa

The 270 Navy men reporting to this Presbyterian school on July 1, 1943, were quartered in Steffans and Severance halls. The Navy office and small stores were also located in Steffans. The sick bay was set up in Van Vliet Hall and the mess hall was in Peters Commons.

The unit at Dubuque benefited from a bit of ecumenical cooperation — the contract for the V-12 laundry service was let to the nearby Catholic Convent of the Good Shepherd.

Football was given up for the duration, but the basketball team, composed mainly of V-12s, went undefeated in the 1943–1944 season. Nearly every Friday night there was a songfest in Peters Commons, with the Navy Chorus providing the leadership.

The "Bluejacket Brevities" was a variety show given by the V-12s on February 11, 1944, and just thirteen days later was the Midshipmen's Ball.

While candlelight was not provided, the V-12s dined with great popular music from their own Navy Band three nights during the week. If they needed additional recreation, they could find it at the USO in town over Neissen's Five and Dime. Diamond's Cafeteria in Dubuque was also a popular gathering place for meals or soft drinks.

The *Que* reported on the week-to-week campus events, while the *Key*, the yearbook, gave a thorough report on the V-12 unit and the typical trainee's life.

Some Dubuque V-12s: Marvin C. Helling, head football coach, University of North Dakota; Roger P. Olesen, president, Jens Olesen and Sons Construction, Waterloo, Iowa, and president, Master Builders of Iowa; Richard M. Ringoen, chairman, Ball Corporation; Dr. Warren R. Rupper, psychiatrist, Ogden, Utah; Roy W. Stevens, president, Hiram Walker; and Dr. Jack B. Watkins, V-12 premed who left medical school to accept a chaplain's commission, now surgeon, Salt Lake City.

University of Dubuque Archives

	1943		1944			1945	
	Jul.-Oct.	Nov.-Feb.	Mar.-Jun.	Jul.-Oct.	Nov.-Feb.	Mar.-Jun.	Jul.-Oct.
Navy	249	260	254	244	198	147	125
C.O.	Lt. C. C. Dunsmoor					Lt. John H. Jacobs	Lt. O. Dahl

Kansas State Teachers College Pittsburg, Kansas
(Now Pittsburg State University)

The V-12s at Pittsburg were first quartered in Willard Hall. In March of 1944 they moved to Walker Hall, and a year later were back in Willard. The college cafeteria served as the mess hall. The V-12s were warmly welcomed in July of 1943 by a "Navy night" band concert for which a crowd of four thousand people turned out. On February 23, 1944, the merchants of Pittsburg took a full-page ad to wish smooth sailing to the departing V-12s and to welcome the newcomers.

The Pittsburg *Collegio* reported in detail the events affecting the campus and the V-12 unit. A weekly column, "Of 'V' I Sing," was a regular feature. The *Kanza* gave yearbook coverage.

The outstanding V-12 event was the annual Navy Day celebration, which extended for three days in October and included a football rally and game, convocation, an open house, a dance, and often a play. A Navy Day queen was also chosen.

Athletics played a big part in the lives of the V-12s at Kansas State Teachers, and the first football team started it off in great style with a six-and-zero season, making it one of the eight undefeated teams in the United States. It scored 165 points to its opponents' 27. But academic work was not forgotten: in May of 1945 the *Collegio* reported that 56 percent of the V-12s were on the honor roll. Navy shows were a regular feature of the V-12 unit. One was called the "Variety Hour," another "Navy Nonsense," and in April of 1945, a third, "Fantail Fantasies," which the *Collegio* described as filled with "drama and corn."

Pittsburg V-12 reunions have been held in Los Angeles and Las Vegas.

Some Kansas State Teachers V-12s: Roy A. Anderson, chairman, Lockheed Corporation; Dr. Roy Lindahl, chairman, Department of Periodontics, University of North Carolina School of Dentistry; Ken Pryor, All-American (A.A.U.), "Phillips 66ers," and State Farm Insurance agency manager, Norman, Okla.; Dr. L. Edwin Scott, Ed Scott Sales Company (wine and spirits), Salt Lake City, and former assistant professor of business at Pittsburg State University; Harry Suker, general manager, Knott's Berry Farm; Dr. Kermit Vanderbilt, professor of English, San Diego State University; Arthur E. Van Leuven, Jr., executive vice president, TransAmerica Corporation; and Irving "M" Ziff, owner, Ziffco, manufacturer of recreational equipment.

	1943		1944			1945	
	Jul.-Oct.	Nov.-Feb.	Mar.-Jun.	Jul.-Oct.	Nov.-Feb.	Mar.-Jun.	Jul.-Oct.
Navy	241	231	247	240	195	96	94
C.O.	Lt. R. E. Baldwin					Lt. Philip E. Taylor	

University of Kansas Lawrence, Kansas

Jack C. Kemp

When the V-12s arrived at the University of Kansas on July 1, 1943, they found many military men already on campus: a large ASTP contingent, V-5 cadets attending the CAA-WTS School, and the Navy Machinist's Mates' School. The V-12s, all of whom were engineering or premedical students, were housed in a variety of fraternity houses, which were called PT boats, such as "PT-7."

The V-12s were a hard-working lot, but like the rest of the students on the Hill they never turned down the opportunity for a party. The *Jay Hawker*, the yearbook, noted that there were seventy-nine parties — which it called "major explosions" — between the first of November and the middle of February of that first winter. The 1944 *Jay Hawker* appeared in three segments, each of which looked like a magazine. Combined, they gave the university the treatment normally accorded by the standard yearbook.

The Jay Hawks played a full schedule in the rigorous Big Six (now Big

Eight), facing some of the best teams in the country. The 1944–1945 basketball squad finished second in the Big Six, and had a twelve-and-five season record.

In spite of all of the activity on the Hill, most Kansas V-12s reported that liberty in Kansas City was "4.0."

Some Kansas V-12s: Kenneth ("Bud") Adams, president, Houston Oilers professional football team; Robert J. Corber, commissioner, Interstate Commerce Commission; Rear Adm. Tyler F. Dedman, USN; Robert F. Ellsworth, deputy secretary of defense; Capt. Paul Hartley, USN; William S. Kanaga, chairman, Arthur Young and Company; Capt. David A. Long, USN, and executive director, Naval Historical Foundation; Rear Adm. Wayne E. Meyer, USN; Willard G. Widder, senior vice president and trust counsel, First National Bank, Kansas City; and Dr. John A. Wildgen, physician and president, American Academy of Family Physicians.

	1943		1944			1945			1946
	Jul.-Oct.	Nov.-Feb.	Mar.-Jun.	Jul.-Oct.	Nov.-Feb.	Mar.-Jun.	Jul.-Oct.	Nov.-Feb.	Mar.-Jun.
Navy	492	507	477	454	328	279	267	# 374	# 273
C.O.	Lt. A. H. Buhl					Lt. A. B. Copping	Capt. Chester A. Kunz		@

@ Capt. John V. Peterson   # Includes NROTC

Washburn Municipal University Topeka, Kansas
(Now Washburn University of Topeka)

The V-12s at Washburn Municipal University were quartered in dormitories and fraternity and sorority houses, which promptly received Navy names. Benton Hall became Yorktown, the Theta House was renamed Concord, the Zeta House turned into Halsey, and the Phi Delt and Alpha Delta fraternity houses became Farragut and Merrimac.

One big improvement that came with the arrival of the V-12s was the relocation of the Washburn Book Store to the Thomas Gymnasium building. Soft drinks, tables, and chairs were added to make the "Green Room" the campus social center.

Navy chow at Washburn was unusually good. The September 24, 1943, issue of the weekly *Washburn Review* concluded a major story about the food service with this comment: "No wonder the guys sing on their way to chow!" The fact that the V-12s were going through the chow line faster than at the beginning was credited in early October as the reason why reveille was moved back to 0600 from 0530.

The *Washburn Kaw* was the annual that recorded all of the wartime campus activity. The 1943 football season started with great promise when the Washburn Ichabods held the favored University of Kansas to a zero-to-zero tie, but the season was downhill from there on. The 1944–1945 basketball team wound up with a twelve-and-eight record.

At the end of the first term, the V-12s achieved representation on the Student Council. The Date Bureau

Washburn University Library

set up in December 1943 helped attendance at the dances, which were called "varsities."

The men of the hall that won Saturday morning room inspections received free tickets to the weekly Wednesday-night wrestling matches at Municipal Auditorium, thanks to the local American Legion Post.

Some Washburn V-12s: Robert L. Berra, senior vice president for administration, Monsanto Company; James D. Head, editor, *Parade* magazine; Dr. Oliver A. Johnson, professor of philosophy, University of California (Riverside); William J. Miller, Jr., president, Security Benefit Life Insurance; and Carl T. Rowan, ambassador to Finland and nationally syndicated columnist.

	1943		1944			1945	
	Jul.-Oct.	Nov.-Feb.	Mar.-Jun.	Jul.-Oct.	Nov.-Feb.	Mar.-Jun.	Jul.-Oct.
Navy	311	326	292	269	196	138	122
C.O.	Lt. O. R. Bontrager						

Berea College Berea, Kentucky

This eighty-eight-year-old college served the Appalachian region. It had a nationally known work-study system and tried to instill students with a sense of "social duty." Some of the 297 V-12s sent there thought they were being ordered to the end of the world, but most of them later realized that their period at Berea was one of the most interesting and rewarding times of their lives. Many married Berea girls, and some thirty-five were permitted to enroll after the war even though they did not qualify for admission because they lived outside the area or had family incomes that exceeded the Berea maximum.

The V-12s were quartered in Blue Ridge, Cumberland, and Howard halls and took their meals in the Boarding Hall which, under Mrs. Welsh's direction, turned out exceptionally good chow.

Some changes came to Berea because of the V-12s. Social dancing was permitted on the campus for the first time (see Chapter 32, "Campus Life"). There was dancing on Wednesday and Saturday nights, and the 1945 *Chimes,* the yearbook, noted, "Dances and 'closed weekends' go hand-in-hand and make the campus go 'round." Many V-12s tried mountain climbing for the first time and were rewarded with the picnics that went with it. During the campus day trainees frequently stopped at the fountain at T. P. Baker's Sundry Store to meet their coed friends.

V-12s took part in all campus activities, from band and glee club to athletics and debate. The sports teams were 100 percent Navy, and Berea won re-

Berea College Archives

spect as a local powerhouse. The *Pinnacle* was the weekly paper that reported campus life.

Berea V-12s have had several reunions.

Some Berea V-12s: Rear Adm. John C. Barrow, USN; the Reverend Fred F. Bergewisch, S.J., assistant professor of religion, Loyola University, Chicago; Dr. Keith L. Broman, chairman, department of finance, University of Nebraska; the Reverend Kenneth R. Callis, D.D., senior minister, Utica United Methodist Church, Sterling Heights, Mich.; the Right Reverend William A. Dimmick,* Episcopal Suffragan Bishop of Alabama; James R. Sherburne, novelist; and Dr. John S. Titus, professor of horticulture, University of Illinois.

	1943		1944			1945		
	Jul.-Oct.	Nov.-Feb.	Mar.-Jun.	Jul.-Oct.	Nov.-Feb.	Mar.-Jun.	Jul.-Oct.
Navy	294	295	295	287	214	125	96
C.O.	Lt. H. R. Dunathan						

University of Louisville Louisville, Kentucky

The University of Louisville was accepted for a V-12 unit even though it did not then have adequate dormitory space or food service. The school — and the Navy — bet on the university's ability to acquire adequate facilities by July 1. The necessary $250,000 was quickly raised from the city of Louisville, the university, and "private business interests." Four dormitories (which the V-12s say were more like barracks) and a mess hall were erected in record time. For the first three months there were no doors on the rooms, per Navy suggestion, but it was impossible to study without doors, and they were added in the fall.

Rear Adm. Randall Jacobs, chief of the Bureau of Naval Personnel, dedicated the new buildings on July 21, 1943. Imagine being inspected by the chief of personnel only twenty-one days after you reported for Navy duty!

The Navy inspectors continually criticized the university for substandard physical training facilities. For swimming class the V-12s were bused to the Henry Clay Hotel's pool in downtown Louisville.

Kentucky Derby day was the highlight of the year, and the V-12s put on a review for the crowd at Churchill Downs. The *Thoroughbred*, the yearbook, gave great coverage to participation by V-12s. The *Cardinal* did a near-professional job in its weekly reporting of campus happenings.

The 1944–1945 basketball team was better than ever before, compiling a sixteen-and-three record.

Some University of Louisville V-12s: John Tolman Burns, president, Vickers Division, Sperry Rand Corporation; Vice Adm. Kenneth M. Carr, USN; Victor M. Corrado, director of technical development, U.S. Government Printing Office; Thomas C. Graham, vice chairman, U.S. Steel; Rear Adm. John S. Kern, USN; William C. Sherman, deputy representative to the Security Council of the United Nations; and Cary Whitehead, real estate developer, Memphis.

	1943		1944			1945			1946
	Jul.-Oct.	Nov.-Feb.	Mar.-Jun.	Jul.-Oct.	Nov.-Feb.	Mar.-Jun.	Jul.-Oct.	Nov.-Feb.	Mar.-Jun.
Navy	475	, 470	439	442	350	263	257	# 445	# 372
C.O.	Lt. S. E. McKerley					@	Capt. John H. Lewis		

Includes NROTC   @ Lcdr. J. Andrew Holley

Alma College Alma, Michigan

Alma College Archives

This Presbyterian school, founded in 1886, housed its V-12s in Wright Hall. The citizens of Alma arranged several social events for the sailors, who arrived in July when most of the coeds were away from the campus. The first event was the "Navy Swing," a dance held on July 31; a second dance followed in two weeks. Later the V-12s returned the favors by putting on a happy hour for Alma's citizens in the Community Center.

The flu epidemic of December 1943 was so severe that the commanding officer successfully pleaded with the higher authorities to end the outdoor early morning calisthenics. He also got extra foul weather gear issued to the Alma unit.

The *Almanian* was the student newspaper, but the V-12s started their own mimeographed sheet called the *Scuttle Butt* (sic). The latter issued a

suggested Christmas book list for families and girlfriends: On the "books you will need" side were *The Blue Jacket's Manual* and *Watch Officer's Guide;* on the "books you will like" side were the *Naval Reserve Guide, Ship's Business,* and *The Navy Reader.*

The student council sponsored regular college dances, and a full intramural athletic program was offered in addition to the varsity program.

Many V-12s returned for a war-era reunion on August 23 to 25, 1985.

Some Alma V-12s: George H. Allen, professional football coach; George Coughlin, vice president, Paine Webber; Louis Hagopian, chairman, N. W. Ayer; and John C. Rosenkrans, president, Eisenhower University, and executive director, Dwight D. Eisenhower Society.

	1943		1944			1945		
	Jul.-Oct.	Nov.-Feb.	Mar.-Jun.	Jul.-Oct.	Nov.-Feb.	Mar.-Jun.	Jul.-Oct.
Navy	197	192	197	213	199	174	155
C.O.	Lt. J. E. Scott						

Central Michigan College of Education Mount Pleasant, Michigan
(Now Central Michigan University)

Central Michigan University faced the prospect of having no mattresses for the bunks just two days before opening of the V-12 program, but the school pulled everything together on its well-equipped campus by the time the 475 V-12s arrived on July 1, 1943. They were housed in the Keeler Union Building and in Ronan Hall, a former girls' dormitory. The dining hall at Ronan had been closed in 1934 because of depression conditions, but it was totally renovated and updated to serve as the V-12 mess hall.

College functions, including dancing and games, were held every Saturday evening in the Keeler Union. An extensive intramural program kept the V-12s busy at other times. In an all-unit tennis tournament the first year, the skipper and the exec took the doubles crown.

The 1944 football team finished five and two, and the 1944–1945 basketball five finished with an eleven-and-four record, making it the most successful squad in Central Michigan's history. It did not lose a game on the home floor. V-12s dominated the marching band, and the campus dance band was known as the "V-12 Thirteen."

Central Michigan Life, the student newspaper, was published regularly when the coeds were on campus, which was generally during the November and March trimesters. The Navy need for news was met by the *Scuttlebutt,* published by the V-12s. The *Chippewa,* the yearbook, reported on the overall picture.

After the unit closed down, Sadie,

Clarke Historical Library, Central Michigan University

the canine mascot of the V-12s, found a permanent home with the family of Lt. Maxwell R. Kelso, the commanding officer.

Some Central Michigan V-12s: Edward J. Chady, vice president for finances and secretary, Thomas Industries; Frank Couzens, Jr., executive vice president, Manufacturers National Bank, Detroit; Jerald Griffin, vice president, Dow Corning Corporation; Dr. John A. Knauss, dean, Graduate School of Oceanography, University of Rhode Island; John J. McHale, president, Montreal Expos professional baseball club; and Richard C. Van Deusen, undersecretary, U.S. Department of Housing and Urban Development.

	1943		1944			1945	
	Jul.-Oct.	Nov.-Feb.	Mar.-Jun.	Jul.-Oct.	Nov.-Feb.	Mar.-Jun.	Jul.-Oct.
Navy	474	456	483	427	352	235	208
C.O.	Lt. Maxwell R. Kelso						

University of Michigan   Ann Arbor, Michigan

University of Michigan Archives

The Marine V-12s were quartered in Wenley House, and most of the Navy V-12s were in the West Quadrangle, where a member of the Naval ROTC was placed in charge of each floor.

Intercollegiate competition was a very important part of V-12-era campus life at Michigan. In 1943 the influx of marines from other Big Ten schools brought Michigan a superabundance of talent, which led to an eight-and-one football record. That was good enough to be ranked third in the nation, behind Notre Dame and Great Lakes Naval Training Station. The record also earned Michigan a share of the Big Ten crown with undefeated Purdue. The 1944 championship baseball team was undefeated in Big Ten play. Winning seasons were recorded in most other sports, too.

V-12s took part in many campus activities and formed an eighty-seven-member V-12 band, the major marching band on campus. Social activities were plentiful and there was always the Ann Arbor USO to fall back on when payday was just around the corner.

The *Michigan Daily* kept the campus up to date on news. The *Ensian*, the yearbook, and the NROTC year-

	1943		1944		1945			1946
	Jul.-Oct.	Nov.-Feb.	Mar.-Jun.	Jul.-Oct.	Nov.-Feb.	Mar.-Jun.	Jul.-Oct.	Nov.-Feb.	Mar.-Jun.
Navy	1031	1046	1002	1108	913	830	796	775	397
C.O.	Capt. R. E. Cassidy			Lcdr. John J. Bronson		Capt. W. V. Michaux			
Marines	300	249	215	129	151	132	141	96	81
O-in-C	Capt. Joseph T. Hoffman				Maj. John P. Wilbern		@	Maj. Harry Calcutt	

@ Capt. Francis H. Bergtholdt

University of Michigan

Edwin Hakala

book, the *Pelorus*, gave historical coverage to V-12 activities.

Some V-12s at Michigan: Charles K. Birdsall, professor of electrical engineering; Lee A. Buck, senior vice president, New York Life Insurance, and Episcopal evangelist; Hal Cooper, television producer and director ("Dick Van Dyke Show," "Odd Couple," etc.); Fenwick J. Crane, chairman, Family Life Insurance Company; Dr. Donald E. DeGraaf, chairman, department of physics, University of Michigan at Flint; Robert N. Dolph, president, Exxon International Company; Robert A. Fuhrman, chairman, Lockheed Missiles; Dr. Frederick W. Gehring, professor of mathematics and chairman, department of mathematics, University of Michigan; Edward E. Hiett, vice president and general counsel, Libby-Owens-Ford; Elroy Hirsch, director of athletics, University of Wisconsin; Thomas V. King, president, Seay and Thomas, Chicago; Donald G. Raymer, president, Central Illinois Public Service Company; and Russell C. Youngdahl, president, Long Island Lighting Company.

Western Michigan College of Education   Kalamazoo, Michigan
(Now Western Michigan University)

Trainees at Western Michigan College walked up a brick street when they reported for duty, and that hill presented a formidable climb twice a day after calisthenics and physical training. The V-12s, however, soon found the unique wooden cable cars on the other side of the hill for their weekend trips up and down.

Sailors and marines made up virtually all of the outstanding Bronco teams. The 1943 football squad lost only two games: to the University of Michigan, which was ranked number three in the nation by the Associated Press, and to Great Lakes Naval Training Station, which was rated number two.

On the hardwood, coach Buck Read's team went fifteen and four and was ranked number four nationally, trailing only West Point, Kentucky, and DePaul. The squad beat the University of Michigan twice and lost only one game to a college team.

The 1944 baseball team finished its ten-and-six season in a blaze of glory by dumping the University of Michigan, the previously undefeated Big Ten champion, five to four and three to two.

V-12s gave wholehearted support to campus activities, including publications, plays, bands, the glee club, and the radio station. V-12s remember the good social life at Western Michigan

Western Michigan University Archives

and happy times at the campus Soda Bar.

The marines never quite got over the sign, "Hall for Women," that remained on the front of Spindler Hall, which they occupied as Barracks One. The Navy shared Barracks Two (Vandercook Hall) with the commanding officer and his family and Barracks Three (Walwood Hall) with the executive officer and his household. The mess hall in Spindler was usually referred to as "one meatball."

The Western Michigan V-12s held a large reunion in August 1984.

Some Western Michigan V-12s: Maurice B. Allen, architect, Bloomfield Hills, Michigan; Rolla Anderson, ath-

	1943		1944		1945		
	Jul.-Oct.	Nov.-Feb.	Mar.-Jun.	Jul.-Oct.	Nov.-Feb.	Mar.-Jun.	Jul.-Oct.
Navy	355	477	491	587	468	275	238
C.O.	Cdr. John T. Tuthill, Jr.			@	Lt. Ernest H. Carl		
Marines	368	291	215	141			
O-in-C	Capt. Ralph E. Britt			2			

@ Lcdr. Frederick S. Bartlett   2. Capt. Grenville Clark, Jr.

Western Michigan College of Education

letic director, Kalamazoo College; Richard T. Burress, associate director and senior fellow, the Hoover Institution; Will M. Caldwell, executive vice president and chief financial officer, Ford Motor Company; Dr. William E. Engbretson, president, Governors State University (Illinois); Rear Adm. James H. Foxgrover, USN; Clifford M. Kiddie, owner, Kiddie Kreations, Citrus Heights, Calif.; William Kowalski, vice president for facility engineering and governmental relations, Western Michigan University; Donald H. Mitzel, president, First Federal Savings of Michigan; Fred L. Stevens, athletic director, State High School, and associate professor of physical education, Western Michigan University; Maj. Gen. Hal W. Vincent, USMC; and Neil W. Zundel, group vice president, Reynolds Metals Company.

College of St. Thomas   St. Paul, Minnesota

College of St. Thomas Archives

Most of the 258 trainees assigned to the College of St. Thomas were strangers to the area. One hundred and eleven came from California, ninety-five from Kansas, and Colorado and Wyoming were the runners-up. Less than a handful came from Minnesota. They were housed in Ireland Hall and the St. Thomas Annex.

The *Aquin,* the college paper, also covered St. Thomas Military Academy, so the V-12s started their own paper to increase the amount of space given to unit activities. The mimeographed *Bowsprite* made its debut on November 18, 1943, with six pages. The second issue came out two months later.

The social schedule at St. Thomas involved lots of dances, including one called the Christmas Formal or "Back to Kansas and California Dance." Girls attending the nearby College of St. Catherine were popular dates. There were also, in quick succession after the Christmas break, the Prom, the Winter Frolic, and the Regimental Dinner Ball, which all took place before the end of the term in February. V-12 variety shows also appeared with some regularity.

In 1943 there was no football, but the team was back in 1944 with a three-and-two record. In 1945 it was seven and zero. The basketball squad for 1943–1944 faced a tough schedule of traditional St. Thomas rivals plus the University of Minnesota, Marquette, and Great Lakes Naval Training Station. The "Tommies" finished with a record of fourteen and four and the following year had fourteen and five. One of the reports by an inspecting officer from the Ninth Naval District noted that the athletic facilities at St. Thomas were "outstandingly superior."

Some St. Thomas V-12s: Addison W. Clark, Jr., partner, Clark Farms, Visalia, California; Ward E. Edwards, vice president for administration, North Memorial Medical Center, Minneapolis; Dr. Dean L. Peterson, professor, University of Kansas Medical School; James R. Peterson, president, Parker Pen Company; Robert H. Shanahan, executive vice president and co-publisher, the *Denver Post;* Ernest W. Toy, Jr., university librarian, California State University at Fullerton; and Joel A. Wentz, assistant state conservationist of Kansas.

	1943		1944			1945	
	Jul.-Oct.	Nov.-Feb.	Mar.-Jun.	Jul.-Oct.	Nov.-Feb.	Mar.-Jun.	Jul.-Oct.
Navy	257	260	237	232	220	146	117
C.O.	Lt. E. B. Womack					@	2

@ Lt. Marston M. McCluggage   2. Lt.(jg) Robert P. Sherman

Gustavus Adolphus College   St. Peter, Minnesota

When the four hundred sailors and marines arrived at this conservative Augustana Synod Lutheran college on July 1, 1943, many on campus worried that this large infusion of servicemen would have an adverse effect upon the school's character. Their concerns were unnecessary, for the military trainees and the civilian students had good rapport and Navy-college relations turned out to be excellent.

The strict social code at GA prohibited dancing on the campus, so the USO in town was frequented by the V-12s. A Navy Service Center installed in the basement of Uhler Hall became an on-campus recreation spot. It was later turned into a student canteen.

An uneven distribution of military units among its members led the Minnesota Intercollegiate Athletic Conference to suspend official league play during 1943 and 1944. As a result, Gustavus Adolphus had difficulty lining up opponents and played only two football games in 1943, both against St. Mary's. In 1944 it was able to schedule seven games, including one with Iowa State and two with Drake, but the competition was too difficult for a successful season. In 1945, league play was back and the team, still mainly composed of V-12s, had a six-and-one record, which brought it the MIAC championship. The 1943–1944 basketball team racked up an eight-and-three record, while the 1944–1945 aggregation won twelve and lost two, which gave it the unofficial conference championship.

The *Gustavian Weekly* was published on a regular basis and gave a good account of unit activities. The

	1943		1944			1945	
	Jul.-Oct.	Nov.-Feb.	Mar.-Jun.	Jul.-Oct.	Nov.-Feb.	Mar.-Jun.	Jul.-Oct.
Navy	193	253	388	344	227	154	145
C.O.	Lcdr. Jesse H. Smith		Lt. Charles P. McCurdy, Jr.				
Marines	195	134					
O-in-C	@	2nd Lt. John W. Faus					

@ 2nd Lt. Ralph L. Cormany

Gustavus Adolphus College

yearbook, the *Gustavian*, became a biennial and appeared only in 1944.

During the life of the V-12 program at Gustavus Adolphus, 213 marines and 739 sailors were stationed there.

Some GA V-12s: Richard J. Durrell, publisher, *People* magazine; Robert L. Gale, president, Association of Governing Boards of Universities and Colleges; Ralph P. Hofstad, president, Land O' Lakes; Wallace J. Jorgenson, president, Jefferson-Pilot Broadcasting Company, Charlotte, N.C.; John E. Pearson, chairman, Northwestern National Life Insurance Company; and Dr. John Roslansky, Woods Hole Marine Research Laboratory, and editor, *Nobel Conferences.*

Saint Mary's College Winona, Minnesota

Allen G. Rossman

The V-12s ordered to this Catholic men's school were quartered in Heffron Hall. They found a warm welcome waiting for them at Saint Mary's and at the nearby campuses of the College of Saint Teresa and the Minnesota Teachers College. Hospitality was also extended by the citizens of Winona, who organized a USO and ran it for the benefit of the trainees and other servicemen in the area. In July of 1944, fifty Saint Mary's V-12s were guests of the Citizens Service Corps of Winona for a two-day party.

Athletics was an important part of life at Saint Mary's and the Redmen were well represented by the V-12s. The abbreviated football season of 1943 produced a three-and-one record, while in basketball the team won eleven and lost five.

The glee club was nearly all Navy; it turned out to be the most active group on campus. It produced a sparkling show called "This Is the Navy" in September of 1943, and an encore was requested for a bond rally in Winona.

Many Saint Mary's V-12s got a chance at leadership through the monthly change of battalion officers.

The student paper, the *Nexus*, appeared semimonthly and covered a lot of news, such as the contest to name the campus soda fountain ("Keel Klub" was finally chosen). The paper also covered all of the musical and theatrical productions, as well as the frequent dances and exchanges with the girls at the nearby colleges.

Some St. Mary's V-12s: Norbert W. Heuel, director of personnel, Loyola Medical Center, Chicago; James F. Heinlen, Winona County juvenile officer and co-developer of nationally recognized voluntary restitution program for juvenile offenders; Melvin R. Laird, secretary of defense; William H. Madden, vice president for industrial mineral products, 3M Company; Robert A. Peterson, vice president for finance, Toro Company; and Allen G. Rossman, chairman, Northprint Company, Grand Rapids, Minn.

	1943		1944			1945	
	Jul.-Oct.	Nov.-Feb.	Mar.-Jun.	Jul.-Oct.	Nov.-Feb.	Mar.-Jun.	Jul.-Oct.
Navy	217	230	212	194	188	114	108
C.O.	Lt. F. B. Andreen		Lt. M. S. Lee	Lt. A. H. Will			

University of Minnesota   Minneapolis, Minnesota

When the more than nine hundred V-12s arrived at the Minnesota campus, they found it full of the military: ASTPs, Navy electrician's mates, Navy machinist's mates, and V-5s. The V-12s were quartered in Pioneer Hall.

One early September noon, an order was posted making the official uniform of the day undress blues. For the next two days there was a strange mixture of whites and blues as V-12s struggled to get their winter uniforms back from the tailor's. October 4 brought a formal inspection by Rear Adm. John Downes, commandant of the Ninth Naval District.

Two years later Vice Adm. Arthur S. Carpenter, then commandant of the Ninth, was the commencement speaker. He had a formal review where he was joined on the reviewing stand by Governor Edward J. Thye and Minneapolis mayor Hubert H. Humphrey. Fleet Admiral William Halsey addressed the students after the war.

Trainees were on all of the athletic teams but most of the U of M's pre-V-12 football squad had enlisted in the Marine Reserve and had thus been sent as V-12s to other Big Ten schools, where they became Minnesota opponents.

The V-12s aided the NROTCs in putting out the *Gopher Log*, a Navy yearbook. The 1944 university yearbook, the *Gopher*, gave an hilarious account of the first two terms of the V-12 program. The *Minnesota Daily* carried the regular campus news.

Social life was good at the university. "Jamborees" brought movie stars such as Betty Hutton and Rosalind Russell to the campus. Other events

University of Minnesota Archives

included the appearance of the Camel Caravan and the Coca-Cola Spotlight Band programs. The Red Cross had a Christmas party for all the boys in Pioneer Hall. A farewell dinner for seniors, usually at the Covered Wagon, became a V-12 tradition. The Navy Ball and the Dream Drag Dance became regular features of campus life. Smokers were held in the field house. The campus soda fountain and coffee shop was the "V."

Some Minnesota V-12s: Dr. Kenneth A. Gilles, assistant U.S. secretary of agriculture; Ernest B. Moffett, Jr., group vice president, 3M Company; Dr. Harry A. Nara, professor and chairman, computer engineering department, Case Western Reserve University; Hicks B. Waldron, chairman, Avon Products; and Winston R. Wallin, president, Pillsbury Company.

	1943		1944		1945			1946
	Jul.-Oct.	Nov.-Feb.	Mar.-Jun.	Jul.-Oct.	Nov.-Feb.	Mar.-Jun.	Jul.-Oct.	Nov.-Feb.	Mar.-Jun.
Navy	730	765	788	739	651	620	452	174	36
C.O.	Capt. J. W. Gates					@	Cdr. J. W. Whaley		Capt. W. C. Holt

@ Capt. John J. Tuthill, Jr.

Central College Fayette, Missouri
(Now Central Methodist College)

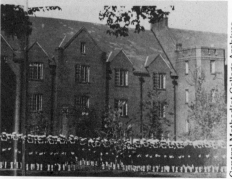

Just twelve hours before the first contingent of V-12s appeared at Central College, their bunks had not arrived. Fortunately, the bunks made it to McMurry Hall just ahead of the sailors.

Although it was one of the smaller V-12 colleges, Central College had many of the attributes of a larger school. The *Central Collegian,* the student newspaper, covered the campus activities exceptionally well. The *Ragout,* the yearbook, gave a good report of the V-12 years. A V-12 dance band was kept busy at the numerous dances at this Methodist school. The campus gathering place was the Hut.

The rigorous physical program kept the men in great shape and both the 1943–1944 and 1944–1945 basketball teams took the Missouri College Athletic Union championship. The 1944–1945 team also made it to the quarterfinals of the National Invitational Tournament in Kansas City.

An indication of the area's friendliness: a sailor leaving Central lingered at the drugstore soda fountain till the last minute and then boarded the local train as it was pulling out of town. He soon discovered that he'd left his orders back in the drugstore booth and reported as much to the conductor, who obligingly had the train backed up to the Fayette station so the sailor could retrieve his important papers.

Some Central V-12s: Lewis B. Fleming, editorial writer, *Los Angeles Times;* Robert L. Hogge, Ford-Mercury dealer, California, Mo.; Willet C. Kubec, president, Industrial Equipment Company, Davenport, Iowa; Clifford B. Maines, president, Safeco Insurance Company; Walter G. Mollman, design engineer, Rockwell International; and Richard McKay Oster, chairman, United Vintners Corporation.

	1943		1944			1945	
	Jul.-Oct.	Nov.-Feb.	Mar.-Jun.	Jul.-Oct.	Nov.-Feb.	Mar.-Jun.	Jul.-Oct.
Navy	342	309	327	304	204	140	102
C.O.	Lt. R. A. Ball					Lt. Carl R. Reng	

Central Missouri State Teachers College   Warrensburg, Missouri
(Now Central Missouri State University)

The 372 men reporting to the Central Missouri V-12 unit represented twenty-six states. They were housed in Yeater Hall and found a warm welcome waiting for them both in town and on campus.

The commanding officer was so highly regarded by the school that after the V-12 unit was deactivated in October of 1945, he was offered and accepted the post of dean of administration and instruction.

The *Student,* the college paper, found a weekly schedule too difficult to sustain under wartime conditions so in the fall of 1943 it was transformed into a monthly combination of student newspaper and yearbook, the *Student-Rhetor.* It featured some excellent pictures of the unit.

Music was a big part of the extracurricular activities. There were two dance bands, the Jolly Rogers and the Rhythm Aces. A Navy choir of forty voices and the Navy marching band met the rest of the musical requirements of the college. Happy hours were conducted regularly, and the Navy Ball each term was the highlight of the college's social life.

Central Missouri competed vigorously in all intercollegiate athletics, and the Mules always gave a good account of themselves. In October of 1944 the V-12s held a house party for their parents.

Some CMSTC V-12s: William B. Bechanan, president, Kentucky Utilities Company; Newton R. Bradley, attorney, Lexington, Mo.; Dr. Sam P. Bradley, optometrist, Warrensburg; Dr. Robert L. Marshall, dean of public services and continuing education, Central Missouri State University, and captain, USNR; Dr. Billie Jo Smith, physician, Windsor, Mo.; Dr. Donald S. Tull, professor of marketing, College of Management and Business, University of Oregon; and Dr. Rhea Walker II, physician, Houston.

	1943		1944			1945	
	Jul.-Oct.	Nov.-Feb.	Mar.-Jun.	Jul.-Oct.	Nov.-Feb.	Mar.-Jun.	Jul.-Oct.
Navy	376	379	394	380	284	169	152
C.O.	Lt. Irving L. Peters						

Missouri Valley College Marshall, Missouri

When the 286 V-12s arrived at this Presbyterian college in 1943, they took over most of the dorms and proceeded to dominate campus life for the next two years.

When they arrived, the new swimming pool the college had promised to install if it received a V-12 unit was under construction. The Missouri Valley teams competed in all sports in the Missouri College Athletic Union.

The Pirates' Den was installed in the basement of Campbell Hall and offered Ping-Pong, a dance floor and juke box, soft drinks, and sandwiches. It was open Saturday and Sunday nights. Dances were held regularly in Morrison Gymnasium. The Navy Swing Band provided the music for many of them.

Campus events were reported by the *Missouri Valley Delta*. In 1945, it produced an issue, *Sabiduria*, to replace the yearbook, which could not be published because of wartime conditions.

Some Missouri Valley V-12s: Joseph Granville, stock market advisor; Herbert E. Harris II, congressman from Virginia; Capt. James D. Hereford, USN; Dr. Robert G. McKinnell, professor of genetics and cell biology, University of Minnesota, and author (*Cloning: Of Frogs, Mice, and Other Animals*); Robert G. Roth, vice president and treasurer, Knowles Electronics; Dr. G. William Skinner, professor of anthropology, Stanford University; and Dr. Harvey Thomas, president, Thomas and Associates, psychological consultants to management.

	1943		1944			1945	
	Jul.-Oct.	Nov.-Feb.	Mar.-Jun.	Jul.-Oct.	Nov.-Feb.	Mar.-Jun.	Jul.-Oct.
Navy	267	266	265	266	203	137	92
C.O.	Lt. Edwin F. Peters				Lt. G. F. W. Boyle	Lt. C. M. Ransom	

Northwest Missouri State Teachers College Maryville, Missouri
(Now Northwest Missouri State University)

Northwest Missouri State University Archives

On July 1, 1943, the arriving V-12s took over the Men's Quadrangle and the Women's Residence Hall, forcing all coeds to utilize off-campus housing. The V-12 office took over the first floor of the library, and all of the Navy men ate at the Quad mess hall.

From the very beginning, the relationship between the civilian and Navy students was excellent. At the start of each term, a mixer was arranged to introduce the new arrivals into the campus social scene. The student senate sponsored a number of functions, including the Ersatz Dance, the Christmas Ball, the V-12 Ball, and a Sadie Hawkins Dance, which climaxed Leap Week in February of 1944.

The Bearcat Den was the campus meeting place. The student body put on "Campus Lights of '44" and 120 V-12s took part in a Navy "happy hour" early in 1944. The marching band was made up entirely of V-12s.

The Bearcats fielded teams in all of the major sports and played a very competitive schedule. The 1944 foot-ball squad went undefeated in a seven-game season, scoring 206 points to their opponents' 21. The team received a bid to the Sun Bowl in El Paso but had to turn it down because many of the starters had already been transferred to other Navy stations.

The *Northwest Missourian,* which appeared semimonthly, was produced by the coeds, except for the sports section. The yearbook was the *Tower,* and an all-girl staff with lots of determination saw that it was published for both 1944 and 1945.

Some Northwest Missouri V-12s: Dr. Arthur E. Bryson, Jr., professor of aerospace engineering, Stanford University; Lawrence A. Hamre, department manager, Sperry Univac; Robert E. Hartmann, vice president and secretary, Alpha Portland Industries; Dr. James B. Ludtke, chairman, department of finance, University of Massachusetts; and Donald R. Morland, career foreign service officer, ambassador to four different nations.

	1943		1944			1945	
	Jul.-Oct.	Nov.-Feb.	Mar.-Jun.	Jul.-Oct.	Nov.-Feb.	Mar.-Jun.	Jul.-Oct.
Navy	366	371	401	380	220	144	128
C.O.	Lt. Ralph K. Brown			Lt. E. O. Olson		Lt. John Kessler	

Park College   Parksville, Missouri

Park College Archives

The hot summer of 1943 is vividly remembered by all of the trainees who arrived at Park College, particularly the many who came from Oregon. The V-12s were quartered in the Copley-Thaw, Woodward, Chesnut, and Nickel dorms, which immediately came to be called "barracks." To accommodate the V-12 swimming classes the college uncovered and rejuvenated the old pool that had been closed in 1914 due to a water shortage.

There was lots of activity on the Park campus on weekends, and the Platt County USO provided another outlet. There were farewell dances each term to honor those departing for other stations, a Sadie Hawkins Day dance, and the annual Snow Ball in December, plus many informal house parties. Still, quite a few Park trainees managed to visit the Play-mor Ballroom in Kansas City, which was a guaranteed way to hear some good bands and meet some girls. The V-12s put on a boxing and variety show and some "happy hours."

There was no football at Park, and the 1943–1944 basketball squad was the first Park cage team in many years. In 1944–1945, it had an excellent season.

The *Park Stylus* gave good weekly coverage of campus affairs and each term published a special edition in magazine form to substitute for the yearbook, which had been discontinued for the duration.

Some Park College V-12s: Robert H. Boykin, president, Federal Reserve Bank of Dallas; Peter R. Elliott, director, Pro Football Hall of Fame; Dr. William D. Phillips, chairman, department of chemistry, Washington University; Richard L. Sejnost, executive vice president, Trade Medical Center; Col. Cecil Sumpter, U.S. Army; and Kenneth Welch, entertainer and television writer (Carol Burnett shows).

	1943		1944			1945
	Jul.-Oct.	Nov.-Feb.	Mar.-Jun.	Jul.-Oct.	Nov.-Feb.	Mar.-Jun.
Navy	395	361	385	337	237	139
C.O.	Lt. H. W. Reninger					

Southeast Missouri State Teachers College
Cape Girardeau, Missouri
(Now Southeast Missouri State University)

The V-12s ordered to Southeast Missouri State Teachers College were quartered in Leming, Albert, and Cheney halls; the mess hall was in Cheney. When quotas were reduced in November of 1944, Leming was returned to the coeds, and later Albert was also given up by the Navy.

Under the V-12 influence the Cape Indians had some excellent intercollegiate teams. The 1943 football squad won its first five games, but at the end of the term (October 31) some regulars moved on to midshipmen's schools and the team lost the final two games. The basketball five that followed that successful football season was undersized, even by the standards of that day. The first eleven men averaged five feet nine inches in height, which caused them to be dubbed "the mighty midgets." It was one of the most exciting and colorful cage campaigns in the Indians' history; the final record was eleven wins and three losses.

The campus events were reported weekly by the award-winning *Capaha Arrow*. Music for the Christmas dance was provided by the V-12 dance band. Just before Christmas, Student Christian Association members saw two movies, "Our Enemy the Jap" and "This Is Everybody's War."

The Winter Dance in February of 1944 was a "backwards" dance, with the women asking the men to the event. The selection of the *Sagamore* queen was also announced at that dance. The *Sagamore* was the yearbook, which gave excellent coverage to the V-12 program.

Anzell O. Lee

The trainees participated in nearly every campus organization, including the Mark Twain Society, which put on a melodrama, "Pure as the Driven Snow," and the Webster Society, which gave as its fifteenth annual production a farce entitled "Is College Dead?"

For V-12s who wanted to get to the big city the St. Louis-Cape bus line ran five round trips daily.

Some Southeast Missouri V-12s: Ray M. Kaegel, real estate broker, Granite City, Ill.; Donald C. Lasater, chairman, Mercantile Bancorporation, St. Louis; Anzell O. Lee, senior engineer, Arizona Public Service Company; Dr. John N. Middelkamp, professor of pediatrics, Washington University Medical School, and president, American Board of Pediatrics; Robert D. Welti, TV weatherman, KSL-TV, Salt Lake City; and Clyde E. Work, associate dean of engineering, Michigan Technical University.

	1943		1944			1945	
	Jul.-Oct.	Nov.-Feb.	Mar.-Jun.	Jul.-Oct.	Nov.-Feb.	Mar.-Jun.	Jul.-Oct.
Navy	328	311	314	307	199	106	100
C.O.	Lt. H. O. Soderquist				Lt. J. Hartt Walsh		

Westminster College   Fulton, Missouri

This Presbyterian men's school, which later gained international fame as the site of Winston Churchill's "Iron Curtain" speech, was the home for hundreds of V-12 students for seven terms. They occupied Reunion Hall and four fraternity houses.

There was no football at Westminster during the V-12 years because the school's uniforms had been sold to other institutions before the unit was established. However, a strong intramural program kept trainees busy.

The town of Fulton established a USO that served as a social center — at least until the fall, when three hundred girls returned to nearby William Woods College. "Happy hours" and Navy dances were held on a regular basis. The unit paraded in downtown Fulton on the twenty-fifth anniversary of the original Armistice Day.

The *Columns* was the biweekly newspaper, which featured a "Now Hear This" column written by the commanding officer.

When a number of the "old salts" decided to "pack it in" during the summer of 1944 and return to the fleet, maintaining the morale of the remaining V-12s was a major problem. It was addressed by both the officers of the unit and by the *Columns* in an editorial, "V-12 Training Essential," in the issue of October 4, 1944.

Some Westminster V-12s: Lt. Gen. Robert J. Baer, U.S. Army; Dr. Hoyt D. Gardner, physician, and president, American Medical Association; Dr. Charles B. Handy, professor of accounting and director of the School of

Westminster College Archives

Business Administration, Iowa State University; Dr. Irving S. Johnson, vice president, Lilly Research Labs; Allan T. O'Toole, vice president, Public Service Company of Oklahoma, and trustee, Westminster College; Richard W. Rogers, vice president and controller, Ralston Purina Company; and Dr. August G. Swanson, director, department of academic affairs, Association of American Medical Colleges.

	1943		1944			1945	
	Jul.-Oct.	Nov.-Feb.	Mar.-Jun.	Jul.-Oct.	Nov.-Feb.	Mar.-Jun.	Jul.-Oct.
Navy	280	276	273	253	189	125	114
C.O.	Lt. Eugene R. Page		Lt. Donald E. Field				

Doane College   Crete, Nebraska

Doane College Library

The V-12s reporting to this Congregational college found that V-5s had preceded them. The V-12s were quartered in Men's Hall and Frees Hall.

Shortly after the V-12 unit's arrival, a drive was begun for donations to install Doane's first swimming pool, which was finally in place by the spring of 1944. Other events of note during the V-12s' life at Doane were the one-week all-campus smoking ban for the men living in Men's Hall because somebody had tossed a lighted cigarette out of an upper window that set fire to an awning outside the sick bay; the installation of a new metal flagpole in the fall of 1943; the one-day flood in the spring of 1944; and the mumps epidemic of the same time.

The *Doane Owl*, the oldest college paper in Nebraska, gave excellent attention to the V-12 unit. The *U.S.S. Doane* was the yearbook put out by the students to record all of the college's activities during 1944.

The 1943 Doane Tigers went undefeated on the gridiron until the final game of the season, racking up a six, one, and one record. The basketball team of 1943–1944 was the best in Doane's history, finishing sixteen and three, including a victory over the powerful Iowa Pre-Flight Seahawks.

Some Doane V-12s: Dr. Richard B. Drake, professor of history, Berea College; Robert H. Fust, executive director, New Jersey League of Municipalities; Everet Gale, district secretary, Merced (Calif.) Irrigation District; Rear Adm. Donald P. Harvey, USN; Capt. Ervin B. Rubey, USN; the Reverend Reuben T. Swanson, corporate secretary, Lutheran Church in America; William B. Tyson, senior vice president, Reading and Bates Drilling Company; and Joseph R. Wong, Roman Catholic priest and rehabilitation counselor.

	1943		1944			1945	
	Jul.-Oct.	Nov.-Feb.	Mar.-Jun.	Jul.-Oct.	Nov.-Feb.	Mar.-Jun.	Jul.-Oct.
Navy	332	326	315	303	205	139	115
C.O.	Lt. W. C. Darrah						Lt. Henry Petty

Peru State Teachers College   Peru, Nebraska
(Now Peru State College)

Don Adamson (courtesy of Alice Swenson Giesecke)

When the 175 V-12s arrived on the beautiful "campus of a thousand oaks," the Peru student body, which before and after consisted of about 90 percent Nebraskans, was instantly diversified — seventy-seven of the men were from the West Coast. Seventeen members of the football squad claimed Los Angeles as their home town, which meant quite a change when they moved to tiny Peru.

Typical of the warm welcome accorded the V-12s was the all-campus reception given in their honor just four days after they arrived. All members of the faculty were there, and the presence of the coeds ensured a successful evening, which finished up with dancing.

The *Peru Pedagogian* reported weekly on the school's activities, which included many dances with music furnished by the Solid Macs, the Navy swing band.

The V-12s provided most of the football and basketball manpower. The Bobcats played full schedules against tough opposition. Intramurals were also prominent in V-12 life.

The Peru V-12s achieved Midwestern recognition for the best average strength test score (71.4) of any unit among the forty-eight in the Ninth Naval District in the October 1943 round of tests.

All the men were quartered in Delzell Hall, which was called "the ship." The mess hall was dubbed "Steiner's Diner" in honor of the cafeteria manager.

One noteworthy occasion: New Year's Eve of 1943 when, according to a V-12 columnist, "The entire crew 'mutinied' and celebrated the coming of the New Year in a fashion which was to bring ten days of restriction."

Some Peru V-12s: C. Neil Ash, vice president and secretary, Signal Company, and president of San Diego USO; Rodolfo Jacuzzi, Jacuzzi Brothers; and Dr. Richard T. Ward, professor and chairman, department of botany and plant pathology, Colorado State University.

| | 1943 | | 1944 | | | 1945 | |
	Jul.-Oct.	Nov.-Feb.	Mar.-Jun.	Jul.-Oct.	Nov.-Feb.	Mar.-Jun.	Jul.-Oct.
Navy	168	157	176	177	177	109	105
C.O.	Lt. R. B. Lowe				Lt. J. W. Lawson		Lt. E. H. Carl

Dickinson State Teachers College Dickinson, North Dakota
(Now Dickinson State College)

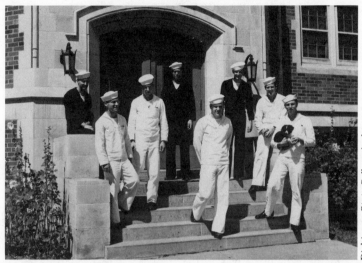

Dickinson State College Archives

Only fifty-three civilian students, most of them women, were on hand to greet the 210 V-12s who arrived on July 1, 1943. The Navy men were quartered in the "U.S.S. South Hall."

Cody, the ship's canine mascot, tried to help the men from warmer climes adjust to the average winter in North Dakota. The trek to class on those days was called the "Murmansk Run," with everyone leaning at a forty-five-degree angle into the never-ending west wind.

The Dickinson V-12s took part in everything. They edited the *Slope Teacher*, and when in the second year a printer could not be found, they started up a mimeographed newspaper called the *Prairie Breeze*. They had an outstanding dance band and presented many fine assembly pro-grams. The student government was reactivated during V-12 days, and the trainees were also instrumental in setting up the first student lounge, the Union Room.

On the athletic field the Dickinson Savages held their own against other service-augmented teams and captured the state basketball championship two years in a row.

Some Dickinson V-12s: George F. Caulfield, senior vice president for public relations, Wells Fargo and Company; Stuart W. Hyde, professor of radio, television, and film, San Francisco State College; Pierre Salinger, presidential press secretary, U.S. senator, and chief foreign correspondent, ABC News; and Wallace M. Scott, Jr., chairman, MSL Industries.

	1943		1944		1945		
	Jul.-Oct.	Nov.-Feb.	Mar.-Jun.	Jul.-Oct.	Nov.-Feb.	Mar.-Jun.	Jul.-Oct.
Navy	186	182	169	166	173	100	121
C.O.	Lt. Gerald C. Bradley						

Minot State Teachers College Minot, North Dakota
(Now Minot State College)

Minot State College Archives

Dakota and Pioneer halls were the barracks for the V-12s at Minot. The mess hall was located on the first deck of Pioneer and the V-12 office was in the administration building.

The civilian students remained on the two-semester schedule, so the full range of campus activities awaited the return of the coeds after the summer vacation. Nearly every weekend there was a dance at the Student Union and every term there was a Seaman's Ball and also a Navy Farewell Formal. The Navy Swing Band played for many of the dances. Other important occasions were the frequent smokers, which featured boxing, wrestling, and the band.

V-12s put on a number of variety shows. One had a gay nineties theme, and another was called "Public Be Pleased." The V-12s organized a marching band and a glee club. The school also fielded football, basketball, and baseball teams, plus cross-country and track. Thanks to the USO, all servicemen could bowl at the Minot bowling alley for five cents a line.

Formal inspections were made by two North Dakota governors and there was vigorous competition for the Red Rooster flag awarded to the most outstanding platoon.

The Navy days at Minot were recorded in the *Navy Picture Annual* issued in the fall of 1945. A trainee publication called the *Sea Breeze* appeared briefly in 1945. The *Red and Green* was the student paper.

Some Minot V-12s: Dr. James H. Dunlevy, physician, Fairfield, Iowa; Ellis T. Gravette, Jr., chairman, Bowery Savings Bank, New York City; H. L. ("Bud") Hoeffel, architect, Minot; Ray G. Olander, vice president, secretary, and general counsel, Bucyrus-Erie Company; Dr. Russell C. Schmidt, consultant, Michigan Department of Education; and Lyle Selbo, attorney, Fargo.

	1943		1944			1945	
	Jul.-Oct.	Nov.-Feb.	Mar.-Jun.	Jul.-Oct.	Nov.-Feb.	Mar.-Jun.	Jul.-Oct.
Navy	310	276	338	301	190	130	119
C.O.	Lt. R. C. Perry			Lt. H. O. Ashton			

Valley City State Teachers College   Valley City, North Dakota
(Now Valley City State College)

Ruth McLain Ployhar

The 223 V-12s ordered to Valley City State College found an interesting campus, which gave them a splendid welcome. The V-12s were quartered in West Hall.

On campus the Grill was the center of daily social life. There a V-12 could meet the coeds and linger in the red leather seats while sipping soft drinks or coffee or eating ice cream. The suspension foot bridge that spanned the Sheyenne River led from campus toward town, where the leading attraction was the Piller Theatre.

The people of Valley City were especially hospitable and invited many of the trainees, particularly those who could not get home for the holidays, to join them for meals and parties.

On the first Thanksgiving Day a heavy snowfall introduced the V-12s from California to what could be expected for the rest of the long North Dakota winter. Because of the demands of the fleet for all of the available foul weather gear, none could be sent to the V-12s in North Dakota where, according to the trainees, there was a crying need for it. Those were long, cold winters!

The Valley City men engaged in intercollegiate athletics, but the competition was limited to the similar schools at Minot and Dickinson.

Some Valley City V-12s: Dr. John D. Corbett, professor, Iowa State University, and senior chemist, Ames Laboratory, U.S. Department of Energy; Dr. Theodore L. Dorpat, clinical professor of psychiatry, University of Washington; Dr. Crawford M. Gates, artist in residence and chairman of the department of music, Beloit College; and Dr. Robert F. Lambert, professor of electrical engineering, University of Minnesota Institute of Technology.

	1943		1944			1945	
	Jul.-Oct.	Nov.-Feb.	Mar.-Jun.	Jul.-Oct.	Nov.-Feb.	Mar.-Jun.	Jul.-Oct.
Navy	223	217	211	198	198	124	122
C.O.	Lt. C. W. McLain						

Baldwin-Wallace College   Berea, Ohio

Most of the 340 V-12s who reported to this ninety-eight-year-old Methodist college on July 1, 1943, were from Ohio, but there was a scattering of others from most parts of the country. They were housed in Merner-Pfeiffer, Kohler, and Hulett halls and the Alpha Tau Omega fraternity house.

The people of Berea made great efforts to have the V-12s feel at home. Two weeks after they arrived the Lintern Corporation of Berea ran a full-page advertisement in the *Berea News* to greet every one of the trainees by name and home town. A group of local women came in on a regular basis to make clothing repairs and alterations, and many invited the V-12s for Sunday dinners.

The Baldwin-Wallace V-12s turned out en masse when fire struck downtown Berea on the afternoon of Tuesday, October 5, 1943. They assisted the firemen, formed fire lines to keep back the four thousand spectators, and spent the night patrolling the devastated area. It was the worst fire in Berea's history, wiping out stores with names typical of small-town America: Art's Men's Store, Bob's Barber Shop, Dick's Oasis, Deluxe Tailors, Berea Cash Market, and Roy's Meat Market.

Like many other units, B-W had a canine mascot. Blackie, a spaniel, had his own uniform — a blue "jacket" lettered with "U.S. Navy V-12." Intercollegiate sports and a wide range of campus activities kept the V-12s busy during off hours. The *Baldwin-Wallace Exponent*, the student paper, and the *Grindstone*, the yearbook, gave excellent coverage to all of the V-12 events.

Baldwin-Wallace College Archives

Some Baldwin-Wallace V-12s: James F. Fitzgerald, president, Milwaukee Bucks NBA basketball team; Robert F. Huber, editor, *Production* magazine; Dr. Stanley J. Idzerda, president, College of St. Benedict; Richard H. Needham, senior vice president, DDB Needham Worldwide; and Dr. Thomas G. Skillman, professor of medicine, Ohio State University.

| | 1943 | | 1944 | | | 1945 | |
	Jul.-Oct.	Nov.-Feb.	Mar.-Jun.	Jul.-Oct.	Nov.-Feb.	Mar.-Jun.	Jul.-Oct.
Navy	343	337	320	322	253	179	161
C.O.	Lt. K. O. Wilson				Lt. Russell H. Seibert		Lt. T. R. Everett

Bowling Green State University Bowling Green, Ohio

The V-12s at Bowling Green were quartered in Williams and Kohl halls; the twenty or so who were left over lived on the third floor of the Training School. The V-12s took part fully in the activities of the BeeGee campus and were represented on all of the student-faculty committees.

The Falcon's Nest was the campus social headquarters; the prewar ban on Sunday dancing was lifted. In May of 1944 the Military Ball replaced the traditional Junior-Senior Prom. In May of 1945, in addition to the Military Ball, the V-12s put on a musical production called "Pitchin' Blue," with proceeds going to Navy Relief.

The 1943 Falcon football season was successful with a five, three, and one record. But it was in basketball that the outstanding results were achieved. The Falcon five turned in a twenty-two-to-three (two losses to Great Lakes Naval Training Station) record in 1943–1944. An invitation to Madison Square Garden for the National Invitational Tournament followed. Weakened by the transfer of three regulars, the Falcons lost the opening game to the defending champs, St. John's

	1943		1944			1945	
	Jul.-Oct.	Nov.-Feb.	Mar.-Jun.	Jul.-Oct.	Nov.-Feb.	Mar.-Jun.	Jul.-Oct.
Navy	190	234	244	282	244	163	137
C.O.	Lcdr. J. Courts		Lt. A. E. Jensen	Lcdr. R. W. Stokes			Lt. H. C. Bold
Marines	183	143	113	75			
O-in-C	Capt. Joseph Anastasio						

Bowling Green State University

of Brooklyn, forty-four to forty. But the following year Bowling Green was back at the NIT and defeated St. John's in the second round, fifty-seven to forty-four. The Falcons lost the championship game to DePaul. The 1944 baseball and track teams had outstanding records, both winning what sportswriters called the "mythical" Ohio championships.

Some Bowling Green V-12s: Dr. Terry Carey, vice president, Central Michigan University; Howard L. Dehnbostel, regional manager, U.S. General Accounting Office; Thomas J. Hermes, vice president, Rand McNally Company; Dr. George W. Knepper, Jr., professor of history, University of Akron; and Thomas A. Luken, congressman from Ohio.

Case Institute of Applied Science Cleveland, Ohio
(Now Case Western Reserve University)

Case Western Reserve University Archives

The Navy V-12 program brought many changes to Case Institute of Applied Science. Foremost was the acquisition of a building on East 105th Street to house, feed, and care for the V-12s. Just a month before the program started Case purchased the four-story Garfield Exchange Building from Ohio Bell Telephone Company and spent approximately eighty thousand dollars to rapidly convert it to a dorm, mess hall, sick bay, lounge, library, and offices for the V-12 unit. It was called "the ship."

The arrival of the 264 trainees also brought Saturday morning classes to Case for the first time. But the Navy helped maintain many of the Case traditions, including intercollegiate athletic competition. The *Case Tech* was the weekly paper.

By all reports, Cleveland was a good liberty town, and the free streetcar rides for servicemen made transportation no problem. In the summer the presence of Lake Erie was a great plus for the V-12s.

Case was an all-engineering unit. When the V-12 program started in July, the seniors had just one semester remaining, so the Navy allowed Case to keep them on the regular term schedule. They graduated on December 20, 1943, and were ordered to the four-month Reserve Midshipmen's School at the Naval Academy.

Those V-12s who graduated from Case in February of 1946 were commissioned directly, ordered to Davisville, Rhode Island, and then sent on a three-month cruise along the east coast on four U.S. Navy cruisers. That served as their midshipmen's school. The thirty-four V-12s remaining on campus were housed in fraternity houses for the final four months of the program. Their commanding officer was located at the new NROTC unit at Ohio State.

Some Case V-12s: Kenneth P. Horsburgh, vice president, Horsburgh and Scott Company, Cleveland; Dr. Irvin M. Krieger, professor of chemistry, Case Western Reserve University; Philip A. Legge, secretary of the corporation, Case Western Reserve University; Robert A. Mattoon, manager of marketing, Lincoln Electric Company, Cleveland; Craig R. Smith, chairman, Warner and Swasey Company; and Genio R. Vitantonio, president, Vitantonio Manufacturing Company, Cleveland.

	1943		1944			1945			1946
	Jul.-Oct.	Nov.-Feb.	Mar.-Jun.	Jul.-Oct.	Nov.-Feb.	Mar.-Jun.	Jul.-Oct.	Nov.-Feb.	Mar.-Jun.
Navy	256	251	256	253	232	218	170	201	37
C.O.	Lt. B. D. Thuma						Lt. John G. Cornwell		Capt. J. D. Shaw

Denison University Granville, Ohio

The Marine and Navy V-12s reporting to Denison found that life in a small college town could be a great experience. The local citizens worked to make their liberty times interesting and pleasant. The Red Shield Canteen, set up by the Salvation Army but operated and sponsored by the town's churches and businesses, became the social center for many V-12s, and summer brought Saturday night street dances on Broadway. This Baptist school also permitted dances, and there were many on the campus.

Although chapel was never compulsory at any V-12 campus, when the name was changed to "convocation," as happened at Denison, the commanding officer approved it as a required V-12 event.

The V-12 unit made Denison basketball teams among the best in the school's history. The 1943–1944 cagers, with an eighteen-and-two record, took the Ohio Conference championship. The 1944–1945 squad went fourteen and four. Football was dropped in 1943, but its resumption in 1944 brought a six, one, and one record.

	1943		1944			1945	
	Jul.-Oct.	Nov.-Feb.	Mar.-Jun.	Jul.-Oct.	Nov.-Feb.	Mar.-Jun.	Jul.-Oct.
Navy	224	259	274	311	286	185	149
C.O.	Lcdr. Maurice VanCleave						
Marines	189	156	120	71			
O-in-C	2nd Lt. Clifford J. Christensen						

Denison University

Denison University Archives

Among the best-remembered events were the annual Christmas parties hosted by the legendary Sally Jones at her nearby Bryn Du Farm, which supplied the milk for the Denison V-12 unit.

Some Denison V-12s: Russell De-Vette, athletic director, Hope College; Louis A. Dudrow, vice president and treasurer, Union Trust Bancorp, Baltimore; Dean I. Gabbert, editor and publisher, *Fairfield* (Iowa) *Daily Ledger;* Ernest L. Grove, Jr., vice chairman, Detroit Edison; Karl G. Henize, scientist and astronaut, NASA; John T. Loehnert, head basketball coach, Denison University, and captain, USNR; Robert N. Mowry, senior vice president, Montgomery Ward and Company; Dr. Paul D. Newland, president, Lake Erie College, Painesville, Ohio; Carl V. Ragsdale, motion picture and television producer, recipient of 1966 Academy Award for best documentary film; Dr. James F. Short, Jr., director, Social Research Center, Washington State University, and president, American Sociological Association; Brig. Gen. Harvey Spielman, USMC; Dr. Howard Webb, higher education administrator, Southern Illinois University; and Dr. George P. Young, superintendent of schools, St. Paul, Minnesota.

John Carroll University Cleveland, Ohio

John Carroll University

The V-12s assigned to this Jesuit men's school took over the dormitory, Bernet Hall, and occupied the finished part of the newly constructed faculty residence, Rodman Hall. The rest of the unit was housed in the adjacent Jewish orphanage, Bellefaire. More than half (190) of the original V-12s came from Ohio; Illinois was second with 99. The rest hailed from twenty-four different states.

Before the V-12s arrived, the university had decided to discontinue intercollegiate athletics "for the duration," and that decision was upheld despite several attempts to have it rescinded. A very extensive intramural program was developed for the JCU V-12s as a substitute.

The physical training program was a rigorous one. The university lacked a swimming pool, so arrangements were made to use the tiny one in the Jewish orphanage. The concentration on physical fitness brought John Carroll trainees up to a very high standard, and the average of sixty-four attained by the trainees on the Navy strength test was claimed to be "one of the highest at any unit in the country."

The academic program maintained the university's traditional high standards. The final summary of V-12 activity showed that more men were sent to V-6 (general duty) than to midshipmen's schools.

On Memorial Day, 1944, a standard review ended with an outdoor mass celebrated by the chief of chaplains of the Ninth Naval District. About one hundred of the V-12s received communion, which indicates that approximately one-third of the trainees at this Catholic school were of that faith.

Some John Carroll V-12s: Dr. Jack A. Kane, medical director, foundry division, General Motors; Richard M. Morrow, chairman, AMOCO Oil Company; Ralph Regula, congressman from Ohio; and Eugene Von Riestenberg, engineering consultant, Des Plaines, Ill.

	1943		1944			1945	
	Jul.-Oct.	Nov.-Feb.	Mar.-Jun.	Jul.-Oct.	Nov.-Feb.	Mar.-Jun.	Jul.-Oct.
Navy	380	401	364	352	228	133	147
C.O.	Lt. Richard P. Raseman						Lt. Howard T. Wood

Miami University Oxford, Ohio

The 629 V-12s reporting to Miami University included both marines and sailors. Preceding them on the campus were V-5, cooks and bakers school, and radio school. One of the pleasant surprises was to find that WAVEs, SPARs and women marines had been sent to the radio school — there were three hundred of them on campus, in addition to all of the coeds.

During the first V-12 year there were nine hundred men and two thousand women on campus, so there were many open houses and parties. There was also a USO in downtown Oxford. The Student War Activities Council set up an introduction bureau called the "date bureau" that was highly useful to both coeds and V-12s.

The marines were quartered in the New Men's Dorm, while the sailors were in Ogden, David Swing, Elliott, and Stoddard halls. There were mess halls in the New Men's Dorm and Ogden, the V-12 office being in Ogden.

The trainees were involved in many university activities and made a fine showing on the athletic teams. The 1944 football squad went eight and one. Ten of the eleven Redskins starters were selected for various all-Ohio teams.

Miami was designated a pre-supply school starting March 1, 1944, which brought many transfers from smaller colleges. The Miami V-12 unit was one of the few that required trainees to march to classes, presumably because the enlisted personnel at other Miami Navy schools had to march to theirs.

	1943		1944			1945			1946
	Jul.-Oct.	Nov.-Feb.	Mar.-Jun.	Jul.-Oct.	Nov.-Feb.	Mar.-Jun.	Jul.-Oct.	Nov.-Feb.	Mar.-Jun.
Navy	370	492	456	535	386	289	254	# 535	# 305
C.O.	Lcdr. J. F. W. Gray					Lcdr. R. W. Stokes		Capt. G. A. Moore	
Marines	233	189	145	106					
O-in-C	Capt. John M. Robb		@						

#Includes NROTC   Capt. J. P. Mehrlust

Miami University

The Navy was pleased with Miami and awarded it one of the twenty-five new NROTC units started in 1945.

Some Miami V-12s: Dr. Carl E. Cassidy, program director, Post-Graduate Medical Institute, Boston; John A. Clawson, president, DuBois Chemicals Division of Chemed Corporation; Harold Deakins, manager of public affairs, Illinois Power Company; the Reverend Gene M. Hummel, bishop and member of the presiding bishopric, Reorganized Church of Jesus Christ of Latter Day Saints; Comdr. Jack A. Jester, USN(Ret.), head, munitions management, Office of the Chief of Naval Operations; Donald J. Kirchhoff,* president, Castle and Cooke; Clarence J. McConville, president, Title Insurance Company of Minnesota, and president, American Land Title Association; Dr. Lawrence E. Payne, professor of mathematics, Cornell University; and Albert D. Schmidt, chairman, Northwestern Public Service Company, Huron, S.D.

Oberlin College   Oberlin, Ohio

Oberlin College Archives

Despite some campus misgivings about the presence of a military unit at this 110-year-old school, the V-12s reporting to Oberlin received a warm welcome from faculty, administrators, students, and townspeople. Oberlin marines and sailors were quartered in the Men's Building, Quadrangle, Baldwin Cottage, Noah Hall, and Talcott Hall. Messing facilities were in the Quadrangle, Talcott, and Baldwin.

Chapel was held twice a week. The Tuesday session was called an "assembly," so it was mandatory for the V-12s. The chapel service on Thursday was optional. The unit also had its own assembly on Sunday nights at 1930, after liberty had ended at 1815.

The 1944 *Hi-O-Hi*, the yearbook, noted, "Probably the V-12 students' greatest contribution . . . was the increased prestige given to Oberlin athletics, football being a notable example. Last fall the Crimson and Gold, bolstered by the trainees, fought through a tough schedule with a rec-

	1943		1944			1945		1946
	Jul.-Oct.	Nov.-Feb.	Mar.-Jun.	Jul.-Oct.	Nov.-Feb.	Mar.-Jun.	Jul.-Oct.	Nov.-Feb.
Navy	353	499	445	559	357	271	140	171
C.O.	Lcdr. Homer Howard		Cdr. R. B. Horner					
Marines	340	209	185	130	134	135	141	89
O-in-C	Capt. LeRoy T. Campbell		Warrant Officer Oscar P. Olson				@	2

@ Capt. Clarence C. Moore, Jr.   2. Capt. Robert E. Brown

Oberlin College

ord blemished only by a scoreless tie with a rugged DePauw eleven." That was the first undefeated season for the Oberlin Yeomen in eighteen years and earned them the All-Ohio Conference championship.

The cross-country team captured the National Junior A.A.U. title, and the swimming team whipped all opponents, including Ohio State. The 1945 gridiron squad, still bolstered by many V-12s, turned in an untied, undefeated season.

When the coeds returned for the beginning of the second term, social life picked up and the trainees no longer deserted the town on weekends. The college's energetic social committee provided a full program of dances, shows, and other entertainments.

Some Oberlin V-12s: Herbert K. Anspach, president, Whirlpool Corporation; Robert M. Best, chairman, Security Mutual Life Insurance Company; Dr. Alonzo J. Fairbanks, Jr., professor of physics, American University, Beirut; Maj. Gen. Harold A. Hatch, USMC; the Reverend Jack Kinkopf, Roman Catholic priest, Chagrin Falls, Ohio; R. A. Michelson, chairman, McNeil Corporation; William O. Nelson, president, J. L. Clark Manufacturing Company, Rockford, Ill.; Dr. George W. Robinson, professor and chairman, department of history, Eastern Kentucky University; James W. Truitt, president of Oberlin Alumni Association, and consultant to industry; and Dr. Thomas H. Wilson, professor of physiology, Harvard Medical School.

Ohio Wesleyan University   Delaware, Ohio

The 390 V-12s arriving at this 101-year-old Methodist school were housed in fraternity houses, which had been deserted as the military draft took its toll of the male student body. Many OWU V-12s were pledged by the fraternities, which were still operating on the campus out of temporary rooms or houses.

The 0545 reveille at OWU was among the earliest in V-12 schools. When the V-12s arrived, they found a V-5 Flight Preparatory School already in place. The two units were rivals until the V-5 school closed down in the fall of 1944.

Saturdays were busy days for Ohio Wesleyan V-12s, with chapel in the morning and either a barracks inspection or a field inspection in the afternoon before liberty was granted. The review often involved some marching through the Delaware streets, with the V-12 Band leading the parade.

Wesleyan V-12s took part in dramatics, a cappella choir, publications, and all the intercollegiate sports. Social activities kept the OWU campus buzzing on the weekends, and there was always Columbus a short ride away as an alternative. But dances, hayrides, open houses, and the like kept most V-12s around campus.

The Student Union was described in the 1944 *Le Bijou* yearbook as "the place to check in and to do some checking."

Some OWU V-12s: Jack F. Meyerhoff, vice president and chief financial officer, Brunswick Corporation; Robert O. Naegele, group vice president, Dow Chemical Company; Kevin O'Donnell, director, Peace Corps, and president, SIFCO Industries; Dr. Robert O. Poorman, president, Lincoln Land Community College, Springfield, Ill.; Avery E. Post, president, United Church of Christ; and Robert J. Simonds, vice president, Ketcham, and national president of Alpha Tau Omega fraternity.

Ohio Wesleyan University Archives

	1943		1944			1945	
	Jul.-Oct.	Nov.-Feb.	Mar.-Jun.	Jul.-Oct.	Nov.-Feb.	Mar.-Jun.	Jul.-Oct.
Navy	383	363	362	456	323	198	127
C.O.	Lt. Trusdell Wisner		Lt. O. Y. Gamel	Lt. B. D. Thuma	Lt. O. Y. Gamel	Lt. K. L. Knickerbocker	

Lawrence College   Appleton, Wisconsin
(Now Lawrence University)

The V-12s at ninety-six-year-old Lawrence College were quartered in Brokaw and Ormsby halls; the latter formerly housed freshman women. The mess hall, V-12 offices, and sick bay were also located in Brokaw, which segregated the strictly Navy activities on the west side of the campus.

The Father-Son Day for V-12s departing for midshipmen's school in June of 1944 was perhaps unique in the entire V-12 program. Seventy-six fathers, some of them in uniform themselves, spent a day and a night bunking alongside their sons, doing calisthenics, and attending classes, but they joined the officers on the reviewing stand for the final inspection. Fathers came from as far as Oregon and New York. A Parents' Day was held on February 17, 1945.

Just prior to the V-12 program Lawrence had its most successful year in intercollegiate athletics, picking up the Midwest Conference championships in football, basketball, track, swimming, and golf. When the Midwest Conference folded for the duration, Lawrence could not find much competition at its level. It took on major universities and service teams such as the Great Lakes Naval Training Station and Fort Sheridan in northern Illinois. The Blue and White gave a good account of themselves in all contests.

V-12s took part in all of the campus activities, including the *Lawrentian* (the student paper), choir, theater, and campus politics. A V-12 became president of the student body. Law-

rence "happy hours" featured V-12s and sometimes traveling USO troupes.

Well-known campus visitors included Wendell L. Willkie, 1940 Republican presidential candidate, and Wisconsin governor Walter S. Goodland, who was the honored guest at the final review.

Some Lawrence College V-12s: John R. Burke, U.S. ambassador to Guyana; Kenneth F. Duchac, director, Brooklyn Public Library, and president, New York Metropolitan Reference and Research Library Agency; Dr. Ralph S. Gage, physician, Kimberly, Wis.; Richard L. Haligas, national sales manager, *Exclusively Yours* magazine; Keith W. Hardacker, research associate, Paper Physics Institute, Appleton; and Dayton G. Howe, manager, Roshek Brothers Department Store, Dubuque, Iowa.

	1943		1944			1945
	Jul.-Oct.	Nov.-Feb.	Mar.-Jun.	Jul.-Oct.	Nov.-Feb.	Mar.-Jun.
Navy	293	290	282	285	203	153
C.O.	Lt. Angus B. Rothwell					Lt. Thomas J. Stritch

Marquette University Milwaukee, Wisconsin

Marquette University Archives

Marquette had to do some scrambling to accommodate the 360 V-12s who arrived there on July 1, 1943. It purchased the Monitor Hotel, leased the Stratford Arms, and assigned Brooks Hall to house the two hundred and sixty engineers and one hundred premeds and predents. Those living in the Stratford Arms ate there, while the rest made the Memorial Union cafeteria their mess hall. Volunteer Red Cross women were in charge of serving the food and cleaning up — there was a severe labor shortage in industrial Milwaukee. Sick bay was located in the Stratford.

Lots of other changes came to the campus with the V-12s. The University Band became the Navy Band. The traditional Friday night dances were abandoned but the slack was picked up with Saturday and Sunday dances in the Memorial Union. When the V-12s had a few spare minutes they could meet their girlfriends at the University Drug Store.

The Marquette basketball squad in 1943–1944 had a good season, proving to be spoilers for several high-ranked teams and for a time holding eighth place in the national ratings. The *Hilltop*, the yearbook, gave excellent coverage to the V-12 program. Current happenings on the campus were reported by the weekly *Marquette Tribune*.

Some Marquette V-12s: Will Holtz, executive vice president and treasurer, Fred Usinger Company, Milwaukee; Dr. Robert B. Pittelkow, dermatologist, Milwaukee; Charles W. Prine, Jr., senior vice president, Ryan Homes, Pittsburgh; and William W. Weide, president, Fleetwood Enterprises.

	1943		1944			1945			1946
	Jul.-Oct.	Nov.-Feb.	Mar.-Jun.	Jul.-Oct.	Nov.-Feb.	Mar.-Jun.	Jul.-Oct.	Nov.-Feb.	Mar.-Jun.
Navy	574	575	618	552	463	417	306	204	258
C.O.	@	Capt. R. A. Dawes					Capt. C. H. Sigel		

@ Capt. D. D. Dupre

University of Wisconsin   Madison, Wisconsin

John B. Opfell

The 446 engineering students assigned to the V-12 unit at the University of Wisconsin found about three thousand military personnel already on campus, including ASTP, Army meteorologists, and various Navy schools, including radio, cooks and bakers, and diesel engineering. The radio school had four hundred WAVEs under instruction.

The engineers were quartered in Gilman, Mack, Showerman, and Turner houses. The Wednesday edition of the triweekly *Cardinal* carried a special section called "The Badger Navy News," which covered all of the naval units on campus. "The Squall," a column devoted to and written by V-12s, reported that during the first term one of the most popular V-12 songs, to the tune of "The Old Grey Mare," was "We'll All Stand Around and Stencil Our Underwear."

The V-12s wasted no time getting the social program under way and had their first big dance on July 30. The University of Wisconsin was a great place for liberty!

V-12s were mainstays on all of the athletic teams and captained the Badger football squads in 1943 and 1945. The 1943–1944 basketball team had seven V-12s, while the 1944 track squad was nearly all trainees.

The Navy was so pleased with the university's facilities and the operation of the V-12 unit that it awarded Wisconsin a postwar NROTC unit.

Some Badger V-12s: Louis Auer, executive vice president and director, Bache, Halsey, Stuart, Shields; George Bunn, dean, University of Wisconsin Law School; William M. Crilly III, president, Bomar Instrument Corporation; Robert B. Liepold, executive vice president, United Telecommunications; Dr. Roy P. Mackal, associate professor of biochemistry, University of Chicago, and U.S. director of the Loch Ness Investigation Bureau; Dr. Henry A. Peters, professor of neurology and rehabilitation medicine, University of Wisconsin; James N. Purse, president, Hanna Mining Company; and Virgil E. Schrock, professor of nuclear engineering, University of California, Berkeley.

	1943		1944			1945			1946
	Jul.-Oct.	Nov.-Feb.	Mar.-Jun.	Jul.-Oct.	Nov.-Feb.	Mar.-Jun.	Jul.-Oct.	Nov.-Feb.	Mar.-Jun.
Navy	514	445	383	443	420	375	320	# 519	# 207
C.O.	Cdr. L. K. Pollard						Capt. J. E. Hurff		

Includes NROTC

Eleventh Naval District

Arizona

114. Arizona State Teachers College

California

115. California Institute of Technology
116. Occidental College
117. University of California at Los Angeles
118. University of Redlands
119. University of Southern California

New Mexico

120. University of New Mexico

Arizona State Teachers College   Flagstaff, Arizona
(Now Northern Arizona University)

Raymond C. Perry

Both Navy and Marine V-12s arrived at ASTC in July of 1943. They were quartered in Morton, Campbell, North, and Taylor halls. The mess hall was located in North, and they attended classes in the Administration and Science buildings.

The marines remained for only two terms and then were transferred to V-12 detachments geographically closer to Parris Island. They were replaced on the ASTC campus by a large group of V-12(a)s, who had enlisted in the V-5 program.

V-12s participated in most of the campus activities, including the Ski Club, which had weekly wintertime outings, and the student paper, the *Pine.* Weekends were filled with dances and other activities. Many V-12s hiked to the bottom of the Grand Canyon.

Under wartime travel restrictions the isolated school had to discontinue intercollegiate athletics, but a rigorous intramural program kept the V-12s busy.

Some ASTC V-12s: Judge Earl H. Carroll, U.S. District of Arizona; Dr. James W. Cobble, professor of chemistry and graduate dean, San Diego State University; William C. Gruber, vice president, California Canners and Growers; Robert H. Johnson, assistant general manager and assistant to the president, Associated Press; Luther R. Marr, vice president, Walt Disney Company; Gen. Kenneth McLennan, USMC; and Keith L. Turley, chairman, Arizona Public Service Company.

	1943		1944			1945	
	Jul.-Oct.	Nov.-Feb.	Mar.-Jun.	Jul.-Oct.	Nov.-Feb.	Mar.-Jun.	Jul.-Oct.
Navy	183	194	366	332	237	173	128
C.O.	Cdr. R. B. Horner		Lt. L. H. Schnell	Lt. R. C. Perry			
Marines	191	136					
O-in-C	Capt. Kirt W. Norton						

California Institute of Technology   Pasadena, California

All of the V-12s at Cal Tech were engineers, who had a very busy academic life. However, the social side of life was not neglected. Friday night on-campus dances were inaugurated by the Pasadena USO very early in the program. The skipper gave a special liberty until midnight for the dances. He also ruled the campus pathways out of bounds at such times. The Associated Student Body sponsored many student activities, including major dances at the Altadena Country Club.

The big event for the first term was the entire unit's attendance at a Bob Hope radio show originating in the Pasadena Civic Auditorium.

The *California Tech* was the weekly paper, which gave excellent coverage of campus activities during the first two terms. Due primarily to the shortage of trainee time, it suspended publication in February of 1944. As a result of special efforts by two students, an abbreviated *Cal Tech Year Book 1943–44* was printed. It was in paperback form, but it covered all the essentials of campus life.

The V-12s brought Cal Tech its biggest year in basketball: the Beavers took the conference championship and also racked up victories over USC, UCLA, and Pepperdine. The intramural program was a vigorous one. The swimming classes were held in "the pea-green pool" of Pasadena Junior College.

V-12 variety shows were held at various times to enliven campus life. The commencement address in February of 1944 was given by Rear Adm. Wilson Brown, naval aide to President Roosevelt.

Some Cal Tech V-12s: Dr. William P. Bair, chairman, department of mathematics, Pasadena City College; Dr. Richard C. Honey, senior staff scientist, SRI International Electromagnetic Sciences Lab; Dr. Alfred G.

	1943		1944		1945			1946	
	Jul.-Oct.	Nov.-Feb.	Mar.-Jun.	Jul.-Oct.	Nov.-Feb.	Mar.-Jun.	Jul.-Oct.	Nov.-Feb.	Mar.-Jun.
Navy	542	533	510	563	463	418	255	373	38
C.O.	Lcdr. E. W. Mantel				Capt. W. H. Osgood		@	2	3

@ Lt. Miles E. Morgan   2. Lcdr. George W. Greene   3. Lt.(jg) W. D. Surgeon

California Institute of Technology

Knudson, Jr., director, Institute of Cancer Research, and discoverer of a class of cancer genes; Dr. Robert W. Lester and Dr. Albert R. Hibbs, members, technical staff, Jet Propulsion Laboratory, California Institute of Technology; Joseph S. Martin, vice president for exploration, Enron Oil and Gas Company; Duane McRuer, president, Systems Technology; Ruben F. Mettler, chairman, TRW, and chairman of the board, California Institute of Technology; Robert C. Pierpoint, CBS news correspondent; Eberhardt Rechtin, president, the Aerospace Corporation; Dr. George G. Shor, Jr., professor of marine geophysics and associate director, Scripps Institution of Oceanography, University of California at San Diego; and Dr. Don R. Swanson, professor, Graduate Library School, University of Chicago.

Occidental College Los Angeles, California

The four hundred V-12s arriving at Occidental College included two hundred sailors and an equal number of marines. The marines were quartered in what their officer-in-charge described as "luxurious Erdman Hall," while the sailors were housed in Wylie and Swan halls. All of them ate in the dining hall at Freeman Union, where the civilian students also ate in another shift.

The severe labor shortage brought one pleasant addition to the dining hall: Occidental coeds working as busboys, servers, and scullery workers on a unique plan through which they converted their wages into war bonds that they then donated to the college. Faculty members and even President Remsen Bird sometimes worked the cafeteria line.

The arrival of the V-12s brought Occidental to its largest enrollment in history. The Military Ball was the big social event; after the marines left it was called the Navy Ball. Most V-12s paid dues to the Associated Students of Occidental College and several headed that student body government group.

Football was discontinued for two seasons, but the basketball teams played a full schedule and the 1944 baseball team won the conference championship.

The *Occidental* appeared weekly and the yearbook, *La Ensina*, covered the year's activities.

Special Collections, Occidental College

In May 1944, an outbreak of polio hit trainees and civilians. One V-12 died. All "fatigue-producing activities" were halted for ten days as medical experts swarmed over the campus. The epidemic subsided but broke out again in August, when several more trainees were afflicted.

Some Occidental V-12s: Charles R. Allen, executive vice president, TRW; Capt. Blake V. Blakey, USN; Crawford Brubaker, deputy assistant secretary, aerospace, U.S. Department of Commerce; Robert H. Finch, secretary, U.S. Department of Housing and Urban Development, and lieutenant governor of California; Dr. Ellis B. Page, professor of educational psychology, Duke University; Wesley E. Redford, vice president and treasurer, Northwest Natural Gas Company, Portland, Oregon; Urban G. Whitaker, Jr., dean of undergraduate studies, San Francisco State University; and Maj. Gen. Edward A. Wilcox,* USMC.

	1943		1944			1945	
	Jul.-Oct.	Nov.-Feb.	Mar.-Jun.	Jul.-Oct.	Nov.-Feb.	Mar.-Jun.	Jul.-Oct.
Navy	188	236	281	304	237	122	128
C.O.	Lcdr. B. C. Wanglin					Lt. Ralph K. Allen	
Marines	181	146	81	63			
O-in-C	@	Capt. John P. Wilbern					

@ 2nd Lt. Paul B. Johnson, Jr.

University of California at Los Angeles Los Angeles, California

UCLA Archives

Approximately half of the six hundred V-12s at UCLA were already students there before the program began. Most of the rest came from California schools. They were quartered in fraternity houses, dorms, and a few apartment buildings. The Navy took over the Kerckhoff Hall cafeteria as its mess hall.

UCLA V-12s soon learned that their commanding officer was a stickler on haircuts. One trainee reported that he had made his weekly visit to a Westwood Village barbershop on Monday, but at the Saturday inspection the skipper restricted him to the campus for the weekend for not having a satisfactory haircut. Thereafter the V-12 got his haircuts on Wednesdays or Thursdays.

The weekly *Bruin* and the yearbook, the *Southern Campus*, covered the busy social and athletic schedules of UCLA trainees. The V-12s were the mainstays of the sports teams during the first two years of the program. The 1944 football squad fought for a Rose Bowl bid down to the final game, when it lost the title to the University of Southern California.

The Navy Dance on December 3, 1943, was typically popular — all of the bids to the dance were sold out the first day.

Some UCLA V-12s: James A. Gambrell, professor of law, New York University; Vice Adm. Samuel L. Gravely, USN; Stephen H. Herron, chief officer, Northwest Group of Companies, Herron Holdings Corporation; William D. Meyer, chairman, Profit Sharing Council of America; Rear Adm. Albert J. Monger, USN; Dr. Robert W. Rand, professor of neurosurgery, UCLA School of Medicine; and William V. Shaw, fellow of the American Institute of Architects, Monterey, Calif.

	1943		1944			1945			1946
	Jul.-Oct.	Nov.-Feb.	Mar.-Jun.	Jul.-Oct.	Nov.-Feb.	Mar.-Jun.	Jul.-Oct.	Nov.-Feb.	Mar.-Jun.
Navy	392	425	458	351	278	181	124	24	0
C.O.	Capt. W. C. Barker						Capt. G. G. Crissman		

University of Redlands Redlands, California

John Scott Davenport

The University of Redlands, a traditional Baptist college, was never quite the same after its encounter with the sailors and marines of the V-12 program. The lively *Bulldog* reported the continuing controversy about dancing with great interest. Nearly every student organization had one or more dances a year, but until six months after the arrival of the V-12s they had to be held off campus. Following the marines' New Year's Eve affair on the chapel steps, permission was finally reluctantly granted for the Navy to use its leased quarters as it liked, and the commanding officer thought dances would be entirely appropriate. (See Chapter 34, "Humor, High Jinks, and 'They Shouldn't Have' " for further details.)

The V-12s were in the thick of campus politics, with the marines taking the leading role. The V-12s were quartered in Grossmont, Melrose, and California halls on this beautiful, sunny Southern California campus. The

"V-12 Varieties" was held in September of 1943; according to the report in the *Bulldog,* the show had the crowd "literally rolling in the aisles." The show was based on campus life under the Navy and featured many easily recognizable college authorities.

When the call came for "volunteers" to set out the smudge pots to protect the orange groves, almost all of the Redlands V-12s reported. The yearbook, *La Letra,* appeared in 1945 and 1946, but due to wartime conditions was not published in 1944.

Some Redlands V-12s: Warren Christopher, U.S. undersecretary of state; Dr. John Scott Davenport, vice president, Bonneville International Corporation, Salt Lake City; H. R. Haldeman, assistant to the president, chief of White House staff; Dr. Van Harvey, chairman of the department of religion, Stanford University; and Dr. Chester O. McCorkle, Jr., executive vice president, University of California systemwide administration.

	1943		1944			1945	
	Jul.-Oct.	Nov.-Feb.	Mar.-Jun.	Jul.-Oct.	Nov.-Feb.	Mar.-Jun.	Jul.-Oct.
Navy	200	284	244	311	228	170	152
C.O.	Cdr. Carlisle H. Thompson			Lcdr. J. Courts			
Marines	190	119	85	55			
O-in-C	2nd Lt. John L. Doyle						

University of Southern California Los Angeles, California

USC Archives

The marines at USC were quartered in Williams Hall (Graduate Lodge) and Reynolds Hall (Shrine Arms Apartments). The sailors were housed in Newkirk (formerly Aeneas), Henderson (Parkshire Manor), and Owens (Sigma Chi House) halls. Later the sailors took over Williams as the number of marines declined. There were two mess halls, one in the basement of Newkirk and the other in the foyer of Town and Gown.

Athletics played a big part in V-12 life at Southern Cal, with the Trojans capturing the Pacific Coast football crowns in both 1943 and 1944 and winning their Rose Bowl appearances against the University of Washington and the University of Tennessee.

Shortly after the arrival of the V-12s the old Trojan men's grill was fitted out as the "USS Poopdeck," which was the on-campus center of social life.

The USC V-12s took leading parts in many campus activities. The *Trojan*, formerly a daily, reduced its publication to three times a week. *Wampus* was the monthly humor magazine, and *El Rodeo*, the yearbook, appeared each year to record the history of the campus.

Some USC V-12s: Dr. Hugo A. Bedau, professor of philosophy, Tufts University; M. D. Borthick, president, Walker Bank, Salt Lake City; Kenneth W. Krause, executive vice president, First Charter Financial Corporation; A. E. Pearson, president, PepsiCo; Dr. Randall C. Phillips, vice president, United States International University; Judge Manuel L. Real, U.S. District of Southern California; and John S. R. Shad, chairman, Securities and Exchange Commission.

	1943		1944			1945			1946
	Jul.-Oct.	Nov.-Feb.	Mar.-Jun.	Jul.-Oct.	Nov.-Feb.	Mar.-Jun.	Jul.-Oct.	Nov.-Feb.	Mar.-Jun.
Navy	786	896	1001	1004	631	479	338	210	300
C.O.	Capt. Reed M. Fawell					Capt. S. Y. Cutler			
Marines	290	217	140	81	103	117	116	72	46
O-in-C	Capt. Reuben M. Welsh					Capt. William H. Godel			

University of New Mexico   Albuquerque, New Mexico

The V-12s reporting to the University of New Mexico in July of 1943 were in the basic, premed, and engineering programs. The V-12s and NROTCs were organized as a battalion consisting of six companies of two platoons each. Four of the companies were V-12s; NROTCs were placed in charge at both battalion and company levels and at the head of some of the platoons. The V-12 companies were, on average, about 60 percent larger than the NROTC companies.

The V-12s were quartered in Hokona Hall and three fraternity houses.

Most of the football players were V-12s. In the fall of 1943 the team managed to line up a four-game schedule, finishing with a three-and-one record. That was good enough to earn it an appearance in the January 1, 1944, Sun Bowl at El Paso, where they faced the tough Southwestern University team. In a hard-fought game, the Southwestern Tigers beat the Lobos seven to zero.

The *Mirage*, the yearbook, appeared in both 1944 and 1945 and gave a good account of V-12 life on the New Mexico campus. The student paper was the *Lobo*.

Capt. Arthur S. Adams, USN(Ret.), who originally headed the V-12 program and then directed the expansion of the NROTC program in 1945, visited the New Mexico campus in the summer of 1945 to explain the upcoming program of phasing V-12 into the NROTC.

Some New Mexico V-12s: Ray W. Ballmer, president, Rio Algom, Limited; Harry E. Kinney, mayor of Albuquerque; William Power, publisher, *Lima* (Ohio) *News;* and Henry M. Willis, director of personnel and personnel services, Sandia Laboratories.

	1943		1944			1945			1946
	Jul.-Oct.	Nov.-Feb.	Mar.-Jun.	Jul.-Oct.	Nov.-Feb.	Mar.-Jun.	Jul.-Oct.	Nov.-Feb.	Mar.-Jun.
Navy	# 455	# 487	# 454	# 421	# 388	# 383	# 350	# 405	# 305
C.O.	Capt. J. B. Will				Cdr. T. S. Daniel				Capt. Joel Newsom

Includes NROTC

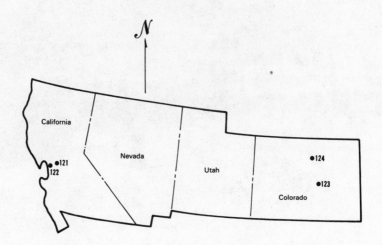

Twelfth Naval District

California

121. College of the Pacific
122. University of California

Colorado

123. Colorado College
124. University of Colorado

College of the Pacific Stockton, California
(Now University of the Pacific)

Holt-Atherton Pacific Center for Western Studies

When the 387 sailors and marines arrived at this Methodist college on July 1, 1943, they were quartered in North Hall and other campus housing. They were fed in Anderson Hall. The arrival of the V-12s changed the most common religious preference of the students from Methodist to Roman Catholic, but harmony seemed to prevail on all fronts.

The 1943 football team has been talked about ever since. The Pacific Tigers became one of the most powerful teams in the country, losing only two contests, to March Field and the University of Southern California. USC went on to win the Rose Bowl. Tackle Art McCaffray was selected on the Consensus All-American and two of his teammates received a number of All-American mentions. The Pacific coach was eighty-one-year-old Amos Alonzo Stagg, then in his fifty-fourth season of coaching. In December he was honored by the Football Writers of America as Coach of the Year. The "Bengal Basketeers" also had an excellent season in 1943–1944.

V-12s took part in all of the campus activities from athletics to the band, orchestra, a cappella choir, and the Pacific Little Theatre. The Student Christian Association was the headquarters for various women's groups that came to do mending and altering of uniforms for the men in Navy blue and Marine green. The Cub House was the campus hangout for soft drinks and meeting friends.

Some College of the Pacific V-12s: Alex Crossan, executive vice president, Occidental Petroleum Corporation; Frank R. Eslinger, executive vice president, Equitable Life Insurance Company; Maj. Gen. Joseph Koler, Jr., USMC; Dr. Richard E. Lininger, psychiatrist, Lafayette, Calif.; John C. McPhee, president, Jumping Jacks Shoes; and John D. Stephens, vice president and senior trust officer, Union Bank, San Francisco.

	1943		1944			1945	
	Jul.-Oct.	Nov.-Feb.	Mar.-Jun.	Jul.-Oct.	Nov.-Feb.	Mar.-Jun.	Jul.-Oct.
Navy	187	239	236	272	217	141	127
C.O.	Cdr. Burton E. Rokes						
Marines	175	134	99	51			
O-in-C	1st Lt. W. A. Seel						

University of California Berkeley, California

The 1,014 Navy V-12 trainees reporting to Berkeley on July 1, 1943, were moved into the International House, which had been built for a maximum capacity of five hundred. It was temporarily renamed Callaghan Hall, in honor of Adm. Daniel J. Callaghan, who died on the USS *San Francisco* in the first Naval Battle of Guadalcanal.

The 350 Marine V-12s who reported on July 1, 1943, were quartered in seven fraternity houses for the first sixteen months. When both Navy and Marine V-12s had diminished in numbers, they were all consolidated in Callaghan Hall, which also served as V-12 headquarters.

The marines proved to be the backbone of the Cal football squads for all of the V-12 years. Three of the Marines were elected president of the student body.

The V-12 sailors held many offices in the Student Union and filled the ranks of the band, glee club, and other campus organizations.

The University of California was as-

	1943		1944			1945			1946
	Jul.-Oct.	Nov.-Feb.	Mar.-Jun.	Jul.-Oct.	Nov.-Feb.	Mar.-Jun.	Jul.-Oct.	Nov.-Feb.	Mar.-Jun.
Navy	969	# 1140	# 1157	# 1160	# 978	# 919	# 691	# 822	# 601
C.O.	Capt. H. E. Kays		Capt. B. L. Canaga					Capt. W. White	
Marines	335	222	153	110	136	146	152	98	42
O-in-C	Capt. Warren P. Gooch, Jr.						Capt. Charles Horn		

Includes NROTC

University of California

sured of being "run by the book" when Capt. Bruce Canaga, USN, arrived on campus during the second term. He came from the Bureau of Naval Personnel, where he had served as director of training. In that position he supervised the entire V-12 program.

Some California V-12s: Myron Du-Bain, chairman, Fireman's Fund; Dr. Jacob P. Frankel, president, California State College at Bakersfield; Alan C. Furth, president, Southern Pacific Company; Dr. Kenneth D. Gaver, commissioner, Texas Department of Mental Health; Phillip M. Hawley, chairman, Carter Hawley Hale; Robert E. Kinsinger, vice president, W. K. Kellogg Foundation; William M. Laub, president, Southwest Gas Corporation; Dr. Karl S. Pister, professor of engineering science and dean, College of Engineering, University of California at Berkeley; Dr. F. James Rutherford, chief education officer, American Association for the Advancement of Science; Hunter Simpson, president, Physio Control Corp.; Hugh F. Swaney, president, Kingsport Press; and John G. Trezevant, executive vice president, Field Enterprises.

Colorado College   Colorado Springs, Colorado

The V-12s reporting to this college located in the shadow of Pike's Peak were quartered in three fraternity houses, which were renamed Grayson, Kirkpatrick, and Berry. They were also housed in Hagerman Hall, Jackson House, and Howbert House. The mess hall was located in Cossit Hall in the old campus dining room, which had been closed for more than ten years. Cossit was the location of the V-12 headquarters.

The 1943 football team was unstoppable. It went undefeated with a seven-and-zero record and scored 199 points to the opponents' total of 27. The season included two victories over the University of Colorado. The team received eight invitations to postseason games but was unable to accept because of travel restrictions. The 1943–1944 basketball Tigers had an excellent record and gained the second round in the national A.A.U. tournament.

The *Colorado College Times* was the paper for the first two and one-half months, when the name was changed to the *Tiger*. The *Nuggets* gave good yearbook coverage to all of the V-12 activities.

Campus life at Colorado College was always interesting. There were many dances, including the V-12 Summer Formal. The Associated Women Students held their annual Gold Digger's Ball at the Broadmoor Hotel.

The Colorado College V-12s held a reunion in 1979.

Some Colorado College V-12s: William D. Eberle, speaker of the Idaho House of Representatives and chairman, American Standard; Donald B. Holbrook, attorney, and chairman, Utah State Board of Regents; Harry W. Hoth, Jr., owner, Pike's Peak Broadcasting Company (television and radio in Colorado Springs and Grand Junction), and mayor, Colorado Springs; Richard P. Lindsay, director of public communications, Church of Jesus Christ of the Latter-day Saints; Edward T. Long, officer, U.S. Foreign Service; Robert H. Rawlings, publisher and editor, Pueblo *Star Journal*; and George C. Scruggs, Federal Bureau of Investigation agent, and mayor, Springfield, Missouri.

	1943		1944			1945			1946
	Jul.-Oct.	Nov.-Feb.	Mar.-Jun.	Jul.-Oct.	Nov.-Feb.	Mar.-Jun.	Jul.-Oct.	Nov.-Feb.	Mar.-Jun.
Navy	214	285	308	311	151	75	51	239	174
C.O.	Lcdr. F. S. Bartlett			Lt. L. D. Bernard				@	2
Marines	178	127	86	75	118	119	102	50	23
O-in-C	3	1st Lt. Hans M. Guenther						Capt. Edward S. McDonald	

@ Lcdr. Elmer C. Darling   2. Lcdr. M. H. Burkholder   3. 1st Lt. Jack C. Finney

University of Colorado   Boulder, Colorado

Western History Collection.
University of Colorado

The University of Colorado was Navy-oriented in 1943. Besides V-12, there were six other Navy units in residence, including NROTC and the Oriental Language Training School. Navy Days was the big celebration, replacing homecoming that fall.

So crowded was the university that four hundred Navy radio trainees were quartered in the Field House. As a result, there was no intercollegiate basketball in the 1943–1944 season. The Navy V-12s were in the Women's Dorm and fraternity houses, while the marines were quartered in the Men's Dorm.

The 1943 football team went five and two and the 1944 squad took the Big Seven championship with a six-and-two record, the only 1944 losses being to top service teams. Physical training was not forgotten at the University of Colorado: it had three "commando courses"!

The 1944 yearbook, the *Coloradan*,

was dedicated to "the men and women of the Naval and Marine Forces at the University." The yearbook claimed that in 1943, "the Navy moved in everything but the ocean."

Boulder's one "hot spot" changed its name in accordance with the times: formerly "the Buff," it became "the Anchorage."

Some University of Colorado V-12s: Steven D. Bechtel, Jr., chairman, Bechtel Group, and recipient of the Distinguished Engineering Alumnus Award, University of Colorado, 1980; Dr. James W. Haun, vice president for engineering policy, General Mills; Dr. Sherman J. Preece, Jr., professor of botany and department chairman, University of Montana; Dr. Roland C. Raustenstraus, president, University of Colorado; and William F. Utlaut, director, National Telecommunications and Information Administration, U.S. Department of Commerce, Boulder.

| | 1943 | | 1944 | | | 1945 | | 1946 | |
	Jul.-Oct.	Nov.-Feb.	Mar.-Jun.	Jul.-Oct.	Nov.-Feb.	Mar.-Jun.	Jul.-Oct.	Nov.-Feb.	Mar.-Jun.
Navy	569	707	561	648	582	399	249	195	189
C.O.	Capt. F. H. Roberts					Capt. Willard E. Cheadle		Capt. N. B. Van Bergen	
Marines	194	163	100	80					
O-in-C	1st Lt. Dale Chamberlain, Jr.		Capt. Derrol E. Huddleson						

Thirteenth Naval District

Idaho

125. University of Idaho (Southern Branch)

Montana

126. Carroll College
127. Montana School of Mines

Oregon

128. Willamette University

Washington

129. Gonzaga University
130. University of Washington
131. Whitman College

University of Idaho (Southern Branch) Pocatello, Idaho
(Now Idaho State University)

The 423 V-12s who reported to the University of Idaho (Southern Branch) on July 1, 1943, were quartered in Graveley Hall, and the basement of Graveley served as the mess hall.

The Idaho *Bengal*, the student newspaper, and the *Dittybag*, a quarterly issued in lieu of the traditional yearbook, kept the student body up to date and recorded the history of that period. Music was a big factor on the Pocatello campus — there was a Navy chorus, a Navy dance band, and the piano selections of a trainee, Louis Weertz, who later became world famous under the name Roger Williams. The band played for the weekly one-hour "coffee dances." Navy "happy hours" and frequent university theatrical presentations kept life interesting.

Because of the scarcity of collegiate competition, the football team, the Battling Bengals, mostly played service teams. The 1944–1945 basketball squad turned in an eleven-and-four performance.

As the V-12 program wound down at Pocatello, Dean E. J. Baldwin had this to say about the V-12s: "They have entered wholeheartedly into our student activities and have been genuinely friendly with our civilian students. They have been on our athletic teams, taken part in our student plays, sung in our choral groups, and edited our student publications. They have added zest to the social life of the campus and have had a thoroughly good time themselves. Mostly they have maintained a serious attitude toward their major objective, and have con-

Idaho State University Archives

ducted themselves as potential officers should. We will miss them when they are gone."

Some University of Idaho (Southern Branch) V-12s: Dr. Max E. Fletcher, chairman, department of economics, University of Idaho; Jay W. Glasman, tax attorney, Washington, D.C.; Jay G. Jensen, dean of student affairs, Idaho State University; Harry F. Magnuson, CPA and prominent Idaho investor; James A. McClure, United States senator from Idaho; Maj. Gen. Herbert L. Wilkerson, USMC; and Roger Williams (Louis Weertz), concert and recording artist.

	1943		1944			1945
	Jul.-Oct.	Nov.-Feb.	Mar.-Jun.	Jul.-Oct.	Nov.-Feb.	Mar.-Jun.
Navy	421	396	428	396	267	169
C.O.	Lt. Louis G. Conlan				Lt. Crawford W. Brubaker	

Carroll College Helena, Montana

The V-12 program was vital to Carroll College. In April of 1943 President Emmet J. Riley, S.J., wired Congressman Mike Mansfield that if the school did not get a college training contract, Montana's only Catholic college would have to close. It received 254 trainees, who were housed in the school's main building. As a result, faculty members had to move to a residence in town. The Montana trainees were outnumbered by the Californians, 121 to 78. During the first major snowfall, the West Coast boys had a festival, which consisted of building snowmen and snow forts, having snowball fights, and sliding down the college hill.

The *Prospector*, the student newspaper, gave excellent coverage to the V-12 program, since its members comprised the vast majority of the students. At one time there were only nineteen civilians enrolled.

There were monthly dances in the gym, weekly dances on Saturday nights at the USO, and plenty of other dances to choose from, including those put on by the cadet nurses at St. John's Hospital. The ice-skating rink at the bottom of the hill was called "Lake Bluff," and its care was turned over to the trainees. Up to 150 men would turn out for skating on a good day.

Because of the distances and lack of competition, no football was played at Carroll during the V-12 years, but the team did well in basketball. In 1943–1944 it had a ten-and-two record and won the mythical Montana State Championship. In 1944–1945, it went twelve and four and shared the title with Montana Mines.

On January 9, 1944, the V-12s helped the Helena Fire Department man the hoses and rescue records and equipment during a fire at the Old National Bank building. On March 23, 1944, the gym caught fire; trainees fought the blaze before the fire department arrived. In January of 1945, the V-12s were saddened by the deaths of two of their close friends, Fubar, the sailors' dog, and Herkimer, "the cigarette-eating goat."

Some Carroll College V-12s: Dr. Robert C. Bain, physician, Seattle; Dr. Neal C. Livingstone, dentist, Helena; B. E. Niedermeyer, managing partner, Niedermeyer-Martin Lumber Co., Portland; Kenneth Stanbury, project foreman, defense installations in Greenland and North Dakota; Dr. William H. Tooley, professor of pediatrics, University of California Medical School; and Nels E. Turnquist, chairman, First Bank of South Dakota, Sioux Falls.

	1943		1944			1945	
	Jul.-Oct.	Nov.-Feb.	Mar.-Jun.	Jul.-Oct.	Nov.-Feb.	Mar.-Jun.	Jul.-Oct.
Navy	253	251	240	226	201	174	140
C.O.	Lt. David McDonald		Lt. Elmer C. Darling				

Montana School of Mines   Butte, Montana
(Now Montana College of Mineral Science and Technology)

The V-12s reporting to Montana School of Mines were in the engineering and basic curricula; they comprised more than 90 percent of the school's enrollment. During the first year, trainees from thirty-four states and the District of Columbia were on campus. Residence Hall was "the ship" for the V-12s.

Their remote location did not keep the MSM "Ore Diggers" from fielding teams in most sports. The 1944 football squad may have been the only V-12 team to play one of its games in Canada, where the miners whipped the Alaskan Clippers of the U.S. Army Air Force Base at Edmonton. The unit's baseball team took top honors in the Copper League of the city of Butte. The 1944 softball team won the Montana State Tournament.

The V-12 paper started on December 13, 1943, should have received an award for an ingenious name: the *Mine's Weeper.*

Social life had an important place in the trainee's weekly routine. "M" Day, the biggest event and always held in May, started off with the detonation of three volleys of dynamite on Big Butte, not far from the letter "M" on the side of the mountain. The rest of the day was spent in the annual student clean-up of the campus, putting a new coat of whitewash on the big "M," and enjoying parties, picnics, and the "M" Day Dance.

The unit had an annual picnic. A Sunday Evening Canteen was provided through the generosity of a Butte couple. The V-12 dance band, the Argies, played for many functions,

Archives of Montana Tech

including a dance known as the "Flunkers' Frolic." Smokers and Ski Club trips added to the interesting life at MSM.

Some Montana School of Mines V-12s: Arthur C. Bigley, Jr., senior member, technical staff, R. M. Parsons Company; Dr. Don S. Gorsline, professor of geology, University of Southern California; George L. Hagen, president, Reichold; T. J. Hallin, vice president, Yellowstone Park Company; William W. McClintock, owner, Queen Alice Gold Mining Company, Fairbanks, Alaska; and D. L. Pinkerton, supervisory cartographer, U.S. Geological Survey.

	1943		1944			1945	
	Jul.-Oct.	Nov.-Feb.	Mar.-Jun.	Jul.-Oct.	Nov.-Feb.	Mar.-Jun.	Jul.-Oct.
Navy	304	307	298	272	197	104	131
C.O.	Lt. Walter Welti						

Willamette University Salem, Oregon

The oldest college in the West was the host to 268 V-12s on July 1, 1943. Most of the men, ninety of whom were premed, were quartered in Lausanne Dormitory, formerly a women's residence; the overflow was housed at the Salem YMCA. The mess hall was in the basement of the USS Lausanne. The V-12 office was established in the College of Law building.

Probably the best coverage of V-12s at any small college was provided by the Willamette yearbook, the *Wallulah*. The *Collegian* was the campus newspaper.

V-12s participated in virtually everything going on at Willamette. Some V-12s headed the Associated Students and many were class officers. They participated in the college choir, band, dramatics, and forensics. The Freshman Glee Club put on the thirty-sixth annual All-University Sing, for which a V-12 wrote the winning song: "You're Everything That a Sailor Dreams Of." The May Weekend was the climax of the college social calendar. The V-12s also put on a number of "happy hours." The student hangout was the Bearcat Cavern.

Everything was not fun and games at Willamette, for trainees remember its obstacle course as one of the toughest anywhere. The paucity of opponents led to a very abbreviated football season in 1943, with the school playing two games with Whitman College. The Whitman game at Salem was the only intercollegiate football contest played in Oregon that year. Travel restrictions and lack of opponents were also the big problems facing the Bearcats basketball squads.

Some Willamette V-12s: William Egan, nurseryman, Salem, Oregon; Robert Donovan, administrator, secondary education, Salem, Oregon; James H. Elliott, director, University Art Museum, Berkeley, Calif.; Samuel A. Godfrey, vice president and controller, Pacific T & T Company; Dr. Ronald Runyan, superintendent of schools, Boise; Vice Adm. James R. Sanderson, USN; Dr. Robert Sheridan, professor, Oregon Health Science University, Department of Dentistry, Portland, Oregon; Jack Strickfaden, lumber and cattle man, Salem, Oregon; Lloyd Sugaski, executive vice president, Bank of America; and Francis Youngers, chairman, Arabian American Oil Companies.

	1943		1944		1945		
	Jul.-Oct.	Nov.-Feb.	Mar.-Jun.	Jul.-Oct.	Nov.-Feb.	Mar.-Jun.	Jul.-Oct.
Navy	260	235	250	224	198	147	124
C.O.	Lt. George C. Bliss				Lt. Marshall E. Woodell		Lt. James F. Kee

Gonzaga University   Spokane, Washington

When the V-12s arrived at Gonzaga they found one of the most difficult obstacle courses in the country, which had been constructed for the V-5 school already on campus. It had twenty-eight different obstacles and ran 470 yards.

The V-12s were housed in Goller and DeSmet halls. For recreation they visited such places as the Canteen, Dutch's, and the Bulldog.

Football had been discontinued for the duration, and although there was some talk of reviving it, almost one-third of the V-12s were beginning freshmen who would have been ineligible for the first term. As a result, the idea was dropped.

But in basketball the "Zags" excelled! They produced a twenty-one-and-two record in the 1943–1944 season, which included three wins out of four games with the University of Washington and a thirteenth ranking among colleges in the nation. They were also recognized as the champions of the Northwest.

EBBS and EDDIES, a monthly magazine written and edited by trainees, contained many feature articles covering the Gonzaga unit. The *Gonzaga Bulldog,* the yearbook, gave a fine summary of the school year. The *Gonzaga Bulletin,* the student newspaper, published a "Farewell to V-12" edition on October 19, 1945, extensively detailing the history of the unit.

While there has been no general V-12 reunion at Gonzaga, annual reunions have been held in San Francisco for the many "Zag" V-12s living in that area.

Gonzaga University Archives

Some Gonzaga V-12s: Robert D. Barbagelata, attorney, San Francisco, and national president, American Board of Trial Advocates; Dr. Edward B. Biglieri, professor of medicine, University of California at San Francisco and president-elect, American Society of Hypertension; Dean Donaldson, free-lance writer, Spokane; Dr. Arthur A. Dugoni, dean, School of Dentistry, University of the Pacific, president, California Dental Association, and president, American Board of Orthodontics; Chief Judge Walter McGovern, United States Court for Western District of Washington; A. T. Paioni, vice president and area manager, Bank of America; Dr. Frank Pavel, Sr., D.D.S., president, American Board of Oral and Maxillofacial Surgery, and vice president, Mayo Medical Alumni Association; Angelo Sangiacamo, builder and landlord, Trinity Properties, San Francisco, Calif.

	1943		1944			1945	
	Jul.-Oct.	Nov.-Feb.	Mar.-Jun.	Jul.-Oct.	Nov.-Feb.	Mar.-Jun.	Jul.-Oct.
Navy	289	268	222	275	196	164	147
C.O.	Lt. Lewis W. Musick		Lt. Lyle L. Morris				

University of Washington Seattle, Washington

U.S. Marine Corps Historical Center

The large contingent of V-12s sent to this school moved in on July 1, 1943, just after the Navy Flight Preparatory School closed down. Sailors were quartered in twelve fraternity houses and ate in the Commons Dining Hall, while the marines and NROTCs lived and ate in the Women's Residence Halls. When the program wound down in the spring of 1946, the sixty-one trainees remaining moved to the *APL-50*, a Navy barracks ship moored in Portage Bay near the campus.

The *Daily*, one of the few college papers to continue as a daily during the war, and the *Tyee*, the yearbook, gave excellent coverage to the unit's activi-

ties. The V-12 Social Council planned many unique activities, including "Sailor Hawkins Day," a splash party, and a Christmas jamboree. They also set up the election of a V-12 queen, who was dubbed the "Restrictees' Dream." The Nautical Knaves was the popular V-12 dance band.

Sororities regularly serenaded the V-12 houses, which, according to the *Daily*, caused "a great deal of comment." Some sailors complained that the girls' singing made them lose two or three hours of sleep, or, if it was earlier, interrupted their study time. But most V-12s liked that new tradition.

	1943		1944			1945			1946
	Jul.-Oct.	Nov.-Feb.	Mar.-Jun.	Jul.-Oct.	Nov.-Feb.	Mar.-Jun.	Jul.-Oct.	Nov.-Feb.	Mar.-Jun.
Navy	659	827	898	900	595	352	251	100	45
C.O.	Capt. Eric Barr							Capt. H. D. McIntosh	
Marines	326	235	169	104					
O-in-C	@	Capt. Paul Moore, Jr.							

@ Capt. Edward L. Katzenbach, Jr.

University of Washington

Although most of its major competitors had dropped out, the University of Washington continued a strong sports schedule, with the 1943 football team playing Southern California in the 1944 Rose Bowl.

Some Washington V-12s: Brock Adams, U.S. Senator from Washington, and U.S. secretary of transportation; John W. Black, director, U.S. Travel Service, U.S. Department of Commerce; Dr. John E. Corbally, president, University of Illinois; Daniel J. Evans, governor of Washington and U.S. senator; Donald E. Petersen, chairman, Ford Motor Company; Dr. Russell Shank, director, University Research Library, UCLA; Donald E. Steele, president, Cooper Energy Services; Dwight L. Stuart, president, Carnation Company; John F. Sullivan, Jr., chairman, Bath Iron Works; and Thomas J. G. Vaughan, director, Oregon Historical Society.

University of Washington Archives

Whitman College   Walla Walla, Washington

The coeds were absent from Whitman when the 208 V-12s reported on July 1, 1943, but at the start of the second term the civilian schedule dovetailed into the Navy trimester plan and the girls returned just before November.

The V-12s in the basic course were quartered in Lyman Hall, formerly a freshman dormitory, and the premeds and predents were placed in the vacated Sigma Chi fraternity house.

The first term was a rough one for V-12s who had grade point averages below 2.0 because that meant the loss of weekend liberty. When the second skipper came aboard in November, the academic disciplinary plan was changed so that instead of penalizing those on the low end of the grade curve, the ones on the top side were given extra liberty. The resulting upturn in grades for the entire unit confirmed the wisdom of the change.

The school competed in most intercollegiate sports, but the distances between schools in the Northwest made scheduling difficult. It was one of only three schools in that region to field a football squad in 1943.

The *Single Striper* was published by the V-12s. At first it was supposed to appear every three weeks, but subsequently it came out on an "irregular schedule." The *Waiilatpu*, the Whitman College yearbook, reported on all of the campus organizations, which found many V-12s taking part in everything from the glee club to intramural sports.

Some Whitman V-12s: Capt. Leonard J. Challain, USN; Gerald E. Gorans, chairman of the Management Group, Touche, Ross and Company; Charles H. Herring, first news director of KING-TV, Seattle, and writer-producer of motion picture and television unit, Boeing Company; James B. King, executive editor, *Seattle Times;* Dr. Walter J. Russell, chief of radiology, Atomic Bomb Casualty Commission, and 1975 recipient of National Academy of Sciences' Medal for Extraordinary Service; and David Stevens, Roger and David Clapp Professor of Economic Thought and chairman of the faculty, Whitman College.

	1943	1944			1945		
	Jul.-Oct.	Nov.-Feb.	Mar.-Jun.	Jul.-Oct.	Nov.-Feb.	Mar.-Jun.	Jul.-Oct.
Navy	197	203	192	178	192	107	99
C.O.	Lt. E. J. Liston	Lt. J. L. Bostwick					Lt. D. H. Frame

NOTES

The following abbreviations have been used in these notes:

V-12 Bulletins   All Navy V-12 Bulletins, No. 1 through No. 344, are found in *U.S. Naval Administration in World War II, Bureau of Naval Personnel, Training Activity Vol. IV, Navy V-12 Bulletins*, Guide Nos. 83d(2) and 83d(3) (Navy Department Library, Washington, D.C.). Most V-12 Bulletins were only one or two pages in length, so page citations will not be given except for bulletins which exceeded a few pages. Titles are given to V-12 Bulletins only when they are manuals or reports of the Columbia Conferences.

BuPers   Bureau of Naval Personnel

C.O.   Commanding Officer

NavAdmin.   *U.S. Naval Administration in World War II, Bureau of Naval Personnel, Training Activity Vol. IV, The College Training Program*, Guide No. 83d(1) (Navy Department Library, Washington, D.C.)

Q   Questionnaire

TR   Trainee

V-12 Corres.   Bureau of Naval Personnel General Correspondence, 1941–45, QR/p11-1/V-12, Boxes 1171–1180 (National Archives)

CHAPTER 1. THE NEED

1. In addition to those at Columbia and Northwestern universities, other reserve midshipmen's schools were later opened at the University of Notre Dame; Cornell University; the Naval Academy; Plattsburgh, N.Y.; Fort Schuyler, N.Y.; Camp Endicott, R.I. (for engineers); and Camp Peary, Va. (for Civil Engineer Corps). The Supply Corps School at Harvard University also served as a midshipmen's school for the V-12s sent there. Those taking the twelve-month course spent the first four months in a midshipman's rank.

2. NavAdmin.

3. Paul V. McNutt (1891–1955) had been governor of Indiana (1933–37), U.S. high commissioner to the Philippines (1937–39), and director of the Federal Security Administration (1939–41). Later he served again as high commissioner (1945–46) and as the first United States ambassador (1946) to the Philippines.

NOTES

4. Dr. Rufus C. Harris, president of Tulane, was added at this time. Original members of the committee in January of 1942 were Dr. Burnham Dell (assistant dean of the college, Princeton University), Dr. Raymond A. Kent (chancellor of the University of Louisville), Dr. Elliott Dunlap Smith (assistant to the president of Yale University), and Dr. Robert L. Stearns (president of the University of Colorado). Later, Dr. Gibb Gilchrest (president of Texas A & M) and the Reverend Edward V. Stanford (rector, Augustinian College of the Catholic University of America) were named to the Council. Files of Presidents Emeriti, Tulane University, and *The Silver and Gold* (University of Colorado newspaper), 1/19/42, 2/20/42, 2/27/42, 3/5/42/, 4/29/42, University of Colorado Library.

5. Letter to author, 3/8/85.
6. NavAdmin.
7. Ibid.
8. *New York Times,* 12/18/42, p. 24, col. 3.

CHAPTER 2. THE PROGRAM TAKES FORM

1. Captain Lake requested assignment as professor of naval science and tactics and commanding officer of the Tulane NROTC unit when his tour of duty at BuPers came to an end on January 5, 1943. After the war when Lake was returned to inactive status, he was offered and readily accepted a position at Tulane as dean of admissions and special assistant to President Harris. He remained at Tulane for ten more years. On March 8, 1985, Harris recalled in a letter that "He [Lake] was the most capable Navy officer I ever saw." That is high praise indeed from a man who dealt with hundreds of high-ranking naval officers during his service on three key committees.

2. Captain Lake's primary role in the establishment of the V-12 program was recognized in a citation issued by James V. Forrestal, secretary of the Navy, in May of 1945:

For outstanding service as Director of Training, Bureau of Naval Personnel, from April 1, 1940, to January 5, 1943. Assuming the responsible task of establishing and developing a training program to meet the increasing demands of our rapidly expanding Navy, Captain Lake exercised keen foresight and broad vision during a period of uncertainty in respect to future requirements. Capably initiating the training of Naval personnel in colleges throughout the country, he inaugurated measures essential to the success of the V-12 program and, by his splendid administrative ability and tireless effort in handling the difficult problems confronting him, conceived and executed progressive plans resulting in the saving of time, instructor personnel, vital building material and funds. He was highly instrumental in effecting specialized training procedures and in organizing the training program for WAVES. Captain Lake's exceptional performance of duty in carrying out these tremendous undertakings was largely responsible for the success of the Navy's vast training project and the efficient functioning of various fields of specialized activity.

Files of Presidents Emeriti, Tulane University.
3. NavAdmin.
4. Ibid.

CHAPTER 3. SELECTION OF SCHOOLS

1. Letter of 1/4/43 to BuPers from Dr. Dale D. Welch, president of the University of Dubuque.

NOTES

2. The American Council on Education, the Association of American Medical Colleges, the Engineers' Council for Professional Development, and the American Institute of Physics. NavAdmin.

3. NavAdmin.

4. Dr. Rufus C. Harris, president of Tulane, in a 4/19/43 letter to Capt. William M. Behrens, wrote, "I have read the list and I am surprised that the roster contains some names the choice of which are mystifying to me as an educator. I will call names if you will answer 'why'!" Files of Presidents Emeriti, Tulane University.

5. Typical of the efforts made by congressmen for the schools in their districts was the keen interest taken by Representative Mike Mansfield of Montana on behalf of Carroll College, as shown by files of President Emmet Riley, S.J.

6. Raymond F. Howes interview, 4/24/82.

7. Doniver A. Lund, *Gustavus Adolphus College: A Centennial History, 1862–1962* (St. Peter, Minn.: Gustavus Adolphus College, 1963) 161–162; and Dr. Walter A. Lunden interview, 5/21/86.

CHAPTER 4. A UNIFORM ARMY/NAVY CONTRACT

1. The main problem with the SATC was that "the lines of authority of academic officials on the one hand and of military officers on the other were not clearly defined. . . . In many institutions there were serious conflicts and misunderstandings." Samuel P. Capen, "The Government and the Colleges in Wartime," *The Educational Record* (October 1942): 638.

2. Files of Presidents Emeriti, Tulane University.

3. W. Glasgow Reynolds interview, 4/10/84.

4. Files of Presidents Emeriti, Tulane University.

5. Minutes of Joint Board meeting, August 18, 1943, p. 5. Files of Presidents Emeriti, Tulane University.

6. Ibid., p. 3.

7. V-12 Bulletin No. 90, "Contract Manual for Navy V-12 Unit," Sept. 13, 1943, pp. 11–16.

8. Ibid.

9. Minutes of Joint Board meeting of November 22 and 23, 1943, pp. 1–3. Files of Presidents Emeriti, Tulane University.

10. Minutes of Joint Board meeting of November 30, 1945. Files of Presidents Emeriti, Tulane University.

11. Dr. Robert B. Stewart interview, 4/18/84; Dr. Rufus C. Harris interview, 9/12/85.

CHAPTER 5. CONTRACTING WITH THE COLLEGES

1. Interviews with H. Struve Hensel, 1/4/86; W. John Kenney, 1/4/86; and W. Glasgow Reynolds, 4/10/84. NavAdmin.

2. W. Glasgow Reynolds interview, 4/10/84; NavAdmin.

3. NavAdmin.

4. Interviews with Kathleen Middleton McAlpin, 3/27/86; Francis X. Reilly, 7/1/85; and W. Glasgow Reynolds, 4/10/84.

5. Ibid.

6. Mrs. Boardman Bump interview, 4/25/86.

7. NavAdmin. Francis X. Reilly interview, 7/1/85.

8. V-12 Corres.

9. Kathleen Middleton McAlpin letter, 11/23/85, interview, 3/27/86.

NOTES

10. Letter to author, 7/9/85.

11. V-12 Corres.

12. V-12 files, Berea College.

13. Kathleen Middleton McAlpin letter, 11/23/85.

14. Robert G. Hawley, "The Army Quits the Colleges," *Harper's Magazine* (April 1944): 419–425. A considerable number of V-12s returning question-naires to the author noted that many of their good friends were among the ASTP soldiers pulled out in early 1944. Many of them were casualties in the Battle of the Bulge in December of 1944.

CHAPTER 6. COLLEGE TRAINING SECTION

1. Adams also wore a "scholastic star" on his collar, which indicated a grade point average of 3.4 or better in his freshman year. The description of Adams at the Academy was distilled from his write-up in the *Lucky Bag* and comments in interviews with and letters from Capt. Miles P. DuVal, USN(Ret.), Vice Adm. George C. Dyer, USN(Ret.), and letters from these other members of the class of 1919: Vice Adm. W. M. Callaghan, Rear Adm. Charles A. Nicholson II, Comdr. Frank Sayre, Dr. Franklin L. Troost, Rear Adm. Malcolm F. Schoeffel, Rear Adm. Richard Tuggle, and Capt. C. Kennin Wildman, all USN(Ret.).

2. Ibid.

3. Jean Paul Mather interview, 4/22/85.

4. Dyer letters to author and interview, 7/14/84.

5. Letter from Dr. George Winchester Stone, Jr., 6/8/86.

6. Letter (in Adams's service record) recommending him for a spot promotion to captain, from Capt. James L. Holloway, Jr., USN, then (4/7/44) director of training, to chief of personnel. Date of Adams's retirement is from his service record.

7. *Current Biography*, 1951, s.v. "Adams, Arthur Stanton"; *Who's Who in America*, 39th ed., s.v. "Adams, Arthur Stanton."

8. Dr. Leonard B. Loeb and Dr. Arthur Adams, *The Development of Physical Thought* (New York: John Wiley and Sons, 1933); Dr. Arthur Adams and Dr. George Dewey Hilding, *Fundamentals of Thermodynamics* (Golden, Colo.: n.p., 1937), and a "complete revision of the 1937 book" by the same authors (New York and London: Harper Brothers, 1945).

9. Adams's service record.

10. Ibid.

11. Interview with John G. Hollister, son of Dean S. C. Hollister, 5/5/86.

12. Adams's service record.

13. NavAdmin. A letter of 1/4/43 about V-12 from the president of the University of Dubuque to BuPers was directed to "Lt. Commander A. S. Adams," so he was apparently functioning as head of the program at that early date.

14. Howes interview, 4/24/82.

15. Stone interview, 3/9/83.

16. Mather interview, 4/22/85.

17. John Wight interview, 9/13/85.

18. Howes interview, 4/24/82.

19. Ibid.

20. Ibid.

21. Reynolds interview, 4/10/84, quoting James A. Fowler, Jr.

22. Copies were also placed in the service records of other key officers, including Howes.

NOTES

CHAPTER 7. THE CTS IN ACTION

1. Howes interview, 4/24/82.
2. George Winchester Stone, Jr., interview, 3/9/83.
3. V-12 Corres.
4. Interviews with Howes, 4/24/82, Mather, 4/22/85, George W. Stone, Jr., 3/9/83, and Wight, 9/13/85.
5. Howes interview, 4/24/82.
6. Mather interview, 4/22/85.
7. Thoma interview, 4/10/83; Howes interview, 4/24/82.
8. Thoma interview, 4/10/83.
9. Narmore interview, 11/22/85.
10. Wyndham S. Clark interview, 9/20/85.
11. Comments by several CTS officers during interviews.
12. Thoma interview, 4/10/83.
13. Howes interview, 4/24/82.
14. Mather interview, 4/22/85.
15. Associates of Adams, in both earlier and later times, felt that "A Christmas Ode" was the kind of thing he would have written, and that he would have made sure to include the name of everyone who was associated with the V-12 section. In a supplement to the *Cosmos Club Bulletin* of April 1982, the memorial to Adams by club member Charles G. Dobbins noted that "staff members and secretaries alike were on a first-name basis and the subjects of personal concern to Adams. He wanted to know even the family members, and followed the fortunes of each with genuine interest. A prodigious writer of birthday greetings, he continued to send them to an astonishing number of former colleagues throughout his life."
16. George W. Hulme, Jr., preserved "A Christmas Ode."

CHAPTER 8. CURRICULUM

1. V-12 Bulletin No. 4, "Conference on the Navy V-12 Program at Columbia University, May 14–15, 1943," June 7, 1943, p. 4.
2. "National Program on Colleges Urged," *New York Times*, Dec. 18, 1942, p. 24, col. 5.
3. Alvin C. Eurich interview, 6/23/83; Milton C. Mumford interview, 4/26/86.
4. Raymond F. Howes, *The Navy Goes To College* (Riverside, Calif.: Raymond F. Howes, 1974), pp. 20–22.
5. V-12 Bulletin No. 22, "Manual for the Operation of All Navy V-12 Units," June 18, 1943, pp. 12, 12A, 12B, 12C.
6. TR Q (trainee questionnaire).
7. Eurich interview, 6/23/83.
8. "Navy College Training Program," *Case Alumnus Magazine* (February 1943): 11.
9. Eurich interview, 6/23/83.
10. Howes, *The Navy Goes*, pp. 7–8; Howes interview, 4/24/82; several other interviews.
11. V-12 Bulletin No. 2, "Curricula, Schedules and Course Descriptions — Supplement," June 1, 1943, p. 22; V-12 Bulletin No. 51, "Physical Fitness Tests and Swimming Requirements," July 23, 1943.
12. At the annual meeting of the Kansas section of the Mathematical Association of America on April 15, 1944, Professor G. W. Smith of the University of

NOTES

Kansas remarked that the mathematics taught in the V-12 program was substantially the same as that included in the usual engineering curriculum. "The Annual Meeting of the Kansas Section," *The American Mathematical Monthly* (November 1944): 550. At a meeting of twenty-eight Eastern V-12 schools on January 22, 1944, the representatives discussed the requirement of calculus for deck candidates and then unanimously adopted the following resolution: "That we request the Training Division of the Bureau of Naval Personnel to re-examine the curricula for deck candidates in the third and fourth terms, looking toward the elimination of required calculus, and to provide more effectively for differences in aptitude." "Eastern Conference on Navy V-12 Programs," *The American Mathematical Monthly* (June–July 1944): 362. Later in 1944 calculus was dropped as a required course. At the same conference Commander Eurich advised the delegates that a new Navy directive would permit the substitution of other advanced courses in physics for the required electrical engineering and elementary heat power in the second college year for the regular deck candidates. Minutes in the library of the American Council on Education.

13. Eurich letter, 9/4/86.
14. NavAdmin.
15. Grant H. Brown interview, 1/11/86.

CHAPTER 9. OFFICERS FOR THE UNITS

1. NavAdmin.
2. Letter of 3/11/43 from chief of personnel to all professors of naval science and tactics (the commanding officers of the NROTC units). V-12 Corres.
3. Russell H. Seibert interview, 8/29/85.
4. Lee Norvelle, *The Road Taken* (Bloomington: Indiana University Foundation, 1980), 283–284; Norvelle interview, 12/3/83.
5. Norvelle interview, 12/3/83.
6. Jane Rollman letter to author, 2/1/86.

CHAPTER 10. SELECTION OF TRAINEES

1. NavAdmin.
2. Howes interview, 4/24/82.
3. NavAdmin.
4. V-12 Corres.
5. NavAdmin.

CHAPTER 11. THE NATIONWIDE EXAMINATION

1. Memo of 3/12/43, V-12 Corres.
2. V-12 Corres.
3. The test was given in over fourteen thousand centers in the continental limits; permission to give it in Alaska was specifically refused, probably because of the uncertain transportation of the examination papers. The cost to the armed forces: $324,000, approximately one dollar per man tested. V-12 Corres.; "The First Qualifying Test for the Army & Navy College Training Programs," File TP/2A4-57-6, p. 1, Archives of the Educational Testing Service, Princeton, N.J.
4. TR Qs.
5. "The First Qualifying Test," p. 2.

NOTES

6. A sample question from the verbal section:
   Opposites: The opposite of:
   FEIGNED: 1 — weak   2 — genuine   3 — paltry   4 — hopeful
               5 — doting.
The CEEB report indicated, from a representative sample of 500 answer sheets, that the percentage of candidates choosing each of the responses was (1) 12.8% (2) 55.2% (3) 7.0% (4) 14.1% (5) 5.0% No answer — 5.2%. (Correct answer underscored.) Ibid., p. 3.

7. A sample question from the scientific section: Which glass is more apt to break when very hot water is poured into it? (a) a thick tumbler (b) a medium thick tumbler (c) a thin tumbler (d) all are equally likely to break.
   The percentage choosing each: (a) 42.0% (b) 2.8% (c) 41.4% (d) 13.4% No answer — 0.4%. Ibid., p. 5.

8. Ibid., pp. 5–7.

9. A sample mathematical question: If 500 feet of cable weigh x pounds, how many feet long is a piece which weighs y pounds? (a) $\dfrac{500y}{x}$ (b) $\dfrac{xy}{500}$ (c) $\dfrac{x}{500y}$ (d) $500xy$ (e) $\dfrac{500x}{y}$.
   The percentage choosing each answer: (a) 24.0% (b) 11.2% (c) 6.4% (d) 6.6% (e) 38.6% No answer — 4.2%. Ibid., p. 8.

10. "The First Qualifying Test," 13, 27.

11. V-12 Corres.

12. Ibid. A trainee from that high school was assigned to Milligan College.

CHAPTER 12. INTERVIEW AND PHYSICAL

1. Office of Naval Officer Procurement letter to author.

2. Author's recollection, confirmed by Wilmer D. Gruelich, who was stationed at the Office of Naval Officer Procurement (ONOP) in Atlanta when it was involved with V-12 selection. He said the V-12 selection board there consisted of an Admiral Allen, officer-in-charge of the Atlanta ONOP, Dr. Harmon White Caldwell, president of the University of Georgia, and a businessman, whose name he does not recall. The Selection Board met weekly. Gruelich was later executive officer at Bloomsburg State and then commanding officer at Muhlenberg College. Interview, 3/22/86.

3. V-12 Corres.

4. Ibid.

5. Letter from Admiral Turner to author, Sept. 11, 1985.

6. Letter from Admiral Denton to author, Sept. 30, 1985.

7. V-12 Corres.

8. Letter to author.

CHAPTER 13. THE COLLEGES PREPARE

1. Archives, Carroll College.

2. Lester E. McGonigle interview, 10/16/85.

3. Howes interview, 4/24/82.

4. Archives, Emory University.

5. "Whereas before the war Occidental had two mathematics instructors, now

NOTES

there are five; before there were only three sections in physics, now there are eleven. Teachers who formerly conducted classes in music, art and education are dividing their time between those classes and the teaching of physics." "The College Goes to War," *Occidental Alumnus* (October 1943): 2.

6. Howes interview, 4/24/82.

7. Sessions interview, 2/2/80; author's recollection; reports from TR Qs.

8. Archives, Muhlenberg College. At Occidental College, President Remsen Bird occasionally helped out in the mess hall serving line, along with Occidental coeds who volunteered their services to alleviate the labor shortage. To properly charge the Navy for their services, the girls were paid a flat salary, which they immediately invested in U.S. War Bonds that were then donated to the college. "The College Goes to War," 2; and Andrew F. Rolle, *Occidental College: The First Seventy-Five Years, 1887–1962* (Los Angeles: Occidental College, 1962), p. 90 and photo after p. 80.

CHAPTER 14. THE COLUMBIA CONFERENCE

1. V-12 Corres.

2. All of the quotations are from Navy V-12 Bulletin No. 4, "Conference on the Navy V-12 Program at Columbia University, May 14–15, 1943," June 7, 1943, which includes a fairly complete transcript of conference proceedings. Admiral Jacobs's mention of previous promises made to the trainees spotlights one of the prime considerations of the Navy during the entire program: it did its best to live up to its promises, and when events prevented that, it usually came up with options which could satisfy many of those who were disappointed. See Chapter 19, "The 'Fly Boys,' " for some examples of those options.

3. This statement was widely quoted in the press, and frequently mentioned by the Navy to calm fears that it was "taking over the colleges." Since Lieutenant Howes wrote most of Admiral Jacobs's speech, the words came out the way the College Training Section wished. Howes interview, 4/24/82.

4. Captain Baughman again reinforced the view that V-12 was a college program. V-12 Bulletin No. 4, "Conference," 7.

5. Ibid., 8–11.

6. As a matter of fact, changes were made in the basic curricula as the program moved along. These were intended to make the program more effective and to avoid the unnecessary attrition of trainees who had good officer potential but were saddled with weak mathematical or scientific backgrounds. See Chapter 8, "Curriculum," for recommendations from professional societies to resolve such problems. After the end of the war, the required curricula were further relaxed.

7. V-12 Bulletin No. 4, "Conference," 11–14.

8. In spite of these instructions by Captain Behrens and similar words in V-12 Bulletin No. 22, "Manual for the Operation of All Navy V-12 Units," June 18, 1943, p. 43, unnecessary watches were established at some units and the regulars marched to classes in a few units.

9. V-12 Bulletin No. 4, "Conference," 15–19.

10. Providing this opportunity for input from the 131 colleges was one of the most important steps the Navy took to rebut the "taking over" charge.

11. V-12 Bulletin No. 4, "Conference," 18.

12. Ibid., 23–25.

13. Ibid., 41.

14. Fowler's remarks, Ibid., 42–51.

15. Attributing the principles to chairman Stewart, the business manager of

NOTES

a major university, was another important step in selling the college representatives on the program. The ten "principles of contract" were sent to all of the prospective V-12 schools. Files of Presidents Emeriti, Tulane University, and Files of President's Office, Manuscripts Division, University of Virginia Library.

16. Captain Webb's remarks are in V-12 Bulletin No. 4, "Conference," 51–56.

CHAPTER 15. V-12 BULLETINS

1. Memorandum, V-12 Corres.

2. The volume for Navy V-12 Bulletins in NavAdmin. concludes with Bulletin No. 344, "Release of NROTC-V-12 Students Who Acquire Sufficient Points Therefor," dated January 9, 1946, but other bulletins were issued at later dates to cover all ongoing matters. Foremost of these were the orderly transfer to the postwar NROTC, the matter of commissioning graduating V-12s (the reserve midshipmen's schools had been closed by then), and the continuing release to inactive duty of men who had accumulated sufficient discharge points. V-12 Bulletin No. 376, dated May 28, 1946, is in the Files of the President's Office, Manuscripts Division, University of Virginia Library. There were undoubtedly a few more V-12 Bulletins, so at the end of the program the number was probably close to 390.

3. The contents of the first one hundred bulletins were apportioned among the subjects in the following numbers: A, curriculum = 8; B, training aids = 1; C, administration = 43; D, finance and contracts = 13; E, procurement = 6; F, physical training = 3; G, medical and dental = 13; H, theological education = 1; I, Marine Corps = 4; J, NROTC = 3; K, general information on the entire program = 5; L, disbursing and supply = 15; and M, Naval Academy = 2. The Navy changed the wording of subject "L" and added "M" with V-12 Bulletin No. 64, Aug. 17, 1943. (The total is more than 100 because many dealt with several subjects.) Navy V-12 Bulletin No. 100, October 7, 1943, p. 23–27.

4. George Winchester Stone, Jr., interviews, 3/9/83 and 3/12/86; NavAdmin.

5. George Winchester Stone, Jr., interviews, 3/9/83 and 3/12/86.

6. Stone recalled carrying policy drafts to other interested offices. He remembered the long discussions with Major Thurston J. Davies, the officer-in-charge of the Marine program, and with Lt. Bruce Buckmaster, "a cheerful accountant" in the Bureau of Supplies and Accounts (BuSandA) as well as with a commander in BuSandA who had come directly from the garment district of New York because of his expertise in materials, supplies, designs, and schedules of production in relation to uniforms. Other Bulletin drafts were taken around to the concerned offices by Stone accompanied by some commanders in the Planning and Control Division, officers of finance and contracting units, Bureau of Medicine personnel, and representatives from the Bureau of Aeronautics. Stone remarked that "No stand-by time existed in the business of college training for young naval officers." Letter to author, 6/8/86.

7. Interviews with, and questionnaires and letters from, more than twenty V-12 commanding officers.

CHAPTER 16. QUOTAS AND ORDERS

1. V-12 Corres.

2. Publications and files at many V-12 units; V-12 Corres.

3. NavAdmin; V-12 Corres.

NOTES

4. Many men who were assigned to the midshipmen's schools in the winter of 1943–44 came directly from civilian life — they were among the two thousand who had chosen to remain on inactive duty so they could graduate from their own colleges.

5. Howes interview, 4/24/82.

6. R. Fred Sessions interviews, 2/2/80 and 9/15/80; author's recollection.

7. John B. Opfell letter, 8/15/84.

8. TR Qs and author's recollection.

9. "1,450 Youths Leave to Get V-12 Training," *New York Times*, July 12, 1943, p. 8, col. 7.

10. Ibid.

11. Archives, Northwestern University.

CHAPTER 17. REPORTING FOR DUTY

1. TR Qs.

2. Robert G. Walsh interview, 2/21/86.

3. Ralph Wright Johnson interview, 6/14/86.

4. TR Q. Some trainees did not have far to travel. Harvey Thomas tells about reporting to the Navy V-12 program: "My orders came for Missouri Valley College, it being all of one mile from my home on the same street but at the other end of town. I well recall my Mother standing at the kitchen door wiping tears from her eyes as I mounted my bicycle and rode off to war." Letter to author, 5/28/85.

5. The long delay was at the University of Oklahoma.

6. TR Q.

7. Lt. James L. Gillard, USNR(MC), "Sick Bay," *Centralight* (September 30, 1943): 10. The University of Richmond unit also had a great number of physical rejections. V-12 Muster Rolls, National Archives.

8. Gillard, "Sick Bay," 10.

9. David A. Long interview, 3/13/86.

10. "Navy Programs In Comparison With River Campus; Hobart, Oberlin, Tufts, Cornell Report on Their V-12 Program," University of Rochester's *Campus*, Aug. 6, 1943, p. 2, col. 1.

11. For more details on the laundry case, see James G. Schneider, "To Son, With Love — and Not Too Much Starch," *Wall Street Journal*, May 8, 1986, p. 26, col. 3.

12. Raymond F. Howes, *The Navy Goes to College* (Riverside, Calif.: Raymond F. Howes, 1974), 12–13.

13. Milligan College V-12 Unit Log Book, June 10, 1943, to October 28, 1943. In author's possession.

14. Trainee Paul M. Lund, "From Sport Coats to Navy Blue," *Centralight*, V-5, V-12 Navy Issue (September 30, 1943): 14.

15. Princeton University.

16. Milligan College V-12 Unit Log Book.

17. John Weaver interview, 7/6/86.

CHAPTER 18. THE "OLD SALTS"

1. Howes interview, 4/24/82.

2. "The Navy College Training Program," *Bureau of Naval Personnel Information Bulletin* (March 1943): 14, 50.

NOTES

3. NavAdmin.
4. Richard B. Eaton interviews, 1/19/86 and 9/13/86.
5. George P. Young TR Q.
6. Morris Mitchell interview, 6/6/86.
7. TR interview.
8. Ralph Wright Johnson interview, 6/14/86.
9. Allen Moss TR Q.
10. Paul Kincade interview, 6/20/86.
11. Robert J. Schrotzberger TR Q.
12. J. H. Copenhaver letter, 11/23/84.
13. B. B. Lucas TR Q.
14. V-12 Corres.

CHAPTER 19. THE "FLY BOYS"

1. V-12 Bulletin No. 213, 4/26/44; NavAdmin.
2. Burton L. Mann interview, 4/14/86.
3. Earlier groups of V-5s went to the Civil Aeronautics Authority (CAA)-War Training Schools operated in many colleges by the Navy and the CAA. These were being phased out in the early part of 1944, however, and shortly thereafter the Navy flight preparatory schools met the same end. On April 26, 1944, an additional term in the V-12 program was prescribed for the V-12(a)s, after which they proceeded directly to pre-flight schools. V-12 Bulletin No. 213.
4. TR Qs.

CHAPTER 20. MARINE V-12s

1. Bernard C. Nalty and Ralph F. Moody, *A Brief History of U.S. Marine Corps Officers Procurement, 1775–1969* (Washington: Historical Division Headquarters, U.S. Marine Corps, 1958; rev. 1970), 6–14.
2. NavAdmin.
3. Ibid.
4. Disbanded on 2/28/44 were the units at Arizona State Teachers College, Emory University, Gustavus Adolphus College, Millsaps College, North Texas Agricultural College, and Northwestern University.
5. The twenty disbanded on 10/31/44 were Arkansas A & M, Bowling Green, Bucknell, College of the Pacific, Denison, Duke, Franklin & Marshall, Louisiana Tech, Miami University, Muhlenberg, Notre Dame, Occidental, Penn State, Redlands, Rochester, Southwestern Louisiana, Southwestern University, University of Colorado, University of Washington, and Western Michigan.
6. They were Colgate, Colorado College, Cornell, Dartmouth, Michigan, North Carolina, Princeton, Purdue, Southern California, University of California, Villanova, and Yale.
7. Marine Corps Historical Center.
8. Jack T. Lytle interview, 6/1/86; John Doyle interview, 6/28/86.
9. Memo in V-12 file, Marine Corps Historical Center.
10. Jack T. Lytle interview, 4/8/84.
11. "Physical Fitness Program at Princeton University for Marine Trainees," two pages, n.d., Princeton V-12 file, Marine Corps Historical Center.
12. Muster Roll, 9/30/43, Duke V-12.
13. "Physical Fitness at Princeton."

NOTES

14. Nalty and Moody, *Brief History*, 14.
15. NavAdmin.
16. Ibid.
17. Harry Tyson Carter letter, 1/17/86.
18. TR Q.
19. NavAdmin.
20. Ibid.
21. Ibid.
22. Ibid.
23. Eugene B. Sledge interview, 2/8/86.
24. Marine Muster Rolls, Emory University and Georgia Institute of Technology V-12 units, 12/31/43, National Archives.
25. E. B. Sledge, *With The Old Breed at Peleliu and Okinawa* (Novato: Presidio Press, 1981), 6–7.
26. Marine V-12 Muster Rolls, National Archives.
27. John Doyle interview, 6/28/86.
28. Memo issued 8/2/43 by Comdr. Maurice Van Cleave, USN (Ret.), C.O. at Denison University, interpreting a letter from the commandant of the USMC on the policy on marriage of privates in V-12 detachments. It noted that there were three married marines in the Denison unit. Denison University Archives. Probably most units had some legally married marines, as was true at the University of Rochester and Arkansas A & M.
29. Paul E. Newland interview, 12/1/85.
30. Harold Van Tongeren interview, 12/1/85.

CHAPTER 21. COAST GUARD V-12s

1. V-12 Corres.
2. Ibid.
3. Muster rolls, Navy V-12 units, National Archives.
4. Ibid.
5. Ibid.

CHAPTER 22. NEGRO V-12s

1. *U.S. Naval Administration in World War II, Bureau of Naval Personnel, The Negro in the Navy*, Guide No. 84, first draft narrative prepared by the Historical Section of the Bureau of Naval Personnel (Navy Department Library, Washington, D.C.).
2. V-12 Corres.
3. Ibid.
4. Alvin C. Eurich interview, 6/23/83.
5. Raymond F. Howes interview, 4/24/82.
6. Walter Johnson, ed., *The Papers of Adlai E. Stevenson*, vol. II, *Washington to Springfield, 1941–1948* (Boston: Little Brown and Company, 1972) 134–135.
7. Memorandum of 9/20/44 from Comdr. R. W. Wood, special assistant to the assistant chief of naval personnel, to Lt. Comdr. W. M. McCarthy, Office of Public Relations, Navy Department. V-12 Corres.
8. Samuel L. Gravely, Jr., was on that date in the midshipmen's school at Columbia University. Gravely Q.

NOTES

9. "First Negro Ensigns," *Life* (April 24, 1944): 44.

10. *The Negro in the Navy,* p. 34.

11. Letter of 4/16/44 from Mrs. Paul H. Goffman to Hon. Frank Knox; reply dated 5/12/44 from Lt. Comdr. Willard Deason, Officer Procurement Division. V-12 Corres.

12. Gravely letter to author, 6/25/86; *Who's Who in America,* 39th ed., s.v. "Gravely, Samuel Lee"; *Who's Who Among Black Americans,* 3rd ed., s.v. "Gravely, Samuel L. (Sam), Jr."; Gravely Q.

13. V-12 muster rolls, National Archives; *Who's Who in America,* 42nd ed., s.v. "Rowan, Carl Thomas."

14. Horace B. Edwards interview, 1/4/86; *Who's Who in America,* 43rd ed., s.v. "Edwards, Horace Burton"; *Who's Who Among Black Americans,* 3rd ed., s.v. "Edwards, Horace B." From trainee Qs it appears that there was at least one additional black V-12 at Union, Louis Henry.

15. V-12 muster rolls; Edwards interview, 1/4/86; Alonzo J. Fairbanks, Jr., interview, 3/24/86.

16. Fairbanks Q and interview, 3/24/86; *American Men of Science,* 11th ed., s.v. Fairbanks, Dr. Alonzo James, Jr.

17. John A. Guy interview, 8/3/85; James E. Ward interview, 11/1/85; Arthur ("Pete") Wilson interview, 2/25/86.

18. "A 'Working Reunion' of Black Alumni," *Princeton Alumni Weekly* (June 27, 1977): 18–19.

19. Wilson interview, 2/25/86.

20. R. Fred Sessions interview, 1/18/86.

21. Frank A. Crossley letter of 6/23/86 to author; Crossley Q; *Who's Who in America,* 42nd ed., s.v. "Crossley, Frank Alphonso"; *Who's Who Among Black Americans,* 11th ed., s.v. "Crossley, Frank A."

22. Richard Walton, unpublished informal history of Swarthmore College (1984), p. 90. Swarthmore Library.

23. Robert L. Randolph Q; *Who's Who in America,* 42nd ed., s.v. "Randolph, Robert Lee."

24. Recollections of various trainees; college publications. From the Purdue *Debris* and the Qs of Virgil G. Trice, Jr., and Charles C. Johnson, Jr., it appears that the following blacks were in the V-12 unit there: Sailors — Eugene F. Mc-Farland, Carl Coggins, and Virgil G. Trice, Jr.; Marines — Frederick C. Branch, Herbert L. Brewer, F. N. Davis, Robert W. Dye, C. Elliott, R. F. Hall, Charles C. Johnson, Jr., J. A. Poindexter, and John E. Rudder. In 1986 Trice was a chemical engineer in the U.S. Department of Energy and Johnson was a consulting engineer, having earlier served in the U.S. Public Health Service as an assistant surgeon general.

25. Dennis D. Nelson, *The Integration of the Negro Into the U.S. Navy* (New York: Farrar, Straus and Young, 1951), 230.

26. Ibid.

27. Gravely Q.

CHAPTER 23. PATHWAYS BEYOND V-12

1. The period at Asbury Park was resented by many of the trainees not only because of the delay in getting to midshipmen's school, but because of the poor housing conditions. As many as eight men were assigned to a small room that would have been close quarters for a prewar tourist couple. Usually there were

NOTES

only two chairs, so the other six had to sit on their bunks to study, write letters, etc. Often the room shared a single bath with another room, so conditions were impossible at reveille and required careful cooperation the rest of the day. While the hotels — the Monterey and the Berkeley-Carteret — had elevators, their use was forbidden to the trainees, so it was double-time up and down the ladders all day long, even for those living on the sixth floor.

2. V-12 Bulletin No. 132, 11/3/43. However, because of changes in the program, especially after the war ended, the NROTC program sometimes involved eight terms and a degree, which was how it was operating when V-12 started. It must again be acknowledged that NROTC was technically a part of the V-12 program, but because of the different scheduling, uniforms, and curriculum, the author made an early decision not to cover it in detail so the size of the book could be kept within reasonable limits.

3. V-12 Bulletins 246 (7/24/44) and 250 (8/11/44).

4. Sometimes, however, the assignment was done on a very unscientific basis. When one trainee reported in 1944 to the Purdue V-12 unit, a yeoman asked him, "Do you like math?" When he was answered "Yes," he asked, "Do you like science?" A second "yes" brought this quick placement: "Okay, we'll put you in engineering." Elsdon Maynard interview, 6/2/86.

CHAPTER 24. PHYSICAL TRAINING

1. Charles Edward Widmayer, "V-12 Physical Training," *Dartmouth Alumni Magazine* (December 1943): 9, 10, 71.

2. Raymond F. Howes, *The Navy Goes to College* (Riverside, Calif.: Raymond F. Howes, 1974), 7–8; Howes interview, 4/24/82; interviews with other officers from CTS.

3. William J. Young interview, 4/18/86.

4. Paul M. Lund, "From Sport Coats to Navy Blue," Central Michigan *Centralight*, V-5, V-12 Navy Issue (September 30, 1943): 14.

5. Howes interview, 4/24/82.

6. Eugene Miller TR Q.

7. Maurice H. Burkholder interview, 5/2/86.

8. At Harvard. Cornelius F. Keating TR Q.

9. Donald K. Mathews, *Measurement in Physical Education*, 3rd ed. (Philadelphia: W. B. Saunders Company, 1968), 122–123.

10. Ibid.

11. This was mentioned by quite a number of trainees.

12. Rufus C. Harris interview, 9/12/85. Several cases of sunstroke were reported from the University of North Carolina.

13. President's file, Carroll College.

CHAPTER 25. ACADEMIC LOAD

1. Ronald V. Sires, "An Experiment in Education: The Navy V-5 and V-12 Programs," *Northwest Science* (February 1945): 22–23.

2. Mentioned by several former faculty members in Qs; recollections of numerous trainees, including author.

3. TR Q.

4. Karl S. Pister TR Q.

5. Comments by Grant H. Brown, former director of training, Ninth Naval

NOTES

District, in interviews, 1/8/86 and 1/11/86; comments by many TRs, including author.

6. Oberlin College Archives. At St. Ambrose College the 4/13/44 issue of the trainee *Sea Breez* reported that 166 of the 284 V-12s were academically restricted.

7. Steve Lacy interview, 8/10/85.

8. Illinois Institute of Technology Archives.

9. Duke University Archives.

10. Mimeographed pamphlet, "Navy-College Conference on the Navy V-12 Program, Columbia University, 12–13 May 1944," p. 11. This transcript of the speeches was apparently mailed to all V-12 units. Files of President's Office, Carroll College Archives.

11. Faculty Qs.

12. Professor C. E. Hix, Jr., (of Central Methodist College, formerly Central College) interview, 8/16/83. President Joel I. Fletcher of Southwestern Louisiana Institute, in attachments to a 10/26/45 letter to Comdr. M. A. Heffernan, director of training for the Eighth Naval District, wrote, "How has the academic work of the V-12 trainees compared with that of the students in peacetime?" "The academic work of the V-12 trainees has been definitely better than that of students in peacetime." University of Southwestern Louisiana Archives.

13. Report of President N. E. McClure to Ursinus Board of Directors, November 20, 1945, p. 4.

14. NavAdmin.

15. "University Votes on Honor Code," *College Topics* (Dec. 9, 1943): 1.

16. Ibid., 12/16/43, p. 1.

17. Ibid., 6/2/44, p. 1.

18. Ibid., 6/6/44, p. 1.

19. Ibid., 6/16/44, p. 1.

20. Virginius Dabney, *Mr. Jefferson's University* (Charlottesville: University Press of Virginia, 1981), 239–240. At the University of California, dean of students E. C. Voorhies noted in a memo of 12/8/43 to Capt. Watson P. Gooch, Jr., officer-in-charge of the Marine detachment, that "During the first final examination period after the V-12 Program started there was not one single case of cheating reported among male students. This is the first time that this has been the case during final examination period, at least in recent years." University of California V-12 file, Marine Corps Historical Center.

CHAPTER 26. ATTRITION

1. NavAdmin.

2. NavAdmin. (*Training Activity*, vol. IV, p. 122.)

3. NavAdmin.

4. NavAdmin. (*Training Activity*, vol. IV, p. 122.)

5. Duke University Archives.

6. Prof. Arthur Dewing, "Teaching Navy Trainees: A Faculty Impression of the V-12 Program at Dartmouth," *Dartmouth Alumni Magazine* (March 1944): 7–9.

7. Grant H. Brown interview, 1/11/86.

8. George W. Hulme, Jr., interview, 9/13/85.

9. Some physics and other science majors who had poorer eyesight (i.e., 12/20 correctable to 20/20) had been enlisted in V-7(S) program and were trans-

ferred to V-12(S), where they were required to meet only the lower vision qualifications.

10. TR Qs. The author was one of those who took the exercises at Day and Day.

CHAPTER 27. DISCIPLINE

1. Southwestern University Archives.

2. Sidney Greeley, Jr., interview, 9/7/86. Examples of "chicken-type" discipline abound. At Dubuque one trainee lost his Easter liberty because his shoeshine was too good! It looked like patent leather. Another Dubuque trainee received a captain's mast for "passing gas after taps." The C.O. was in the passageway at the time. Related in Roger Olesen TR Q. At Union College, V-12 George Fellendorf playfully placed his hat on a teen-aged girl's head while they were eating hamburgers at the Little Tavern after the Armistice Day parade in 1943. Unfortunately, CPO Carson observed it through a window, so Fellendorf drew extra guard duty. Fellendorf letter, 9/20/84.

3. Dean Gabbert TR Q. The socks-for-gloves caper was pulled at Tufts. Letter from Richard D. Bunker, 11/6/84.

4. Gordon Shillinglaw TR Q.

5. "Thanks, Sgt. Botti," *The Campus* (August 13, 1943): 6.

6. TR Q.

7. TR Q.

8. TR interview, 8/16/83.

9. R. Fred Sessions interview, 2/4/80.

10. Russell H. Seibert interview, 8/29/85.

11. TR Q.

12. Wilmot N. Hess TR Q.

13. V-12 Bulletin No. 9, June 15, 1943.

14. TR Q.

15. TR Q.

16. V-12 Bulletin No. 241, July 18, 1944.

17. TR Q.

18. Arthur S. Postle, "Conserving Human Resources: Implications for Postwar Higher Education Found in the Administration of the V-12 Program," *Journal of Higher Education* (November 1944): 407–12. Postle was C.O. at Carson-Newman College, and was dean of students at the University of Cincinnati in civilian life.

CHAPTER 28. NAVY-COLLEGE RELATIONS

1. Letter is available in files of many colleges.

2. Mimeographed pamphlet, "Navy-College Conference on the Navy V-12 Program, Columbia University, 12–13 May 1944," p. 16. Files of President's Office, Carroll College Archives.

3. Representative of that view were the few schools, such as the University of Richmond, that kept all of their civilian students on the traditional two-semester and summer-school schedule. This split schedule meant that V-12 irregulars had a rather meager choice of upper-level courses.

4. Carroll College Archives.

5. That telegram was sent to all V-12 schools, but it is likely that the situation

NOTES

at Virginia brought it about. Lt. R. F. Howes made a special August 24 visit to the University of Virginia. Howes's service record.

6. E.g., a January 1944 letter from Sen. Scott Lucas to Rear Adm. Randall Jacobs about a food problem at Northwestern University brought a swift investigation. Northwestern University Archives.

7. At Emory University a plumbing mistake resulted in two marines being severely scalded in the showers. But the usual complaints at most schools centered around the lack of adequate hot water.

8. Comments were made on September 10, 1943, followed by President Snyder's letter of the 11th and Captain Cobb's three-page letter of the 13th. Northwestern University Archives.

9. Grant H. Brown interview, 1/11/86.

10. "Before 1 July 1943, many of the older people wanted to know how we intended to control the service men and what time in the evening the girls would have to be checked into their homes. They soon realized after 1 July that the quality and caliber of our soldiers has changed since the last war." Excerpt from report of Capt. L. T. Campbell, officer-in-charge of Marine detachment, Oberlin College, to Marine *Headquarters Bulletin,* December 1943. Oberlin College V-12 file, Marine Corps Historical Center.

11. In a December 11, 1943, report to the *Headquarters Bulletin,* Oberlin College librarian Julian S. Fowler wrote, ". . . the properly maintained discipline which benefits the men of the Marine Corps may have some good effect on the civilian students who appear to come to college each year with less and less sense of responsibility or self-discipline." On December 7, 1943, the Oberlin dean of men wrote, "I am glad to have a Marine contingent in our V-12 unit. These men have been and are most welcome. Their influence has been a good one. They have proven themselves to be well-disciplined gentlemen and have taken an active, co-operative part in campus life, especially in athletics." Oberlin College V-12 file, Marine Corps Historical Center.

12. A majority of the V-12 schools provided such certificates.

13. "Report of the Treasurer," *The Ursinus College Bulletin* (No. VI, Report of Officers, Academic Year 1944–45): 17.

14. Ibid.

15. Gustavus Adolphus Archives. The Reverend Thomas J. Donnelly, S.J., president of John Carroll University, wrote in "Carroll Says Farewell," *Carroll News* (November 1945): 33, "Two things have impressed me . . . in the progress of this important undertaking for officer training. First, the careful and intelligent planning which went into the inauguration of this program. . . . All was calculated to make the work that the colleges were asked to do fit in smoothly and efficiently with their traditional academic procedure. Then there was something very impressive and reassuring in the consistently high type of character in the official Navy personnel with whom as an institution we had to deal. This, I am sure, is chiefly responsible for the excellent mutual relations which have prevailed here at Carroll for the twenty-eight months of Navy occupancy."

16. Officer Q, 5/1/86.

17. "A War Program — Report and Appraisal," *Whitman College Bulletin* (September 1944): 1.

18. Interview, 1/11/86. At the Second Columbia Conference, May 12, 1944, Vice Adm. Randall Jacobs said, "From the Navy's point of view, the V-12 Program has more than met our highest expectations." "Navy-College Conference," p. 3.

19. Joel L. Fletcher, president, Southwestern Louisiana Institute. The University of Southwestern Louisiana Archives.

NOTES

CHAPTER 29. THE COMMANDING OFFICERS

1. Interview, 9/12/85.
2. "The Little Guy—Junior 'Exec.,' " *Gonzaga Bulletin*, Oct. 19, 1945, p. 3, col. 6.
3. Rollman letter, 2/1/86.
4. Ruth Heath Reeves interview, 9/23/82.
5. NavAdmin and archives at various schools visited by author.
6. Information on Dartmouth and Yale from various interviews, including William V. Weber, 5/1/86, and Raymond F. Howes, 4/24/82; Northwestern University Archives.
7. Howes, 4/24/82, Weber, 5/1/86, and trainee interviews.
8. Weber interview, 5/1/86.
9. Howes, 4/24/82, and Weber, 5/1/86, interviews.
10. Northwestern University Archives.
11. Various trainee interviews and Polly Stone Buck interview, 4/28/85.
12. Walter A. Lunden interview, 5/21/86.
13. Charles P. McCurdy interview, 3/9/85.
14. Weber interview, 5/1/86; V-12 Corres.
15. Oberlin College Archives.
16. Lee Norvelle interview, 12/3/83, and Lee Norvelle, *The Road Taken* (Bloomington: Indiana University Foundation, 1980), 285–289.
17. R. Fred Sessions interview, 2/2/80.
18. Interviews with Sessions, 2/2/80 and 9/15/80, Steve Lacy, 8/10/85, and Virgil Elliott, 9/19/80.
19. Jack T. Lytle interview, 4/8/84.
20. Ibid.
21. Lt. George F. Howe, C.O. at Hampden-Sydney College, June 1945.
22. Capt. Eric Barr became director of summer schools at Washington, while Capt. Forrest U. Lake was made dean of admissions and special assistant to the president at Tulane.
23. "Training for Peace Is Wartime Policy, Nason Announces," *Swarthmore Phoenix*, December 15, 1942, p. 3, col. 1.
24. Everett L. Hunt, "Of the Faculty and Administration," *Garnet Letter* (October 1945): 6–7.
25. Mrs. Glenn Bartle interview, 5/24/86.
26. Weber interview, 5/1/86.
27. NavAdmin., V-12 Corres.
28. Russell H. Seibert interview, 8/29/85.
29. McCurdy interview, 3/9/85.
30. Maxwell Kelso interview, 2/17/86.
31. Seibert interview, 8/29/85.

CHAPTER 30. THE DISTRICT TRAINING OFFICERS

1. "Lieut. Field Inspects Unit," *Columns*, May 24, 1944, p. 1., col. 3.
2. Grant H. Brown interview, 1/11/86.
3. This happened in the Thirteenth Naval District.
4. NavAdmin.
5. Lt. J. L. Bostwick (commanding officer), *Historical Report of Operation* (of Navy V-12 Unit), March 20, 1945, p. 19. Whitman College Archives.

NOTES

CHAPTER 31. THE TRAINEE AND THE COLLEGE

1. TR Qs.

2. Letter from Dr. Richard H. Barrett, 6/13/86.

3. The author and his classmates benefited greatly from Dr. Gergen's help. A V-12 from a later class reported that Professor Gergen gave them the same kind of assistance. Robert D. Plunkett TR Q.

4. Q. from Prof. John M. Boltan.

5. Polly Stone Buck interview, 4/28/85.

6. "Problems," *Williams Record,* May 2, 1945, p. 2, col. 1.

7. TR Qs.

8. University of California V-12 file, Marine Corps Historical Center.

9. The V-12 era marked the first time that smoking had been permitted at some colleges. But the Navy's arrival sometimes resulted in a tightening of campus regulations, even for civilians. "College Enrolls 361," *Dartmouth Alumni Magazine* (August 1943): 31, reported, "New rulings prohibit the drinking of liquor in dormitory rooms at any time and bar women visitors from the dorm rooms after 7:00 P.M."

10. Raymond F. Howes interview, 4/24/82. Raymond F. Howes, *The Navy Goes to College* (Riverside, Calif.: Raymond F. Howes, 1974), 34–35.

11. TR Q.

12. Author's recollection.

13. "New Faculty Members," *Dartmouth Alumni Magazine* (August 1943): 33.

14. A composite answer distilled from faculty questionnaires.

15. Miss Jones's comments were written following her attendance at the first Milligan V-12 reunion in 1980.

16. Letter to author, 10/3/85.

CHAPTER 32. CAMPUS LIFE

1. P. 24.

2. TR Q.

3. See Chapter 34, "Humor, High Jinks, and 'They Shouldn't Have.' "

4. "National Program on Colleges Urged," *New York Times,* Nov. 28, 1942, p. 28, col. 5.

5. "Students–Alumni Oppose Proposal to Move USC," *Gamecock,* Jan. 5, 1945, p. 1, col. 5.

6. Editorial, *Collegian,* October 20, 1944, p. 2, col. 1.

7. At Illinois Institute of Technology, trainee editor Alan J. Grant of *Tech News* had the temerity to criticize by name those professors who held classes past the dismissal bell, thereby making trainees late for their next class, which could result in demerits. One of those named was Capt. D. McGregor, USN, who was professor of naval science and tactics and also the commanding officer. Grant received a captain's mast punishment of several weeks restriction, and his punishment would probably have been more severe had not IIT president Henry Heald interceded. He wrote the C.O. that he assumed full responsibility because at the start of the term he had personally assured the *Tech News* staff of their complete freedom to write as they saw fit. Alan J. Grant interview, 9/15/86.

8. E.g., trainee Marvin L. Stone, who had previously worked on a West Virginia paper, was made editor of the Emory and Henry *White Topper* during the first term. Stone interview, 11/2/84.

NOTES

9. Mahard interview, 11/29/85.

10. H. Melvin Swift, Jr., interview, 4/24/82.

11. "Four Navy V-12 Men Cited for Fire Duty," *Hartford Times*, July 24, 1944, sec. 2, p. 1, col. 1.

CHAPTER 33. INTERCOLLEGIATE ATHLETICS

1. Raymond F. Howes interview, 4/24/82.

2. Raymond F. Howes, *The Navy Goes to College* (Riverside, Calif.: Raymond F. Howes, 1974), 7–8.

3. The policy on intercollegiate athletics was announced by Secretary of the Navy Knox on August 1, 1943, and was reported in virtually every newspaper in the country. "Bowl Trips Barred to Naval Elevens," *New York Times*, Aug. 2, 1943, p. 10, col. 2.

4. Howes, *The Navy Goes*, 7–8.

5. According to Col. John A. Gunn, USMC(Ret.), an authority on Marine Corps football.

6. Jack T. Lytle interview, 6/1/86.

7. Ibid.

8. Ibid.

9. V-12 trainees were permitted to play in the bowl games because they were on leave for the holidays and could travel to Houston or Pasadena if they wished.

10. Stagg was named coach of the year by the Football Writers Association.

11. John A. Gunn.

12. The Redlands football program appeared to have come to an abrupt halt when it was reported on October 30, 1943, that the season was terminated because three-fourths of the team had become ineligible for scholastic reasons. "Redlands Drops Football," *New York Times*, Oct. 31, 1943, sec. 3, p. 2, col. 1. But the Redlands student paper disputed that, alleging travel difficulties as the real reason for cancellation of the College of the Pacific game at Stockton. However, the Bulldogs did play another game, holding the Yuma Army Air Base to a 0–0 tie on November 5, 1943. "Bulldogs meet army team," *Bulldog*, Nov. 4, 1943, p. 3, col. 5, and Nov. 11, 1943, p. 3, col. 3.

13. John A. Gunn.

14. Howes, *The Navy Goes*, 13.

15. Joseph F. Shea TR Q.

16. John A. Gunn.

17. Several Oberlin trainees mentioned this in their questionnaires. The 1943 Oberlin team had a 7–0–1 record, while the 1945 squad, which included sixteen V-12s, was undefeated and untied.

18. John A. Gunn.

CHAPTER 34. HUMOR, HIGH JINKS, AND "THEY SHOULDN'T HAVE"

1. TR Q from Robert T. Hegler, who witnessed the event.

2. James Vollmer interview, 7/12/86.

3. Paul Kincade interview, 6/20/86.

4. TR Qs. Anonymity at this point protects both the innocent and the guilty.

5. Letter from the civilian student.

6. TR Q from William A. Adler.

7. TR Q (including exhibits) from Blair Smith.

NOTES

8. Jane Meldrum Reid interview, 10/29/85.

9. Vollmer interview, 7/12/86.

10. Interview, 3/8/86, and letter, 1/17/86, Harry Tyson Carter.

11. Author's recollection.

12. Paul Kincade interview, 6/20/86.

13. Cecil E. Ingram, at Milligan reunion, 1980.

14. TR Qs.

15. Letter from Janet Wilson Schoenduke, 1/2/85.

16. Kenneth ("Bud") Adams interview, 6/10/86.

17. John Scott Davenport interview, 1/9/86.

18. John Scott Davenport, "Operation Redlands," *Redlands Report* (Spring 1985): 23.

19. "Winter Military Ball Will Honor Seniors Saturday in Commons," *Bulldog*, Feb. 18, 1944, p. 1, col. 4.

CHAPTER 35. LIBERTY AND LEAVE

1. Many TR Qs.

2. "Christmas Leaves Hampered By Transportation Difficulties," *The Link*, Nov. 13, 1943, p. 1, col. 1.

CHAPTER 36. V-12 AND THE PUBLIC

1. V-12 Corres.

2. R. Fred Sessions interview, 2/2/80.

3. University of Rochester Library.

4. V-12 Corres.

5. Ibid.

6. Bloomsburg State University Archives.

7. Jack T. Lytle interview, 6/1/86.

8. At Milligan V-12 reunion, August 10, 1985.

9. Richard Coon interview, 12/15/84; George D. O'Brien interview, 4/24/82.

10. Interview with Alice B. Whitten, mother of trainee George E. Whitten, 2/2/80.

11. At Tulane the group was organized by Mrs. Rufus Harris, wife of Tulane's president.

12. Letter from Margaret S. Zeigler, 2/25/85.

13. Grant H. Brown interview, 1/11/86.

14. Robert E. Kearney at Milligan College V-12 reunion, August 10, 1985, referring to the people of Johnson City, Tenn.

CHAPTER 37. CHANGES IN THE PROGRAM

1. NavAdmin. and Navy and Marine Corps V-12 Muster Rolls, National Archives.

2. Ibid.

3. Ibid.

4. Ibid.

5. Arthur S. Adams's service record and V-12 Corres.

6. V-12 Corres.

7. Interviews with Jean Paul Mather, 4/22/85, George Winchester Stone, Jr., 3/9/83, and John W. Wight, 9/13/85.

NOTES

8. Interviews with Raymond F. Howes, 4/24/82, and Jack T. Lytle, 4/8/84.

9. Mather interview, 4/22/85.

10. Howes interview, 4/24/82, and service record.

11. V-12 Corres.

12. NavAdmin. and Navy and Marine Corps Muster Rolls.

13. Ibid.

14. Ibid.

15. Ibid.

16. Ibid.

17. Ibid.

18. Marine Corps Muster Roll, Colorado College.

19. NavAdmin.

20. "With the March Semester," *Chanticleer* (1945): 222.

21. "Barracks Ship Provides Temporary Housing for Washington Unit," *Training* (June 15, 1946): 21.

22. Maurice Burkholder interview, 5/2/86.

23. NavAdmin.

24. Reported by several schools in response to author's questionnaire.

CHAPTER 38. V-12 AND POSTWAR OFFICER TRAINING

1. "For Navy Training In Fifty Colleges," *New York Times,* November 23, 1944, p. 21, col. 1.

2. "V-12s Being Shifted to NROTC," Bureau of Naval Personnel *Training Division Letter* (March 1945): 73–74.

3. "NROTC Expansion Approved," BNP *Training Division Letter*:1.

4. Ibid., 2.

5. "25 More Colleges Get Naval ROTC Units," *New York Times,* May 2, 1945, p. 26, col. 5.

6. "To End V-12 Training for 24,000," *New York Times,* Dec. 12, 1945, p. 21, col. 2.

7. "Congress Refuses to Cut Its Recess," *New York Times,* Dec. 21, 1945, p. 12, col. 6.

8. Admiral James L. Holloway, Jr., USN(Ret.), with Jack Sweetman, "A Gentlemen's Agreement," *Proceedings* (September 1980): 71–77.

9. Ibid.

10. Ibid.

11. Ibid., p. 74.

12. Arthur S. Adams file, American Council on Education Library.

CHAPTER 39. WINDING DOWN

1. Photographs of sailors (apprentice seamen) at both Oregon State University and the University of Missouri, both newly selected NROTC schools, establish that fact. Missouri was awarded a V-12 scroll signed by Secretary of the Navy Forrestal on June 6, 1946. "Dear Alumni Friends," *Missouri Alumnus* (June 1946): 1.

2. "Release System Set Up By The Navy," *New York Times,* July 25, 1945, p. 1, col. 4.

3. "Our 3 Armed Services Plan Demobilization," *New York Times,* Aug. 16, 1945, p. 1, col. 6.; "Text of Services' Demobilization Statements," *New York Times,* Aug. 16, 1945, p. 11, cols. 4–5.

NOTES

4. "Navy to Speed Discharges; 550,000 Men Its Peace Total," *New York Times*, Aug. 28, 1945, p. 1, col. 2.

5. "Reserve Training Cut Down By Navy," *New York Times*, Aug. 25, 1945, p. 24, col. 4.

6. V-12 Bulletin No. 322, Sept. 1, 1945.

7. Many TR Qs.

8. Ibid.

9. Ibid.

10. Navy V-12 Bulletins Nos. 344, Jan. 9, 1946, and 347, referred to in "V-12s Given Opportunity to Remain On Duty Until 1 July, Get Commissions," *All Hands* (March 1946): 70.

11. Hundreds of questionnaires received by the author attest to that attitude.

CHAPTER 40. THE KOREAN WAR

1. Based on questionnaires received by author.

2. According to many marine questionnaires.

3. TR Q from Clarence L. French, Jr.

4. Grant H. Brown interview, 1/11/86.

5. Ibid.

CHAPTER 41. V-12 OFFICERS AFTER WORLD WAR II

1. Charles P. McCurdy interview, 3/9/85.

2. Mrs. Glenn Bartle interview, 5/24/86.

3. The President of the United States takes pleasure in presenting the LEGION OF MERIT to

CAPTAIN ARTHUR STANTON ADAMS
UNITED STATES NAVY, RETIRED

for service as set forth in the following:

CITATION:

"For exceptionally meritorious conduct in the performance of outstanding services to the Government of the United States as Officer in Charge of the Curriculum Section, Officer in Charge of the College Training Section, Director of the Field Administration Division and special Assistant to the Director of Training, from November 1, 1942, to November 1, 1945. Discharging with tact, foresight and initiative his important duties throughout this period, Captain Adams consistently advocated and administered policies and procedures which insured cooperative relations between the Navy Department and American colleges. A central figure in the planning and administration of the Navy V-12 Program, he rendered invaluable assistance in training 150,000 officer candidates enrolled in colleges and universities, of whom more than 50,000 qualified for commissions during the war, and, in addition, assumed a leading role in shaping the course of the post-war Naval Reserve Officers Training Corps. By establishing mutual confidence between the Navy and the educational institutions, Captain Adams contributed to the greatest wartime training program ever undertaken by the Navy and to the creation of a solid foundation for effective peacetime officer training."

For the President,
James V. Forrestal
Secretary of the Navy
27 November 1945

Board of Decorations and Medals, Navy Department

NOTES

4. *Who's Who in America*, 39th ed., s. v. "Adams, Arthur Stanton"; and *Current Biography*, 1951, s. v. "Adams, Arthur Stanton."
5. Page Thomson Steele interview, 1/29/84.
6. Mrs. Lewis K. Adams interview, 3/14/82.

CHAPTER 42. DID THE NAVY ACHIEVE ITS GOALS?

1. The story was carried by the wire service to papers across the land. "War May Last Three or Four Years, Knox Says," Johnson City, Tenn., *Press-Citizen*, July 1, 1943, p. 6, col. 8.
2. Marvin L. Stone, editorial: "A Broader Scope," Emory and Henry *White Topper*, July 29, 1943, p. 2. cols. 1–2. Also, Rear Adm. I. C. Johnson, director of naval officer procurement for the Eleventh Naval District, addressing the V-12s at Occidental College in October of 1943, assured them, "This war will last long enough for all of you to see active service." *Occidental*, 10/6/43, p. 1.
3. NavAdmin.
4. Letter from Grant H. Brown to author, 1/15/86.
5. Raymond F. Howes interview, 4/24/82.
6. "Baxter, Newhall, McLaren Comment On Probable Duration of War in Pacific," Williams College *Record*, May 16, 1945, p. 1, cols. 2–3.
7. Vincent C. DeBaun, "25 years ago — V-12 remembered," Union College *Symposium* (Fall 1968): 11–15.
8. Comments in many TR Qs. One trainee, a staunch Republican, flies his flag on the first Monday of every August to honor Harry Truman for making the decision to drop the bomb.
9. Mimeographed pamphlet, "Navy-College Conference on the Navy V-12 Program, Columbia University, New York, 12–13 May 1944," p. 7. This was mailed to all V-12 schools. Carroll College Archives.

CHAPTER 43. BENEFITS TO V-12 COLLEGES

1. Carroll College Archives.
2. Letter to author, 6/23/86.
3. Officials and trainees at Alma College, St. Lawrence University, and Rensselaer Polytechnic Institute noticed that beneficial effect of the V-12 program on town-college relations.
4. This conclusion is supported by the many favorable reports to college trustees and to the Navy itself at the end of the program. At North Texas Agricultural College, Dean E. E. Davis wrote Admiral Denfeld on October 17, 1945,

Our relationship with the V-12 Unit . . . has been a genuine delight. The trainees sent here have been above the average in personality and maturity of mind for lads of their age. They have entered freely into the spirit of the institution and its student activities. They have been a worthy asset to the college campus. It has been a pleasure to work with the commanding officers and other members of the Navy's official personnel in charge of this Unit. It has been a real privilege for this college to have a part in this patriotic educational undertaking. The teamwork with the Bureau of Naval Personnel has

NOTES

been all that one could desire. We are grateful to the Navy for this contact and acquaintance with its great organization.

Archives of University of Texas at Arlington.

CHAPTER 44. IMPACT ON HIGHER EDUCATION

1. Letter to author, 6/24/86.
2. Arthur S. Adams files, American Council on Education Library.
3. There were many marriages between V-12s and coeds or other young women from the area near the colleges. Swarthmore College was called "the Quaker matchbox" in recognition of Cupid's work there. V-12s were forbidden to marry until completing their training, and most of them waited as required. There were, however, a number of secret marriages, probably at nearly every unit. TR Qs and interviews.
4. Letters to author by Lillard, 6/19/86, and Poorman, 6/17/86.
5. Letter to author, 6/24/86.
6. Letter to author, 6/24/86.

CHAPTER 45. TRAINEE BENEFITS

1. One or two trainees at Illinois Institute of Technology and Denison University took as many as twenty-five academic hours that first term, and no doubt there were similar examples at many other schools. At Tufts College, trainee Samuel R. Watkins was allowed to take twenty-seven hours so he could complete graduation requirements (at Murray State Teachers College, Ky.) in the one term he was allotted in V-12. Watkins Q.
2. TR Q.

CHAPTER 46. V-12s LATER

1. At the end of the war the Navy wanted thirty thousand reserve officers to transfer to the regular Navy. Rear Adm. Louis E. Denfeld, who had already been announced as Vice Adm. Randall Jacobs's successor as chief of personnel, effective September 15, stated, "There is no room in the present Navy or in the Navy of the future for any distinctions between one group and another. Our determination is to assure those reserve officers who transfer to the regular Navy absolute equality of treatment in assignments, promotions and in the development of their careers." "Navy to Speed Discharges; 550,000 Men Its Peace Total," *New York Times*, Aug. 28, 1945, p. 13, col. 5 (carry over from p. 1, col. 2).

There may be many more admirals and Marine Corps generals from the V-12 program than those listed herein. The Navy and the Marine Corps do not categorize officers by their origin, so only those whom the author was able to discover are mentioned. No doubt other flag- or field-rank officers will be located after this book has been published.
2. Nowhere in the nation — either in the Department of the Navy or elsewhere — is there a list of former V-12s who have achieved significant places in American life. All of the names listed come from the author's research. Undoubtedly there are hundreds more who should be listed but are not because they were not discovered by the author before the completion of the book.

NOTES

Whether or not to list a man in this chapter was strictly a judgment call, based upon incomplete information and governed by only rudimentary rules. How does one compare a well-known political figure with perhaps the best surgeon, attorney, professor, or architect in a state or region? The professional man is widely regarded by his peers, but inclusion in a general listing such as this would require documentation that would not only be difficult to provide but would be impossible to use because of space and reader interest considerations. Thus, a former trainee's position or public recognition has usually been the deciding factor on whether to include him in this chapter.

Many additional V-12s are mentioned in the individual school pages in the appendix. But those listings, too, do not adequately recognize the leadership provided to the nation by former V-12s.

3. Thomas Heggen, *Mister Roberts*. (Boston: Houghton Mifflin Company, 1946).

CHAPTER 47. THE MELODY LINGERS ON

1. Copyright 1927, Irving Berlin Music Corporation.
2. NavAdmin.
3. Blair Smith letter, 3/12/86.

BIBLIOGRAPHY

In NEARLY all of the 131 undergraduate V-12 schools I made considerable use of the yearbooks, student newspapers, college catalogs or bulletins, and alumni publications. To list them all in the bibliography would add tremendously to the size of this portion of the book, and for little purpose. Many student publications, however, are mentioned by name in the appendix pages for the various schools. The decision not to list them here does not indicate a lack of appreciation of the many students, faculty members, and administrators who put together those wartime publications. Without their conscientious efforts there would be precious little evidence remaining on any campus of the V-12 days, and they deserve the thanks of all of us.

INTERVIEWS BY AUTHOR

Key to abbreviations

BuCounsel	Officer, Office of Counsel, Bureau of Naval Personnel
BuPers	Officer, Bureau of Naval Personnel
CO	Commanding officer
CTS	Officer, College Training Section
FIN	Officer, Finance Section of Planning and Control
F	Faculty member or administrator
M	Marine
MTR	Marine V-12 trainee
N	Navy
NTR	Navy V-12 trainee
O	Officer
O-in-C	Officer-in-charge
PR	College president
XO	Executive Officer

BIBLIOGRAPHY

Person	Type	Date
Adams, Kenneth ("Bud")	NTR	6/10/86*
Adams, Mrs. Lewis K.	Widow, CTS	3/14/82*
Adams, Lynn	Daughter-in-law of Arthur S. Adams	8/16/86*
Bartle, Mrs. Glenn	Widow, CO, Swarthmore	5/24/86*
Bell, Robert	NTR	10/14/85
Betz, Edward	F, College of the Pacific	11/12/83
Biersted, Robert H.	XO, Mercer	2/17/86*
Blake, William	NTR	4/27/83
Brown, Grant H.	Director of Training, Ninth Naval District	1/8/86* 1/11/86*
Buck, Polly Stone	Widow, dean of Yale	4/28/85
Bump, Mrs. Boardman	Widow, FIN (civilian)	4/25/86*
Burkholder, Maurice	CO, Oberlin	5/2/86
Burrill, Meldrim	CO, Illinois State Normal	1/18/86*
Carter, Harry T.	MTR	3/8/86
Case, Everett N.	PR, Colgate	1/1/84*
Chitty, Elizabeth N.	F, University of the South	4/20/84
Clark, Alice L.	Regarding A. S. Adams	4/25/86*
Clark, Wyndham S.	Classmate, W. S. Thomson	9/20/85
Coon, Richard	NTR	12/15/84*
Davenport, John Scott	MTR	1/9/86*
Davis, Kathryn	PR's Secy., Tulane	8/27/84
Doyal, Eugene	NTR	7/26/85
Doyle, John	M, O-in-C, Redlands	6/28/86*
DuVal, Miles P.	Classmate, A. S. Adams	10/30/84
Dyer, George C.	Classmate, A. S. Adams	7/14/84*
Eaton, Richard B.	N O	1/19/86* 9/13/86
Edwards, Horace B.	NTR	1/4/86*
Elliott, Virgil	PR, Milligan	9/19/80
Eurich, Alvin C.	O-in-C, Curriculum	6/23/83 2/6/86*
Fairbanks, Alonzo J., Jr.	NTR	3/24/86*
Fowler, James A., Jr.	Counsel, BuPers	3/11/84*
Goodwin, John B.	FIN	5/5/86*
Grant, Alan J.	NTR	9/15/86
Greene, George	CO, Arkansas A & M	1/6/86*
Gruelich, Wilmer D.	CO, Muhlenberg	3/22/86*
Guy, John A.	O, Princeton	8/3/85*
Harris, Rufus C.	PR, Tulane	9/12/85
Hensel, H. Struve	O, Procurement, Legal Div.	1/4/86*
Hix, C. E., Jr.	F, Central College	8/16/83
Hogge, Robert L.	NTR	8/16/83
Howes, Raymond F.	O-in-C, CTS	6/13/81* 4/24/82

BIBLIOGRAPHY

Person	Type	Date
Hulme, George W., Jr.	CO, Howard; CTS	3/27/82*
		9/12/85
Hurst, Robert E.	NTR	4/25/82
Jackson, Charles A.	Cousin, W. S. Thomson	11/17/85
Jensen, A. E.	CO, Emory and Henry, St. Ambrose	2/4/86*
Johns, Theron	NTR	4/24/82
Johnson, Ralph Wright	NTR	6/14/86*
Kelso, Maxwell	CO, Central Michigan	2/17/86*
Kenney, W. John	Spec. Asst. to Undersecy. of Navy	1/4/86*
Kincade, Paul	NTR	6/20/86*
Labrie, Isabel	Regarding A. S. Adams	4/25/86*
Lacy, Steve	F, Milligan	8/10/85
Lewis, Mae	F, Arkansas A & M	4/16/83
Long, David A.	NTR	3/13/86
Longley, Gordon J.	CO, Bethany	1/11/86*
Lunden, Walter A.	PR, Gustavus Adolphus	5/21/86
Lytle, Jack T.	M, O-in-C, Arkansas A & M	4/8/84
		6/1/86*
Mahard, Richard	F, Denison	11/29/85
Mann, Burton L.	NTR	4/14/86
Mather, Jean Paul	CTS	4/22/85
Matheson, R. G.	CO, Mercer	9/28/85*
Maynard, Elsdon	NTR	6/2/86
McAlpin, Kathleen M.	BuCounsel	3/27/86*
McCurdy, Charles P.	CO, Gustavus Adolphus	3/9/85
McGonigle, Lester	NTR	10/16/85
Mitchell, Morris	NTR	6/6/86*
Mumford, Milton C.	BuPers	4/26/86*
Nagler, Gordon	NTR	3/14/85
Narmore, Philip	CTS	11/22/85*
Norvelle, Lee	XO, College of the Pacific	12/3/83*
O'Brien, George D.	NTR	4/24/82
Oleson, Loyd	F, Doane	8/15/86
Pardee, Graham F.	NTR	4/26/83
Perry, R. C.	CO, Minot State and Arizona State Teachers	9/25/86*
Pine, R. Dean	BuCounsel	5/10/86*
Rakov, Clayton	NTR	4/23/82
Randolph, Esther	F, Westminster	8/17/83
Reeves, Ruth Heath	Ship's company, Milligan	9/23/82
Reid, Jane Meldrum	Coed, Miami University	10/29/85*
Reilly, Francis X.	BuCounsel	7/1/85
Reynolds, W. Glasgow	BuCounsel	4/10/84
Saylor, Galen	O, University of Oklahoma	2/4/86*

* = Telephone interview

BIBLIOGRAPHY

Person	Type	Date
Seibert, Russell H.	CO, Baldwin-Wallace	11/17/84*
		8/29/85
Sessions, R. Fred	CO, Milligan, IIT	2/2/80*
		9/15/80
		1/18/86*
Shine, Henry	NTR	10/31/84
Shirley, Walter W.	NTR	4/23/82
Sledge, Eugene B.	MTR	2/8/86*
Sloss, Brooks	F, Westminster	8/17/83
Steele, Page Thomson	Daughter, W. S. Thomson	1/29/84
Steirs, Lawrence	NTR	7/26/85
Stewart, Robert B.	Chairman, Uniform Contracts	4/18/84
Stone, George W., Jr.	CTS	3/9/83
		3/12/86
Stone, Marvin L.	NTR	11/2/84
Swift, H. Melvin, Jr.	NTR	4/24/82
		9/10/86
Taylor, Dwight	BuPers	1/4/86*
		1/11/86*
Thoma, Henry F.	CTS	4/10/83*
Thomson, Mrs. W. S.	Widow, W. S. Thomson	1/29/84
Toomey, T. Murray	MTR	11/2/84
Van Tongeren, Harold	MTR	12/1/85*
Vollmer, James	NTR	7/12/86*
Walsh, Robert G.	NTR	2/21/86
Ward, Frances Brant	Secy. to W. S. Thomson	3/11/84*
Ward, James E.	NTR	11/1/85
Weaver, John	NTR	7/6/86*
Weber, William Valdo	CTS	2/11/84*
		5/1/86
Wellborn, Gordon R.	CO, Milligan	8/19/80
		4/17/83
Whitten, Mrs. Alice B.	Mother, NTR	2/2/80*
Wight, John W.	CTS	9/13/85
Wilson, Arthur "Pete"	NTR	2/25/86*

BOOKS

Ageton, Arthur A. *The Naval Officer's Guide.* New York: McGraw-Hill Book Company, Whittlesey House, 1943.

Alley, Reuben E. *History of the University of Richmond, 1830–1971.* Richmond, Va.: University of Richmond, 1971.

Barron's Profiles of American Colleges. Vol. I, *Descriptions of the Colleges.* 9th ed. Woodbury, N.Y.: Barron's Educational Series, 1974.

Beach, Edward L. *The United States Navy: 200 Years.* New York: Henry Holt and Company, 1986.

BIBLIOGRAPHY

Beal, Merrill D. *History of Idaho State College.* Pocatello: Idaho State College, 1952.

Belsheim, Osbourne T. *The Story of Dickinson State College.* Dickinson, N.D.: Dickinson State College, 1968.

Bishop, Morris. *A History of Cornell.* Ithaca, N.Y.: Cornell University Press, 1962.

Bluejackets' Manual: United States Navy. 11th ed. Annapolis: United States Naval Institute, 1943.

Blum, John Morton. *V Was For Victory.* New York: Harcourt Brace Jovanovich, 1977.

Brewer, Kara Pratt. *Pioneer or Perish.* Fresno: Pioneer Publishing Co., 1977.

Buck, Polly Stone. *We Minded the Store: Yale Life and Letters During World War II.* Privately printed. New Haven: Polly Stone Buck, 1975.

Burchard, John. *Q.E.D.: M.I.T. in World War II.* New York: Technology Press, 1948.

Burns, James MacGregor. *Roosevelt: The Soldier of Freedom.* New York: Harcourt Brace Jovanovich, 1970.

Chicago Manual of Style. 13th ed. Chicago: University of Chicago Press, 1982.

Connery, Robert H. *The Navy and Industrial Mobilization in World War II.* Princeton: Princeton University Press, 1951.

Cooper, Jackie (with Richard Kleiner). *Please Don't Shoot My Dog.* New York: William Morrow and Co., 1981.

Costello, John. *The Pacific War.* New York: Rawson, Wade Publishers, 1981.

Cunningham, John T. *University in the Forest: The Story of Drew University.* Florham Park, N.J.: Afton Publishing Company, 1972.

Current Biography, 1951 and other years. New York: H. W. Wilson Co.

Dabney, Virginius. *Mr. Jefferson's University: A History.* Charlottesville: University Press of Virginia, 1981.

Dykes, Mattie M. *Behind the Birches.* Maryville, Mo.: Northwest Missouri State College, 1956.

Edwards, Eda Bessie. *Profile of the Past, A Living Legacy: Bloomsburg State College, 1839–1979.* Bloomsburg: Bloomsburg State College Alumni Association, 1982.

Farrell, Anthony. *Bees and Bur Oaks: 100 Years of St. Ambrose College.* Davenport, Iowa: St. Ambrose College, 1982.

Fetridge, William Harrison, ed. *Abbott Hall.* Chicago: Abbott Hall Publications Committee, n.d. (circa 1946).

Field, James A., Jr. *History of United States Naval Operations: Korea.* Washington, D.C.: U.S. Government Printing Office, 1962.

Fleming, Charles A.; Austin, Robin L.; and Braley, Charles, III. *Quantico: Crossroads of the Marine Corps.* Washington, D.C.: History and Museums Division, Headquarters, U.S. Marine Corps, 1978.

Gavin, David P. *History of John Carroll College: A Century of Service.* Kent, Ohio: Kent State University Press, 1985.

Gregg, Robert W. *Chronicles of Willamette.* Vol. II. Portland, Oreg.: Durham and Downey, 1970.

Guide to United States Administrative Histories of World War II, Naval History Division, Department of the Navy, 1976.

Hamilton, Raphael N. *The Story of Marquette University: An Object Lesson in the Development of Catholic Higher Education.* Milwaukee: Marquette University Press, 1953.

Heggen, Thomas. *Mister Roberts.* Boston: Houghton Mifflin Company, 1946.

BIBLIOGRAPHY

Hershey, Charlie Brown. *Colorado College, 1874–1949.* Colorado Springs: Colorado College, 1952.

History of Columbia College on Morningside. New York: Columbia University Press, 1954.

Hollingsworth, Lloyd. *Gustavus Athletics: A Century of Building the Gustie Tradition 1880–1980.* St. Peter, Minn.: Gustavus Adolphus College, 1984.

Howes, Raymond F. *A Cornell Notebook.* Ithaca, N.Y.: Cornell Alumni Association, 1971.

————. *Important to Me.* Privately printed limited edition of one hundred copies. Riverside, Calif.: Raymond F. Howes, 1980.

————. *More Cornell (And Other) Notes.* Privately printed limited edition of one hundred copies. Riverside, Calif.: Raymond F. Howes, 1979.

————. *The Navy Goes to College.* Privately printed limited edition of one hundred copies. Riverside, Calif.: Raymond F. Howes, 1974.

Hoyt, Edwin P. *Closing the Circle: War in the Pacific: 1945.* New York: Van Nostrand Reinhold Company, 1982.

Johnson, Walter, ed. *The Papers of Adlai E. Stevenson.* Vol. II, *Washington to Springfield, 1941–1948.* Boston: Little, Brown and Company, 1972.

King, Ernest J. *U.S. Navy at War.* Washington, D.C.: United States Navy Department, 1946.

Klein, H. M. J. *History of Franklin and Marshall College, 1787–1948.* Lancaster, Pa.: Franklin and Marshall Alumni Association, 1952.

Knox, Dudley W. *A History of the United States Navy.* Rev. ed. New York: G. P. Putnam's Sons, 1948.

Lee, Robert Edson. *To the War.* New York: Alfred A. Knopf, 1968.

Lovejoy, Clarence E. *Lovejoy's College Guide.* 12th ed. New York: Simon and Schuster, 1974.

Lund, Doniver A. *Gustavus Adolphus College: A Centennial History, 1862–1962.* St. Peter, Minn.: Gustavus Adolphus College, 1962.

Manchester, William. *Goodbye, Darkness: A Memoir of the Pacific War.* Boston: Little, Brown and Company, 1979; Dell, 1982.

Manhart, George B. *DePauw Through the Years.* Vol. II, *DePauw University, 1919–1962.* Greencastle, Ind.: DePauw University, 1962.

"Marine Corps Ground Training in World War II." Marine Corps Historical Branch, 1956. Typescript.

Marshall, Helen E. *Grandest of Enterprises.* Normal, Ill.: Illinois State Normal University, 1956.

Mathews, Donald K. *Measurement in Physical Education.* 3rd ed. Philadelphia: W. B. Saunders Company, 1968.

McLemore, Richard Aubrey, and Pitts, Nannie. *The History of Mississippi College.* Jackson, Miss.: Hederman Brothers, 1979.

Millett, Allan R. *Semper Fidelis: The History of the United States Marine Corps.* New York: Macmillan Publishing Co., 1980.

Millis, Walter, ed. *The Forrestal Diaries.* New York: Viking Press, 1951.

Nash, Ray. *Navy at Dartmouth.* Hanover, N.H.: Dartmouth Publications, 1946.

Nelson, Dennis D. *The Integration of the Negro into the U.S. Navy.* New York: Farrar, Straus and Young, 1951.

Norvelle, Lee. *The Road Taken.* Bloomington, Ind.: Indiana University Foundation, 1980.

BIBLIOGRAPHY

Oliphant, J. Orin. *The Rise of Bucknell University.* New York: Appleton-Century-Crofts, 1965.

Palmer, Edgar A., ed. *G.I. Songs: Written, Composed and/or Collected by the Men in the Service.* New York: Sheridan House, 1944.

Parrish, William E. *Westminster College: An Informal History, 1851–1969.* Fulton, Mo.: Westminster College, 1971.

Pease, Royal S. *Navy Correspondence and Report Forms.* Boston: Houghton Mifflin Company, 1943.

Peckham, Howard H. *The Making of the University of Michigan, 1817–1967.* Ann Arbor: University of Michigan Press, 1967.

Peterson, Conrad. *Remember Thy Past: A History of Gustavus Adolphus College, 1862–1952.* St. Peter, Minn.: Gustavus Adolphus College, 1953.

Powell, William S. *The First State University: A Pictorial History of the University of North Carolina.* Chapel Hill: University of North Carolina Press, 1972.

Register of Alumni. 1984 ed. Annapolis: United States Naval Academy Alumni Association, 1984.

Rogow, Arnold A. *James Forrestal.* New York: Macmillan Company, 1963.

Rolle, Andrew F. *Occidental College: The First Seventy-Five Years, 1887–1962.* Los Angeles: Occidental College, 1962.

Schneider, James G. *Milligan College Navy V-12 Unit, July 1, 1943–June 30, 1945.* Kankakee, Ill.: Milligan College V-12 Reunion Committee, 1980.

Schoor, Gene, ed. *A Treasury of Notre Dame Football.* New York: Funk and Wagnalls Co., 1962.

Sledge, E. B. *With The Old Breed at Peleliu and Okinawa.* Novato, Calif.: Presidio Press, 1981.

Smith, Warren Hunting. *Hobart and William Smith: The History of Two Colleges.* Geneva, N.Y.: Hobart and William Smith Colleges, 1972.

Smythe, Mabel M., ed. *The Black American Reference Book.* Englewood Cliffs, N.J.: Prentice-Hall, 1976.

Stevenson, George J. *Increase in Excellence: A History of Emory and Henry College.* New York: Appleton-Century-Crofts, 1963.

Swain, James E. *A History of Muhlenberg College, 1848–1967.* New York: Appleton-Century-Crofts, 1967.

Harvey, Robert S., ed. *These Fleeting Years: Wabash College, 1832–1982.* Crawfordsville, Ind.: Wabash College, 1982.

Thompson, Robert E., and Myers, Hortense. *Robert F. Kennedy: The Brother Within.* New York: Macmillan Company, 1962.

Tucker, Frank C. *Central Methodist College, One Hundred and Ten Years.* Nashville, Tenn.: Parthenon Press, 1967.

U.S. Naval Administration in World War II, Bureau of Naval Personnel, Training Activity. Vol. IV, *The College Training Program,* Guide No. 83d(1), and many other volumes in the 115-volume series, including *The Negro in the Navy,* Guide No. 84. Washington, D.C.: Bureau of Naval Personnel, 1945.

U.S. Naval History, A Bibliography. 6th ed. Naval History Division, Department of the Navy, 1972.

U.S. Naval History Sources in the Washington Area and Suggested Research Subjects. 3rd ed. Washington, D.C.: U.S. Naval History Division, 1970.

Waldron, Charles Newman. *The Union College I Remember: 1902–1946.* Privately printed. Boston: Charles Newman Waldron, 1954.

BIBLIOGRAPHY

Who's Who in America. (Various editions, especially the 29th, 42nd, and 43rd.) Chicago: Marquis Who's Who.

Williams, Howard D. *A History of Colgate University, 1819–1969.* New York: Van Nostrand Reinhold Co., 1969.

Writing Guide. Rev. ed. Washington, D.C.: History and Museums Division, Headquarters, U.S. Marine Corps, 1983.

PERIODICALS

All Hands (and its predecessors, *TraDivLetter* and *Bureau of Naval Personnel Information Bulletin*), Bureau of Naval Personnel. Nearly every issue between February 1943 and July 1946.

Estabrooks, G. H. "Campus Revolution." *Saturday Evening Post* (September 18, 1943): 14–15, 74, 77.

"First Negro Ensigns." *Life* (April 24, 1944): 44.

Forrestal, James V. "Will We Choose Naval Suicide Again?" *Saturday Evening Post* (June 24, 1944): 9–11, 90.

Hawley, Robert G. "The Army Quits the Colleges." *Harper's Magazine* (April 1944): 419–425.

"Hobart Under V-12." *Newsweek* (August 2, 1943): 72.

Holloway, James L., Jr. (with Jack Sweetman). "A Gentlemen's Agreement." *Proceedings* (September 1980): 71–77.

Hopkins, Ernest Martin. "Shall It Be the Old College Again?" *New York Times Magazine* (August 15, 1943): 7, 38.

Periodicals of the 131 colleges and universities involved in the undergraduate Navy V-12 program.

MISCELLANEOUS

Correspondence files of the presidents of many V-12 schools.

Marine Corps Historical Center. Files for Marine V-12 units at various schools.

National Archives. Bureau of Naval Personnel General Correspondence, 1941–1945, QR/p11-1/V-12, Boxes 1171–1180.

National Archives. Muster Rolls for Marine and Navy V-12 units.

ACKNOWLEDGMENTS

I AM greatly indebted to thousands of people for assistance in making this book possible.

During the course of my research I visited more than one hundred V-12 schools. With but a few exceptions, the cooperation was superb. The diligence of archivists, librarians, alumni directors — and their assistants — in digging through long-dormant records was heart-warming. It led to an occasional surprise. One assistant in a Southern college wrote to regretfully inform me that there had only been Army programs on that campus, citing as her authority the present military science department. Both the assistant and the department were amazed when supplied with proof of that school's Navy V-12 program.

At the National Archives, Elaine Everly helped me locate the invaluable correspondence files of the College Training Section. The National Archives holds miles upon miles of World War II Navy files, and finding the right one is not easy.

In the Army and Navy Records Section, William E. Lind was most helpful in gathering the microfilms of V-12 unit muster rolls and making arrangements for me to use them in his office.

At the Marine Corps Historical Center, Danny J. Crawford, head of the Reference Section, provided excellent assistance in locating materials and providing access to photographs.

At the Navy Department Archives, Dr. Dean C. Allard and his staff met my every need. In the Navy Department Library, Barbara Lynch and John Vajda used their tremendous knowledge of the Navy files to suggest which materials would be most helpful and to locate them. Whether I made my request by phone, letter, or in person, it was met with prompt action.

Capt. David A. Long, USN(Ret.), a V-12 from the University of Kansas and now executive director of the Naval Historical Foundation, made my tasks much easier, and on occasion helped me with some preliminary research.

The more than one thousand former V-12s who responded to the many questionnaires I sent out were of incalculable value, not only in

ACKNOWLEDGMENTS

reinforcing my belief in the success of the V-12 program but in supplying interesting sidelights, anecdotes, and opinions about the program in all of its facets. One of the amazing things about the questionnaires is that approximately two-thirds of those who responded took time to write additional comments ranging from a few words to five typewritten pages. Those lengthy replies provided a great deal of encouragement and convinced me that this history was long overdue. Their inquiries as to how they could obtain a copy of the book helped assure me of the commercial viability of the volume.

Many V-12s were reaching retirement age at the time most of the questionnaires were mailed out. As a result, a substantial number were returned because the addressees had moved and the postmaster was unable to forward them. Not every V-12 who received a questionnaire replied to it, but an amazing 75 percent did respond. Of the trainees who replied, only two refused to provide any information.

The cooperation of retired faculty members who taught in the V-12 program was also excellent. I had the addresses for many professors, whom I did not write to because of the tendency for memories of student groups to blend together over a lifetime of teaching. But those who were contacted responded fully and helpfully.

There are undoubtedly more former unit officers still alive than those I found. I followed up leads only as time permitted and only when I had information that was especially helpful in following their trails. I was in contact with more than thirty former officers of the program. They were extremely friendly and cooperative, and they supplied a wealth of information in personal interviews, telephone interviews, letters, and questionnaires. Without their assistance this history of the V-12 program would have been quite incomplete.

I also received excellent cooperation from some members of ship's company, the enlisted personnel who staffed the 131 V-12 units. I learned many things from them that have been helpful in giving the complete picture.

Among the most important interviews were those with the officers who helped set up the program and then assisted in running it from the Bureau of Naval Personnel. They gave willingly of their time, and all had excellent recall.

The longest interview, and one that really provided the impetus to begin diligent work on the book, was with Raymond F. Howes at his home in Riverside, California, on April 24, 1982. Howes's marvelous recall and lively sense of humor made the six-hour interview a delight. Since he was the *de facto* exec for the first two years of the program and was the officer-in-charge during the third year, his recollections provided a vital base for presenting the history of the program.

581

ACKNOWLEDGMENTS

The interviews with John W. Wight, Dr. Jean Paul Mather, Dr. George Winchester Stone, Jr., Francis X. Reilly, Jr., and William Glasgow Reynolds were all of major importance. Telephone and personal interviews with Henry F. Thoma, George W. Hulme, James Alexander Fowler, Jr., John B. Goodwin, Kathleen Middleton McAlpin, and R. Dean Pine were extremely helpful in filling out the story.

My initial telephone interviews, personal visit, and 1980 videotaped interview with my original V-12 skipper, Dr. Royal Fred Sessions, provided the encouragement necessary to carry this idea through to a book.

Hundreds of trainees were also interviewed during the writing process. The story could not have been told without them.

My thanks go to the following people, who reviewed chapters about which they had special knowledge or background. Their verifications of facts and their helpful suggestions were important contributions.

Chapter	*Reviewed by*
1. The Need 2. The Program Takes Form	Dr. Rufus C. Harris, president of Tulane University, member of Navy Advisory Educational Council, and member of Joint Army and Navy Board for Training Unit Contracts Miss Kathryn Davis, Dr. Harris's secretary (1937–54) and assistant to the president (1954–60)
4. A Uniform Army/Navy Contract	Dr. Rufus C. Harris Miss Kathryn Davis Dr. Robert B. Stewart, controller of Purdue University and chairman of the Joint Army and Navy Board for Training Unit Contracts
5. Contracting with the Colleges	John B. Goodwin, officer of the Finance Section, Division of Planning and Control, Bureau of Naval Personnel (1943–45) Francis X. Reilly, officer in the Office of Bureau Counsel, Bureau of Naval Personnel (1943–45)
6. The College Training Section 7. The CTS in Action	Dr. Jean Paul Mather, officer in the College Training Section (1943–46) Dr. George Winchester Stone, Jr., officer in the College Training Section (1943–46)
19. The "Fly Boys"	Rear Adm. Thomas A. Kamm, USNR(Ret.), V-12(a) at Wabash College Burton L. Mann, V-12(a) at Milligan College

ACKNOWLEDGMENTS

20. Marine V-12s

Jack T. Lytle, officer-in-charge, Marine Detachment, Arkansas A & M

Harry Tyson Carter, Marine V-12 at Dartmouth College

John Scott Davenport, Marine V-12 at University of Redlands

Dean Gabbert, Marine V-12 at Denison University

Danny J. Crawford, head of the Reference Section, Marine Corps Historical Center

21. Coast Guard V-12s

Robert G. Walker, Coast Guard V-12 at Duke University

22. Negro V-12s

Vice Adm. Samuel L. Gravely, Jr., USN(Ret.), V-12 at UCLA

James E. Ward, V-12 at Princeton University

24. Physical Training

Gordon R. Wellborn, athletic officer and commanding officer, Milligan College

William J. Young, chief athletic specialist, John Carroll University

28. Navy-College Relations

Grant H. Brown, V-12 administrator, district training officer, Ninth Naval District

29. Commanding Officers

Meldrim F. Burrill, commanding officer, Illinois State Normal

Dr. Everett Case, president, Colgate University

Dr. Rufus C. Harris

Dr. Russell H. Seibert, commanding officer, Baldwin-Wallace College

Dr. R. Fred Sessions, commanding officer, Milligan College and Illinois Institute of Technology

30. District Training Officers

Grant H. Brown

33. Intercollegiate Athletics

Col. John A. Gunn, USMC(Ret.), authority on Marine Corps football

Jack T. Lytle

Gordon R. Wellborn

This book would have taken much longer to get to the final manuscript phase had it not been for the diligence, great interest, and high degree of accuracy of my two secretaries during the time we were work-

ACKNOWLEDGMENTS

ing on the book. Working after hours, Carol Hilgert Hoekstra compiled the lists of trainees to whom questionnaires would be sent and handled the early correspondence. When she moved to Texas early in 1985, Lynn Gregoire O'Brien took over and showed the same enthusiasm for the project. She transformed my dictation and scribbled editing into the finished manuscript, which proved to be longer than either of us had expected.

My thanks go to both of those fine ladies!

My wife, Phyllis, accompanied me on many of the trips, taking over part of the research at the National Archives and at many of the libraries. While I would be reading the newspaper microfilms, she would be going through the yearbooks and making the appropriate photocopies, always calling my attention to other possible sources of V-12 information.

When the manuscript started to take form, she became my "Editor of First Resort," going over each chapter revision after I had reviewed it myself and making comments and suggestions in pencil. I then reread the manuscript and adopted probably 75 percent of the changes she proposed; in the other 25 percent, we would discuss which word, phrase, or approach best fitted a particular situation.

When the returned questionnaires started to pile up into rather unworkable files, Phyllis undertook to sort them alphabetically into four large notebooks. I had read each questionnaire as it came in over the course of several years, but once they were all assembled she reread each of them, making notations on those that had especially helpful comments and categorizing them for me. This was a great advantage when I made my final review of the questionnaires. For this type of work she also earned the title of "Worthy Keeper of the Questionnaires."

Her encouragement all through the long project was a vital ingredient in bringing it to completion. For all of this she has my undying thanks.

I thought V-12 readers would also enjoy the cartoon reproduced on page 338. For forty years it has been the first page of my World War II photo album. It was drawn by Ralph E. Ricketts for the *Gangway* yearbook at the Pre-Midshipmen's School at Asbury Park, New Jersey, in January 1945. Ralph and I worked on that book and I selected the cartoon from the discarded photos and drawings after publication. It is used with permission of Ricketts, who is now a free-lance artist in Atlanta.

The V-5 "purge" cartoon on page 132 is used with permission of cartoonist Emil M. Jecmen, who is now a real estate broker in St. Louis.

For most of the photos in the book, I am indebted to more than one hundred schools and many individuals. A credit is given alongside each

ACKNOWLEDGMENTS

photograph. Copy negatives were made from many of those pictures by G and G Studios, Bradley, Illinois.

The maps in the appendix for locating the V-12 units were created by Ellis Gravlin of G and G Studios.

I acknowledge with appreciation the permission received from the following publishers to reproduce extended quotations from copyrighted works: Charles E. Widmayer, "V-12 Physical Training," *Dartmouth Alumni Magazine,* December 1943, from *Dartmouth Alumni Magazine;* and Admiral James L. Holloway, Jr., USN(Ret.), with Jack Sweetman, "A Gentlemen's Agreement," *Proceedings,* September 1980, from United States Naval Institute.

I am most appreciative of Houghton Mifflin Company's recognition of the need for this first book about the V-12 program and its faith in contracting with a first-time author to bring it about. It has been a pleasure to work with all of the people at Houghton Mifflin, and especially my editor, Larry Kessenich, who has been extremely helpful and patient and turned out to be a good friend. Manuscript editor Daniel Otis's skill and patience contributed a good deal of improvement in the wording and flow of the copy.

My only serious regret in writing this volume was that I did not have a chance to meet Arthur Stanton Adams. When I made the first call to his home in November of 1979 he was ill and unable to come to the phone. When I called a year later, he had died. By all accounts from every source, he was a rare individual: a pleasure to know, a joy to be around, brilliant, and brim full of workable good ideas. He had enthusiasm, idealism, and determination and he passed those qualities on to the V-12s.

On behalf of nearly 125,000 American men I acknowledge the great debt we all owe to Arthur Stanton Adams.

James G. Schneider
Kankakee, Illinois

INDEX

INDEX

INDEX

INDEX

INDEX

INDEX

INDEX

INDEX

INDEX